Read this book online today:

With SAP PRESS BooksOnline we offer you online access to knowledge from the leading SAP experts. Whether you use it as a beneficial supplement or as an alternative to the printed book, with SAP PRESS BooksOnline you can:

- Access your book anywhere, at any time. All you need is an Internet connection.
- Perform full text searches on your book and on the entire SAP PRESS library.
- Build your own personalized SAP library.

The SAP PRESS customer advantage:

Register this book today at www.sap-press.com and obtain exclusive free trial access to its online version. If you like it (and we think you will), you can choose to purchase permanent, unrestricted access to the online edition at a very special price!

Here's how to get started:

1. Visit www.sap-press.com.
2. Click on the link for SAP PRESS BooksOnline and login (or create an account).
3. Enter your free trial license key, shown below in the corner of the page.
4. Try out your online book with full, unrestricted access for a limited time!

Your personal free trial license key
for this online book is:

qv7x-judr-8sye-akz6

Creating Dashboards with Xcelsius — Practical Guide

SAP PRESS is a joint initiative of SAP and Galileo Press. The know-how offered by SAP specialists combined with the expertise of the Galileo Press publishing house offers the reader expert books in the field. SAP PRESS features first-hand information and expert advice, and provides useful skills for professional decision-making.

SAP PRESS offers a variety of books on technical and business related topics for the SAP user. For further information, please visit our website: www.sap-press.com.

Jim Brogden, Heather Sinkwitz, Mac Holden
SAP BusinessObjects Web Intelligence
2010, 583 pp.
978-1-59229-322-3

Mike Garrett
Using Crystal Reports with SAP
2010, 442 pp.
978-1-59229-327-8

Ingo Hilgefort
Reporting and Analytics with SAP BusinessObjects
2009, 655 pp.
978-1-59229-310-0

Larry Sackett
MDX Reporting and Analytics with SAP NetWeaver BW
2009, 380 pp.
978-1-59229-249-3

Ray Li and Evan DeLodder

Creating Dashboards with Xcelsius — Practical Guide

Bonn • Boston

Galileo Press is named after the Italian physicist, mathematician and philosopher Galileo Galilei (1564–1642). He is known as one of the founders of modern science and an advocate of our contemporary, heliocentric worldview. His words *Eppur si muove* (And yet it moves) have become legendary. The Galileo Press logo depicts Jupiter orbited by the four Galilean moons, which were discovered by Galileo in 1610.

Editor Erik Herman
Technical Reviewer Larry Sackett
Copyeditor Ruth Saavedra
Cover Design Graham Geary
Photo Credit iStockphoto.com/sebastian-k, domin_domin, winterling
Layout Design Vera Brauner
Production Editor Kelly O'Callaghan
Assistant Production Editor Graham Geary
Typesetting Publishers' Design and Production Services, Inc.
Printed and bound in Canada

ISBN 978-1-59229-335-3

© 2012 by Galileo Press Inc., Boston (MA)
1st edition 2011; 1st reprint, with corrections, 2012

Library of Congress Cataloging-in-Publication Data
Li, Ray.
  Creating dashboards with Xcelsius — practical guide /
Ray Li, Evan DeLodder. — 1st ed.
      p. cm.
  ISBN-13: 978-1-59229-335-3
  ISBN-10: 1-59229-335-2
  1. Xcelsius (Computer file) 2. Dashboards (Management information systems)
I. DeLodder, Evan. II. Title.
  HD30.213.L52 2011
  005.4'37—dc22
                                                      2010028732

All rights reserved. Neither this publication nor any part of it may be copied or reproduced in any form or by any means or translated into another language, without the prior consent of Galileo Press GmbH, Rheinwerkallee 4, 53227 Bonn, Germany.

Galileo Press makes no warranties or representations with respect to the content hereof and specifically disclaims any implied warranties of merchantability or fitness for any particular purpose. Galileo Press assumes no responsibility for any errors that may appear in this publication.

"Galileo Press" and the Galileo Press logo are registered trademarks of Galileo Press GmbH, Bonn, Germany. SAP PRESS is an imprint of Galileo Press.

All of the screenshots and graphics reproduced in this book are subject to copyright © SAP AG, Dietmar-Hopp-Allee 16, 69190 Walldorf, Germany.

SAP, the SAP-Logo, mySAP, mySAP.com, mySAP Business Suite, SAP NetWeaver, SAP R/3, SAP R/2, SAP B2B, SAPtronic, SAPscript, SAP BW, SAP CRM, SAP Early Watch, SAP ArchiveLink, SAP GUI, SAP Business Workflow, SAP Business Engineer, SAP Business Navigator, SAP Business Framework, SAP Business Information Warehouse, SAP inter-enterprise solutions, SAP APO, AcceleratedSAP, InterSAP, SAPoffice, SAPfind, SAPfile, SAPtime, SAPmail, SAPaccess, SAP-EDI, R/3 Retail, Accelerated HR, Accelerated HiTech, Accelerated Consumer Products, ABAP, ABAP/4, ALE/WEB, Alloy, BAPI, Business Framework, BW Explorer, Duet, Enjoy-SAP, mySAP.com e-business platform, mySAP Enterprise Portals, RIVA, SAPPHIRE, TeamSAP, Webflow and SAP PRESS are registered or unregistered trademarks of SAP AG, Walldorf, Germany.

All other products mentioned in this book are registered or unregistered trademarks of their respective companies.

Contents at a Glance

1	Introduction to Xcelsius 2008	17
2	Get Familiar with Xcelsius 2008	31
3	Get Started	77
4	UI Component Basics	91
5	UI Components – Advanced	185
6	Data Connectivity Basics	293
7	Advanced Data Connectivity	331
8	Special Features	393
9	A Comprehensive Hands-On Example	439
10	Introducion to the Xcelsius SDK	461
11	Get Started with Custom Component Basics	475
12	Implement Advanced Custom Add-On Component Features	505
13	Hands-On: Develop Your Custom Add-On Component	527
A	Tips for Using Xcelsius in SAP BusinessObjects Enterprise or other SAP Environment	545
B	The Authors	581

Contents

Acknowledgments 15

1 Introduction to Xcelsius 2008 17

1.1 What's Xcelsius? 17
    1.1.1 Installation 18
    1.1.2 Relationship with Excel 19
    1.1.3 History 19
1.2 What Can Xcelsius 2008 Do? 19
    1.2.1 Data Visualization Capabilities 20
    1.2.2 Data Connectivity Capabilities 26
    1.2.3 Distribution 27
1.3 Reasons to Choose Xcelsius 27
1.4 Xcelsius in the SAP BusinessObjects Portfolio 28
1.5 Summary 29

2 Get Familiar with Xcelsius 2008 31

2.1 Menu 31
    2.1.1 File 31
    2.1.2 Edit 50
    2.1.3 View 51
    2.1.4 Format 56
    2.1.5 Data 59
    2.1.6 Help 62
2.2 Toolbar 64
    2.2.1 Standard 64
    2.2.2 Export 65
    2.2.3 Themes 65
    2.2.4 Format 66
    2.2.5 Quick Start 66
    2.2.6 Summary 66
2.3 Components Browser 68
    2.3.1 Category 68
    2.3.2 Tree 69

Contents

	2.3.3 List	70
2.4	Canvas	71
2.5	Embedded Excel Spreadsheet	71
2.6	Property Sheet	72
2.7	Object Browser	74
2.8	Summary	75

3 Get Started ... 77

3.1	Introduction	77
3.2	Choose the Right UI Components	78
3.3	Bind Data	79
	3.3.1 Bind Data for Pie Chart	80
	3.3.2 Enable Drill-Down for the Pie Chart	82
	3.3.3 Bind Data for Label	84
3.4	Connect to External Data	85
3.5	Formatting	85
3.6	Distribute the Output	88
3.7	Summary	89

4 UI Component Basics ... 91

4.1	Working with Charts	92
	4.1.1 Pie Chart	92
	4.1.2 Column Chart	110
	4.1.3 Line Chart	128
	4.1.4 Bar Chart	136
	4.1.5 XY Chart	137
	4.1.6 Bubble Chart	141
	4.1.7 Area Chart	144
4.2	Selectors	147
	4.2.1 Introduction to Xcelsius Selectors	147
	4.2.2 Select a Single Item	147
	4.2.3 Filter	153
	4.2.4 Checkbox	157
	4.2.5 Toggle Button	158
	4.2.6 Ticker	158

		4.2.7	Picture Menus	160
		4.2.8	List Builder	165
	4.3	Represent a Single Value		166
		4.3.1	Introduction to Single-Value Components	166
		4.3.2	Slider	167
		4.3.3	Progress Bar	171
		4.3.4	Dial and Gauge	172
	4.4	Use Containers to Wrap Several Components		176
		4.4.1	When to Use a Container	176
		4.4.2	How to Use a Container	177
	4.5	Build Backgrounds to Assist Layout		180
		4.5.1	When to Use Backgrounds	180
		4.5.2	How to Use Backgrounds	181
	4.6	Summary		184

5 UI Components – Advanced ... 185

	5.1	Advanced Charts		185
		5.1.1	Stacked Column Chart	186
		5.1.2	Stacked Bar and Area Chart	189
		5.1.3	Combination Chart	189
		5.1.4	OHLC Chart	191
		5.1.5	Candlestick Chart	202
		5.1.6	Radar Chart	203
		5.1.7	Filled Radar Chart	206
		5.1.8	Tree Map	208
	5.2	Advanced Selectors		210
		5.2.1	Accordion Menu	210
		5.2.2	Icon	217
		5.2.3	Play Selector	219
		5.2.4	Calendar	225
	5.3	Advanced Single-Value Components		228
		5.3.1	Dual Slider	229
		5.3.2	Spinner	230
		5.3.3	Play Control	231
		5.3.4	Value	233
	5.4	Displaying Data in a Table		235
		5.4.1	List View	235

	5.4.2	Spreadsheet Table	239
	5.4.3	Grid	243
5.5	Using Art		246
	5.5.1	Image Component	246
	5.5.2	Shapes	248
	5.5.3	Lines	252
5.6	Use Maps for Geographical Representation		253
	5.6.1	Map Components	253
5.7	Web Connectivity		262
	5.7.1	Connection Refresh Button	262
	5.7.2	URL Button	264
	5.7.3	Reporting Services Button	268
	5.7.4	Slide Show	271
5.8	Others		273
	5.8.1	Local Scenario Button	273
	5.8.2	Trend Icon	275
	5.8.3	Trend Analyzer	277
	5.8.4	History	279
	5.8.5	Print Button	282
	5.8.6	Reset Button	283
	5.8.7	Source Data	284
	5.8.8	Panel Set	287
5.9	Summary		292

6 Data Connectivity Basics 293

6.1	Embedded Excel Spreadsheet		294
	6.1.1	How to Use Excel	295
6.2	Import Data from an Excel File		298
	6.2.1	When to Use	298
	6.2.2	How to Use	298
6.3	Security Issues Related to Accessing External Data		299
6.4	XML Data		301
	6.4.1	When to Use XML Data	304
	6.4.2	How to Use XML Data	305
	6.4.3	Practice	314
6.5	Web Service Connection		322
	6.5.1	When to Use a Web Service Connection	322
	6.5.2	How to Use a Web Service Connection	323

	6.6	Excel XML Map	326
		6.6.1 When to Use an Excel XML Map	327
		6.6.2 How to Use an Excel XML Map	328
	6.7	Summary	330

7 Advanced Data Connectivity — 331

	7.1	Query as a Web Service	331
		7.1.1 When to Use Query as a Web Service	333
		7.1.2 How to Use Query as a Web Service	334
	7.2	Live Office Connection	339
		7.2.1 When to Use SAP BusinessObjects Live Office Connection	340
		7.2.2 How to Insert SAP BusinessObjects Reports to Excel	342
		7.2.3 How to Use SAP BusinessObjects Live Office Connection	343
		7.2.4 Practice	348
	7.3	Crystal Reports Data Consumer	351
		7.3.1 When to Use the Crystal Reports Data Consumer Connection	352
		7.3.2 How to Use the Crystal Reports Data Consumer Connection	352
		7.3.3 Practice	359
	7.4	Flash Variables	362
		7.4.1 When to Use Flash Variables	364
		7.4.2 How to Use Flash Variables	364
	7.5	FS Command	368
		7.5.1 When to Use FS Command	369
		7.5.2 How to Use FS Command	369
		7.5.3 Practice	372
	7.6	External Interface Connection	375
		7.6.1 When to Use an External Interface Connection	376
		7.6.2 How to Use and External Interface Connection	376
		7.6.3 Practice	378
	7.7	LCDS Connection	382
		7.7.1 When to Use an LCDS Connection	384
		7.7.2 How to Use an LCDS Connection	384
	7.8	Portal Data	387

	7.8.1	When to Use Portal Data	387
	7.8.2	How to Use Portal Data	388
7.9	Summary		391

8　Special Features　393

8.1	Drill-Down		393
	8.1.1	When to Use Drill-Down	394
	8.1.2	How to Use Drill-Down	395
	8.1.3	Drill Down from One Chart to Another	396
	8.1.4	Drill-Down on the Same Chart	399
8.2	Make Smart Use of Dynamic Visibility		405
	8.2.1	When to Use Dynamic Visibility	406
	8.2.2	How to Use Dynamic Visibility	408
	8.2.3	Practice	411
8.3	Alerts		416
	8.3.1	How to Use Alerts	417
	8.3.2	Practice	418
8.4	Export		424
	8.4.1	How to Use the Export Functionality	425
8.5	Themes and Colors		430
	8.5.1	How to Use Themes and Color	430
8.6	Summary		438

9　A Comprehensive Hands-On Example　439

9.1	Planning the Dashboard		441
	9.1.1	Plan the Workflow	441
	9.1.2	Plan the UI	442
9.2	Preparing Data		443
	9.2.1	The U.S. Map	444
	9.2.2	The Gauge	445
	9.2.3	The Column Chart	445
	9.2.4	The Line Chart	447
	9.2.5	The Radio Button	450
	9.2.6	The Pie Chart	450
9.3	Organizing Data in Excel		451
9.4	Designing the Dashboard		455

		9.4.1	Position the UI Components	456
		9.4.2	Import the Excel File	456
		9.4.3	Connect to External Data	458
		9.4.4	Adjust the Appearance	459
	9.5	Summary		460

10 Introduction to the Xcelsius SDK ... 461

	10.1	About the Xcelsius SDK	461
	10.2	About Flex	462
	10.3	When to Use the SDK	463
	10.4	How to Use the SDK	464
	10.5	What Can be Done with the SDK?	468
	10.6	SDK Best Practices	471
	10.7	Summary	473

11 Get Started with Custom Component Basics ... 475

	11.1	Developing Basic Add-On Property Sheets		475
		11.1.1	Property Sheet Data Binding	476
		11.1.2	Explicitly Setting Property Values	479
		11.1.3	Explicitly Getting Property Values	480
		11.1.4	Property Sheet Styling	480
		11.1.5	Basic Property Sheet Overview	480
		11.1.6	Proxy.Bind Explained	490
	11.2	Developing Basic Add-On Components		491
		11.2.1	Custom Component Code Walkthrough	491
	11.3	Creating Basic Component Packages		500
	11.4	Summary		503

12 Implement Advanced Custom Add-On Component Features ... 505

	12.1	Implementing Advanced Property Sheet Features		505
		12.1.1	Sub-Element Binding	505
		12.1.2	Persisting Property Sheet Values	508
		12.1.3	Retrieving Persisted Property Sheet Values	509
		12.1.4	Setting Custom Component Property Values	510

Contents

        12.1.5   Retrieving Custom Component Property Values 510
        12.1.6   Generating Reusable Property Sheet Patterns 510
        12.1.7   Communicating with External Data Services 513
        12.1.8   Implementing Advanced Component Features 513
        12.1.9   Additional Packaging Features 524
  12.2 Summary 526

13 Hands-On: Develop Your Custom Add-On Component 527

  13.1 Custom Properties Explained 527
  13.2 Creating the Flex Component and Property Sheet Project 528
  13.3 Creating the Flex Property Sheet 534
  13.4 Creating the Flex Component 540
  13.5 Creating the Flex Test Container 543
  13.6 Creating the Packager and Xcelsius XLX Add-On 543
  13.7 Summary 544

Appendices 545

  A   Tips for Using Xcelsius in SAP BusinessObjects Enterprise or
      other SAP Environment 545
  B   The Authors 581

Index 583

Acknowledgments

Ray Li

The publishing of this book is inspiring to me, but the authoring process was rather challenging. I'd like to take this opportunity to show my sincere appreciation to my family, friends, colleagues, and all those who have helped me during my writing time.

I'd like to say thank you to Evan DeLodder, the co-author of this book. It's my honor to have worked with Evan. His excellent contributions helped to make this a 100% complete book.

Many thanks go to my family for their understanding, support, and happiness for me, which was a great help and endless source of encouragement during my work. Each time I felt tired or in trouble, my family helped calm me down and cheer me up.

Special thanks go to two of my colleagues and best friends, Chris Cai and Robin Guo, who helped me research and develop useful, valuable content. Without their help, I would have spent countless more nights writing the book and keeping it on schedule. Buddies, I can't thank you too much.

I'm also grateful to the many other people who helped me during the process of writing this book, including Erik Herman and Mico Yuk. Erik was so kind and provided support throughout the entire publishing process. He patiently helped me understand and follow the complex process of writing the book. And many thanks to Mico for her help in discussing with me the scope and positioning of this book and recommending it to a group of professionals.

I also want to thank you, the reader of this book. It's my biggest prize when you tell me this book has really helped you.

Evan DeLodder

Writing this book was a great experience made possible by the thorough support and expert knowledge contributed by my co-author Ray Li and by our outstanding editor, Erik Herman at Galileo Press.

Acknowledgments

I'd also like to thank Mico Yuk, SAP Mentor and Xcelsius community champion, who introduced me to Galileo Press and helped to align this writing opportunity.

Finally, I would like to thank the readers of this book. I sincerely hope that the SDK-focused content presented in this book is helpful to those who are new to the Xcelsius 2008 SDK and serves to jumpstart your understanding of the SDK.

Xcelsius® is an outstanding and easy-to-use data visualization tool to create interactive, attractive, and powerful analytics or dashboards with secure and live connections to your real data.

1   Introduction to Xcelsius 2008

This chapter provides a general introduction to Xcelsius 2008, including what it is, what you can do with it, and how it is positioned in the SAP® BusinessObjects™ portfolio. After reading this chapter you should have a basic understanding of Xcelsius 2008 and know whether it's the right tool for your analytic and dashboard requirement.

1.1   What's Xcelsius?

Xcelsius is a flagship product of SAP BusinessObjectsthat allows users to transform plain data into interactive Adobe® Flash®–style visualization. Simply speaking, it's a tool to design dashboards and connect to live data.

As a dashboard designer, you may want to use it to create interactive dashboards to visualize your data and turn data into information. Xcelsius adopts Adobe Flash technology to represent such information which is a cutting-edge technology now widely used in frontend development for its nice visualization and excellent user experience.

The end user, often the decision-makers in a company or department, uses the output of Xcelsius, which is a Flash file or a PowerPoint® slide where the data is represented in a straightforward and attractive way, to make wise decisions either in business or in daily life.

Xcelsius mainly targets enterprise users as an enterprise-level business intelligence (BI) visualization tool. However, no matter who you are, you may find it very useful and easy to use. The users of Xcelsius can be divided into three categories as below:

▶ Enterprise users
Enterprise users, typically the business user and IT department in a large company, can use it to create reliable, visually stunning and accurate dashboards to access timely and relevant business data.

▶ Common users
Common users, such as students, can use it to create fantastic dashboards about anything they're interested in and share it with friends or colleagues.

▶ Developers
The developers or programmers can develop plug-ins or new components using Xcelsius Component SDK for their specific use scenarios. They can then either share the new plug-in with others for free or sell them at some marketplace.

Xcelsius bridges the gap between data analysis and data presentation, empowering anyone who can point and click a mouse to create a professional and compelling dashboard. It's the most powerful data visualization tool in the world, with plenty of users. Both enterprise users and individuals can use it to present data in a clearer style so that information can be delivered in a more effective way. Everyone is a data analyst to some extent.

1.1.1 Installation

Xcelsius can only be installed on Windows systems from Windows® XP, Vista, to Windows 7, either 32-bit or 64-bit edition. However, its output, a Flash file (.swf) or something else containing the Flash file such as HTML and Adobe PDF (Portable Document Format), is supported by all platforms including Mac OS®, Linux®, and so on. You can run it as a stand-alone application using Adobe Flash Player or Adobe AIR® or through a web browser such as Internet Explorer® or Firefox®. To run the flash files, you need have Adobe Flash Player 9.0.151.0 or above installed.

Xcelsius is a multilingual product, supporting more than 10 languages including English, French, German, Spanish, Chinese, Russian, and Korea. It provides an intuitive integrated development environment (IDE) with which you can easily design the dashboard you want by simply dragging and dropping user interface (UI) elements. The user doesn't need to have any programming skill to create a powerful dashboard, thus saving much time for users to get hands-on. Throughout this book you will see exactly what you can do with Xcelsius to present your data, and how.

1.1.2 Relationship with Excel

Xcelsius has much to do with Excel®, as you may have guessed from its name. In fact, Xcelsius treats Microsoft Excel as its one and only direct data source. It was originally designed to turn Excel spreadsheet data into dashboards.

Now Xcelsius is used for creating straightforward and engaging dashboards to convey information in the best way. Some business users may have used Excel spreadsheets to do this, to represent data with tables and graphs. Compared to Excel, Xcelsius provides a better look and feel, is more powerful, and is easier to use. In the meantime, users can benefit from their experience with Excel, because Xcelsius uses Excel as its direct data source, where Excel experts can write Excel formulas (for example, HLookup) to make a powerful visualization.

1.1.3 History

Xcelsius was originally developed by Infommersion, which was founded by Santiago Becerra, Sr., a Harvard MBA and former Booz Allen & Hamilton management consultant, in 2002. In 2005, Infommersion was acquired by BusinessObjects, and in 2006, BusinessObjects released Xcelsius version 4.5, named Crystal Xcelsius. Then in 2008, with SAP's acquisition of BusinessObjects, Xcelsius became a product of SAP. Now the latest version is Xcelsius 2008, which SAP released in 2008, with Service Pack 3 released in December 2009.

With Xcelsius, you can realize the slogan "Your business, visualized."

1.2 What Can Xcelsius 2008 Do?

You can use Xcelsius to create dashboards to visualize information for others or for yourself. The dashboard can be attractive, interactive, and powerful, with rich intuitive information that the consumer can act upon immediately. This can help executives and business users to better understand their business situations and then make wiser decisions. It applies to both enterprise and individual uses of data visualization. For example, a sales manager can use Xcelsius to create a dashboard illustrating the sales info in each region and/or for each product so that the general manager can see the sales info at one glance, and an individual can use Xcelsius to show the monthly expenses and consumption distribution for himself or his family.

Under certain circumstances, the functionalities of Xcelsius 2008 may have some limitation in satisfying your needs. To solve such problems, Xcelsius 2008 provides Flex®-based software development kit (SDK), which you can use to create Xcelsius add-ons for your specific requirements. To do this, you need be familiar with Adobe Flex programming language.

In a word, Xcelsius is used to help you create interactive dashboards to present your data in a fancy way. You can design your dashboard with UI elements connect to your live data with some kinds of data connectivity, and distribute it to others by either exporting it to a local file and sending it to others or hosting the output in a web application server so that the information consumer can access it with a web browser.

Briefly, with the help of Xcelsius 2008, you can:

- Create attractive and interactive dashboards, using several kinds of UI controls such as charts and gauges
- Connect dashboards to your real and live data, using many kinds of data connectivity provided by Xcelsius such as web service connections and XML data
- Distribute dashboards through several media including Flash, Microsoft Office Word and PowerPoint, and SAP BusinessObjects Enterprise
- Develop an Xcelsius add-on component using the Xcelsius SDK when the existing features have limitations for your specific requirement

In the three sections below, we'll talk more about each of Xcelsius' capabilities of UI components, data connectivity, and distribution.

1.2.1 Data Visualization Capabilities

The traditional way to represent data is in tables, including vertical tables, horizontal tables, and cross-tables. When there's too much data, it's difficult to understand and hard to remember. By visualizing data, the consumer can easily and quickly understand the data and even the information behind the data (such as the relative difference between two items) and have an intuitive impression of the visualization, and thus can remember the data easily.

Data visualization transforms data into a form that is comprehensible to the eye, allowing you to analyze data through the sense of sight. An Xcelsius visualization provides insight into complex data and delivers confidence to those who will use it to make decisions. Xcelsius 2008 provides several types of UI elements such as charts, gauges, and maps for data visualization. Each type of UI element may again contain several kinds to satisfy different situations. For example, the elements of type "chart" include pie chart, stacked column chart, and bubble chart. You can use them to convert data from plain sheets or tables to attractive dashboards.

Most charts support drill-down ability, which means that you can drill from summary level to more detailed level. This is very important and helpful in data analysis. By using drill-down, the user can drill from the top level to the more detailed level to find the de facto cause of a problem.

As described in Figure 1.1, using Xcelsius, you can convert data presentation from a static and difficult-to-understand Excel worksheet to a dynamic, visualized, and easy-to-understand presentation.

Figure 1.1 Typical Dynamic Dashboard Created with Xcelsius 2008

In Chapters 4 and 5 you will see detailed descriptions of UI elements provided by Xcelsius 2008. To help you get acquainted with Xcelsius UI elements, here we'll show you some simple examples, categorized into percentage, comparison, and interactivity.

Remember, choosing the right UI element as your display medium is one of the most important steps during the design of a good dashboard.

Percentage

Sometimes you may want to see the percentage or contribution of each item to get a rough idea about who's doing well and who's doing badly at a glance. For example, you can use a pie chart to show the contribution of each region to the company's total sales revenue. Xcelsius 2008 provides pie charts and radar charts for this situation. Figure 1.2 and Figure 1.3 are examples of these two kinds of charts.

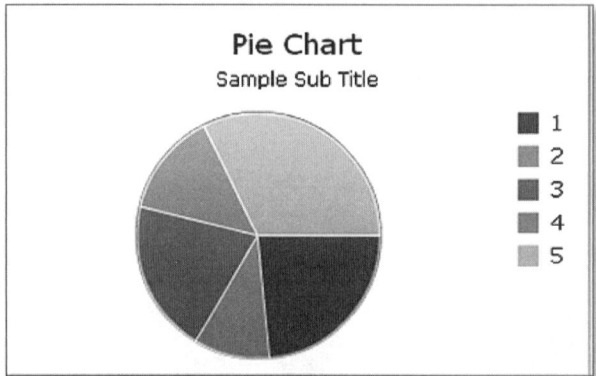

Figure 1.2 A Pie Chart to Visualize Contributions

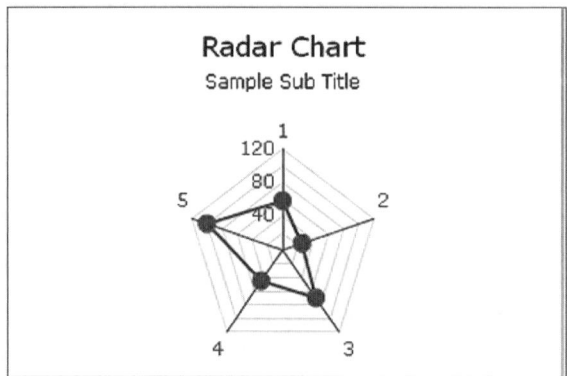

Figure 1.3 A Radar Chart to Visualize Percentages

These figures are just two examples. Note that the title, subtitle, color, legend, and so on can all be customized according to your real data. For more information about these charts and how to use them, please refer to Chapter 4.

Comparison

You use comparison charts when you want to show the differences among several items instead of the contribution of each item.

Xcelsius 2008 provides several charts for comparison such as column charts, bar charts, and stacked bar charts. For example, you can use a column chart to show the sales amounts of all regions or to see the difference between region 1 and region 2. Figure 1.4 and Figure 1.5 show a column chart and a stacked bar chart, respectively.

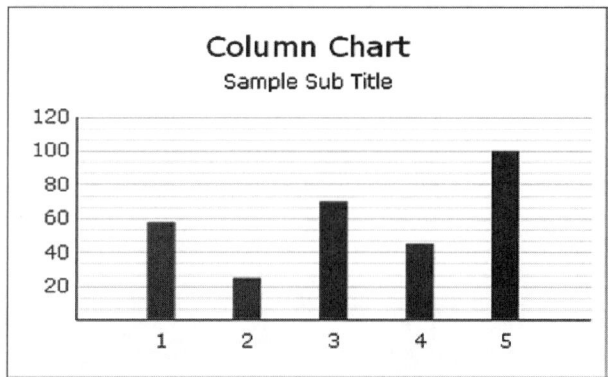

Figure 1.4 A Column Chart to Show a Comparison

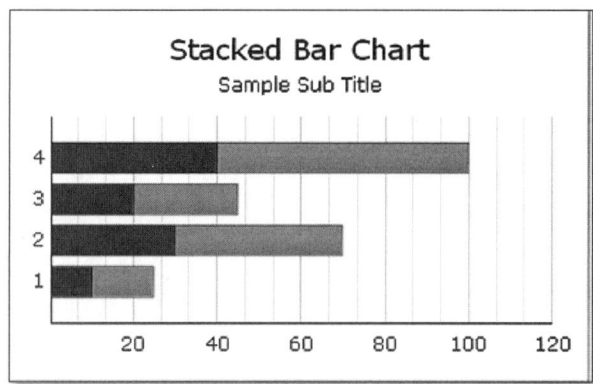

Figure 1.5 A Stacked Bar Chart to Show a Comparison

Xcelsius 2008 also provides bubble charts and XY charts for multidimensional comparison and analysis. For example, you can use a bubble chart to compare a group or series of items based on three different parameters. It has an X-axis and Y-axis to represent the item location over the chart area, and a Z value to represent the item size. For example, you can use this chart to represent market composition, with the X-axis representing the return on investment (ROI) by industry type, the Y-axis representing the cash flow, and the Z-axis representing the market value. Note that the bigger the bubble is, the higher the Z-value is. Figure 1.6 shows a simple bubble chart.

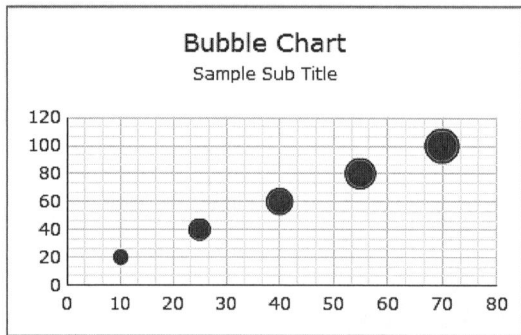

Figure 1.6 A Bubble Chart to Show a Multidimensional Comparison

Interactivity

Xcelsius 2008 provides several UI elements to make your dashboard interactive, including combo boxes, sliders, gauges, maps, fisheye picture menus, and calendars, which are like parameters or filters. The user can see information fit to him by setting corresponding values for these elements. Essentially, such UI components all act as selectors.

For example, you can create a dashboard with a combo box of regions, as shown in Figure 1.7. The end user can then see the information for a specific region instead of all of it by selecting one region from that combo box.

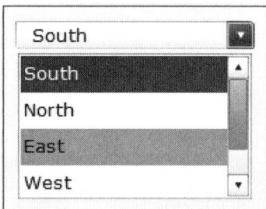

Figure 1.7 A Combo Box for User Selection

Xcelsius 2008 provides maps of many countries as selectors. With these maps, the user can select what region he is interested in in a quite obvious way. Imagine that you need to select a region or city without a map; you have to select from a large list, either a combo box or a radio box. Figure 1.8 shows an example of a U.S. map.

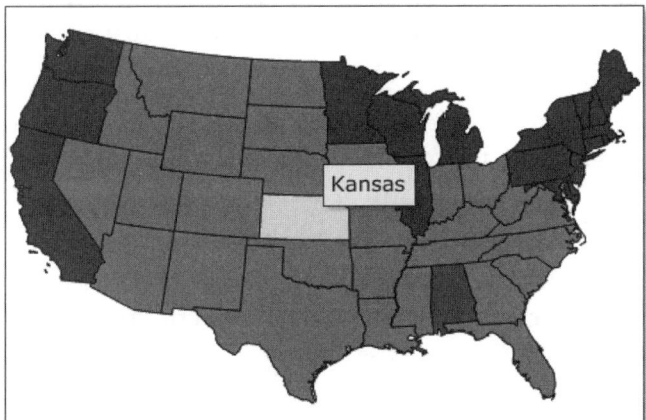

Figure 1.8 A Map for User Selection

A map is a very good choice to display geographical data.

You can also create a gauge-based dashboard, in which gauges are available for the user to set values interactively. Such dashboards are usually used for what-if analysis, when you need to change the conditions on the fly to see what will happen in a particular situation. See Figure 1.9 for an example of gauge usage.

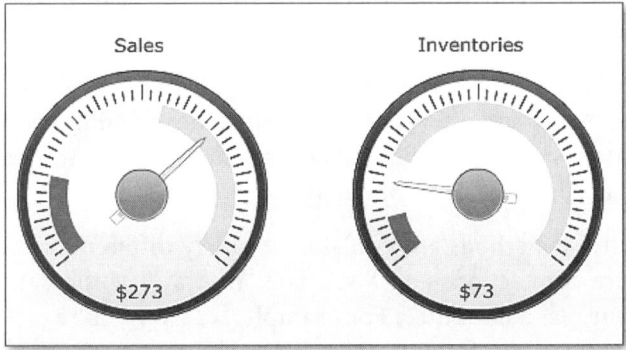

Figure 1.9 A Gauge for Displaying and Setting a Numeric Value

1.2.2 Data Connectivity Capabilities

In the section above we have seen that we can create robust dashboards with Xcelsius 2008 using its rich and attractive UI elements. However, it is not enough to create a dashboard with only static UI elements, which is just a beautiful picture but far from an interactive dashboard. To make it really useful and meaningful, you need to bind the UI elements to your real and live data source. In this way, you enable the dashboard to reflect the real status and convey the accurate, up-to-the-minute information.

Data connectivity is a part of Xcelsius 2008 to solve such a problem. Xcelsius provides several kinds of data connectivity for your specific data sources. In this way you can provide everyone in your organization with live data and manage multiple data sources by controlling all data connections from one central interface.

Generally, there are two ways to reflect real data in your dashboard: Put data in the embedded Excel spreadsheet at design time, or connect to the external data source using one or more kinds of data connectivity.

An Excel spreadsheet is embedded into Xcelsius as the direct data source for UI elements. You can write your data in an Excel spreadsheet file and then import it into Xcelsius, put the data directly into the built-in Excel in Xcelsius' workspace, or connect to dynamic data through data connectivity but map the returned data into the built-in Excel spreadsheet. Remember, Excel is the one and only direct data source for all UI components. You can bind UI elements to a single cell or a range of cells in the embedded spreadsheet.

You can write the data that you know at the time you create the dashboard (design time), such as the metadata of the dashboard like the titles, directly in the built-in Excel spreadsheet and bind it to UI elements. This is usually the case for one-time visualization, when you know the data in advance.

However, in most of the cases, the data will not be available until runtime. Sometimes the data must be processed by some server before being consumed in your dashboard. Sometimes the data resides in another data source such as an XML file. To connect to such data, you need to use data connectivity.

A wide range of data connectivity methods are available to satisfy different environments, such as Web service connections and XML data. You can use the data connectivity to connect to your real data source. For example, let's say you're creating a dashboard to show the sales info for each region in each quarter. The data resides in the database and a Web service hosted in a Web application server at your company is providing the data you require. In this case, you can create a Web service connection to that Web service to request data.

1.2.3 Distribution

Your dashboard is designed to communicate information in the best way. Usually, the dashboard is designed is to be consumed by someone else. With Xcelsius 2008, you can export your dashboard into many formats so that it can be distributed through several kinds of media. The available distribution methods are explained below.

- You can export the dashboard to Macromedia Flash, Adobe AIR, or HTML so that it can be viewed stand-alone or from a web browser.
- You can also export it to PDF or Microsoft Office documents including Word, Outlook, and PowerPoint so that you can send your dashboard via email or present your dashboard during a speech. In this way you can leverage the large installation base of Microsoft Office.
- If you are an SAP BusinessObjects Enterprise user, you can also export it to the SAP BusinessObjects platform. By doing so you can make use of the security settings provided by SAP BusinessObjects Enterprise, so that only people you permit have the right to access your dashboard, and the data they see will depend on their roles.

1.3 Reasons to Choose Xcelsius

So far, you have gotten some idea about what amazing dashboards you can create with Xcelsius 2008 with its rich UI elements and data connectivity. In the following chapters you will see more detailed information about what you can do with Xcelsius 2008 and how. Before that, let's check some reasons to choose Xcelsius as your dashboarding tool.

- It's powerful.
  By using cutting-edge technology, Xcelsius provides the best visualization effect and user experience. With several kinds of data connectivity, such as Web services and XML data, you can connect to almost any kind of data source.
- It's easy to use.
  Xcelsius offers a wide range of UI components such as pie charts, candlestick charts, accordion menu, and maps, and you need simply drag and drop the

components to create a professional dashboard. It uses almost everyone's daily tool, Microsoft Excel, as its direct data source and provides a built-in Excel. In this way, you can easily bind the UI components to a single cell or a range of cells in the Excel spreadsheet.

- It's extensible and growing.
  Xcelsius brings with it a wide range of UI components and data connectivity methods, but sometimes you may encounter a scenario where you need something new. Xcelsius is extensible in that it provides a software development kit (SDK), which you can use to create your custom UI components and data connectivity. Moreover, some companies are working on developing a new component, and there are many active forums about how to use Xcelsius. Also, SAP keeps releasing new features to Xcelsius.

1.4 Xcelsius in the SAP BusinessObjects Portfolio

Xcelsius is the dashboard and visualization component in the SAP BusinessObjects portfolio. In the reporting category, SAP BusinessObjects provides three outstanding tools: Crystal Reports®, SAP BusinessObjects Web Intelligence, and Xcelsius. Among them, Crystal Reports is for enterprise reporting, SAP BusinessObjects Web Intelligence is for ad-hoc query designer, and Xcelsius is for analysis.

Xcelsius can work with several other SAP BusinessObjects products in a business intelligence (BI) solution, such as Crystal Reports, SAP BusinessObjects Web Intelligence, SAP BusinessObjects Universe Designer, and BusinessObjects Enterprise, as explained below.

Xcelsius can consume data from Crystal Reports or SAP BusinessObjects Web Intelligence with the help of SAP BusinessObjects Live Office. You can create a Crystal Reports report within a Microsoft Excel document after installing SAP BusinessObjects Live Office. The Excel document can then be used as a data source for Xcelsius. Of course, you can also export your Crystal Reports report directly into an Excel file.

A special kind of data connectivity, Crystal Report Data Consumer, can also be used to integrate Xcelsius with Crystal Reports 2008, as will be explained in Chapter 7.

Xcelsius can also consume data from a universe with the help of Query as a Web Service (QaaWS), another SAP BusinessObjects product that exposes data from a universe query into a standard Web service.

Xcelsius can be exported to an SAP BusinessObjects Enterprise system, thus distributing the dashboards to other users in the organization and making use of SAP BusinessObjects Enterprise security mechanisms to control users' access. Other SAP BusinessObjects Enterprise users can access then the dashboard through a browser from the BI portal, if they are permitted to.

1.5 Summary

In this chapter we introduced Xcelsius 2008 as a powerful yet easy-to-use tool to design dashboards and its targeted designer and end user. As to its functionalities, we talked about its rich set of UI elements and included some figures in the hope of giving you a rough idea about what it can do. We also talked about its data connectivity to connect to external live data and how to distribute it to other users in several kinds of formats.

As a designer, you need to understand how to use Xcelsius 2008 to create efficient, attractive, and powerful dashboards.

2 Get Familiar with Xcelsius 2008

Xcelsius provides an intuitive integrated development environment (IDE) for creating dashboards. You lay out the UI components, create data connectivities, and do the data binding with the embedded Excel spreadsheet, all inside the IDE. This chapter will illustrate all of the elements of Xcelsius 2008 that you will work with to help you get acquainted with it, including menus, toolbars, and the canvas.

After reading this chapter you will understand the purpose of each command in Xcelsius 2008 and know how to adjust settings in your dashboard.

Figure 2.1 shows the components of Xcelsius 2008, including the menus, toolbar, Components Browser, canvas, Properties sheet, and embedded Excel spreadsheet.

In the rest of this chapter, we'll explain all of these features separately, including their purposes and how to use them. Now, let's begin the exploratory journey.

2.1 Menu

The menu area lies in the first row of the Xcelsius 2008 designer workspace. We explain the items in the following sections.

2.1.1 File

This is the most comprehensive menu in Xcelsius 2008. You can create, open, save, export, or print your dashboard through this File menu, as shown in Figure 2.2. Xcelsius preferences such as language, default theme, and preset size are also set here.

2 | Get Familiar with Xcelsius 2008

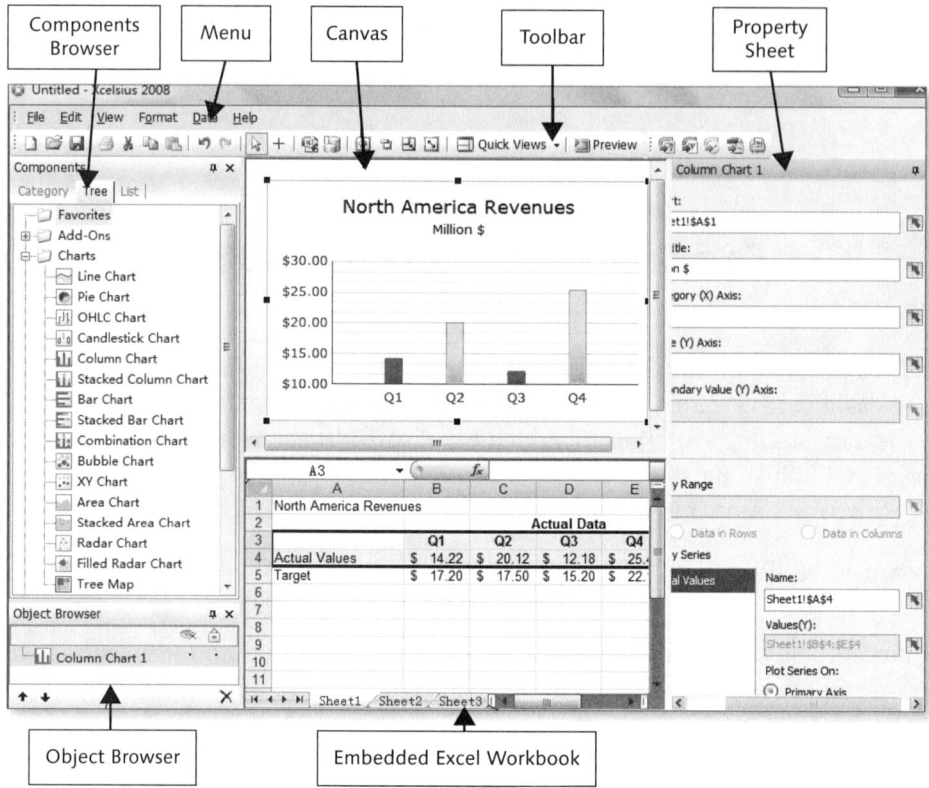

Figure 2.1 Components of an Xcelsius Workspace

New

This is a command group including New and New With Spreadsheet. You use the New command to create a new dashboard from scratch. After selecting this command, you will see an empty canvas and empty Excel spreadsheet embedded in your Xcelsius workspace, often below the canvas.

By selecting New With Spreadsheet, you are to create a new dashboard and in the meantime import data from an existing Excel file (.xls or .xlsx) into Xcelsius. After selecting this command, you will see an empty canvas and be prompted to select an Excel file, the data of which will then be imported into the embedded Excel spreadsheet.

Note that the existing Excel file is only used at import time. When the data has been imported, Xcelsius has nothing to do with it any more. Changes to that file will not affect your dashboard. You can even delete the original file. This also means that changes to the original Excel file will not be reflected in Xcelsius. If you want to get the latest content in the Excel file, you have to import it again from the Data menu, which we'll explain shortly.

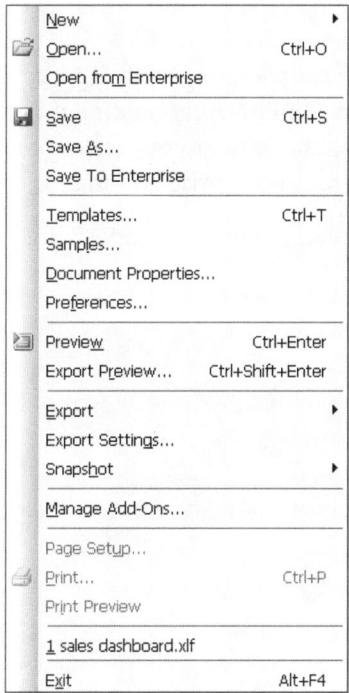

Figure 2.2 The File Menu

Open/Save/Save As

You use the Open command to open an existing Xcelsius dashboard definition file (.xlf) from your file system, either locally or on a network location. Similarly, you use the Save or Save as… command to save your design as an Xcelsius dashboard definition file.

After you select the Open command, a dialog will prompt you to choose an Excel file. What folder is displayed by default can be customized in the Preferences menu item, to Last Folder Open or always to a specified folder.

If the Xcelsius dashboard definition file you opened is not of the same version as your Xcelsius software, you will see a warning message showing the risk.

Open from Enterprise/Save To Enterprise

The "enterprise" here refers to an SAP BusinessObjects Enterprise system. Besides a file system as mentioned above, you can also open an existing Xcelsius dashboard definition file (.xlf) from your SAP BusinessObjects Enterprise system with the command Open from Enterprise or save it to an SAP BusinessObjects Enterprise system using the command Save to Enterprise.

You may want to use these commands when you are collaborating with your colleagues in designing a dashboard. You can use the Save to Enterprise command to save your design to SAP BusinessObjects Enterprise so that you or your colleagues can open it in Xcelsius Designer later via the Open From Enterprise command.

When you select either command, you will be prompted to log on to an SAP BusinessObjects Enterprise system, as shown in Figure 2.3.

Figure 2.3 The Dialog to Log on to SAP BusinessObjects Enterprise

> **Note**
> You need the license of the Xcelsius Enterprise edition to use this command. Otherwise, it will be disabled (in gray).

Templates

Xcelsius 2008 provides several well-designed templates so that you can give your dashboard a strong start. Obviously, the layout, including the color, size, and position, is very important to an attractive and professional dashboard. Xcelsius 2008 provides templates in several categories such as finance, government, HR, and sales.

A template is a fully functional dashboard with predefined layout and data. In some cases, all you need to do before using a template as your working dashboard is update the data in the embedded spreadsheet.

When you select this command, you will see a dialog showing all available templates, as shown in Figure 2.4.

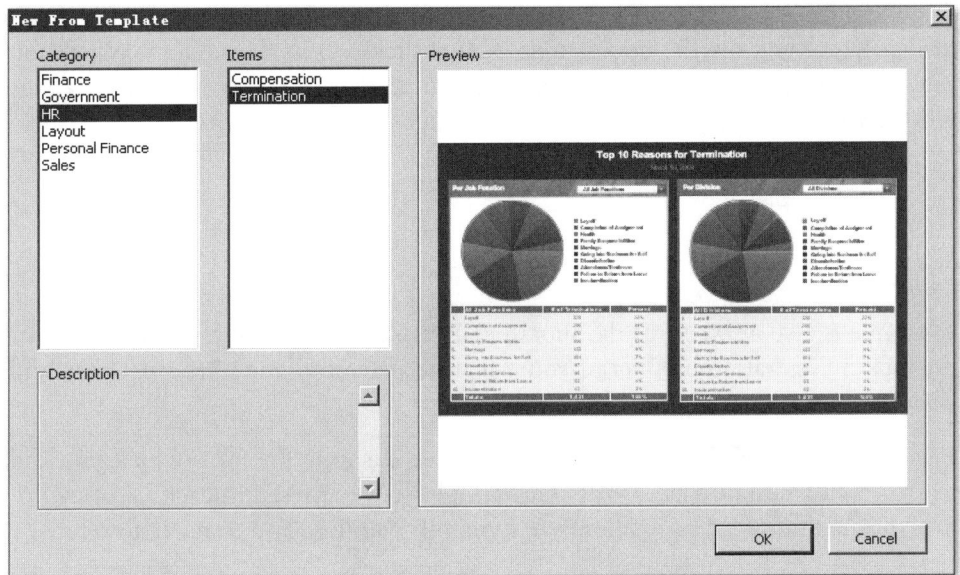

Figure 2.4 Available Templates in Xcelsius 2008

You can navigate through the dialog to find the template that best fits your requirements. When you have selected a template and clicked the OK button, the template, as a common Xcelsius dashboard, is opened in your workspace with all of the UI elements copied to your canvas and the data to your embedded spreadsheet.

Choosing a template means creating a new dashboard from the template. You may treat this operation as New from a Template, compared to the New menu item, which means a new dashboard from scratch. If you are clicking this menu item when editing your own dashboard, you will be asked if you want to save your changes to the old dashboard. That is, if you want to take advantage of a template in the process of designing your dashboard, you have to start from the template to begin with.

As mentioned before, Xcelsius 2008 templates are common Xcelsius dashboard source files with the .xlf extension. They are copied to your file system during installation. Typically, you can find them in *XCELSIUS_INSTALL_DIR/assets/template*, for example, C:\Program Files\Business Objects\Xcelsius\assets\template.

You can add your custom template or category to Xcelsius 2008 by adding a dashboard definition file (.xlf) and its corresponding output, a Flash SWF file, to a folder in the template directory as mentioned above. The next time you launch Xcelsius, you will see the new template after clicking this menu item. When you select this template, the corresponding definition will be opened in your Xcelsius workspace.

Note that for this to work, the name of the Flash file should be identical to that of the definition file.

Samples

A sample is also an Xcelsius dashboard source file with an .xlf extension. Its purpose is to illustrate the effect of some feature delivered with Xcelsius 2008 and how to use it.

Xcelsius 2008 provides many kinds of sample dashboards, from which you can learn how to design dashboards. The samples cover most important features of Xcelsius, including alerts, drill-down, dynamic visibility, and trend analyzer.

These samples are also fully functional, with both UI components and data. You can preview one to see the effect, and check the properties of each component to find out how it's designed. You can then use that feature in your future design.

When the Sample command is selected, a dialog will prompt you by showing all of the available samples, as illustrated in Figure 2.5. You can click any category in the Category list to see items belonging to that category displayed in the Items list. To the right of the dialog is a preview of the sample dashboard, and on the bottom left is the description.

When you have selected a sample and clicked the OK button, the sample dashboard will be opened in Xcelsius, as displayed in Figure 2.6. You can then check how it's designed to learn from it or continue your design on top of it.

Menu | 2.1

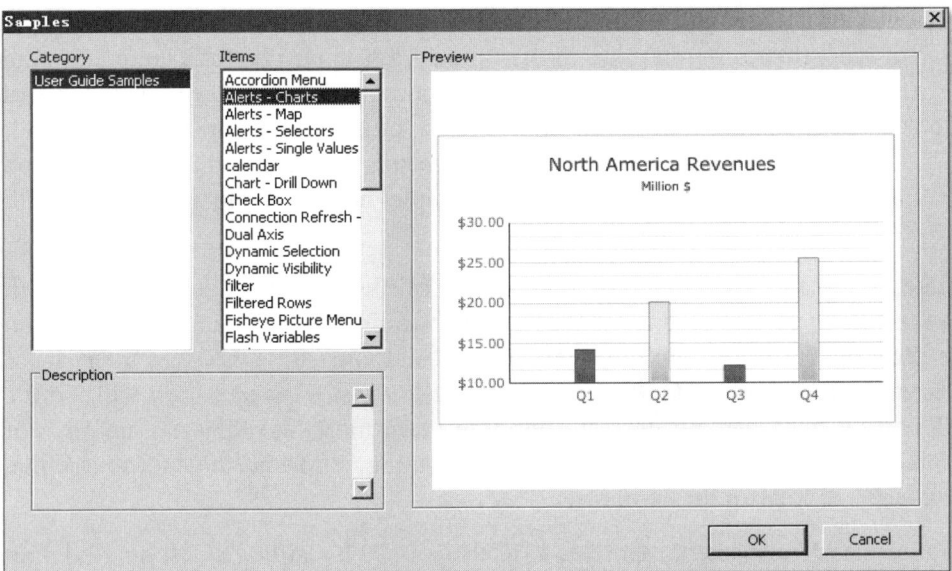

Figure 2.5 Available Samples in Xcelsius 2008

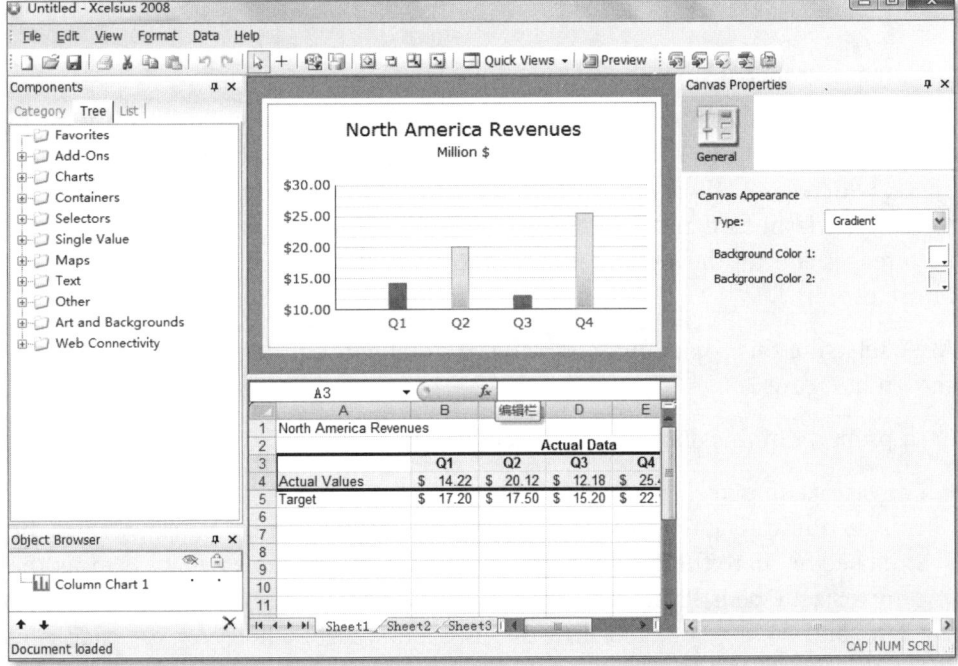

Figure 2.6 Your Workspace After Selecting a Sample

37

You may find that samples are similar to templates and wonder why they are separated. Well, their difference lies in their purpose. The purpose of a template is the appearance, showing how to define the dashboard layout to make your dashboard look professional. It focuses on high-level layout. Samples, on the other hand, focus on some specific functionalities of Xcelsius 2008, showing you what you can achieve with Xcelsius and how, for example, how to create a dashboard with drill-down and trend analysis capabilities.

Like a template, a sample is also a common Xcelsius dashboard definition file with an .xlf extension. These files are copied to your file system during the installation of Xcelsius 2008. You can find them at *XCELSIUS_INSTALL_DIR/assets/samples*, for example, *C:\Program Files\Business Objects\Xcelsius\assets\samples*. You will see the definition file (.xlf) and its corresponding Flash file (.swf) for each sample. For some samples with external data sources, you may also find the data source file, typically an XML or an Excel file.

You can add your custom samples to Xcelsius 2008 by adding a dashboard definition file (.xlf) and its corresponding Flash file (.swf) to the samples directory as mentioned in the paragraph above. The next time you launch Xcelsius, you will see the new sample with the name of the Flash file.

Document Properties

You use this command to set the document properties of the dashboard you are currently working on, such as canvas size and description. Compared to preferences, which we'll talk about later, your changes to document settings only affect the current dashboard and will disappear the next time you start up Xcelsius, while Preferences control the global settings of Xcelsius that will be always effective for future use.

After selecting this command, you will see a dialog to set document properties as shown in Figure 2.7.

Each property of this dialog is explained below.

- Canvas size in pixels
    You set the canvas size of your current dashboard here. The canvas will be stretched or cut to the specified size. Xcelsius 2008 provides two ways to set the canvas size. One is Preset Size, including 160 * 160, 320 * 320, 640 * 640, 800 * 600, and 1024 * 768, and the other is Custom Size, where you can manually set the width and height to fit your requirements. Note that the size is in pixels.

You may only want to set the canvas size here when there's some strict requirement for the size of your dashboard. Most of the time, to adjust the canvas size, you can use the four buttons of Increase Canvas Size, Decrease Canvas Size, Fit Canvas to Components, and Fit Canvas to Window, on the toolbar which will be explained in Section 2.3.

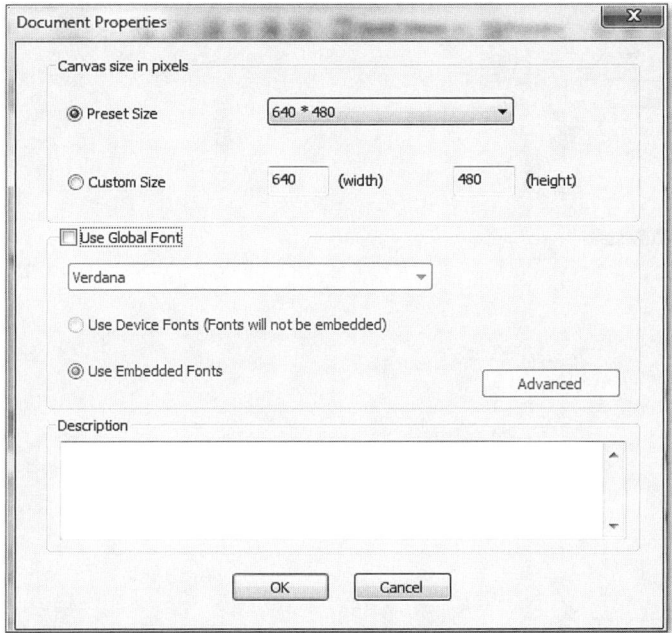

Figure 2.7 Properties in the Document Properties Dialog

- Description
  You can write some words here to describe the current dashboard, such as the purpose and the development status, so that when you or someone else opens your dashboard later in Xcelsius, you can recall what it's about.

> **Note**
> The description will only appear here when the user selects the Document Properties with your dashboard opened in Xcelsius. It will not appear anywhere in the exported Flash file or the file properties.

- Font
  With Xcelsius 2008, you can set fonts for all texts in your dashboard to make it

look better and easier to read. After selecting the option Use Global Font, you can set the default font for the texts of all of the UI components, which is Verdana by default. For example, if you select this option and select the font Arial as illustrated in Figure 2.8, then the font of all of the text parts, such as title and text, of all of the UI components in this dashboard will be Arial. You can check this in the Appearance – Text in the Properties panel of any UI component.

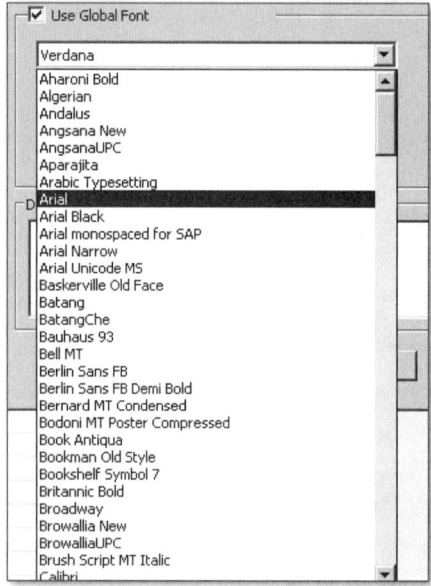

Figure 2.8 Customize the Default Font for All UI Components

After selecting Use Global Font, you can choose whether to use device fonts or embedded fonts for your dashboard, as displayed in Figure 2.9.

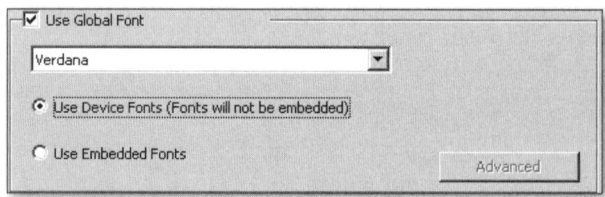

Figure 2.9 Using Device or Embedded Fonts

Use Device Fonts (Fonts Will Not Be Embedded) is the default option used by Xcelsius 2008. It is recommended when creating dashboards that require the extended character set as defined by Unicode.

As the label "Use Device Fonts" indicated, the fonts are not embedded into the generated SWF file. At runtime, the Adobe Flash player will render the True-Type font you selected for each UI component, using those installed on the machine where the Flash player is installed. Device fonts also let you use different fonts for different components within one dashboard.

However, depending on the TrueType fonts installed on the end user's machine, the fonts may not display properly. For example, if you choose Courier New for the title of a pie chart and select Use Device Fonts, but the end user's machine has no such font installed, the text may behave badly at runtime.

The Use Embedded Fonts option generates the characters from the TrueType font you select and embeds them into the output SWF file. Because the font is embedded in the SWF file, it displays properly regardless of whether the user has the TrueType font installed. What's more, the texts of your dashboard display exactly the same on any machine.

However, this option increases the size of the output file and the time required to load or render the dashboard.

> **Note**
> Asian character sets are not supported with embedded fonts due to the large number of characters they require. You must select Use Global Fonts for situations where you are using Asian characters in your dashboard.
>
> Also, if you select Use Embedded Fonts, you cannot change text fonts through the Property panel of a UI component. All texts in your dashboard will use the default font you selected.

Preferences

You set Xcelsius global preferences through this command, such as the display language, the default theme, and the default open folder. Let's talk about them each.

Document

Figure 2.10 shows the available properties you can set in this tab.

Similar to document properties, you can set the canvas size here, which will take affect not only in the current dashboard you are designing but also each time Xcelsius is launched.

2 | Get Familiar with Xcelsius 2008

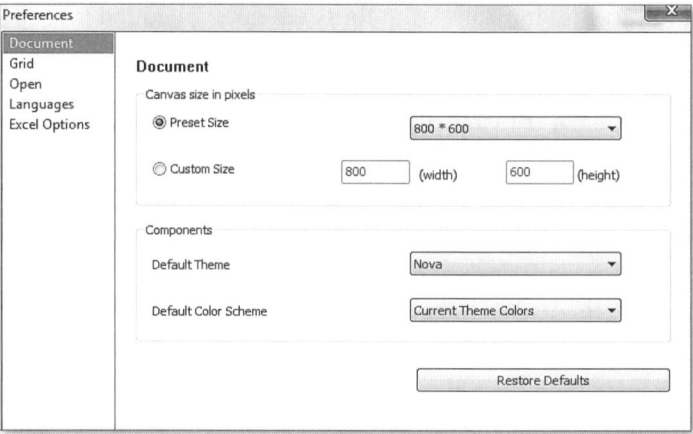

Figure 2.10 Document Preferences

When the canvas size is set both here and in document properties, the one set in document properties takes precedence.

You can also set the default theme and default color schema here. For an explanation of the theme and color schema, please refer to Section 2.2.3 and Chapter 8.

If you have accidentally made any changes to the settings, you can click the Restore Defaults button to revert to the default settings. This button is always available in the Preferences window.

Grid

Here you set whether to show gridlines on the canvas and snap components to them. The width and height of the grid are also set here (Figure 2.11).

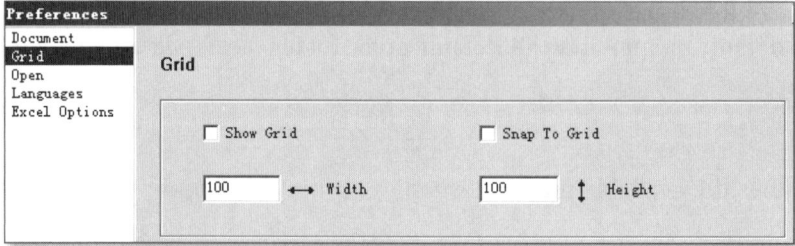

Figure 2.11 Properties to define for Grid.

If you want to show the grid in the canvas to help position and align the UI components, select Show Grid. After that, you can set the width and height of the grid.

For example, if Show Grid is selected with a width of 20 and height of 30 (pixels), the canvas will be filled with rectangles of the size 20 * 30. Figure 2.12 shows the grid on the canvas and the Preferences window.

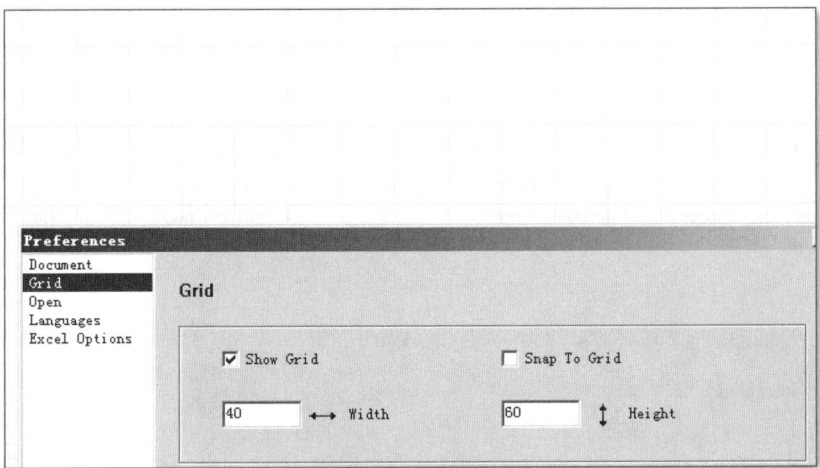

Figure 2.12 The Definition of Grid and the Canvas

You can enable Snap To Grid to help align components on the canvas. When this option is selected, the components have to be aligned to the gridlines. This can help you align components in a particular direction.

Open

With this command you can set the default folder that you will be prompted to open when you select FILE • OPEN. There are two options.

One option is Last Folder Open, which means the folder you opened the last time you used Xcelsius. You may want to use this option if you always want to see related dashboards.

The other option is Folder, for you to specify the path you want. With this option, each time you click the Open command, you will see the same folder here. This option is helpful if you are working on several dashboards for one project.

Languages

Xcelsius 2008 is internationalized for users in different countries or regions. English is the default language. You can also use one or more language packs on one machine to see menus and commands for your language. There are more than 10 languages available including French, Germany, Chinese, Japanese, and Russian.

You can use this command to switch the language for your Xcelsius system. This will affect all user interface texts, including the labels of buttons, menus, chart names, and Xcelsius help. Changes to language will take effect when you restart Xcelsius 2008.

> **Note**
>
> The available languages depend on the language packs you selected during Xcelsius 2008 installation. Figure 2.13 shows that one language pack, simplified Chinese, has been installed.

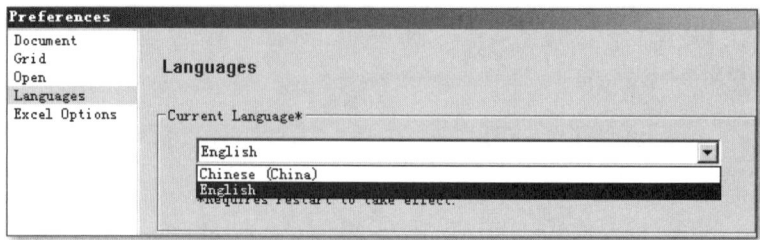

Figure 2.13 Available Languages Depending on Language Packs Installed

Excel Options

Microsoft Excel is the foundation of Xcelsius. Each UI element can only bind to data in the embedded spreadsheet. In other words, Excel acts as the only and direct data source that an Xcelsius element can bind to. You can write data directly in the embedded Excel workbook, put data in another Excel file then import it into Xcelsius, or connect to an external data source using some form of data connectivity and then map it to a cell in the embedded Excel spreadsheet. From this perspective, Excel acts as the bridge between visualization and the backend data.

No matter what way you choose, you are working closely with the embedded Excel. The Preferences window includes some Excel options as displayed in Figure 2.14.

You can set the Maximum Number of Rows that any Excel formula or binding in your dashboard can refer to. For example, you cannot calculate the sum of values across more than the defined rows with the Excel sum function. For data connectivities, you cannot bind the output values to a cell range of more than the defined rows either.

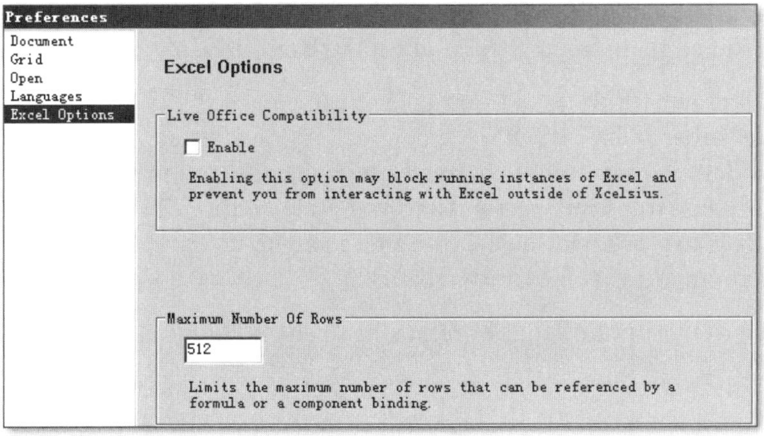

Figure 2.14 Available Excel Options to Customize

One more complex example: Suppose you are using several combo box components in your dashboard for the user to make selections. For the convenience of the end user, you want to limit the size of the candidate items of each selector to 10. Suppose the candidates are listed in rows in the embedded spreadsheet. You can set Maximum Number of Rows to 10. When the user tries to bind a selector to more than 10 rows, Xcelsius will automatically apply the restriction with the warning "Your range has been reduced to the maximum rows allowed."

Note that this number only restricts the maximum rows that can be used in an Excel formula and the bindings of a data connectivity or a UI component. The embedded spreadsheet can still contain as many rows as you want. By default, the number is 512. You can increase or decrease it according to your specific requirements.

The Live Office Compatibility option is only useful for SAP BusinessObjects Enterprise users. You need to enable Live Office compatibility if you want to use data in a Live Office–enabled Excel spreadsheet, which means the data in the Excel spreadsheet is actually a view created from either managed Crystal Reports or managed SAP BusinessObjects Web Intelligence documents deployed on an SAP BusinessObjects Enterprise system.

After you have imported a Live Office–enabled Excel spreadsheet into Xcelsius 2008, you can also make it refreshable against the source data by configuring the Live Office connection in the Xcelsius 2008 Data Manager. In this way you can get live data from a Live Office–enabled Excel file from your dashboard, compared to importing data from a common Excel file, where the data is static after it's imported, and you need to reimport the file to get the latest data.

However, there's a drawback to this. When Live Office compatibility is enabled, the performance of other Microsoft Office programs may be affected, and Microsoft Office files might not open or work correctly. If you choose not to enable Live Office compatibility but still want to use data from a Live Office document, the recommended way is to work with Live Office in a stand-alone Excel file outside of Xcelsius and then import that file into Xcelsius.

Note that a change to this option requires restarting Xcelsius 2008 to take effect.

Preview

You can switch from design mode to preview mode by clicking this command. In preview mode you can see how your dashboard will behave for the end user. This can help you adjust the design of your dashboard. If you have experience in code debugging, you may find these modes to be very similar.

The Adobe Flash Player is required to preview your dashboard. To return to design mode, just click this command again.

Export Preview

You can click this command to quickly view how your dashboard behaves in a stand-alone Adobe Flash Player. Xcelsius generates a temp Flash (.swf) file and launches Adobe Flash Player in a separate window to play it. The generated Flash (.swf) file is located in a temporary folder in your user directory, for example, *C:/Users/ray/AppData/Local/Temp/XC_124/*.

Export

Export is an important feature of Xcelsius 2008. The dashboard is designed to communicate information with others. You can export your dashboard to a file in several kinds of media. Depending on the consumer's environment, you need to select one medium to export your dashboard to. You can rest assured that no matter what type you choose, the exported dashboard will behave completely the same as what you see in Preview or Export Preview.

After clicking this command, you will see a list of available media types as displayed in Figure 2.15.

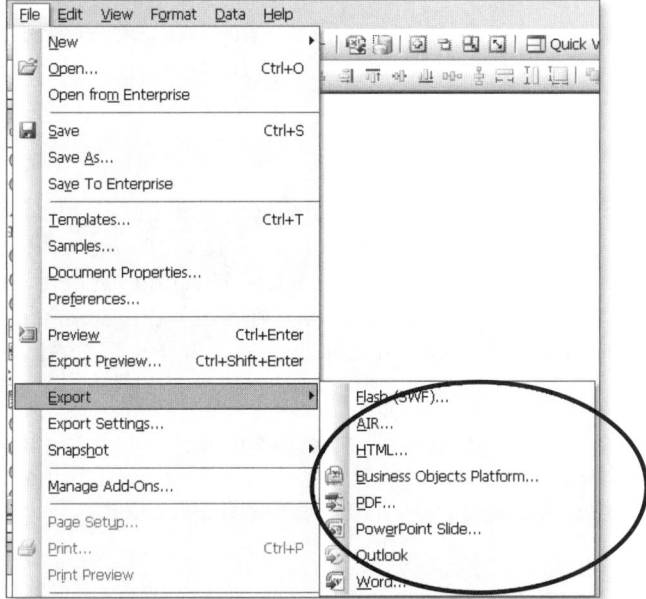

Figure 2.15 Available Media Types for Export

You can choose an appropriate type based on your requirement and the environment in which it will be used. we'll provide detailed explanations about when and how to use each type in Chapter 8.

Export Settings

This command is used to specify what data in what Excel file you want to use for the exported dashboard. You can choose to use current Excel data or in another external Excel file, as displayed in Figure 2.16:

Figure 2.16 Choose Data for the Exported Dashboard

Use Current Excel Data
This is the default option. The exported dashboard will use the data you see in the embedded Excel spreadsheet, and it will function exactly the same as what you see in Preview mode.

Use Another Excel file
Sometimes, the data source for the dashboard is unavailable to you, the dashboard designer, at first. In this case, you can work against sample data in the embedded spreadsheet, which has exactly the same format as the actual Excel file. When the real data is ready in another Excel file, you can specify it through this command and then export the dashboard. The end user will then see your dashboard reflecting the actual data.

For example, you may need to create a sales distribution dashboard for the month. You know what the data is like in Excel, but the data has not come yet. You can create the dashboard with sample data and export it when you get the data.

Snapshot

You use this command to take a snapshot of your dashboard. In preview mode, you can interact with the visualization the same way an end user will. If you find a scenario or combination of settings interesting or useful, you can take a snapshot of the visualization to save the specific status.

Snapshot is similar to Export in that both commands export the dashboard to a certain type of file such as Flash or PDF. The difference lies in the initial scenario for the consumer: The default values and what components are visible for an exported dashboard are set in design mode, while you set those for a snapshot in preview mode. Another difference is that the Export command is only available in design mode, while Snapshot is only available in preview mode.

The export methods include:

- Current Excel Data
  Xcelsius will generate an Excel spreadsheet file (.xls) with the current data values. This file may be different from what you see in the embedded Excel spreadsheet. For example, if you bind a text input to an Excel cell and change its value in preview mode, the generated Excel file will have the value you entered. This can be a very useful tool for diagnosing dashboards that are not performing as expected.

- PDF

  An Adobe PDF file is generated with the current state of the components. The dashboard is still interactive, with all of the functionalities.

- PowerPoint Slide

  A Microsoft PowerPoint file with one slide that contains a Flash (SWF) file with the current state of the components is generated. Similar to what you see via the menu path EXPORT • POWERPOINT SLIDE, one PowerPoint file and one SWF file are generated.

- Outlook

  A Microsoft Outlook email that attaches the Flash (SWF) file with the current state of the components is generated. Similar to what you see via EXPORT • OUTLOOK, Xcelsius generates a temp SWF file, launches Outlook to create a new email message, and attaches the SWF file.

- Flash

  A Flash (SWF) file with the changes made in preview mode is generated.

- HTML

  Similar to what you see via EXPORT • HTML, one HTML file and one Flash (SWF) file with the current state of the components are generated. You may choose this option to put the HTML file in a Web server so that others can access your dashboard with a web browser.

Manage Add-Ons

An add-on is an Xcelsius extension for UI or data connectivity. It can be developed by SAP BusinessObjects, SAP BusinessObjects partners, or customers using Xcelsius 2008 Component SDK, which will be covered in Chapters 10 to 12. An add-on, either a custom UI component or a data connectivity, is a file with an .xlx extension.

After clicking this menu item you will see the Xcelsius Add-On Manager, where you can install a new Xcelsius add-on by clicking the Install Add-On button and browsing to the .xls file.

Note that there's a link, Get More Add-Ons, on the bottom left. Clicking this link will direct you to the Xcelsius Add-On Marketplace website at *http://www.ondemand.com/information/xcelsius.asp*, where you can download add-ons for your unique business requirements or sell add-ons that you have developed.

You can also view the details of an existing add-on by simply clicking on it. As shown in Figure 2.17, the name, description, and other information are displayed so that you can easily understand the purpose of that add-on and then decide whether or not to use it.

To uninstall a custom add-on, just click the Remove Add-On button. You will be prompted to confirm before actually removing an add-on.

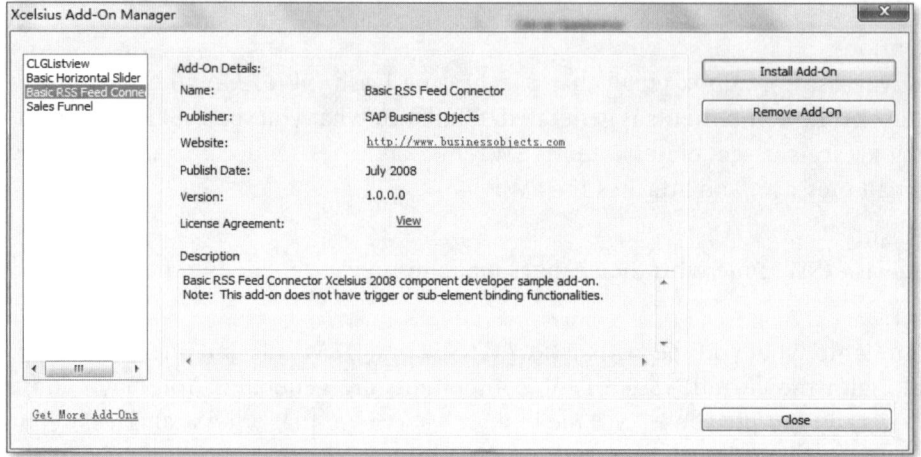

Figure 2.17 Details of an Installed Custom Add-on

2.1.2 Edit

The Edit menu is used to undo and redo and other copy and paste operations.

Undo/Redo

Xcelsius 2008 supports many levels of undo and redo. For example, you may want to use the Undo command to cancel an operation when you delete a component by accident.

These operations are similar to those in other daily applications, such as Microsoft Office Word. The hotkeys are also common: [Ctrl] + [Z] for Undo and [Ctrl] + [Y] for Redo.

Copy/Paste/Cut/Delete/Select All

These operations are also very common. You may want to copy or cut a component in the canvas and then paste it to move or duplicate it. For example, when multiple Input Text components in the logon screen of your dashboard need to have the same styles, it's easier to adjust the appearance of one component and copy it for others, instead of dropping new components into the canvas and adjusting them again.

Xcelsius also provides a command to select all components in the canvas: Select All. You can use this command when you want to operate on all of the components, for example, to delete or make alignments.

The hotkeys are also the same as those in other daily applications such as Microsoft Office Word, for example, [Ctrl] + [C] for Copy, [Ctrl] + [X] for Cut, [Ctrl] + [V] for Paste, [Del] for Delete, and [Ctrl] + [A] for Select All.

2.1.3 View

Commands in this menu are used to show or hide certain parts of Xcelsius 2008, such as the Components Browser and Toolbars, as shown in Figure 2.18.

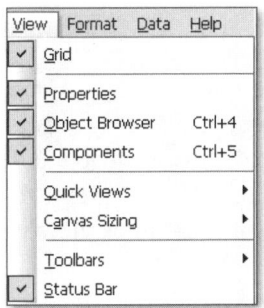

Figure 2.18 View Menu Commands

Grid

Use this command to show or hide grids in the canvas. When this command is selected, you will see grids in the canvas as we showed in Figure 2.12. The grids will disappear when this command is unselected.

Note that the width and height of the grid are set via FILE • PREFERENCES as explained in Section 2.2.1 above.

Properties/Object Browser/Components

There are three important views in the Xcelsius workspace during your design time, which we'll explain in more detail later in this section. Briefly, the three views are:

- Properties
  This view displays the Properties panel to show the properties of the canvas (when no component is selected) or one or more selected components, including titles, data, and colors.
- Components Browser
  This view lists all available Xcelsius components in categories, in trees, or in a list.
- Object Browser
  This view lists all in-use components that have been dragged into the canvas of your dashboard.

You can show or hide each view by selecting the corresponding command. For example, you may want to hide all of them for a larger canvas to position your components but show Object Browser when there are many components in the canvas and you want to select some.

Quick Views

At different design stages, you may want to focus on different aspects of your dashboard. For example, you may focus on adjusting the positioning of all components or the properties of a single component or how the data is retrieved and mapped in the embedded spreadsheet. You can use commands in this menu to only display components you're interested in. The meaning of each quick view is explained below.

- Canvas Only
  As the name indicates, only the canvas is displayed in the center of the screen, allowing you to focus on positioning the components, as shown in Figure 2.19. This is similar to the effect of hiding the views of Properties, Object Browser and Components, and then drag the embedded Excel spreadsheet to the lowest.

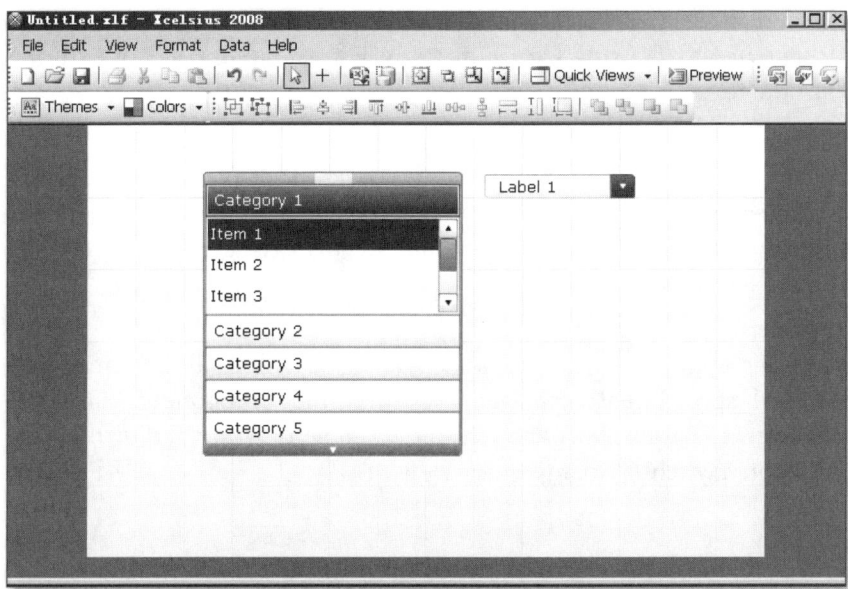

Figure 2.19 Xcelsius Workspace with Canvas Only

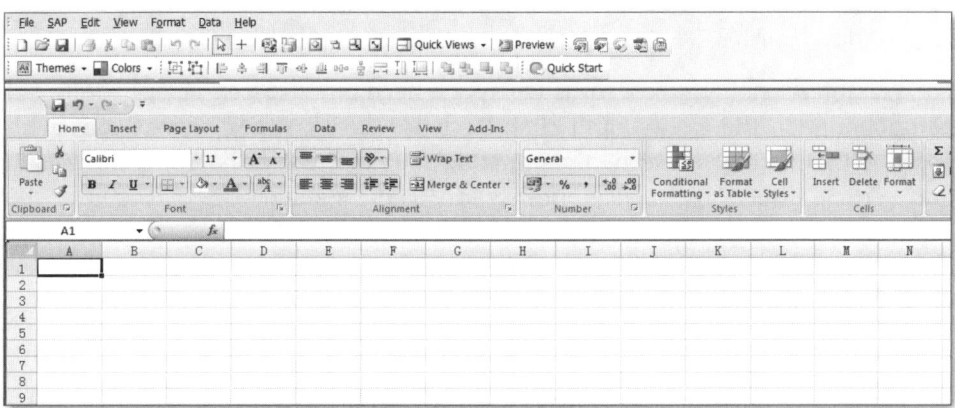

Figure 2.20 Xcelsius Workspace with Spreadsheet Only

- Spreadsheet Only
  When you switch to this quick view, only the embedded Excel spreadsheet is displayed in the screen, as shown in Figure 2.20. You can then focus on:
  - Data binding
    To bind properties of UI components to cells or cell ranges in the spreadsheet, or to map input and output of a data connectivity to the spreadsheet.

- Excel formulas
  To calculate new data using Excel functions. For example, you can edit one cell with the formula =Sum(B1:B5).
- Canvas and Spreadsheet
  As indicated by the name, with this quick view, both the canvas and the embedded spreadsheet are displayed. You may want to switch to this view when you want to check whether the UI components are displaying the right data as entered in the Excel spreadsheet.
- My workspace
  You can use this option to return to the default view, with both the canvas and the embedded spreadsheet displayed. Whether the Components Browser, Object Browser, or Properties panel are shown depends on whether they are displayed before switching to any quick view.

Canvas Sizing

From this menu, you can select Increase Canvas or Decrease Canvas to increase or decrease the canvas size (both in width and in height). You may want to use these commands to adjust the canvas size based on how many components are included in your dashboard.

For example, click Increase Canvas when you need more space to place additional components on the canvas, and click Decrease Canvas when there's too much space left. Note that these two commands alter the size in both the horizontal and vertical directions. That is, both width and height will be changed at the same time. To adjust either width or height but not both, you can use some other methods, either changing the canvas size in Document Properties or using a rectangle component to define the layout and then clicking Fit Canvas to Components, which we'll explain below.

Another two commands, Fit Canvas to Components and Fit Canvas to Windows, are ways to auto-adjust the canvas size. You can first place your components at will on the canvas and then use Fit Canvas to Components so that the canvas is just large enough to hold your components. Sometimes, to make the dashboard look better, you may use Increase Canvas to leave some space or gap at the borders.

Fit Canvas to Windows, on the other hand, adjusts the canvas to the current window size, that is, the size of the current space left for the canvas surrounded by the toolbar and other parts, as illustrated in Figure 2.21.

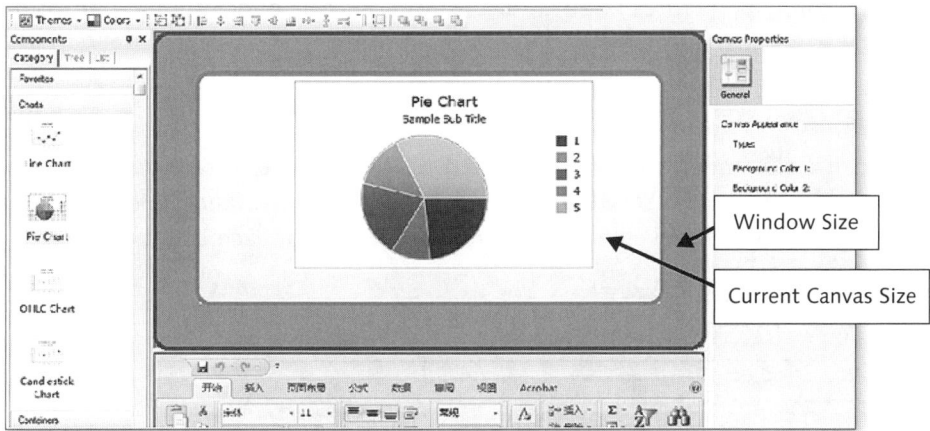

Figure 2.21 Canvas Size and Window Size in Xcelsius Workspace

In this figure, the current canvas size is in the white background color, and the window size is larger, surrounded by the Components Browser to the left, the embedded Excel spreadsheet at the bottom, the Properties sheet to the right, and the toolbar at the top. If you click Fit Canvas to Windows now, the canvas will extend to the whole window, as shown in Figure 2.22.

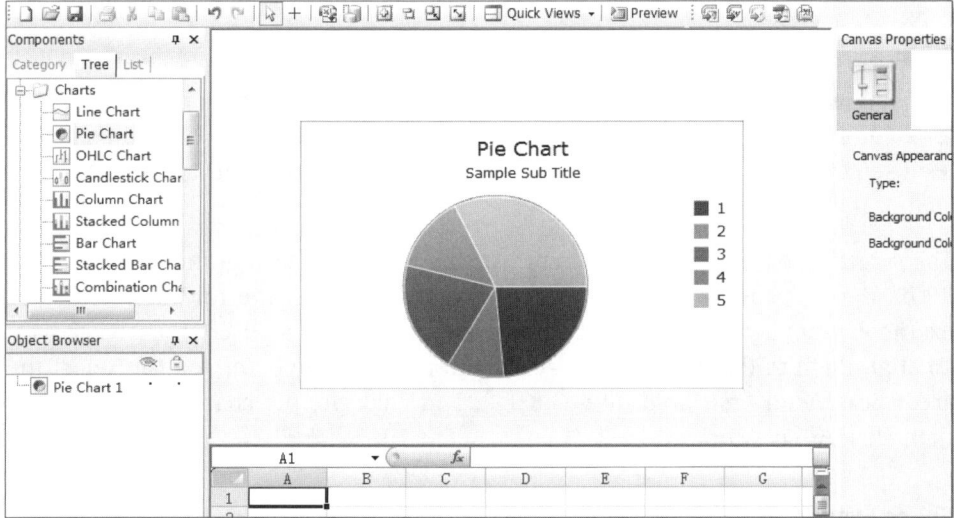

Figure 2.22 Fit Canvas Size to Window

You can compare Figures 2.22 and 2.21 to see the effect of Fit Canvas to Window.

Toolbars

You can use this menu to customize what to display in the toolbar. This menu includes five submenus: Standard, Themes, Export, Format, and Quick Start. See Figure 2.23 for the corresponding parts in the toolbar for each command.

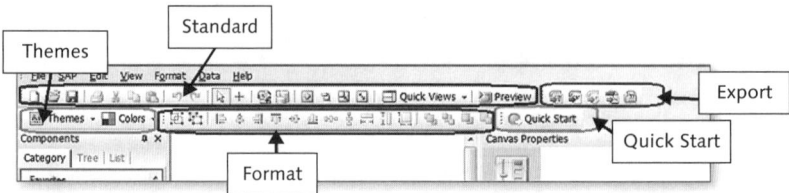

Figure 2.23 Parts of the Toolbar

2.1.4 Format

Commands in this menu are very helpful in positioning the UI components. We'll explain them separately.

Align

Sometimes you may want to make the components align to each other for a neat look and feel. In Xcelsius 2008, you can first select two or more components and then set alignment through the Align command, including align to the left, right, center, top, bottom, and middle.

The selection order is very important for the result of the alignment. In Xcelsius 2008, the first component you select becomes the base line for alignment. For example, you may have dropped an accordion menu and a pie chart in the canvas. To align them to the top with the accordion menu as the base, you can select the accordion menu first, hold down Ctrl, and click the pie chart to select it and then click Align – Top.

Space Evenly

You use this menu to adjust spaces between the center points of multiple UI components so that the spaces are equal. There are two commands in this menu, one to adjust spaces horizontally (Across) and the other to adjust spaces vertically (Down).

Xcelsius adjusts the spaces by summing the horizontal (or vertical if Down is selected) spaces between the center points of every two horizontally (or vertically) adjacent components and calculating the average. Then Xcelsius rearranges the components horizontally (or vertically) with the average space. As a result, you need to select at least three components to use this command. Otherwise, the commands in this menu are disabled.

If you select components that are vertically aligned and click Space Evenly – Across or select components that are horizontally aligned and click Space Evenly – Down, no change is made, because the spaces in that direction are all zero.

> **Note**
>
> The commands will adjust spaces between the center points of components, not their edges.

Make Same Size

As indicated by the name, you can use commands in this menu to make multiple components the same size — width, height, or both. For example, let's say you have dragged one pie chart and one column chart into your dashboard, either reflecting the same data or in a drill-down scenario. For a neat look and feel, you want to make the two components the same size. Instead of resizing them incrementally using the mouse, you can select them and then click Make Same Size and then select Width, Height, or Both.

Similar to alignment, the first component you select becomes the base. For example, if you click component A and then press [Ctrl] to multiselect components B and C and then click Make Same Size – Width, the width of components B and C will be adjusted automatically to be equal to that of component A.

Center in Canvas

There are three commands in this menu: Vertically, Horizontally, and Both. As indicated by the name, you can put your components in the center of the canvas using this menu, centered by width, height, or both.

You may want to use this command to leave equal gaps to the borders of your dashboard. To do this, select one or more components and click this menu. You can easily try this out to better understand the feature.

Order

If you place multiple UI components on the canvas, they may overlap, and parts of certain components become invisible to the user when there's any component in front. In addition to the X (width) and Y (height) coordinates, each component on the canvas has depth that is in the Z direction. The overlapping among components is determined by the relative depths, the default value of which is defined by the order it's dropped into the canvas. With the Order menu, you can change the relative depth of a component, thus changing the overlap relationship.

You use the Command Bring to Front to bring the selected component(s) to the foremost, or the top, level. Correspondingly, Send to Back sends the selected component(s) to the backmost, or the bottom, level, so that it acts as the background of other components. For example, let's say you dragged several components including a pie chart and a background (or image component) to the canvas. You may want to set the background component as the dashboard background by selecting it and clicking Send to Back, and select the pie chart and click Bring to Front.

To change the depth slightly, you can use Bring Forward to move the component one layer closer to the top from its current position. On the other hand, you use Send Backward to move the component one layer closer to the bottom layer from its current position. You may want to use these commands to switch the relative depth of two adjacent components.

Group/Ungroup

You can gather multiple components into one group so that you can move them together without worrying about changing the relative positions by accident. For example, let's say you have perfectly adjusted the relative position of several combo boxes as selectors. Now you want to move them a little down or left. You can select all of them by holding down `Ctrl` and then moving them together. But this is error-prone, and in the future when you want to move them again, you will have to select all of them again. A better solution is to organize them into one group and then click on any of the components to move them all.

To organize multiple components into one group, just select them all and click Group. Then, each time you click one of the components and move it, all components in the group get moved. To ungroup them, just select any component in the group and click Ungroup.

2.1.5 Data

To make your dashboard reflect real and live data, you need to map your real data to the embedded Excel spreadsheet and bind it to UI components with the help of data connectivity. With the Data menu, you can import real data from an Excel file or connect to live data. The available commands in the Data menu are described as follows.

Import

You can use this command to import data from an existing Excel file into the embedded Excel spreadsheet of your design workspace. You may want to use this command when the data is already in an Excel file, typically provided by another department in your company or a third-party provider, and the data will not be updated frequently. For example, maybe the HR department in your company used to use Excel to store employee info such as salary and number of days on leave. Now your company is considering using Xcelsius to visualize data, and you are to create a demo dashboard using the data provided by the HR department.

For SAP BusinessObjects Enterprise users, you can insert the data from Crystal Reports or SAP BusinessObjects Web Intelligence documents into a Live Office-enabled Excel file and use this command to import it into the embedded spreadsheet.

You have to use this command when the data is only available in Excel format but cannot be provided through any of the data connectivities that will be covered in Chapters 6 and 7. For example, the data exists in an old legacy system that provides no application programming interface (API).

On clicking this command, you will be prompted to select an Excel file on your local machine or on a network. The Excel file can be either Office 97-2003 (with an .xls extension) or Office 2007 (with an .xlsx extension). After you have selected an Excel file, the data in all sheets of the file will be copied to the built-in Excel spreadsheet in Xcelsius. Any change you have made to the built-in Excel spreadsheet will be lost.

Note that after import, Xcelsius has nothing to do with that existing Excel file. This has two consequences. First, you can delete or move that file without affecting your dashboard. Second, changes to that existing Excel file will not be reflected automatically in your dashboard. To solve this, you can import the Excel file again, but any changes made to the built-in Excel spreadsheet, such as formulas, will be overwritten by the imported Excel file.

Import from Platform

Sometimes the existing Excel file is not sent to you directly or located in a network. Instead, for security reasons, it may be stored in SAP BusinessObjects Enterprise so that only certain people with required rights can access it. You can use the Import from Platform command to import such an Excel file.

On clicking this command, you will be prompted to enter credentials to log on to an SAP BusinessObjects Enterprise system. On a successful logon, you will see the folder hierarchy in that SAP BusinessObjects Enterprise system where you can navigate to and select an Excel file. After you have selected an Excel file, the data in all sheets of the file will be copied to the built-in Excel spreadsheet in Xcelsius, and any changes you have made to the built-in Excel file will be lost, the same as above.

Export

As mentioned in the two previous sections, you can import the data of an existing Excel file into Xcelsius. On the other hand, you can also export the data in the embedded spreadsheet of your design to another Excel file with this command.

You may want to use this command when you have adjusted the Excel file format, such as what data is put in what ranges within Xcelsius to satisfy the dashboard needs, and you want the data provider to enter data in that format.

For example, let's say you, as a dashboard designer, are working with the HR department, the data provider, to create a dashboard. The HR department delivers the data in an Excel file, but it is very difficult to use in Xcelsius. You then work in Xcelsius to design the UI and where to put the data in the Excel file, such as the employee names, salaries, and last year's average salary. Then you export the data to an Excel file and send it to the HR department. They can then enter the data you require.

Connections

The three commands just described concern data in Excel files. Xcelsius 2008 provides many more ways to connect to external data sources other than Excel, such as Web services and XML data. They can be accessed through this menu.

After clicking this command, you will see the Data Manager, where you can define connections. You can click Add Combo Box to select a connection type, as shown in Figure 2.24.

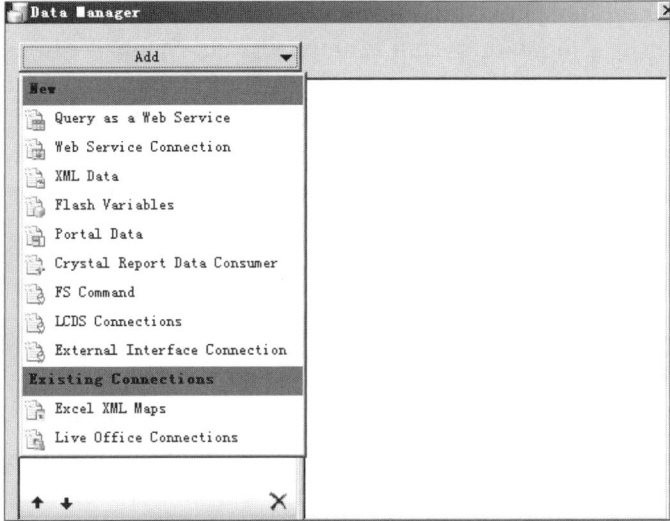

Figure 2.24 Available Connection Types in the Data Manager

You can select a connection type according to your environment and fill in the required parameters in the corresponding pages to define your connection. For example, you need define the service URL, where to bind the input parameters and output results in the embedded Excel spreadsheet, and when to refresh the connection.

You can define several connections of one type such as Web services or XML data. However, for some other types of connection, such as Flash variable, you can only define one connection of that type.

Defined connections will be listed in the Data Manager, where you can change their sequences or delete them. To delete a connection, just select it and click the Delete button at the bottom: ⊠.

2 | Get Familiar with Xcelsius 2008

If you have several connections that are all set to refresh on load, Xcelsius will load them in the sequence defined in the Data Manager. You can change the sequence by selecting a connection and clicking the Move Up or Move Down buttons at the bottom: ↑ ↓. Detailed explanations of the connections will be provided in Chapters 6 and 7.

2.1.6 Help

Like many other SAP products, Xcelsius provides a help document with rich information about how to use Xcelsius 2008. You can launch it from the Xcelsius Help menu. The help document is a file with a .chm (Compiled Help Manual) extension copied to your file system during your Xcelsius installation. You can find it at *%Xcelsius_DIR%/assets/help/locale/%LANGUAGE%/Xcelsius.chm,* for example, *C:\Program Files\BusinessObjects\Xcelsius\assets\help\locale\en\xcelsius.chm.* Based on the language packs you have installed, you may find the help document in each language.

Quick Start

Quick Start is a view that shows resources about how to quickly get familiar with Xcelsius and create simple dashboards with step-by-step guides. When this command is selected (enabled), you will see the Quick Start window in the main window of Xcelsius, often in the bottom right. You can then learn from the resources listed in the window, as displayed in Figure 2.25.

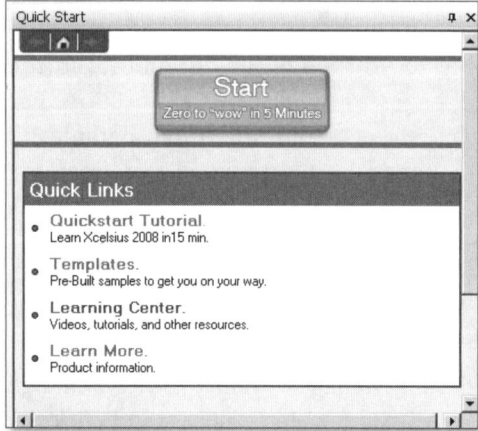

Figure 2.25 Quick Start Window of Xcelsius 2008 SP1

The quick start is a group of HTML files copied to your file system during your Xcelsius installation. You can find them in the folder *assets/quickStart/%LANGUAGE%*, for example, *C:\Program Files\BusinessObjects\Xcelsius\assets\quickStart\en*. You can refer to these HTML files directly to quickly get started with Xcelsius.

License Manager

You use this command to update the license for your Xcelsius system. After clicking this command, you will see a window pop-up where you can enter your Xcelsius key code.

The Xcelsius license is written to the registry, at *HKEY_LOCAL_MACHINE\SOFTWARE\BusinessObjects\Suite 12.0\Xcelsius\Keycodes*. On a 64-bit machine, there's an extra node, *Wow6432Node*, between *SOFTWARE* and *Business Objects*. You can also update your license there.

About Xcelsius

You can use this command to check what version of Xcelsius you are using. You may want to do this when working with someone else to create a dashboard or explaining how to reproduce a problem. After clicking this command, you will see the dialog shown in Figure 2.26.

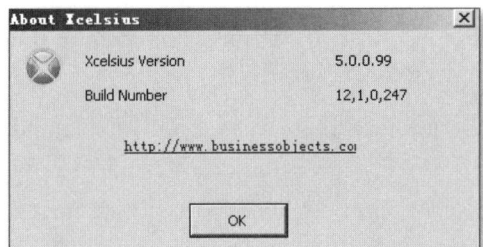

Figure 2.26 Version Info of Your Xcelsius System

From the first line, Xcelsius Version 5.0.0.0, you can see that you are using Xcelsius 2008 without any service pack or fix pack installed. The number structure is [Product Version].[Service Pack Number].[Fix Pack Number].0.

The second line shows the build number of your Xcelsius system, from which the software developers can know the source code version your Xcelsius system is built upon. The SAP website lists the version and build number for each release of Xcelsius, as listed in below:

Xcelsius Release	Xcelsius Version	Build Number
Xcelsius 2008 (RTM)	5.0.0.99	12,1,0,121
Xcelsius 2008 SP1	5.0.0.99	12,1,0,247
Xcelsius 2008 Fix Pack 1.1	5.1.1.0	12,1,1,344
Xcelsius 2008 SP2	5.2.0.0	12,2,0,608
Xcelsius 2008 Fix Pack 2.1	5.2.1.0	12,2,1,66
Xcelsius 2008 SP3	5.3.0.0	12,3,0,670

2.2 Toolbar

The toolbar area is below the menus and above the canvas. It lists some commands that are also accessible from the menus but are more convenient to use, like shortcuts. The commands are categorized into several groups, as displayed in Figure 2.23.

To show or hide toolbar icons, go to the menu VIEW • TOOLBARS and click the corresponding toolbar category name. A checkmark before a toolbar name indicates that the toolbar is currently displayed.

To use a command, just click on it. Depending on your currently selected components, some commands may be disabled. For example, if nothing is selected in the canvas, the Copy and Paste commands are disabled.

The purpose of each command in the toolbar and how to use it are briefly explained below, organized by category.

2.2.1 Standard

The Standard category includes the following commands:

- Create, Open, and Save a dashboard
- Print the SWF file
  You use this command to print the current state of the dashboard, which is only available in preview mode. It is disabled if you don't have a printer installed.
- Cut, Copy, and Paste one or more UI components
- Switch the mouse between a select tool and a component tool
  When the mouse is a select tool, you can click on the canvas to select a compo-

nent. If it's a component tool, when you click on the canvas, and the component selected in the Components Browser will be created on the canvas.

- Import Spreadsheet and Manage data connections
- Change the canvas size
- Quick Views
- Preview
  This command toggles between design mode and preview mode.

2.2.2 Export

This category includes commands to export the dashboard to several file types, including PowerPoint, Word, Outlook, and Adobe PDF and to SAP BusinessObjects Enterprise.

If PowerPoint, Word, Outlook, or PDF is selected, a temp file containing the dashboard content is created, and you can save it to another location you prefer.

If SAP BusinessObjects Enterprise is selected, you will be prompted to enter credentials to log on to an SAP BusinessObjects Enterprise system and select a folder to save your dashboard in.

Using these commands to export your dashboard is a little different from using the menus. For example, after following the menu path FILE • EXPORT • PDF, you can choose whether to use Acrobat 6.0 (PDF 1.5) or Acrobat 9.0 (PDF 1.8), but if you do this from the toolbar, the exported document will always be in format Acrobat 9.0.

2.2.3 Themes

The Themes category includes commands to change the current theme and the color scheme of your dashboard. Themes and color schemes are a big topic in Xcelsius 2008. Chapter 8 will provide detailed explanations of them. Here we just say a little about how to use them.

- Themes
  Similar to many applications such as the Microsoft Windows operating system, a theme defines the global visual styles and properties of all components. It provides an easy way to customize the components and maintain a consistent look and feel among all components throughout your dashboard. This concept

is called Skins in some other applications. To change the theme of your dashboard, you can click the Themes dropdown list and select a theme.

- Colors
Colors define the color schema of your dashboard. The colors of the canvas background; the titles, labels, and values of a text component; and the mouseover and selected color are defined in the color scheme. For example, a pie chart may have many parts, and the color of the first, second, and other parts are defined in the color scheme. A color scheme is also included in a theme, but you can further customize your components by changing the color scheme, without changing the theme.

Sometimes you may want to create your own color scheme and reuse it in your dashboards. Xcelsius supports this. You can create a custom color scheme by clicking Create new Color Scheme... in the Colors dropdown list.

2.2.4 Format

This category includes commands to:

- Group or Ungroup more than one component
- Align more than one component to the Left, Right, Top, or Bottom
- Center more than one component Horizontally or Vertically
- Space more than two components Evenly Across or Down
- Make more than one component the Same Width, Height, or Both

These commands are also accessible from the Format menu. For a detailed explanation of each command, please refer to Section 2.1.4.

2.2.5 Quick Start

This category includes one command, which is used to show or hide the Quick Start view. Its effect is similar to selecting HELP • QUICK START.

2.2.6 Summary

As a summary of the commands in Toolbar, Table 2.1 shows the toolbar button and the corresponding purpose of that command.

Button	Description
	Create a new dashboard
	Open an Xcelsius dashboard definition file (.xlf)
	Save the Xcelsius dashboard design to an .xlf file
	Print the current SWF
	Cut the selected components
	Copy the selected components
	Paste the selected components
	Undo an operation
	Redo an operation
	Change the mouse to the select tool
	Change the mouse to the component tool
	Import data from an external Excel file (.xls or .xlsx)
	Manage data connections
	Increase the canvas
	Decrease the canvas
	Fit the canvas to components
	Fit the canvas to the window
	Export the dashboard to Microsoft Office PowerPoint
	Export the dashboard to Microsoft Office Word
	Export the dashboard to Microsoft Office Word
	Attach the dashboard to Outlook
	Export the dashboard to SAP BusinessObjects Enterprise
	Group selected components
	Ungroup components in a group

Table 2.1 Toolbar Buttons and Their Functions

Button	Description
	Align components to the left border of the first selected component
	Center components horizontally
	Align components to the right border of the first selected component
	Align components to the top border of the first selected component
	Center components vertically
	Align components to the bottom border of the first selected component
	Space more than two selected components evenly across the canvas
	Space more than two selected components evenly down the canvas
	Make selected components the same width as the first selected component
	Make selected components the same height as the first selected component
	Make selected components the same width and height as the first selected component
	Bring the selected component to the front
	Send the selected component to the back
	Bring selected component(s) one layer forward
	Send selected component(s) one layer backward

Table 2.1 Toolbar Buttons and Their Functions (Cont.)

2.3 Components Browser

The Components Browser lists all available UI components in Xcelsius 2008. Some UI components may be excluded if they are not available to your license. The browser provides three kinds of view to list the components.

2.3.1 Category

The components in this view are listed by category with a thumbnail above, including charts, selectors, and maps, as shown in Figure 2.27.

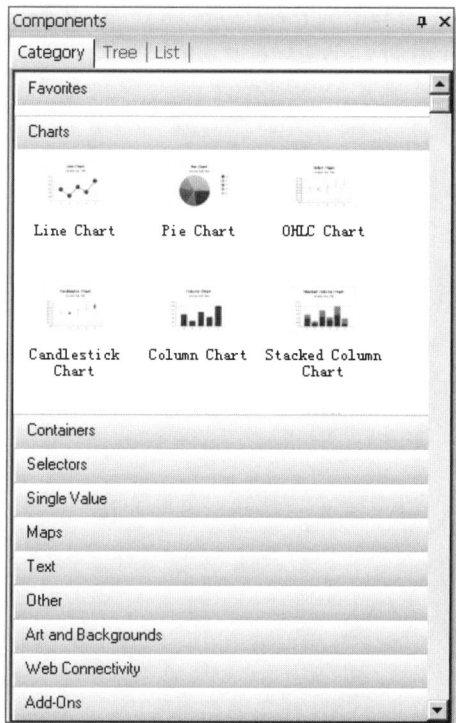

Figure 2.27 Components Displayed by Category

You can drag its right border to adjust the width of this view. Depending on its width, there may be one or more components in one row.

This view is helpful to find the right component when you know what type you want to use during design but are not sure what components of that type are available. For example, when you want to use a chart, expand the Charts category in this view and see what is inside.

Note that there are two special categories, Favorites and Add-Ons. Favorites lists the components that you frequently use, for quicker access. Add-Ons lists the add-on components that you have installed via the menu path FILE • MANAGE ADD-ONS, as illustrated in Section 2.1.1.

2.3.2 Tree

This view is very similar to the Category view except that the thumbnail for each component is smaller, as shown in Figure 2.28.

A component in this view occupies less space than in the Category view. If you want to see more components in one screen, this view ispreferable.

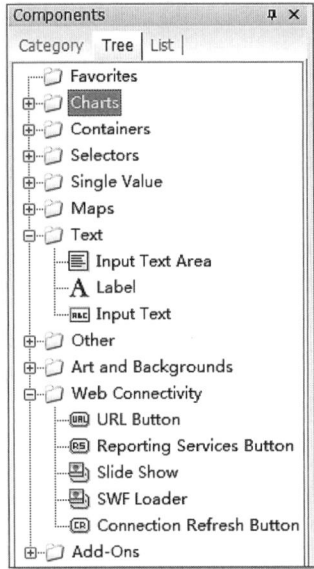

Figure 2.28 Components Displayed in a Tree Structure

2.3.3 List

This view lists all components in alphabetical order, as displayed in Figure 2.29.

Figure 2.29 Components Displayed in a List

You can switch to this view when you want to locate a UI component by its name, for example, if someone told you that a List view component can be used to display a wide range of data but you don't know what category it falls into. You can quickly find it in List view, by its starting letter L.

2.4 Canvas

The canvas is the area where you drag and drop and manipulate UI components to build your dashboard. You can place, position, and resize them on the canvas.

To change the canvas size, you can use the Increase Canvas, Decrease Canvas, Fit Canvas to Components, and Fit Canvas to Windows commands. The default canvas size is set in the menu path FILE • PREFERENCES • DOCUMENT OR FILE • DOCUMENT PROPERTIES.

To help arrange your components, you can show grids on the canvas by selecting VIEW • GRID. You can set the grid properties via the menu path FILE PREFERENCES.

The canvas background can be a solid color, gradient colors, an image, or no background. To change the canvas background color, or to use an image as your dashboard background, you can click the canvas (not on any component) and in its corresponding Properties sheet, set its type, background color, or import background image, as shown in Figure 2.30.

Figure 2.30 Properties of the Canvas

2.5 Embedded Excel Spreadsheet

As mentioned before, Xcelsius has used Excel as its only direct data source and has embedded an Excel spreadsheet along with it since Xcelsius 2008. You can see some sample data in the embedded Excel spreadsheet during dashboard design, which is very intuitive, and this may save a lot of time for you.

There's no command to directly show or hide the embedded Excel spreadsheet. However, you can click on the borders between it and the adjacent views to resize its space, as displayed in Figure 2.31.

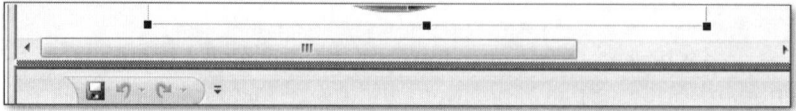

Figure 2.31 Drag the Border to Resize the Embedded Spreadsheet

2.6 Property Sheet

Each UI component, including the canvas, is related to a Properties sheet where you can set its properties including data and appearance. For example, to set the title of a pie chart, you can click to select the chart in the canvas and then enter your text for its title or bind it to a cell in the embedded spreadsheet in the Properties sheet.

Many properties can be bound to a cell or a range of cells in the embedded Excel spreadsheet, including but not limited to:

- Texts
- Colors
- Data
- Dynamic visibility
- Drill-down

To bind properties to a single cell or a cell range in the embedded spreadsheet, click the Bind button to the right of the property. Then you will be prompted to enter a range. You can enter it directly in the prompt dialog or select cells in the embedded Excel spreadsheet and then click OK.

For example, to set title of a pie chart, you can click on it to open its Properties sheet and click the Bind button to the right of the chart title text box, as shown in Figure 2.32.

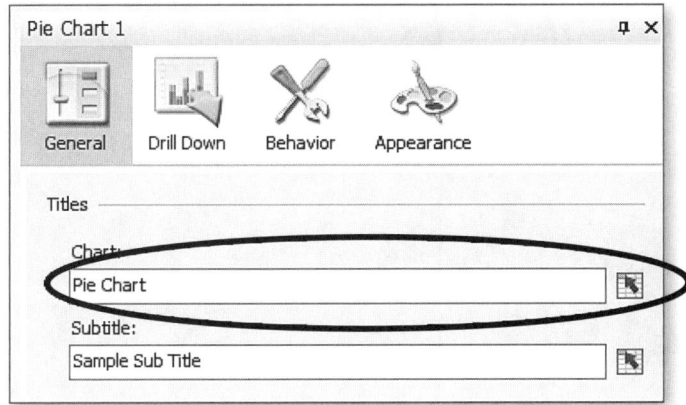

Figure 2.32 Bind Title of a Pie Chart

Then you will see a dialog pop up asking you to Select a Range, as illustrated in Figure 2.33. Note that, though the prompt is Select a Range, you can also select a single cell, which is the case here. So you just click the embedded Excel spreadsheet to select a single cell or a range of cells and then click OK in the dialog.

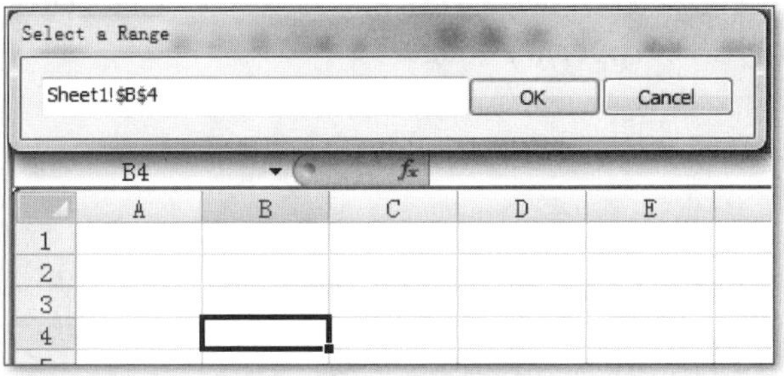

Figure 2.33 The Dialog to Select a Range

You can also enter the definition of the cell or cell range directly in the dialog. For example, enter "Sheet1!$B$4" directly.

When multiple components are selected, the Properties sheet will display properties that are common to all. In this way you set the same property of multiple components at the same time. For example, when two charts are selected, you can set the Dynamic Visibility property of both in the Property panel, but you cannot set the titles, as shown in Figure 2.34.

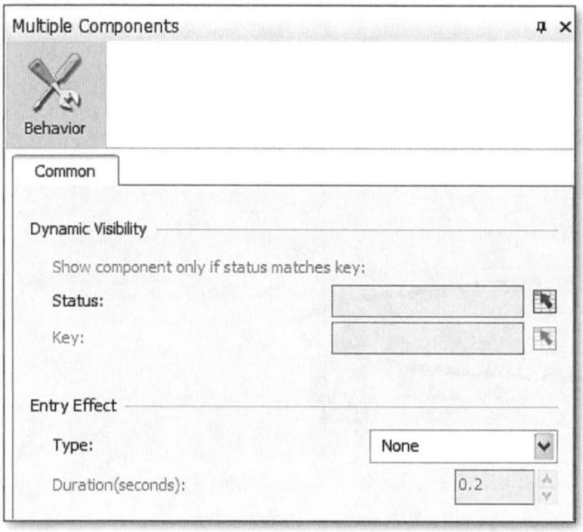

Figure 2.34 Property Panel for Multiple Components

As mentioned above, what properties are displayed in the Properties sheet depends on the selected component(s). A detailed explanation of the Properties sheet will be given in later chapters, where we'll discuss the UI individual components.

To show or hide the Properties sheet, select VIEW • PROPERTIES. You can also click the Close button ✕ in the top right of Properties sheet to close it.

2.7 Object Browser

The Object Browser lists all components existing in your dashboard design in a tree hierarchy and in the order of depth. You may want to use this command when you have several components in the canvas and you want to:

- Find one component quickly
- Lock some components to avoid changing their positions
- Hide some components to focus on the others

As shown in Figure 2.35, you can Hide, Lock, Delete, Send Backward, or Bring Forward a component by clicking the corresponding button in the Object Browser.

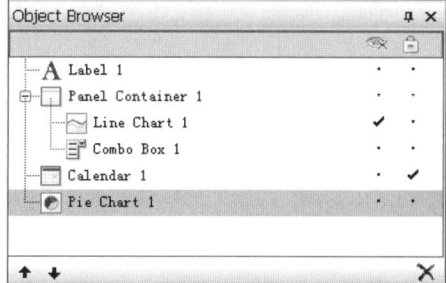

Figure 2.35 The Object Browser Showing All UI Components of Your Dashboard

As mentioned before, the components are listed by hierarchy and in order in the Object Browser. As you can see from this figure, the label component is higher than the pie chart, meaning that the label is at the back of the pie chart. That is, if they are overlapped, part of the label may be invisible, while the pie chart will always be visible. Also, the line chart and the combo box are displayed as children of the panel container, which means they are inside the panel container.

If it's hard to select one or more UI components from the canvas, for example, when there are too many components, you can easily select them here. What's more, if a component is hidden or locked in a container, you have to select it here, because it's unselectable in the canvas.

2.8 Summary

The workspace of Xcelsius 2008 consists of several parts, such as menus, the canvas, and the Components Browser. In this chapter we have illustrated all of the parts and commands you will use during your work with Xcelsius. Being familiar with each part and a having good understanding of what they are used to will be very helpful for you in designing your dashboard and will save you a lot of time.

Xcelsius 2008 is easy to use and powerful. In this chapter, you'll follow a simple tutorial on how to create a simple dashboard to quickly get started.

3   Get Started

So now you know what Xcelsius is and are familiar with its environment and commands. Maybe you cannot wait to try it out and get a quick hands-on experience with it. Before diving into the complex UI components in Chapters 4 and 5, we'll guide you through a simple example to quickly get you started.

In this chapter we'll present a tutorial on how to create a simple dashboard. After reading this chapter you will be able to:

- Describe the steps of creating a dashboard using Xcelsius 2008
- Know where to start to create a dashboard

3.1   Introduction

In this chapter we'll show you the basic steps of creating a dashboard using Xcelsius 2008. You can also follow these steps when creating more complex dashboards. Generally, the required steps to create a dashboard are:

1. Design – Understand the purpose, audience and data
2. Development I – Choose data visualization methods
3. Development II – Choose data connectivity
4. Development III – Format
5. Distribute

Of course, the first thing you need to understand is the business scenario, including but not limited to:

- The purpose of the dashboard
- Who will use it

- The location of the data
- What the data is like
- How the user will use the dashboard

This applies to complex requirements and simple ones. Only when you thoroughly understand them can you choose the right UI components to deliver information, find the way to bind and retrieve data, and finally help the user analyze the business and make a wise decision.

The following sections will guide you through a simple dashboard design process. Suppose now that one of your friends asks you to create a dashboard showing the area of each of the continents so he can get a clearer idea. You decide to use a pie chart to show the area for each continent. When the user clicks on one continent, a label below displays text showing the area — very simple, but informative enough. Now let's begin.

3.2 Choose the Right UI Components

Once you have made clear the purpose and audience of the dashboard, the first step is to choose suitable UI components to visualize your data. You choose the right components based on the business scenario or the end user's preferences. It's a best practice to think about what UI components to use and how to lay them out outside Xcelsius. For example, you can first draw the dashboard on a piece of paper, thinking about the use scenario and user interactions that will affect the design of the layout. Then you can drag the component from the Components view and drop it onto the canvas and position it.

In our case, we need a pie chart to show and compare each continent's area and a label to show some general info about the selected continent. We've provide detailed explanations of available UI components and cover when to choose what in Chapters 4 and 5.

After dropping one or more components onto the canvas, you need position them to build a logical layout. You can use the mouse to move and resize them. If you have too many components, you may want to use the Object Browser to hide, lock, or delete them, as illustrated in Section 2.7.

You can customize each component in its Properties panel by changing elements such as the colors, font styles, and entry effect.

For this tutorial, you begin by launching Xcelsius 2008. Open the Components view, and in the Category tab, drag a pie chart from Charts and a label from Text and drop them onto the canvas. You can position them as displayed in Figure 3.1, with the label below the pie chart.

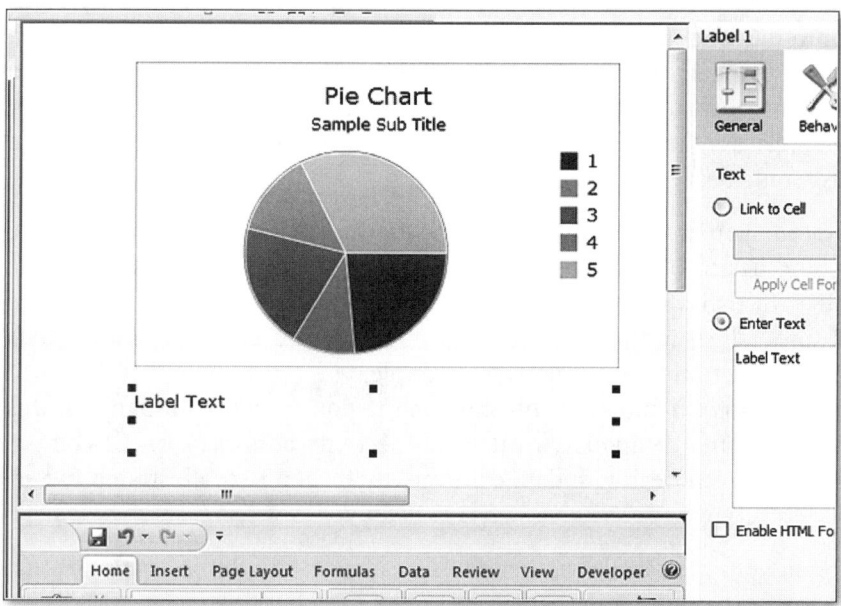

Figure 3.1 The Components of Our Sample

For a better layout, you can align them to the left and make them the same width by selecting both and then selecting FORMAT • ALIGN • LEFT AND FORMAT • MAKE SAME SIZE • WIDTH.

These are all of the components in our simple dashboard. To make it look professional, you can adjust the canvas size by clicking the Fit Canvas to Components button on the toolbar to make it just big enough to hold them. You can then click Increase Canvas to increase it a little bit, leaving some gap around the borders to make the user feel more comfortable.

3.3 Bind Data

The second step is to bind the UI components to data to reflect real information. For static data, you can directly enter it into the embedded Excel spreadsheet or import it from an existing Excel file (with an .xls or .xlsx extension). For dynamic data, you need to go one step further by mapping the real data to a cell or a cell range in the embedded spreadsheet through some kind of data connectivity and then bind the UI components to them.

In our tutorial, the continents' areas are static. For simplicity, we directly enter such data into the embedded spreadsheet. For information about how to use the embedded spreadsheet, including the naming convention of each sheet, where to put the data, and how to use color to show different data, please refer to Chapter 6 where we'll discuss the embedded Excel spreadsheet, and the Appendix, where we'll discuss some best practices of Xcelsius.

Most of the time you are using dynamic data, the actual, live data resides outside of Xcelsius and has to be retrieved with the help one or more of Xcelsius' data connectivities. In such cases, you can write some explanative sample data in the embedded spreadsheet in this step and wait until the next phase of binding data to map the real data to this cell range. For example, you can assume that the range Sheet1!$B$2:$C$4 is for the sales info for each region in your company. In this way you eliminate the complexity of data connectivity and focus on UI components for now. You can deal with data connectivity in step 3, as illustrated in Section 3.4.

In our tutorial, your data in the embedded spreadsheet should be similar to that in Figure 3.2.

	A	B	C	D	E	F	G	H
1								
2			Area for the 7 continents					
3								
4								
5		Africa	Antarctica	Asia	Europe	North Am	Oceania	South America
6		30.2	14	44	10.16	24.22	8.97	17.97
7								

Figure 3.2 Data in the Embedded Spreadsheet of Our Sample

3.3.1 Bind Data for Pie Chart

The two components we have dropped onto the canvas are empty. In this step, let's enrich the pie chart with some meaningful data. To do this, click the pie chart to open the Properties panel, and in General tab, we can bind properties such as Title and Data Source to some cells in the embedded spreadsheet. If the Properties panel is not displayed, double-click the pie chart or select Properties in the View menu.

The binding can be divided into three categories, as illustrated below.

To a Single Cell

To bind a single-value property to a cell in the embedded Excel spreadsheet, click the Bind button to the right of the property and select a single cell. For example, in our tutorial, we need bind the Title property of the pie chart to cell Sheet1!$C$2, where the title is stored, as displayed in Figure 3.3.

Figure 3.3 Title of the Pie Chart Bound to a Cell in the Spreadsheet

You can also enter the title directly in the Input field. However, binding it to a cell makes it easier when you need to update it later.

To a One-Dimensional Cell Range

This is appropriate if you need to bind some property, such as the labels of a combo box, to a one-dimensional list of values, that is, a row or a column in the embedded spreadsheet. To do this, click the Bind button to the right of that property and drag the mouse to select a range of cells in one row or in one column. If you select cell ranges in multiple rows or columns, only the data in the first row or column is used.

In our tutorial, we need bind the Values property of the pie chart to the cell range Sheet1!$B$6:$H$6, where the sizes of the continents are stored. Similarly, bind the Labels property to the cell range Sheet1!$B$5:$H$5, as shown in Figure 3.4.

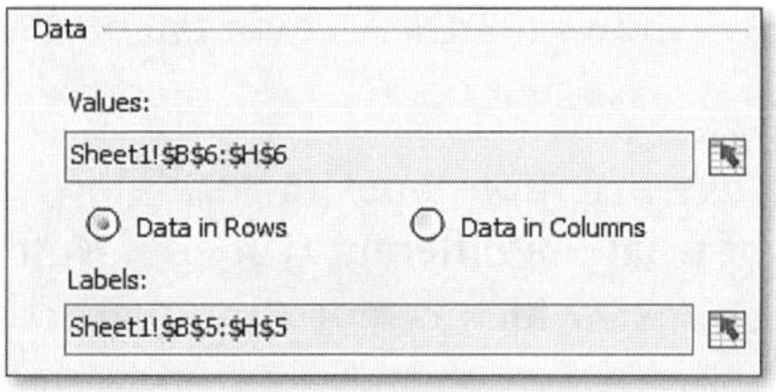

Figure 3.4 Data Binding for the Pie Chart

To a Two-Dimensional Cell Range

To bind a two-dimensional list of values to a cell range (multiple rows and columns), click the Bind button to the right of that property and drag the mouse to select a two-dimensional range of cells. Xcelsius will then automatically parse the data using its own mechanism and divide it into categories and series or into several series. For example, you may want to bind the data of a column chart to a two-dimensional cell range in the embedded spreadsheet.

Xcelsius does not support data binding in more than two dimensions.

Now the pie chart displays the data your friend is interested in. You can click Preview to have a look at the effect. Let's move on to make it more interactive by adding drill-down ability to the dashboard.

3.3.2 Enable Drill-Down for the Pie Chart

By now the pie chart is displaying the size of each continent. You can get a rough idea of the percentage of each continent at a glance and know the concrete size by moving your mouse over an item. To make the dashboard clearer and more intuitive, we use a label component under the pie chart to show the area of the selected continent in an obvious way.

The purpose behind this is to use another component to show more info about the selected item in a pie chart. It can be as simple as a label or as complex as another chart showing the countries in the continent.

In our example, we enable drill-down on the pie chart so that the name and the area of the selected continent can be inserted somewhere in the spreadsheet. Then we can use that data to form the text for the label.

To enable drill-down, you can click on the pie chart to open its Properties panel and in the Behavior tab, select Enable Drill Down. You then have the option to insert something into another location in the embedded Excel spreadsheet, based on the user selection in the pie chart. Figure 3.5 shows the Drill Down tab of the pie chart.

As displayed in the dropdown list, there are five insertion types for drill-down. You can click the help icon to get an idea of what the different types do. Note that the help is like a live video instead of plain text, which is more intuitive and easier to understand.

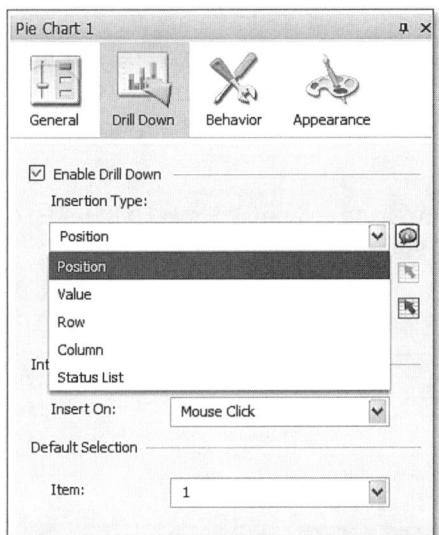

Figure 3.5 Configure Drill Down Behavior of the Pie Chart

You can choose the type depending on the requirement. We'll provide detailed explanations of each insertion type in Chapter 4 when we talk about how to use a pie chart in more detail.

In Interaction Options, you can configure when the drill-down happens, either on mouse-over or on mouse-click. There's no strict rule about what to choose, and you can just follow your preference. By default, Mouse Click is selected.

Xcelsius also provides a way to specify what item is selected by default. When the component is displayed, the drill-down action will happen automatically on the item you have selected here. You set the default item by setting its index, starting from 1, as shown in Figure 3.6.

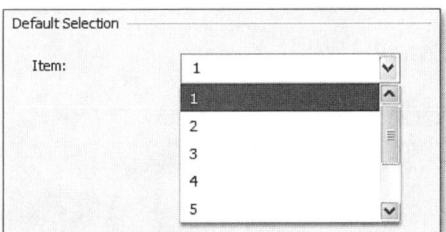

Figure 3.6 Default Selected Item of a Drill Down

Note that you have to select a default item. That is, a drill-down always happens immediately when the pie chart is displayed. However, in certain cases, you may want to display nothing until the user explicitly clicks on the pie chart to select an item. To fulfill this requirement, you need to install Xcelsius 2008 Service Pack 3 where this feature is supported.

In this simple tutorial, we need to insert a column from cell range Sheet1!$B$5:$H$6 into column Sheet1!$C$8:$C$9, as shown in Figure 3.7.

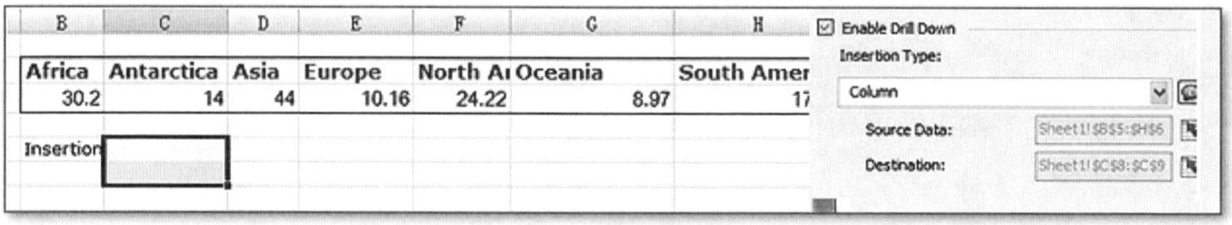

Figure 3.7 Drilldown Definition of the Pie Chart in this Example

Note that the destination is a cell range with two rows and one column, highlighted in yellow. The cell range containing the source data is also highlighted with a thick box, so you can easily distinguish the data from other cells in the embedded spreadsheet.

3.3.3 Bind Data for Label

As mentioned above, we will add a label below the pie chart to display info about the selected continent for the user's better understanding. For example, when Asia is selected, the label displays, "The area of Asia is 30.2 million kilometers."

You either bind a the text of a label to a cell or enter constant text directly — meaning you cannot concatenate constant texts with Excel cells. To form the sentence you need, you have to use a string function in the Excel spreadsheet. For example, you select a cell and set its value to:

=CONCATENATE("The area of ", C8, " is ", C9, " million kilometers.")

> **Note**
>
> Sheet1!$C$8 stores the name of the selected continent, and Sheet1!$C$9 stores its area, which is a number.

You then bind the label to cell Sheet1!$F$8 through the label's Properties panel, as displayed in Figure 3.8.

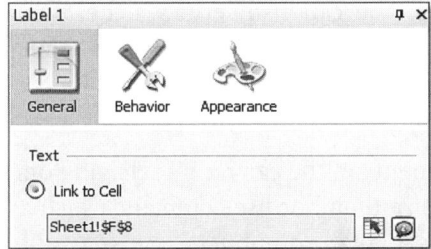

Figure 3.8 Binding the Label to a Cell with Excel Formulas

By now the dashboard has provided all of the functionalities you wanted: the pie chart displays each continent's area, and the label displays an explanation text of the selected item when the user clicks on the pie chart.

In the future you can format the dashboard to make it look better, which we'll discuss in Section 3.5. You can set the color, font, and animation.

3.4 Connect to External Data

This step is required if your data is not known at design time and has to be retrieved through some kind of data connectivity such as a Web service.

In this step, you define the data connectivity in the Data Manager, which is accessible from the menu DATA • CONNECTIONS, where you map the input and output data to a cell or cell range in the embedded Excel spreadsheet and define when and how to trigger the connections to load the live data.

Because the data in our tutorial is static, we'll skip this step. For information about how to use data connectivity in Xcelsius 2008, refer to Chapters 6 and 7.

3.5 Formatting

The steps described above focus on the functionality of the dashboard: choosing the right UI components to visualize data and retrieving the accurate and live data. In this step we focus on the visual appearance, including the sizing, alignment, positioning, fonts, colors, and so on. If you like, you can also add a background to it or choose a different theme or color scheme to make it more customized.

You change the canvas size by using the four commands of Increase Canvas, Decrease Canvas, Fit Canvas to Components, and Fit Canvas to Window in the toolbar or via the menu VIEW CANVAS SIZING. You can also set it via the menu FILE • DOCUMENT PROPERTIES, but setting it will resize the canvas without taking into account existing UI components. Judging by our experience, these four buttons on the toolbar are frequently used.

You change the sizes and alignment of components in the canvas by selecting one or multiple components and use mouse to resize them, or use commands such as Align to Left and Align to Top. The commands to align components are accessible from either the toolbar or the menu FORMAT • ALIGN and are disabled if zero or only one component is selected.

> **Note**
> During aligning components and making them the same size, the first component you selected becomes the base.

Properties such as fonts, colors, and text alignments are set in the Appearance tab in the Properties sheet of the selected component(s), as shown in Figure 3.9.

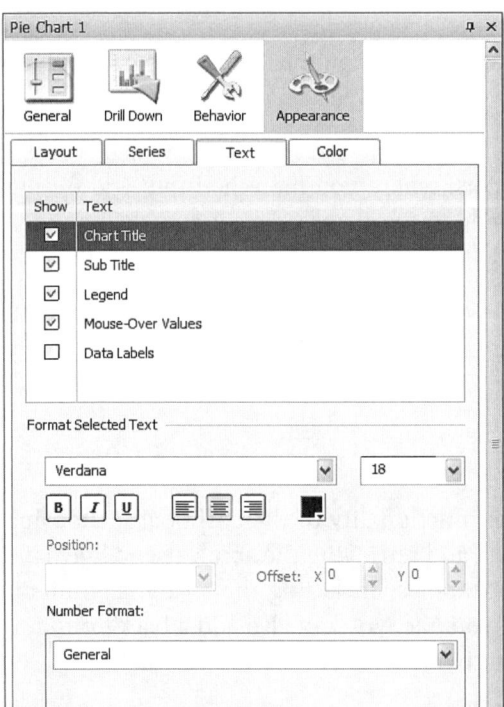

Figure 3.9 The Format of Text Is Set in the Appearance Tab

We give detailed explanations of each property related to the text formats Chapters 4 and 5. Here we'll just go through an example by setting the font, size, style, and color of the pie chart's title.

To do this, click the pie chart on the canvas to open its Properties sheet. Select the Appearance tab and then select Text, and you will see a list of texts that are available for formatting. Here we want to format the title of the pie chart, so click Chart Title, set its font to Verdana, size to 20, style to Bold, alignment to Center, and color to Cyan. Your property sheet should look similar to Figure 3.10.

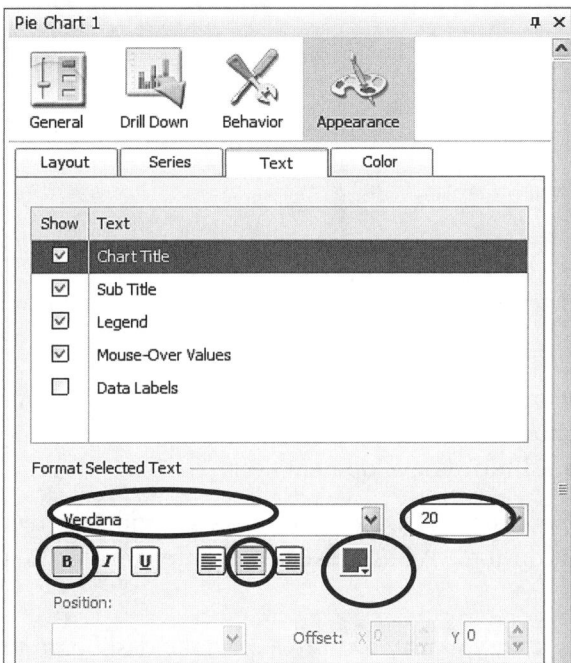

Figure 3.10 Title Formats of the Pie Chart in this Example

Pay attention to the checkbox in front of each text. If it's unselected, the corresponding text will not be displayed in the chart.

3.6 Distribute the Output

By now you have created a professional dashboard, not only in appearance, but also in the information it conveys. When you click Preview to have a look at your dashboard, it should look like Figure 3.11. If not, go back to the sections above to check what you did.

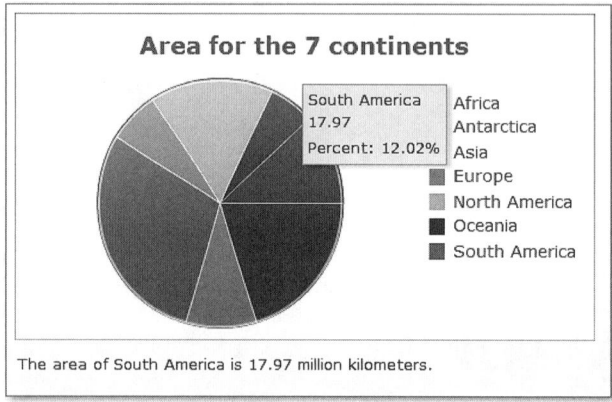

Figure 3.11 Final Effect of this Example

As mentioned before, the purpose of a dashboard is to help with communication, so we need to distribute the dashboard to others in some manner. Most of the time, this is the last step of your dashboard development cycle.

Distribution is achieved via the menu FILE • EXPORT. Xcelsius 2008 supports two methods of distribution: distribution to SAP BusinessObjects Enterprise or to a local file.

If you are an SAP BusinessObjects user, you may want to export the dashboard to SAP BusinessObjects Enterprise so that other SAP BusinessObjects Enterprise users can access it through the BI portal, if they are permitted to. In such a case, a Flash file will be created in your SAP BusinessObjects Enterprise system.

In some other cases, you may want to export the dashboard to a file and then either send it directly to others or store it in a web application (for example, your personal website or your company's portal) so that others can access it through a web browser.

In our tutorial, we simply export it to an SWF file. To do this, after saving the dashboard, select FILE • EXPORT • FLASH (SWF), as shown in Figure 2.15.

After setting the file location and file name, you will find an SWF file generated in your file system. You can then send it to your friend to wait for his "Wow!"

3.7 Summary

We have just created a professional though simple dashboard with Xcelsius 2008. Now let's look back. In this chapter we explained the typical steps to design a dashboard, and for each step, we illustrated what we need do and how to do it.

Dashboards created with Xcelsius 2008 can be visually stunning, thanks to its rich set of UI components. Some are very easy to understand, while others are more complex. In this chapter let's begin with some commonly used components.

4   UI Component Basics

So, the example in Chapter 3 is too simple to meet your requirements? Don't worry. Xcelsius can be more powerful. It provides a large range of UI components to create attractive and powerful data visualizations. In this chapter we'll describe some commonly used UI components and what you can do with each of them, including creating charts, menus, selectors, and so on. After reading this chapter you will have a clear idea of what UI component you can use in certain scenarios and how to use them.

Some properties are common to most components, such as dynamic visibility, drill-down, text formats, and alerts. Discussing them in a separate section may look clearer but will cause the misunderstanding that they are common to all components and confuse the readers about what functionalities are available to what charts. So, instead, we'll discuss them as we meet them. For example, drill-down is covered in Section 4.1.2 when cover pie charts, while alerts appear in Section 4.1.3 about column charts, because they are unavailable for pie charts.

In this chapter you will see:

▶ A list of available UI components including charts and menus

▶ What you can do with each of them, when to use them, and how

After reading this chapter you will be able to:

▶ Describe the UI components provided by Xcelsius 2008

▶ Create a more attractive dashboard with more UI components

4.1 Working with Charts

The chart is the most widely used UI component in data visualization, thanks to its intuitive and attractive appearance. A chart can organize and represent a set of numerical or qualitative data. The data in a chart is represented by symbols, such as bars in a bar chart, lines in a line chart, and slices in a pie chart.

Charts are used to represent data in a way that provides easier and better understanding to the end user. The main benefits of using a chart are that it eases the understanding of the relationships among multiple parts of the data. You can use them to show, compare, and analyze the values of several items.

In Xcelsius 2008, you can find many kinds of charts such as bar charts, pie charts, radar chart, and so on. All charts share some common purposes, while each chart has its specific purpose and use scenario. For example, you may want to use a pie chart to explain the percentages of different data parts, while a line chart may be a better candidate to show data at discrete time points over a period.

To use charts in Xcelsius 2008, just select one from the Charts category in the Components view, drag and drop it onto the canvas, adjust its position, and set its properties.

In this chapter, we'll explain some basic as well as commonly used charts, including what the chart is, its advantages and disadvantages, under what conditions you may want to use the chart, and how to use it.

In the next chapter we'll discuss some more complex or less frequently used charts such as the radar chart.

4.1.1 Pie Chart

A pie chart is a circular chart that resembles a pie. It uses slices with different colors to represent data. The part-to-whole relationship is built into the pie chart in a quite obvious way. The user can learn the percentage of each part and relative size by simply looking at or moving the mouse over the pie slices and decode the ratio (half, quarter etc.) in his head.

When to Use a Pie Chart

You may want to use a pie chart to show the relative size and especially the contribution or distribution of each data part. For example, when you want to explain the sales revenue of each branch and its contribution to the total sales revenue of the entire company, a pie chart is the best candidate.

You may think that some other kinds of charts, such as a column chart or a bar chart, can also show the size and contribution of each data part. You are partly right. Yes, they can show the size of each part but are not the best way to show the contribution or percentage. For example, in the pie chart showing sales revenue in Figure 4.1, you can easily find out at one glance that Q4 takes up almost exactly one-quarter of the yearly sales revenue, and Q2 takes up a little more than one-third.

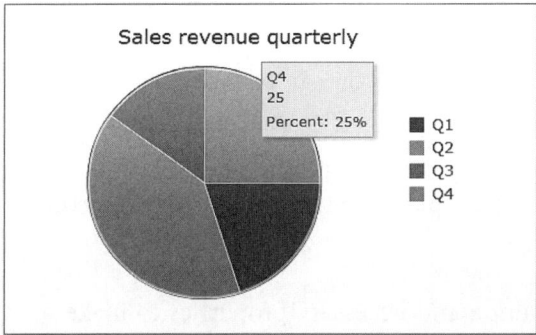

Figure 4.1 A Pie Chart Showing the Contribution of Each Quarter

However, if you use a bar chart (or column chart, which is very similar) in this situation, as displayed in Figure 4.2, it will be difficult to find such info.

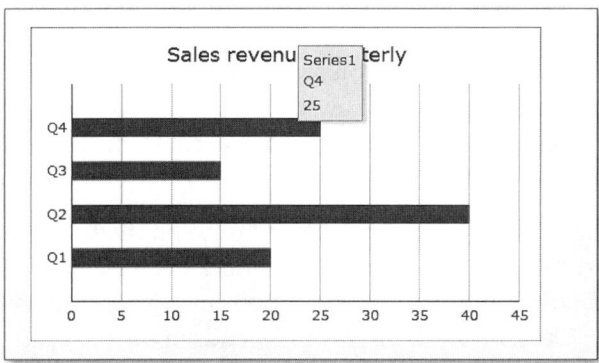

Figure 4.2 The Contribution of a Quarter is Not Intuitive Enough in a Bar Chart

We'll explain the use scenario where a bar chart is more appropriate in the section on bar charts.

How to Use a Pie Chart

To use a pie chart in your dashboard design, first select it in the Components view and drag it to the canvas.

To set its position and size, use the mouse to move or resize it by clicking on it, holding the mouse and moving.

A pie chart, and each of the other charts, has a rich set of properties including titles, data, and dynamic visibility. You can set the properties of a pie chart in the Properties panel, which will display when you have selected the pie chart and the Properties view is enabled (VIEW • PROPERTIES). You can also see the Properties panel by double-clicking the chart.

The properties of a pie chart are categorized into four groups, corresponding to the four tabs in it's the Properties view. Let's explain them in the following sections.

General

This category includes the most common and necessary properties to make up a chart — titles and data.

A pie chart has both a title and a subtitle. Either can be constant text (enter text directly in the fields) or be bound to a cell in the embedded Excel spreadsheet.

Generally, the title tells the overall purpose of the chart, and the subtitle gives some additional information. For example, in a quarterly sales revenue report, you can use "Sales Revenue by Quarter" as the title, and show the year such as "2009" as the subtitle so that others can know what year you are talking about. Similarly, if your dashboard contains parameters, you can show the parameter values that the user has entered in the subtitle area. This is also a best practice to make your dashboard clear, exact, and easy to understand.

The data of a pie chart contains labels and values, which need to be bound to a row or column in the Excel spreadsheet. The labels are dimension attributes such as "Q1" and "Q2," while the values are numbers such as "25,000" or a percentage of a measure such as sales revenue. The labels will display as legends in the pie chart, and the values will appear when you move the mouse over the slices.

To bind data, click the Bind button to the right of Labels or Values, and then select a cell range in a row or column in the Excel spreadsheet. You can also enter the cell range directly in the input field, such as "data!$D$5: $D$10."

Note that the data parts are arranged clockwise, starting from the fourth quadrant. That is, the first data part appears from the horizontal rightward radius, and the remaining parts follow it clockwise, as illustrated in Figure 4.3.

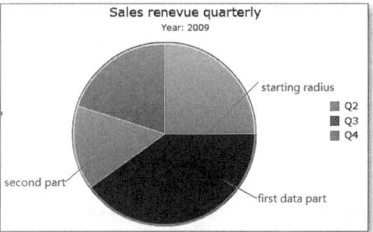

Figure 4.3 Data Parts of a Pie Chart Arranged Clockwise (Starting from the Fourth Quadrant)

Understanding this helps you make a better dashboard by adjusting the order of the data parts.

Figure 4.4 illustrates the properties in this category and how they relate to the pie chart and the embedded spreadsheet:

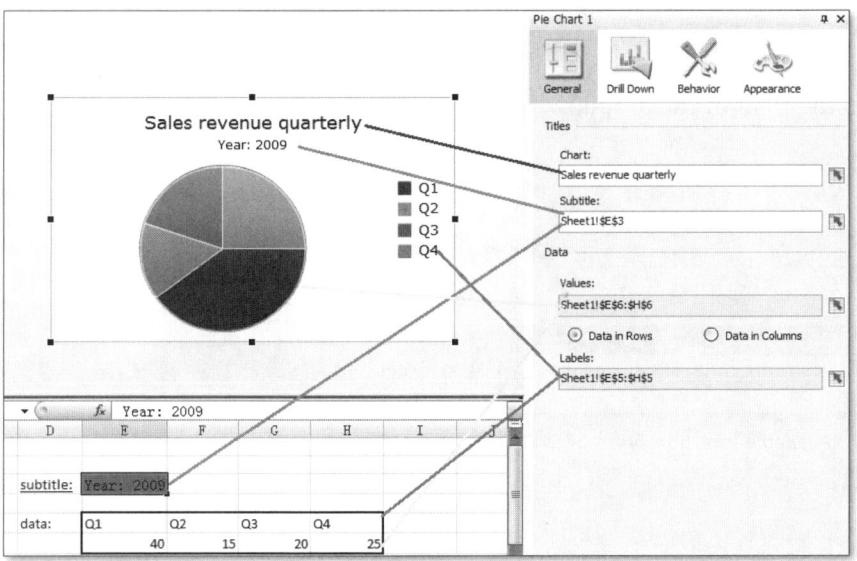

Figure 4.4 The UI Properties in the General Tab

Drill Down

To drill down means to move from high-level summary information to more detailed data. The purpose is to understand or find out the reason for something. For example, in a pie chart showing the quarterly sales revenue, you can drill down from a quarter to see more detailed data, such as the monthly data, about that selected quarter.

A useful drill-down often occurs along a hierarchy, for example, from year to quarter to month or from country to region to state. This is to some extent similar to navigating through the file system in your computer, from the root folder (e.g., My Computer) to the drivers (C:) to folders (My Documents) and files.

Sometimes you may use drill down along no hierarchy. Instead, you just use it as a selector. That is, when the user clicks on a slice on the pie chart, some other information related to your selection is displayed on some other components. The information is updated according to your selection.

In the rest of this section, we'll discuss the features of drill-down and explain the properties and its effects. We'll discuss more advanced usage of drill-down, and how to use this functionality to create a useful dashboard, in Chapter 8, Section 8.1, which focuses on drill-down as a special feature.

Enable Drill-Down

In Xcelsius, you can insert the position, value, or status list of the selected slice, or a row or column of a two-dimensional cell range, to a cell or cell range in the embedded Excel spreadsheet. As shown in Figure 4.5, you can click the Help button 🔘 to the right of the dropdown list to see how to use it.

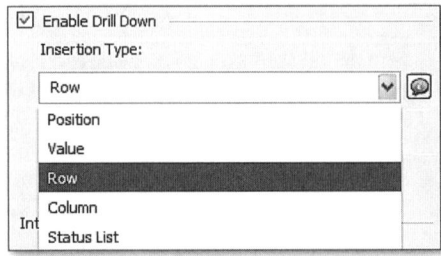

Figure 4.5 Available Insertion Types of Drill-Down on a Pie Chart

By default the drill-down functionality of a pie chart is disabled. To use it, you need first to enable it by selecting the Enable Drill Down checkbox.

Detailed explanations of each insertion type are covered below.

Position

You can choose this option if you want to know the index of the selected slice in the pie chart. With this selection, you insert the position of the selected slice into a cell. The position corresponds to the order of each data part in the Excel spreadsheet, starting from 1. You can also count the position by looking at the pie chart. Do you remember that we mentioned that the data parts are arranged from the horizontal rightward radius clockwise?

You need to specify a target cell in the embedded spreadsheet to store the position. With each selection, the position of the selected slice is inserted into that cell. For example, if you click the Q2 slice, the content of the target cell becomes 2.

Value

You can choose this option if you want to show the value of the selected slice. With this selection, you insert the value of the selected slice into a cell. The values are specified in the Values property in the General tab.

Similar to position, you need specify a target cell in the embedded spreadsheet to store the value. With each selection, the value of the selected slice is inserted into that cell. For example, if you click the Q2 slice, the sales revenue of Q2 will be inserted.

Status List

The status of a data part refers to whether it's currently selected: 1 for yes and 0 for no. You need to specify a cell range to store the statuses of all data parts. The number of cells should be the same as that of the data parts. With each selection, the corresponding cell contains value 1, while all other cells are set to 0.

You may be a little puzzled about the difference between position and status list. You can use both to check what item is selected, and most of the time, you can use position instead of status list. However, sometimes you need show different components for different parts in the pie chart, and you need to control their dynamic visibilities. In such a case, it's easier to use a status list and control the dynamic visibility of each child component based on the corresponding cell. You can contact the author for a sample of this usage.

Row/Column

With the three options above, you insert something related to the selected slice into a single cell or a cell range. The value in the target cell(s) might be the text of the label, the value of the selected data part, or a number indicating what data part is currently selected.

However, with Row or Column, the pie chart behaves like a selector. Based on the index of your selected slice, you select a row or a column from a two-dimensional cell range (the source data) and insert it into another row or column (the target). The source data can be anywhere else in the embedded Excel spreadsheet and can have nothing to do with the pie chart. Let's emphasize that again: The pie chart here is just a selector, similar to a combo box or a menu.

With this option, you specify a two-dimensional cell range in the Source Data field and a row or column in the Destination field. The source data is related to the pie chart, and with each selection, the corresponding row or column is inserted into the Destination field. For example, in Figure 4.6, the pie chart shows the total sales for each city in Q1.

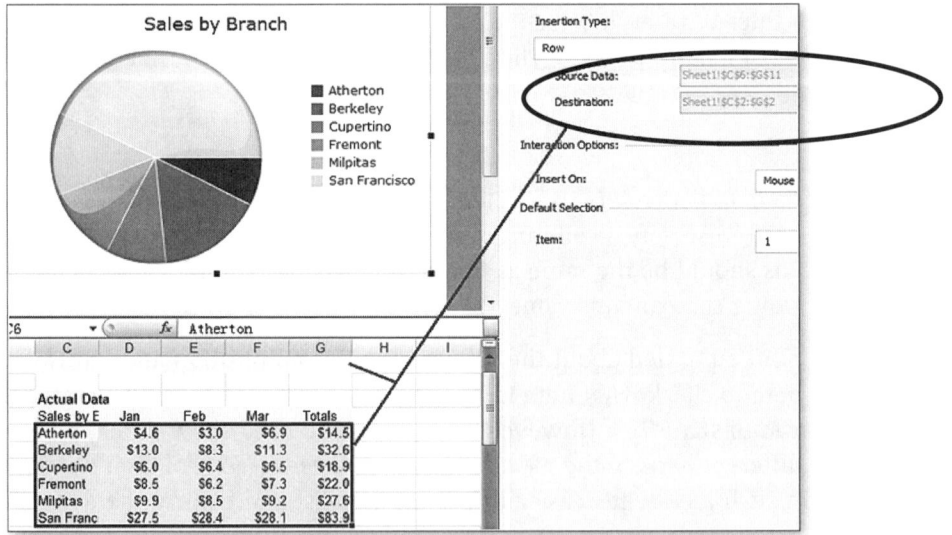

Figure 4.6 Use a Pie Chart to Select a Row or Column from a Cell Range

When the user selects a city, the monthly sales revenue for that city is inserted into another row, which can in turn be used as the data source for another component. In this example, the source data is in cell range Sheet1!$C$6:$G$11, and the destination in row Sheet1!$C$2:$G$2.

- Interaction Options
  The Interaction options refer to when the drill-down happens: on a mouse click or mouse over a slice, as you can see from Figure 4.7.

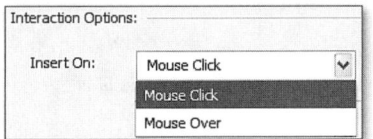

Figure 4.7 Available Interaction Options for Drill-Down of a Pie Chart

You make a selection based on your requirement or preference. The default option is Mouse Click, which is most frequently used. With this option you can move your mouse over the slices to see the value and percentage of each data part and click the one you are interested in to see more detailed data.

Otherwise, drill-down is triggered on each mouse-over action. Select this option if you want the user to see the corresponding detailed data immediately on mouse over, without an additional action of clicking the slice.

- Default Selection
  Default selection refers to what item is selected by default, without user interaction. By default, the default selection is 1, which means the position or value of the first item is inserted into the target cell or the first row or column in the cell range specified as source data is inserted into the destination. You can assume that Xcelsius "clicks" on that item immediately after the pie chart is displayed.

Behavior

In this category you set the behaviors of the pie chart, as explained below.

- Ignore Blank Cells
  Check this option if you want to ignore the data parts with an empty value (if any) at the end of the range, so that those with a blank value will not be displayed in the pie chart. For example, let's say you are creating a dashboard showing the sales revenue of each quarter and you want to ignore the quarters with 0 sales revenue (of course, this is impossible; just take it as an example).

Let's assume that the sales revenue in Q4 is 0. Figure 4.8 shows the difference between the pie charts with and without this option selected.

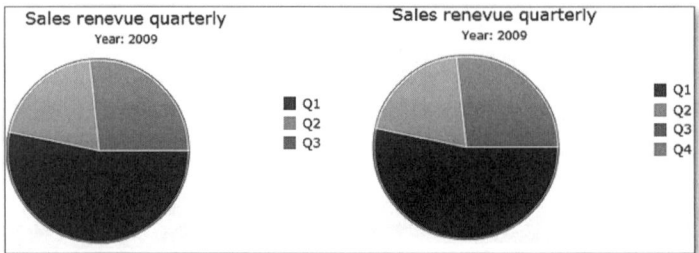

Figure 4.8 The Last Data Parts with 0 Value Are Not Displayed when Ignore Blank Cells Is Selected

Whether the label for the blank cell, Q4, is displayed depends on whether Ignore Blank Cells is selected.

Note: Only the blank cells at the end of the range are ignored. In the sample above, if the sales revenue for Q2 is empty, it will not be ignored because it's not at the end. Of course, if the sales revenues of Q3 and Q4 are both empty, both will be ignored.

If you want to ignore all data items with an empty value, not only these at the end, you can create a workaround to do this. For example, you can use some Excel formulas to rearrange the data for the pie chart, so that the items with an empty value are all placed at the end of the range. Then when this option is selected, all of such items will be ignored.

One more note: Whether a cell is considered blank is determined by its value, not its label. That is, if the sales revenue of Q4 is not empty but you forgot to type Q4 in the Excel spreadsheet, it will not be ignored, though it will have an empty legend.

▶ Dynamic Visibility
This property is common to all UI components. With this property, you have the ability to show one or more components only under a certain condition, when the value of a certain cell is equal to a constant or that of another cell.

To make use of it, select a cell in the Status field. Then the Key field is enabled and you can enter a constant or select another cell to compare with in it. The pie chart will only show when Status matches Key.

If you have set dynamic visibility before, and now you want to remove it, simply click the Bind button of the Status field and empty the Select a Range field.

The constant or cell you specified in the Key field will be automatically removed.

In our example of the sales revenue dashboard, a pie chart is used to represent the data. You may want to enhance it by adding a column chart representing the same info and ask the user to select whether he wants to see the pie chart or the column chart. In such a situation, you use a cell to control the visibility of the two charts. Note that the status cell is bound to a selector such as a combo box from which the user selects what chart to see.

In your future development, you will find dynamic visibility to be a very useful property and will use it a lot. For example, to introduce your dashboard and show others how to use it, you need provide a help document. You can write the help info in a label and put it in a panel container (let's name it the Help panel). Obviously, you add a toggle button labeled Help to the dashboard and only show the Help panel when the user clicks the Help button. To achieve this, you insert a certain value to a cell when the user clicks the toggle button and set dynamic visibility of the Help panel based on that cell.

- Enable Data Animation
  When this option is selected, the slices of the pie chart appear on the screen with an amination effectOtherwise, all of the slices of the pie chart appear all of a sudden and at the same time. You can try it out with a simple test, by dropping a pie chart on the canvas and previewing it with and without this option selected.

  For a better user experience, we suggest that you always choose this option by selecting Enable Data Animation. As the name indicates, the animation is for the data, or the slices of the pie chart, not the pie chart itself, which is defined by Entry Effect, as described in the section below.

- Entry Effect
  You use this option to configure how the chart appears on the screen. You can select one effect from the Type dropdown list. None means no effect, which is the default option.

  The other three options are Fade-In, Wipe Right, and Wipe Right-Down. You can select one based on your preferences.

  With any effect you select, you need to specify the duration in seconds that the entry effect will last. You can enter the duration directly or use the spin button to increase or decrease it at 0.1–second intervals. The suggested duration is 0.2 – 1 second.

In the meantime, for a consistent user experience, we recommend setting the same entry effect for all the charts in one dashboard.

Appearance

This category is divided into four subcategories as illustrated below.

1. Layout

    ▶ Chart Area

    You can set whether or not to show the chart background on the canvas by setting the property Show Chart Background. The background is a solid area with borders behind the chart, as shown in Figure 4.9.

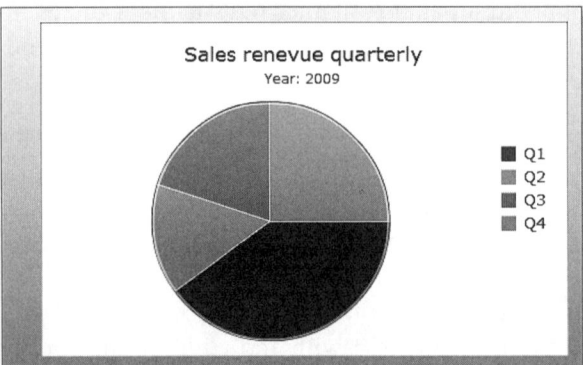

Figure 4.9 The Chart Background of a Pie Chart

The chart background of the pie chart in Figure 4.9 is the white rectangle area with borders. Note that for a clear look, we changed the canvas background color from white to light gray.

You can then set the margin to control the space between the chart and the edge (border) of the background, by entering a number directly in the Margin field or clicking the Up or Down arrow in the spinner. You can set the color of the background on the Color tab.

Showing the chart background is a good way to identify the chart area and make it stand out from other components. The chart then appears somewhat above the canvas. If you don't like this effect and want to provide a user experience in which the chart is integrated into the canvas, you can choose not to show the chart background. Then the user will see a transparent chart, as displayed in Figure 4.10.

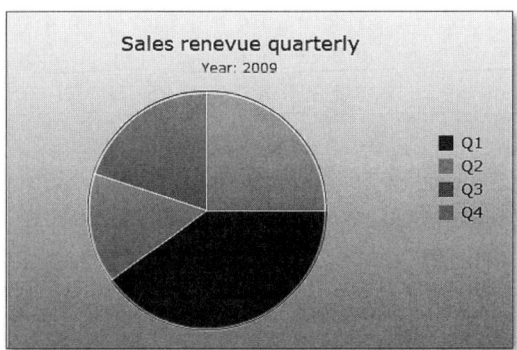

Figure 4.10 The Pie Chart Appears Embedded In the Canvas with the Chart Background Not Shown

▶ Plot Area
The Plot Area is where the pie chart lies, determined by its axes. You can configure whether or not to Show Fill, which displays a background to the plot area, and Show Border, which displays borders around it.

You can set the color of the fill or the border when it's enabled via the Color Picker button to the right of each property.

When Show Border is selected, you have the option to set the Border Thickness, by entering a number directly in this field or clicking the Up or Down arrow of the spinner. Only an integer is accepted here.

Figure 4.11 shows how these settings affect the look and feel of the chart.

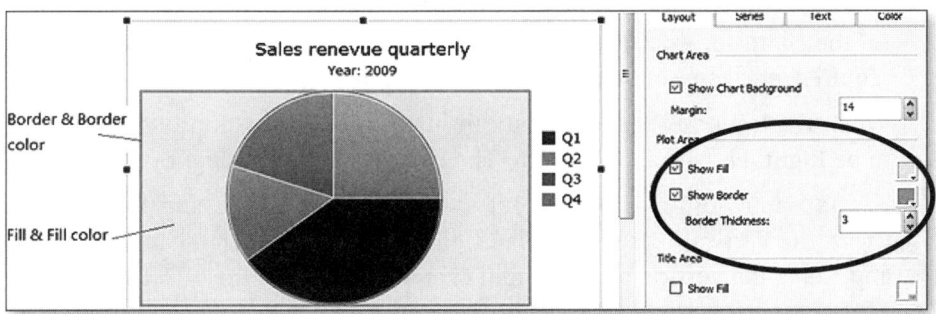

Figure 4.11 Effects of Settings in the Plot Area of a Pie Chart

▶ Title Area
Similar to the Plot Area, the Title Area is where the titles (including both the

chart title and the subtitle) lie. You can also configure whether or not to Show Fill (background) or Show Border and choose their colors and set Border Thickness when enabled. You make your settings through the corresponding fields.

Figure 4.12 shows how these settings affect the look and feel of the chart.

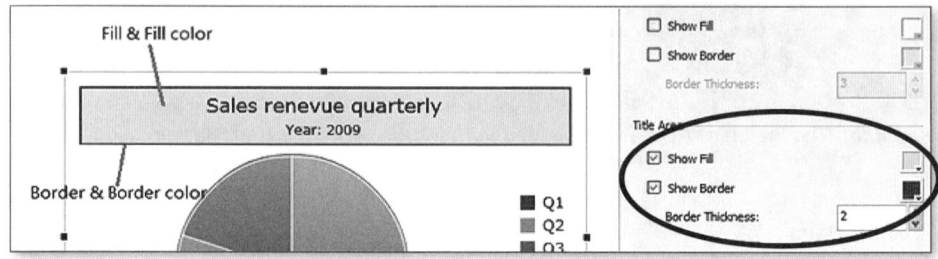

Figure 4.12 Effects of Settings in the Title Area of a Pie Chart

- Legend
  The legend is an explanatory list of the symbols on the chart, typically an inscription or title with an image as an indicator. In the screen shots of our pie chart above, the list on the right (e.g., ■ Q1) displays the legend.

  The legend can help the user know the label of each slice from its color, for example, what quarter the slice stands for. Without it, the user has to move the mouse over a slice to know its label. As a result, you may want to display the legend to prompt the user by selecting Enable Legend.

  However, sometimes you may choose not to show the legend to save space for the chart, for example, when the label of some slice is very long and thus requires much space for the pie chart and looks ugly.

  When the legend is enabled, you can further set its position in the pie chart to be Right, Left, Top, or Bottom. The default position is Right.

  For Top and Bottom, you can set the Horizontal Offset, and for Left and Right, the Vertical Offset. By default, the offset is 0, which means the legend appears in the vertical or horizontal center. You can set the offset by entering an integer in the field or increasing or decreasing it using the Spin button with increments of 1.

  The purposes of the offset are explained below.

Horizontal Offset:

– N > 0: N pixels to the right

– N < 0: N pixels to the left

Vertical Offset:

– N > 0: N pixels to the top

– N < 0: N pixels to the bottom

Similar to the Plot Area and Title Area, You can also configure whether or not to Show Fill (background) or Show Border and set their colors and Border Thickness when Border is enabled.

Generally speaking, you may choose to show the rill or border to emphasize the legend, and not when you want a tidy and clean appearance.

Figure 4.13 shows the effect of these settings, where the legend is displayed at the top with a horizontal offset of 24 and a border thickness of 3.

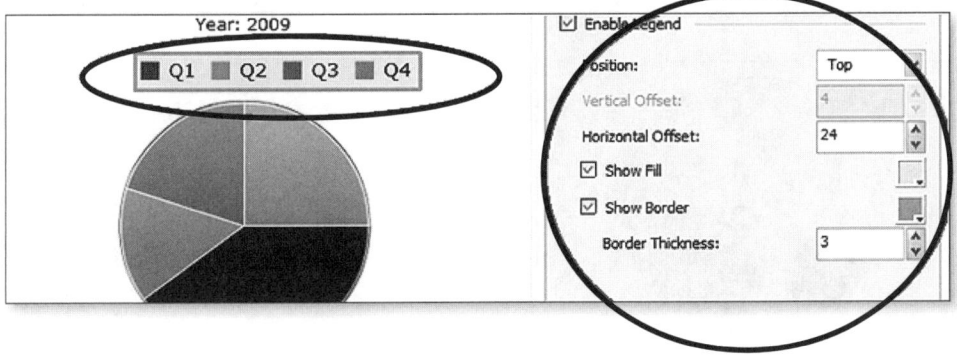

Figure 4.13 Effects of Settings for the Legends of the Pie Chart

2. Series

▶ Data Point
In this list area, the color of each data point, or slice, of the pie chart is displayed. The default colors of the pie chart are defined by the color scheme you are currently using. You can customize the color of each data part by clicking the color picker and choosing a color you prefer. This property is useful if you want to use specific colors for certain data parts.

4 | UI Component Basics

- Transparency

  By default, the pie chart is solid. With the Transparency property you can set the transparency level. The minimum value is 0, which means solid (no transparency), and the maximum is 100, meaning it's fully transparent and thus no slice is visible.

  You can move the slider bar to adjust the transparency or directly enter an integer in the field. If you want a transparency level of 50%, enter "50." Note that decimals are not accepted here. If you enter a decimal such as "32.6," Xcelsius will round it to 33.

- Lines

  You can use this option to control whether or not to show a line between every two adjacent slices and around the pie. If Show Lines is enabled, you have the option to set the color and thickness of the lines.

  Figure 4.14 shows the effect of these settings where Show Lines is enabled with a thickness of 2 in red (it looks ugly, but it's just for explanation here). Pay attention to the lines between every two slices and around the pie.

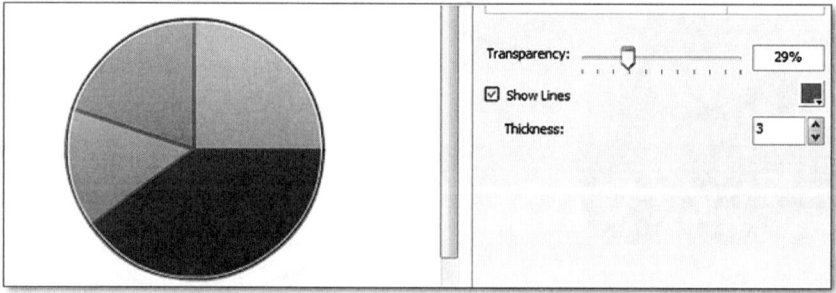

Figure 4.14 Lines Between Every Two Adjacent Slices of the Pie Chart

3. Text

   In this tab you can set the format for all texts that will appear in the pie chart, including the chart title and subtitle, the legend, mouse-over values, and data labels.

   For each item you can set the format including font, font size, style, alignment, and color. For legends and data labels you can set the properties of Position and Offset so they will appear where you want them. Note that you cannot customize the position for the chart title or subtitle, which is fixed by Xcelsius 2008 itself.

Figure 4.15 shows the text properties for the legend of a pie chart.

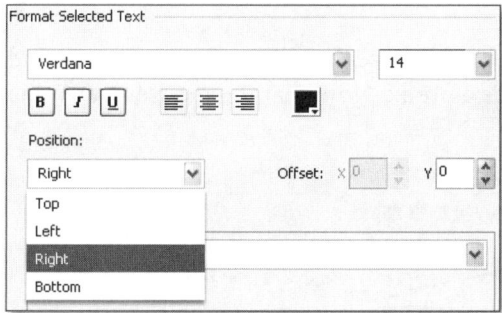

Figure 4.15 Available Properties to Format the Legend of a Pie Chart

Number Format defines how the value is displayed. The available options, such as Numeric and Currency, are explained one by one below.

- General
  Choose this option if you want to display the value as a string.

- Numeric
  Choose this option if you want to display the value as numeric such as 3.14.

  You can configure how a negative value is displayed, the number of digits after the decimal point, and whether or not to show a thousand separator, as displayed in Figure 4.16.

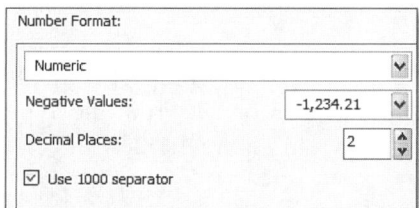

Figure 4.16 Customize the Display Format of a Numeric Value

- Currency
  Display the value as a currency value, for example, the sales revenue. Similar to the Numeric option, you can also configure how a negative amount is displayed and the number of digits after the decimal point.

  Using the thousand separators is required here, and you cannot change it.

To display the value in a meaningful way, you can also set Prefix and Postfix. For example, you can display the currency symbol (eg. $, USD) as the prefix or postfix.

Figure 4.17 shows the effect of setting Mouse-Over Values to Currency and displaying the currency symbol $ as a prefix. Note that the mouse-over value on Q4 is now displayed as $25.00.

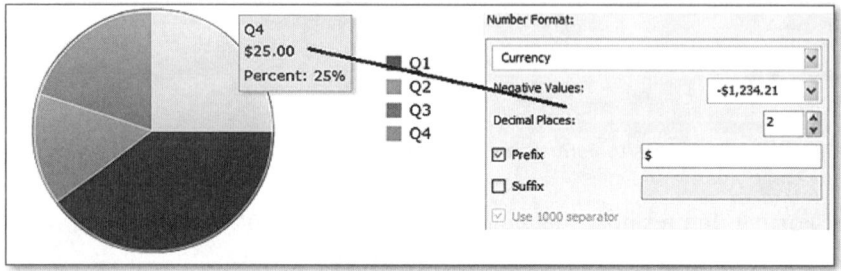

Figure 4.17 Customize the Display Format of a Currency Value

- Percent

  Choose this format if you want to display your value as a percentage, for example, if you are showing the year-to-year growth in sales revenue. The value is calculated inside the embedded spreadsheet as (this year's sales revenue – last year's sales revenue) / (last year's sales revenue), such as 0.13. Instead of displaying 0.13 on mouse over, you want the user to see 13%. Then you need set Number Format for Mouse-Over Values as Percentage.

  You can set the number of digits after the decimal point.

- Date/Time

  You can customize how to display a date or time with this property, for example, whether to show the month as March or 3 or 03. From the Type drop-down list, you can select a format, as shown in Figure 4.18.

4. Color

   In this tab you set the colors of all elements of a pie chart, including the background, the slices, the lines between slices, the title area, the plot area, the legend area and so on.

   If you have enabled Chart Background in the Layout tab, you can set the background color here, by clicking the Color Picker button to the right of the label Background Color, with the same steps apply to Title Area, Plot Area, and Legend Area. You can also set their fill color and border color here.

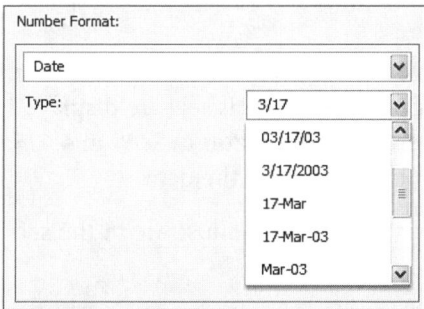

Figure 4.18 Choose a Display Format for the Date

Similar to what you do in the Series tab, you can also customize the slice colors here, by clicking the color picker to the right of each data part.

You can also set the line color between every two adjacent slices in this tab.

Figure 4.19 shows the configuration items in this tab. Note that Title Area is configurable, while Plot Area is disabled, due to the different settings in the Layout tab.

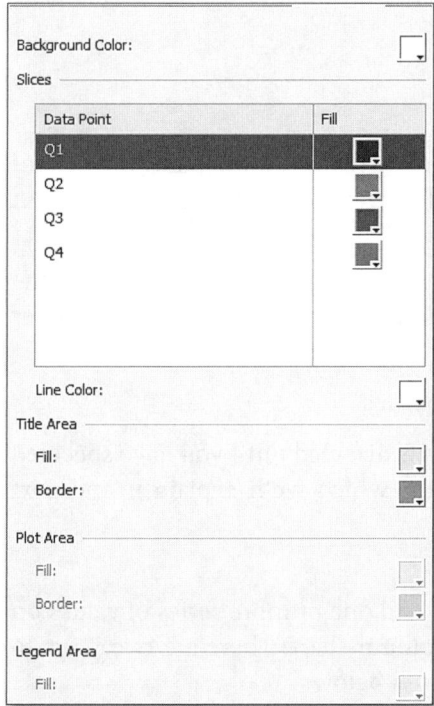

Figure 4.19 Configuration Items in the Color Tab

4.1.2 Column Chart

A column chart uses a column (vertical, tall, and relatively thin) to represent the data for each data part, compared to slice in a pie chart. The labels are displayed in the horizontal X-axis and the values in the vertical Y-axis. Later in Section 4.1.5, you will see bar charts, which use a horizontal bar to display the data.

A column chart can also have a secondary Y-axis, which we'll illustrate in the sections below.

When to Use a Column Chart

A column chart is mainly used to show and compare the values for different counterparts in a range, for example, to show and compare the sales revenue in each quarter or in each branch. Remember, we use a pie chart to show the percentage or contribution to the total sales revenue of each quarter. This is the difference between a pie chart and a column chart.

How to Use a Column Chart

The Properties panel of a column chart is arranged in five subcategories, as explained below.

General
- Titles
  Similar to a pie chart, you can set the chart title, the subtitle, and the title of each axis here. You can either enter a text directly into the corresponding input field or click the Bind button to bind it to a cell in the embedded spreadsheet.

  A column chart contains an X-axis to display the category, a Y-axis to display the value, and possibly a secondary axis (vertical) to display the value of another series. You can also set titles for the two or three axes.

  Figure 4.20 shows the effects of these properties.

  Note that the field Secondary Value (Y) Axis is disabled until you have specified a data series plotting on the secondary axis, which we'll explain in the next section.

- Data
  You need to specify the labels on the X-axis and one or more series of values on the Y-axis (or the secondary Y-axis) for a column chart. There are two ways to specify the data source for them, as illustrated below:

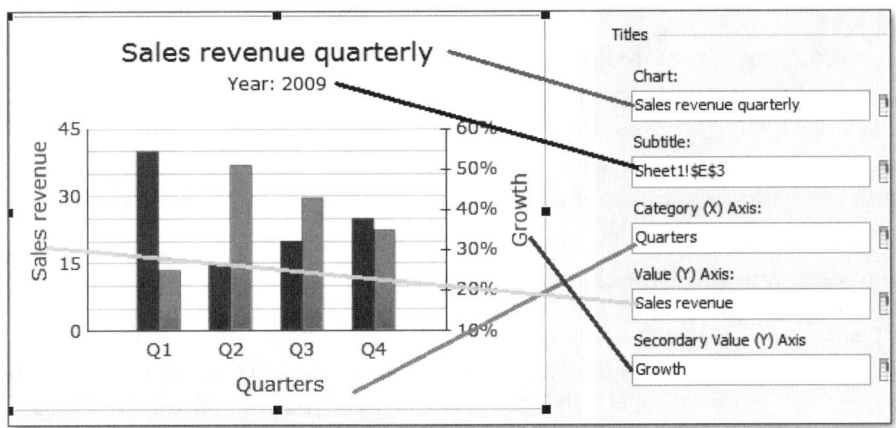

Figure 4.20 Effects of Setting the Titles of a Column Chart

▸ By Range
You click the Bind button to select a cell range as the data source, and depending on the way your data is arranged, select either Data in Rows or Data in Columns.

As Figure 4.21 shows, the labels (quarter names) are in the fifth row, and the values (sales revenue and growth) are in the sixth and seventh rows, so we select the range "Sheet1!$F$5:$I$7" as the data source and select Data in Rows.

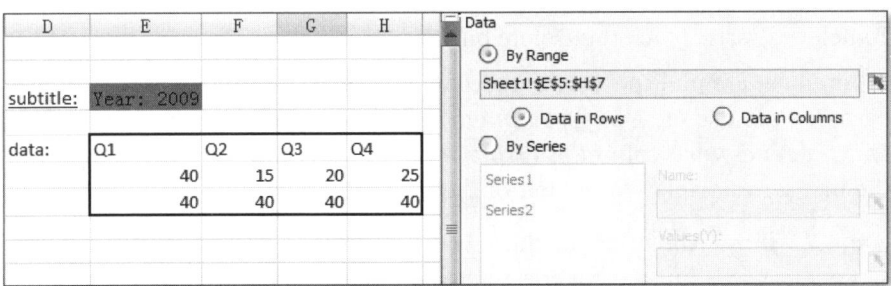

Figure 4.21 Specify a Cell Range as the Data Source of a Column Chart

Xcelsius will automatically treat the first row (or column, if Data in Columns is selected) as the label (category) and others as values that will appear in the Y-axis. The data will appear in the column chart immediately so that you can quickly check whether it's what you want.

- By Series

  This option provides more flexibility but more complexity than By Range. Here you need to manually specify a row or column for labels, add one series for each kind of value (or measure, if you are familiar with data warehouse), and bind it to another row or column. You can specify the series name that will appear in the legend area and on mousing over the columns, which is impossible when By Range is selected.

  The typical steps for using this option are:

  - Specify a cell range for Category Labels that will appear on the X-axis by clicking the Bind button in the bottom. In our case, click the Bind button and select cell range Sheet1!$F$5:$I$5, where the names of Q1 to Q4 are stored.
  - Click the Add Series button [+] to add one series for values that will appear in the Y-axis. Then you have the option to set the series name by either entering a text directly or binding it to a single cell, specify a cell range for it, and configure whether to show the values on the primary or secondary axis.
  - In our case, enter "Sales Revenue" in the Name field, select the range Sheet1!$F$6:$I$6 as the data source for Values(Y), and plot it on the primary axis. You can also bind the name to a cell such as Sheet1!$D$5.
  - Repeat step 2 if you want to show other value series. In our case, we'll add a second series named Growth to show the year-to-year sales revenue growth and plot it on the secondary Y-axis.
  - To delete a series, click the Delete button [-].
  - When there are multiple series, there will be multiple columns for each data part. You can use the Up [^] or Down [v] button to change the series order, which defines what column is displayed to the left. Note that the columns of the first series display to the left of those of the second and later series.

  Figure 4.22 shows the effect of these settings. In this example we specified a label for the X-axis but not for the Y-axis (neither primary nor secondary). The sales revenue for each quarter is displayed on the primary Y-axis in cyan, and growth on the secondary Y-axis in orange.

  Note that the columns for sales revenue are displayed to the left of those for growth, based on the series order you defined in the list.

Figure 4.22 Effects of Setting the Data Source for a Column Chart By Series

Drill-Down

Similar to what we discussed for pie charts, you can insert the position or value into a cell, or the status list, or a row or column from a cell range to another row or column.

In addition, you can insert the series name of your current selection into a cell. You define the series names in the General tab. When you click on a column in the column chart, its series name is inserted into the target cell.

The drill-down behavior is per series. That is, when there are multiple series, the drill-down can be triggered on each series. You may want to use this option to insert a row or column from different ranges into the target. This is different from pie charts, where there's only one series.

However, there can only be one insertion type in a column chart, no matter how many series there are. As shown in Figure 4.23, you can select one insertion type and then specify the destination and the source data (if available) for each series.

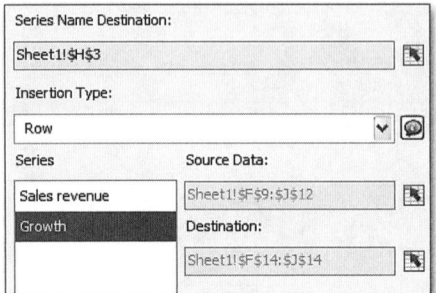

Figure 4.23 Drill-Down Behavior for Each Series with One Insertion Type

The interaction options and default selection are the same as those for pie charts. For more info about what they are and how to use them, please refer to the corresponding subsection in Section 4.1.2. The difference is that you can set the default item for each series here.

Behavior

By default, this category is divided into three tabs: Common, Scale, and Animations and Effects. When there's any series plotting on the secondary Y-axis, the Scale tab is subdivided into a Primary Scale tab and a Secondary Scale tab.

- Ignore Blank Cells
  You can choose to ignore cells at the end of the range that are blank In Series, In Values or both. Note that for a pie chart, you can only ignore cells blank in Values.

  If cells blank In Values are not ignored, the spaces for them will still be left in the chart, resulting in an unfriendly user experience. For example, if we select two more empty columns in the quarterly sales revenue column chart, Figure 4.24 shows the difference when Ignore Blank Cells – In Values is selected and not selected.

As you can see from this figure, the space for the two empty items is still displayed in the left-hand column chart, resulting in a confusing appearance.

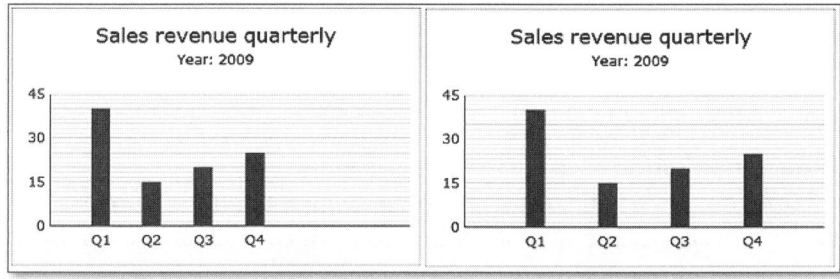

Figure 4.24 Effects of Ignoring End Blank Cells in a Column Chart

We recommend that you always select the two options here to ignore cells at the end of the range that are empty either in series or in values. This is useful especially when you are not sure about the actual size of the data. For example, the sales revenue of each branch is returned from a data connectivity such as a Web service that is mapped to a cell range in the embedded spreadsheet. The number of rows, or the branches, changes every year or month. As a result, you have to talk to the user to agree on the maximum number of branches in the next one or two years and bind the data to a cell range with that number of rows. However, currently there may be fewer branches, and the last few rows are empty. In such a case, you need to ignore the end blank cells.

As mentioned previously, a data item that is empty in value or in series but is not at the end of the range will not be ignored. As a result, you will see a blank column, or a column without a label, displayed in the column chart. To solve this problem, move the blank cells to the end of the cell range either using Excel formulas or in the backend so that such cells are placed at the end.

▶ Enable Run-Time Tools
When you select this option Xcelsius offers a set of functions to enable data scale configuration at runtime. As chart data changes at runtime, you can adjust the scaling options with these tools.

When you select the Enable Run-Time Tools checkbox and three subordinate checkboxes, an icon will be displayed at the top-left corner of the column chart at runtime. When you move your mouse over that icon, a menu list will pop up. What menu items are available is based on your selection of the subordinate checkboxes here.

The options that are available when you select Enable Run-Time Tools are explained below.

- Show Focus Button

  With this option selected, a focus button will be displayed in the popup menu. By clicking the focus button, you rescale the chart axes based on current data.

- Show Reset Scale Button

  A Reset Scale button will be displayed in the popup menu if you select this option. You can clickthe Reset Scale button to rescale the chart axes to those that were initially loaded.

- Show Scale Behavior Options

  Three status buttons will be displayed in the popup menu if you select this option. The three buttons are Grow, Off, and Auto, as explained below:

  — Grow: Auto (Y) axis with Allow Zoom Only selected

  — Off: Manual (Y) axis

  — Auto: Auto (Y) axis with Allow Zoom Only unselected

You can switch to one of the three options at runtime to change the scaling options. The option you set at Scale tab at design time will be the default option at runtime. For example, if you select "Manual(Y) Axis" at Scale tab, the default option at runtime will be "Off".

▶ Scale

In this tab you define how the Y-axis behaves, including the minimum and maximum limits, number of major and minor divisions, and so on. Note that this tab is divided into Primary Scale and Secondary Scale.

▶ Auto (Y) Axis

When you select this option, Xcelsius will automatically calculate the minimum and maximum limits and number of divisions based on the values at run time. The scale will grow and shrink automatically as data changes.

You can select this option if you are not sure about the values at design time or you just want to leave it to Xcelsius, for example, if you don't know whether the sales revenue is several tens of thousands or millions of dollars.

You can select Allow Zoom Out Only if you want the Y-axis to grow without shrinking when data changes, thus minimizing chart scaling, for example, if you are using a column chart to display the quarterly sales revenue every year, with a combo box for the user to select one year. In 2000 the sales revenues are very low, say, less than 100, and in 2009, revenues are more than 100 and less than 500. The maximum limit of the Y-axis an grow from 100 to 500 on your selection. If you do not select this option, you will see an obvious shrinkage, or change, of the Y-axis, and the change or shrinkage may happen on every change. In contrast, if the change happens gently without any shrinkage, the user may not even notice it. You may want to check this option when your chart is used in an animation.

Note that the shrinkage will only happen when the scale is growing higher and will not happen when it's decreasing. That is, the scale will change from 100 to 500 when you change the year from 2000 to 2009. But when you change it back to 2000, the scale will remain 500.

With this option selected, you can tune the zoom sensitivity via the slider beneath it. The value determines how much the Y-axis scale will grow on data changes. Moving the slider to the left results in the axis scale increasing by a small factor when the scale of the Y-axis changes. On the other hand, the axis scale increases by a larger factor on data change when you move the slider to the right.

- Manual (Y) Axis
  Select this option if you are not satisfied with the result of selecting Auto (Y) Axis and want more flexibility. You can manually set the minimum and maximum limits and number of major and minor divisions by directly entering an integer in the corresponding field or clicking the Bind button to bind to a cell in the embedded spreadsheet.

  The advantage of this option is that it provides more flexibility. For example, when all of the values are very large (e.g., larger than 1,000,000), you can choose not to start from 0 but from 1,000,000 or 500,000. You can also configure how to display the divisions, which we'll explain in the next section.

  However, the minimum and maximum limits of the chart are fixed with this option. So don't use this option if you are not sure about the values, in other words, if the values might vary quite a lot in different situations. For example, let's say you are showing the quantity of a product sold every quarter. The user needs to select one product from a large list of products your company sells. Some products may have very few units sold every quarter, say, fewer than 100, and others may have more than 1,000 sold. In this situation, if you set the limits to be 0 to 100, products with more than 1,000 units sold will not be displayed. If you set the maximum limit to 10,000, the columns for the less-sold products will be very short and thus meaningless.

If you still want to use this option in the situation above, you can achieve a perfect chart by binding the limits to cells whose values are dynamic. But this is more complex and requires more time. We recommend choosing Auto (Y) Axis in such scenarios.

▶ (Y) Axis Scale
Here you define how to position the major and minor divisions on the vertical axis, by selecting Linear or Logarithmic from the dropdown list.

Linear means to dividing the axis into divisions on a linear scale. The divisions are plotted at evenly spaced intervals.

On the other hand, Logarithmic means plotting the divisions on a logarithmic scale instead of linearly. The divisions are plotted at intervals of the logarithm of the value, instead of the value itself. The spaces between every two adjacent divisions are not even: Smaller values have larger space intervals, while larger values have smaller intervals.

Figure 4.25 shows the difference between these two methods by displaying the same data in two column charts.

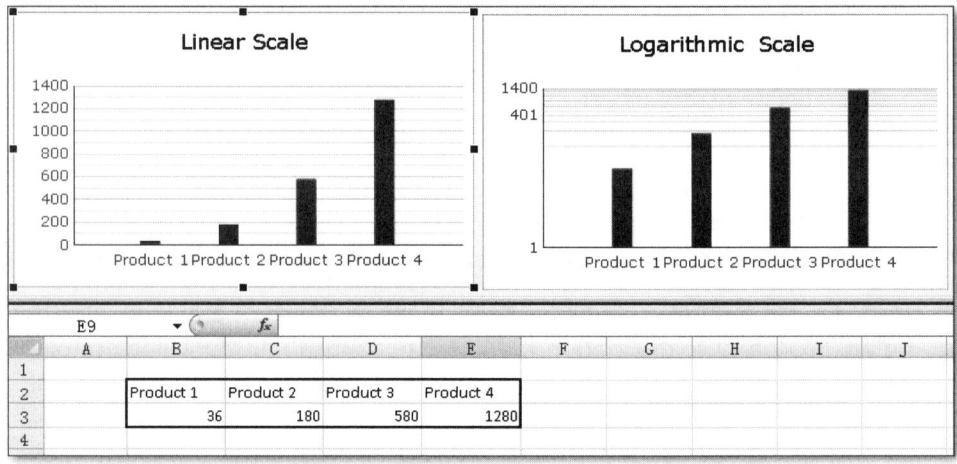

Figure 4.25 Difference Between Linear and Logarithmic Y Axis Scale

Linear is most commonly used in daily life. You may only want to choose Logarithmic when the values are vastly different, covering a large range of data, for example, if the values include 10, 200, and 40,000. If you select Linear, the value 10 will be a tiny column. Choosing Logarithmic can reduce the scale to a more manageable range that's more suitable to display on the Y-axis.

- Fixed Label Size

  In a column chart, the label for some value points on the Y-axis may be longer than others (e.g., 40,000 is much larger than 100). For a consistent look and feel, you can select this option to lock the width of the Y-axis labels so that they will not change when the scale changes.

  Sometimes the value is very big (e.g., larger than 1,000,000). With Fixed Label Size selected, you can choose to display abbreviations of the values as labels. For example, instead of displaying 45,000, you can display it as 45K. You can click the Label Abbreviations button to customize the abbreviations, that is, what symbol is used to represent thousand, million, billion, and trillion, as shown in Figure 4.26.

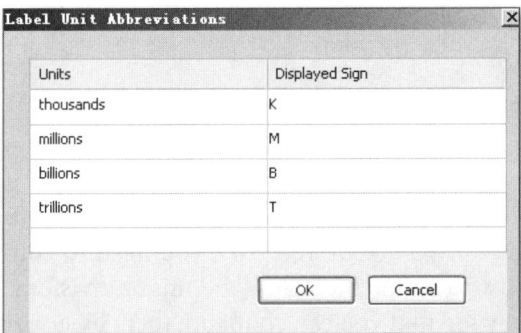

Figure 4.26 Manage Label Abbreviations for Quantitative Values

  You can click the Displayed Sign field to change the abbreviation. However, you cannot create new abbreviations.

  Figure 4.27 shows the comprehensive effect, with Logarithmic Y axis scale and Fixed Label Size selected. Note that the letter K is used to abbreviate thousands.

- Divisions

  In a column chart, the values are represented by columns. The higher the column is, the bigger the value is. Aside from the minimum and maximum limits, you need to display some major and minor divisions so the user can easily understand the value of a data part through its height.

  You can define how the divisions are displayed by specifying either the number or the size. Note that this option is only available if you have selected Manual (Y) Axis. Xcelsius will then automatically calculate where to position the divisions.

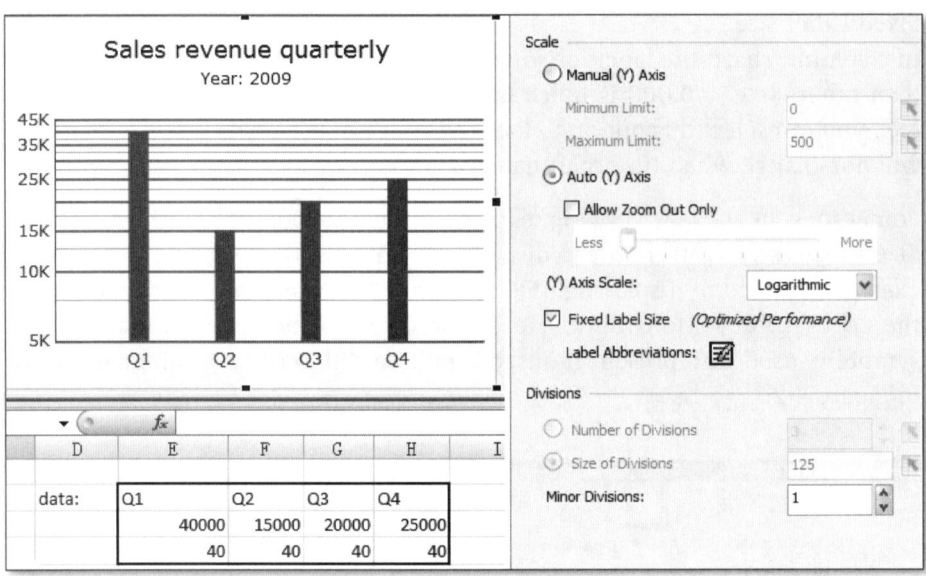

Figure 4.27 Effects of Setting Scale Properties of a Column Chart

You can also define how many minor divisions will appear between every two adjacent major divisions. Depending on your requirements, you need to consider thoroughly before choosing how to define the major and minor divisions. In the Properties panel, you can easily see that you can configure them by either directly entering an integer in the field or by clicking the Bind button.

Figure 4.28 is a column chart with three major divisions and one minor division in between. Pay attention to the three horizontal lines of value 20, 40, and 60 and the one horizontal line in between.

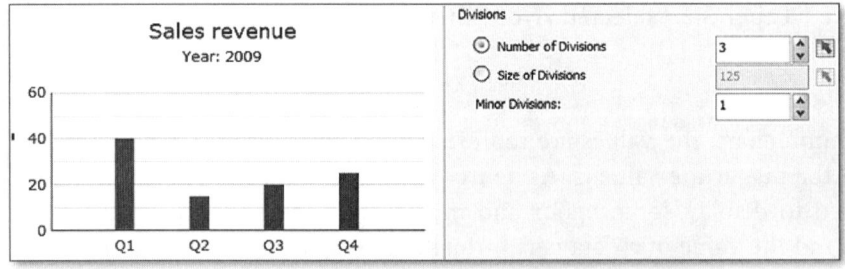

Figure 4.28 A Column Chart with Three Major and One Minor Divisions

- Animations and Effects

    The properties here are the same as those of a pie chart, and we'll ignore them here and in any later UI components. For more info about them, please refer to the corresponding part in Section 4.1.2. To be more exact, in section 4.1.2 when we are talking about How to use a Pie chart – Behavior – Enable Data Animation and Entry Effect.,

Appearance

- Layout

    This is the same as the settings for a pie chart. Here you can configure:

    - Whether to show the chart background and the margin between the chart and, if so, the background border.

    - Whether to show the fill in the plot area or title area and, if so, the color. The fill is a solid background.

    - Whether to show the border in the plot area or title area and, if so, the color and thickness.

You can also configure whether and how to display the legend. For a pie chart, the legends are labels with images, while for a column chart, they are series names with images. When you select Enable Legend, you can set the position where it will appear and the vertical and horizontal offset and whether and how to show the fill and border.

Figure 4.29 shows the effects of these settings, where the fill is shown in both plot and title areas, and the border is shown in title area with a thickness of 2, and legend is positioned on the right with both fill and border.

Now that you understand the effects of each property, you can customize these settings on your dashboard based on your requirements.

- Series

    You set the color and transparency level of each series here, through the corresponding color picker and slider. For a pie chart, each data part is a series, while for a column chart, each measure (sales revenue or growth) is a series, and all data parts in the measure are columns (markers) in the same series. That is, all columns (markers) in the same measure are of the same width, color, and transparency, though different in height which is used to represent the value.

    You can also set the width of the columns for each series, with the Marker Size field. This option is helpful when you have several items, making the column very crowded. For a better user experience, you can reduce the marker size when there are too many items (e.g., over 20 products) or increase it when they are too few (e.g., four quarters) for a better look and feel.

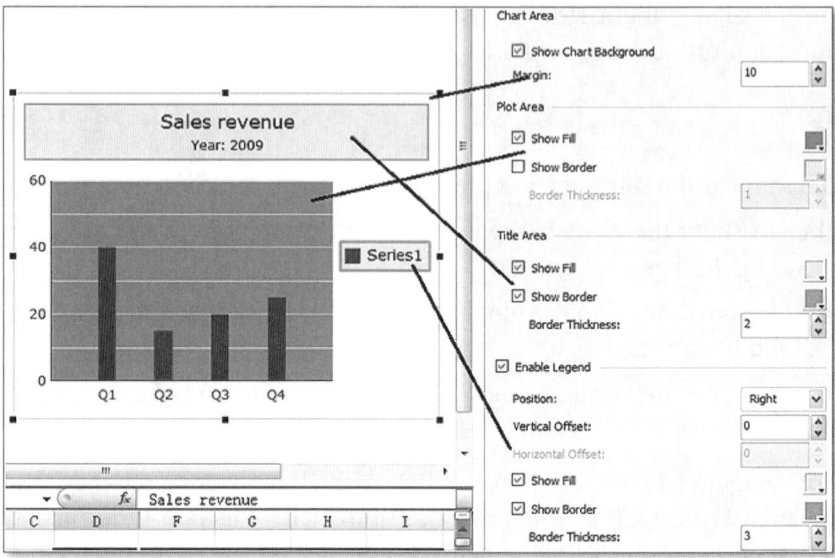

Figure 4.29 Effects of Settings in the Layout of a Column Chart

▶ Axes
You can configure whether or how to show the horizontal axis and the primary or secondary vertical axis here. When there's a series plotting on the secondary vertical axis, this tab is divided into Primary Axes and Secondary Axes.

When the primary vertical, the secondary vertical, or the horizontal axis is enabled, you can set its color by selecting one from the corresponding color picker and its thickness via the corresponding spinner.

You can choose to display a tick mark for each major or minor division on the vertical axes. Whether to show the major or minor ticks is also configured here.

You can also define whether or how to show the major and minor gridlines by selecting the corresponding checkboxes. When these checkboxes are selected, the color and thickness of the gridline can also be set via the corresponding color picker and spinner. Figure 4.30 shows the effects of these properties.

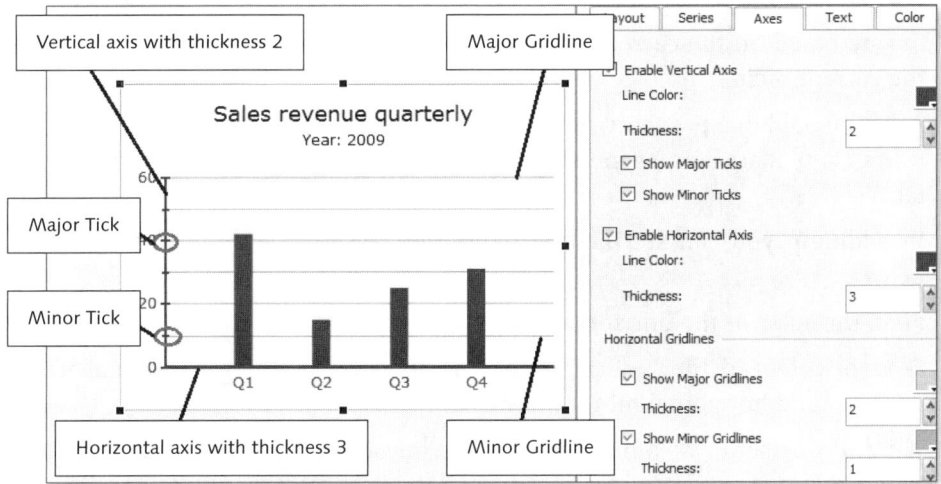

Figure 4.30 Effects of Settings in the Axes Tab

As shown in this figure, the primary vertical axis is enabled in cyan with a thickness of 2, and the horizontal axis is enabled with a thickness of 3. Both major and minor gridlines are enabled in the same color but of different thicknesses, and both major and minor ticks are displayed.

► Text
Here you set the formats of all texts that will appear in the column chart, including the title and subtitle, titles and labels of the horizontal (X, for categories) axis and the primary and secondary vertical (Y, for values) axes, legend, and mouse-over values.

The format includes font, size, style, alignment, and color. For some texts you can also configure where to display them by setting the positions and offsets. Your changes will be reflected in the chart immediately.

Like the settings for a pie chart, you can customize the format to display the value if it's a numeric, currency, percentage, date, or time value. For more details about these formats, please refer to the corresponding section about pie charts in Section 4.1.2.

► Color
You can set colors for all parts of a column chart here. If Show Chart Background is enabled (in the Layout tab), you can set the background color with the Color Picker button.

Like the Series tab, you can also set colors for each series here. The default colors are based on the current color scheme, which is by default determined by the current theme.

As you would in a pie chart, you can set the colors for the fill and border of the title area, plot area, or legend area here, if you have enabled them in the Layout tab.

In addition, you can set the colors for the axes and gridlines, as explained below.

First, the color of the horizontal X axis.

Second, colors of the vertical Y-Axis and its corresponding horizontal major gridlines and horizontal minor gridlines.

Third, if one series or more is plotted on the secondary vertical axis, you can also specify colors related to it, including the vertical (secondary) axis, its corresponding horizontal (secondary) major gridlines and horizontal (secondary) minor gridlines.

Alerts

In the beginning of this section, we mentioned that in a column chart, all markers of one series share the same color, in contrast to a pie chart, where each data part has a different color. However, you can also show different colors for different data parts of the same series in a column chart. In the following paragraphs you will learn how to show different colors for markers of one series, based on its value.

An alert is used to highlight values under certain conditions by displaying the markers in colors that stand out. This is a very useful feature. For example, you may want to highlight the quarters with a quantity sold that is higher than the yearly average or products with a sales revenue growth less than -10% so that at a glance you can determine the outstanding items that need looked into. Typically, you can display the poor items in red, and the good ones in green.

- Enable Alerts
  You need to select this option before making use of alerts.

  Note that Alert cannot be enabled when there's more than one series on the column chart. This is easy to understand, because markers in another series are in a different color, which makes it confusing with colors representing alerts.

  Alerts are an important and very useful feature of Xcelsius 2008. In Chapter 8, we'll discuss alerts in general instead of in relation to a specific kind of chart. In this section, we'll discuss in detail the meaning of each property and how to use it in a pie chart.

The condition to define alerts is based on the value, either the quantity itself or its percentage, of a target. You can choose one based on the business requirements of your dashboard.

There are three options to specify the target if you have selected As Percentage of Target.

- A single cell
  You select a single cell after clicking the Bind button. The value in that specified cell will be used as the target for all values. That is, the percentage of each category item, which will be used in the condition to determine its color, is calculated by dividing the value by that in the target cell.

- A cell range
  You also select a cell range by clicking the Bind button. The cell range can be either in a row or in a column and should be the same size as the values. For example, in our quarterly sales revenue sample, there are four category items, so the number of cells in this range should also be four. The percentage of each category item will be based on the value in the corresponding cell in the range, by its index.

If you select more cells than there are category items, redundant cells are ignored. On the other hand, if fewer cells are selected, the remaining targets will be the same as the last one in the specified cell range. Moreover, if there are empty or nonnumeric cells in between, the percentage for the corresponding category item will be 100%.

- Directly entering values
  Instead of binding to a cell or a cell range, you can directly enter values as the target by clicking the button next to the Bind button. In the prompt window, you can enter the target value for each category item. As for the cell range, redundant values are ignored, and remaining targets will have the same value as the last specified value. And if there are any empty or nonnumeric cells in between, the percentage for the corresponding category item will be 100%.

In the prompt window you can add, modify, or delete a target value. You can also change the target orders with the Up and Down buttons, as shown in Figure 4.31.

4 | UI Component Basics

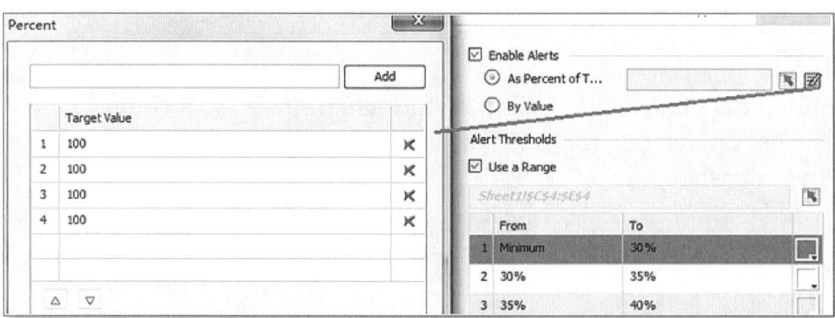

Figure 4.31 Manually Specify Target for Each Data Item

▶ Alert Thresholds
Under Alert Thresholds you can set the level for each threshold and the color for each level. A level is defined in a condition that is based on the absolute value or the calculated percentage of each data item.

By default there are three levels, based on a 30-70 division by percentage, that is, three levels of less than or equal to 30%, larger than 30% but less than or equal to 70%, and higher than 70%. Values larger than the From value and smaller than or equal to the To value fall into the corresponding level.

Note that there's a level called No Data at the end, which is used to handle exceptions. If any cell contains an unexpected value, for example, a string when a number is expected, the corresponding data item will fall into the No Data level and consequently will be displayed in the color defined for that level.

You can double-click any field to change its value. Its adjacent levels will be updated automatically according to the new value. The starting and ending limits, Minimum and Maximum, cannot be edited. For example, as displayed in the left part of Figure 4.32, 30% appears in both level 1 and level 2. If you change either of them to 40%, the other will be changed automatically to 40%.

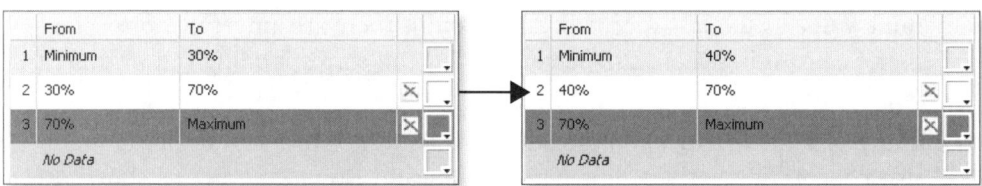

Figure 4.32 Alerts Definition Is Updated When a Threshold is Manually Updated

To add a level, click the input field on top of the level list and enter a value. Based on its value and the existing levels, a new level will be inserted. For example, in Figure 4.32, if you enter "50" in the input field and click the Add button or press ⌈Enter⌉, the existing level 30% to 70% will be divided into two: 30% to 50% and 50% to 70%. This happens because 50% falls into the level 30% to 70%. The result is illustrated in Figure 4.33.

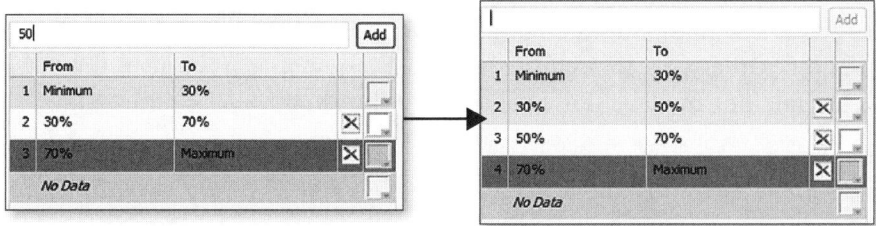

Figure 4.33 Enter a Threshold to Define New Levels

Note that for a percentage-based threshold, you enter the value without the percent sign. That is, to add a threshold of 50%, enter "50" instead of "50%" or "0.5." In fact, if you enter "0.5" in the field, Xcelsius will think that you are in fact asking for 0.5%.

For value-based thresholds, also enter the value directly.

To delete a level, click the Delete icon of the corresponding level. Its adjacent levels will be adjusted automatically so that the existing levels cover all data points. For example, if you delete level 30% to 50%, the To value of the first level will be changed to 50% immediately.

You can click the color picker on the right to set the color for each level. This option is disabled if Enable Auto Colors is selected, and the colors for each level are defined by Xcelsius and according to the theme.

You may have noticed that the methods above use static constant numeric values to define the thresholds or levels. Sometimes dynamic thresholds are required. For example, you might want the user to define the threshold. To achieve this, you need to bind the thresholds to cells in the embedded Excel spreadsheet. To do this, select Use a Range and select a cell range. Xcelsius will create levels based on the threshold values defined in the cells. For example, say you have 18 in cell F8, 30 in cell G8, and 35 in cell H8. Then the levels will be less than or equal to 18, larger than 18 but less than or equal to 30, larger than 30 but less than or equal to 35, and larger than 35.

With Use a Range selected, you can specify the colors if Enabled Auto Colors is not selected, but you cannot change the values by double-clicking it.

The values in the cells of the range should be in incremental order. That is, the value of the right-hand cell should be bigger than that of the left-hand cell. Note that in the example above, the values are in incremental order (18, 30, 35). If the cell range is in a column, the value of the lower cell should be bigger than that of the upper cell. Otherwise, though the levels definition appears correct, the markers will not fall into any level for a value-based threshold.

- Color Order
  This option is useful to generate colors for levels automatically. You can choose whether low values, middle values, or high values are good, which will be displayed in a more agreeable color (e.g., Green). Note that option Middle Values Are Good is only available for percent alerts, that is, for a percentage-based thresholds definition.

  By default, Low Values Are Good is selected. If you change it to High Values Are Good, colors of each level will be switched, in a reverse order. That is, given T levels, the color of N-th level will be switched with that of the (T-N)-th level, where T is the number of levels and N is a integer between 1 and T.

4.1.3 Line Chart

A line chart uses a series of data points to represent values. Every two adjacent points are connected by one straight line. Similar to the column chart, the category items, or labels, are displayed in the horizontal X-axis. The Y-axis displays the value scale. You can get the value of a label from the Y-coordinate of its corresponding data point.

The line chart is a basic type of chart that is commonly used in many fields. It's an extension of the scattered graph, produced by connecting the scattered data points with line segments. A line chart can also display values of several measures, or series. Figure 4.34 shows a typical line chart.

Essentially, a line chart is very similar to a column chart in configuration and usage. The only difference between them, aside from their different purposes, is that a line chart uses points to represent values, while a column chart uses columns or bars to do so.

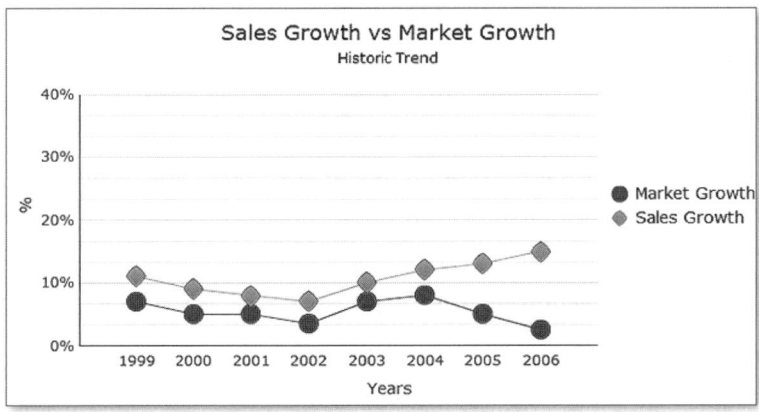

Figure 4.34 A Typical Line Chart with Two Series

In the How to Use section below, we'll explain only the properties specific to a line chart. We'll ignore the parts that are the same as those in a column chart or explained them very briefly. For more details, please refer to the corresponding parts in the "How to Use" sections in Section 4.1.1 about pie charts or Section 4.1.2 about column charts.

When to Use a Line Chart

A line chart is often used to illustrate the trend of changes in data of certain measures over a period of time. Its focus is the trend of data change over intervals of time. So, the labels are often time intervals, such as days, months, or years. That's why the line segments are often drawn chronologically.

For example, when you want to see the change, or trend, in sales revenue over quarters this year, you can choose a line chart. In Figure 4.34 above, you can easily get an idea about the growth trend in the two measures (sales growth and market growth) over the years from 1999 to 2006.

As mentioned in Sections 4.1.2 and 4.1.3, the focus of a pie chart is to illustrate the percentage or contribution of each data part to the whole, while that of a column chart is to display and compare a range, and the purpose of a line chart is to show the trend of data over a period of time.

How to Use a Line Chart

You can drag a line chart from the Components view to the canvas and resize it using the mouse, which is the same for all charts. You can set its properties in the Properties panel, which, like a column chart, is divided into five categories.

General

Similar to the column chart, you can set the data source of all parts in the line chart, including the chart title and subtitle, titles of the category (X) axis and value (Y) axis, labels of the category (X) axis, and values of the Y-axis.

You can add as many series as you want, plotted on either the primary Y-axis or the secondary Y-axis. If a series is plotted on the secondary axis, you can set its title.

The way to set the data items is the same as for a column chart and is explained in the How To Use – General subsection in Section 4.1.2.

Drill-Down

The functionality and configuration of drill down here are exactly the same as those of a column chart, as explained in the How To Use – Drill-Down subsections in Section 4.1.2. The only difference the end user will encounter when he uses this functionality at runtime is that he clicks or puts the mouse over a point, instead of a column or marker.

Behavior

The properties in this category and their usages are exactly the same as those of a column chart, as explained in the How to Use – Behavior subsections of Section 4.1.2, including whether to ignore empty cells at the end of a range in series or value, set the axis scale manually or automatically, and show the major or minor gridlines.

Appearance

As indicated by the name, you can set how the chart appears through this category, including the font of all texts, the color and thickness of all axes and gridlines, and whether and how to show fill and border in the chart, title, plot, and legend areas. They are configured the same way as a column chart, which has been illustrated in Section 4.1.2.

All settings and usages are the same as those of a column chart, except in the Series tab, where you can select a shape for the data points as markers per series, selection from a circle, diamond, star, triangle, and cross. For each series, Fill defines the color of the markers and Line defines that of the line segments connecting the markers.

Figure 4.35 shows an example of this setting.

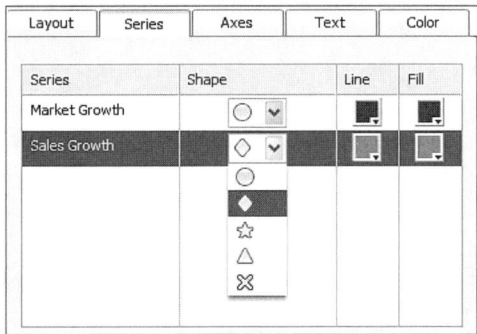

Figure 4.35 Customize Shape and Color of Each Series in a Line Chart

Alerts

Like in column charts, you can enable alerts to highlight outstanding (very good or very bad) items by displaying them in special colors, based on their quantities or their calculated percentages against targets.

Note that with alerts enabled, the color of a marker is defined by the level it falls into, but the color of the line segments will not be changed.

Practice

Now let's go through a simple hands-on example to get a deeper impression of line charts. Suppose the director of the sales department in your company asks you to create a dashboard showing the change in sales revenue over each quarter in 2009 and the growth rate on a year-to-year basis.

A line chart is best fit to satisfy his requirement to show the change trend over a period of time. So we begin by dragging a line chart from the Components panel and dropping it onto the canvas and resizing it a little bigger. Now let's move on, step by step.

1. Prepare the Data

The director has sent you the data in an Excel file. You can either pick up the data you want and enter it into the embedded Excel spreadsheet or import it directly by selecting DATA • IMPORT.

You can calculate some data that is required in the chart but not provided in the original data source using some Excel formulas. For example, the growth over a quarter is not provided by default but is calculated with a formula. The content of cell F8 is =(F6-F7)/F7. One more word here: You can format the cell in the embedded spreadsheet to be a percentage.

Briefly, your data is similar to that displayed in Figure 4.36.

	A	B	C	D	F	G	H	I
2								
3				subtitle:	Year: 2009			
4								
5				Sales revenue	Q1	Q2	Q3	Q4
6				This year	40,000	52,000	35,000	44,000
7				Last year	32,000	46,000	32,000	48,000
8				Growth	25.00%	13.04%	9.38%	-8.33%
9								

Figure 4.36 Data in the Embedded Spreadsheet of this Hands-On Example

Note that the subtitle is blue and the data area has a bold border. We highlight each kind of data for a clear understanding of the data structure during our design time.

Pay attention to the cell index, which we'll refer to shortly in the data binding phase.

The Excel file is available on this book's web page at *www.sap-press.com*. You can import it to try it out on your own.

2. Specify Data in the General Tab

To make the chart easy to understand, we display some useful info in the titles.

The chart title conveys the main purpose of the line chart. Here, we directly enter the name "Sales revenue quarterly trend."

The chart subtitle provides supplementary information about the chart. Here, we'd like to show what year we are talking about. The year may be dynamic, for example, selected by the user from a combo box. So we bind it to a cell, by clicking the Bind button next to the input field, and click the OK button in the prompt window after selecting the cell Sheet1!$F$3 in the embedded spreadsheet.

The titles of the X- and Y-axes are also displayed, providing additional hints about what each axis is showing. These titles are also directly entered into the input fields.

We want to customize the series names, so we select By Series instead of By Range.

On the X-axis, we want to display the four quarters. So we click the Bind button at the bottom, next to Category Label(X), and hold the mouse to select range Sheet1!$F$5:$I$5, where the four quarters are stored.

To show the sales revenue for each quarter of this year, click the Add button to add a series. Then enter its name, "Sales revenue," in the input field of the Name property, click the Bind button next to Values(Y), and select the range Sheet1!$F$6:$I$6, where the values for this year are stored. We want them to display on the primary Y-axis, so we leave the default selection Primary Axis to plot the series on.

The director also wants to see the growth, in percentage. We have calculated the growth in Excel using formulas, and now we need to add one series. To do this, click the Add Series button to add another series, bind its name to the cell Sheet1!$D$8 and its values(Y) to cell range Sheet1!$F$8:$I$8, where the growth values are stored. Here we need to select Secondary Axis to plot this series on, because the growth is less than 1 or 100%, but the sales revenue, which is plotted on the primary Y-axis, is over 10,000. You can imagine that if data in these two series is plotted on the same Y-axis, the growth will be almost invisible.

By now your chart and the General tab should be like what's displayed in Figure 4.37.

Figure 4.37 The Line Chart with Two Series Plotted on Different Y-Axes

4 | UI Component Basics

3. Set Behavior

We don't need a drill-down for this chart, so ignore category Drill Down.

In the Behavior category, as a best practice, always select In Series and In Values for Ignore Blank Cells if blank cells are not specially required.

As shown in Figure 4.37 above, the sales revenues are in the tens of thousands, which should be abbreviated. So, in Primary Scale, select Fixed Label Size. Then 60,000 will be displayed as 60K, which is more agreeable to the eye. This is very useful when the number is too large, for example, 60,000,000.

And we don't want to see too many gridlines in the chart, so we decrease Minor Divisions from the default 2 to 1.

In Figure 4.37, the divisions on the secondary Y-axis are too dense. So in the Secondary Scale tab, select Manual (Y) Axis to manually set the minimum and maximum limits, and set them to -0.2 and 0.5, respectively.

By default, the major divisions are defined with a size of 10, which is not suitable for percentages. We can change Size of Divisions to 0.1 or 0.05 or something like that or just specify how many major gridlines we want. Here we select Number of Divisions and set it to 5.

Figure 4.38 shows the dashboard now and the properties in the Secondary Scale tab.

Figure 4.38 The Line Chart after Customizing the Primary and Secondary Scale Tabs

4. Set Appearance

By default, the legend area appears to the right of the line chart. The dashboard seems to be too wide and not very tall so far. So we want to decrease width and increase height. One way to do this is to show the legend area on the top instead of to the right. To do this, set Position to Top under Enable Legend in the Layout tab.

In the Series tab, we can set the series shape, line color, and fill color. We don't want to make any customizations here, so just leave them alone. However, we want a smaller marker size, so decrease Marker Size from 17 to 12.

We don't want to show the minor gridlines, so unselect Show Minor Gridlines in both the Primary Axes and Secondary Axes tabs.

To highlight the current year, we want to display the subtitle with an underline. To do this, in the Text tab, select Sub Title and then click the Underline button [U].

Finally, in preview mode, your dashboard should be similar to the one in Figure 4.39.

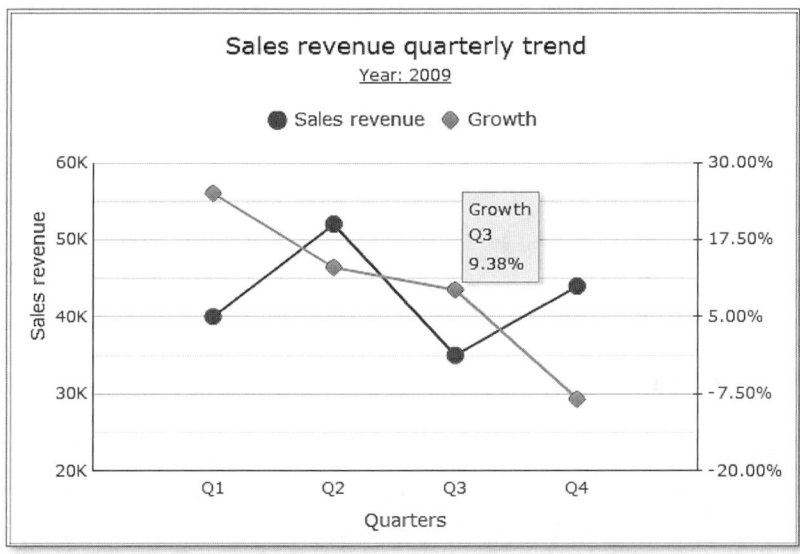

Figure 4.39 The Final Appearance of the Line Chart in this Hands-On Example

You can then export the dashboard and send it to the director of the sales department. From the chart, the director can easily find out that the sales revenue in

2009 keeps bouncing, which is not a good sign. Though the sales revenue in Q4 has increased a lot compared to Q3, the growth keeps going down.

You can find the source file for this example on this book's web page at www.sap-press.com.

4.1.4 Bar Chart

A bar chart uses horizontal bars to represent the data values of one or more series, rather than the vertical columns in a column chart. As a result, the horizontal axis (primary or secondary) shows the values, while the vertical axis shows the category labels. Except for this, a bar chart is very similar to a column chart, not only in the usage and configuration, but also in focus. You will find that their Properties panels are very alike.

You can regard the bar chart as a transposition of column chart, as illustrated in Figure 4.40.

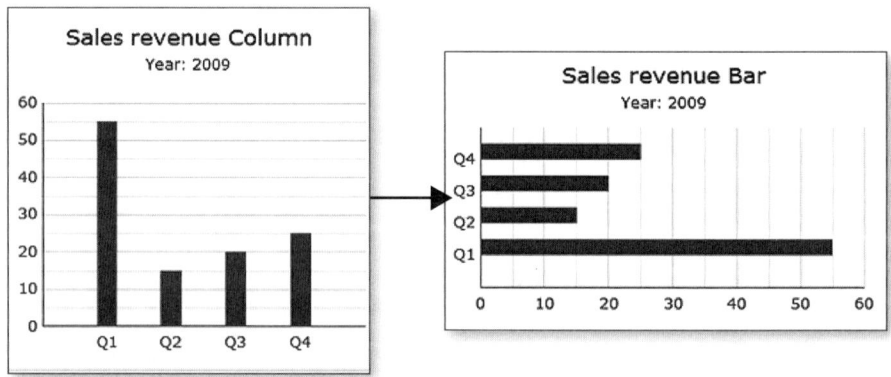

Figure 4.40 A Bar Chart Looks Like the Transposition of a Column Chart

When any series are plotted on the secondary axis, there will be a horizontal X-axis on the top, compared to a vertical Y-axis on the right side of the column chart. The new axis is used to show the values of the secondary axis.

The direction of the markers (columns or bars) is the main difference between a column chart and a bar chart, though you can call the vertical column in a column chart a bar if you want. However, for consistency, we will call the marker a bar when it's horizontal and column when it's vertical.

When to Use a Bar Chart

A bar chart is often used to compare the values of different category items, which is the same as a column chart. For example, you can use a bar chart to compare the sales revenue of every quarter in a given year.

It's hard to choose one between a bar chart and a column chart. Basically, you can make your choice according to your, or the end user's, preferences. Some people like the visualization of a bar chart, while others like the other.

As shown in Figure 4.40 above, when the numeric values vary much, a bar chart requires a wider space, while a column chart requires a taller space. Similarly, when there are many category items, a bar chart takes up a taller space, while a column chart takes up a wider space. You need to take this into consideration when there are many UI components on the canvas and limited free space.

How to Use a Bar Chart

How to use a bar chart, including moving, resizing, and setting its properties, is exactly the same as for a column chart, as described in Section 4.1.2. Instead of repeating ourselves, we will simply ignore those details here.

4.1.5 XY Chart

From the name, you can see that there are two axes in an XY chart, X and Y, and there will never be a secondary Y-axis. In contrast to other charts such as the column chart, there's no category data. Instead, both axes show values of some measures.

The X-axis of a column chart represents the category labels and is discrete. However, both the X- and Y-axes of an XY chart are continuous.

The XY chart shows a data point at each intersection of the X- and Y-values. The data points might not appear in the order that the values appear in the cell range. Instead, the points are shown along the X-axis in ascending order. All points are of the same size, shape, and color. Similar to other charts, you can enable alerts to set different colors for items that you want to stand out. Unlike the line chart, there's no line segment between every two points.

Figure 4.41 shows a typical XY chart, where sales revenues are displayed on the X-axis and the cost is on the Y-axis.

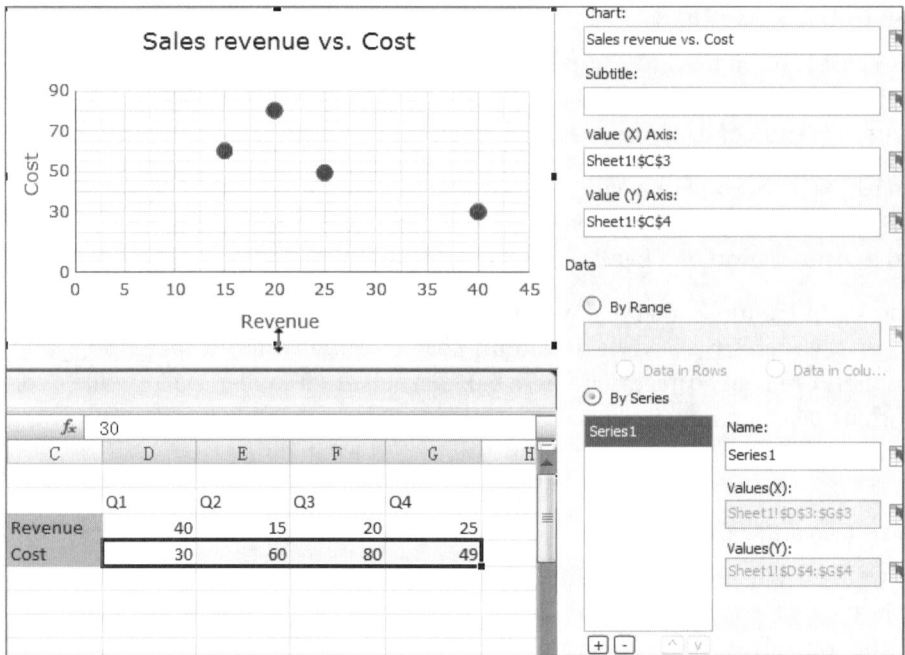

Figure 4.41 A Typical XY Chart with Two Series

In this figure, there are four points in the chart, one for each quarter, plotted at the intersection of two values of the X- and Y-axes. At each data intersection, that is, for each quarter, a point is shown with an X-coordinate of the sales revenue and a Y-coordinate of the cost. From the figure you can tell that in Q1, the cost is the highest, but its sales revenue is the poorest.

When to Use an XY Chart

An XY chart is mainly used to compare the values of different measures of one category item. For example, you can use an XY chart to show the sales revenue against the number of sales persons involved every month. You can display the number of sales persons on the X-axis and the sales revenue on the Y-axis. This way, you can determine roughly whether it's worth adding more sales persons for a higher sales revenue.

How to Use an XY Chart

Most functionalities and properties of an XY chart, including titles, drill-down, fonts, colors, and alerts, are the same as those of a line chart. You will find the Properties panels to be very similar. For explanations of each property and how to use it, please refer to the corresponding section for the line chart. Here we will only go through some properties that are specific to an XY chart.

General

You set the data source for all data parts of an XY chart here, including the chart title and subtitle, the title of the X- or Y-axis, and data.

However, you cannot set category labels for the chart. That is, when you select By Range to specify data, don't include any category labels. If you select By Series, you can manually set the series names and values on the X- and Y-axes. One more word: Both the X- and Y-axes display values but no categories.

There's no secondary Y-axis here. That is, though you can specify multiple series in this XY chart, they are plotted on the same Y-axis. So pay attention to the minimum and maximum limits of the series when there're multiple.

For charts like a column chart, you display the category labels on the X-axis and values on the primary or secondary axis. No matter how many series there are, the category labels remain the same. That is, you cannot set category labels per series. However, for an XY chart, you can set values for the X-axis per series, in the Values(X) field of each series.

Figure 4.42 shows an example of the effects of these settings, where the sales revenues are plotted on the X-axis, and the costs in the current as well as the last month are plotted on the Y-axis.

Note that the Values (X) field can be bound to different cell ranges for different series.

Behavior

All settings in this tab are the same as for a line chart, except that in the Scale tab, you can set the minimum and maximum limits and the scale algorithms of both the Y- and X-axes, as displayed in Figure 4.43.

4 | UI Component Basics

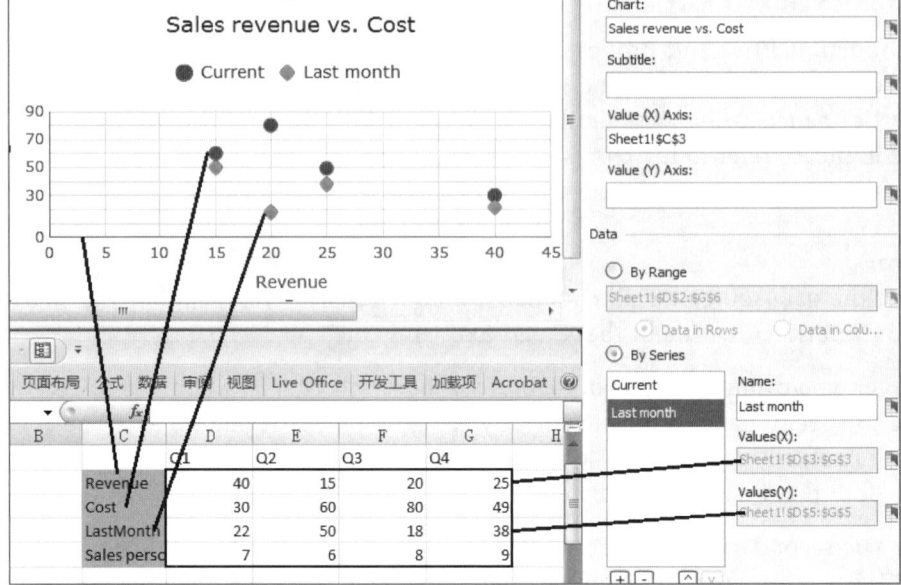

Figure 4.42 Effects of Settings in the General Tab of an XY Chart

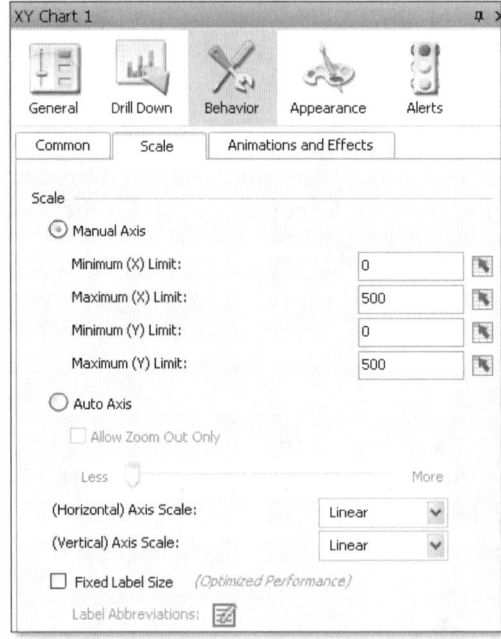

Figure 4.43 The Scales of Both the X- and Y-Axes Can Be Configured, Unlike a Line Chart

You can have a look the source file of this example, which you can download at our website.

Similarly, the limits can be automatically or manually set and can be constant numeric values or bound to a cell in the embedded Excel spreadsheet. This is easy to understand, because both axes show numeric values.

Appearance

Here you set how each part of an XY chart appears, including whether and how to show fills and borders, gridlines and ticks, and the font and color of each text. Because these settings were discussed previously, we will not repeat them here.

As for a line chart, you can set the shape, size, and color of the points (markers) but not the line segments connecting them.

4.1.6 Bubble Chart

A bubble chart looks very similar to an XY chart in that both:

- Show values in both the X- and Y-axes without category labels
- Have no secondary X- or Y-axis
- Use a circle point to represent the value at each intersection of X and Y values
- Have no line segments connecting the points
- Are continuous in both the X- and Y-axes

However, a bubble chart is very different from, and more powerful than, an XY chart. The points or markers of a bubble chart are always round, with variable sizes. Each point in a bubble chart is defined in terms of numeric values on three distinct measures, making it possible to be used in three-dimensional analysis. Because both the X- and Y-axes of the bubble chart are numeric scales, the position of each point is nothing but an indicator of the two values. The size, or area, of the point (marker) depends on the magnitude of the third numeric measure. That is, you can tell whether one item is bigger than another by the markers' sizes.

A bubble chart uses the circle size to represent its quantity value, which should always be above zero. If the value is negative, a tiny dot is displayed, and its size never changes. As a result, the size makes little difference in such a situation. A workaround for such a situation is to duplicate the numeric values into another row with the negative values changed into positive ones and to display them as a series in the chart. For example, if the values of a measure are (1,2,-3,4), you can duplicate them into another row with values (1,2,3,4) and add both series to the chart. The bubble for value -3 will be displayed twice, once a tiny dot in the original series and then as a bubble with a size proportional to its value in the new series. Figure 4.44 shows the effect of such a situation at runtime.

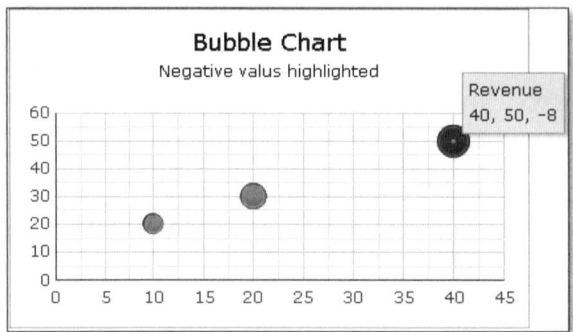

Figure 4.44 Use Two Series to Highlight the Negative Values with an Appropriate Bubble Size

The markers (referred to as circle points or bubbles) are different in size, big or small, just like bubbles from a fish. That's why it's called a bubble chart.

You can think of a bubble chart as three-dimensional: X-axis, Y-axis, and the size of the point as the Z-axis. Graphically, it has an X-axis and a Y-axis to represent the item location and a Z-value representing its size. This is a very clever way to fulfill the requirement for a multidimensional analysis.

When to Use a Bubble Chart

A bubble chart is often used to compare a group of items based on three different measures on one dimension (category), providing a three-dimensional analysis. For example, you can use a bubble chart to analyze the market share of each vendor by showing the sales revenue on the X-axis and the number of products on the Y-axis. Here the category items are the company names, with three measures of number of products, sales revenue, and competitive ability.

When using a bubble chart, you need think a lot about what measure is associated with the X-axis, the Y-axis, or the bubble size.

Figure 4.45 shows an example of chart just described. From it you can easily find out that, though the sales revenue of the third bubble is not the largest, it has the biggest market share. B has the largest sales revenue; its market size is top 1.

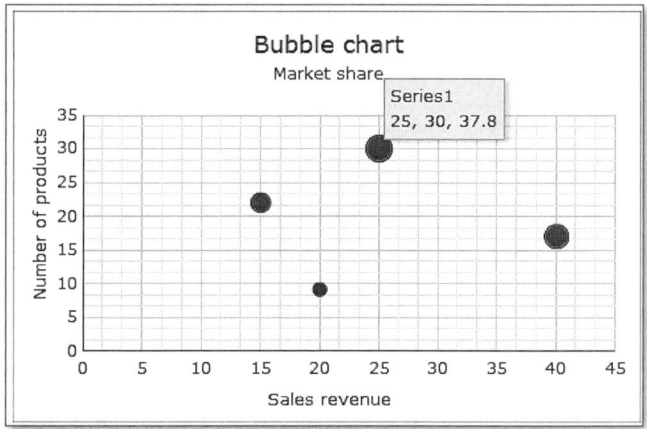

Figure 4.45 A Typical Bubble Chart to Analyze the Relationship Among Market Share, Sales Revenue, and Number of Product Lines

How to Use a Bubble Chart

How to use a bubble chart is very similar to how to use an XY chart, including its data, appearance, drill-downs, and alerts. Its property panel is also divided into five categories: General, Drill Down, Behavior, Appearance, and Alerts. Instead of discussing them in five separate sections, we'll just briefly cover them here.

In the General tab you set the data source for all data parts. Note that you specify three data sources for values of the X-axis, Y–axis, and size. If By Range is selected, you need to select three rows or columns that will be the values of the X-axis, Y axis, and size, sequentially, with the data in the first row or column being the value for the X-axis, the second for Y, and the third for size.

The drill-down functionality is the same as that of other charts. You can set drill-down operation per series, similar to that of a column chart.

In the Appearance tab you can set the marker size for each series. The size of each bubble is not fixed, and the setting here is just a reference. You can try to understand the effect of setting the marker size here by displaying a bubble with a size of 1.

One more word about the size of the marker, or the bubble: The bubble is a circle, the area of which is sequential to the square of its radius. As a result, if the size of one data item is four times larger than that of another; the radius of the bigger one will just be twice that of the smaller one.

The Legend area displays the name of each series such as Market size, not the name of each category item such as Company A. So when you mouse over a bubble, you don't know what company the value combination represents. As a workaround, you could use a spreadsheet component to show the data in a table, as a supplementary explanation. Figure 4.46 shows an example.

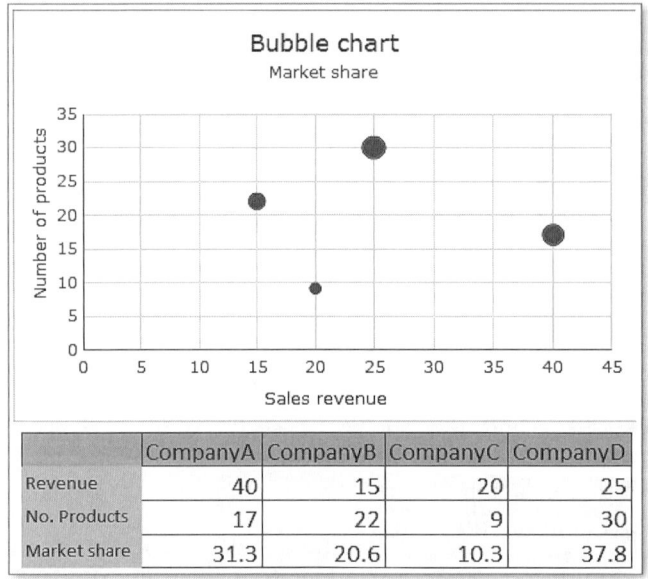

Figure 4.46 A Bubble Chart with a Spreadsheet Showing the Actual Data

4.1.7 Area Chart

Like a line chart, an area chart uses points plotted on the vertical axis to represent quantitative values on one or more measures of a category. The category items are plotted on the horizontal X-axis. The points are connected by line segments. An area chart is different in that:

- The first point of an area chart is displayed on the Y-axis
- The last point is displayed on the right edge
- The area between the X- and Y-axes and the lines is filled

- The point size is the same as the line size
- No drill-down is supported

Figure 4.47 displays an example of an area chart. Note that the first item, Q1, is displayed in the same position as the minimum limit of the Y-axis, which is different from any other kind of chart, where the first item is always displayed some distance away from the starting point of the X- or Y-axis.

Another difference is that in an area chart, there's no point or marker for each data part, which, for example, is a bubble in a bubble chart or a bar in a bar chart. The reason is that an area chart focuses on the total, not the individual.

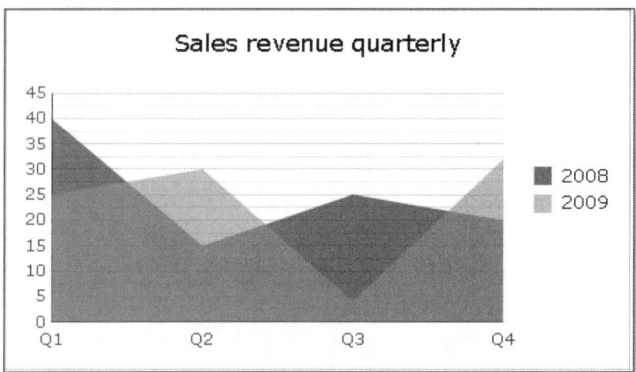

Figure 4.47 A Typical Area Chart

The filled area between the X- and Y-axes and the line segments of one series indicates a quantitative approach to the total value of the measure and over the category items of that series. In Figure 4.47, that chart shows the total sales revenue over four quarters in 2009. Of course, in the figure, the area size is not equal to the total, which is the entire year's sales revenue. However, when the sales revenue of multiple years or products is displayed together, you can compare the total of each series from their areas.

If there are multiple series in one area chart, they are stacked vertically, as we displayed in Figure 4.47, where there are two series, one for year 2008 and the other for 2009.

When to Use an Area Chart

You may choose an area chart when you want to show and compare the value of each category item, especially to compare the cumulated total value over a period.

The filled area often indicates a cumulative total over time, for example, to display the sales revenue of each quarter, with the area size indicating the total sales revenue each year. You can then compare the sales revenue of each year by the area sizes in different colors.

When there are several series in one area chart, which is usually the case, it's recommended that you display the slower-changing series on the bottom. The reason is that a vastly changing series may introduce the illusion that all series are changing a lot.

How to Use an Area Chart

The Properties panel of an area chart is divided into three categories: General, Behavior, and Appearance. This is quite different from the previously discussed charts, because it does not include drill-down functionalities or alerts. This is easy to understand, because the focus of an area chart is the total, not the individual, and there's no marker for you to click on.

Most properties and their functionalities are the same as those of other charts, we we'll ignore them here. For details about how to configure them, please refer to the corresponding How to Use sections of other charts. In this section we'll only explain some properties that are specific to area charts.

General

This tab is the same as that of many other charts including the column chart and the line chart. You set the data sources for all data parts of an area chart, including the chart title and subtitle and the titles of the X-, Y-, and secondary Y-axes.

Also, you specify cell ranges in the embedded spreadsheet of category items to display on the X-axis and of values for each series to display. You can choose whether to plot each series on the primary or secondary Y-axis.

If you specify data by range, the first row or column should be the category items, and each of the subsequent rows or columns will be treated as series.

Appearance

Like in other charts, here you set the appearance, including fonts, colors, styles, and alignments of all parts that will appear in the area chart. However, for each series, you can only set the fill color and no shape or color of the markers, because there are not any.

4.2 Selectors

Selectors are UI components that the user can use to make a selection from several items. Typical selectors include the radio button and the combo box. To build an interactive dashboard, you need to provide a UI with selectors so that the user can choose to see only the data that he is interested in.

4.2.1 Introduction to Xcelsius Selectors

The basic functionality of a selector is to provide the user with a way to select something from a list of candidates. From the implementation perspective, a selector inserts the selected values into the destination.

Xcelsius 2008 provides a rich set of selectors, as you can see in the Selectors category in the Components view. Most selector components provide a similar functionality, with different appearances and different use scenarios.

Instead of repeating descriptions of the similar characteristics of the selectors one at a time, we'll will divide them into several categories, based on their usage, as in the section below.

Some properties are common to all selectors, such as data insertion and dynamic visibility. Very simply put, you use dynamic visibility to show the component only when the content of a specified cell is equal to a constant value or that of another cell in the embedded spreadsheet.

Data insertion, similar to that in the drill-down tab of a chart, plays a critical role in Xcelsius interactive models. It's a common property of all selector components. At design time, data insertion concerns specifying three elements: data insertion type, source data (if applicable), and destination. At runtime, data insertion inserts some data into the destination cell(s) according to the specified insertion type when the selector is selected. There are various types of data insertion, including position, label, value, row, column, filtered rows, and status list, as explained in the How To Use a Pie Chart section above.

Note that not all insertion types are applicable for all selector components. The available types are listed in the corresponding dropdown list in the Properties panel.

4.2.2 Select a Single Item

This section covers some selector components used to select a single item from a list, including combo boxes, radio buttons, list boxes, and label-based menus, as shown in Figure 4.48.

4 | UI Component Basics

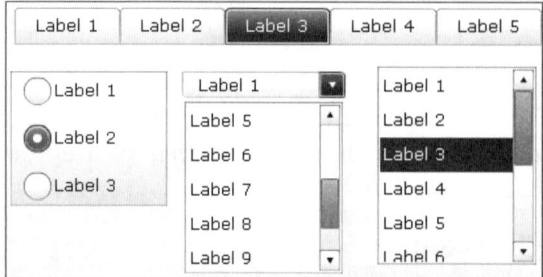

Figure 4.48 Selector Components to Select a Single Item

A combo box is a standard UI component in which a vertical dropdown list of items displays when it's clicked. The user can then select one of them. The dropdown list will collapse after the user clicks his selection, and the selected item is displayed in the box. A list box is very similar to a combo box.

A radio button, on the other hand, lists all candidates vertically or horizontally, with a radio button next to each item. The user can click one of them to select.

A label-based menu displays the candidates in a vertical or horizontal group of buttons and can be used as a menu for the user to choose from.

When to Use a Single-Item Selector

These selectors are very common in our daily life, and you might already be very familiar with them. You can use one of them when you want the user to select a single item from a list of candidates.

Based on your dashboard layout or your preferences, you can choose the one that best fits your design and requirements.

How to Use a Single-Item Selector

To use a selector, drag it from the Components view and drop it onto the canvas. Moving it is similar to moving other components, but you may not be able to resize some selectors horizontally or vertically. For example, you cannot drag a combo box to make it taller. Instead, you can only adjust its height by changing the font size of the label.

The various single-item selectors are used and configured almost identically. Basically, you need to specify its data source (named Labels) and then define data insertion behavior.

The Properties panel is divided into the categories General, Behavior, Appearance, and Alerts. Note that a radio button has no Alerts category.

General
In this tab you set the title, labels, and data insertion behavior for the selector currently selected in the canvas, either a combo box, a radio button, or a label-based menu. For radio buttons and label-based menus, you will see an additional option to set its orientation to either horizontal or vertical.

Figure 4.49 shows the effects of these settings. Note that the labels are displayed horizontally.

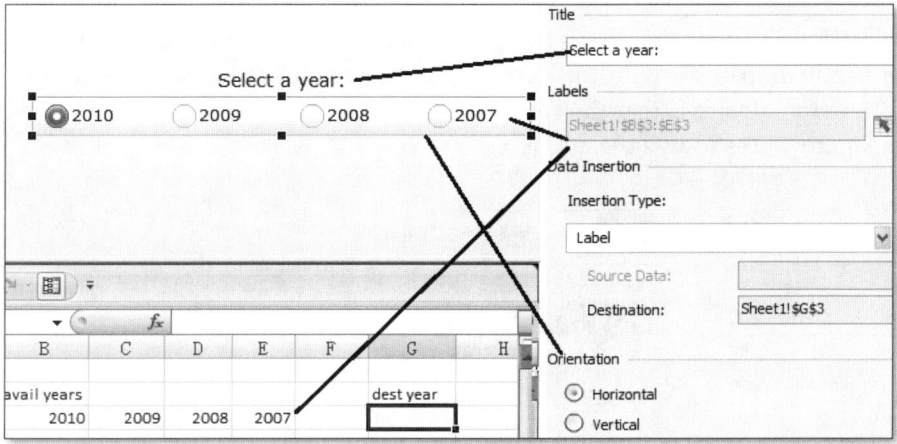

Figure 4.49   Effects of Setting the General Properties of a Radio Button

The insertions types position, row, column, and status list are the same as those of a chart, as explained in Section 4.1.1 when discussed pie charts. Three more types need mentioning here:

- Value
  The insertion type "value" is different from that of a pie chart. Instead of inserting one of the Values specified for a chart, here you need to specify an array of cells as source data, and the content of the selected cell will be inserted into the Destination field.

You can click the Hint button to the right of the Insertion Type field to see an illustration of this option.

- Label

  The insertion type "label" is similar to the Value insertion type of a pie chart in that it inserts one of the Labels you have specified For example, in Figure 4.49 above, if the user clicks on 2009, the label 2009 is inserted into the destination as a text.

Note that, unlike values, you cannot specify source data with this option.

- Filtered Rows

  This is a special insertion type used to insert one or more rows from a cell range specified as source data to the destination. The main point here is that this type can select multiple rows from source data, while in drill-down of a chart, you only have the ability to select one row or column from source to destination.

Basically, Xcelsius does the filtering of a cell range based on the value in the first column and compares it with the currently selected label of the selector component. The prerequisite is that the selector is bound to the first column of this cell range. Figure 4.50 shows an example.

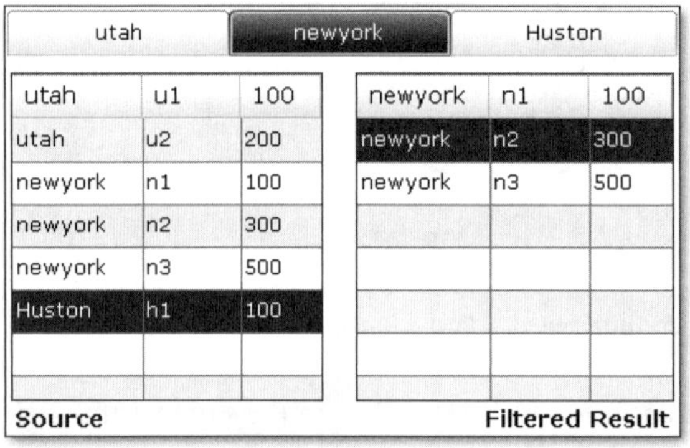

Figure 4.50 Effect of Using the Filtered Rows Insertion Type

Note that we used two list view components in this sample, one to show the source data in the embedded spreadsheet and the other to show the filtered rows. The labels of the label-based menu are bound to the first column of the source data, which contains six cells. You only see three distinct values in the menu because of the insertion type you have chosen.

You can find the source file of this example on this book's website, *www.sap-press.com*.

Behavior

▶ Selected Item

You can set the default selected item here. By default, the first item is selected. You can change it to the *N*-th item by selecting Label N in the dropdown list.

You can also bind it to a cell. At runtime, the content of that cell will be compared sequentially against all items of the selector, and the first match will be selected by default. The first item will be selected if no match exists. In Figure 4.49 above, we can pass the current year from a flash var (a data connectivity that will be introduced in Chapter 7) to a cell and bind the selected item of the radio button to that cell. Then, no matter when the user views this dashboard, the current year is always selected by default.

Binding the selected item to a cell is also useful for multiple components interaction. As one more example, say you have a combo box and a list box and they share the same labels, and you want to synchronize their selected items. That is, when the user selects one item on the combo box, the selected item of the list box will change accordingly, and vice versa. You can follow the steps below to practice this example

1. Drop a combo box and a list box onto the canvas.

2. Bind their labels to the same range, as shown in Figure 4.51.

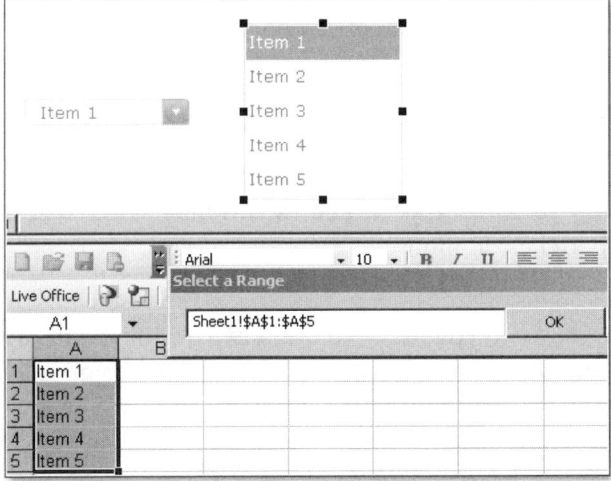

Figure 4.51 Data Binding for the Two Selectors

3. Set the insertion type of both of the components to Label and set the destination to cell Sheet1!$B$1.

4. For both components, on the Behavior tab, bind Selected Item to cell B1, as displayed in Figure 4.52.

Figure 4.52 Bind the Selected Item of Both Components to the Same Cell

5. To test the selected items, click Preview to run the dashboard, and you'll find that the selected items of two selector components are synchronized.

   ▶ Interaction Options
   For label-based menus and list boxes, you can configure whether the data insertion happens on mouse over or mouse click. Either option has advantages and disadvantages. You can select one based on your requirements.

   ▶ Animations and Effects
   In this tab, besides Entry Type and Duration, which we explained in Section 4.1.1, you can also check Enable Sound to play a sound each time the user makes a selection. However, the sound file is provided by Xcelsius and cannot be customized.

Appearance
Here you set the formats such as font, color, and position of all texts including the title and the labels, similar to the Text and Color tabs in a chart.

For each label you can set its default color, selected color, and mouse-over color, if applicable. This is an easy way to indicate what item is currently selected and provides an enjoyable user experience on mouse over.

Note that if you have configured data insertion to be triggered on mouse over for a combo box or label-based menu, when you move your mouse over the items, its color is first changed to the mouse-over color and then to the selected color.

For some components, you can also set the colors of the label background and the horizontal or vertical scroll bar, if any. However, the title of a label-based menu will not be displayed, though you can set its text and format.

The Layout tab is a little different among different selector components. A common property is transparency, which controls the transparency level of the entire component. You can adjust the value then check the effect in preview mode.

Some properties are specific to each component in the Layout tab. For example, you can configure Number of Labels Displayed for a combo box when the user clicks to display the items list, Button Separation space between every two adjacent buttons of a label-based menu, and Marker Size of the circle next to each label of a radio button.

4.2.3 Filter

Xcelsius 2008 provides a component called filter to conditionally select a row from a cell range in the embedded spreadsheet. The filter component looks at a range of cells with multiple fields of data and categorizes the dimension columns by unique data entries. The dimension columns then form a group of combo boxes, one for each dimension (column), with all of the unique values listed. The number of dimension columns included in the filter is configurable. When the user makes a selection in the filter, the row of data with all dimension values meeting the filter is inserted into the target row. You may find it somewhat similar to the filtered rows insertion type of the selectors described above.

Let's go through a simple example to better understand how to use this component. Suppose you have a data table of sales measures for different regions and products, as displayed in Figure 4.53.

Region	Product	Sales Revenue	Sales Quantity
East	Phone	350,000	2,350
East	PC	580,000	1,830
West	Phone	425,000	2,815
West	PC	660,000	2,268

Figure 4.53 A Data Table Showing Sales Info for Regions and Products

Now you need select a combination of one region and one product to show the specific sales figures. For example, you want to see the measures for product PC in region East.

The filter component is designed for this kind of scenario: filtering data from multiple columns of conditions. Note that the visual presentation of a filter is a set of combo boxes, each of which represents one column of conditions. For this example, when you specify the number of filters as two, the filter component includes two combo boxes for the user to select a region and a product, as shown in Figure 4.54.

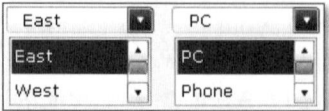

Figure 4.54 The Filter Appears as Two Combo Boxes as You Configured

If the user selects West and Phone, the corresponding row [425000, 2815], as displayed in Figure 4.53, will be inserted into the destination cells. You can then use a chart or some other component to show the measures of the specific PC product in the specific East region.

When to Use a Filter

You might choose a filter component when you have plenty of data, with several dimensions and measures, and you want the user to be able to select a single row by making his choice from a group of combo boxes.

You can achieve the same goal by manually creating several combo boxes and using complex Excel functions including HlookUp or VLookUp, which is more complex and does not perform as well. A filter is designed to do this and thus makes it much easier.

How to Use a Filter

The Properties panel of a filter is divided into three categories: General, Behavior, and Appearance, as explained below. We'll ignore Behavior because it contains nothing special.

General

Title defines the title of each combo box in the filter component. You can click the Bind button to bind the title to a row or column, whose number of cells should be the same as the number of filters (described below). Otherwise, the titles of the last few combo boxes will be empty. You can also manually edit the title for each combo box after clicking the 🖉 button.

Data insertion is a little different from other components here. For Source Data, you specify a range of data including both the dimension columns and the values.

For Destination, you specify a row to store only the values, without the dimension columns.

You set Number of Filters to define how many combo boxes that the user can choose from appear in the filter. If you set it's the Number of Filters value to N, Xcelsius generates one combo box for each of the first N columns and lists the distinct items in it. So, if we denote the number of columns of source data as Ns and that of the destination as Nd, then we should have an equation such as:

$Ns = Nd + N$.

You then know how many columns there should be in the cell range you specified in the Destination field.

Figure 4.55 shows a sample effect of these settings.

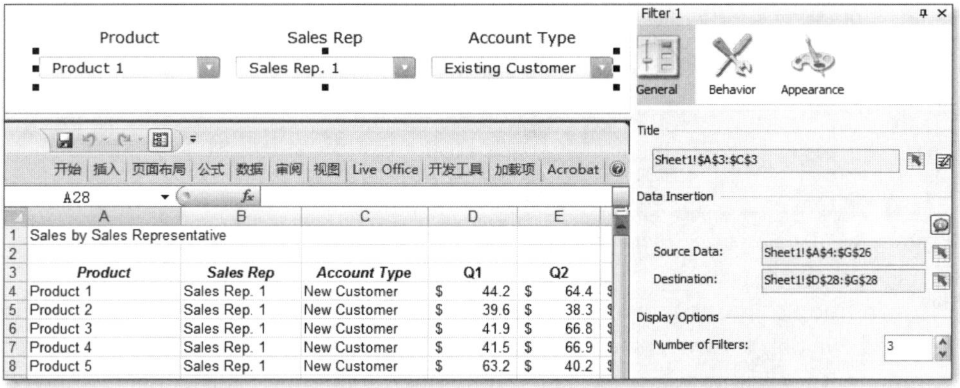

Figure 4.55 The Effects of Using a Filter Component against a Large Range of Data

As you can see from this figure, the entire cell range, including the products, sales representatives, account type, and sales revenue in each quarter, is specified as source data, but the destination is only a row with four columns to store the sales revenues for four quarters. The first three columns are used as filters, so we set Number of Filters to 3.

As a result, the user chooses one product, one sales rep, and one account type from the filter, and Xcelsius inserts the rows corresponding to these selections, the data of which can then be illustrated in another UI component.

Note that the candidates of each combo box are unique. Unlike other selector components, you don't need to specify labels for a filter. Instead, the labels are determined by the data table specified as source data. In other word, labels for the selector and data for insertion are combined together as the source data.

Appearance

Most properties here, including transparency, text formats and positions, and colors, are similar to those of other components. The difference is that you can configure the colors of the combo boxes in a filter, including the dropdown button color and its arrow color when it's selected or not selected.

Used in Hierarchical data

With the filter component, we can work with hierarchical data to let users select conditions hierarchically. For example, we have a data table as shown in Figure 4.56.

Year	Quarter	Sales Revenue	Sales Quantity
2008	Q1 08	23900	6300
2008	Q2 08	26385	7398
2008	Q3 08	25760	6932
2008	Q4 08	31738	7690
2009	Q1 09	32630	7802
2009	Q2 09	33476	8090
2009	Q3 09	32983	8006
2009	Q4 09	34081	8683

Figure 4.56 Data Arranged Hierarchically

The condition columns Year and Quarter are a hierarchical structure. When 2008 is selected, we don't want to see Q1 09 in the combo box for quarter. With this filter component, once one year is selected, only quarters in that year will be displayed in the quarter combo box, as displayed in Figure 4.57.

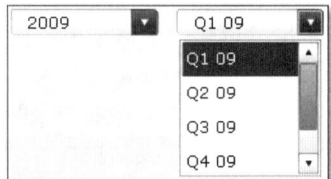

Figure 4.57 Cascading Display of Combo Boxes in the Filter Component

That is to say, with a hierarchical data structure, the later combo box in the filter will only list the candidate values based on the selected value in the previous combo boxes.

4.2.4 Checkbox

A checkbox in Xcelsius 2008 is a square box that contains white space (for false, not selected) or a tick mark (for true, selected) with a caption describing its meaning displayed adjacent to it, which can be on the top, left, right, or bottom.

To toggle the state of a checkbox, simply click the square but not the caption.

When to Use a Checkbox

A checkbox is often used to show the state (selected or not, yes or no, true or false, 1 or 0, etc.) of something. For example, you can use a checkbox to control the dynamic visibility of another component. The user can click the checkbox to show that component and uncheck to hide it.

How to Use a Checkbox

In the General tab of the Properties panel, you can set Title of a Check Box by directly entering a constant string or binding it to a cell. Quite simple.

In Data Insertion, you need to bind Source Data to a row or column with two and only two cells and Destination to a single cell in the embedded spreadsheet.

Note that the first cell is the one for unselected, and the second, for selected. That is, if the default Selected Item is Unchecked, which can be set in the Behavior tab, the content of the first cell is inserted into Destination by default, and when the user clicks the checkbox to change its state, the second value is inserted. In contrast, if Checked is selected as the default Selected Item, the second cell is inserted into Destination by default.

In the Appearance tab, you can set the font size, style, color, and position of the caption. You can also set the colors of the square when it's selected and not selected.

Figure 4.58 shows an example of a checkbox, with the caption Show Chart displayed on the top, that is selected by default.

Figure 4.58 A Typical Checkbox

4.2.5 Toggle Button

A toggle button is very similar to a combo box in that both have only two options. It's often used for the user to toggle between two states: on and off. The differences are:

- The caption of a combo box can be either a constant string or bound to a cell, while the caption of a toggle button must be bound to two adjacent cells in a row or column, which defines the label of the toggle button when it's selected or unselected. For some special purposes, you may make the two cells identical.
- The caption of a combo box can be on the top, left, right, or bottom of the square, while the caption can only be in the center of a toggle button. That is, you cannot set the position for the caption.

In addition, in the Behavior tab of the toggle button's Properties panel, you can select Enable Sound to play a sound when the user clicks the toggle button. In the Appearance tab you cannot set the font family for the labels, but you can set the on and off colors of both the button and the labels. You can change the colors and check the effects in preview mode.

4.2.6 Ticker

A ticker component displays a group of scrolling texts horizontally. One outstanding feature of the ticker is that its candidates continue scrolling until the user hovers the mouse over the labels.

When to Use a Ticker

When the ticker is not wide enough to display all of the candidates in one screen, the texts scroll but no scroll bar is displayed. This makes the ticker the best-fit component when you want to present many candidate items within a limited space, for user selection or just display. For example, you might use a ticker in your dashboard to list the current prices of some stocks that you are interested in.

Figure 4.59 shows a typical ticker.

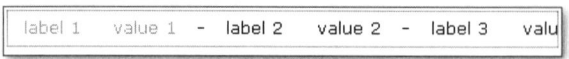

Figure 4.59 A Typical Ticker

How to Use a Ticker

In the canvas, you can use mouse to resize the width of a Ticker component, but you cannot adjust the height. To change the height, change the font size of Labels in Text tab of the Appearance category in the ticker's Properties panel.

General

Here you specify the title, labels, and value labels of a ticker component. The labels or value labels need be bound to a cell range in a row or column. Each label corresponds to one value label in a one-to-one relationship.

Behavior

Most properties here are similar to those of other charts, except one specific group of properties, ticker options, where you set the item separator, scroll direction, and scroll speed, as displayed in Figure 4.60.

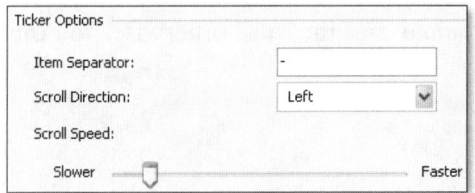

Figure 4.60 Options Specific to a Ticker

The item separator is a symbol with one or more letters that's used to separate different labels. Typical separators are "-" and "|". Of course, you can use any letters as item separator for your needs.

The other two options control the scrolling behavior of the labels. You can choose whether the scrolling occurs to the left or right. To adjust scroll speed, move the Scroll Speed slider from Slower (leftmost) to Faster (rightmost).

Alerts

Unlike most other selector components, you can enable alerts for a ticker to show labels in different colors based on their corresponding values.

Alerts and their effects work the same as those of other components, so we'll ignore them here. If alerting is enabled, there will be a leading icon for each item, the color of which is defined in Alert Thresholds according to its corresponding value. Figure 4.61 shows a ticker with both the label and value displayed, a minus sign "-" as the item separator, and alerts enabled:

Figure 4.61 Ticker with Alerts Enabled

Alerts are usually used to display KPI (Key Performance Index) for large amounts of members or to indicate whether stock prices are going up or down.

For example, when using a ticker to display stock prices, you can show the stock codes in labels, the current stock prices in value labels, and use alerts to show whether each stock price is going upward or downward.

One more word about this example: You store the stock prices of the last trading day in another row that is used as the percentage target in the Alerts category and set the threshold at 100%. As a result, the stock falls into the first level if its price has gone down, the second if there's no change, and the third otherwise. You can refer to Figure 4.62 for the configuration.

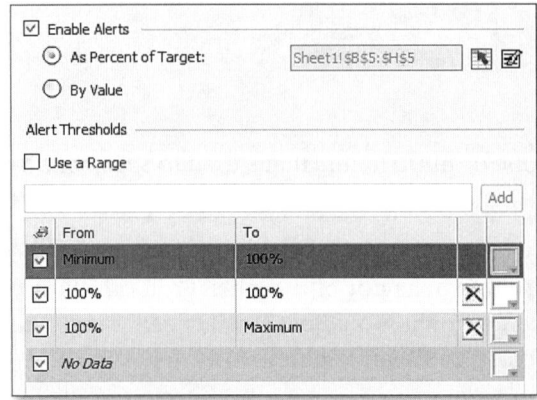

Figure 4.62 Alerts Definition of the Ticker

4.2.7   Picture Menus

Picture menus are similar to a label-based menu or a ticker. In terms of functionality, they are essentially the same. All are used to select one option from a list of candidates and insert the position or value or a row to the destination cell(s). The difference is that, instead of showing literal labels, images are displayed in picture menus.

Xcelsius 2008 provides two kinds of such menus, sliding picture menu and fisheye picture menu. Both use images to display options, with slight differences in appearance and user experience that we'll cover shortly.

When to Use a Picture Menu

You can choose a picture menu when you want to construct a more visual and stunning UI for selection. For example, to show the financial status of various countries, you can use a sliding picture menu so that the user can choose a country from a list of vivid flags, instead of from a combo box listing the country names.

How to Use a Picture Menu

General

In this tab you define the title, label, and images to display in the sliding or fisheye picture menu.

The images to display in the menu can be either in your local file system or on the Internet. For images in your local file system, you select Embedded, click the Import button, and browse to the file in the prompt window. In this window, to add more images, click the Click to Add Images button to browse to them one by one, as shown in Figure 4.63.

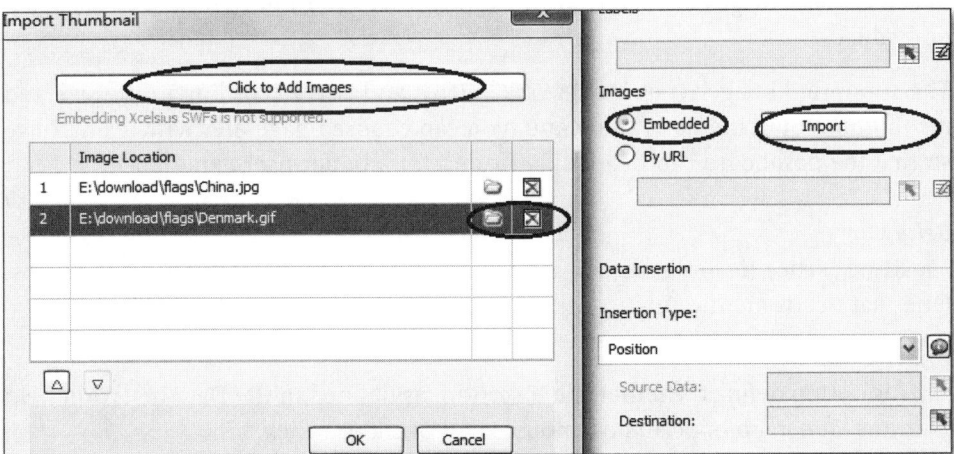

Figure 4.63 Manage Image Locations in Import Thumbnail Window

As displayed in this figure, you can click the red Delete icon to delete an image.

Instead of embedding the images as part of the dashboard, causing the output to have a bigger file size, you can request the images through URLs at run-time. You may want to do this because:

- Sometimes the images are not available locally. Instead, they are on your company intranet or the Internet.
- The images are dynamic images that may change from time to time, and you cannot fix them at design time.

To do this, select By URL and bind to a cell range containing the image URLs. With this option, you put the URLs of the images in a sequence of cells in the embedded spreadsheet and click the Bind button to bind to them. Or you can click the 🖉 button next to the Bind button to manually enter the URLs, without writing them in Excel and then binding to them.

Both Embedded and By URL have advantages and disadvantages. If the images are embedded, the output visualization file can be used and distributed without those image files. On the other hand, for By URL, the visualization will not work when those URLs are not accessible, but the file size will be smaller.

Figure 4.64 shows the effects of setting these properties of a sliding picture menu. Pay attention to where the title and label are displayed and how the image URLs are stored, bound to, and displayed.

In this example, the three countries are represented by their flags in a very intuitive way. The images are referred to by URLs over the Internet instead of being embedded.

The supported image types include JPG, PNG, and GIF. According to the size and resolution requirements of the menu, you can choose image files with a small size so that the dashboard can be quickly loaded for a better user experience.

Behavior

Most properties in this category are the same as those of other UI components. One that needs mentioning is interaction options.

- Insert On
  This option defines whether the insertion, as defined in the Data Insertion field in the General tab, occurs on mouse over or mouse click.

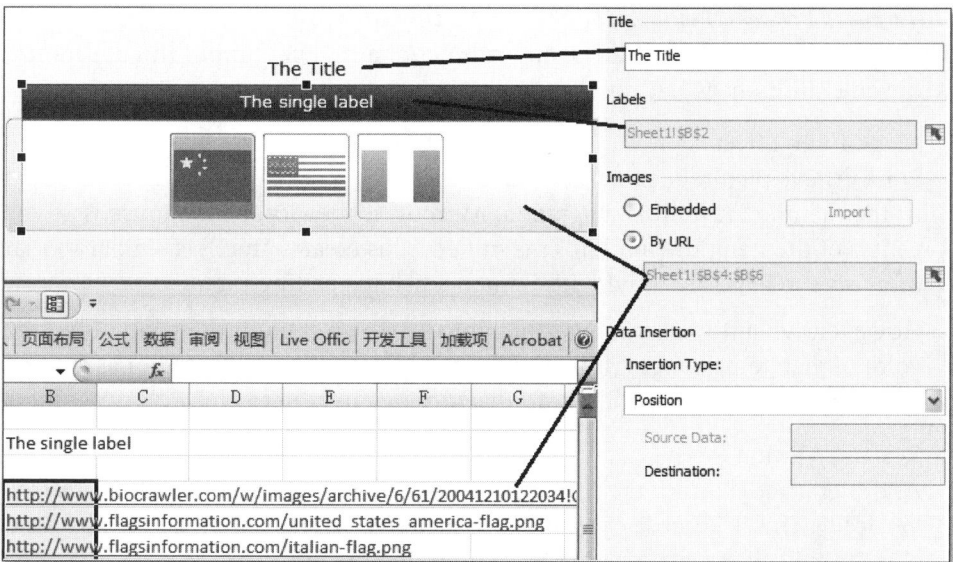

Figure 4.64 Effects of Settings in General Tab of a Sliding Picture Menu

- Slider Method
  This option is only applicable to sliding picture menus, and you may want to spend some time on it when the menu is not wide enough to display all of the images at the same time.

  It controls how to make visible the images that are invisible at first due to the menu width. When Buttons is selected, you see two arrows to the left and right, which you can click to see more images. If the menu is wide enough to display all images, the two arrows are still displayed but cannot be clicked.

  Otherwise, if Mouse is selected, the two arrows are not displayed, and the invisible images appear when you move the mouse over the right or left corner of the menu.

- Scroll Speed and Zoom Speed
  You adjust the slider to set how fast the invisible images appear for a sliding picture menu or how fast the images are zoomed for a fisheye menu.

- Zoom Size
  This option is only applicable for a fisheye picture menu, and it controls how an image is magnified on mouse over. The minimum size is 1, meaning no magnification. You can adjust the slider bar to change this size.

Differences between Fisheye and Sliding Picture Menus

These two menu types are the same in functionality and similar in appearance, with some differences illustrated below.

- Magnifying Effect

  For a fisheye picture menu, as the user moves the mouse over each item (image) in the menu, that item is magnified. Moreover, the closer the mouse is to the center of the item, the more it's magnified. This creates an effect similar to that of a fish-eye lens. That's why it's named a fisheye picture menu.

  However, when the user moves the mouse over an item in the menu, only the color of that item changes (from the default color to mouse-over color as defined in the Appearance tab). There's no magnifying effect here.

- Resizing Option

  At design time, neither the fisheye nor the sliding picture menu can be resized vertically. This is because each image in them has a fixed height defined by Xcelsius 2008 itself, no matter how big the original image is.

  The sliding picture menu is a little more flexible here, because you can resize it horizontally, thus change its width, at design time. But you cannot resize a fisheye menu, neither horizontally nor vertically. Xcelsius controls the width of a fisheye menu, depending on how many images it contains. That is, a fisheye menu is just wide enough to display all of the images at the same time.

  At run time, all images are visible at one glance of a fisheye menu. On the other hand, if the sliding menu is not wide enough to show all images, you can use the arrows to the left or right to scroll through the images. You can also configure the sliding menu to scroll through the images automatically as the user moves the mouse, by changing Slider Method from Buttons to Mouse in the Behavior category in the Properties panel.

  Figure 4.65 shows the difference between these two methods, both showing flags of three countries.

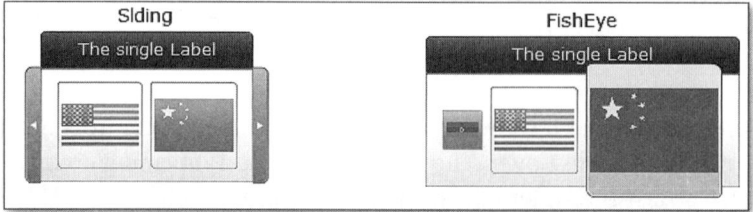

Figure 4.65 The Difference Between the Appearance of a Fisheye and a Sliding Picture Menu

Pay attention to the arrows in the sliding menu and the different sizes of the three flags in the fisheye picture menu in the right side of this figure.

4.2.8 List Builder

A list builder is a component that allows the user to choose one or more options from a list of candidates. This is different from all of the other selectors we have discussed so far, which support selecting only one item at a time.

Moreover, there are two areas in a list builder component: One lists the candidates that have not been selected yet, and the other lists the selected items. Figure 4.66 displays a typical list builder.

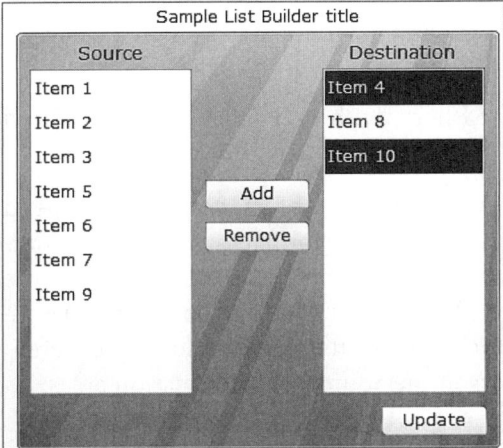

Figure 4.66 A Typical List Builder

When to Use a List Builder

You can use a list builder when you want the user to be able to select one or more items at the same time. For example, you have a chart showing the sales information of various products, and the user can choose one or more products to see.

How to Use a List Builder

At runtime, the user can select one or multiple items in the Source area and click the Add button to move them to the Destination area or select one or more items in the Destination area and click the Remove button to delete them. When the user has finished the selection, he click the Update button to commit the changes, and data insertion will be triggered.

At design time, you can move or resize a list builder component on the canvas.

The Properties panel is divided into the four categories General, Behavior, Appearance, and Alerts. There are no special property here, and their names are self-explanatory.

In the next few paragraphs, we'll briefly discuss what you can do in each tab.

In General tab, you will see many more configurable properties than many other components have. Here you specify a data source for all data parts that will appear in a list builder component, including the titles of the list builder itself, the Source area and the Destination area. You can also specify the texts for the three buttons Add, Remove, and Update. And, of course, you need to specify a data source for the labels that will appear in the Source area.

Fewer data insertion types are supported here, with only label, value, row, and column.

To build an attractive dashboard with a good look and feel, you need to spend some time in the Appearance category, setting the text formats and colors at different states for all texts. Xcelsius 2008 provides the ability to set the default, mouse over, and selected colors of the labels and backgrounds of the Source and Destination areas. In addition, you can set the colors of the three buttons in different states (selected or not) and the scroll bars in the Source and Destination areas.

4.3 Represent a Single Value

You may often want to display a single numeric value, either for display or for the user to change. Xcelsius provides a special category for such UI components, called "single value," which includes dials, sliders, progress bars, and spinners.

4.3.1 Introduction to Single-Value Components

A single-value component is always bound to a single cell in the embedded Excel spreadsheet. When you run the visualization (in runtime), you can see or modify the value in that cell. The content in that cell can only be a numeric value.

All single-value components are born output controls. That is, any of them can be used to represent some value.

However, not all of them can be used as input to allow user interaction. This depends on the content in the cell the component links to. If the cell contains a formula of any type, the component is interpreted as an output only and allows no user interaction, which means the user cannot change the value. For example, if you have a spinner linked to a cell that does not contain a formula, you can modify the value by clicking the Up or Down arrow of the button, thereby modifying the cell value. However, if the cell the spinner is linking to does contain a formula, such as =SUM(B4:C4), it becomes output-only and you cannot modify the value.

As a common property, most single-value components have minimum and maximum limits. For some components, you can also enable alerts to show a different color based on the value they stand for. This is a very useful feature. For example, you can use a gauge to show the current debt of your company or family and show it in red when it reaches some limit.

Moreover, different from most other components, a single-value component has no mouse-over values. That is, the current value will not be displayed when you move your mouse over it.

In the rest of this section, we'll discuss most of the UI components of this category in detail.

4.3.2 Slider

A slider, either horizontal or vertical, provides a slider for the user to move to change its value within the range defined by the minimum limit and maximum limit.

When to Use a Slider

You can use a slider component to represent some unit or base value, so that the user can adjust it to see its effects. For example, in a dashboard for budget and planning, you can use a horizontal slider for the user to adjust the price, which affects the potential sales revenue in another chart.

Xcelsius 2008 delivers two horizontal and two vertical sliders. There is little difference in the shape of the marker in these sliders. You can drop both kinds onto the canvas and have a look at them before choosing the one that suits your needs.

How to Use a Slider

Xcelsius 2008 offers four sliders: Horizontal Slider, Horizontal Slider2, Vertical Slider, and Vertical Slider2. After dropping any one of them onto the canvas, you can move or resize it as you want.

The Properties panel of a slider is divided into four categories, which we'll discuss in the sections below.

General

Here you set data source of the title and data for the slider component. For data, you input a single numeric value directly or bind it to a single cell in the embedded spreadsheet. Its value can be either an integer or a decimal. If an invalid value, such as a string, is specified as the data, the string will still be displayed as data, but the slider will be in its leftmost position, treating the invalid value as zero.

Two more options are available for the scale, that is, the minimum and maximum limits. With Manual selection, you need to specify the minimal and maximum limits by entering constant numeric values manually or via data binding. With Auto selection, there are four options to determine how Xcelsius automatically calculates the scale range.

- Value Based
  A range around the value.

- Zero Based
  A range with 0 as the lower limit and a value larger than the value as the upper limit

- Zero Centered
  A range that includes the value and its negative, with zero at the center point

- Alert Based
  A range based on the selected alert method

You can choose one of these methods based on your specific requirements or just use the default one, Value Based.

Behavior

You use this tab to control user interaction options. You may find that there are many more properties available here than there are in this category of other components.

- Slider Movement
  This property specifies the increment by which the value increases or decreases when users move the needle, progress bar, slider, or spinner. There are three options.
  - Increment
    You manually input an increment value or bind it to a cell.
  - Major Ticks
    With this option, the value progress moves incrementally only on the major ticks but cannot be finer. That is, the end user can never set a value other than that indicated by any major tick.
  - Major and Minor Ticks
    With this option, the value progress moves incrementally only on the major and the minor ticks.
- Limits
  This controls how the maximum limit and minimal limit specified in the General tab work. There are three options for each limit.
  - Fixed:
    The end users is not allowed to change the limit set on General tab. Value can only be within the fixed limit.
  - Adjustable:
    The limit set on the General tab will be the default limit and displayed visually. Users can adjust the limit at runtime, through a Value component displayed beneath the corresponding limit.

Figure 4.67 shows an example of a horizontal slider where the minimum limit is fixed, while the maximum limit is adjustable.

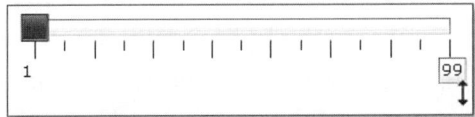

Figure 4.67 A Value Component is Displayed Below the Maximum Limit, Which Is Adjustable

Pay attention to the value component below the maximum limit. The user can hold the mouse and drag it higher or lower to increase or decrease the maximum limit.

- Enable Play Button

  Play means the value increases automatically once the Play button is clicked and stops once the Pause button is clicked, which makes up a play sequence. If the Enable Play Button checkbox is selected, a Play button will show on the component, and more options are available as well.

  - Play Time

    This option determines the duration of the play sequence in seconds. The duration should be within the range of 1 to 100 seconds.

  - Auto Rewind

    This property determines whether the value should rewind to the minimum after reaching the maximum limit.

  - Auto Replay

    This option determines whether the play sequence replays automatically.

  - When the Play Button is enabled, you will see a Play button ▶ displayed near the component. When the user has clicked on it, the value will be updated automatically, with the increment defined earlier. The duration for each step is defined by Play Time divided by the total number of steps in the scale.

Appearance

You use this category to control the layout of a slider component. Similar to the Appearance category in many other components, here you can set the text formats and colors of all data parts in the component.

You may feel a little strange about the Layout tab as it's unique to the Slider component. Here you can control whether or not to show the ticks. If the Enable Ticks checkbox is selected, ticks will be displayed on the component. The ticks can be automatically scaled, with the Auto Scale option. Or you can determine how they scale with the Manual option.

Similar to the gridlines in a column chart, there are two kinds of ticks, major and minor, as displayed in Figure 4.68.

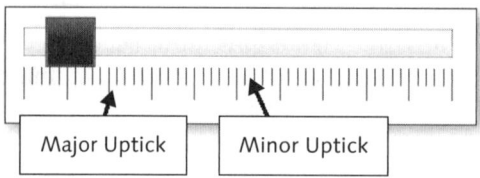

Figure 4.68 *Major and Minor Ticks in a Horizontal Slider Component*

There are two methods to manually control tick scaling: by number of ticks or by size of divisions. For each option you can set the major ticks and minor ticks.

Number of Ticks

The Major spinner defines the total number of major ticks on the component, while the Minor spinner determines the number of minor ticks between every two adjacent major ticks.

Size of Divisions

The major and minor ticks are defined by the value between them.

Concerning the Text tab, you can set whether and how to display the title, current value, and limits of the slider. By default, the current value is displayed to the right. Sometimes you may want to display it on the top. When you have such a requirement, don't forget to set the Position and Offset ere.

As mentioned previously, there's no mouse-over value for such a component.

4.3.3 Progress Bar

A progress bar is very similar to a slider in representing a single numeric value. However, no slider is displayed in the bar, and the user needs to hold and drag the mouse to decrease or increase the value. Another difference is that the space from the minimum limit to the current value is filled, as shown in Figure 4.69.

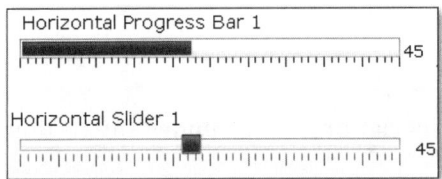

Figure 4.69 A Progress Bar Compared to a Slider

A progress bar is often used to convey the progress of a task, such as how much of the sales target has been met. If you are familiar with finance, you may notice that the progress bar is widely used in the Du Pont System, to represent some values such as turnover rate of capital.

Two progress bars are available in Xcelsius 2008, one horizontal and the other vertical.

4 UI Component Basics

How to Use Progress Bar

The configuration of a progress bar component at design time is exactly the same as that of a slider. Please refer to Section 4.3.2 for details.

The only difference at runtime is that, here no slider is displayed in the component, and the user needs to hold and drag the mouse to change its value.

4.3.4 Dial and Gauge

Dials and gauges are very similar. Both have minimum and maximum limits, with a cursor or pointer indicating the current value, which is displayed in the bottom center. The user drags the cursor upward or downward to adjust its value.

Xcelsius 2008 provides many dial and gauge components. They look almost the same, with slight differences in the shapes and markers. You can drag and drop them onto the canvas to have a look, and choose the one you like. Generally, you can simply make your choice based on the requirements or your preferences.

How to Use Dials and Gauges

To use a dial or gauge component, find it by name in the category Single Value, which is further divided into subcategories such as Dial and Gauge in the Tree of the Components tab view.

The usage, both at design time and at runtime, is very similar across all single-value components. Here we will only list the properties that are specific to a dial or gauge component.

General

In this category, you will see some more special properties under Interaction Options, as displayed in Figure 4.70.

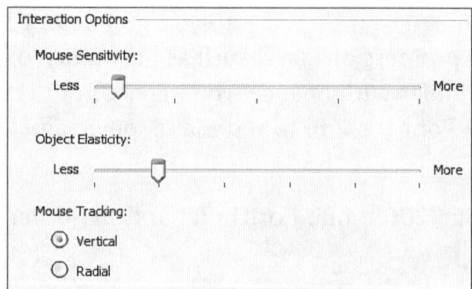

Figure 4.70 Specific Properties of Interaction Options of a Dial or Gauge

The meaning of each property is explained as below.

- Mouse Sensitivity
  This property controls how sensitively the value change reacts to the pointer movement. You can drag the slider to change the value. When the setting is high, small pointer movements can change the value by large increments.

  This option is available for value, gauge, and dial components in the category Single Value.

- Object Elasticity
  This property controls the elasticity of the movement of the needle. You can drag the slider to adjust the value. When the setting is low, the needle will snap to the new value. When the setting is high, the needle will bounce around the new value and finally settle in place. This option is only available for gauges.

- Mouse Tracking
  You select one option from Vertical and Radial. With Vertical, users increase the value by dragging the mouse up and decrease the value by dragging the mouse down. With Radial, users increase the value by dragging the mouse clockwise and decrease the value by dragging the mouse counterclockwise.

  This option is available for gauges and dials.

Appearance

In the Layout tab you will see the property Radial Definition, that is, the minimum and maximum angles of the minimum and maximum limits. By default the range is –130° to 130°. You can change it to any integer you want. For example, Figure 4.71 shows the effect of changing the angle range of a gauge to -90° to 150°.

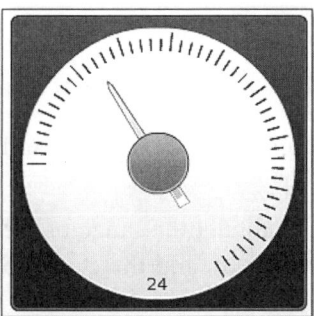

Figure 4.71 Effects of Changing the Minimum and Maximum Angles of a Gauge

Practice

A gauge is a very useful component in a professional and good-looking dashboard. In this section, we'll create a simple visualization to demonstrate the use of gauges and sliders through a simple hands-on example.

Consider a simple business scenario: We have revenue and cost data, and we want to calculate and display the margin. You can follow the steps below to create such a visualization.

1. Drag a gauge component and two slider components from the Components view, drop them onto the canvas, and assign titles for them, as displayed in Figure 4.72.

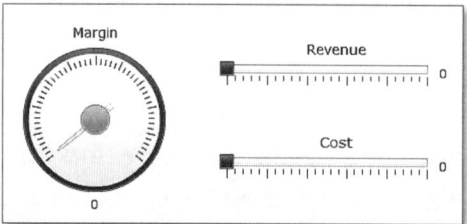

Figure 4.72 Layout of this Hands-On Example

2. In the embedded spreadsheet, enter the values for revenue in cell Sheet1!$B$1 and cost in cell B2, and calculate the margin in cell B3 with Excel formulas (B1-B2)/B1. Your data in the embedded spreadsheet should look like Figure 4.73.

	A	B
1	Revenue	5000
2	Cost	4000
3	Margin	0.2

Figure 4.73 Data in the Embedded Spreadsheet of this Hands-On Example

3. Bind the data of the revenue slider to cell B1, of the cost slider data to B2, and of the gauge to B3.
4. Set the data range for each component in the General tab. Set the range of the revenue Slider to [0, 10000], the cost slider to [1000, 8000], and the gauge to [0, 0.5].

Enable alerts for the gauge component as follows. On the Alerts tab of the gauge component, select the Enable Alerts checkbox, and select the By Value option. Because a higher margin is better, select the High Values Are Good option for Color Order. In the Alert Thresholds section, define level [minimal, 0.1] to be red, [0.1, 0.3] to be yellow, and [0.3, maximum] to be green. Figure 4.74 below shows what the alerts definition looks like.

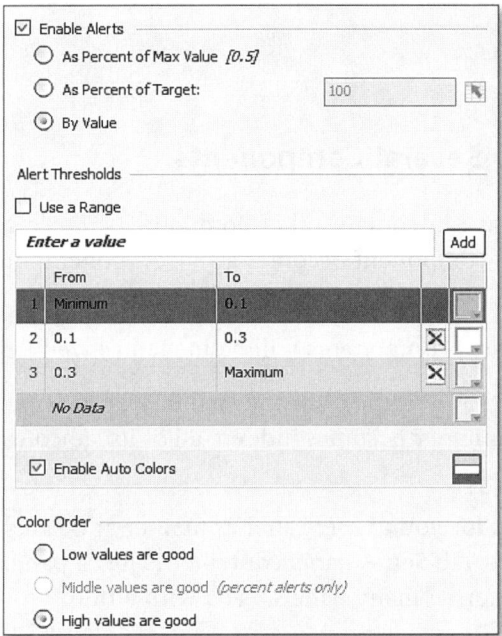

Figure 4.74 Alerts Definition of the Gauge Component in this Hands-On Example

5. Set the display format of the gauge to Percent. On the Appearance - Text tab of the gauge component, select Value on the list, and set Number Format to Percent.

6. Click Preview to test the visualization. You can adjust the values of revenue and cost with the two sliders, and gauge will display the margin. The color on the gauge will give the user a clear sign whether the current combination is good or bad, as shown in Figure 4.75.

4 | UI Component Basics

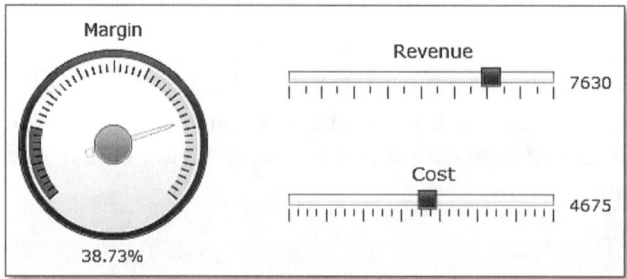

Figure 4.75 Our Hands-On Example at Runtime

4.4 Use Containers to Wrap Several Components

A container is a special component that can contain other components. Once a component is placed in a container, the component becomes a subcomponent, or child, of the container.

When the container is moved, all of its subcomponents will be moved as well.

All subcomponents in the container will inherit the dynamic visibility of the container component. That is, when the container becomes hidden, all of its subcomponents will also be invisible.

Xcelsius 2008 provides three containers for you to use: Panel Container and Panel Container2, which are quite similar, and Tab Set. A panel container is just a panel with a title. A tab set is like a combination of many panels, each with a title.

In this section, you'll see how to put groups of UI components into containers so that they can be moved or placed together, just like a single component. In addition, you can set dynamic visibility for a group of components by setting that of the container alone. This not only saves a lot of work at design time, but also provides a better, more integrated user experience.

4.4.1 When to Use a Container

You may want to use a container component to contain other components when you have a group of components that will work together and, especially, will display or hide together. For example, let's say you want to implement a dialog box that pops up on some situations. In this case, you can use a container as the dialog box to hold other components. This way, all components of the dialog will show when the dialog pops up and disappear when the dialog is closed. You only need to set the dynamic visibility once, for the container component.

A typical usage of container components is the logon screen, where the user enters his credentials. You create the logon screen using a panel container to host the input fields of username, password, and so on. The entire screen will be hidden when the logon succeeds.

Moreover, at design time, it's much easier to adjust the position of a container instead of each individual component.

4.4.2 How to Use a Container

It's very simple to use containers. Briefly, you just move some components into the container. If there are many components on the canvas and you find it difficult to move some components to the container to form a parent-child relationship, you can use the Object Browser view, where you can drag and drop components.

In the Object Browser, you'll observe that containers and their subcomponents are organized in a tree view, as shown in Figure 4.76.

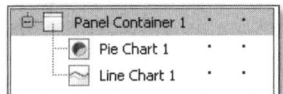

Figure 4.76 Components of a Container Displayed Below It in the Object Browser

Panel Container

To use a panel container, find the component called Panel Container or Panel Container2 in the Components view and drop it onto the canvas. Then, on the canvas or via the Object Browser, you can drag other components and drop them onto the container, to make them subcomponents of it.

When you are dragging a component onto the panel container, there will be a visual effect of a semi-transparent rectangle to indicate that the component will be placed "into" the container, as illustrated in Figure 4.77.

The Properties panel of a panel container is very simple. On the General tab of the Properties sheet of a panel container, there's only one option: Title.

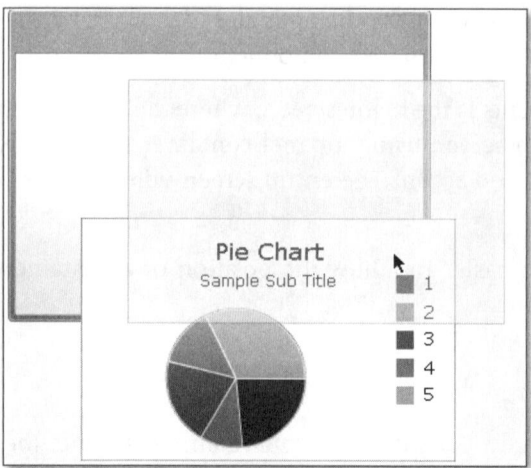

Figure 4.77 Before Dropping the Container onto the Canvas

On the Behavior - Common tab, you can control the scroll bar options of the panel container. There are three options for both the horizontal scroll bar and the vertical scroll bar.

- Auto
  With this option selected, the scroll bar appears automatically only when it's needed, for example, when the container is not wide or tall enough to hold all of the components inside.
- On
  Always show a scroll bar.
- Off
  No scroll bar is shown.

The title of a panel container always displays in the center of the title area on the top. Its position cannot be changed, though you can configure it to not be shown, by unselecting the Title in Appearance - Text checkbox.

Tab Set

It's common to use tabs as the navigation tool on UI design. A tab set is a container component you can use to build a tab-based UI with great ease. You can put different UI components in different tabs and click the title to switch among tabs. Only one tab is displayed on the canvas at a time.

A tab set can be considered as multiple panel containers put together, and you can switch from one tab to another.

By default, there's only one tab in the tab set component. You can add new tabs by clicking the add sign (+) of Tab Set. Assign a name for the newly added tab in the prompt window, as shown in Figure 4.78.

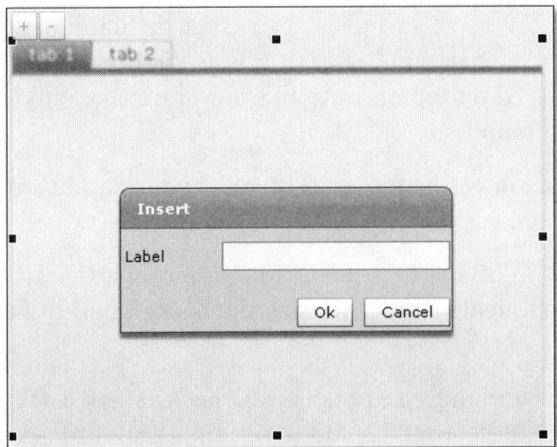

Figure 4.78 Add a New Tab

To delete a tab, first click its name to select it and then simply click the minus sign (-) on the top left of the tab set. Note that all components belonging to that tab will be removed at the same time.

You can activate, or display, one tab by clicking the tab label. You can then add components to this active tab by dragging one or more UI components from either the canvas or the Object Browser and drop them into it. To exclude components from one tab, drag them out of the tab with your mouse or change its depth after clicking to selecting them, using commands such as Send to Back, Bring Forward, or Bring to Front.

The Properties panel of a tab set component is also very simple. On the General tab, there's only one option: Tab Alignment. Tab labels can be placed on the left, center, or right.

On the Behavior tab of the Properties sheet, you can set the default tab to show when the visualization is loaded. To set the scroll option and tab labels, you first need to select the canvas of one tab. You can do this in the Object Browser, as displayed in Figure 4.76 above.

You can click on the area of each tab below the tab name to select a certain tab, not the tab set itself. You can then set some properties specific to that tab, such as the label of the tab, the scroll bar options, and their colors.

4.5 Build Backgrounds to Assist Layout

A background is prebuilt artwork such as an image used to assist the dashboard layout and improve your design. As the name indicates, it acts as the background scenery of other UI components placed on top of it. As a result, those UI components appear to be within the background.

With the help of backgrounds, you can easily and quickly make your dashboard cohesive, visually stimulating, and professional.

The backgrounds can also be used to divide the canvas into several parts, each designating a group of related components. You can resize the background to fit its included components.

Xcelsius 2008 provides several background components in the Arts and Backgrounds category, called Background, Background2, and so on. Note that the background is related to the theme and color scheme. This has means to things.

▶ A background can appear in different a color under different themes or color schemes.

▶ Some backgrounds may be unavailable for certain themes.

For example, you may notice that there are six background components in the Nova theme, but only two in iTheme.

This section describes some available backgrounds. After reading this section you will know the differences among the backgrounds provided by Xcelsius 2008 and how to use them to assist your layout and improve your design.

4.5.1 When to Use Backgrounds

You can add one or more backgrounds to the canvas when you want your dashboard to look better or more professional or to make some UI components appear as parts of a whole. By putting some components on top of one background, you provide the appearance that together they form an integrated component. Moreover, you can use backgrounds to divide the canvas into several meaningful parts, for example, one background on the top including the company info such as its name and logo, another on the bottom including a list builder to select measures and a chart showing the values.

For a better layout, it's recommended that you always use backgrounds. And, of course, overusing backgrounds will make the dashboard a disordered mess.

4.5.2 How to Use Backgrounds

A good way to use backgrounds is to design and position them before adding other UI components. That is, design your dashboard against a plain canvas and then position UI components on it.

To add a background to a group of UI components, simply choose one from the Components view, drag it to the canvas, and then drag the components on top it.

If you add backgrounds to UI components already on the canvas, and the positions of those components have been adjusted, you can also drop the background onto the correct place. The background will overlap and block those components, however. To solve this, select the background in the Objects Browser and click Send to Back or Send Backward to move it behind the components.

Moving or resizing a background is the same as moving or resizing other UI components.

The Properties panel of a background is very simple, with two categories.

General
Here you set properties such as the background color, transparency, border scale, and whether or not to block mouse events, as displayed in Figure 4.79.

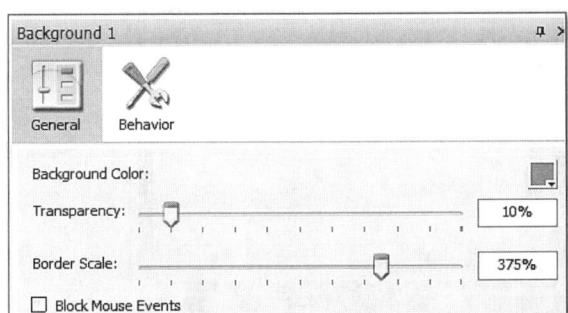

Figure 4.79 Available Properties in the General Tab of a Background

The meaning of each property and how to use it are explained below.

- Background Color
  The default background color of a background component is determined by the color scheme. You can change it with the color picker.

- Transparency
  This property defines the transparency level of the background. By default it's 0; that is, it's opaque and all UI components behind it are invisible. You may want to change this value for a cooler user experience.

  To change the transparency, move the slider or directly enter an integer in the input field. If you enter a decimal, Xcelsius will automatically round it up to an integer. Entering a nonnumeric value will not change the value.

- Border Scale
  The border scale defines the width of the background component's border. You can move the slider to adjust this value, or directly enter an integer in the input field. The smaller the value is, the thinner the borders are.

  For most background components, changing this property only affects the border width and nothing else. However, for certain background, its shape is also changed. Figure 4.80 shows an example of a background component called Background6 in the Components view, with a border scale of 100% (left) or 300% (right).

  Pay attention to the boundaries of the background component and the round corners in the right part of this figure.

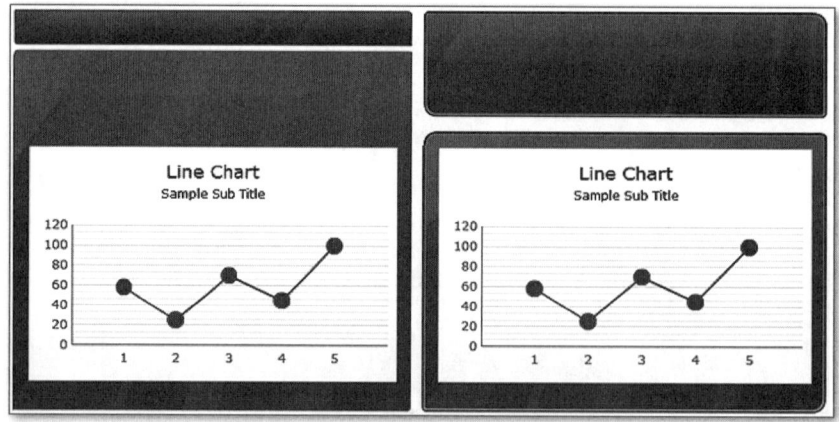

Figure 4.80 Effect of Changing a Background Border Scale

▶ Block Mouse Events
This option refers to whether a mouse-over or mouse-click action on the background component will be passed along to the UI components behind it. You could select this if you want to use the background as a mask to prevent the user from clicking some other components. That is, the user can see the components but cannot interact with them.

Two aspects need be considered before using this functionality. First, to prevent the user from clicking the components, the background component should be layered on top of other components. Second, to make the components visible, you need set the transparency of the background to less than 100%.

Figure 4.81 shows an example. The user can see the combo box and the line chart but cannot select one from the box or drill down through the chart.

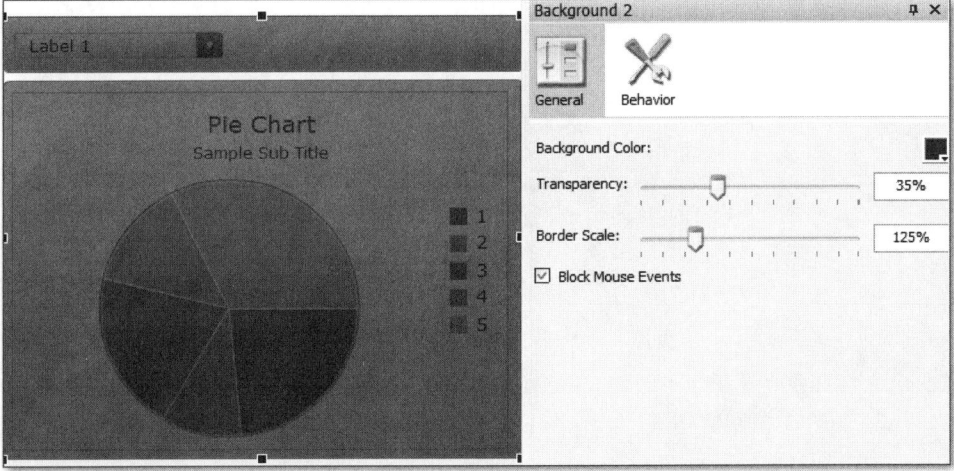

Figure 4.81 A Background Used as a Mask with Block Mouse Events Selected

You can adjust the transparency according to your use scenario for a better look and feel. For example, if you just want the chart to display some information and keep the user unaware of the background, you can set Transparency to 100%. As a result, the background component is completely invisible to the user, and the components behind it accept no user interaction.

Behavior
This tab is very simple, providing the ability to configure properties such as dynamic visibility, entry type, and duration.

How to use them and their effects are the same as for the various kinds of charts. For more details, please refer to the corresponding section of other charts such as the pie chart.

4.6 Summary

In this chapter, we discussed in detail some basic and commonly used UI components provided by Xcelsius 2008. The topics include what the components are, when and how to use them, and some best practices for using them. For some components, we also included a simple hands-on example for you to quickly get acquainted with it.

The rich set of UI components in Xcelsius 2008 contains more than we discussed in Chapter 4. We'll now cover some of the more complex and advanced components for some special scenarios.

5   UI Components – Advanced

In Chapter 4, we looked at some commonly used UI components such as charts, selectors, single values, containers, and backgrounds. With these components, you are already able to build complicated and interesting interactive dashboards. Yet in some cases, we just want more. In this chapter, we are going to introduce some more advanced components including some more charts, art, maps, and some components that provide special functionality such as trend analysis, history preservation, and local scenarios.

In this chapter you will see:

▶ More advanced UI components including more charts, art, maps, and special components

▶ What you can do with each of them, when to use them, and how

After reading this chapter you will be able to:

▶ Describe these advanced UI components

▶ Create a complicated interactive dashboard using advanced UI components

5.1   Advanced Charts

Xcelsius 2008 provides a wide range of charts in the Charts category. Chapter 4 covered some basic charts such as the column chart. Here we'll show you the rest, some of which are more complex such as the stacked and combination charts. The others may be not that complex but are less frequently used such as the OHLC chart.

5.1.1 Stacked Column Chart

In Chapter 4, we discussed the column chart, which uses a vertical column to display the value of a data item. The category labels are plotted on the X-axis, and the values, on the primary or secondary Y-axis. If you need to display values of multiple measures (or series) in one column chart, there will be one column for each measure of a category item.

A stacked column chart is very similar to a column chart. The differences are that a stacked column chart:

- Has no secondary vertical axis
- Displays only one column per category item, regardless of how many measures are to be displayed
- Divides each column into segments in different colors, one for each measure

The segments of a column are stacked vertically, so this chart is called stacked.

Figure 5.1 compares a column chart and a stacked chart, both showing the expenses for each category every month.

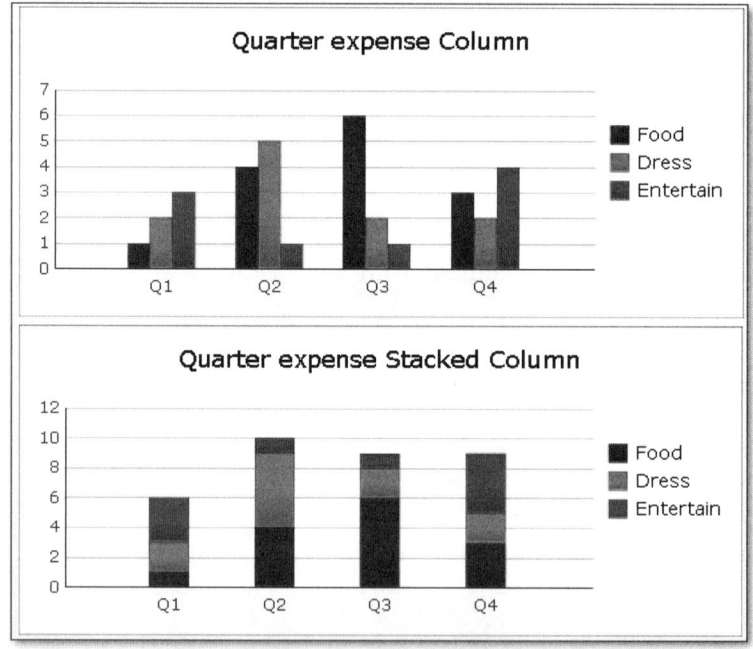

Figure 5.1 A Stacked Column Chart Compared to a Normal Column Chart

The chart on the top is a column chart, while the one below is a stacked column chart. Pay attention to the way the expenses in each category are displayed.

When to Use a Stacked Column Chart

Basically, a stacked column chart is used to show the values of different series in one column and in the meantime to compare the totals among category items.

It's often used to compare totals over a period of time (Q1, Q2, etc.). However, you can also use it to compare data on other dimensions, for example, over different branches or people. As displayed in Figure 5.1 above, you can change the category labels from quarters to people, thus comparing the consumption info of each person.

In Figure 5.1, you may have noticed the difference between a normal and the stacked column chart and got some idea about when to use which. In a column chart, you can compare the values of different measures and of different category items over a period of time, but cannot compare the total. In a stacked chart, however, each measure of one item is displayed in a different color in one column. Each column represents the total of each item, making it easy to see and compare the total values of all category items.

In a word, use a column chart if you want to compare the individuals, and a stacked column chart to compare the totals.

How to Use a Stacked Column Chart

How to add, move, and resize a stacked column chart and set its properties is very similar to a column chart. This section will only cover the different aspects.

General

In this tab you set the data sources for all parts of the chart, including the titles and data for axes.

To set the titles, enter a text directly into the field or bind it to a single cell in the embedded spreadsheet after clicking the corresponding Bind button.

To set the data, either select a cell range by selecting By Range or manually set the labels to display on the X-axis and series on the Y-axis by selecting By Series.

- By Range
  For By Range, the cell range that you choose as the source should be similar to

that displayed in Figure 5.2. After binding, the chart will be updated immediately.

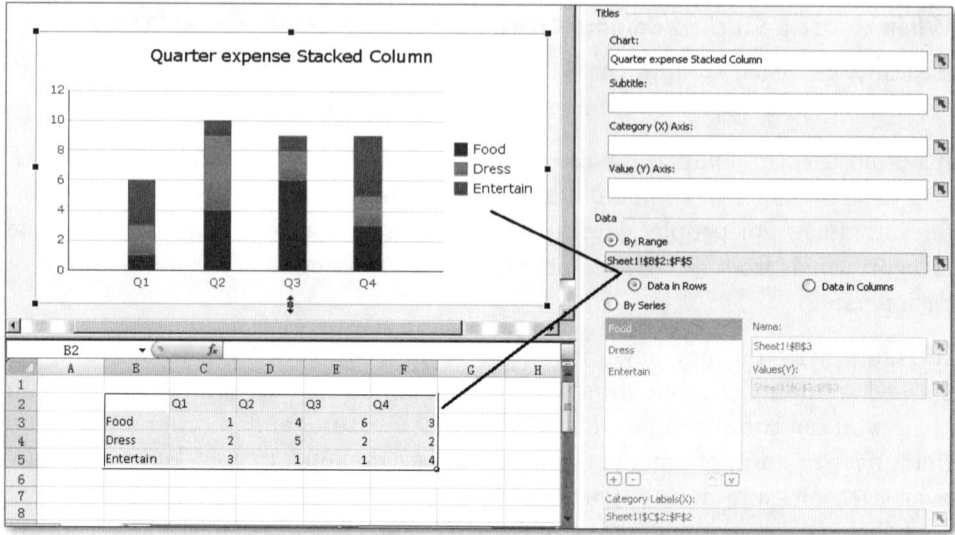

Figure 5.2 The Data Binding of a Stacked Column Chart

The first row is treated as a category if it contains nonnumeric values. Otherwise, the category labels will be 1, 2, 3, and so on. Similarly, if Data in Columns is selected, the first column is treated as series names if it contains nonnumeric values. Otherwise, the names of each series will be series1, series2, series3, and so on.

In Figure 5.2, you can check the difference by selecting range Sheet1!$B$3:$F$5 (without category labels), Sheet1!$C$2:$F$5 (without series names), or Sheet1!$C$3:$F$5 (with neither category labels nor series names) as the data source.

By default, Data in Rows is selected, indicating that the data is read row by row. Depending on your data, you can change it to Data in Columns, thus transposing the rows and columns. For the data in Figure 5.2, if you switch to Data in Columns, the category labels will become Food, Dress, and Entertain, while Q1–Q4 will become series names.

▶ By Series
This part will be updated automatically after you select a cell range for By Range.

You can select this option to adjust the result of selecting a range or manually set the category labels and series from scratch.

Pay attention to the series orders here. The series defined on the top in the data series area will be displayed on the bottom of the column in the chart. As you can see from Figure 5.2, the series Food is defined on the top, while its values are displayed on the bottom of the columns.

Alert

Similar to a column chart, the Enable Alerts check box is disabled if more than one series is defined in the General tab.

How to use alerts is thus completely the same as for other charts. If you want to know more, please refer to the corresponding subsection of Section 4.1.2 in Chapter 4 when we are talking about the Column chart.

5.1.2   Stacked Bar and Area Chart

A stacked bar chart is to a stacked column chart what a bar chart is to a column chart. There's only one bar for each category label. For each category label, values of different measures are stacked horizontally in a bar, in different colors.

Similarly, a stacked area chart is to an area chart what a stacked column chart is to a column chart. The areas are stacked vertically, with each area adding up to the total.

5.1.3   Combination Chart

A combination chart can show series in either columns or points. You can regard it as a combination of a column and a line chart.

When to Use a Combination Chart

As mentioned in Chapter 4, a column chart is often used to show and compare values for different counterparts in a range, and a line chart is best suited to show the trend of data change over a period of time. Sometimes you may want to take advantages of both. That's when a combination chart comes into play. Briefly, a combination chart displays a range of values with a trend line for all of them.

For example, you can use a combination chart to display the trade volumes of a stock every day in columns, with a trend line to show the historical prices over the month.

How to Use a Combination Chart

How to use a combination chart is very similar to using a column or a line chart. Its Properties panel is also divided into the five categories General, Drill Down, Behavior, Appearance, and Alerts.

General

In this tab we set the chart's data source. The series can be plotted on either the primary or secondary Y-axis. On a typical combination chart, there are often two series in different scales (e.g., one for volume itself, which is often very large, and the other for growth, which is very small), plotted on different Y-axes. Of course, you can add as many series as you want and display each series as either a column or a line chart.

In our example to illustrate a combination chart, we use the volumes and stock prices of SAP AG in the last 10 trade days in 2009, taken from Yahoo Finance. After setting the chart title and specifying its labels and values, the chart and the General tab are displayed as in Figure 5.3.

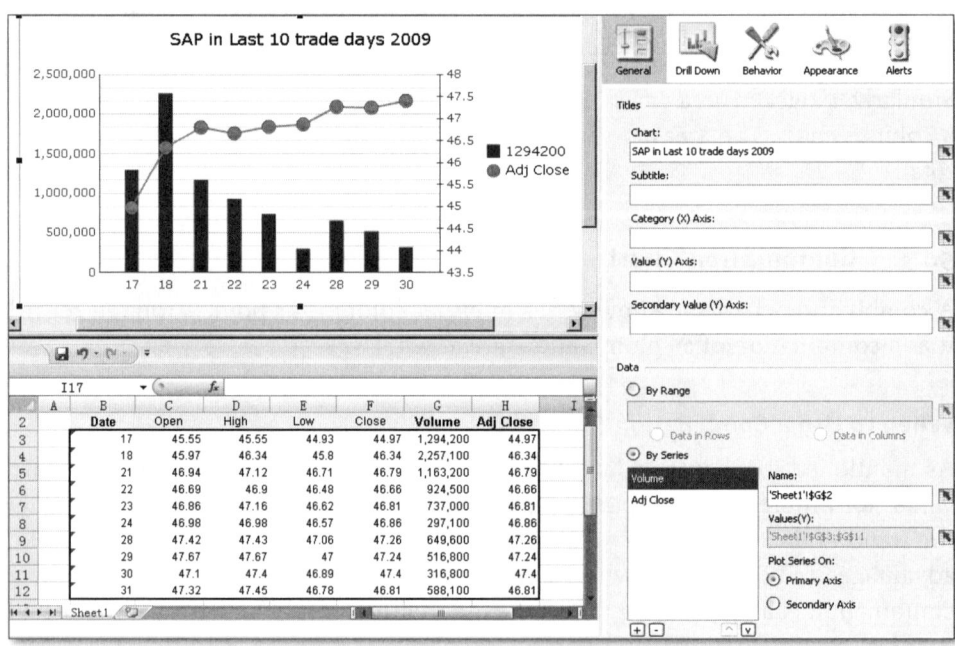

Figure 5.3 Data Binding of a Combination Chart

Appearance

In the Appearance tab, you set the fonts, colors, and so on of all text parts and configure whether and how to show the fills, borders, and gridlines.

One thing we need to mention here is that, in the Series tab, you can define how to display each series, either as a column or as a line, but there is not a third option.

If you choose to display the values of some series in a line, you can further set other properties such as the marker shape, as displayed in Figure 5.4.

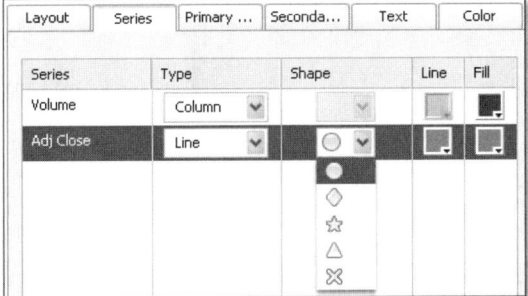

Figure 5.4 Choose How to Display a Series, Column, or Line

The Drill Down, Behavior, and Alerts tabs are almost the same as those of other charts. In the Alerts tab, note that the Enable Alerts checkbox is disabled if more than one series is defined in the General tab.

5.1.4 OHLC Chart

OHLC stands for open, high, low, and close. An OHLC chart is a special kind of bar chart that is used to illustrate the movements in the price of a stock over time. Each vertical bar shows the price range (the highest and lowest prices) over one unit of time, for example, one day or one hour, with two horizontal hash marks indicating where the open and close prices were for the stock in that time period.

Figure 5.5 shows an example of an OHLC chart that shows the weekly prices of the stock of the New York Stock Exchange–listed company, SAP AG. People familiar with the stock market could easily read this chart. For those who are not, the vertical bar illustrates the highest and lowest traded price. The hash mark to the left of the bar illustrates the opening trades, and the hash mark to the right illustrates the closing trades. The blue bars represent higher closing prices, while the red bars represent lower closing prices.

The colors in Figure 5.5 are the default colors defined by the theme being used. Of course, you can customize the colors in the Appearance tab, similarly to what you do to other charts.

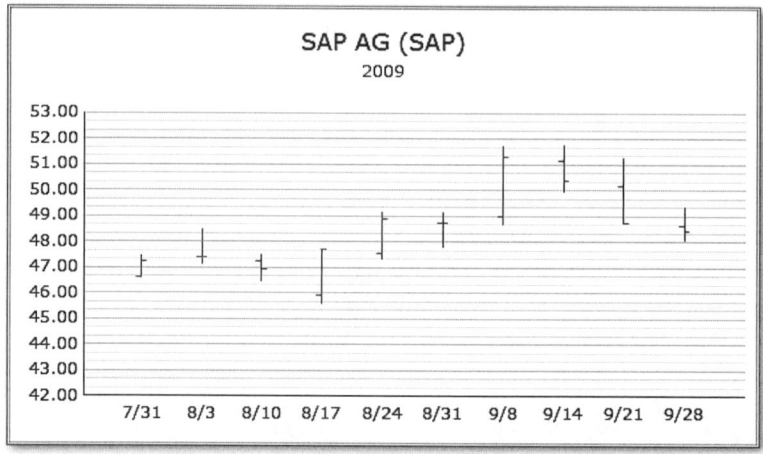

Figure 5.5 Weekly Prices of SAP AG from July 31 to September 28, 2009 in an OHLC Chart

When to Use an OHLC Chart

You use an OHLC chart when you need to show the prices and trends of a stock. For example, say you are creating a dashboard for a listed company. On the homepage of the dashboard, the CEO of the company wants to see the recent prices of their stock. An OHLC chart could be your choice.

There are other types of charts that are commonly used to show stock prices. Some users prefer the simplest line chart, which connects the closing price of the each period to the closing price of the previous time period and the closing price of the following time period. A candlestick chart is another type of chart that is very similar to the OHLC chart.

A line chart is simple, but it conveys less information. The user can only see one series of data, the closing trade of the security. A candlestick chart brings the same amount of information to the user. The only difference between the OHLC chart and the candlestick chart is the appearance of each bar. We already know how to use a line chart, and we'll discuss candlestick charts in a later section in this chapter.

How to Use an OHLC Chart

As we mentioned before, the OHLC chart is a special kind of column chart or bar chart, so they share a lot of properties in common, but an OHLC chart cannot have a secondary Y-axis. It cannot have alerts. And most importantly, there must be four series of data to be displayed, and each bar must consist of four values, so this means the OHLC chart has some special behaviors that are unlike an ordinary column chart or bar chart.

General

- Titles

    The titles properties are very similar to those of the column chart or the bar chart. You can set chart title, the subtitle, the category (X) axis title, and the value (Y) axis title here, as displayed in Figure 5.6.

    The only difference is that the OHLC chart doesn't support a secondary Y-axis, so there isn't a secondary Y-axis title here.

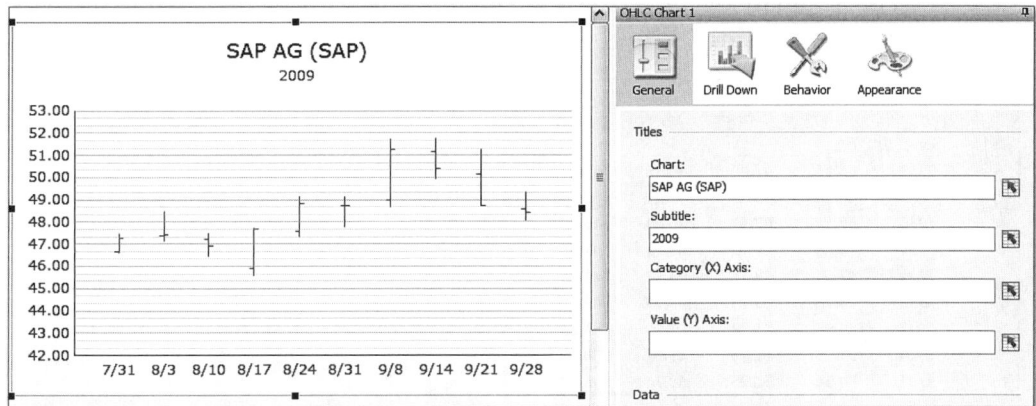

Figure 5.6 The Titles Properties of an OHLC Chart

- Data

    The OHLC chart always needs exactly four series of data, no more and no less, which are the opening, the highest, the lowest, and the closing trades.

    Like what you do in the column chart or the bar chart, you also have two ways to bind data: By Range or By Series. You already know how to use these two methods in column charts and bar charts. Here we explain the difference between these two types in more detail.

5 | UI Components – Advanced

Generally, you bind the data by range when the data is in a range of continuous cells and, of course, in a table form that Xcelsius can recognize. If your data is arranged this way, by range is the easier way to bind data, but if your data is not in a range of continuous cells, for example, different series of data are not arranged together or they are even in different Excel sheets, you have to bind the data by series and manually bind each series and the category label.

Now let's see how to bind data for the OHLC chart.

- By Range

  Again, your data should be in a continuous range of cells, so the four series of data and the category label should be in adjacent cells.

  In Figure 5.7, you can see how the data is arranged in the embedded Excel worksheet. Column A is the category label, in this case, the date. Column B to column E are opening, highest, lowest, and closing prices, respectively. The sequence of these four series should exactly match the acronym OHLC. And in cell $B$1, we put in the series name that appears when the user hovers the mouse over the data point on the chart. Usually this is set to the symbol of some stock.

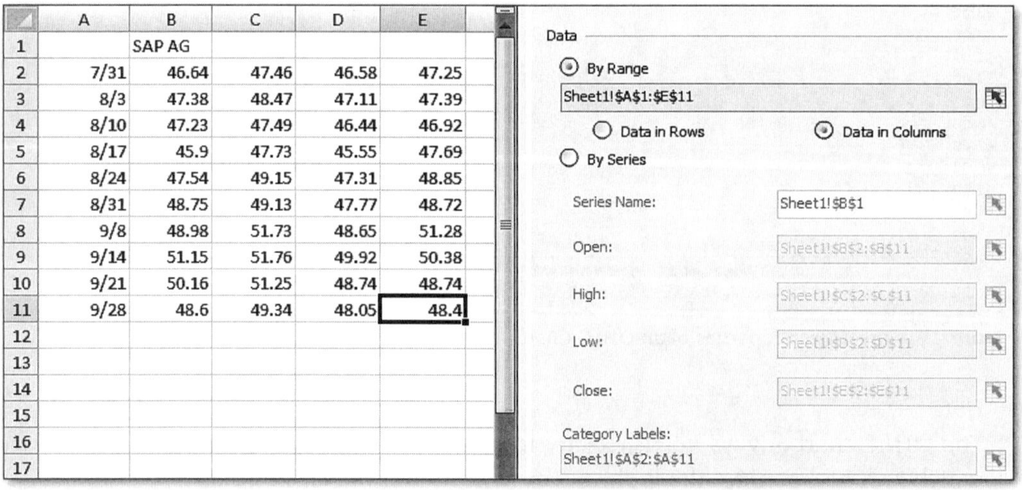

	A	B	C	D	E
1		SAP AG			
2	7/31	46.64	47.46	46.58	47.25
3	8/3	47.38	48.47	47.11	47.39
4	8/10	47.23	47.49	46.44	46.92
5	8/17	45.9	47.73	45.55	47.69
6	8/24	47.54	49.15	47.31	48.85
7	8/31	48.75	49.13	47.77	48.72
8	9/8	48.98	51.73	48.65	51.28
9	9/14	51.15	51.76	49.92	50.38
10	9/21	50.16	51.25	48.74	48.74
11	9/28	48.6	49.34	48.05	48.4

Data
- By Range: Sheet1!$A$1:$E$11
  - Data in Rows
  - Data in Columns (selected)
- By Series

Series Name: Sheet1!$B$1
Open: Sheet1!$B$2:$B$11
High: Sheet1!$C$2:$C$11
Low: Sheet1!$D$2:$D$11
Close: Sheet1!$E$2:$E$11
Category Labels: Sheet1!$A$2:$A$11

Figure 5.7 Binding Data for OHLC Chart by Range When Data Is in Columns

Figure 5.7 shows an example when the data is in columns, so you select the By Range radio button, bind the cell range $A$1:$E$11, and select Data in Columns if Xcelsius has not done that by itself. Then Xcelsius will automatically set up the series name, the open series, the high series, the low series, the close series, and the category labels for you.

- By Series
  Sometimes, your data is not arranged in continuous cells, so you have to bind individual series and other properties yourself. You need to select the By Series radio button, bind the Series Name property, the four series of data and the category label. The process is similar to when you bind data by series for a column chart.

  In some cases, your data doesn't have a column for category label or it's separated from the OHLC series, or you don't have the proper series name in the corresponding cell. As long as the OHLC series are in continuous cells, you can use the By Range option and the By Series option together for easier data binding.

  First, let's assume that in Figure 5.7, we've inserted another column, Volume, between column A and column B, which makes it impossible to bind the whole range together. The sample data is presented in Figure 5.8. Knowing that the category label is not mandatory for binding by range, you can first select the By Range radio button and bind the range $C$1 to $F$11, which is highlighted in blue in Figure 5.8.

	A	B	C	D	E	F
1			SAP AG			
2	7/31	1,638,300	46.64	47.46	46.58	47.25
3	8/3	931,300	47.38	48.47	47.11	47.39
4	8/10	586,000	47.23	47.49	46.44	46.92
5	8/17	648,900	45.9	47.73	45.55	47.69
6	8/24	744,200	47.54	49.15	47.31	48.85
7	8/31	799,700	48.75	49.13	47.77	48.72
8	9/8	1,711,500	48.98	51.73	48.65	51.28
9	9/14	1,809,200	51.15	51.76	49.92	50.38
10	9/21	1,092,600	50.16	51.25	48.74	48.74
11	9/28	1,891,400	48.6	49.34	48.05	48.4

Figure 5.8 Binding Data when the Category Labels Column and OHLC Data Are Not Continuous

Xcelsius will bind everything except the category label. But now you are not able to bind the category label because this property is under the By Series option and

5 | UI Components – Advanced

is currently disabled. To do this, you switch to the By Series option. Notice that Xcelsius doesn't discard what is already bound, and the category label is now enabled. As a final step, you bind the category label $A$2 to $A$11, which is highlighted in red in Figure 5.8.

Now, let's consider another change to the data in the embedded spreadsheet shown in Figure 5.7. This time, the category label and the four series of data are still continuous, but there isn't any series name cell. The sample data are presented in Figure 5.9.

	A	B	C	D	E	F	G	H	I	J
1	7/31	46.64	47.46	46.58	47.25					
2	8/3	47.38	48.47	47.11	47.39					
3	8/10	47.23	47.49	46.44	46.92					
4	8/17	45.9	47.73	45.55	47.69					
5	8/24	47.54	49.15	47.31	48.85					
6	8/31	48.75	49.13	47.77	48.72					
7	9/8	48.98	51.73	48.65	51.28					
8	9/14	51.15	51.76	49.92	50.38					
9	9/21	50.16	51.25	48.74	48.74					
10	9/28	48.6	49.34	48.05	48.4					
11										
12										
13										
14										
15										

Figure 5.9 Binding Data when the Range Doesn't Contain a Series Name Cell

To easily bind the data, you first bind the cell range $B$1 to $E$10, which is highlighted in blue in Figure 5.9, using the By Region option. Do not include the category label column; otherwise, your chart won't display the correct data. Remember, if the range doesn't include a series name, it must not include the category label either. So you only bind the four series of data.

Now that they are properly bound, you switch to the By Series option and bind the category label to the range $A$1 to $A$10, which is highlighted in red in Figure 5.9. As with the series name, you can manually enter the name you want or bind it to another cell in the embedded spreadsheet.

Drill-Down

The OHLC chart also supports the drill-down functionality. Even though it's a chart that displays four series of data, it has drill-down behavior that's very similar to the pie chart, which can only display one series of data, but unlike the column chart, the bar chart, and the line chart. The reason for this is that each vertical bar in the OHLC chart consists of four values, and it isn't practical to click on each value.

In the Insertion Type dropdown list, you can select either Position, Value, Row, Column, or Status List, which are almost the same as for a column chart.

But when you select Value as the insertion type, which value will be inserted? There's no way for Xcelsius to know which value you want unless you tell it, so when you select the Value insert type, there is an extra options list, Value Set, for which you can select Open, High, Low, or Close, so that the corresponding value is inserted (Figure 5.10). The other operations are similar to what you do for other charts, so we'll ignore them here.

Figure 5.10 The Value Set Option for the "Value" Insertion Type

Appearance

The appearance settings for the OHLC chart are almost identical to the column chart, with some slight differences as covered below.

- Layout
  In the Layout tab, you can enable the legend for the OHLC chart. The legend for the OHLC chart is a little bit special, because it always shows two legend items: Up and Down.

Figure 5.11 shows the effect of showing the legends in an OHLC chart.

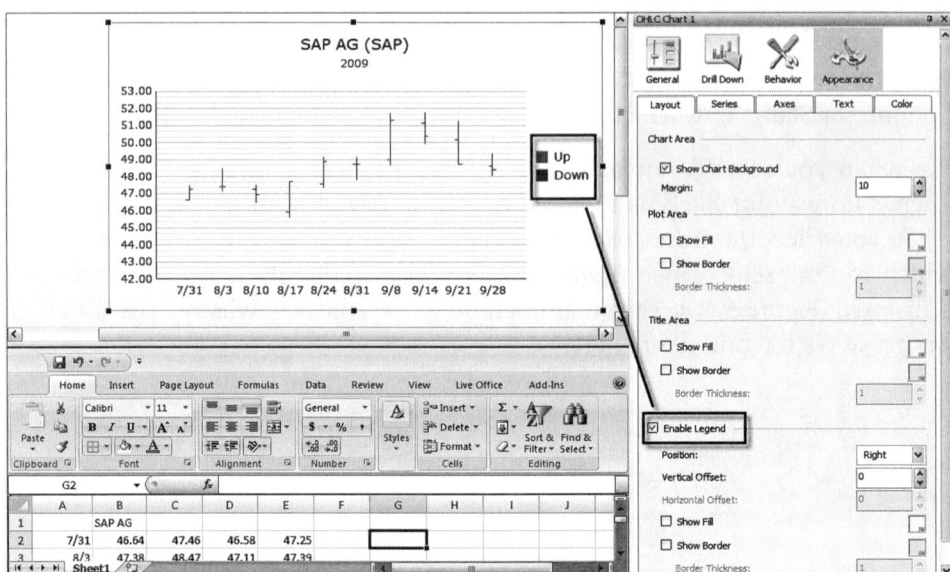

Figure 5.11 An OHLC Chart that Has its Legend Enabled

- Series
  To change the colors of the vertical bars and the markers in the legend, you go to the Series tab. As you can see from Figure 5.12, you can change the Positive Color, Negative Color, and Transparency level settings to customize the appearance of the series and legend items.

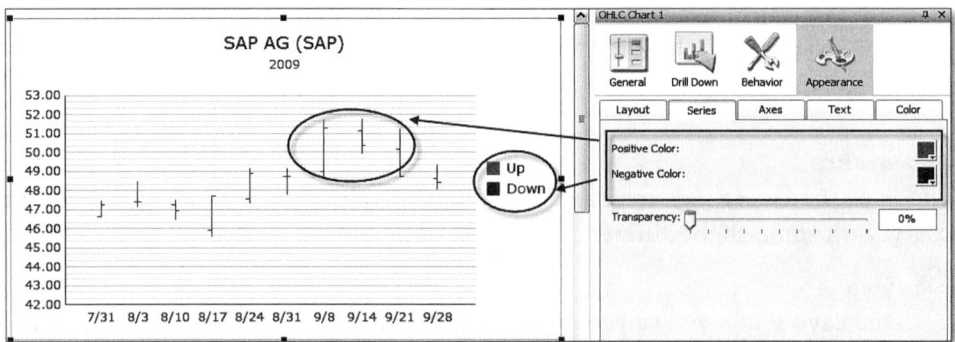

Figure 5.12 Changing Series Color Options for an OHLC Chart

Practice

Now let's go through a simple hands-on example to get more familiar with this component. Suppose that you need an OHLC chart to display your company's stock prices for the past three months. As a practice here, we'll choose Google as our example and plot the daily price from June 2009 to August 2009.

1. Get the stock prices.

   You can get the historical prices of Google stock from Yahoo Finance, at *http://finance.yahoo.com*. On the homepage of Yahoo Finance, enter the Google symbol, GOOG, into the search box, and click the Get Quotes button. You now go to the GOOG page. Select Historical Prices in the left-hand panel, enter the Start Date and End Date, and click the Get Prices button. The table shown in Figure 5.13 will be updated according to the dates specified.

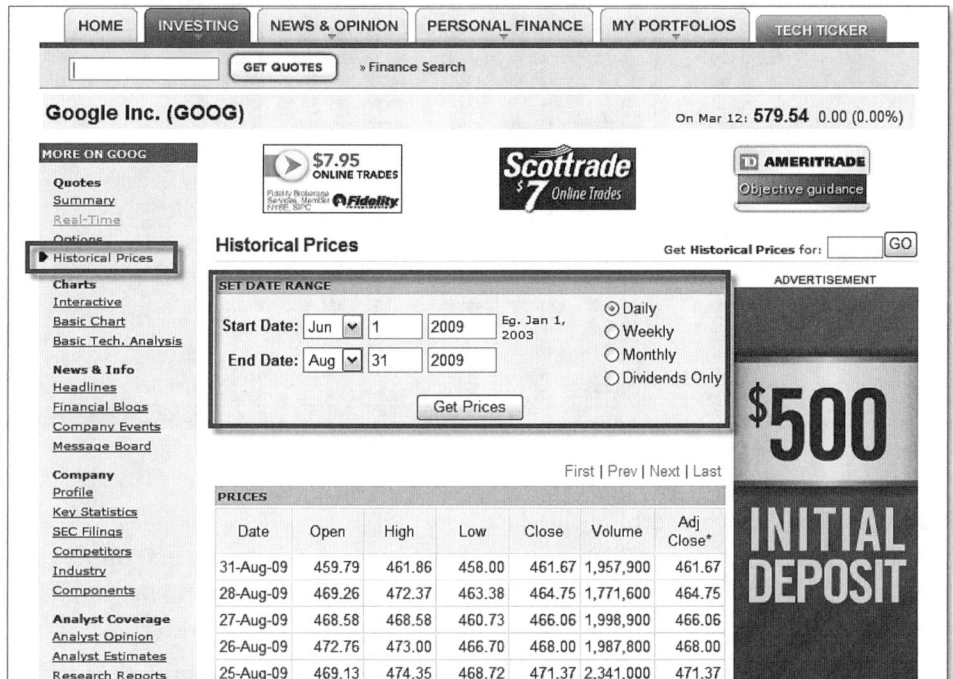

Figure 5.13 Getting Prices of GOOG from June 1, 2009 to Aug 31, 2009

2. Prepare the data source.

   You can then copy the whole price table from the web page into an Excel worksheet. Because Yahoo Finance lists historical prices retrospectively, you need to sort the data from oldest to newest so that they can be correctly plotted on the OHLC chart.

To do this, select any cell in the data column. Right-click to pop up the context menu. In the Sort submenu, select Sort Oldest to Newest. Now that the data is correctly sorted, you can add some descriptive text in the Excel worksheet.

Figure 5.14 shows an example Excel worksheet that has the data organized. We'll add some text so that they can be used as the titles of the chart.

	A	B	C	D	E	F	G	H	I	J	K	L
1			Symbol	GOOG								
2			Date Range	From 6/1 to 8/31								
3												
4				Date	Open	High	Low	Close	Volume	Adj Close*		
5				6/1/2009	418.73	429.6	418.53	426.56	3,322,400	426.56		
6				6/2/2009	426.25	429.96	423.4	428.4	2,623,600	428.4		
7				6/3/2009	426	432.46	424	431.65	3,532,800	431.65		
8				6/4/2009	435.3	441.24	434.5	440.28	3,638,100	440.28		
9				6/5/2009	445.07	447.34	439.46	444.32	3,680,800	444.32		
10				6/8/2009	439.5	440.92	434.12	438.77	3,098,700	438.77		
11				6/9/2009	438.58	440.5	431.76	435.62	3,254,900	435.62		
12				6/10/2009	436.23	437.89	426.67	432.6	3,358,900	432.6		
13				6/11/2009	431.77	433.73	428.37	429	2,865,200	429		
14				6/12/2009	426.86	427.7	421.21	424.84	2,918,400	424.84		
15				6/15/2009	421.5	421.5	414	416.77	3,736,900	416.77		
16				6/16/2009	419.31	421.09	415.42	416	3,049,700	416		
17				6/17/2009	416.19	419.72	411.56	415.16	3,490,100	415.16		
18				6/18/2009	415.68	418.69	413	414.06	3,085,200	414.06		
19				6/19/2009	418.21	420.46	414.58	420.09	4,259,100	420.09		
20				6/22/2009	416.95	417.49	401.89	407.35	4,124,400	407.35		
21				6/23/2009	406.65	408.99	402.55	405.68	2,899,600	405.68		
22				6/24/2009	408.74	412.23	406.56	409.29	2,457,800	409.29		
23				6/25/2009	407	415.9	406.51	415.77	3,044,500	415.77		
24				6/26/2009	413.68	428.23	413.11	425.32	3,256,700	425.32		

Figure 5.14 GOOG Stock Prices Organized in an Excel Worksheet

3. Add an OHLC chart and bind the data.

   Now you launch Xcelsius 2008 and create a new dashboard. You first import the Excel file created in the last step into the embedded spreadsheet, via the menu path DATA • IMPORT.

   Then you add an OHLC chart to the canvas. Now you need to bind data to the chart to make it display the stock prices.

   The format of the data in Figure 5.14 is similar to that in Figure 5.9. There is not a proper series name cell for you to bind everything in one shot, so first, in the General tab of the Properties panel, select the By Range radio button and bind data to the range $D$5 to $G$69. Then select the By Series radio button. You can rest assured that the data you specified for the chart in By Range will be carried over to the series. You then bind the series name to the cell $D$1 and bind the category label to the range $C$5:$C$69.

Now the data are properly set up. You can see the result in Figure 5.15.

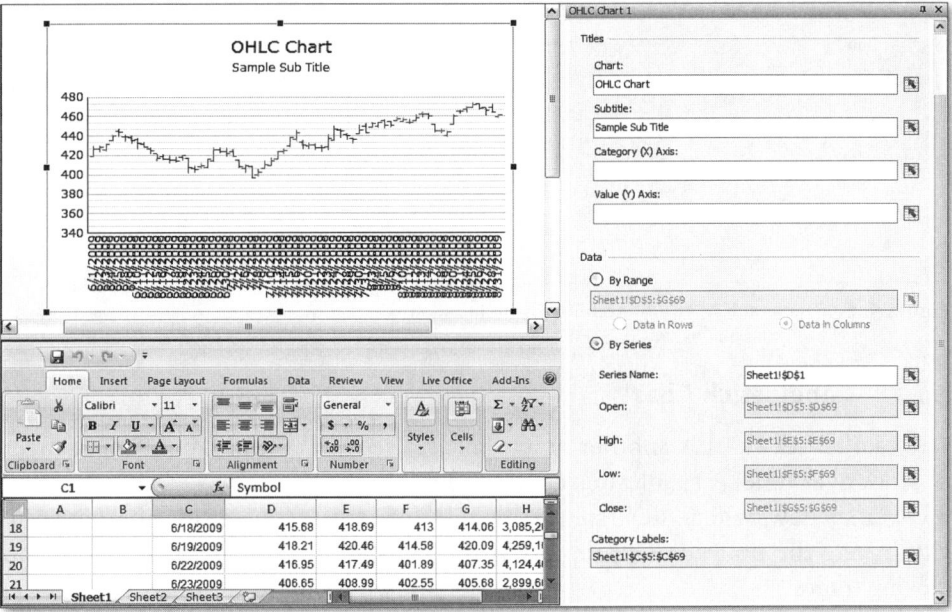

Figure 5.15 Binding Data for the Chart

4. Add titles and change the appearance.

   You can see that the OHLC chart on the canvas is already showing stock prices as you want, but there are still some problems in the chart.

   First, the chart titles contain default text and are not very informative. Second, the category labels, the dates in the date range, take up too much space and will not be very useful. Lastly, the series colors are not the ones you are used to.

   Now let's solve these problems. In the General tab of the Properties sheet, bind the title to the $D$1 cell and the subtitle to the $D$2 cell, so that now you can easily understand what the chart is showing, which is the Google stock prices in June, July, and August. Then you switch to the Appearance tab to change the appearance of the chart. In the Series tab, change the positive color to green, which usually represents higher closing prices. In the Text tab, unselect Horizontal (Category) Axis Label so that the dates won't appear.

Figure 5.16 displays the final result of this hands-on example.

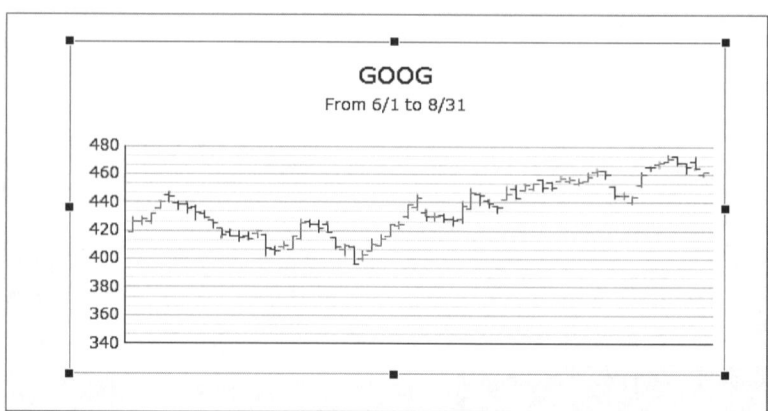

Figure 5.16   The Result of the Hands-On Example

5.1.5   Candlestick Chart

The candlestick chart is another kind of chart used to illustrate the price changes of stock over time. A candlestick chart is composed of the body and an upper and a lower shadow, which illustrate the highest and lowest traded price of that security during the time interval represented. The body illustrates the opening and closing trades.

Figure 5.17 shows an example of a candlestick chart that displays the same stock price information as shown in Figure 5.5.

When to Use a Candlestick Chart

When to choose the candlestick chart and when to choose the OHLC chart is usually determined by the user's preference. In terms of functionality, they are almost identical.

The only difference between these two charts is in the way each data point is represented. In most cases, they can be used interchangeably for the best look and feel.

How to Use Candlestick Chart

How to use a candlestick chart, including moving, resizing, and setting its properties, is exactly the same as for an OHLC chart, as illustrated in Section 5.1.4.

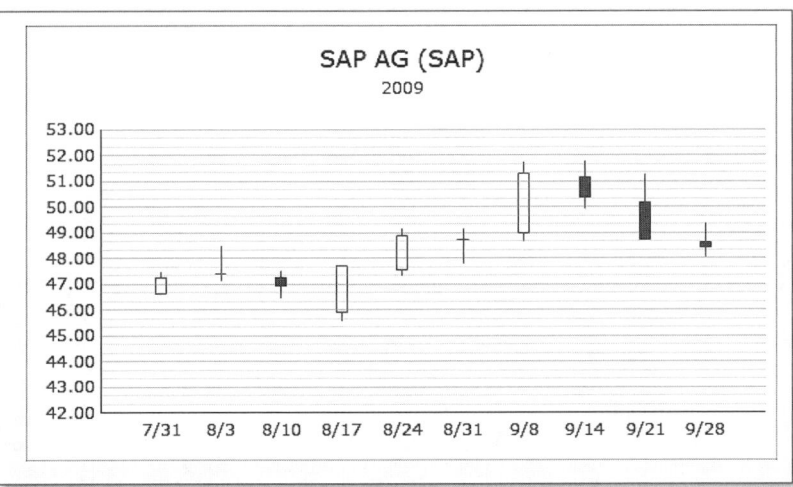

Figure 5.17 Weekly Prices of SAP AG Stock from July 31 to September 28, 2009 in a Candlestick Chart

5.1.6 Radar Chart

The radar chart displays data in a radial layout, which makes it a very interesting type of chart. Almost all of the charts we've discussed so far have a category (X) axis and a value (Y) axis. The radar chart doesn't have a category axis but has multiple value axes. In a radar chart, these axes are called vertical axes. The vertical axes in a radar chart have the following properties.

- All of the vertical axes start from the same center point and end at the perimeter.
- All of the vertical axes are the same length.
- The separation angles between adjacent axes are all equal.

This makes the radar chart a polygon shape. The number of sides of the polygon or the number of axes is determined by the number of data points each data series has. Each data point is plotted on one vertical axis. The value of the data point is represented as the distance from the center of the chart, where the center represents the minimum value, and the chart edge is the maximum value. And all of the data points in a series are connected by straight lines, which makes a series a closed circuit in a radar chart.

Figure 5.18 shows an example of a radar chart that is used to illustrate a company's performance in six different areas. We can see that for financial and growth

203

metrics, this company gets quite low scores but quite high scores for the internal process and community metrics.

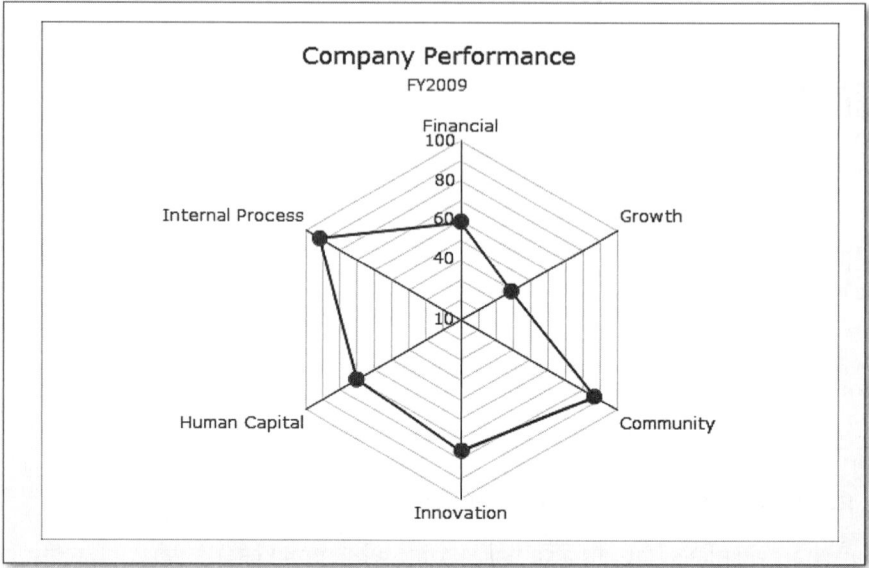

Figure 5.18 Performance Metrics Plotted on a Radar Chart

In Xcelsius 2008, the radar chart component also supports multiple series and alerts. However, as mentioned before, you cannot enable alerts when you have multiple series of data displayed in a radar chart, just like the other charts that have alerts capabilities.

When to Use a Radar Chart

From the description of the radar chart above, you can see that a radar chart is essentially a line chart wrapped into a circle, where the value (Y) axis starts at the center and ends at the perimeter, and category (X) axis becomes the perimeter. Technically, this makes using a radar chart quite similar to using a line chart in Xcelsius, but actually, the radar chart usually doesn't fit situations in which the line chart works very well.

We've already learned that the line chart is very good at visualizing trends in the data. In Section 4.1.3, in Chapter 4, we saw an example of a line chart displaying the historical trends of the market growth and sales growth of a company. Let's see how well the radar chart shows the same data.

Figure 5.19 shows the growth in sales and market share over several years.

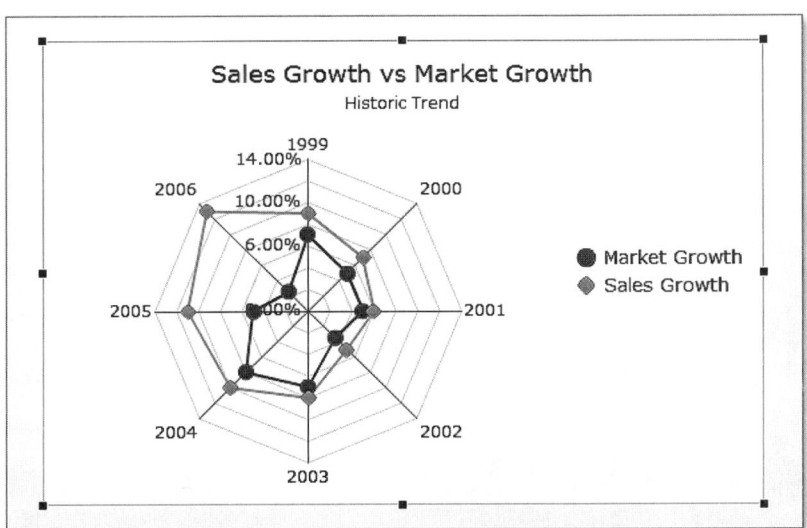

Figure 5.19 Market Growth and Sales Growth Trends from 1999 to 2006 Plotted on a Radar Chart

In this figure, we see a radar chart displaying exactly the same data as that in Figure 4.34. The question is, is it possible for you to describe the trends of our market growth and sales growth from a single glance at the line chart. We believe it's impossible. Now you may want to go back to Figure 4.34 in Chapter 4, Section 4.1.3 to compare the two charts.

The radar chart is often used to display several different aspects of something under investigation. Usually each axis represents a different measure. You can compare values in a single series of data to determine which factor is dominant, or you can compare multiple series of data to find the differences among these items. For example, you can use a radar chart to compare the individual as well as overall ability of some NBA players, with each radius representing ability in rebounds, steals and assists, and so on, as displayed in Figure 5.20.

A more typical application of the radar chart is to display the performance metric of an organization. Usually the radar chart displays several important categories of performance and makes visible concentrations of the overall strengths and weakness. Typically, you need first to create several categories or measures to describe the performance. Next, you come to a more important step, standardizing the performance definition. Each category must have a consistent scoring range, for example, 0 to 100. After evaluating and rating each category, you can construct the chart by plotting the ratings on a radar chart. Finally and the most important step is to analyze and interpret the results.

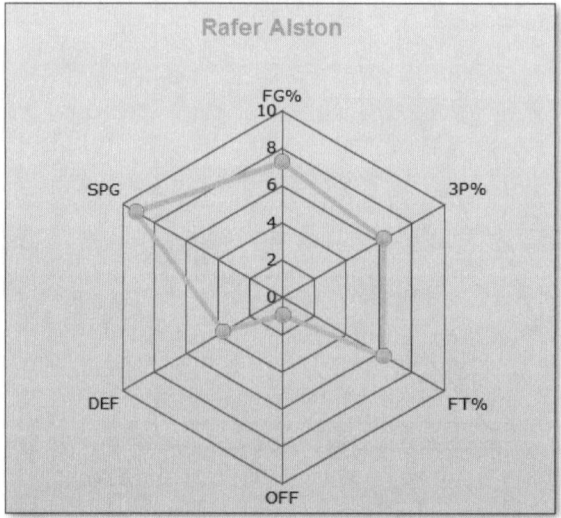

Figure 5.20 NBA Player Abilities in a Radar Chart

How to Use a Radar Chart

Because the radar chart is a essentially another kind of line chart, the methods to bind the display data, change the appearance, enable alerts, and so on are exactly the same as those illustrated in Chapter 4, Section 4.1.4, Line Chart. We'll ignore them here.

5.1.7 Filled Radar Chart

The filled radar chart is essentially a radar chart whose area is covered by data series filled with a color. The filled radar chart doesn't provide series markers, so it is impossible to enable alerts on a filled radar chart, even if it displays only one series of data.

Figure 5.21 is an example of a filled radar chart that compares the performance of two departments.

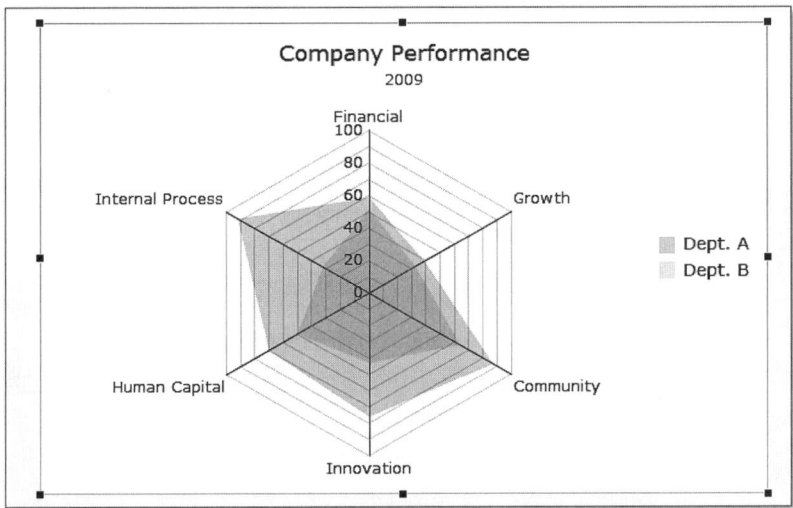

Figure 5.21 Performance Metrics Plotted on a Filled Radar Chart

As you can see from this figure, it's quite obvious that the performance of department A exceeds that of department B in all aspects.

When to Use a Filled Radar Chart

The filled radar chart is very similar to the radar chart. Unless you want to highlight some abnormal values in a single data series, you can always use these two charts interchangeably. Sometimes a filled radar chart may be preferable because you can compare the areas of two series more easily on a filled radar chart. Generally, the larger the area is, the better the overall performance is.

How to Use a Filled Radar Chart

How to use the filled radar chart is very similar to how to use the radar chart. For the filled radar chart, you can also set the filled colors of series.

Appearance
- Series
  You can change the filled colors of series in the Series tab in the Appearance tab in the filled radar chart's Properties sheet, which is quite straightforward. The Transparency option is also very important here. As in Figure 5.22, the transparency is set to 70% by default. Usually, you need a higher transparency value. Otherwise, the department A series will be barely visible because it's covered by the department B series.

5 | UI Components – Advanced

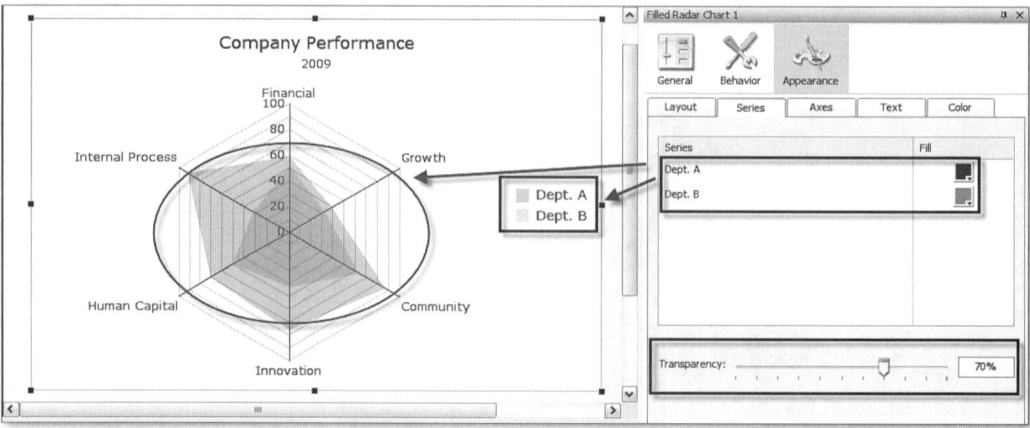

Figure 5.22 Changing Series Color Options for a Filled Radar Chart

5.1.8 Tree Map

The tree map is another interesting chart. It displays a rectangle, which is tiled with small rectangles. The size of each rectangle is proportional to a measure of the data. Also, each rectangle is filled with a color, the intensity of which is related to another measure. The tree map manifests the correlation of two measures, which is very similar to what the XY chart does. Moreover, a tree map appears to be more intuitive to some extent. After all, the differences in color and size are easier to distinguish visually.

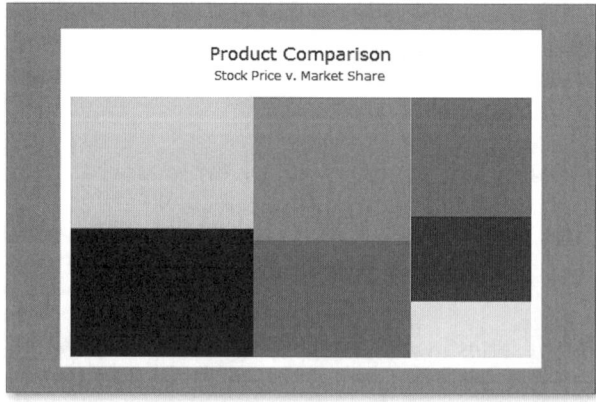

Figure 5.23 Product Comparison in a Tree Map

Figure 5.23 shows an example of a tree map that compares seven products in two measures: stock price and market share. The size represents the stock price, and the color intensity represents the market share. From this chart, we can easily discover the following facts.

- The company that has a product with a high market share could have a very high stock price (the rectangle at the bottom-left corner).
- The company that has a product with a high market share could have a very low stock price (the rectangle at the upper-left corner).
- The company that has a product with a low market share could have a very high stock price (the rectangle at the bottom-right corner).
- The company that has a product with a low market share could have a very low stock price (the rectangle at the middle right).

Such facts are quite extreme. Maybe the company with a high market share product and low stock price is doing worse than before, so people don't want to keep their stock. And maybe the company with a low market share product and high price has an amazing new product that hasn't taken the market share yet, so people have high expectations for the company. Anyway, you get the idea that the tree map reveals the correlation of two different measures.

When to Use a Tree Map

When you want to analyze a situation using two different measures, you can choose either an XY chart or a tree map. The tree map may seem more intuitive and more interesting, but it doesn't support alerts, so if you want to highlight data points conditionally, you should choose an XY chart.

How to Use a Tree Map

The ways to bind data and set most of the properties for a tree map is identical to that for an XY chart. You can refer to Chapter 4, Section 4.1.5 for details. The only special property for the tree map is the series color.

Appearance
- Series
  You need to specify two colors for each series in the tree map. One is the high color, which is usually a dark color, and the other is the low color, which is usually a light color. Based on these two colors, Xcelsius automatically calculates all

of the other colors for each rectangle by interpolation so that the intensity of all of the colors is within the range of the high and low colors.

In Figure 5.24, you can see how the colors of the series are specified. We've changed the high color to purple and low color to yellow. We've also added red lines around the perimeter of the whole rectangle and increased their thickness to make it clearer.

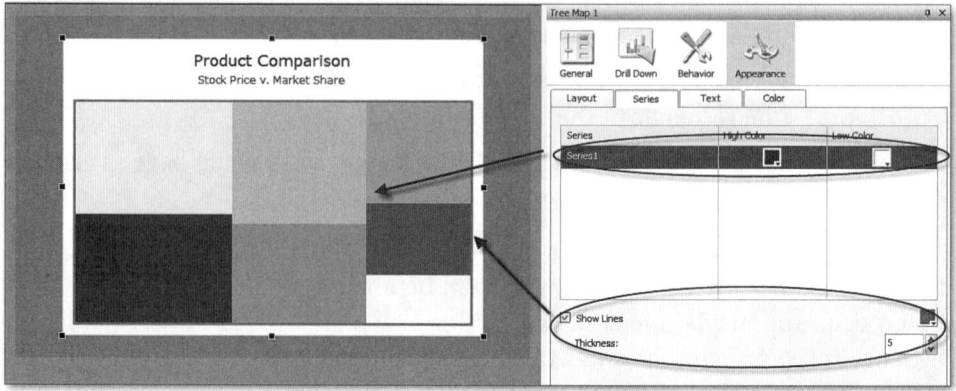

Figure 5.24 Effects of Setting Series Colors in the Appearance Tab

5.2 Advanced Selectors

Xcelsius 2008 provides a wide range of selectors in the Selectors category, some of which we covered in Chapter 4. In this section, we'll show you the rest, such as the accordion menu and play selector.

5.2.1 Accordion Menu

An accordion menu is a two-level menu in which items are categorized into groups. The user can first select a category and then select one of the items within it. The categories are stacked vertically and can be expanded or collapsed. In fact, in the Category tab of the Components view, all Xcelsius 2008 components are listed in an accordion menu.

When to Use an Accordion Menu

You may want to choose this component when there are too many items to choose from, and they can be categorized into groups. For example, say you are creating a dashboard showing values such as sales revenue of each branch in your company, which requires the user to select a branch first. The branches in your company are too numerous. To help with user selection, you can list them in an accordion menu where the user first selects a sales district and then a branch.

You can select only one item each time. The category cannot be selected; clicking on it will just expand it to list its labels.

How to Use an Accordion Menu

The Properties panel of an accordion menu is divided into three categories as explained below.

General
- Titles
  The title tells the user about the menu and what he needs do. You can customize its location in the Appearance tab by choosing a location from the Position dropdown list.

- Categories
  As mentioned above, the accordion menu is a two-level selector with candidates divided into categories. The typical steps to set up the labels of an accordion menu are:
  - Add a category
    You do this by clicking the Add button (with a plus (+) sign) below the Categories list. You can then enter the name of the category directly in the Name field or bind it to a cell in the embedded spreadsheet with the Bind button.
  - Add labels of the category
    The labels will appear within the category when it's selected. You add the labels by clicking the Bind button to bind them to a row or column in the embedded spreadsheet.

Figure 5.25 shows an accordion menu with one category. Pay attention to the Properties panel.

5 | UI Components – Advanced

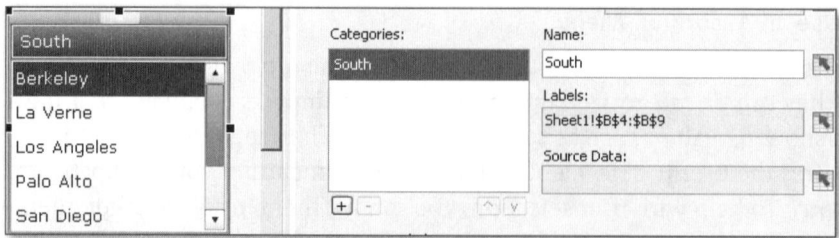

Figure 5.25 An Accordion Menu with One Category

To add more categories, follow the steps above. To delete a category, click to select it and click the Delete button (with a minus (–) sign).

At runtime, the categories are displayed in the order defined here, from top to bottom. You can click the buttons to the bottom right of the Categories list with a up or down symbol to move a category up or down.

▸ Data Insertion
You use a selector component to insert something into a destination. The accordion menu is not an exception. Similar to other components, you can select from the Insertion Type dropdown list. The options are Row, Value, Column, Filtered Rows and Status List. We explained their meanings in Chapter 4, when we discussed the pie chart in Section 4.1.1 and selectors in Section 4.2.

Depending on what insertion type you have chosen, you can bind the destination to a cell or a cell range in the embedded spreadsheet. Each time the user makes a selection in the menu, the corresponding value or rows is inserted into that cell or cell range.

An accordion menu is more powerful than a normal selector such as a Combo box Only one insertion type and destination can be defined in an accordion menu, but you can define source data for each category. The source data can be a row or a column, or even a cell range with multiple rows and columns. For example, you can display the monthly sales revenue of each branch in a cell range, one row per branch. With this range being the source data, and selecting Row as the insertion type, you insert the monthly sales revenue of the selected branch to a target row, which can also be used in a column chart.

In Category Label Destination, you can insert the category name of the current selected item to a cell in the embedded spreadsheet.

Clicking the category name will not trigger any data insertion. The user needs to click the items inside each category.

Behavior

▶ Slide Speed
When the user clicks a category that is not currently expanded, it rolls up to expand its labels. The slide speed controls how fast a category expands when clicked. You can adjust it with the slider, from Slower on the left to Faster on the right.

▶ Selected Item
Similar to the default selection of a chart or a combo box, you define what category and what label within that category is selected by default. You do this by selecting one from the corresponding Category or Item dropdown list. That category will then be expanded by default.

▶ Ignore Blank Cells
If you don't want to display a category or an item if it's empty, select In Categories or In Values. *Empty* means that the category, or value, of a certain item is blank.

Just one more word: This option will only ignore the last empty categories, or the last few empty items of each category. As mentioned before, if you want to hide all of the cells that are blank in categories or values, move all such cells to the end of each category, which is achieved either in the backend server, or in the embedded spreadsheet with Excel formulas.

Practice

Now let's go through a simple hands-on example to reinforce how to use an accordion menu. Suppose you want to create a dashboard to show and compare the sales revenue and quantity sold of each branch over a period of quarters. Instead of asking the user to select one branch from many in a combo box, we'll use an accordion menu and a column chart to its right to show the values.

1. Prepare the data.
   Display the values of two measures, sales revenue and quantity sold, of each branch in a range, with one row per branch. Display the sales revenue in each quarter in front of the quantity sold. Display the branches in a column, categorized into sales districts.

   Your data should be similar to that displayed in Figure 5.26.

	A	B	C	D	E	F	G	H	I	J
1										
2										
3					Sales revenue				Quantity sold	
4		South	Q1	Q2	Q3	Q4	Q1	Q2	Q3	Q4
5		Branch 1	282	309	435	283	15	18	22	10
6		Branch 2	363	447	171	403	17	20	20	18
7		Branch 3	322	112	260	273	22	28	36	26
8		Branch 4	318	330	325	158	25	32	38.7	34
9		Branch 5	114	217	274	146	22	37	45	42
10		Branch 6	167	496	213	420	32	42	25	60
11										
12		North								
13		Branch 7	435	443	130	147	18	10	33	38
14		Branch 8	474	260	362	160	11	17	22	39
15		Branch 9	454	387	339	128	15	20	30	14
16		Branch 10	377	625	439	268	22	24	19	28

Figure 5.26 Data in the Embedded Spreadsheet in this Hands-On Example

2. Set up the accordion menu.

   Having planned the data, now let's focus on the UI components. We'll use an accordion menu for the user to select a branch in a quarter, and we'll use a column chart to display the sales info under that condition.

   In this step, drag an accordion menu from the Selectors category in the Components view and drop it onto the canvas. Move and resize it as you want. In the step 4 we'll focus on setting up the column chart.

   We give the accordion menu the title "Please select a branch" to prompt the user, and set it to display on the top left. To do this, click the Appearance tab in the Properties panel, select the Text tab, and then select Title and select Top Left in the Position dropdown list.

   Now let's set the categories and labels. Click the Add button (with a + sign) below the Categories list. Select the new category, bind its name to cell Sheet1!$B$4, which is sales district South, and bind Labels to cell range Sheet1!$B$5:$B$10, which contains the branches in the South sales district.

   Follow the steps to add categories and labels for the sales districts North, East, and West.

   Now the accordion menu can display properly. You can click each category to see its contained items.

3. Implement data insertion.

   Before this step, nothing happens when the user makes selections in this menu. The menu is used for the user to select a branch to see its sales info. So we'll set Insertion Type to Row and bind the source data of each category to the cell range containing the sales info of that category.

To do this, select the category South and click the Bind button next to Source Data to bind to range Sheet1!$B$5:$J$10, where the branch names and their sales info are stored. Repeat this step for other categories.

The inserted data is inserted into a row, and here we bind Destination to cell range Sheet1!$B$2.

It's better to display the sales district next to the branch name in the column chart, so we'll also insert the category name by binding Category Label Destination to cell Sheet1!$A$3.

4. Arrange the column chart.
Now it's time to set up the column chart. After positioning it to the right of the accordion menu and making them the same height and aligning to the top, let's set properties for the column chart.

In the General tab of the chart's Properties panel, select By Series to manually set its category labels and values. Bind its category labels to range Sheet1!$C$4:$F$4, where the quarter's names are stored. Add one series called "Sales revenue," bind its values to range Sheet1!$C$2:$F$2, which is the destination of the accordion menu, and plot it on the primary Y-axis. Add another series called "Quantity sold," bind its values to range Sheet1!$G$2:$J$2, and plot it on the secondary Y-axis.

We'd like to show the current branch to avoid confusion about what the data is for. Insert the name of the current sales district, which is the category name of the accordion menu, into cell Sheet1!$A$3 as defined in step 3. Also, the branch name is the first cell of the destination of the menu, Sheet1!$B$2. So we'll use a formula to format a meaningful subtitle for the column chart:

=CONCATENATE("Sales district: ",A3," Branch: ",B2)

Save it in a cell and bind the subtitle of the column chart to it.

Now we are all done. You can refer to the website for the sample model definition file (.xlf). Figure 5.27 shows the Properties panels of both the menu and the chart.

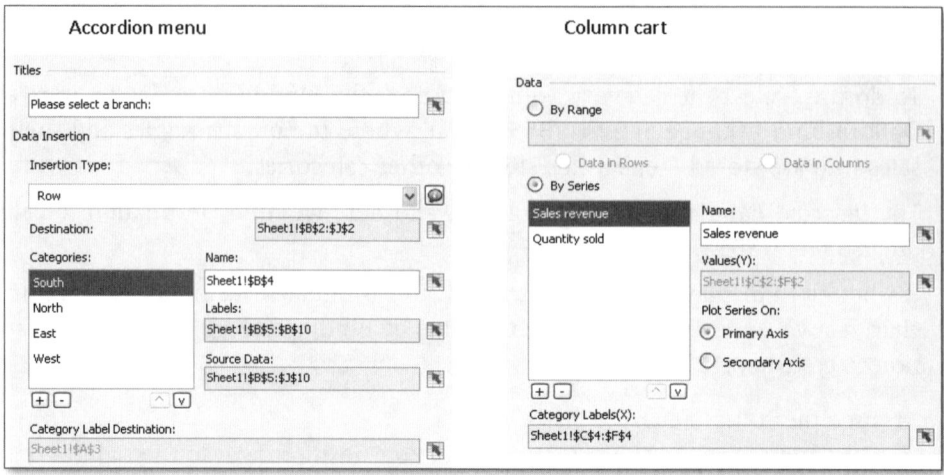

Figure 5.27 Properties Panels of the Two UI Components in this Hands-On Example

The final result of this hands-on example is as displayed in Figure 5.28.

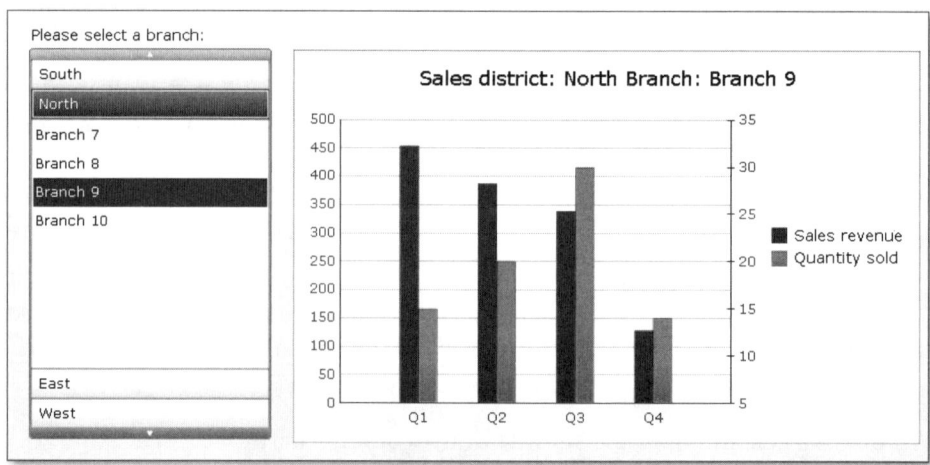

Figure 5.28 Final Result of the Accordion Menu

At runtime, each time the user clicks a category (sales district), its branches are listed below it. When the user selects one branch, its corresponding values are inserted into Destination, shown in the column chart.

5.2.2 Icon

The visual appearance of an icon component is a colorful circle. It is a very useful and unique UI component.

When to Use and Icon

With alerts enabled, an icon is a good way to show whether the value it's bound to is good or bad. You can use it in combination with other components such as a label or a gauge, where the label or gauge component displays the actual value, while the icon indicates its status. An icon the ideal component to represent the traffic light, in green, yellow, or red.

An icon component can have two states, on and off, similar to a checkbox, making it a selector component. In this case, the user can click it to switch its state and see different data or components.

Based on these two functionalities of icons, you may want to use this component either to indicate the status of some data field or to switch between two states, showing different values when it's selected or not.

How to Use an Icon

You can move or resize an icon component on the canvas. For example, you can resize it from a circle to an ellipse. Its Properties panel is divided into four categories, as explained below.

General

If you want the icon component to display a certain value, you can set its label to indicate what value it represents. You can either enter a text directly in the input field of Label or bind it to a cell in the embedded spreadsheet. The label will not appear anywhere next to the icon. Instead, it will only be displayed as a hint on mouse over.

The display value, naturally, is a constant value entered by the designer here or bound to a cell storing the data. It's used in Alerts Threshold to determine the color of the icon.

Figure 5.29 shows how the label and display value of an icon component are displayed at runtime. You can customize whether and how to show them in the Appearance tab, which we'll discuss shortly.

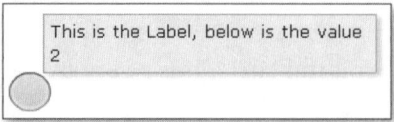

Figure 5.29 Label and Display Value of an Icon at Runtime

If you just want to use an icon as an on/off selector, you can leave the label and the display value empty.

As a selector component, the icon also provides data insertion functionality, to choose one from two candidates. At this point it's the same as a checkbox. The source data is a row or column with two cells, and the destination is a single cell to store the selected value. The first cell in the row or column specified in source data indicates the unselected status, while the second row or column indicates selected. Therefore, if the default selected item is unselected, the content in the first cell will be inserted into the destination when the user launches the dashboard. You can configure the default selected item in BEHAVIOR • COMMON.

Behavior

The properties is this tab are similar to those of other components. You can set whether the data insertion occurs on mouse over or mouse click, configure the default selected item, and set dynamic visibility.

If you want to add more fun to your dashboard, you can also choose to play a sound on user interaction, by selecting Enable Sound.

Appearance

Here you set the transparency level of the component. In the Text tab, you set the formats of the label and display value, which will display on mouse over if enabled. However, note that you cannot specify their positions.

One property specific to icons is Show On/Off. An icon component has two states, on (for selected) and off (for unselected). By default, Show On/Off is selected, and the icon appears in different colors for the different states. If Show On/Off is not selected, the data insertion can still work perfectly on user interaction, but the color of the icon will not change between the on and off states. Note that Xcelsius automatically calculates the on color based on its off color, and you cannot specify it. You can unselect Show On/Off if you have enabled alerts and you don't want the on color to make the colors defined in alerts confusing.

You can set the default color (for unselected) in the Color tab only when alerts is not enabled.

> **Note**
> The color you specify here is for unselected, no matter what is selected as the default selected item.

Alerts

How to use alerts is exactly the same for all components. You can select Enable Alerts if you want to use the icon component as an indicator of the value it represents. For example, you can display the actual value in a label or a single value component, with an icon component alongside to show its status.

5.2.3 Play Selector

A play selector looks like the controller you use when listening to the music or playing movies. Typically, it has buttons to play or pause an item, move to the previous or next item, and move to the first or the last item.

Xcelsius 2008 provides such a UI component with the five buttons mentioned above to continuously insert a row or column from a cell range such as the source data to another row or column such as the destination. With the play selector component on your dashboard, the user can see data from a large number of items without clicking on each selection. The play selector can automatically insert items one at a time from a large list to a destination, with a movie effect. The user can go backward or forward or pause the play at any time with a simple click.

Figure 5.30 shows an example of a play selector. The slider bar is the progress indicator that shows what item is currently selected, and the five buttons are, respectively, Previous, Rewind, Play/Pause, Forward, and Next.

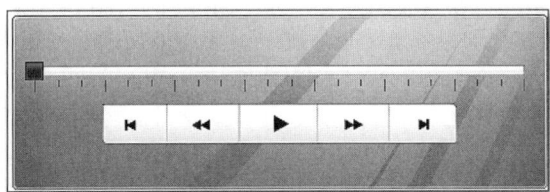

Figure 5.30 A Simple Play Selector Component

When to Use a Play Selector

You may choose a play selector component when you want to display a large list of data one at a time, without requiring user interaction to select them or when you just want to simulate the effect of a media player.

How to Use a Play Selector

The Properties panel of a play selector component is very simple, as you can see from the following description.

General

In this tab, you define how the data insertion occurs, by choosing from the Insertion Type dropdown list, and bind the source data to a cell range and the destination to a row or column, depending on what insertion type you have chosen.

Behavior

In this tab, you can configure interaction options as displayed in Figure 5.31.

Figure 5.31 The Interaction Options of a Play Selector

The following properties are available.

- Play Time
  This is the amount of time needed for the entire sequence to play, from the first item to the last item, if the play selector is configured to play automatically. If you use another UI component such as a column chart to show data in the destination, the display time of each item will then be the play time divided by the number of items. Of course, you can click Pause at runtime to stay on the current item and click one of the other four buttons to quickly leave it.

- Auto Play
  As indicated by the name, if this option is enabled, the component will play automatically when the dashboard is launched.

- Auto Rewind
  If you want the play to rewind automatically, select Auto Rewind.

▶ Auto Replay
If you want the play to automatically repeat from the first item after reaching the end, select Auto Replay. With Auto Replay enabled, the sequence will keep repeating when you have launched the play, and will never stop until you click the Pause button.

Appearance
In this tab, you can configure whether or not to show the background, the progress indicator, the Rewind and Forward buttons, and the Previous and Next buttons. These parts are displayed in Figure 5.30 above. You can unselect all of them, leaving only the Play button on the screen.

However, you cannot customize the shape of the progress indicator, nor can you configure whether or how to show its major and minor ticks. The reason is that they are fixed by Xcelsius, with 11 major and 4 minor ticks, which are the default settings of a horizontal slider, when Manual is selected in the play selector's Properties panel.

Practice
Now let's go through a simple hands-on example to see a play selector in use. Suppose you, as the sales director, are to present the sales data and some basic information about each of your company's 10 major branches at the year-end company meeting. It's straightforward to illustrate the sales data in a fancy chart and show the basic information such as location and number of employees in a big label. The best way to talk about the 10 branches one by one would be to use a play selector component, which selects the info from each branch automatically at intervals, and you can go on with your presentation without stopping to select another branch.

Prepare Data
All of the data is placed in a range (either directly input into the embedded spreadsheet, or mapped from the output of some type of data connectivity, which we'll cover in the next two chapters), with one row for each branch. The sales data includes sales revenue for each quarter and the basic info such as the location and number of employees of each branch. Each column represents a data field.

We'll use a column chart to show and compare the sales revenue, and two label components to show the basic info, of the selected branch. No matter what selector component is used, we need to insert the data of a branch from the range to a new row.

The two label components will show the location and the number of employees of the branch. We'll use Excel formulas to make a meaningful name. Set cell G2 to:

=CONCATENATE(G5,": ",G3)

and cell H2 to:

=CONCATENATE(H5,": ",H3)

As a result, the data in the embedded Excel spreadsheet should be similar to what's displayed in Figure 5.32.

	A	B	C	D	E	F	G	H
1								
2		Sales revenues by Branch						
3	Insertion							
4								
5				Q1	Q2	Q3	Q4	Location	No. of Employees
6		Branch 1	27.00	34.60	48.70	54.80	Houston	32
7		Branch 2	43.30	52.50	33.50	30.70	Washington	36
8		Branch 3	46.80	23.10	41.80	50.90	London	44
9		Branch 4	36.90	51.90	50.50	54.50	Memphis	48
10		Branch 5	23.60	34.00	32.80	50.70	San Jose	23
11		Branch 6	45.10	35.90	27.70	37.30	City 1	27
12		Branch 7	39.00	28.30	25.30	49.00	City 2	33
13		Branch 8	33.40	47.70	43.80	40.70	City 3	19
14		Branch 9	23.40	24.30	23.30	47.30	City 4	11
15		Branch 10	28.90	49.90	40.90	52.10	City 5	20
16								

Figure 5.32 Data in the Embedded Spreadsheet for the Play Selector

Add Selector

Now that we have planned the data, let's work with the play selector. From the Components view, drag a play selector component from the Selector category and drop it onto the canvas. Move it to the bottom of the canvas if you like

We'll use the play selector for the user to select a row from the cell range and insert it into a destination row. For this, in the tab General of the play selector's Properties panel, we'll set Insertion Type to Row and bind the source data to cell range Sheet1!$B$6:$H$15 and the destination to row Sheet1!$B$3:$H$3, as displayed in Figure 5.33.

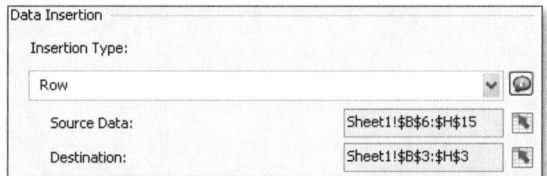

Figure 5.33 Bindings for Data Insertion of the Play Selector

We don't want the presentation to play automatically, but it's good if we can go backward and forward. For this, unselect Auto Play and Auto Replay in Behavior and leave Auto Rewind selected.

It takes about 20 seconds to talk about each branch. There are 10 branches here, so we'll set Play Time to 20 * 10 = 200 seconds in the Behavior tab. Pay attention to the way we calculate the play time here.

In the Appearance tab, make sure Show Rew/Fwd and Show Prev/Next are selected. You can configure whether or not to show the background or progress indicator as you want.

Add Components for the Selected Branch

By now the play selector is displaying properly and has been configured to insert the data of the selected branch into a row. In this step, we'll add the necessary components to display the data. Let's use a column chart and a label. You can choose other components to represent the same data based on your preferences.

This phase can be divided into three steps as illustrated below.

1. Lay out the required UI components.
   Drag a column chart and two label components onto the canvas. Put them on the top of the canvas, above the play selector, with the column chart to the right of the labels. Position the labels vertically. Resize them for an agreeable look and feel.

2. Set the properties for the column chart.
   Bind the title to cell Sheet1!$B$2, and the subtitle to cell Sheet1!$B$29, which stores the name of the selected branch. Select By Series for Data, bind the category labels to Sheet1!$C$5:$F$5 which stores the names of the four quarters, add a series named "Sales revenue," and bind its values to Sheet1!$C$3:$F$3, where the sales revenues of the selected branch are stored.

   The General tab of the Properties panel of the column chart should be similar to what's displayed in Figure 5.34.

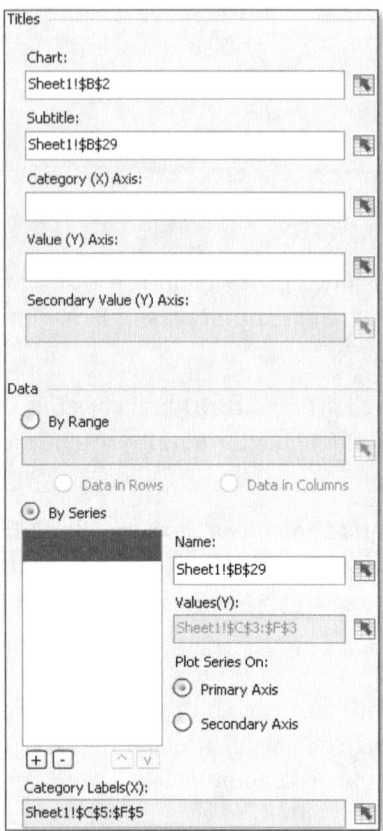

Figure 5.34 The Configuration of the Column Chart in this Hands-On Example

3. Set properties for the labels.

   This step is rather simple. Bind the two label components to cells Sheet1!$G$2 and Sheet1!$H$2, to show the basic info of the branch. If you want to display more info about the branch, add more labels.

Now we are done. At runtime, after you have clicked the Play button to begin the presentation, the data of each branch will be displayed on the chart along with the labels, in sequence, starting from the first branch. Each lasts for 20 seconds. If you want to spend more time on one of the branches, click the Pause button. To quickly go to the next or previous one, click the corresponding buttons.

Figure 5.35 shows the dashboard at runtime. The left side shows a screenshot from the beginning of the presentation, while on the right side shows the selector has stepped to the fifth branch.

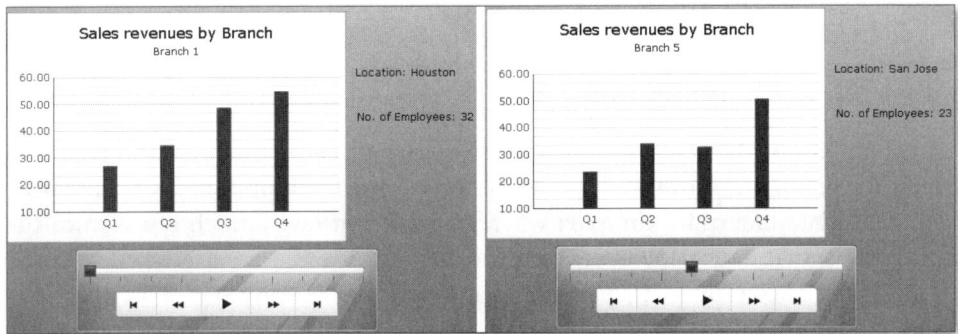

Figure 5.35 The Final Result of the Play Selector Hands-On Example

5.2.4 Calendar

A calendar is often used to display dates in years, months, and weeks. A calendar component in Xcelsius 2008 is designed for the user to select a single date from a visually intuitive dashboard.

This component is located in the Other category in the Components view of Xcelsius 2008. However, essentially, it can be regarded as a selector for the user to choose one date from many. That's why we talk about it here.

There are an almost unlimited number of dates to choose from, making it impossible for a combo box to display the dates for the user to choose from. A calendar component solves this problem by displaying the days of a month in a fixed area, with inside buttons to go to another month or year, as displayed in Figure 5.36.

Figure 5.36 A Typical Calendar Component in Xcelsius 2008

As you can see from this figure, you can click the ◄ or ► button to go to the previous or the next month, and the ◄◄ or ►► button to go the previous or next year.

When to Use a Calendar

You can use a calendar control in your dashboard when you want to provide a way for the user to select a date from a large list of candidate dates.

Of course, if you like, you can achieve this with three or four cascading combo boxes for years, months, weeks, and days or with several input fields for the user to enter a date in a quite complex way. Moreover,, it takes much effort in calculating the actual date. However, a calendar control is the most elegant tool for this purpose. Not only is it agreeable to the user, but it also saves a lot of design time.

How to Use a Calendar

You can give the calendar component a title to provide the user a hint about it, for example, "Please select the start date." For a clean look and feel, we often leave this property empty.

General

As a selector component, a calendar supports data insertion, enabling you to insert either the day or date into a single cell as the destination.

- Day
  The day of the month of the selected date is an integer. For example, if the currently selected date is 12/31/2009, the day is 31.
- Date
  The value of the selected date is a variable of the type date. To make the insertion work, you need to set the format of the destination cell in the embedded spreadsheet by right-clicking on it and selecting Set Cell Format and setting its type to Date. You can then configure how to display the date, such as 03/14/01, 14-Mar-01, and so on.

You make your choice based on the requirements. If you want to display the selected date in a label with a customized format, select Date and set the destination cell's format. If you just want the numeric value of the day in the month, select Day.

You can also insert the month or year of the selected date into a single cell in the embedded spreadsheet, also as an integer. However, you cannot insert the week of the selected date into the destination.

Behavior

▶ Default Date
You configure what date is displayed by default when the dashboard is launched through Default Date. If you want it to display the current date each time the dashboard is launched, select Use Current Date and leave it to Xcelsius to calculate the selected date.

Otherwise, select Use Custom Date, which provides more flexibility. With this option, you can enter either the year, month, and day directly in the input fields, thus hard-coding the default date, or bind each of them to a single cell, the value of which can be either calculated or passed from Flash Vars or something like it. In a word, if you want more flexibility in controlling the default date, select Use Custom Date.

▶ Calendar Limits
No matter what date is displayed and selected by default, the user can select an arbitrary date from the calendar at runtime. If you want to restrict what date can be selected, thus only passing a valid date to the backend, you can select Enable Calendar Limits and specify the date range that the user can choose from. For example, say you are to compare the sales revenue of each branch on a year-to-year basis, thus requiring the user to select a month first. The month thus shouldn't be earlier than when your company was founded or later than today. Assume that your company is founded in May 2001. Then you can set the calendar limits to May 2001 to December 2099.

With Enable Calendar Limits selected, Xcelsius enables you to set the start and end year and month, as displayed in Figure 5.37.

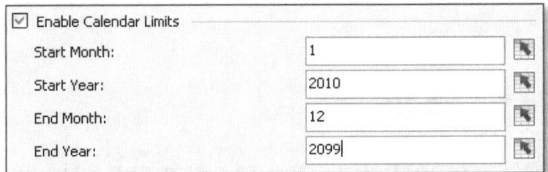

Figure 5.37 Setting the Minimum and Maximum Year and Month of a Calendar

As you can see from this figure, for each of the four properties, you can either directly enter a valid integer or bind it to a single cell in the embedded spreadsheet.

Note that you can only define the range in months, not in weeks or days.

Appearance

In tab Text, you set the formats of each part of the calendar component. The formats include font family, size, style, alignment, and color. Position is only available for the title.

In the Color tab, you set the colors or background colors of the many parts of the calendar component, such as the mouse-over color for a date and the button and symbol color of the four buttons (Previous and Next Year and Month).

You can get the meanings of most properties simply from their names.

> **Note**
> The disabled symbol color and disabled button color are used to show the buttons when the currently displayed month or year is the first or last available one.

For example, if we have defined the calendar limits as January 2010 to March 2010, and the calendar currently displays March 2010, the buttons for previous year, next month, and next year will be disabled, in green background and gray color, as displayed in Figure 5.38.

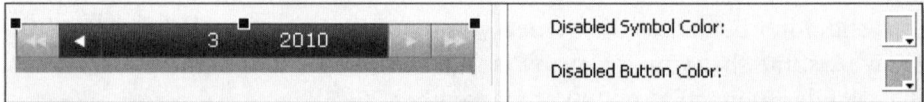

Figure 5.38 Buttons Are Displayed when out of Range

In this figure, pay attention to the different colors of the four buttons of the calendar.

5.3 Advanced Single-Value Components

In Chapter 4, we discussed some basic components used to represent a single numeric value such as a gauge that are provided with Xcelsius 2008 in the Single Value category. We'll cover the rest of those components such as the spinner in this section.

5.3.1 Dual Slider

As mentioned in Chapter 4, Xcelsius 2008 provides four sliders, two horizontal and two vertical, which can be used both as input components to represent a single value and as output for the user to adjust the value.

A dual slider, as the name indicates, can represent two values. The user can adjust the two values in the same component by moving the sliders.

Xcelsius 2008 provides two dual sliders in the Single Value category, which are almost identical, differing in the marker shape only, as displayed in Figure 5.39.

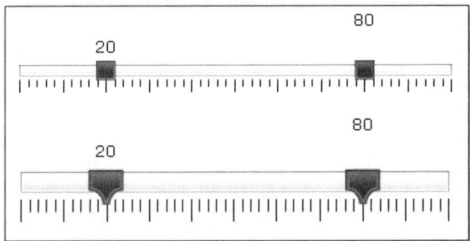

Figure 5.39 Dual Sliders

You can see from Figure 5.39 that the high value is displayed higher that the low value. This is done to avoid overlapping when the low and high values are equal or very near. Otherwise, the user may have difficulty reading the values.

When to Use a Dual Slider

A dual slider component is often used to represent the minimum and maximum values of some field. It makes little sense to represent two unrelated fields. You can choose this component if you want the user to adjust both the minimum and the maximum values, as a range. For example, say you are to create a dashboard where the user can search products with a quantity sold within a certain range. You can use a dual slider for the user to specify the lowest and highest values of quantity sold.

How to Use a Dual Slider

The Properties panel of a dual slider component is very similar to that of a slider, including the scale, slider movement, and whether and how to show ticks and alerts.

One difference is that for a dual slider, you need to specify both the low value and the high value. If you bind either to a cell, the corresponding new value will be inserted into that cell when the user moves the corresponding low or high marker.

The low value can be equal to, but never greater than, the high value. At runtime, you cannot move the low marker in front of the high marker. The case is similar for the high value.

The minimum limit and maximum limit define the scale of the entire slider, similar to a slider.

The values should conform to the rule that the low value shouldn't be greater than the high value, and both should be within the scale defined by the minimum limit and maximum limit. Though the default values can break this rule, at runtime, the user will never have a chance to break it after moving the markers.

Another difference is that you cannot select Enable Play Button for a dual slider, while you can do it for a common slider.

5.3.2 Spinner

A spinner is an input component through which the user adjusts the value by clicking the up or down arrow or by directly entering a numeric value. Compared to a slider, it takes up less space to display.

A spinner can never be used alone, but must be used together with other components. It helps analyze the impact of one value on some other measures.

When to Use a Spinner

You may choose a spinner component if you want the user to adjust the value more accurately. With a slider, the user moves the mouse to change the value, making it difficult to make slight adjustments. For example, with the same scale of 1 to 100, it's difficult to decrease or increase the value by 1 with a slider, while it's very easy with a spinner.

How to Use a Spinner

To use a spinner, find it in the Selector category or by its name in the Components view and drag and drop it onto the canvas. You can use the mouse to resize its width but not to change its height. If you want to change the height, go to the Appearance tab and set the font size for Value.

The Properties panel of a spinner is very similar to that of a slider. Some properties specific to spinners are explained below.

General

In the General tab, you can set a title for the spinner, which can show the user what value the spinner represents.

You can enter a numeric value in the Data field, either an integer or a decimal, as the spinner's default value. You can also bind it to a single cell in the embedded spreadsheet, the value of which is used as the default. At runtime, the new value changed by the user will be inserted into this cell.

You need define the scale for a valid value by setting the minimum limit and the maximum limit.

Behavior

Pay attention to Increment property here, which defines how much the value changes when the user clicks the up or down arrow. At runtime, the user can only change the value to a multiple of the increment you define here. That is, if the default value is 0.2 and the increment is 1, clicking the up arrow will take you to 1, not 1.2. Similarly, if the default value is 3 and the increment is 10, clicking the up arrow will take you to 10, not 13.

One more word: Make the increment smaller if you want to provide a slighter and thus more accurate adjustment of the value.

Appearance and Alerts

The properties in these two tabs are very similar to those of other components. Pay attention to alerts, which are very useful to display the status of the current value.

5.3.3 Play Control

A play control is an input component for the user to set a numeric value. It looks like a media player, with five buttons: Previous, Rewind, Play/Pause, Forward, and Next, similar to the play selector described in Section 5.2.3.

Figure 5.40 shows a sample play control component in Xcelsius 2008, with the current value on the top, a horizontal slider as the progress indicator in the middle, and the play buttons on the bottom.

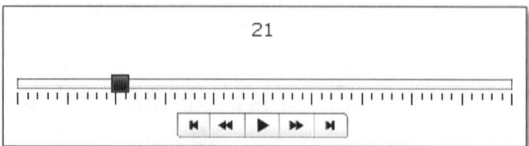

Figure 5.40 A Play Control Component

You change the value by clicking the Previous, Rewind, Forward, or Next button. There is no way to enter a value directly. When you click the Play button, the component will automatically increment the value. You can click the Pause button to remain on the current value for a longer time, or the other four buttons to quickly jump to another value.

A play control differs from a spinner in appearance, but is similar in representing and manipulating a single numeric value. On the other hand, its appearance is very similar to that of a play selector, with the difference being that it inserts the current numeric value to a single cell, while a play selector inserts a row or column from a cell range in the embedded spreadsheet to another row or column.

When to Use a Play Control

You may choose a play control component either for its unique appearance, or because it increments the value at equal intervals automatically without user interaction.

The value you adjust with a play control component is often used in another component. For example, you can use a play control to adjust the product price and analyze the corresponding sales revenue and quantity sold in another chart. Within a reasonable range, the play control automatically increases the price with your specified increment, and the charts help you analyze the impact on sales revenue and quantity sold on each price.

How to Use a Play Control

General
Here you set the data and scale of the component, the same way you do for a spinner or a slider. For more info, please refer to Section 5.3.2.

Behavior

Here you set the user interaction behavior. The increment is the smallest amount that the value can be changed. For example, if the default value is 0 and the increment is 3, then you cannot set the value to 2.

When you click the Previous or Next button, the value is decreased or increased by the amount of the increment. If you click Rewind or Forward, the value is changed an amount that is four times the increment amount.

To set the increment, you can either directly enter a numeric value, integer or decimal, in the Input field or bind it to a cell in the embedded spreadsheet.

The play options, including Play Time, Auto Play, Auto Rewind, and Auto Replay are exactly the same as for a play selector. For more info about their meanings and how to use them, please refer to the corresponding part in Section 5.2.3.

Appearance

In this tab you can configure whether or not to show each part of a play control component, including the title, the current value, the slider, the Rewind and Forward buttons, and the Previous and Next buttons.

As with a play selector, you cannot configure whether or not to show the ticks. There will always be 11 major ticks and 4 minor ones.

If you want to show both the title and the value, choose a different position for each of them to avoid overlap.

5.3.4 Value

A value component displays a numeric value in a rectangle. It's very similar to a spinner, described in Section 5.3.2, in appearance and properties. However, the user adjusts its value by dragging the mouse up or down or double-clicking it and then editing its value inside the component.

You can regard a value component as a grid in the grid component, which we'll described in Section 5.4.3.

How To Use a Value

You may choose a value component when you want to display a single numeric value in your dashboard, and in the meantime allow the user to adjust the value in an especial way by dragging the mouse higher or lower.

A value component is the same as a spinner in functionality. The difference is that with a spinner, the user can adjust the value incrementally by clicking the up or down arrow, while with a value, he can just drag the mouse to change the numeric value. Usually, you can choose between them based on your preferences.

How To Use a Value

The Properties panel of a value is almost the same as that of a spinner, with some differences in Behavior tab, as displayed in Figure 5.41.

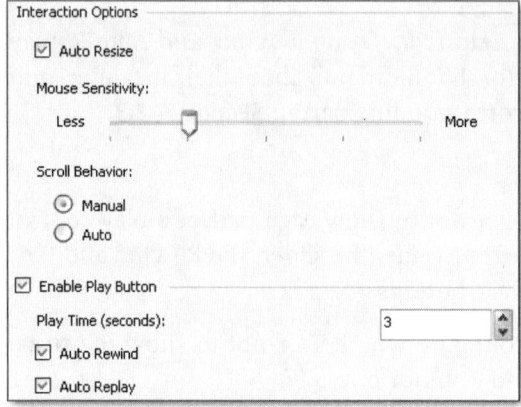

Figure 5.41 The Behavior Tab of a Value Component

- Auto Resize
  You can select Auto Resize if you want the component to resize automatically based on the length of the value it's displaying. Figure 5.42 shows two screenshots of one value component with Auto Resize selected, one with a value of 2 and the other 100. Pay attention to their lengths.

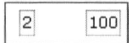

Figure 5.42 The Length of a Value Component is Auto Resized to be Just Enough to Display the Current Numeric Value

- Mouse Sensitivity
  Mouse Sensitivity defines how sensitive the mouse is during dragging up or down to change the value. You can adjust it by moving the slider, from less sensitive on the left to more on the right. Basically, if you want the values to be changed slowly, make the mouse less sensitive. When designing your dash-

board, you can try out the least sensitivity, by moving the slider all the way to the left, and the most sensitivity, to find out the best-fit sensitivity for you.

- Scroll Behavior
This property controls how the value is changed when you drag the mouse — either Auto or Manual. Manual is the default, which means the value is increased or decreased each time you drag the mouse up or down, and stops when you stop dragging, regardless of whether your mouse button is released or still being held down.

If you select Auto, the value will keep increasing or decreasing when you hold down the mouse and will stop when you release it. You can choose based on the users' preferences.

Unlike a spinner, you can select Enable Play Button here, allowing the value to be changed automatically.

5.4 Displaying Data in a Table

Xcelsius 2008 provides three UI components to display a range of data in a table style: list view and spreadsheet table in the Selectors category and Grid in the Other category.

5.4.1 List View

A list view component displays a range of data in a list view, similar to a table. You can use it both as a display component and as a selector.

As a display component, it displays data in a cell range in the embedded Excel spreadsheet, treating the first row as the header. At runtime, the user can adjust the width of each column but cannot adjust the width of each row. He can also sort the rows by each data field, in either ascending or descending order, by clicking on the column header.

As a selector component, the user can click on a row to choose it, thus triggering the data insertion action. Only one row can be selected at a time.

When to Use a List View

You may choose this component when you want to display data in a table-like style, as a supplement to the charts. For example, say you have used a line chart to show the trend of changes in the price of some stock over a period of time. Now you add a list view below the chart to list the prices (or compare them to that of another stock), giving user more detailed information.

How to Use a List View

The Properties panel of a list view component is divided into three categories: General, Behavior, and Appearance. Most properties are similar to those in other components. In the section below, we'll explain some properties in General and Appearance table.

General

▸ Title
You can specify a title for a list view, giving the user an idea of what it's about. You either enter a text directly in the input field or bind it to a cell in the embedded spreadsheet. By default, the title appears in the top center of the component. You can customize where to display it by selecting APPEARANCE • TEXT • TITLE • POSITION.

▸ Display Data
You bind display data to a cell range with *N* rows *M* columns in the embedded spreadsheet that contains the data you want to display. Xcelsius will automatically treat the first row as the column headers and list the rows below in sequence.

Xcelsius automatically defines the width of each row and each column. It determines the width that is exactly enough to display the data. If the width of the list view component is bigger than what's enough to display all data fields, the last column will be stretched wider. If the height of the component is bigger than what's enough, more rows will be added below the last row, as shown in Figure 5.43.

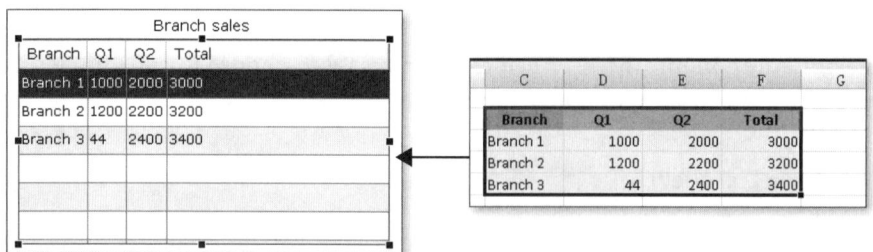

Figure 5.43 Blank Rows are Displayed if There's Extra Space in the List View

In Figure 5.43, the embedded spreadsheet is displayed on the right, and the list view component in the canvas is displayed on the left. Pay attention to the redundant rows and extra space in the last column.

If the list view component is too small to display the data, a scrollbar will appear horizontally or vertically or both. When you resize the list view on the canvas at design time, the columns widths will not change.

Data Insertion

As a selector, a list view also supports data insertion, although only three insertion types are available as listed below.

- Position
  You insert the position of the selected row into a cell which is bound to Destination. The position of the first row is 1.

> **Note**
> The position here is the position of the row in the cell range specified for display data, not that of the selected row in list view at runtime. That is, at runtime, you can change the order of rows by sorting on a column. For example, in Figure 5.43 above, you can sort by Total in a descending order, and thus Branch 3 will be displayed in the first row. If you click to select the row of Branch 3, the position is still 3, not 1.

- Value
  Similar the method for other components, you select a row or column as the source data and insert its value into a single cell as the destination.

- Row
  As for other components, you select a cell range as the source data and insert a row into the destination. The number of rows in the source data should be equal to that of display data.

Appearance

As mentioned above, Xcelsius automatically calculates the default width of each column. Here you can also manually set its width, by selecting Custom Column Widths, clicking the button to the right of it, and then setting the width of each column in pixels, as displayed in Figure 5.44.

If you set zero (0) for the width or leave it empty, Xcelsius will display the column with the minimum width. Of course, this isn't the case for the last column, which will occupy all the space left.

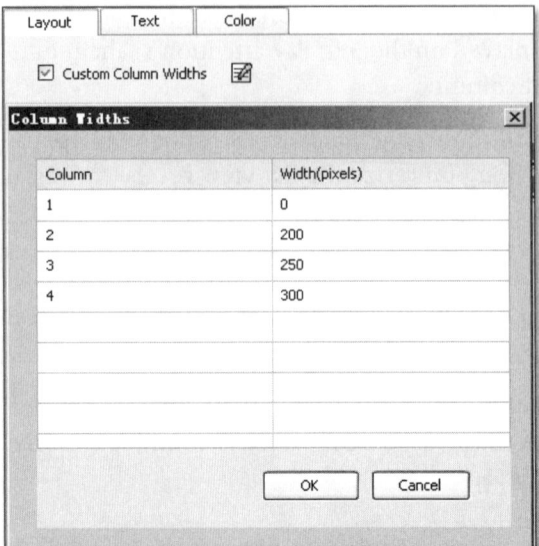

Figure 5.44 Manually Customize the Width of Each Column

The settings here only affect the default width of each column. Despite this, you can adjust their width at runtime by moving the gridlines between adjacent columns.

You can configure whether to show the vertical or horizontal gridlines in the view by selecting corresponding checkbox. If gridlines are enabled, you can also set their color. However, your changes here will not affect the gridlines in the column; they will always display with default colors.

In Text tab you can format the title ("Branch sales" in Figure 5.43 above), the headers (Branch, Q1, Q2, and Total in Figure 5.43), and the labels. You can also configure whether and where to show the title.

For a better look and feel, you can set colors for a rich set of items in the Color tab. Typically, you may want to set the header background color to make it stand out. The rows are displayed in alternative colors with a frequency of 1. That is, the even- and odd-numbered rows are of the same color. You can configure the colors of the odd or even rows by specifying row 1 color and row 2 color, respectively. When you click on a column header, you will see a sort symbol displayed on it, the color of which can be customized in this tab through Symbol Color.

Practice

Figure 5.45 shows a sample list view component at run time, with the title displayed on the top center, headers centered, and the colors of the header label, header background, row 1 color, and row 2 color customized.

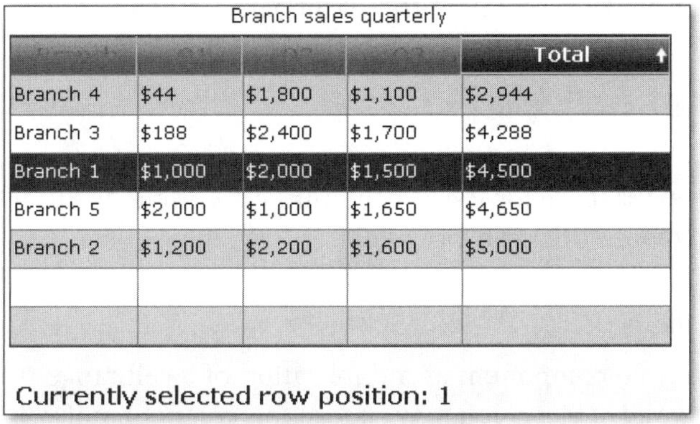

	Branch sales quarterly				
	Q1	Q2	Q3	Total	↑
Branch 4	$44	$1,800	$1,100	$2,944	
Branch 3	$188	$2,400	$1,700	$4,288	
Branch 1	$1,000	$2,000	$1,500	$4,500	
Branch 5	$2,000	$1,000	$1,650	$4,650	
Branch 2	$1,200	$2,200	$1,600	$5,000	

Currently selected row position: 1

Figure 5.45 A Practical List View at Runtime

In this screenshot, the rows are sorted by total, in ascending order, as indicated by the up arrow in the Total column header. Currently, the third row is selected, which is the first row in the embedded spreadsheet. That's why the label below says the currently selected row position is 1, not 3.

Achieving this is in fact very simple, so we'll ignore the steps here. The purpose of Figure 5.45 is just to give you an idea about how to use a list view.

5.4.2 Spreadsheet Table

A spreadsheet table component is similar to a list view in that both display data stored in a cell range in a table style. It can also be used as a selector.

A spreadsheet table is a real what-you-see-is-what-you-get component. What you see in the embedded spreadsheet is almost exactly what you get in the spreadsheet table. Most formats of the cells in the embedded spreadsheet, including the color and size, are reflected in this component. This is what a list view component cannot do. It only displays the data of the cell range, with all formats ignored.

One limitation of a spreadsheet table is that it currently only supports the font Verdana, which results in some minor differences between the spreadsheet table component and the embedded Excel spreadsheet.

However, a spreadsheet table is not as configurable as a list view. Generally, a spreadsheet table component:

- Doesn't have a title
- Doesn't have any column headers
- Spaces the columns evenly and doesn't allow the dashboard designer to customize their widths
- Provides no alternative color

In contrast to a list view, there are no redundant rows in a spreadsheet table component, nor will there be any extra space for the last column. At runtime, the user cannot adjust the width of a column or sort by any field.

When to Use a Spreadsheet Table

You can regard a spreadsheet table component as a duplication of a cell range in the embedded spreadsheet. Like a list view, you may choose this component if you want to display some data in a table style.

The list view and the spreadsheet table components have both advantages and disadvantages. With their different functionalities in mind, you can choose one based on your requirements. For example, if you want the user to be able to sort the records by some data field or display the records in alternative colors, you would choose a list view. On the other hand, if there are specific requirements for the cell formats, especially when you want to display different cells of one row in different formats such as color and data format, you have to use a spreadsheet table, format each cell in the embedded spreadsheet and then bind the display data of the spreadsheet table to that cell range

With any other UI component in Xcelsius 2008, you cannot display a row of data in different formats. As you can see from Figure 5.46 below, the second cell in the second row is black text with a yellow gray and aligned to the middle, while the third cell in the third row is in a different color and aligned to the right

If there's too much data to display (for example, over 100 rows and 10 columns), using a spreadsheet table may introduce a severe performance problem because it will bring the format of the many cells. In this case, if it's not necessary to retain the formats of the cells, you should use a list view instead.

Figure 5.46 shows a case when a spreadsheet table has to be used.

Branch	SalesRevenue				Quantity sold		
	Q1	Q2	Q3	Total	Q1	Q2	Q3
Branch 1	1000	2000	1500	4500	34	22	28
Branch 2	1200	2200	1600	5000	49	88	30
Branch 3	188	2400	1700	4288	12	19	15
Branch 4	44	1800	1100	2944	66	39	71
Branch 5	2000	1000	1650	4650	42	33	29

Figure 5.46 A Spreadsheet Table view at Runtime

Pay attention to the different colors of the cells, and note that the column headers are in two rows. No other component in Xcelsius 2008 can achieve the same effect.

To better understand the differences, you can compare Figure 4.46 to Figure 5.45 in the section above, where we discussed list views.

How to Use a Spreadsheet Table

To use a spreadsheet table component, drag it from the Selectors category and drop it onto the canvas. You can move or resize a spreadsheet table component in the canvas.

If scroll bars are not enabled in the Properties panel, the resizing happens both horizontally and vertically simultaneously; you cannot resize it on one direction only. Unlike in a list view, when resized, the width and the height of each column and row are increased or decreased in proportion. For example, there will be no more redundant rows when the spreadsheet is stretched very tall.

The Properties panel is divided into three categories: General, Behavior, and Appearance.

General
- Display Data
  Here you bind display data to a cell range in the embedded spreadsheet. Note that there will be no column header in the table. If you want to show the column headers, often in the first row of the component, set the background color in the embedded Excel spreadsheet.

  For example, to display a spreadsheet table as displayed in Figure 5.46 above, the source data in the embedded Excel spreadsheet should be as displayed in Figure 5.47.

	B	C	D	E	F	G	H	I	J
1									
2		Branch	SalesRevenue				Quantity sold		
3			Q1	Q2	Q3	Total	Q1	Q2	Q3
4		Branch 1	1000	2000	1500	4500	34	22	28
5		Branch 2	1200	2200	1600	5000	49	88	30
6		Branch 3	188	2400	1700	4288	12	19	15
7		Branch 4	44	1800	1100	2944	66	39	71
8		Branch 5	2000	1000	1650	4650	42	33	29

Figure 5.47 Data in the Embedded Spreadsheet Should Already Be Formatted

Keep in mind that you can select any range you want in the embedded spreadsheet, and the spreadsheet table will display it almost exactly the same. Note that the colors of each cell are retained, but bold and italic are not. However, underlining is retained, though it works a little strangely. You may notice that underlining is not displayed at first, and you need resize the spreadsheet table component a little to see it.

- Data Insertion
  As a selector, the spreadsheet table supports data insertion operations. Only two types are available: position and row. Their meanings and how to use them are the same as those of a list view, as explained in section 5.4.1.

Behavior
- Row Selectability
  One property specific to the spreadsheet table is row selectability, which indicates what rows can be selected. Only a selectable row can be selected to trigger data insertion and changes into another color when selected. Typically, you may want to unselect the header rows to make them unselectable, so that it makes no difference when the user clicks on them. For example, in Figure 5.47 above, you may want to make the first two rows (used as headers) unselectable, with the rest selectable.

- Enable Scroll Bars
  This property is very interesting. By default, scroll bars are disabled when the component takes up just enough space to hold its contents. If you resize the spreadsheet table component to make it smaller, the entire component, including the width, height, and font sizes, are reduced in proportion to adjust to the new size.

  When you select this option, resizing the component to make it smaller or larger will not affect its size. Instead, the component remains it's the same size, and a scroll bar is displayed when necessary. In a word, what you are resizing is a transparent "container" to display the table, not the component itself. You can test this by resizing the spreadsheet table with Enable Scroll Bars selected.

You can set the horizontal and vertical scroll bar to On, Off, or Auto. The scroll bar will always show if On is selected, and never show if Off is selected. If Auto is selected, the scroll bar will only show when the space is insufficient to display the entire component. For a clean look and feel, it's suggested that you select Auto.

The property "Table Scale" defines how much space is used to display the spreadsheet table component. Increasing it will increase the size of the component, while decreasing it will also decrease its size. The size of the component is related to the increase or decrease and has nothing to do with its actual value. However, changing this value will never affect the size of the space, or "container", that holds the component.

You can try this out by making changes to these settings and then previewing to check the effects.

Appearance

Xcelsius will automatically insert a gridline for each row and each column when Show Gridlines is selected. Otherwise, there will be no gridlines in the component. However, if you have defined gridlines for cells in the embedded spreadsheet, these gridlines will always appear, whether Show Gridlines is elected or not.

You can customize the colors in many parts of the spreadsheet table component in the Color tab, including the gridline color and the row selected color.

5.4.3 Grid

In terms of visual appearance, a grid component displays a range of data in a table style. You can tell from the name that each cell is the same size, in contrast to a list view or a spreadsheet table. Moreover, there's no column header concept in a grid.

As to the functionalities, a grid component differs from a list view or a spreadsheet table in that besides representing the data in a table format, the user can modify the values. As a result, a grid can act as both an input and an output component.

Figure 5.48 shows such a grid, where the sales revenues of each branch in the last five years are listed together in a grid. You could create a chart on top of the grid for your specific purposes, and change the values for any variable in the grid to analyze its impact.

	FY05	FY06	FY07	FY08	FY09
Atherton	$19.7	$17.1	$18.3	$14.8	$19.8
Berkeley	$14.4	$17.0	$16.4	$16.7	$19.3
Carmel	$18.8	$13.5	$18.7	$13.9	$15.7
Cupertino	$12.0	$16.2	$17.5	$17.8	$13.8
Fremont	$19.2	$15.6	$19.6	$15.9	$14.4
Irvine	$18.9	$14.6	$16.7	$12.1	$13.9
Milpitas	$18.7	$17.8	$14.0	$18.5	$13.7
Orange County	$17.0	$19.4	$17.1	$17.3	$17.3
San Francisco	$14.4	$14.0	$13.9	$15.4	$18.3

Figure 5.48 A Typical Grid Showing Multiple Values

When to Use a Grid

You may choose a grid if you want to display multiple values together, and/or give the user the ability to change values at runtime. For example, when making your budget plan, you can display the relative expenses and incomes in a grid, which the user can modify to analyze the budget on the fly. Besides the numeric values, you can also use a grid to show some texts, such as the names of branches in your company.

How to Use a Grid

You can use a grid as an output component to represent data in a table, similar to a list view or a spreadsheet, but you cannot use it as a selector.

You can also use it as an input component, allowing the user to manipulate each value. To change the value, the end user can either drag you're his mouse up or down to make the value bigger or smaller in that cell or double-click the value and then modify it directly. From this perspective, a grid is similar to a gauge or a dial, which can also be either input or output components. However, a gauge can only display one value, while a grid can display more.

The grid's Properties panel is divided into four categories, as explained below.

General
Click the Bind button below Data and bind it to the cell range in the embedded spreadsheet containing the values you want to display. At runtime, when the user

makes changes to the values of certain cells, the new values are written back to the cell range defined here. This property is for the Grid as an output.

Scale, on the other hand, is for the grid as an input. You can edit the value of a cell in the grid by either dragging your mouse up or down or double-clicking the value and entering a new value. Scale here defines the range of a valid value. That is, you cannot enter a value, or drag the value to, less than the minimum limit or greater than the maximum limit. If you enter a value beyond the scale, the new value will not be accepted.

The original data may not fall into the scale you define here. For example, if some value is 120.3, and the scale you define here is 0 to 100, when launched, the grid will show 120.3. However, if you change the value to be within that range, you will have no chance to revert to the original value, which is beyond the scale.

To define the limit, enter an integer directly or bind it to a cell in the embedded spreadsheet.

Behavior
- Increment
  As mentioned above, you can change a value in the grid by dragging the mouse up or down. Increment defines how much the value is increased or decreased on each move. You can either enter a constant integer directly in the input field, or bind it to a cell in the embedded spreadsheet, which contains the step value. For example, you can let the user customize this value through an input control, pass it to the embedded spreadsheet through Flash Var or something else, and bind the increment to that value.

- Limits
  As mentioned in the General section above, you can set the limits of a valid value that the user can change the old value to. If you don't want to set maximum or minimum limits for the values, you can set it to Open instead of Fixed in the corresponding dropdown list.

  When Open is selected, the corresponding limit property in the General tab is disabled.

- Enable Interaction
  If you want the user to be able to change the values, thus making a grid an input component, you can select Enable Interaction. Then you have the option to control mouse sensitivity and scroll behavior, which controls the way the user uses the mouse to change the value.

These two properties are exactly the same as those of a value component, as described in Section 5.3.4. Briefly, mouse sensitivity defines how sensitive the mouse is when you drag up or down to change the value, and scroll behavior controls how the value is changed when you drag the mouse; you can select either Auto or Manual. For more info, please refer to Section 5.3.4.

Appearance

Two properties specific to a grid component are the vertical margin and horizontal margin, which control the space between every two vertically or horizontally adjacent grids. By default, they are both 0, leaving a minimal space between every two adjacent grids. You can adjust them to create an agreeable look and feel.

In the Text tab you can set the number format of the values. Note that there's one special format called From Spreadsheet, which uses the format you specify for each cell. Only the number format you set in the embedded spreadsheet is kept — not the color, font style, or alignment.

Alerts

You can enable alerts in this tab to show different colors for different values, based on the alert thresholds you define here.

How to use alerts is the same as for other components such as a column chart. You can refer to the corresponding sections for more info.

5.5 Using Art

Xcelsius provides some special UI components, in the Art and Backgrounds category to enhance your design. In Chapter 4, we introduced some backgrounds, and here let's talk about arts.

5.5.1 Image Component

You can use the image components to add graphics, logos, custom JPG backgrounds, and SWF movies to your dashboard. Adding artwork makes your dashboard more appealing and professional.

The image component supports the following file formats.

- JPG
- PNG

- GIF
- BMP
- SWF

> **Note**
> An SWF file can also be generated by Xcelsius 2008 itself, but these SWF files can only be linked out of the main presentation rather than embedded in it. This will be further explained in the next section.

When to Use an Image Component

You use image components to enhance your dashboard. There is really no restriction on using images, but keep it in mind that too many images may distract the users from the really useful information they need, so we recommend using images only when necessary.

How to Use an Image Component

To use an image component in your dashboard, first drop it onto the canvas. Then click the Import button to select the external image or flash file you want to import into the Xcelsius model.

General

Prior to selecting the file, if you select the Resize Image to Component option, the image will automatically fits itself to the current size of the image component. Otherwise, the image component will be resized to show the image at its actual size.

When importing external files into the image components, you may choose whether or not to embed the file. If you choose to embed a loaded image, it becomes a part of the completed model, so you can publish and distribute your model as a stand-alone file. If you choose not to embed the file, at runtime the file will be loaded into the exported dashboard as needed. Xcelsius will generate a subfolder with the same name as the SWF file during export and put the images in that folder.

The main advantages of embedding files are as follows.

- Embedded files let you distribute your entire dashboard in a single file.
- Dynamic visibility is faster because reloading is not necessary.
- Embedded files maintain their state when hidden with dynamic visibility.

The main advantages of not embedding files as follows.

- ▶ Runtime performance might increase because the external files are unloaded when they are hidden with dynamic visibility.
- ▶ Load times will be shorter for the application because external files are loaded only when necessary.
- ▶ The dashboard does not need to be re-exported if the external file changes.

So you can choose whether to select the Embed File option. If you are importing an SWF file generated by Xcelsius, Xcelsius 2008 will prompt a warning message informing you that this kind of file can't be embedded into the model you are editing and can only be linked into it.

You can change the transparency level of the image and block the mouse event on it. To hide the background color of the SWF file so that the components behind it are visible, you can select the Hide SWF Background Color checkbox.

5.5.2 Shapes

In addition to images and flash movies, sometimes you might want some simple drawings on your canvas. Xcelsius 2008 provides shapes and lines components. We'll discuss lines in the following section. Here we'll show you two shape components, the rectangle component and the ellipse component. As their names suggest, you can draw rectangles and ellipses on you canvas. You can also fill them with colors.

When to Use Shapes

Shapes are often used to assist in layout they same way background components do, but background components all have their own visual styles. They could have rounded corners, shadow effects, special drawings on them, and fixed gradient patterns. So, what if you want pure shapes or you want the gradient pattern you like to group relevant components together?

Figure 5.49 is an example of using shapes to assist in layout.

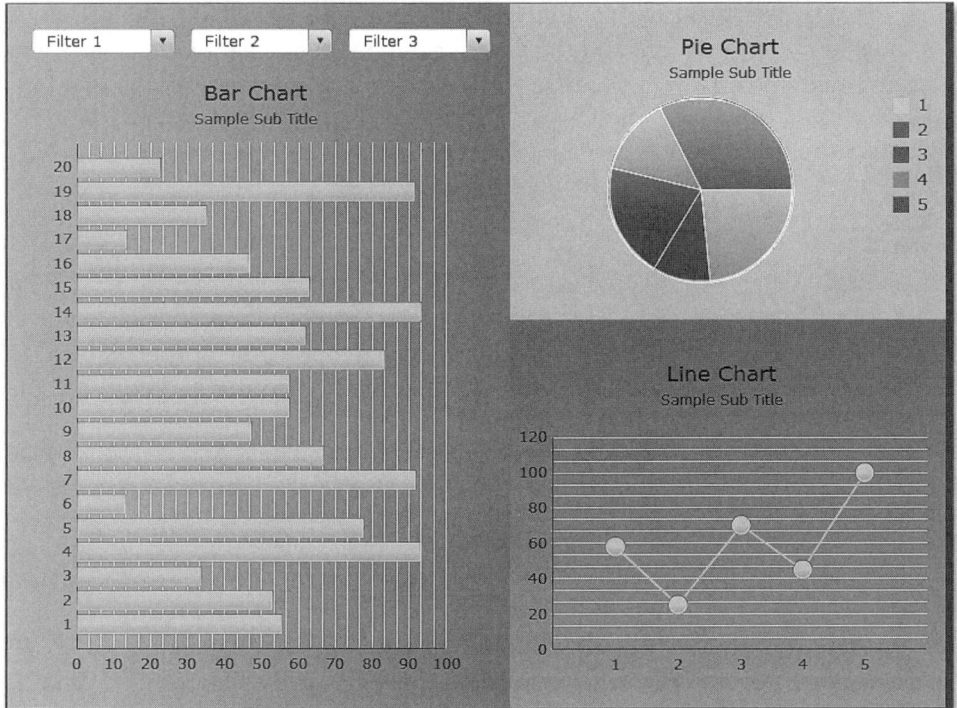

Figure 5.49 Using Shapes to Assist in Layout

As you can see from this figure, we used three rectangle components to divide the canvas into three sections and we set gradient fills inside them. The idea is basically the same as using background components, but with shapes everything is nice and clean. There are no fancy effects at all, just rectangles with fills. Sometime less is more, because it's the information that user cares about the most, not the artwork, so it could be a good idea if there is no flashy artwork to distract them from the most important information on the dashboard.

How to Use Shapes

You add the rectangle component and the ellipse component the same way you add other components, but there is a trick to how to resize them. If you want to maintain the ratio of the two sides of a rectangle or the two axes of an ellipse, you can hold down [Shift] while you resize the component on the canvas. The ratio is now locked. This is particularly useful when you want to create a square or a perfect circle. First, add the component to the canvas. By default, the rectangle component creates a square and the ellipse component creates a perfect circle, so you just hold down [Shift] to resize the component to the size you want and it's done.

Now let's take a look at the properties specific to shapes components.

General

▶ Enable Border
By default, rectangles and ellipses have a black border of thickness 1. You can change the color, the thickness, and the transparency of the border as well. In Figure 5.50, we've created an ellipse with an orange border and adjusted the border's thickness to 6 and transparency to 80%.

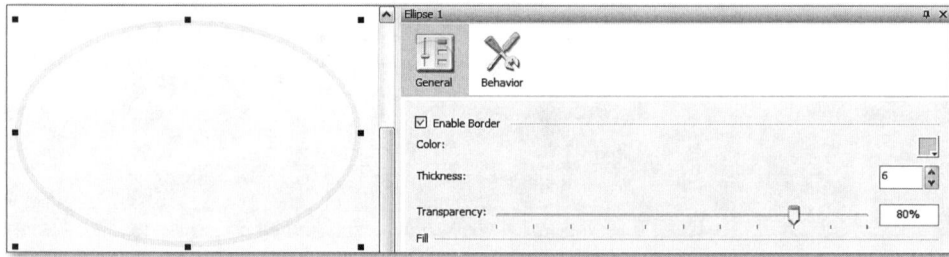

Figure 5.50 The Border Properties for the Rectangle and the Ellipse Components

▶ Fill
You can fill the rectangle or the ellipse with color. There are four fill types, as illustrated below.

This first type is None, which simply means not to fill the shape with anything. With nothing filled, the inside of the shape is transparent. Another component that overlaps with the shape component is visible even if it lies beneath the shape.

The second type is Solid. This fill type is also very simple. It just fills the shape with a single color. You can choose the color you want. And if you still want to see the overlapped components that lie beneath the shape, you can give the fill a higher transparency setting. Figure 5.51 shows an example of a solid fill, with transparency.

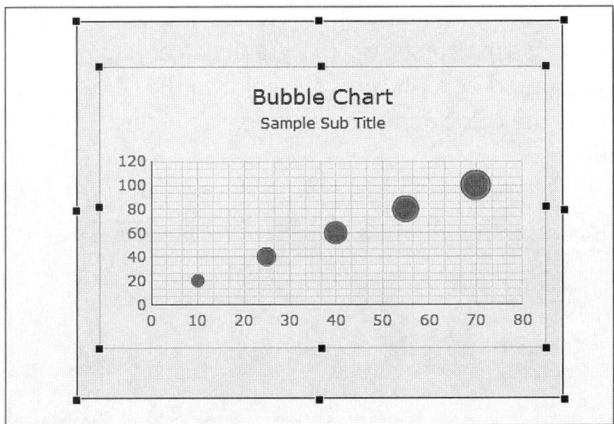

Figure 5.51 A Rectangle Filled with 50% Transparent Solid Light Gray that Covers a Bubble Chart

The third type is Linear(gradient). When you select this fill type, the Gradient Preview property and the Rotation property are enabled. To define the gradient, you use the markers under the color stripe in the Gradient Preview property. You click on each marker to set the color to the transparency of the corresponding position on the color stripe. You can also add more markers by clicking on the position you want on the color stripe. To remove redundant markers, simply drag these markers away, and they'll disappear instantly. You can also rotate the gradient to create a tilted gradient. You can refer to Figure 5.52 to see this type of fill.

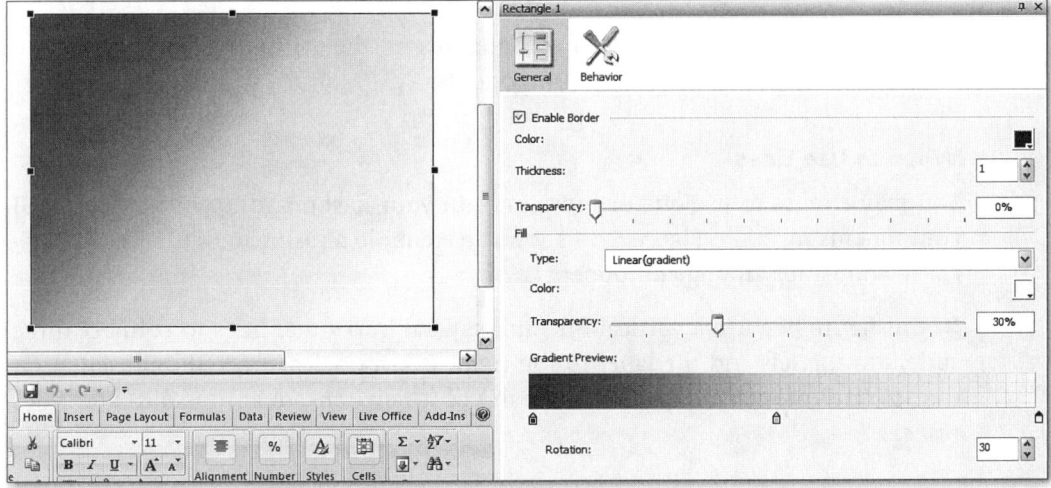

Figure 5.52 A Rectangle Filled with Linear Gradient Colors

The last type is Radial(gradient). It works similarly to the linear gradient type. You should work with the color stripe to set up the gradient colors. For the radial gradient type, the leftmost marker represents the color in the center, and the rightmost marker represents the color on the outer ring. See Figure 5.53 for an example of this type of fill.

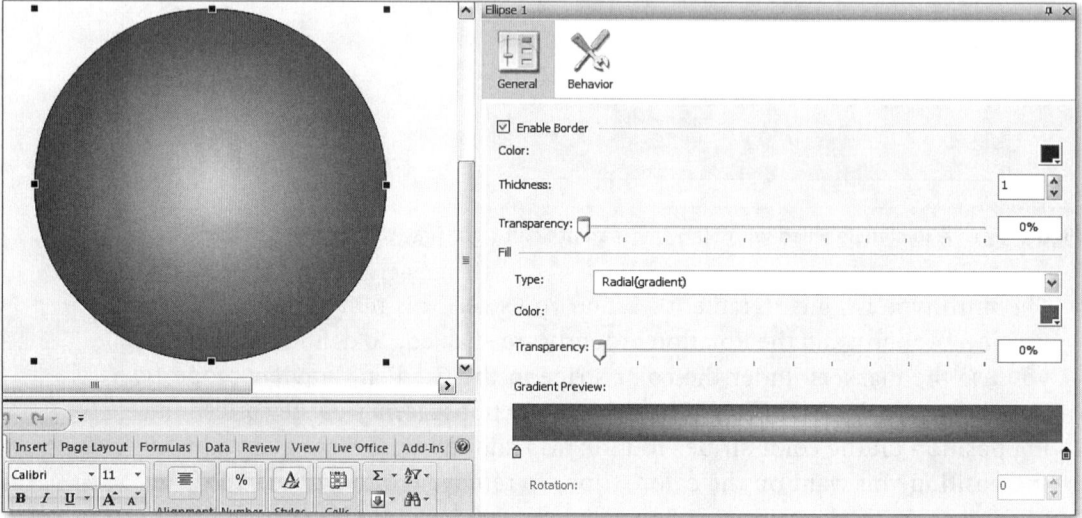

Figure 5.53 A Circle Filled with Radial Gradient Colors

5.5.3 Lines

You can use lines as separators of components on the canvas. They can also indicate logical relationships among components.

When to Use Lines

You may choose to use one or more lines in your dashboard to connect some UI components together. Figure 5.54 shows an example of using lines to indicate logical relationships among components.

In this figure, we use a vertical line and several horizontal lines to connect three sliders to the left and the label to the right. It's very clear from the presentation that the net profit is calculated from the cost per item, quantity sold, and sales price.

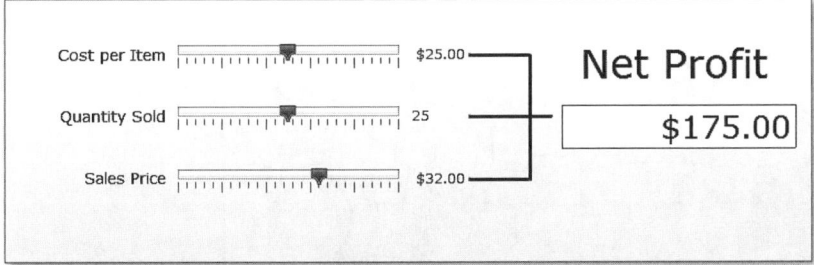

Figure 5.54 Using Lines to Indicate Logical Relationships Among Components

How to Use Lines

To use a line component, drag a vertical or horizontal line from the Components view and drop it onto the canvas, where you can change the its length.

Lines are very simple to use. There are not many properties you need to set for them. You may want to change the line color and thickness in the Properties panel, which is very straightforward, so we'll ignore it here.

5.6   Use Maps for Geographical Representation

A map component is a graphical representation of a region, either a continent, a country, or a state, from which the user can choose one place. It's widely welcomed due to its intuitive and visual representation of each candidate item. Imagine the experience of choosing a state from a plain combo box compared to a vivid U.S. map.

5.6.1   Map Components

Xcelsius comes with map components for many countries and continents. You use maps components for geographical representation.

The map components act like a combination of charts and selectors. They display data for each region when you point the mouse over the region, and when you select one of the regions, data insertion occurs so that you can get additional information about the region selected.

You can also create alerts on a map component, thus displaying different colors for different regions based on their values of some measure, as displayed in Figure 5.55.

5 | UI Components – Advanced

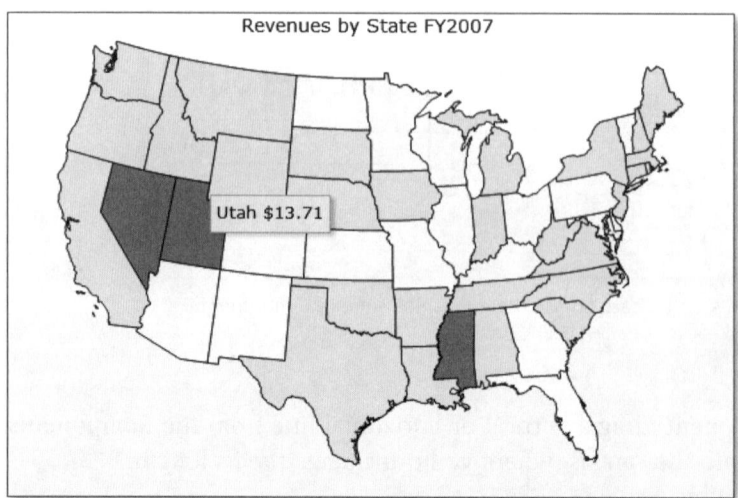

Figure 5.55 A Map Showing Revenues by State in FY2007 with Alerts Enabled

For easy reference, the supported countries and regions are listed below, in alphabetical order:

- **Continents**
    - Africa by country
    - Asia by country
    - Asia Pacific by country
    - Oceania by country
    - Australia by region
    - Central America by country
    - Europe by country
    - European Union by country
    - North America by country
    - South America by country
- **Asia Pacific countries**
    - Cambodia
    - China
    - Indonesia

- Japan
- Kazakhstan
- Kyrgyzstan
- Laos
- Malaysia
- Mongolia
- Myanmar
- New Zealand
- North Korea
- Papua New Guinea
- Philippines
- South Korea
- Thailand
- Turkmenistan
- Uzbekistan
- Vietnam

▶ **European countries**
  - Albania
  - Andorra
  - Armenia
  - Austria
  - Azerbaijan
  - Belarus
  - Bosnia and Herzegovina
  - Bulgaria
  - Croatia
  - Cyprus by District
  - Czech Republic
  - Denmark
  - England

- Estonia
- Faroe Islands
- Finland
- France
- Georgia
- Germany
- Gibraltar
- Greece
- Hungary
- Iceland
- Ireland
- Italy
- Latvia
- Liechtenstein
- Lithuania
- Luxembourg
- Macedonia
- Malta
- Moldova
- Monaco
- Netherlands
- Northern Ireland
- Norway
- Poland
- Portugal
- Romania
- Russia
- San Marino
- Scotland
- Serbia and Montenegro

- Slovakia
- Slovenia
- Spain
- Sweden
- Switzerland
- Turkey
- Ukraine
- United Kingdom
- Vatican City
- Wales

▶ **North American countries**
- Canada
- United States

▶ **Other**
- World by continents
- California (U.S. state) by county

When to Use Maps

When you have data concerning different regions, how are you going to present it? Maybe you'd use ordinary charts such as a pie chart or column chart, or you'd simply put the data in a spreadsheet table, but in some cases, displaying this data on a map is more appealing.

Instead of plain text in a table, slices in a pie chart, or columns in a column chart, the user gets a real map to look at. It's easier for him to get the information for a specific region.

For example, if we need to know the sales revenue for California last year, we simply point to the bottom-left corner region of the map for the United States to get the answer. On the other hand, if a spreadsheet table or a chart is used, we may need to search for the label California to get the same information.

In a word, you can consider map components for better geographical representation.

5 | UI Components – Advanced

How to Use Maps

General
▶ Title
The map can have a title. By default, the title is the name of the component itself. For example, in Figure 5.56, the map component USA has the default title, USA. Of course, you can change it to anything you want, for example, "USA Population Distribution."

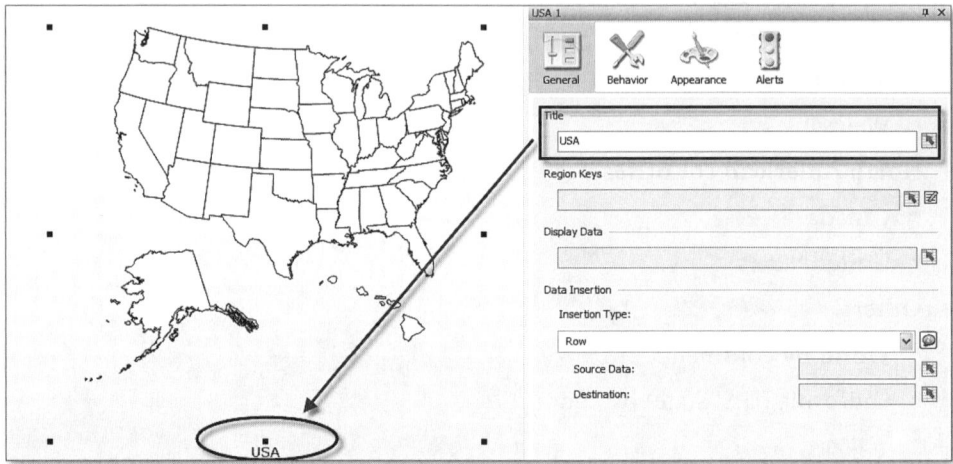

Figure 5.56 The Title Property of a Map Component

▶ Region Keys
This property is unique to the map components. To understand what this property means, we first need to explain how the map components work internally.

We already know how a pie chart arranges its data parts (to recall, data items are arranged clockwise, starting from the fourth quadrant), but how does the map components associate data with each region? Each region in the map has its own identifier, which is called the region key in Xcelsius. To populate the map with data, your data must include a row or a column associated with the rest of the data to match the region keys defined in the map.

Figure 5.57 shows an example of how the regions keys are related to the map.

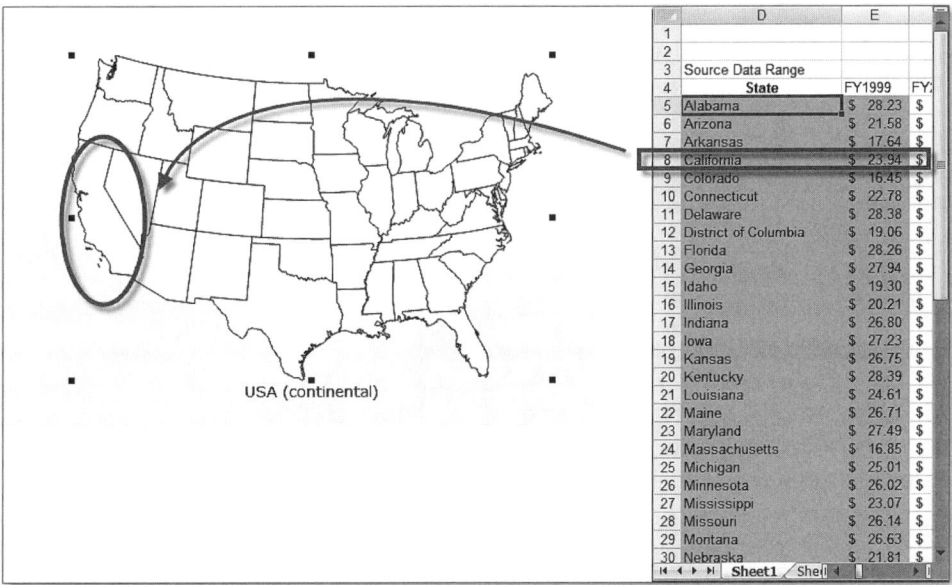

Figure 5.57 Region Key that Is Used to Populate the Map with Data

In Figure 5.57, you can see an example of how data is organized in the embedded spreadsheet and how the map is populated with data. We'll discuss the display data soon. At the moment, you need to understand that the region key enables the map to know which value is set to which region.

Each region in the map has a default region key, but it is likely that the regions in your data don't match the default region keys defined by the map component. For example, you have postal abbreviations for the states in the United States in your data, but Xcelsius uses the full names of the states as region keys. You don't need to manually change the regions in your data because Xcelsius allows you to enter your own region keys, or, in other words, to change the default region keys. That's also what the region keys property does. You can do this by clicking the list icon to the right of the Region Keys field and manually editing the names in the Region Key column for each item in the window popped up as illustrated in Figure 5.58.

You can also bind the region keys to specific cells. This saves a lot of typing, but it's only possible when your data is sorted in the same order as the regions listed in the Region Keys dialog box. Otherwise, you may still have to edit the region keys manually.

5 | UI Components – Advanced

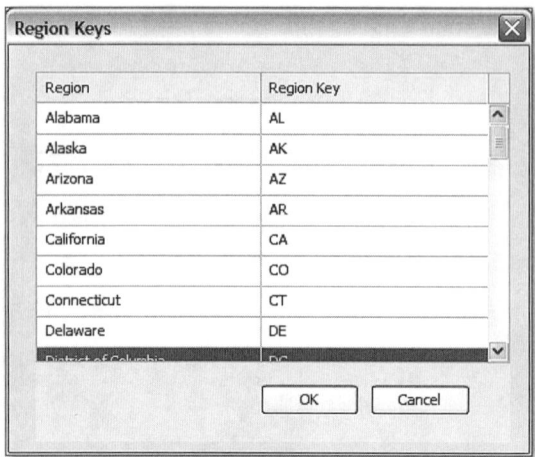

Figure 5.58 Customized Region Keys with United States Postal Abbreviations

You can find all of the default region keys in the Excel file MapRegions.xls in the folder *C:\Program Files\BusinessObjects\Xcelsius\assets\samples\User Guide Samples*, assuming you've installed Xcelsius in the default location. This Excel spreadsheet is organized in several worksheets. Each map component has a corresponding sheet listing all of the regions in the map. The first sheet is a map index that makes it very easy to navigate to a specific map.

▶ Display Data
You should already know that your data must include an extra region key column or row, so your data will always contains two columns or rows, the first one of which is the region key column or row. It's worth noting that your data doesn't need to be sorted in any order, nor does it need to cover all of the regions defined in the map.

▶ Data Insertion
The map components support two insertion types: row and column. This is similar to other kinds of selectors, but the key to correctly setting up data insertion is that the source range has to include the region row or column so that when you click a region on the map, Xcelsius knows which corresponding row or column in the source region to insert.

Appearance

- Text

  Unlike other charts that only show mouse-over values when you point to a data point, map components also show mouse-over labels when you point to a region on the map, so in the Text tab, you can set text appearance of both.

- Color

  You can have five different colors on the map, as illustrated in Figure 5.59.

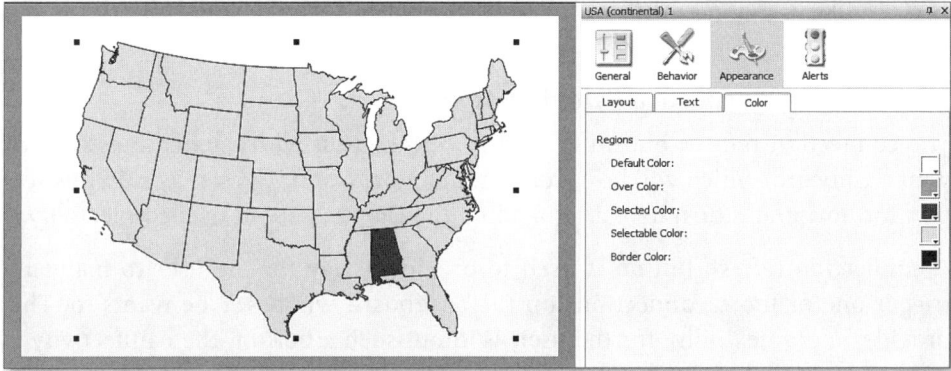

Figure 5.59 Changing Colors of the Map

When the map is used for output only, that is, when data insertion is not enabled for the map, all of the regions are filled with the default color. In this case, you cannot interact with the map, so the color won't change when you point your mouse over a region or click on a region. Regions are always filled with the default color.

If you've enabled data insertion, regions are filled with the default color when there are no values associated with them and are filled with the selectable color when there are values associated with them. Regions with associated values change to the over color when you point your mouse over them and to the selected color when you selected them by clicking on them.

The lines that separate individual regions are drawn in the border color.

Alerts

You use alerts similarly to the way you use them with other charts, but notice if you select the As Percent of Target option, the cells that you bind for this option must also include the region key column or row.

5.7 Web Connectivity

Xcelsius 2008 web connectivity functionality allows you to further extend the reach and usefulness of your dashboards. In this section, we'll explain the features of web connectivity.

5.7.1 Connection Refresh Button

A connection refresh button is a normal rectangular button with a label on top of it. Unlike a toggle button, it has only one state. Each click on it has the same effect.

When to Use a Connection Refresh Button

The connection refresh button is used in conjunction with data connectivity of your dashboard, which will be covered in Chapters 6 and 7. You may skip this section for now and return here after reading the chapters about data connectivity.

A connection refresh button is used to provide a way for the user to manually trigger one or more connections on the dashboard whenever he wants to. This provides more flexibility for the user. Without such a button, the connectivity is triggered on loading the dashboard or at intervals, or when the value of a certain cell in the embedded spreadsheet has changed or has become equal to something. With a connection refresh button on the dashboard, the user can click the button to trigger the related connections whenever he wants to. If there's a logon panel in your dashboard, you can add such a button in the logon panel for the user to submit his logon info.

With a connection refresh button you can also set the trigger behavior of multiple connections together, or in batch, instead of setting it for the connections one by one. That is, if some connections are triggered in the same way, you can set the trigger behavior for all of them here instead of repeating the same steps for each.

Now that you understand what a connection refresh button can do, when to use it will be obvious.

How to Use a Connection Refresh Button

To add a connection refresh button to your dashboard, simply drag one from the Components view and drop it on the canvas. You can move or resize it at will.

Its Properties panel is divided into three categories, as illustrated below.

General

In this tab you define the label and related data connectivities of this button, as displayed in Figure 5.60.

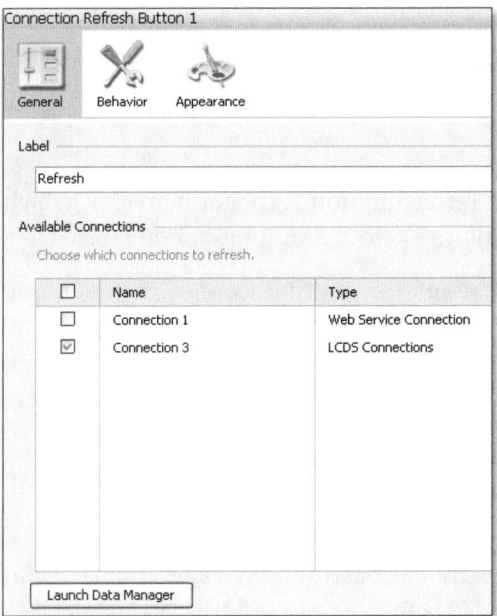

Figure 5.60 Properties in the General Tab for a Connection Refresh Button

- Label
  Here you set the label of the button, which will display on top of it. You can set it by either entering a text in the Label field directly, or clicking the Bind button to bind it to a single cell in the embedded spreadsheet. By default, the label is Refresh, indicating its purpose. You can customize it to make it more meaningful or easier to understand, such as "Click to Refresh" and so on. Most of the time, you can bind it to a cell with a localized name for it.

- Available Connections
  All data connectivities that you have defined in this dashboard through the Data Manager will be listed in the table here, with their names and types. You can select the checkbox in front of each connectivity to select it, or unselect the checkbox to unselect it. This button will then be linked with all of the selected connections. As a result, clicking this button at runtime will trigger all related connectivities at the same time.

The Data Manager, where you define the data connectivities, can be accessed by either selecting DATA • CONNECTIONS, clicking the Manage Connections button in the toolbar, or pressing `Ctrl` + `M`. Another way is provided here: the Launch Data Manager button below the Connections table, which, when clicked, will also launch the Data Manager.

Additions or deletions of data connectivities in the Data Manager will be reflected here when you return to this Properties panel.

Behavior

One property specific to the connection refresh button is trigger behavior, which defines how to trigger all of the connectivities selected in the General tab.

On this tab you can set the trigger behaviors for multiple connectivities in one place, without repeating the action for each such connectivity. For example, if multiple connections are triggered by the same cell, you can use a connection refresh button to set this trigger behavior for them all here. To avoid users triggering them manually, you can hide the button at runtime.

If you want all selected connectivities to be triggered on loading the dashboard, select Refresh On Load.

If you want to trigger the selected connectivities based on the value change event of a certain cell, click the Bind button of Trigger Cell to bind it to a single cell in the embedded spreadsheet. You then have the option to set the connections to be triggered either on value change, or when the value of that cell has become equal to something – either a constant text or that of another cell.

Appearance

If you don't want to display the rectangle of the button, unselect Show Button Background.

The transparency defines how transparent the button's background is. You can adjust it by moving the slider from 0 on the far left to 100% on the far right. If you set Transparency to 100%, the effect is the same as unselecting Show Button Background.

5.7.2 URL Button

The URL button component allows you to add a link to your dashboard. It looks like a normal button, similar to the connection refresh button described above. However, it can open the URL specified when clicked. Clicking on it makes no change but redirects the user to another URL, either in the same window or in a new window.

The URL can be either manually entered or dynamically determined if it's bound to a cell in the Excel worksheet. More interestingly, it is also possible to trigger the link without the user actually clicking the button, with the help of a Trigger Cell. With a Trigger Cell, you can configure to trigger the link when the content in that cell changes or becomes equal to something.

When to Use a URL Button

Usually, your dashboard provides high-level, aggregated information. Xcelsius, as a data presentation tool, is not very good at processing data or displaying a large quantity of data. Hence, it is not a good idea to display a large volume of data or performance-extensive data processing with Xcelsius. When the user wants to drill down to more detailed information, the URL button components enables the user to navigate to the right information from the dashboard. For example, you can create a dashboard showing high-level data, using Xcelsius with a URL button, which will redirect the user to a report with more detailed information, which is created using Crystal Reports.

In a word, you may choose a URL button when you want the user to see the content of one URL at runtime.

How to Use a URL Button

General
- Label
  This is the label on the button. You can manually enter the value or bind it to a cell in the Excel worksheet.

- URL
  Similar to the label property, you can also manually enter the value or bind it to a cell in the Excel worksheet for the URL property.

- Window Options
  The window options controls where the URL will be opened. Normally, the New Window option is selected, so that when the URL button is clicked, a new browser window will be launched and navigate to the URL.

  Another option here is This Window. If This Window is selected, when the link is clicked, the target URL will be opened in the same window as the dashboard. There is no way that you can return to the previous state of the dashboard. You can use the Back button of the web browser to load the dashboard's SWF again, but you'll lose the interactions you've done. All the components on the canvas will return to their initial state.

Behavior
- Trigger Behavior
  Normally, you click on the button to open the target URL, but the trigger behavior allows you to open the URL without actually click on the button. You can trigger the URL button when a cell in the Excel worksheet changes or becomes a specific value.

Appearance
- Layout
  Sometimes you don't want the URL button to look like a button. You might want to make it look more like a traditional link, for example. If that is the case, you can unselect the Show Button Background checkbox to make the button disappear. Only the label is left.

- Color
  You can change the default color and pressed colors for both the button and the label. That makes four color options. The button and label are in default colors when the button isn't pressed, while they're in pressed colors when the mouse is pressed down on the button.

Practice

Now let's go through a simple hands-on example to get more familiar with a URL button in use. Suppose you need to create a column chart to compare the sales revenue in the fourth quarter in 2009. The user would like a link to the homepage of the company's website on the upper-right corner of the column chart. In the meantime, user wants to be able to click on the columns in the column chart to open the detailed sales reports of the corresponding quarter. The detailed sales reports are hosted on your web application server, and you have access to them with a parameterized URL.

Adding a link to the homepage is pretty straightforward, but it seems impossible to open a URL when you click on the column chart. Nevertheless, we can click on columns in a chart when the column chart enables drill-down. And when the column chart has enabled drill-down, it can insert data corresponding to the column clicked to some target range of cells. This would result in changes to some cells, and these cells could in turn be used as trigger cells of the URL button, which in turn opens the URL. Understanding this, we can start building this dashboard.

1. Create the column chart.

    You should already be very familiar with the column chart component. Figure 5.61 shows the column chart that we have built. Notice that you need to enable drill-down so that the columns respond to mouse clicks. In our case, we insert the row that contains both the label and the value into some destination cells.

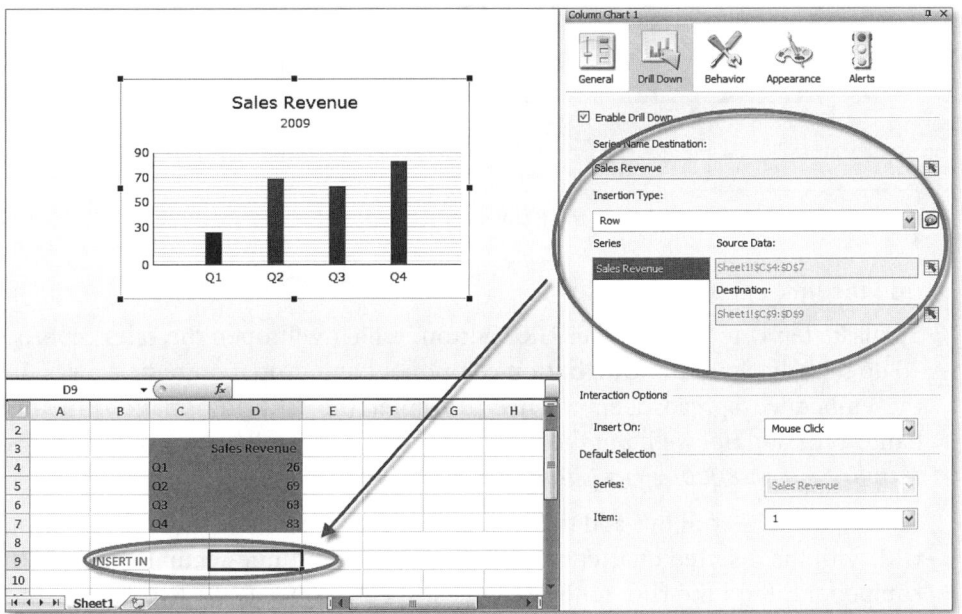

Figure 5.61 A Column Chart with Drill-Down Enabled

2. Add the link to the homepage.

    Drag a URL button component to the canvas and move it to the upper-right corner of the column chart. Keep the URL button component selected and edit the label and URL properties. For example, we set the label to Homepage and the URL to something like "*www.mycompany.com*" as illustrated in Figure 5.62.

    Here we want a hyperlink-like button as shown in Figure 5.62 so we continue to edit the appearance of the URL button. In the Appearance property sheet of the URL button, we unselect the Show Button Background checkbox in the Layout tab, underline the label text and make it blue in the Text tab, and change the pressed color for the label to the same blue as the default color. Now we've properly set up a link to the company's homepage.

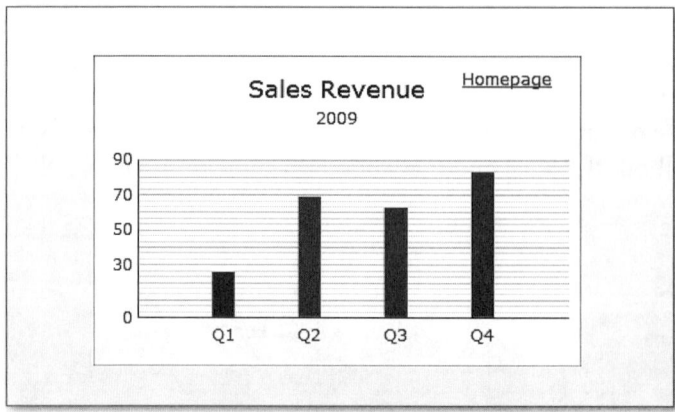

Figure 5.62 A URL Button Linked to the Homepage

3. Add the link to the sales reports.

    The last step is to add another URL button, which will open the sales reports. To do this, drag another URL button component and drop it onto the canvas. In the embedded spreadsheet, we need to enter the URL information. In this hands-on example, we'll put the base URL in the $F$8 cell, which in our case is "*http://localhost:8080/report.jsp?quarter=.*"

    Then in the $F$9 cell, we add the formula =$F$8&$C$9 to concatenate the base URL with the inserted quarter name. Now we can continue set up the new URL component. Bind the URL to the $F$9 cell, specify $F$9 as the trigger cell, and select the option to trigger when the value changes.

Now you can preview the dashboard and try clicking on the columns in the column chart. It will work, but there's another problem. We don't need the second URL button on the canvas. There are two ways to hide it. The first way is to put the URL button beneath the column chart. The other way is to prevent the button from showing its background and its label. You can choose whichever way you like to hide the URL button.

5.7.3 Reporting Services Button

You use a reporting services button component to connect your dashboard to the Xcelsius Reporting Services (XRS) server, from which you can then select the report that will be used to populate the dashboard.

The XRS server is a Web service that allows Xcelsius to communicate with your Microsoft SQL Server Reporting Services (SSRS) server. This is a powerful integration between Xcelsius and the Microsoft products family, combining Xcelsius' award-winning data visualization capabilities with point-and-click connectivity to the Microsoft SQL Server Reporting Services platform. As a result, users can take advantage of Reporting Services features such as full role-based security, server-side caching, and proactive notification. Refer to Microsoft website for more info about SSRS and its features.

You need to have the Xcelsius Reporting Services server installed to use this functionality. After installation, you can find more info about it at *<drive>:\inetpub\wwwroot\xrs*. In the Web.Config file here, you need make some important configurations such as the URLs of each service, as displayed below.

```
<appSettings>
  <add key="ReportingServicesUrl" value="http://xrsdemo-sd/ReportServer" />
  <add key="ReportServerUrl" value="http://xrsdemo-sd/Reports" />
  <add key="XrsServicesUrl" value="http://xrsdemo-sd/xrs" />
</appSettings>
```

When to Use a Reporting Services Button

Very simply put, you may choose to add such a button to your dashboard when you want to connect your dashboard to a report in the Xcelsius Reporting Services server.

How to Use a Reporting Services Button

To add a reporting services button to yourdashboard, simply drag one from the Components view and drop it on the canvas. You can move or resize it as you like.

Its Property panel is divided into three categories, as illustrated below.

General
- Label
  This is the label that will be displayed on top of the button. You can either manually enter the value directly or click the Bind button to bind it to a cell in the embedded spreadsheet.

- Select Report

  You need to select a report from the XRS server here. Clicking on this button will launch the Select Report window, where you type in the Xcelsius for Reporting Services URL or choose one from the dropdown list. You then click the Import button to display all of the reports available at the given URL. In Chapter 6 when we discuss the Web service connectivity, you will find the Import buttons very similar.

  You then select one report from the Select Source Report area, if any. The Report Parameters area then lists all parameters in the selected report, with names and types. Meanwhile, the area at the bottom of the Select Report window displays the raw data contained in the report in columns by parameters.

  To check the report, you can click the Launch Report in Web Browser button to preview the selected report in your default web browser.

- Reporting Parameters

  If you want to display the report parameters on the dashboard at runtime, select the Display Parameters at Run Time checkbox.

  The list box below this checkbox lists all of the report parameters. For each parameter, you can either click Use Service Values to use a value in the report for the selected parameter by selecting one from the dropdown list, or click Link to Cell to use values from a single cell or a row or column in the embedded spreadsheet.

- Data Mapping

  If you want to keep default data mapping, select Default. Otherwise, select Advanced. You will then see two separate list boxes.

  Below Mapped Ranges, ranges that have been mapped are listed. You can click the Add button (plus sign) or the Delete button (minus sign) to add or delete ranges from this list.

  This Selected Columns area lists the columns for the selected range. You can click the up and down arrows to change the sort order of the highlighted column, or click the X button to remove a column from the list.

  In the Name field, you enter a text as the name of the selected range.

  The data from the report is to be inserted into your dashboard. In the Range field, you click the Bind button to select a cell range in the embedded spreadsheet where the report data will be inserted.

▶ Use Report History
As the name indicates, you can select this box to use the report's history.

Behavior
Similar to other UI components, you set the dynamic visibility property and specify its entry effect type and duration in this tab.

Similar to other data connectivities, which we'll cover in Chapters 6 and 7, you define how to trigger the service here. You can configure whether to trigger the service on loading the dashboard or at intervals or when the value of a certain cell in the embedded spreadsheet has just changed or has become equal to something.

You can also set the messages when the service is loading or idle, and insert either message to a cell. This message can be used to tell the user the current status of the service, to avoid confusion about what the service is doing.

Appearance
Properties in this tab are rather common and simple. You adjust the transparency level, set the format of the label in the Text tab, and set the colors of the label and the button, for when they are pressed or not, in the Color tab. Note that in Text tab, you cannot change the position of the label.

5.7.4 Slide Show

As its name implies, you can create slide shows by using this slide show component. The slide show component is used to display images and SWF movies, but unlike the normal image component, the slide show component doesn't require you to import the source file. Instead, the slide show component will load the image or SWF movie from the URL that you specify at runtime. By binding this URL to a cell in the Excel worksheet, it's pretty easy to create dynamic slide show effects.

When to Use a Slide Show

It's pretty obvious from the previous section that you use the slide show component when you want to display a slide show of a number of pictures. If you only need to display a static image, you can use the normal image component, which we covered in Section 5.5.1.

How to Use a Slide Show

To add a slide show button to your dashboard, simply drag one from the Components view and drop it on the canvas. You can move or resize it as needed.

Its Properties panel is divided into three categories, as illustrated below.

General

In the URL text box, you can manually enter the URL of the image or SWF movie. Or you can bind the URL to a cell in the Excel worksheet using the Bind button to the right of the URL text box.

Behavior

You can set the transition behavior here.

- Transition Type
  You can choose among different styles of transition between each slide. This is similar to the transition animation in PowerPoint. Actually, all of the transition types the slide show component supports have their counterparts in PowerPoint.
- Easing Type
  There are three easing types that you can choose from.
  - Slow In
    The transition begins slowly and accelerates as it progresses.
  - Slow Out
    With this option selected, the transition begins quickly and slows down as it progresses.
  - Slow In and Out
    The transition begins slowly and increases in speed until the middle of the transition. The transition then decelerates until it is finished
- Transition Time
  This is the amount of the time for the transition between two slides. A smaller number is better for smooth transitions, while a larger number may be better for performance.

Appearance
- Sizing Method
  Usually the original size of your image will not be the same as the size of the slide show component, so the Sizing Method option lets you choose how the

images are sized within the bounds of the slide show component. There are three options: Original Size, Stretch, and Scale.

You select the Original Size option if you want your image to maintain its size. If the slide show component is not as large as the image, the areas of the image that extend outside of the slide show component are not shown. This is often used when you want to highlight only part of the image, and you don't want to lose the resolution of the image. Combining the Horizontal Alignment and Vertical Alignment options, you can choose which part of the image will be visible.

If you select the Stretch option, the image will be stretched to fit the bounds of the slide show component. You can ensure that the whole image is displayed, but you will make the image blurry. Moreover, the image could also be distorted if its aspect ratio is changed.

However, the Scale option will ensure that the aspect ratio of the image is maintained. Hence, to fit the image into the bounds of the slide show component, the slide show component may not be fully filled. There could be blank space at the top and bottom or at the left and right of the slide show component.

- Horizontal Alignment
  This option defines how images are horizontally aligned to the bounds of the slide show component. You can choose from center, left, and right.

- Vertical Alignment
  This option defines how images are vertically aligned to the bounds of the slide show component. You can choose from middle, top, and bottom.

5.8 Others

In this section, we discuss some UI components in Other category in the Components view of Xcelsius 2008. There are two exceptions here: Calendars are covered in Section 5.2.4 about advanced selectors, and grids are covered in Section 5.4.3 as a component to display data in a table.

5.8.1 Local Scenario Button

A local scenario button is used to save the status under certain conditions to or load it from your local computer, making it perfect to save states of a what-if analysis. No new dashboard is created on your file system. It's just the status that is saved to the dashboard file.

When you click the local scenario button, it appears as a button with three menus: Load, Save, and Delete, as displayed in Figure 5.63.

Figure 5.63 Buttons in a Local Scenario Button

Note that the Load and Delete buttons are disabled if you haven't saved any scenario to your local machine. You can click Save to save the current configuration of your dashboard, including the values you have adjusted or items you have selected. You can save many scenarios, each with a unique and meaningful name. Later you can load it to restore it to that state, even after closing the dashboard.

You need keep in mind that these scenarios are saved to the user's local machine, so they are unavailable to load if the dashboard is opened on a different machine.

When to Use a Local Scenario Button

You may choose to use this component when the user will be performing some interactive analysis with your visualization. For example, in a what-if analysis, you may want to save some analysis results or snapshots for later use.

With the local scenario button component, you can save current dashboard states on your local computer and then load these states later.

How to Use Local Scenario Button

The Properties panel of a local scenario button is very simple at design time, though it is divided into three categories.

In the General tab, you set the label that will appear as the button title by either entering a text directly or binding it to a single cell. You may have noticed that you can customize only the label, which is Scenario by default, but cannot customize the other three labels, Save, Load, and Delete. This is a limitation of Xcelsius 2008.

There is little to do with the local scenario button at design time. At runtime, the user can make full use of it for a complete analysis.

The functionalities of the Save, Load, and Delete buttons are explained below.

Save

When the user clicks the Save menu item, a dialog will prompt him to enter the scenario name. Current states of the dashboard can be saved for future use. The saved scenario is stored on the local computer and associated to the dashboard file (swf file). If that file is renamed or moved on the same computer, the scenario is still available. However, if the visualization file is emailed or copied to other computers, saved scenarios will not be available on the destination computer.

Load

When the user clicks the Load menu item clicked, a dialog will prompt him to pick one saved scenario from a list. The dashboard will be restored to the previously saved state.

Delete

Clicking the Delete item clicked results in a dialog prompt. Users can select a scenario to delete. This operation is unrecoverable, so be cautious here.

If you are a PC game fan, you may find this button and the save/load operation very familiar. It's widely used in PC games, especially in role-playing games.

5.8.2 Trend Icon

A trend icon is an output component that represents a single numeric value. It looks like a colored circle or ellipse with an icon inside indicating whether the value is positive, not changed, or negative. Compared to the icon component discussed in Section 5.2.2, which can be used as both an input and an output, a trend icon component can only act as an output.

A trend icon is often used to show the trend of a value change. For example, to show whether the sales revenue is going up or down compared to the previous month or year. This is different from an icon component, which is used to show the status of a current value, indicating whether it's acceptable or in danger.

When to Use a Trend Icon

You may choose to use one or more trend icon components in your dashboard when you want to show the trend of some value change. A typical usage is in the Du Pont Financial analysis system, to indicate whether each measure such as asset-liability ratio or rate of return is getting better or worse.

A trend icon is often used in conjunction with a single-value component such as a horizontal slider or a horizontal progress bar to show the trend together with the actual value of the current (or previous) period. Moreover, you can also add in an icon component to further show the status of the value, indicating whether it's good or bad.

How to Use a Trend Icon

You can move or resize a trend icon on the canvas. Its Properties panel is very simple. Bind its data to a single cell in the embedded spreadsheet that contains the value of a certain measure, and set colors of the icon for when the value is positive, zero, and negative.

Figure 5.64 shows the design and data and the Properties panel of the trend icon of one measure in a Du Pont system, retained profit. In this dashboard, the horizontal progress bar shows the current value, and the trend icon on the top right indicates whether it's higher or lower than that of the previous period.

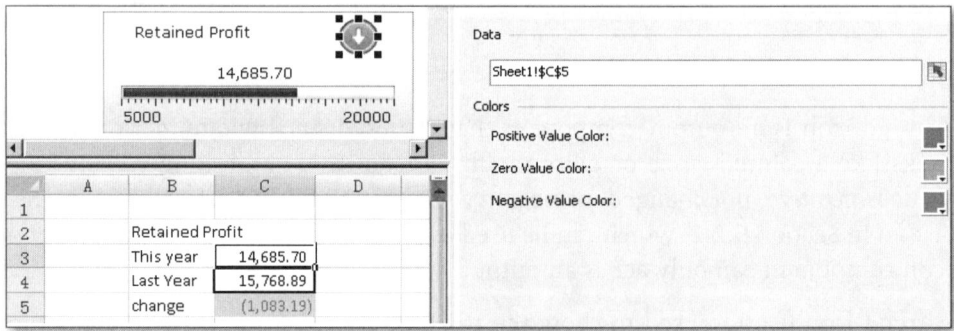

Figure 5.64 Use of a Trend Icon in a Du Point System

Note that the trend icon is bound to cell Sheet1!$C$5, which stores the difference between this year and last year.

5.8.3 Trend Analyzer

A trend analyzer is a background component that will not appear in the dashboard, like the history component, which we'll describe in Section 5.8.4.

This component is more complex and powerful that a trend icon. At runtime, it reads input numeric data and generates output with a predefined trend analysis algorithm such as linear, logarithmic, and power. If the data pattern is unknown, the trend analyzer has the option to determine the best fit data trend line for the input data. It then inserts the output to a row or column in the embedded spreadsheet, which can be used in your dashboard as a trend line.

The calculation only occurs at runtime. Each time the source data changes, Xcelsius will re-calculate the trend.

When to Use a Trend Analyzer

You can use a trend analyzer when you want to analyze the trend of a series of numeric values using some mathematical method and display it in your dashboard next to the actual values themselves.

How to Use a Trend Analyzer

There's only one tab in the Properties panel of a trend analyzer component: General.

Data refers to the source numeric values the trend that will be analyzed. You set Data by clicking the Bind button to bind it to a row or column containing the values.

You then select a Trend/Regression Type as the algorithm to use for the analysis. If you are not sure about what you should choose, select Best Fit to leave it to Xcelsius to choose one for you. Otherwise, select one from the six types listed below:

- Linear
  A linear function is used to calculate the values distribution. The output values of a linear regression are distributed in a straight line in the dashboard. If the goal of your dashboard is prediction or forecasting, you can use linear regression to fit a predictive model to an observed data set.

- Logarithmic

  Select this if your focus is probability analysis. Unlike linear regression, the output values of this and the other four methods are distributed in a curved line to fit the values.

- Polynomial

  You may choose this type to help analyze gains and losses over a large data set. If you select this type, you have another option to specify the order, between 2 and 6. An Order 2 polynomial trendline generally has only one hill or valley. Similarly, Order 3 generally has one or two hills or valleys.

- Power

  Choose this type if you want to compare values that increase at a specific rate. Note that you cannot use Power if your data contains zero or negative values

- Exponential

  Choose this type when your data values rise or fall at increasingly higher rates. Same as Power, don't use this type if your data contains zero or negative values.

Some knowledge of mathematics is required to understand each trend and regression type. Alternatively, you can get a rough idea about how each type processes data by looking at the sample shapes of the lines, as displayed in Figure 5.65.

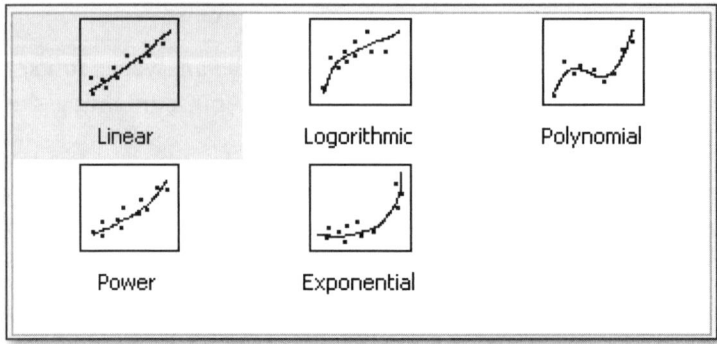

Figure 5.65 Available Algorithms to Calculate Trends

If you trust the ability of Xcelsius, select Best Fit.

Figure 5.66 shows a sample with two trend analyzer components to analyze the trend of a stock price, one with Best Fit and the other with Logarithmic selected. A combination chart is used to show the two trends and the actual values. The trend calculated with best fit is displayed in a circle, while that calculated with the logarithmic algorithm is displayed in a cross.

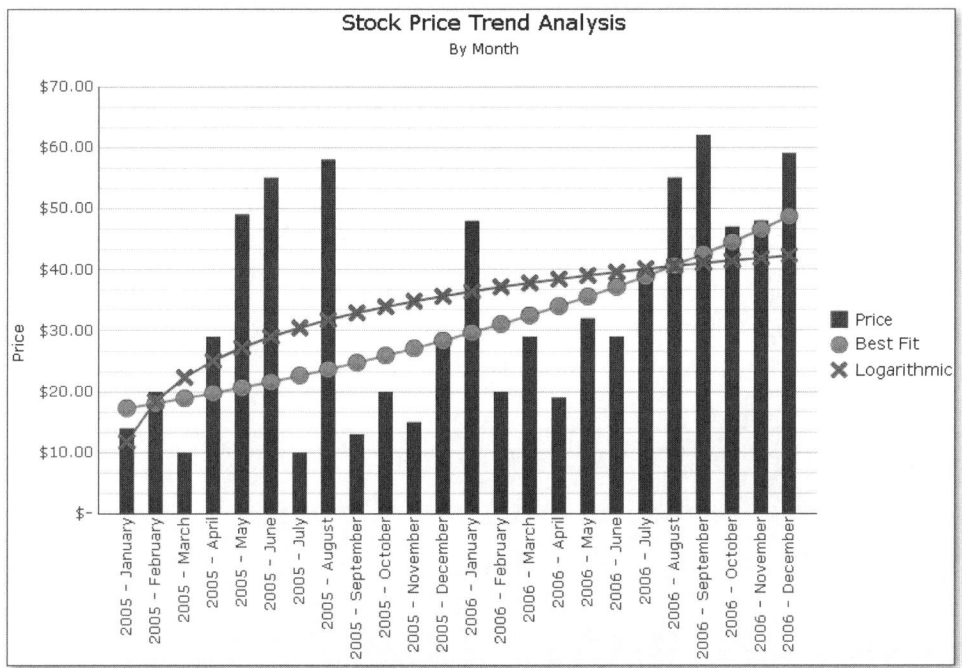

Figure 5.66 Trend Lines of the Same Data with Two Different Algorithms

5.8.4 History

You use a history component to track and display the history of changes of a selected cell. At runtime, the value of a certain cell may change over time.

History is a background component without a visual presentation at runtime. It just tracks value changes of one specified cell and stores the history in an array.

When to Use History

With a history component, you can capture and store the history of value changes. Sometimes you use a single input control to receive multiple values. In such a case, history can be used to store all values entered via the same input control for further processing.

How to Use History

To use history in your dashboard, find the History component under the Other category in the Components view and then drag and drop it onto the canvas.

Unlike any other UI components, it can be placed anywhere on the canvas, and it will not show up at runtime. Moreover, it cannot be resized because it's meaningless to do so.

Its Properties panel is rather simple, with only a General tab. Data refers to the cell you want to monitor. You bind it to a single cell in the embedded spreadsheet. If multiple cells are selected, the first cell will be used.

You bind Data Destination to a row or column of cells to store the history of the value change, as displayed in Figure 5.67

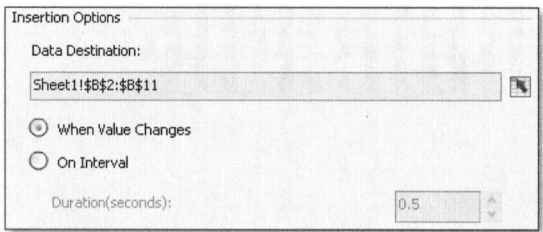

Figure 5.67 The Number of Cells in the Destination Determines How Many History Values Will Be Kept

The length of array you specify as the data destination determines the maximum number of values that will be stored for history tracking. Once the data change history entries exceed the length of the data destination array, the earliest value will be eliminated. This is a kind of first–in, first-out behavior.

As displayed in Figure 5.67 above, you need to select one from the two options below Data Destination. If you select the When Value Changes option, a new entry of data change history will be created only when the monitored value changes. Otherwise, if you select On Interval, a new entry will be created on the specified interval basis, even if no changes are made to the monitored value. Generally, you can choose based on the actual business requirement.

Practice

Now let's go through a simple hands-on example to see how to use a history component. To show the data-change-tracking function, we need a value that changes over time. This can either be accomplished by manual input at runtime or by setting up the automatic value change.

In this hands-on example, we'll choose a play control component to enable automatic value change, which we covered in Section 5.3.3.

Set Up Play Control
First, place a play control component on the canvas and insert its value into a single cell by binding its data property to Sheet1!$B$3. Leave other properties of the play control unchanged. The properties of this play control component are displayed in Figure 5.68.

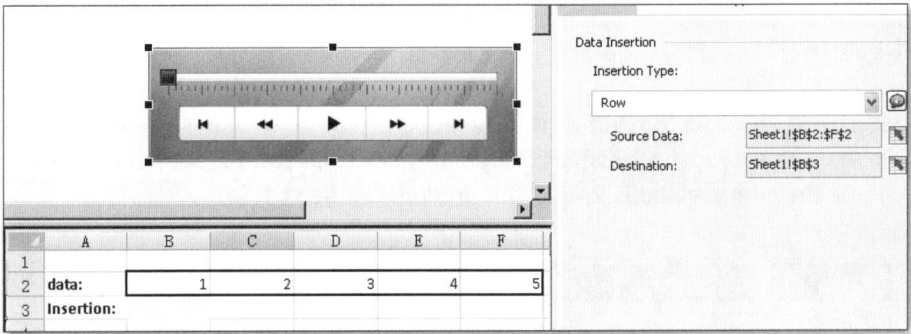

Figure 5.68 The Bindings of the Play Control in this Hands-On Example

Set Up History Component
With the monitored value set up, we can proceed to track data changes with the history component. To do this, add a history component to the canvas and simply bind the Data field to the monitored cell Sheet1!$B$3. For the data destination, we'll bind it to a row with three cells, thus tracking the last three values of that cell. If you want to track more changes, simply bind to a row or column with more cells.

Because the data changes automatically, we'll select the option to insert a new entry When Value Changes. The Properties panel of the history component is displayed in Figure 5.69.

We're almost done. To display the history tracking at runtime, we'll add a spreadsheet table component to the canvas and bind its display date to the data destination of the history component, which is Sheet1!$B$4:$D$4.

Now you can click Preview to test the dashboard, and click the Play button of the play control component. As the value of the monitored cell changes, a new entry

281

of data is inserted into the destination array and pushes the others out. The three most recently changed values are stored in the data destination array because the length of destination array is three.

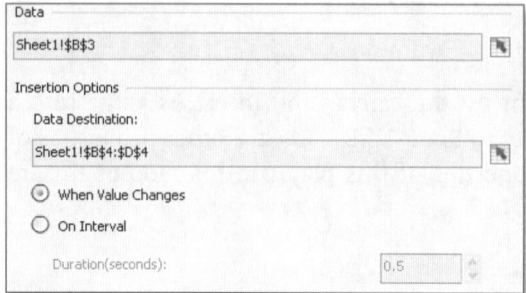

Figure 5.69 Properties of the History Component in this Hands-On Example

Figure 5.70 shows a screenshot of this dashboard when the play selector steps to 2. Note that the spreadsheet displays three numbers, 0, 1, and 2, which means the current, or the latest, value is 2, and the previous value is 1.

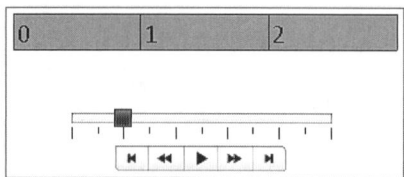

Figure 5.70 Final Result of this Hands-On Example

As you can see from this figure, as the play control plays, the content of the destination cells, as shown in the spreadsheet table component above, changes from "empty empty empty" to "empty empty 0" to "empty 0 1," and so on.

5.8.5 Print Button

The print button is a button used to print your visualization. It will appear in your dashboard, but not in the printed result (either a PDF or a physical paper). Moreover, all components that do not appear in the visualization at runtime, such as the history and the trend analyzer, will not be printed.

You may add a print button to your dashboard if you want to provide the end user such an ability. The user can then click it to print the dashboard to paper and send it to others for further processing.

A print button looks like a regular a button, so its Properties panel is very simple. One property specific to this component is print scale, in BEHAVIOR • COMMON.

By default, Scale to Fit Page is selected so that the dashboard will always be printed to one page. If the dashboard crosses over a page, either in width or in height, Xcelsius will automatically zoom it out to fit on one page. Otherwise, the dashboard will just be printed as is.

If you want to always zoom the dashboard in or out with a constant percentage, select Scale To and specify a percent as the zoom value. Xcelsius will always zoom it in or out to that scale, regardless of its actual size. For example, you can set Scale to 100% to always print it as is, without fitting it to the page. As a result, if the visualization is wider than the page you are using, it will be split into two pages.

5.8.6 Reset Button

You use a reset button to return the dashboard to its original state. When using this component, keep in mind that "original state" means the original scenario when you ran it, including the values in the embedded spreadsheet and what components are displayed. This sounds very simple, but may cause confusion.

You may add a reset button to your dashboard if you want the user to be able to revert to the original state. For example, in a what-if analysis, the user may adjust the values of several variables to analyze their impacts. Sometime later, he gets in a mess and wants to see the default values. Instead of rerunning the dashboard, he can simply click the Reset button.

Another example is when your dashboard requires the user to select a value for a parameter before retrieving live data for it. The user may need to set another value for the parameter. In such a case, instead of using dynamic visibility, a reset button will be better.

Suppose you want to show the sales revenue and some other values of each branch, among many branches of your company. Instead of retrieving all of the data at once, you provide a parameter prompt panel with a combo box for the user to select a branch first. When the user runs the dashboard, what he see immediately is a combo box listing all branches. When he has made his selection and clicked the Submit button (often a connection refresh button), another request is sent to the server requesting live data of that branch. On data return, the parameter prompt panel disappears, and the charts showing the values display. If he wants to see data of another branch, clicking the Reset button will direct the user to the parameter prompt screen.

The Properties panel is very simple, similar to that of a print button. To name a few variables, you set the label, color and background color of the button, text format, transparency level, and dynamic visibility.

5.8.7 Source Data

You use a source data component to push data into other cells by changing the component's selected index. You can push the value of a single cell in the source row or column to another cell such as the destination, or a row or column from the source range to another row or column.

At runtime, this component will not be displayed in the dashboard, like a history or a trend analyzer.

When to Use Source Data

You may choose this component if you want to display the content of an arbitrary cell or row, based on the user's selection or some other criteria.

An example is a simple dashboard of a quiz. You have a cell range containing many questions from several categories, such as How long will the grass stay alive without water? in the category Nature. Each category corresponds to a row or column. At runtime, questions from a random category are displayed.

To do this, you generate the index by either using the Excel function Rand() or the user's age, preference, and so on. You then use a source data component to insert the row or column with the questions of that category to another row or column, which will be displayed by components in the dashboard. The source data component makes the insertion based on the value of some cell that stores the user's selection.

You may think that you can achieve the same thing with complex Excel functions such as HLookup(). However, it's more difficult, and thus error-prone, and results in poor performance at runtime because HLookup() is very expensive to run.

How to Use Source Data

The Properties panel of a source data component is very simple. In the General tab, you define the data insertion behavior by selecting an insertion type from Value,

Row, and Column, and do the binding for the source data and destination correspondingly. If you are to insert a single value, select the insertion type Value, and bind Source Data to a row or column and Destination to a single cell. Otherwise, bind Source Data to a cell range and Destination to another row or column.

In the Behavior tab, you set the selected item index by either entering an integer directly or binding it to a single cell that stores the index. The item index begins with 1. In the example given in "When to Use Source Date" above, we bound Selected Item Index to the cell that contains the formula to calculate a random integer, for example, =ROUND(RAND() * 10, 0).

Practice

If you are not very clear about when or how to use a source data component, this hands-on example may help you. Suppose you want to add a saying to an existing dashboard so that each time the user runs the dashboard (or every day), he will see a proverb. This also brings more individuality to your dashboard.

1. Prepare the data.

    As displayed in Figure 5.71, many proverbs are placed in row 'Sheet1'!$B$2:$B$12 (you can add more interesting proverbs if you like). Only one of them will be selected each time. We plan to insert it into cell 'Sheet1'!$B$1. Also, we need to generate a random integer each time the user runs the dashboard, so we'll calculate it in cell 'Sheet1'!$D$1, which is a formula, =ROUND(RAND() * 12, 0).

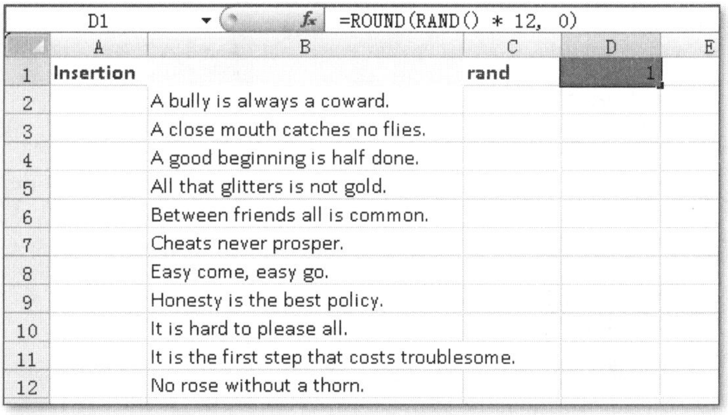

	A	B	C	D	E
1	Insertion		rand	1	
2		A bully is always a coward.			
3		A close mouth catches no flies.			
4		A good beginning is half done.			
5		All that glitters is not gold.			
6		Between friends all is common.			
7		Cheats never prosper.			
8		Easy come, easy go.			
9		Honesty is the best policy.			
10		It is hard to please all.			
11		It is the first step that costs troublesome.			
12		No rose without a thorn.			

Figure 5.71 Data Structure in the Embedded Spreadsheet for this Hands-On Example

2. Set up the source data component.

   We'll use the source data component to insert one proverb from a column, so we'll select Value as the insertion type, and bind Source Data to column 'Sheet1'!$B$2:$B$12 and Destination to cell 'Sheet1'!$B$1, as we planned in the first step.

   The insertion is based on the random integer stored in cell 'Sheet1'!$D$1, so in the Behavior tab, we'll bind Selected Item Index to this cell.

   Figure 5.72 shows the Properties panel of the source data.

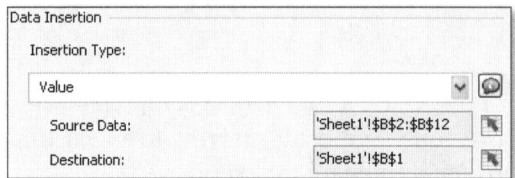

Figure 5.72 Data Bindings of the Source Data Component

3. We're almost done. Finally, add a label to show the randomly selected proverb. Figure 5.73 shows the final screenshot. Note that the proverb displayed is selected randomly.

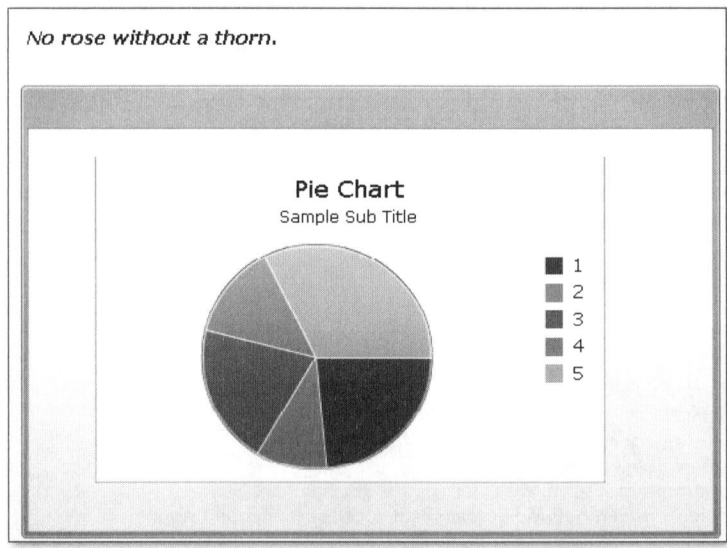

Figure 5.73 Final Result of this Hands-On Example

5.8.8 Panel Set

You can use a panel set to display several dashboards or images within one scene, making it possible for users to navigate among multiple visualizations without leaving the presentation.

You can keep an SWF or a JPEG image inside one panel set component. You can either embed the files into the dashboard or simply link to them to reduce the dashboard size.

Xcelsius provides several kinds of layouts for you to position the SWF or image files, each of which can be maximized for the user to focus on a certain aspect at runtime.

When to Use a Panel Set

You may choose a panel set when you want to display several dashboards or images in your presentation. For example, say you have created several dashboards for different sales districts or different product categories. Traditionally, you would open them one after another during your presentation. With a panel set, you can display all of them together in one screen, thus explaining all without leaving your presentation.

How to Use a Panel Set

General

- Layout
  First, you need define what the panel set looks like by choosing one layout from the list. There are 27 kinds of layouts available in Xcelsius 2008. Each divides the panel set component into several child panels, each of which can then contain an SWF or a JPEG image.

- Panel Titles
  To name the child panels, you bind Panel Titles to a single cell or a row or column, depending on the layout you have chosen. Briefly, the number of cells you bind Panel Titles to should be equal to the number of child panels the chosen layout divides the panel set into. For example, if you select Layout4, which divides the component into three child panels, you need to bind Panel Titles to a row or column with three cells. If the row or column contains only two cells, the name of the last child panel will be empty.

▶ Content
Depending on the selected layout, one or more panels may be displayed in the Panels list. You can click on one of them to set its content and the dropdown menu Labels.

There are three kinds of content types as explained below.

▶ None
If you want to leave the panel empty, select None.

▶ Embedded JPEG or SWF
Select this type if you want to embed the SWF or JPEG file into the current dashboard. Then you can click the Import button to launch a window where you select one or more JPEG or SWF files to display in this panel, as shown in Figure 5.74.

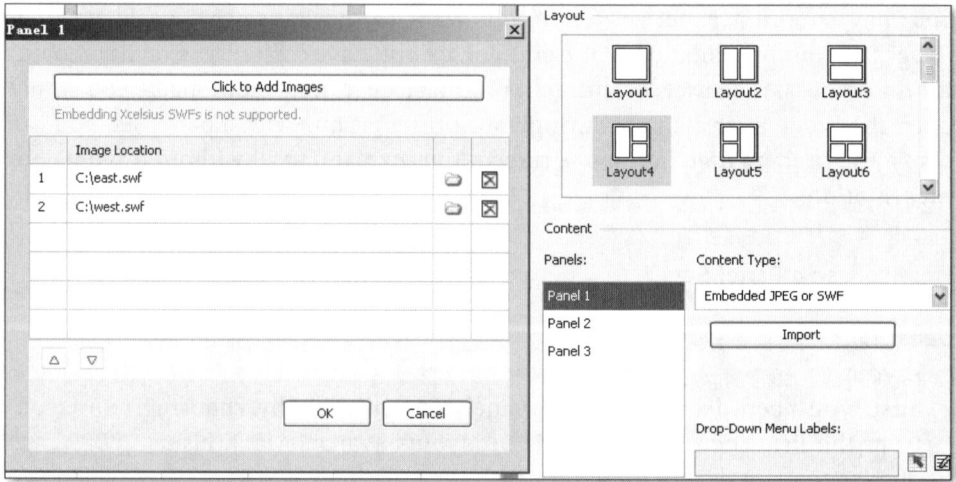

Figure 5.74 Choose Images to Add from your File System

In the window in Figure 5.74, click the Click to Add Images button to create a new entry for a JPEG or SWF file.

As noted in this window, embedding SWFs created by Xcelsius is not supported. If you click the Folder icon to browse to an SWF file, Xcelsius will check if it's exported from Xcelsius and reject it with an error message as displayed in Figure 5.75.

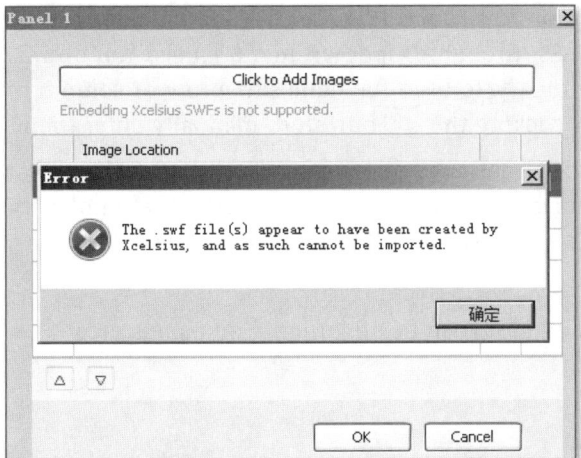

Figure 5.75 An Error Message Is Displayed if You Choose an SWF Created by Xcelsius

This is very frustrating, because usually the SWFs we want to embed or link here are created by Xcelsius. However, there's a workaround. The steps are:

1. Click the Click to Add Images button.
2. Browse to a JPEG or an SWF file not created by Xcelsius.
3. Click OK to close the browse window.
4. Double-click the Image Location field and edit it to the path of the SWF you want, which is created by Xcelsius.

When in Preview mode, you will find that the SWF, though created by Xcelsius, is successfully loaded in the panel set with full functionalities.

Some available operations in this window are that you can double-click the location or click the Folder button to edit it, click the Delete button to delete an image or SWF, or click the up or down arrow on the bottom to change the orders of the imported items.

▶ By URL
If you want to create a link to the SWF or JPEG files instead of embedding them into the current dashboard, select this type. You can then click the Bind button to bind the URL's property to a row or column in the embedded spreadsheet containing the absolute or relative file paths. If you don't want to store the URLs in the spreadsheet, click the button to enter the URLs directly in the pop-up window.

When you select either By URL or Embedded JPEG or SWF, you can further set the names of the SWFs or JPEGs through dropdown menu labels. You do this by either clicking the Bind button ![] to bind the names to a row or column in the embedded spreadsheet, or clicking the ![] button to manually enter them.

These names will appear in the dropdown menu of each child panel, so that you can choose one SWF or image from the menu. Obviously, the number of names should be the same as the number of SWFs or JPEGs you defined for this child panel.

You can repeat the steps listed above for each of the other child panels.

Behavior

- Panel Behavior

  With Enable Maximize Button selected, a Maximize button ![] will be displayed on the top right of each child panel. The user can click it to expand that child panel to display it on the entire panel set component. When the child panel is maximized, the user can click the button again to revert it to the normal size. A window animation is played on each click. This feature is useful when you want to emphasize different sets of data at different times during a presentation.

  The zoom speed defines how fast it takes window animation to go from normal to maximized. You can adjust this setting by moving the slider below, from slower on the left to faster on the right.

- Selected Item

  The selected item defines what SWF or JPEG is displayed by default for each child panel. You do this by selecting a panel first and then selecting the default item for it.

- Ignore Blank Cells

  With this option selected, the SWF or JPEG will not be listed in the dropdown menu if its corresponding label is blank. Its label is regarded as blank only when it's bound to a cell in the embedded spreadsheet and that cell is blank. If you haven't bound the dropdown menu labels to any cell or cell range, or the length of the target is less than that of the SWFs or JPEGs, the labels are not blank but will be generated automatically by Xcelsius. As a result, items will not be ignored in this situation.

  One more word: If the number of cells of the row or column the dropdown menu labels are bound to is higher than that of the included SWFs or JPEGs, the extra labels will be ignored.

Appearance

By default, a header on the top of a child panel shows its name and the name of the currently selected SWF or JPEG (if any). If you don't want to display this, either to save space or based on your preferences, unselect Show Panel Headers.

The property Number of Labels Displayed defines how many labels are listed in the dropdown menu of each child panel. If the number you specify here is smaller than the actual number of labels, a vertical scroll bar will appear.

Figure 5.76 shows a sample panel set component at runtime.

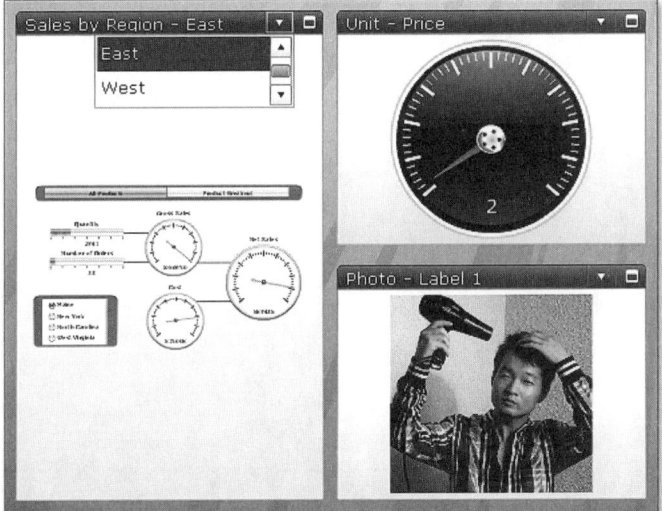

Figure 5.76 A Panel Set Used to Divide the Canvas into Several Parts

As you can see from this figure, this panel set uses a layout with three parts. The left shows the sales info for each region, where the user selects a region from the dropdown menu. The top right part shows a gauge the user can use to adjust the unit, and a photo is displayed on the bottom right. You can operate on each SWF as normal.

5.9 Summary

In this chapter, we discussed some complex and less-frequently-used UI components in Xcelsius 2008. Some components share most common properties with others such as data binding and alerts, so we did not explain them here. Others have many specific properties such as rectangles, play control, and OHLC charts, which we illustrated extensively. Having looked at all of the UI components provided by Xcelsius 2008 SP1, we hope you have a big picture of what amazing dashboards you can create with Xcelsius and that you choose the best-fit UI components for your own dashboard.

No matter how good your dashboard looks, without reflecting the live, actual data, it's just a beautiful, static image and will not be useful. Xcelsius 2008 provides several kinds of data connectivity to retrieve live data, to make your dashboard not only attractive but powerful.

6   Data Connectivity Basics

In Chapters 4 and 5, we discussed all of the powerful UI components in Xcelsius 2008. However, a dashboard is not only a UI. To make real business sense, you need to provide meaningful data to it. Xcelsius 2008 provides a wide range of methods to access your data, called data connectivity, which are accessible from the Data Manager.

The data connectivity provided by Xcelsius 2008 can be divided into several categories. Some are specific to the SAP BusinessObjects environment, such as Query as a Web Service and Live Office. Some are used for communication between the SWF and its container (either Adobe Flash Player or a web browser) such as Flash Variables and External Interface Connection. Some are for Xcelsius to retrieve live data from a web application server, such as Web Service Connection and XML data. If license permits, you can use several kinds of data connectivity in a single dashboard.

In this chapter, we'll illustrate some types of data connectivity that you can use to connect the dashboard to your own data, including local Excel file, remote Web service, and XML data.

After reading this chapter you will be able to:

- Describe some basic data connectivity methods
- Know how to connect to an external data source using one or more types of data connectivity

6.1 Embedded Excel Spreadsheet

An Excel spreadsheet can be embedded into the Xcelsius 2008 workspace below the canvas. Supported versions include Microsoft Office Excel 2003 and 2007. This is a fully functional instance of Excel, where you can add, delete, or modify data directly without having to import or reimport an Excel spreadsheet file, just like in a normal stand-alone version of Excel.

The appearance of the embedded Excel spreadsheet is the same as that when you launch Excel directly as a stand-alone application. Your customization of Excel will be reflected here, including the language and layout. All of the menus and toolbars are also available here, and you can create as many sheets as you like.

During installation, Xcelsius will detect whether Excel is installed on your machine. If Excel is not detected, Xcelsius will not be installed.

Excel is only required at design time, for data manipulation and binding. The data in Excel is incorporated into the dashboard output, and it's not required at runtime. That is, the designer cannot function without Excel, but the user can. This helps the wide distribution of the output, not only in Windows, but also in other operating systems such as Linux or Unix.

An idle, or "rogue," Microsoft Excel process hanging in the computer will block Xcelsius from starting up, with the error message displayed in Figure 6.1, when you try to launch Xcelsius.

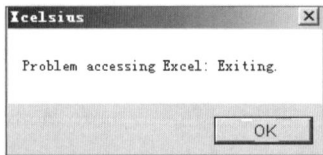

Figure 6.1 Xcelsius Cannot Start Up if an Idle Excel Instance Is Running

This situation may occur when you have launched Excel or Xcelsius before, and it crashed and stopped improperly. As a result, a rogue Excel process is still there, though you cannot see it. To solve this, press [Ctrl] + [Alt] + [Del] to launch the Task Manager, locate the idle Excel process, and end it. You can then launch Xcelsius successfully.

Role of Excel

The embedded Excel spreadsheet is the only direct data source for all UI components of your dashboard and the only interface for all external data sources. That is, you bind a property of a UI component to a cell or cell range in the embedded Excel, and all external data sources should be mapped here. In a word, the embedded Excel spreadsheet is the bridge between Xcelsius components and data connectivity. From this perspective, Excel acts as a *data model* of Xcelsius.

In the meantime, Excel can also act as a *calculation engine* of Xcelsius, to calculate new fields based on the existing data. Most Excel formulas are supported here, providing the dashboard designer more flexibility in calculating new data from existing fields. This is helpful when some data is unavailable or shouldn't be provided by the data source but should be calculated on top of it, for example, to calculate some percentages. A list of supported Excel formulas is provided in the appendix.

As you will see shortly, some types of data connectivity can be triggered when the value of a cell changes or becomes equal to something. From this perspective, Excel acts as an *eventing model* for Xcelsius.

6.1.1 How to Use Excel

You can bind the properties of UI components, and map the input and output of external data sources, to a cell or cell range in the embedded Excel spreadsheet.

Plan First

It's recommended that you define cells for each purpose first, before data binding and mapping. That is, before designing your dashboard, you plan how many sheets you need, what cell will be used for what purpose, and so on. During this planning time, you need to think not only about the cells for the UI components' properties and for data input and output, but also about your calculation and rearrangement of them.

It's a best practice to give descriptive names to the sheets and explanatory labels for a cell or a cell range and to use colors and borders to highlight and distinguish them. For example, you use a data connectivity to access external data, the output of which is a cell range with 4 columns and 10 rows. Before binding the output in the Data Manager, you plan what area will be used to store the output and highlight the columns and rows with colors or borders. Then in the Data Manger, you can easily see where to bind the output. Here, we'll just provide an overview of how to use Excel, and we'll cover it in more detail in the appendix.

6   Data Connectivity Basics

Figure 6.2 shows an example of a well-planned design in Excel.

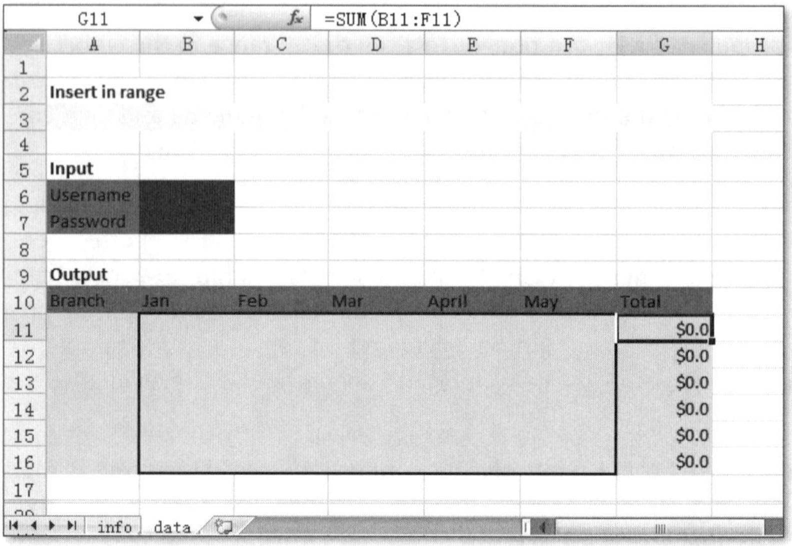

Figure 6.2 Example of a Well-Planned Design in Excel

As you can see from this figure, some metadata, such as the author and the purpose of this dashboard, is placed in a sheet called Info. The actual data, including input, output, and calculated data is placed in the Data sheet and highlighted with colors and cell borders. Note that the destination cells of data insertion or drill-down of UI components are also highlighted, for easy understanding of the design.

Sometimes it's difficult to design on an empty Excel spreadsheet and imagine the business meaning and format of a cell. To make the design simpler, you can write some sample values next to the mapped cells, in another row or column or range.

The data of the embedded Excel spreadsheet can also be exported, with all sheets included. To do this, first switch to preview mode and then follow the menu path FILE • SNAPSHOT • CURRENT EXCEL DATA.

If you use data connectivity and map the output of the external data source to the embedded Excel spreadsheet, the output is not really written to Excel. Remember, the data is only mapped, not written. That means the content of the embedded Excel spreadsheet will not be changed after a preview, and you will not be able to see the output data in the spreadsheet.

Resize

You can resize the area to display the embedded Excel spreadsheet can be resized, both in width and in height. The behavior is a little different for Excel 2007 and 2003. If you are using Excel 2007, the ribbon area, the toolbars, and the menus are all visible by default when the space is high enough. However, they will disappear when the height is decreased to some limit, to save more space for the cells. If you decrease the width, the menus and the ribbon area will shrink. For Excel 2003, this is simpler: The toolbars just show or hide depending on the space size, and a horizontal scrollbar will appear if the width is not adequate.

Working with the embedded Excel spreadsheet here is no different from what you would normally do. You can fill in texts or numbers in a cell, set its formats including fonts and colors, set border styles, create calculated cells, and so on. You can also create multiple sheets to store different data and give them descriptive names. For example, you can have an Info sheet to store some metadata such as the author, the purpose, and the target audience of the dashboard and another sheet called Data to store the input and output values of a data connectivity.

Copy and Paste

You can copy and paste some texts or formulas from or to the embedded Excel spreadsheet. The copy and paste operation can happen between two Xcelsius instances or between Xcelsius and another stand-alone Excel instance. Note that both the data and its format are copied. It's helpful when your data resides in multiple Excel files and that you want to copy it into the embedded Excel spreadsheet to design your dashboard.

However, formulas cannot be copied between the embedded Excel spreadsheet and a stand-alone one. Only the result data is copied. For example, in Xcelsius, you have letter A in cell Sheet1!B2, letter B in Sheet1!B3, and formula =CONCATENATE(Sheet1!B2, Sheet1!B3) in cell Sheet1!C2. When you copy cell Sheet1!C2 and paste it into a cell, say Sheet1!D1, in a stand-alone Excel file, the copied content is "AB" instead a formula.

Copying and pasting between two Xcelsius instances is also supported. That is, you can design two dashboards simultaneously by running two Xcelsius instances at the same time and copy and paste data between them. You will find this functionality useful when you are learning from a dashboard designed by an expert, and you try to create an excellent dashboard from scratch. However, if the two dashboards are not opened at the same time, copy and paste between them is not supported. That is, when you have copied something from one Xcelsius instance, and then you open or create another Xcelsius file (.xlf) via the menu path FILE • OPEN OR FILE • NEW, or restart Xcelsius, the copied data cannot be pasted.

6.2 Import Data from an Excel File

You can import data from an existing Excel file into the embedded Excel spreadsheet. The Excel file can be either Office 97-2003 (with an .xls extension) or Office 2007 (with an .xlsx extension), located either on your local machine, on a network, or in an SAP BusinessObjects Enterprise system. Once imported, the embedded spreadsheet will be identical to the source file, with all changes you have made to it lost. Xcelsius will try to maintain the binding relationship between a UI component and the embedded spreadsheet. However, the bindings will also be lost if the sheets have different names.

6.2.1 When to Use

You may want to use this option when the data source of your dashboard is an Excel file, for example, if the director of the sales department asks you to build a dashboard showing the sales status of the year and gives you the data in an Excel file. You may also use this option when the Excel file containing the source data is unavailable at design time, and you, the dashboard designer, cannot wait until it's ready. In such a situation, you can agree with the data provider on what data is stored in what cells in the Excel file. Then you can begin your design, and import data from the Excel file when it's ready.

You have to use the command "Import Data" when the data is only available in Excel format but cannot be provided through any of the data connectivity methods in the Data Manager. For example, the data might exist in a legacy system that provides no application programming interface (API) for external calls. Imagine the case when your data is in an SAP R/3 system.

6.2.2 How to Use

Importing data from an Excel file is very easy and straightforward in Xcelsius 2008. You can do this by selecting DATA • IMPORT to locate a file on your local file system or a network. You can also import data from an Excel file on an SAP BusinessObjects Enterprise system, via the menu path DATA • IMPORT FROM ENTERPRISE.

This options requires that you have the right to log on to the SAP BusinessObjects Enterprise system and to access the Excel file.

After being imported, the data in all sheets of the Excel file will be copied to the embedded Excel spreadsheet in Xcelsius. You need do this with caution as all data that existed in the embedded Excel spreadsheet will be overwritten, and any change you have made to the spreadsheet will be lost. Moreover, this operation is unrecoverable.

If you already have some UI components bound to cells in the embedded Excel spreadsheet, Xcelsius will try to maintain the binding relationship. The binding will work perfectly after importing data if the names of the cells or cell ranges are still available. For example, let's say you have bound the title property of a pie chart to cell Sheet1!$B$2. It will still be bound to Sheet1$B$2 after import if there's such a cell. However, if there's no sheet named Sheet1 in the source Excel file, the binding will be removed because Xcelsius cannot find such a cell.

Note that after you have imported data from an existing Excel file, Xcelsius has nothing to do with that file any more. This means two things. First, you can delete or move that file without affecting your dashboard. Second, changes to the existing Excel file will not be automatically reflected in your dashboard. To solve this, you can import that Excel file again, but any changes made to the built-in Excel spreadsheet, such as formulas, will be overwritten by the imported Excel file.

6.3   Security Issues Related to Accessing External Data

In the sections below we'll discuss some basic data connectivity types that you use in the Data Manager to connect your dashboard to external data. The external data source can be an XML file on your local file system or a Web service via HTTP.

Your dashboard can either be run locally as a Flash or a PowerPoint or be hosted on a web server. At runtime or in preview mode, an Adobe Flash Player is used to play the output. This is where the security issue arises.

The Adobe Flash Player of version 9 or later includes security restrictions that restrict the output (Flash, PDF, or PowerPoint, etc.) to access local files or HTTP services. If you don't grant the output permission to access the resources, you will get an error message on launching the dashboard or in preview mode, as displayed in Figure 6.3 (Adobe Flash Player 10 is used here).

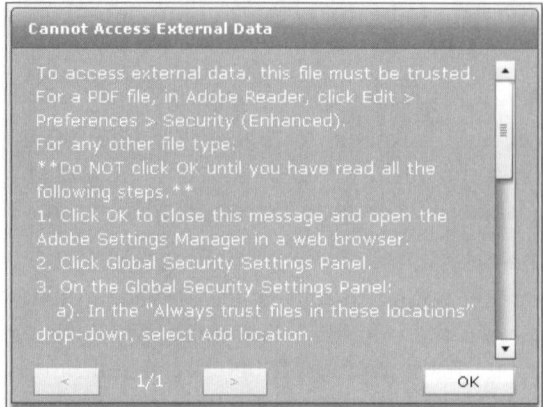

Figure 6.3 Error Window When Flash Player Is not Granted Access

The security issue includes two situations, when your dashboard is run locally or on a Web server, as explained below.

Run Locally

If your dashboard is exported to a file on your local file system, such as a Flash or PowerPoint, you need to add that file to the trusted locations in Adobe Flash Player Settings Manager so it can access other files or HTTP services.

The Adobe Flash Player Settings Manager is not a tool or setting on your local machine. Instead, you have to set it over the Web. To open the manager, go to *http://www.macromedia.com/support/documentation/en/flashplayer/help/settings_manager04.html*.

Then either click Global Security Settings Panel in the Table of Contents area on the left of the page, or click the third icon in the Settings Manager on the right. In the window, select Always Allow, click Add Location, and browse to the folder or the dashboard file (SWF, PowerPoint, HTML, etc.).

Then you are done. You have marked your dashboard as trustworthy, and it can access external resources now. You can reopen the dashboard to have a try.

Run on a Web Server

Sometimes you'll export the dashboard to a Flash or an HTML file and host it on a web server. The user can then access it through a URL such as *http://webserver:port/xxx/dashboard.html*. If it connects to an HTTP service hosted on another server, you must provide a cross-domain policy file (typically, a cross-domain.xml file) in the web server root. Otherwise, you will get an error message. The reason is that the Adobe Flash Player doesn't allow an SWF file to access data that resides in a domain different from the web domain from which the SWF originated.

The cross-domain policy file grants the Adobe Flash Player permission to access data in a given domain. It controls what SWF files, running on what domains, can access resources on your web server. It's a simple XML file placed on a folder in your web server. The folder differs for each kind of web server. For example, the folder is *TOMCAT/webapps/root* if you are using Tomcat to host your dashboard.

For more details about the cross-domain file, search for it over the Internet or refer to *http://kb.adobe.com/selfservice/viewContent.do?externalId=tn_14213&sliceId=2*.

A sample cross-domain.xml is shown below, which allows any SWF file from any domain to access resources in the web server.

```
<?xml version="1.0"?>
<!DOCTYPE cross-domain-policy SYSTEM
   "http://www.macromedia.com/xml/dtds/cross-domain-policy.dtd ">
<cross-domain-policy>
<allow-http-request-headers-from domain="*" headers="*" secure="false" />
<allow-access-from domain="*" secure="false" />
</cross-domain-policy>
```

6.4 XML Data

XML is a set of rules for encoding documents electronically. It can be used to represent almost arbitrary data structures, not only XML files, but also web resources, with great simplicity, generality, and usability. That's why it's now widely used in many situations. For example, you can get the stock price of one or more companies from Yahoo! Finance with one URL, which provides the data in an XML format.

In Xcelsius, XML data means any data source in an XML format, either from a file or over the Web available in HTTP protocol. With this data connectivity you can connect your dashboard to a wide range of external data sources.

The XML data connectivity is identified as a URL, pointing to either a file or a service starting with *http://*. The URL can accept input parameters, which enables you to use one URL for different user inputs. Don't undervalue this property. This enables you to write back to your data source. For example, you can bind user input to one or more cells in the embedded spreadsheet, concatenate them to the URL in key-value format, and trigger the connectivity. The server will then get the user input and write them to the data source after processing. If you are familiar with web programming, you may know this is achieved by the http GET method.

The standard XML schema can be very flexible and complex, as you will see in the next section about Web service connections. In Xcelsius 2008, the data from XML data connectivity needs be mapped to a cell range in the embedded spreadsheet with a row-column structure. Xcelsius provides limited support for XML data, with some requirement to the XML data format. Generally, to be able to be consumed by Xcelsius, the XML data should be in the format illustrated below.

```
<?xml version="1.0" encoding="UTF-8"?>
<data>
<variable name="any string here">
  <row>
    <column> column value 1 </column>
    <column> column value 2 </column>
    ...
  </row>
  ...
</variable>
...
</data>
```

The principals for using XML data in Xcelsius 2008 are:

- The XML data may or may not contain the header `<?xml version="" />`. However, if there are some Asian characters in the XML data, you need the header to specify the encoding type to read them correctly.
- The XML body should be within a node named `data`.
- The first row below node `data` should be `<variable name="any string here">`. In `name` you can put anything to explain the meaning of this data. You can have several variable nodes in the XML data.
- Inside the tag variable are a list of row nodes. A row indicates a row of data, mapped to a row in Excel. A row can contain one or more columns, mapped to a column in Excel. There're can be as many rows as you want, but the number of columns should not exceed 256.

- Inside each row is a list of columns. The content of each column node represents the content of the mapped cell.

If the data source resides in an XML file, the file content should be the same as shown above. If it's exposed as an HTTP service, the service should also return exactly the same content in its output stream. This is easy and natural to understand: Excel is two-dimensional, and Xcelsius can only bind data to a cell range, with N rows and M columns.

For example, let's say you are going to show the sales revenue and quantity sold of two companies. To be consumed by Xcelsius, the content in XML format should be:

```
<data>
<variable name="any string here">
  <row>
    <column>Company A</column>
    <column>300,000</column>
    <column>1200</column>
  </row>
  <row>
    <column>Company B</column>
    <column>420,000</column>
    <column>1560</column>
  </row>
</variable>
</data>
```

The data will be mapped to a cell range B3:D4 with two rows and three columns in the embedded Excel spreadsheet, as shown in Figure 6.4.

	A	B	C	D	E
1					
2					
3		Company A	300,000	1200	
4		Company B	420,000	1560	
5					

Figure 6.4 Output of XML Data Connectivity Mapped to a Cell Range in an Embedded Spreadsheet

When you use XML data in your dashboard, you can configure how and when the data will be refreshed against the source. We'll provide a detailed explanation about how to use it in Section 6.4.3.

6.4.1 When to Use XML Data

You can use this data connectivity type when the data source is provided in XML format, either as a file or as a service with an HTTP protocol. You can also use it to send data to external applications in an XML format, for example, to export data in the spreadsheet to an XML file.

XML File
This is the case when someone collects the data and put it in an XML file or when the data is generated automatically by some program and saved into an XML file. The file can located either in a file system or on a network.

XML Service over HTTP
Sometimes it's not practical to save data in a physical file. For example, the data is dynamic and varies a lot depending on different conditions. In such situations, you can expose the data as an HTTP service.

If you are familiar with Java, you can simply write a Java Servlet to expose the data. The Java Servlet can be hosted in any Java Web Application Server such as a Tomcat. In addition to returning data as an XML string, it can also accept input parameters.

This is very powerful. It enables Xcelsius to connect to almost any data source, only if it can be access and processed by the Java programming language and exposed as an XML string. This is also a practical combination of experts in dashboard designing and experts in Java programing, which work together to create a fancy and powerful dashboard.

For example, say your sales data is stored in the database (either transactional or data warehouse) and you want to create a dashboard showing some measures about sales, where the user can choose what years, branches, or products to see. To achieve this, the Java experts write code to access the database, calculate the required values, and return the data in a Java Servlet. The dashboard designer then creates a dashboard connecting to the servlet.

The user's default web browser may cache the URL defined in the XML data connectivity. That is, if you request data with the same URL (its parameter included) twice within a short period (before the web browser considers the cached URL as expired), the web browser will not send the request to the web application server. Instead, it returns the cached page content. To avoid this, you can simply disable your web browser from caching. A better way is to append a redundant parameter with `Rand()` as its value. For example, you can update the URL for the XML data connectivity by concatenating `&redundant_param=RAND()` to the real URL in the cell in the embedded spreadsheet.

6.4.2 How to Use XML Data

To connect to XML data, you need to first add one such connectivity by launching the Data Manager, clicking Add, and selecting XML Data from the dropdown list, as displayed in Figure 6.5.

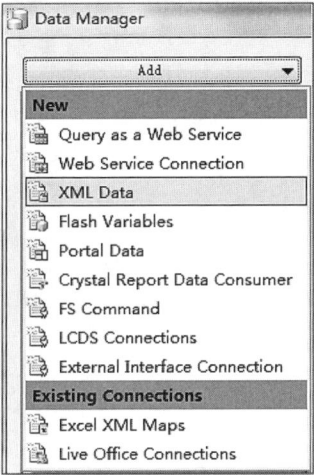

Figure 6.5 Add One XML Data Connectivity from the Data Manager

The Data Manager can be launched either from the menu DATA • CONNECTIONS, from toolbar, or from the keyboard shortcut Ctrl + M.

You can create as many XML data connectivities in one dashboard as you want and set their properties.

You set the properties of an XML data connectivity in the Properties panel to its right. In the sections below, we'll illustrate the purposes of the properties.

Definition
In this tab you define the location and format of the XML data connectivity, as displayed in Figure 6.6.

6 | Data Connectivity Basics

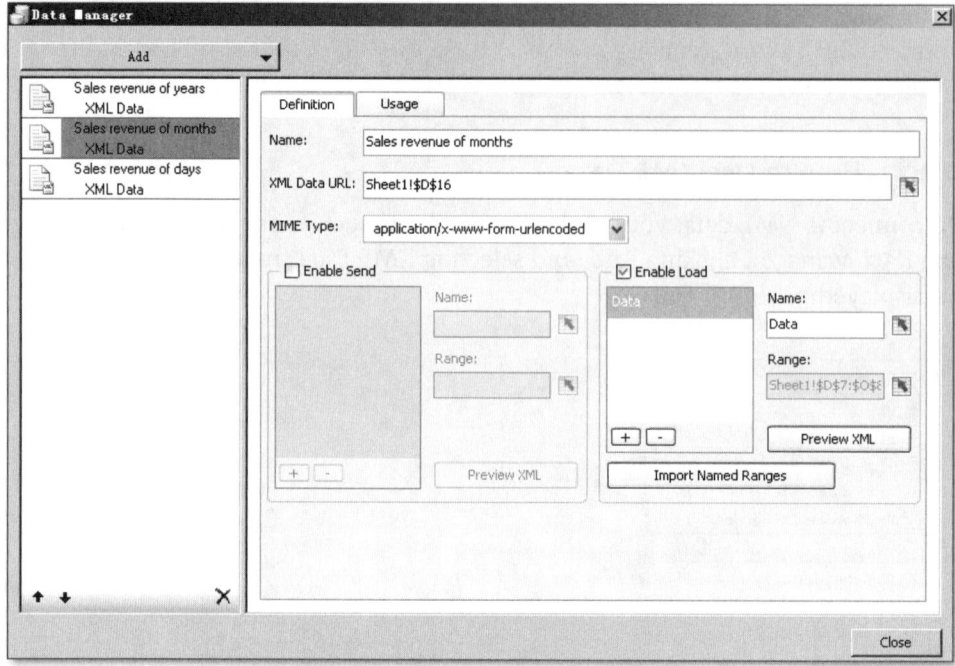

Figure 6.6 Defining XML Data Connectivity

The properties for the XML data are explained below.

▶ Name

Here you specify the name of this connectivity. The name can be any string, but should be meaningful enough to explain what it's about. It will also appear in the connectivity list, where the name will help you easily locate the one you want.

▶ XML Data URL

Here you specify where the XML data source resides. You can directly enter the URL in the input field or bind it to a cell in the embedded Excel spreadsheet. When the URL has to be concatenated by the values in several cells or be passed in from a Flash variable, you need save it in a cell and bind the URL to it.

If the source is an XML file on the file system, the URL should be something like *file:// D://salesXMLdata.xml*, *D://salesXMLdata.xml*, or *\\my-file-server\data\salesXMLdata.xml*. The prefix, *file://*, is not required. You can also use a relative path here, such as *../data/salesXMLdata.xml*, which locates the file in folder Data in the same directory as the output at runtime. For example, if you specify the URL as *../data/salesXMLdata.xml* and export the dashboard as an SWF file to the folder *E:/samples,* then to make it work, the file salesXMLdata.xml should be available in the folder *E:/samples/data.*

If there's space in the file name, you can either leave it alone or encode it as %20. For example, you can use either *D:/sales XML data.xml"* or *D:/sales%20 XML%20data.xml.*

The content of the XML file is not burned, or embedded, into the output, which means the XML file should be available at the dashboard's runtime. If you use a relative or network path to locate the XML file, ensure that it's accessible when the user launches the dashboard.

To be able to access the XML file, the output (SWF, PDF, PowerPoint, etc.) must be declared as trusted. Refer to Section 6.3 for how to do this.

If the source is an HTTP service such as a Java Servlet, you need to specify the full URL such as *http://myserver:poart/context/salesXMLdata.do*. Unlike for an XML file, the *http://* prefix is required.

You can also use a relative path such as *.../salesXMLdata.do*. The path is relative to where the dashboard originates.

If the HTTP service resides on a domain other than the dashboard, you need a cross-domain policy file to grant access to the dashboard. Refer to Section 6.3 for more information.

▶ MIME Type
You select a MIME type from the dropdown list for the data source. There are two options here, text/xml for human-readable text that is defined in RFC 3023 (available at *http://tools.ietf.org/html/rfc3023*), and application/x-www-form-urlencoded for nonstandard files documented in HTML 4.01 Specification, Section 17.13.4.1 (available at *http://www.w3.org/TR/html401/interact/forms.html#h-17.13.4.1*). You can refer to these websites for an in-depth understanding of the two types.

If the data source is an XML file, there's no difference between them. On the other hand, if it's an HTTP service such as a Java servlet, you make your selection based on the content type specified in the source. Usually, either is all right, and you can just leave it unchanged, to use the default type.

▶ Enable Load

Select this option if you want the XML data specified in the URL to be loaded into Xcelsius when the connection is triggered. It may seem strange that you have to select this option to get data from the URL: Why do you add an XML data connectivity if you don't want to load into data into Xcelsius? Well, most of the time you don't have to, but imagine a scenario in which you want to submit some info to the server through this URL and don't need to get the result. In this case, you just need to select Enable Load, which we'll explain shortly.

The XML data is loaded into Excel cell ranges. Each variable node, as explained in Section 6.4.1, corresponds to one range.

To add a range, click the button with a plus (+) sign below the range list.

The range name should be the same as the one specified in the variable node. For example, if you have a node <variable name="Sales info"> in the XML data, you need to specify "Sales info" as the range name here. Similar to many other properties, you can directly enter the name in the input field or bind it to a cell.

In addition to the name, you need to specify a cell range in the embedded Excel spreadsheet to store the data within that variable node. The numbers of rows and columns in the cell range should match those inside the variable node.

If there is more than one variable node in the XML data, you can repeat the steps above to add more ranges.

To delete a range, click to select it from the list and then click the button with a minus (-) sign. The Preview XML button is used to show you what your data should be like, not to preview the data specified in the URL. Clicking it will generate a temp XML file in your system's TEMP directory (for example, *C:\Users\Ray\AppData\Local\Temp*) according to the settings here and open it in your default Internet browser. For example, let's say you have defined two ranges here, one called Range_0 bound to cell range Sheet1!$E$3:$G$4, which has two rows and three columns, and the other called Range_1 bound to range Sheet1!$E$5:$E$6 with two rows and one column. Clicking the Preview XML button now will direct you to a web page that shows a temp XML file. Figure 6.7 displays the content of the XML file and the settings.

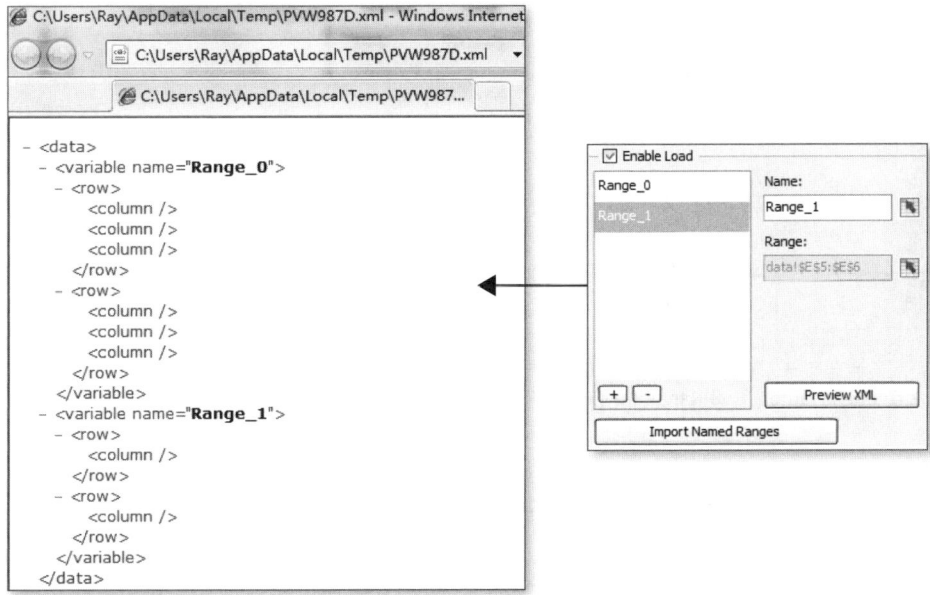

Figure 6.7 Accepted Structure of the XML Content Displayed in a Browser Window after Clicking Preview XML

This functionality is helpful for troubleshooting, when you think the format of your XML data is correct but it just cannot be displayed properly in your dashboard. You can then check the format of your data to see what Xcelsius asks for.

You use the Import Named Ranges button to import all named ranges you have created in the embedded Excel spreadsheet. A named range is a cell range with a name, which you can create with the following four steps.

1. Select the cell range to be named.
2. Click the Excel Name box to the left of the formula bar.
3. Type a one-word name for the list, for example, FruitList. No spaces are allowed.
4. Press Enter.

Figure 6.8 shows some named ranges.

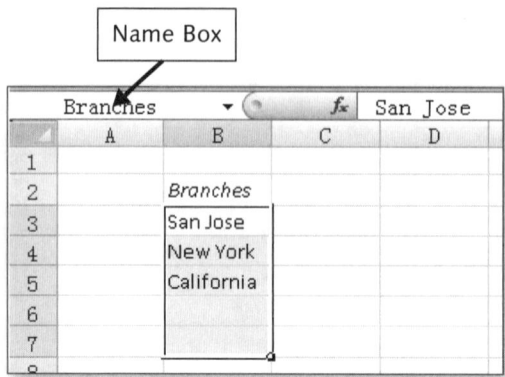

Figure 6.8 Name a Cell Range for Future Reference

After creating a named range, you can select a name in the Name Box drop-down list to select its corresponding cell range. The name can also be used in formulas, such as a SUM calculation.

As we mentioned before, it's a best practice to plan ahead what cells are used for what purpose. For example, you can first define a cell range, Sheet2!$B$3:$B$7, to store all branches and another range for all products. The cells may later be used as the source of a combo box, for the user to choose what branch he wants to see. Then in the Data Manager, instead of selecting the ranges one by one, you can click the Import Named Ranges button to automatically import all of them.

Note that clicking this button makes no change if there's no named range in the Excel spreadsheet.

- Enable Send
  Select this if you want to send some data to the URL. For example, you can send the username and password you entered in the logon panel to the URL, or you can export data from the embedded Excel spreadsheet to an external service. You define what data to send by adding one or more ranges, just like what you do in the enable load step.

  You can click Preview XML to see the format of the data that will be sent to the URL. However, you cannot import named ranges here.

  All of the data will be included and wrapped into an XML string, the format of which is the same as that discussed in the section above. Name the ranges with care. They will be part of the generated XML string, so the URL should be able to parse them.

This option is very useful if you want to export data to an external service at runtime. A typical use is to export the data to an Excel file. To do this, define the cell ranges containing the data you want to export, and write an HTTP service (e.g., a Java servlet if you are familiar with Java Enterprise Edition [JEE]) to process the sent XML string and export it to an Excel spreadsheet.

Usage
In this tab, shown in Figure 6.9, you configure when to trigger the data connectivity and how to inform the user about the status.

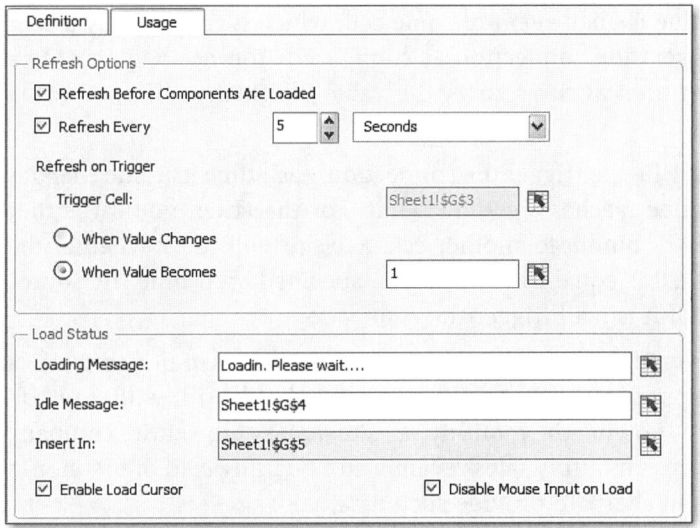

Figure 6.9 Usage Tab of an XML Data Connectivity

The available properties in this tab are illustrated below.

- Refresh Before Components are Loaded
  Select this option if you want to trigger this data connectivity (in other words, load the data) automatically each time before any component is loaded. Xcelsius will then load data from the specified URL first, before building the UI components. When the UI components appear on the screen, they will be filled with data.

  You may select this option when the user is not required to interact with specific values. Instead, you load data under default conditions to the dashboard.

- Refresh Every

    Select this option if you want to trigger the data connectivity at intervals. A typical usage is listing stock prices, which requires up-to-date data. When this option is selected, you can specify the interval as *N* seconds, minutes, or hours. Xcelsius will then load data at each interval, from the time when the dashboard is loaded.

- Refresh on Trigger

    The two options above require a user interaction to trigger the connection. In other words, the user cannot control when to load data. Refresh on Trigger provides the user with the ability to control when to load the data. Basically, Xcelsius listens to the value-change event of some cell, which is triggered by a user interaction, and triggers the connection as configured. You need to provide a trigger cell, which is used as the source, the value of which is listened to by Xcelsius.

    Then you can choose when to trigger the connection: each time its value changes or only when the value reaches a certain point. For the latter, you can either enter a value directly or bind it to another cell. Xcelsius will check whether the value of the source cell is equal to the one you specified each time the source cell is updated and , if it is, will trigger the connection.

    You can use the first type of trigger in many situations, for example, to create a drill-down chart. Suppose you are going to create a dashboard, with one column chart on the top showing the monthly sales revenue of the entire company and one pie chart for the monthly sales revenue and quantity sold of the month selected in the column chart. To provide such data, you:

1. Create an XML data connectivity to retrieve yearly sales revenues for all all branches, and select Refresh Before Components are Loaded.
2. Bind the data for the pie chart. Enable drill-down for it, and insert the identifier of the selected branch to a cell (say, cell Sheet1!$D$2).
3. Create another XML data connectivity to retrieve monthly sales revenue and quantity sold for a given branch. The URL of this connectivity should contain the value of the cell in step 2, which stores the identifier of the selected branch (for example, *http://server:port/services/getBranchData?branchId=xx*). Set this connectivity to trigger on cell Sheet1!$D$2 when the value changes.
4. Bind data for the column chart.

Figure 6.10 shows an example where the user clicks on a month in the column chart on the top, and then the pie chart on the bottom left is updated to show the info of each branch in that month; when the user clicks on a branch in this pie chart, the pie chart on the bottom right is updated to show the quantity sold every week at that branch in that month. Each time the user clicks on a different month in the column chart, the second data connectivity is triggered, and the pie chart on the bottom left is updated. For the second pie chart, the steps are similar.

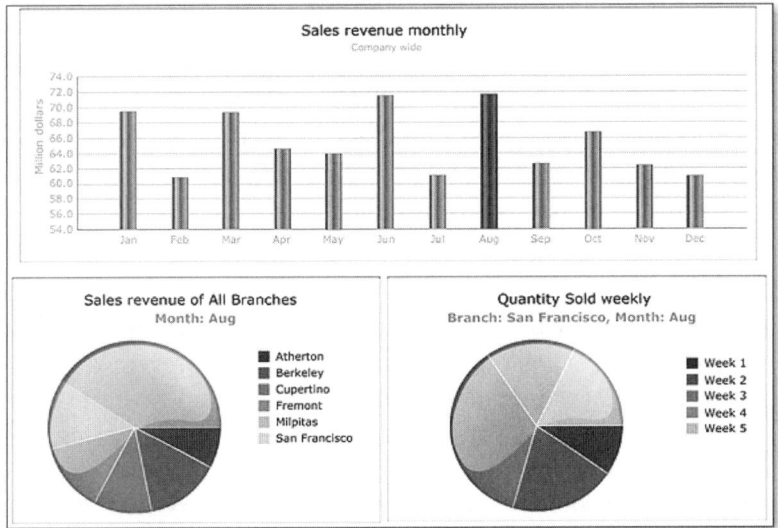

Figure 6.10 XML Data Connection Triggered Whenever the Content of Some Cell Changes

You can also achieve this by returning the monthly data for each branch along with the yearly data, but this may cause performance problems if it takes a lot of time to query and parse the monthly data for each branch in the backend. What's more, what if the user wants to drill down from the column chart to see the daily sales revenue of a selected branch in a selected month?

Here's one more example, of the When Value Becomes option. Suppose there's an XML Data connectivity requesting some confidential data in your dashboard. Not all people who can see the dashboard have the right to access data from this specific connectivity. You achieve this with a shared secret. You and the user who have the right to access the data agree on a shared secret (a text). In your dashboard you provide an input field for the user to input the shared secret, and for that connection, you select Refresh on Trigger and When Value Becomes the shared secret. In this way, only users who enter the correct shared secret can trigger the connection.

▶ Load Status
An XML data connectivity is either loading or idle. When it has been triggered and the result XML has not returned, it's in loading status. Otherwise, it's idle. Here you can set the loading message and the idle message, by either entering some text directly in the input field or binding it to a cell.

You use the Insert In field to select a cell in the embedded Excel spreadsheet where either the loading or the idle message will be inserted, depending on the load status of the connectivity. You can then bind a label component to this cell, thus displaying the status of the connectivity on the screen.

Select Enable Load Cursor if you want to display a busy cursor when the connectivity is loading. Then, the cursor will become a busy cursor ⌛ when the connectivity is loading and go back to its usual shape when the connectivity is idle. This allows the user to know by the shape of the cursor that the connectivity is being loaded.

Select Disable Mouse Input on Load if you don't want the user to take any action while this connection is loading. You can select this to prevent the user from sending another request unintentionally while the previous request is still being loaded. For example, let's say you have a pie chart showing the sales revenue of each branch, and each time the user selects a branch, another connectivity is triggered to request some other info about that branch. When the info from one branch is being loaded, you may want to disable the user's ability to click on the pie chart to select another branch. Otherwise, if the info of the latter branch returns before that of the former one, the user will see incorrect data.

Load status can be very useful to create an interactive dashboard. For example, the user may get confused when the connection takes a lot of time to return the XML data and he can see nothing indicating the load status: Is it still loading, or has already finished with nothing returned? Displaying a Loading... label and/or showing the cursor as busy is a simple way to reassure the user that the system is still processing the data. With the help of dynamic visibility and some other functionalities, you can make the interface better: showing the loading status in an image in front of all other UI components and preventing user interaction during loading.

6.4.3 Practice

It's easy to understand how to set up an XML data connectivity, but that doesn't mean it's a simple function. It can be very powerful and flexible. In a word, with

XML data connectivity, you can connect your dashboard to almost any kind of data source and create a dashboard with infinite levels of drill-down.

Let's go through a simple hands-on example to see how to fetch live data using XML data, with a three-level drill-down. After this hands-on example, you might be able to drill down four or more levels.

Suppose your boss wants to see the sales revenue of each year since the company was founded. On clicking a year, he wants to see the value of each month in that year; on clicking a month, he wants to see the sales revenue and/or the quantity sold each day. Now, let's begin.

Plan the Data
The scenario is almost unachievable by placing all of the required data in the embedded spreadsheet at design time or by retrieving data from all years, all months, and all days of all measures with one request, mapping it to cell ranges in the embedded spreadsheet, and binding each chart to them. Instead, we'll request data for each chart separately, passing the selected year or month to the server.

There will be three ranges in the embedded spreadsheet, one for each chart. Drill-down is enabled for each chart (not necessary for the last one). Your embedded spreadsheet should be like Figure 6.11.

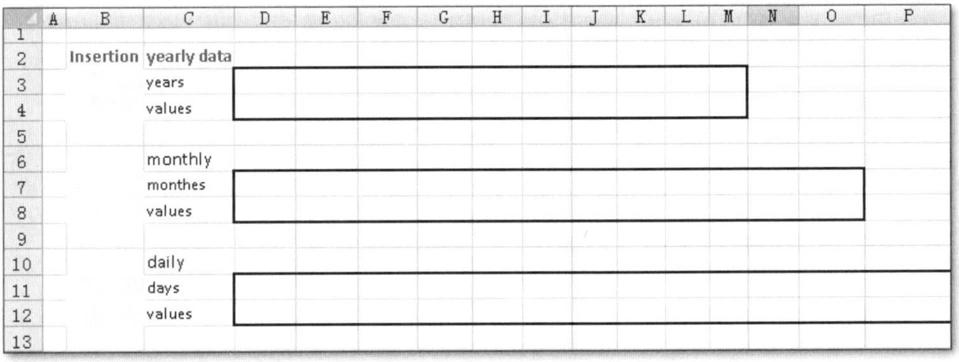

Figure 6.11 Data Structure in the Embedded Spreadsheet

In this hands-on example, only the values of one measure are returned, so each range has only two rows, the first for labels and the other for values. Assume our company is less than 10 years old, so we simply leave 10 columns for the yearly data.

Similarly, there are 12 and 31 columns for monthly and daily data, respectively. Note that for some months, there are fewer than 31 days. We choose the maximum number here to avoid missing any data.

For each chart, the selected year, month, or day will be passed to the backend server for further processing to retrieve data for the next level. So we insert the selected item into a column, as highlighted in yellow.

Write Java Servlets in Server Side

After planning the data, we need something to provide data that is accessible over HTTP. Here we choose Java Servlet to process input parameters and return data in an XML format, assuming that you are familiar with Java Enterprise Edition (JEE).

The logic is the following:

- If no parameter is passed in, return data of all available years.
- Otherwise, if only a year is passed in as an input parameter, return data of all months of that year.
- Otherwise, if both year and month are passed in, return data of all days in that month.

The following shows the sample code to process this logic, using Apache Struts 1 Framework. For more information about it, please refer to *http://struts.apache.org/*.

```
import org.apache.struts.action.Action;
public class GetSalesRevenueAction extends Action {
   public ActionForward perform(ActionMapping actionMapping, ActionForm form, HttpServletRequest request, HttpServletResponse response) throws IOException, ServletException {
      int year = request.getParameter("year") == null ? 0 : Integer.parseInt(request.getParameter("year"));
      int month = request.getParameter("month") == null ? 0 : Integer.parseInt(request.getParameter("month"));
      List<SalesRevenue> resultData = new Array List<SalesRevenue>();
        if(year == 0) resultData = getDataOfYears();
       else if(month == 0) resultData = getDataOfMonths(year);
       else resultData = getDataOfDays(year, month);
```

```
      String ret = wrapToXML(resultData);
   response.setContentType("text/xml");
      response.getWriter().println(ret);
      response.getWriter().flush();
      response.getWriter().close();
}

   protected String wrapToXML(List<SalesRevenue> resultData) {
   StringBuffer ret = new StringBuffer();
   ret.append("<?xml version=\"1.0\" encoding=\"UTF-8\" ?>");
   ret.append("<data>");
   ret..append("<variable name=\"Data\">");
   ret.append("<row>");
   for(SalesRevenue item : resultData) {
      ret.append("<column>").append(item.label).append("</column>");

      ret.append("<column>").append(item.value).append("</column>");
   }
   ret.append("</row>");
   ret.append("</variable>");
   ret.append("</data>");
   }
}

class SalesRevenue {
   public String label;
   public String value;
   …..
}
```

The three methods of getDataOfYears(), getDataOfMonths(String year) and getDataOfDays(String year, String month) all return a list of SalesRevenue. Their content is omitted. Briefly, what they do is something like querying the data source and wrapping the result into structures of SalesRevenue. You can enrich the class SalesRevenue to include more data fields on your own.

Pay attention to the function wrapToXML(), which wraps a list of SalesRevenue to an XML string that conforms to the format required by Xcelsius. After programming, you need deploy it as a web application hosted on a web application server such as a Tomcat. Let's assume the URL to call this servlet is *http://localhost:8080/sales/getSalesRevenue.do*.

Set Up XML Data Connectivity

Now that the server is ready, let's define the XML data connectivities that will retrieve live data for us. There will be three such connectivities in our dashboard, one per chart.

Before adding the three connectivities in the Data Manager, we need to build the URLs for them. We store the servlet in a cell for reference, for example, Sheet1!$D$14.

The URL to get data of all years is the same as the base URL. The URL to get data of all months is the base URL with "&year=[selected year]" appended, so the formula in the cell for the second connectivity is:

=CONCATENATE(D14,"&year=",Sheet1!$B$3)

Sheet1!$B$3 stores the numeric value of the selected year.

The URL to get data of all days in a month is similar. Figure 6.12 shows the URL definitions in the embedded spreadsheet.

	D17			f_x	=CONCATENATE (D14, "&year=", B3, "&month=", B7)						
	A	B	C	D	E	F	G	H	I	J	K	M
13												
14			base URL	http://localhost:8080/sales/getSalesRevenue.do								
15			year URL	http://localhost:8080/sales/getSalesRevenue.do								
16			month URL	http://localhost:8080/sales/getSalesRevenue.do&year=								
17			day URL	http://localhost:8080/sales/getSalesRevenue.do&year=&month=								
18												

Figure 6.12 Concatenate URLs for XML Data Connectivities

Pay attention to the formula for cell D17, which stores the URL to get daily values.

Now let's launch the Data Manager and select ADD • WEB SERVICE CONNECTION to create the connection to get yearly values. In the connection's Properties panel, name it "Sales revenue of years" to distinguish it from the other two, bind XML Data URL to the cell containing its value (Sheet1!$D$15), select Enable Load and name the range "Data," and bind to range Sheet1!$D$3:$M$4, as defined in the planning phase. The range is named Data as defined in the XML returned from the Java Servlet, "<variable name=\"Data\">".

We want to show the sales revenue of all years when the user launches the dashboard. In the Usage tab, select Refresh On Load.

Repeat the steps above to add and configure the other two connectivities, but set the refresh options of the second connectivity to When Value Changes of Trigger Cell Sheet1!$B$3, which contains the selected year, and that of the third connectivity to When Value Changes of Trigger Cell Sheet1!$B$7, which contains the selected month.

Figure 6.13 shows the Properties panel of the XML data connectivity to retrieve monthly data of a particular year.

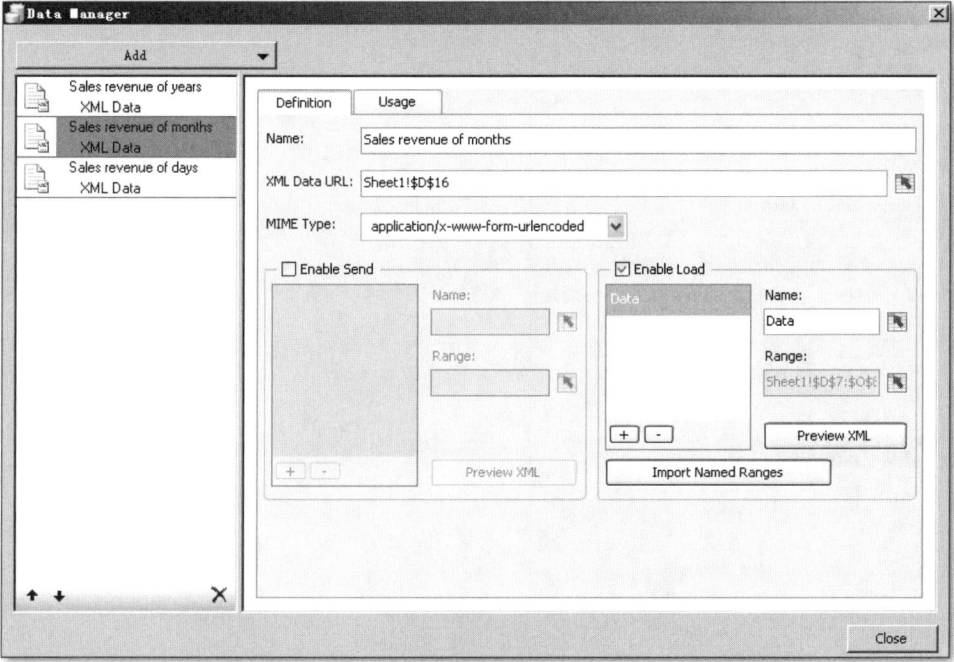

Figure 6.13 Configuration of an XML Data Connectivity

Set up Charts
In this phase, we focus on adjusting the visual appearance and configuring the charts, including data binding and drill-down behavior.

We drag three column charts to the canvas, two on the top with equal size to show data of years and months and one on the bottom to show daily data. Select the top two charts and follow the menu path FORMAT • MAKE SAME SIZE • BOTH AND FORMAT • ALIGN • BOTTOM. Select the chart on the top left and the one for days and select FORMAT • ALIGN • LEFT.

The chart on the top left is for years, so in its Properties panel, enter the name "Sales revenue yearly," select By Series, and bind its category labels to row Sheet1!$D$3:$M$3, where the years are mapped. Click the button with a + sign to add a series, and bind its values to Sheet1!$D$4:$M$4, where the sales revenues of all years are mapped.

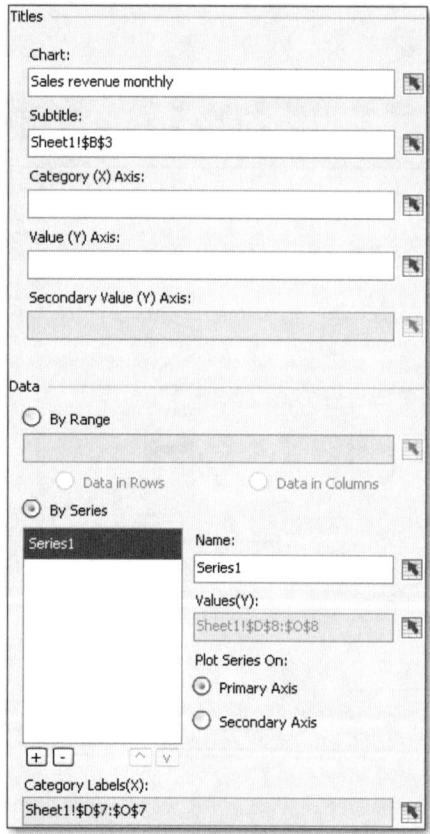

Figure 6.14 Configuration of the Column Chart Showing the Monthly Value

The number of years may be less than 10, so the last few cells may be empty in range Sheet1!$D$3:$M$4. To avoid empty markers on the column chart, select IGNORE BLANK CELLS • IN SERIES AND IN VALUES in the Behavior tab.

It makes little sense to display series names on the chart. Moreover, showing them is a waste of space. So in APPEARANCE • LAYOUT, unselect Enable Legend to hide them.

The most important thing is drill-down. Select Enable Drill Down in the Drill Down tab. We want to insert both the name and sales revenue of the selected year, so we'll select Column as the insertion type, click Series1, and set the source data to range Sheet1!$D$3:$M$4 and the destination to column Sheet1!$B$3:$B$4, as defined in the planning phase.

Repeat the steps above to set data and binding for the other two charts. To show the user the context of the other two charts, bind the subtitle of the second chart to Sheet1!$B$3, which contains the selected year, and that of the third chart to Sheet1!$B$7, which contains the selected month.

Figure 6.14 displays the Properties panel of the chart of monthly sales revenues.

Now we're done! At runtime, the sales revenues for each year, for each month of the first year, and for each day of the first month of the first year are displayed in the three charts by default. When the user selects another year from the first chart, the values in the other two charts are changed accordingly. Figure 6.15 shows a screenshot at runtime.

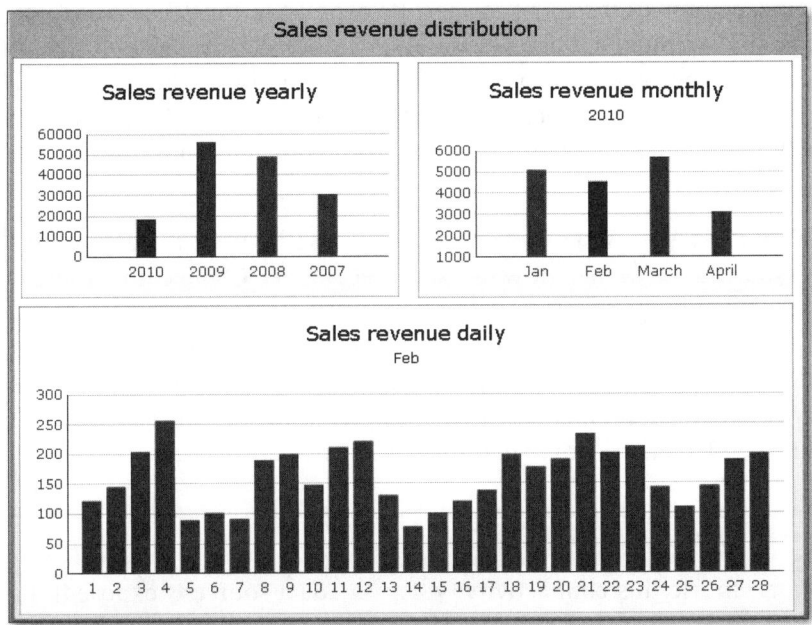

Figure 6.15 Final Effect of this Hands-On Example

Pay attention to the subtitles of the second and third charts, which are the selected year (2010) of the first chart and the selected month (February) of the second one.

6.5 Web Service Connection

A Web service is a service hosted by a web server over the HTTP protocol. Its messages are in XML (or JSON, often used in the RESTful Web service) format, following the SOAP (Simple Object Access Protocol) standard. It can be developed in many kinds of programming languages and hosted in many web application servers. There's often a machine-readable description of its operations and message structures written in WSDL (Web Service Description Language).

In Xcelsius, the Web service connection is somewhat similar to the XML data connectivity in that both use XML to format the return data. However, Web service is more complex. The return data of XML data connectivity just follows XML format. It doesn't need to follow the SOAP standard or provide a WSDL description. And there are significant limitations to its format: Its root node must be "data," followed by a node hierarchy of variable, row, column. Nothing else is permitted. A Web service is more powerful here. It's just required to follow the XML standard, with no restriction to the node names or hierarchy. Compared to XML data, a Web service connection provides a more sophisticated structure and more control over the output.

Similar to XML data, a Web service connection can also be used for data source write-back. As you will see in the "How to Use a Web Service Connection" section, this connectivity accepts input parameters that can be bound to cells in the embedded spreadsheet. That is, you can save user input into the embedded spreadsheet and send it to the server. The server can then write the data back to the data source after processing. If you are familiar with web programming, you may know that this is the HTTP POST method, compared to GET in XML data connectivity.

6.5.1 When to Use a Web Service Connection

It's obvious when to use this connectivity: when the data source is exposed as a standard Web service. One exception here is Query as a Web Service, which is a product of SAP BusinessObjects that also exposes data as a Web service, as we'll explain in the appendix. For such data, you choose connectivity of the type Query as a Web Service instead of a Web service.

6.5.2 How to Use a Web Service Connection

To add a Web service connectivity, launch the Data Manager and select Web Service in the Add dropdown list. A Web service connection will then be added to the connection list. You can create as many Web service connectivities as you want in one dashboard and set their properties respectively. You can click a Web service connectivity to open its Properties panel to set its properties.

Definition

In this tab you define the URL of the Web service, set values for input parameters, if any, and bind the output values to cell ranges in the embedded spreadsheet, as displayed in Figure 6.16.

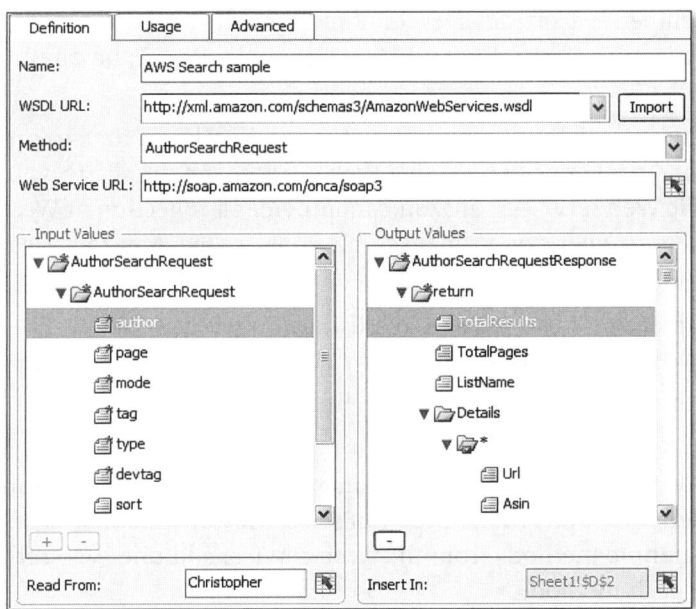

Figure 6.16 Definition of the Web Service Connectivity

The configuration items in this tab are explained below.

- Name
  As for XML data, you enter a descriptive name for the Web service such as its purpose. This can help you quickly identify a connectivity in the list to the left if there are many connections on your dashboard.

- WSDL URL

    To use a Web service, you need know its WSDL URL and enter it here. The WSDL describes the available methods and structure of both input and output.

    You click the Import button after entering the WSDL URL. Xcelsius will then connect to and parse it. If it's unavailable or doesn't have a valid format, Xcelsius will send an error message saying, "Unable to load URL". If everything is all right, Xcelsius will list all methods in the Method dropdown list below and all input and output values in the corresponding lists.

    Note that each time you modify the WSDL URL, even just adding or deleting a character in the field, all methods and input and output values of the previous WSDL will be removed. If you have bound the input or output values to a cell or cell range in the embedded spreadsheet, the binding will also be removed; you have to re-bind them. So if you don't want to change the WSDL, be careful not to modify the URL.

    If you are learning how to use this connectivity, it may take a lot of time to set up an environment and programs to publish a Web service. For simplicity, you can use existing public Web services. Amazon.com provides a collection of Web services for developers to query or to manage his shop, called Amazon Web Service (AWS). For more details, please visit *http://aws.amazon.com/*.

    In the rest of this chapter, we'll use an AWS to illustrate how to use Web service connectivity. Here we enter the WSDL URL *http://xml.amazon.com/schemas3/ AmazonWebServices.wsdl*, which we can use for searching.

- Method

    After importing the WSDL URL, Xcelsius will parse it and list all methods (or operations) in the Method dropdown list. You can select only one method here. If you want to use multiple methods from this Web service, add one Web service connectivity for each method.

- Web Service URL

    The available Web service URLs are also defined in the WSDL, so you will see this field filled after clicking Import. If there are many, you need to select the one you want to use for this connection from the dropdown list. However, the WSDL just defines the methods and structures. At runtime, the request is sent to the Web Service URL, not the WSDL URL.

    You can also bind the Web service URL to a cell, giving you the ability to change it at runtime. For example, you can copy the default Web service URL to a cell and then replace the host with another cell (e.g., use an Excel formula to change the URL to =CONCATENATE("http://", Sheet1!$A$2," /onca/soap3"). At runtime, you can then ask the user to select the host from a combo box and insert it into Sheet1$A$2 (you can use this method when migrating from a development environment to testing). Or you can pass the Web service URL through Flash Variables, which we'll explain in Chapter 7, Section 7.4. You may want to bind Web Service URL to a cell to make it dynamic when you need migrate your dashboard from development environment to production environment.

▶ Input Values
The mandatory and optional input variables or parameters of the Web service are listed here. For each variable, you can either enter the value directly in the Read From field or bind it to a cell in the embedded spreadsheet by clicking the Bind button. For example, you may want to add an input label to the dashboard for the user to enter an author name and send it to the Web service so that only books by that author are returned.

All values are treated as text, whether it's an integer, date, currency, and so on. For the Web service to work perfectly, you need to make be clear about the accepted format of each value. For example, if the Web service requires a month for the search to begin with, you need know whether you should enter 200910 or 2009.10 or something else.

All values you specify here will be passed to the Web service URL, as key-value pairs.

▶ Output Values
A Web service may return several data fields, categorized into classes, which are all listed here. A folder icon next to a field indicates a class, and a file icon indicates a field. You can choose the data you are interested in and insert it to the embedded spreadsheet.

Some fields have only one value, such as the TotalResults field, as we have shown in Figure 6.16 above. As a result, this field should be bound to a single cell. On the other hand, other fields, such as Details in Figure 6.16, may have several values and should be bound to a column.

If you want to insert all fields of a class into the embedded spreadsheet, click on the class and bind it to a cell range. The number of columns of the range should be the same as the number of fields within the class, and the number of rows should be the same as the number of returned records. If you are not sure about how many records are returned, use the maximum number that will return or that you want. You need pay attention to the maximum number of rows supported by Xcelsius. By default, Xcelsius allows up to 512 rows to be retrieved and inserted into the embedded spreadsheet. If you want to increase the number of rows allowed, go to FILE • PREFERENCE and modify the setting in Excel Options, as explained in Section 2.1 in Chapter 2.

Microsoft Excel is two-dimensional, so you cannot insert a class with subclasses into a cell range. That is, you can either bind a field to a cell or a column, or bind a class with no subclass to a cell range, in the embedded spreadsheet.

Usage

In this tab you define when to trigger the connection and how to deal with load status. This is exactly the same as for XML data, so we'll ignore it here. For more details, please refer to Chapter 6, Section 6.4.3.

Advanced

This tab is specific to this connectivity. You may want to use this tab when the Web service requires some information to be passed in the SOAP header. That information should be as defined by the Web service you are requesting.

You can either directly enter the information in HTML format in the SOAP header field, or click the Bind button to bind it to a cell in the embedded Excel spreadsheet containing the required information. For example, the Web service may require user credentials to be passed in the SOAP header, and you can enter something like the following to the field.

```
<soap:Header>
<userName>Ray</userName> <password>abcd</password>
</soap:Header>
```

If the data is bound to a cell, Xcelsius will automatically insert the SOAP header tag to it. That is, in the cell you don't need to include the <soap:Header> tag, but only:

```
<userName>Ray</userName> <password>abcd</password>
```
.

6.6 Excel XML Map

One powerful feature of Microsoft Office Excel (2003 and 2007) is that it supports user-defined XML schemas. You can map data from one or more XML files into cell ranges in an Excel file, with or without the XML Schema (.xsd files). Excel automates most of the processes for you, including XML parsing and filtering.

When we discussed Xcelsius data connectivities such as XML data and Web services, we mentioned that XML is widely used in representing and storing data. For example, sales revenue may be exported into an XML file from your SAP ERP system. By mapping XML elements into an Excel file, you can further process the data without leaving Excel, which might be your everyday tool, and refresh it to retrieve the latest data.

Xcelsius 2008 provides an Excel XML map connectivity so you can create dashboards based on data in an XML file, by mapping data from XML files into an Excel file and then importing the Excel file into Xcelsius. Xcelsius will retain the link to the original XML files. Similar to other connectivities, you can define when to trigger such connections to get the latest data. To get the data, the XML file must be available when the connection is triggered.

6.6.1 When to Use an Excel XML Map

You may want create connectivities of this kind on your dashboard when the data source is always XML files, which may or may not need further processing in Excel. A typical usage is when, for example, the sales department asks you to create a dashboard showing monthly sales status, but they have no way to expose the relative data through a Web service or Java Servlet. Instead, their application can only export the data into an XML file. The sales department has agreed with you on the location of the exported XML files. You can then connect to the XML files in your dashboard through Excel XML map connectivities. At runtime, the XML file is updated monthly, when the user exports data to it. The latest data will be updated in the dashboard immediately after the user clicks a Refresh button or does anything else that will trigger the connections, without the need to reimport the Excel file.

You are really creating dashboards based on data in XML files. At design time, the Excel spreadsheet acts as a visualization tool in the workspace, so you can better understand the XML schema and easily bind UI components to cells. At runtime, Excel acts as a bridge between your dashboard and the data source — XML files in a specified location.

6.6.2 How to Use an Excel XML Map

Generally, the steps to use an Excel XML map connectivity in your dashboard are as follows.

- Import Data from XML File(s) into Excel

  How to import XML files into an Excel file is not the focus of this book. Very simply put, you first open the XML file in Excel, from the menu path FILE • OPEN. If you are using Excel 2007, you will see more options available in the XML group in the Developer tab, which is unavailable by default. To enable it, you need launch Excel outside Xcelsius and click the Microsoft Office Button . Then click Excel Options at the bottom right, and select Show Developer Tab in the Ribbon in the Popular category. For more detailed information about this subject, please refer to the Microsoft website, at:

  http://office.microsoft.com/en-us/excel/HP102063971033.aspx for Microsoft Office Excel 2007, and:

  http://office.microsoft.com/en-us/excel/HA011019641033.aspx for Excel 2003.

  You can also import XML files directly into the embedded spreadsheet in Xcelsius. In this case, for Excel 2007, you have to access the XML file via the Developer tab in the ribbon area. For Excel 2003, the process is a little different, in that you need click the XML Source button. To show this button, right-click your Excel toolbar and click Customize, Navigate to the Commands tab, and then select Data, and scroll down to the XML Data source option. Click and drag the XML Source button onto your toolbar.

- Import the Excel File into Xcelsius

  This step is required if you launch Excel outside Xcelsius and import data from one or more XML files into an Excel file.

  To import the Excel file, simply click the Import Spreadsheet button in the toolbar, or select menu DATA • IMPORT/IMPORT from SAP BusinessObjects Enterprise. We discuss this subject in more detail din Chapter 2, where we cover menus.

- Add Excel XML Map Connections

  After importing the Excel file, or the XML file directly, you will see the data in the embedded spreadsheet. You can then create dashboards based on such data. However, this is just a static snapshot of the source XML file and cannot be

refreshed to retrieve live data, because by now, Xcelsius doesn't know that the data is in fact from an external XML file.

To solve this problem, as for other connectivities, you add Excel XML map connections by clicking Excel XML Maps in the Add dropdown list after launching the Data Manager. However, if you do this when the embedded spreadsheet contains no mapping to any XML file, nothing will happen. Clicking Excel XML Maps triggers Xcelsius to detect any existing mapping to XML files in the embedded spreadsheet and creates one connectivity for each mapping. Later when cover Live Office Connection, you'll find them very similar.

Properties Panel

In our example, we assume that the finance department exports the data about monthly reimbursement amounts into an XML file called Expense.xml in the folder *D:/finance*. Figure 6.17 shows the Properties panel of the detected Excel XML map connection.

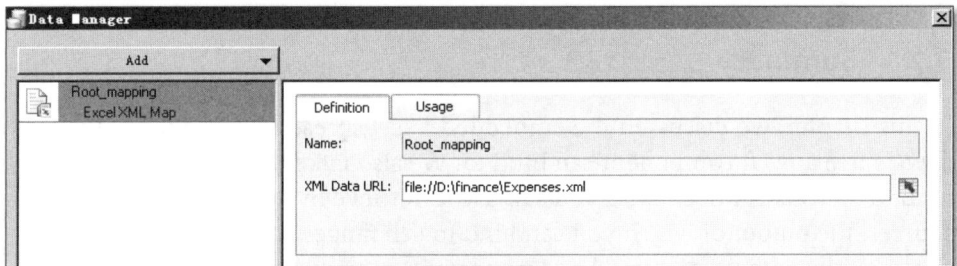

Figure 6.17 Definition of an Excel XML Map Connection

The properties in this tab are very simple. The Name fields displays the name of the XML mapping, which cannot be changed here. Taking Excel 2007 as an example, you can change the name by clicking Source in the XML group of the Developer tab, in the ribbon area.

The XML data URL defines where to locate the XML file. You can specify it by either entering a constant file path directly in the input field or clicking the Bind button to bind it to a cell in the embedded spreadsheet.

The URL can be of any protocol as long as it's valid. As displayed in the figure, the default URL is the one selected on mapping the XML file, which is:

file://finance\Expenses.xml.

You can also point it to a network place, such as:

\\192.168.0.4\finance\Expenses.xml.

This is helpful if you are working in a corporate environment, where different departments can share folders over a file server.

By binding the URL to a cell, you make it possible for it to be dynamically based on some condition. For example, you can point to different XML files based on the user selection via some selectors such as a combo box, using if...then...else logic in Excel. If the information about the user who is viewing the dashboard can be passed in, you can also point to different files based on the current user, thus controlling the data security inside your dashboard.

The Usage tab is exactly the same as that of any other connectivity, where you control how to trigger this connection. For more information about this tab, please refer to the corresponding paragraphs in Section 6.4, where we discussed the XML Data connectivity.

6.7 Summary

In this chapter, we discussed the embedded Excel spreadsheet, which is the only data source any UI component can bind to. We also talked about some commonly used, basic data connectivities you can use to retrieve live data from external data sources, the output of which you can bind to cell ranges in the embedded spreadsheet. With the help of such data Connectivities, you enable your dashboard to reflect real and live data.

In addition to being user friendly and visually engaging, Xcelsius 2008 is also very powerful in connecting to external data. Such advanced connectivity allows you to connect to data in an SAP BusinessObjects Enterprise environment system or consume data from an HTML page or Flash Player.

7   Advanced Data Connectivity

In Chapter 6 we discussed the embedded Excel spreadsheet in the Xcelsius 2008 workspace, where acts as the only direct data source each component binds to. To connect to external data, we discussed importing data from an external Excel file and using XML data and Web service connectivity, which returns data in a simple or standard XML format over HTTP.

These are not the whole story. Xcelsius 2008 provides several more types of data connectivity for you to pass data to or from your dashboard, such as Query as a Web Service which is specific to an SAP BusinessObjects environment, and Flash Variables which is common to all environments.

In this chapter, we'll illustrate all of data the connectivity methods we covered in Chapter 6, including Query as a Web Service, Flash Variables, FS Command, and External Interface connection.

After reading this chapter you will be able to:

▶ Describe all data connectivity methods available in Xcelsius 2008

▶ Understand the use scenario of each type of data connectivity

▶ Know when to use what type of data connectivity and how

7.1   Query as a Web Service

This connectivity is specific to SAP BusinessObjects users. Without an SAP BusinessObjects system, you have no way to use it.

It connects your dashboard to data provided by Query as a Web Service, an SAP BusinessObjects application that allows business users to quickly create queries and publish them as a Web service. The queries are created with data fields (dimensions or measures) from an SAP BusinessObjects universe, a semantic layer between reporting and database that translates the complexities of the database into business-friendly terms for end users. Using a designer tool provided by SAP BusinessObjects, you can create a universe from almost all kinds of commonly used data sources, either relational database or multidimensional data warehouse, including but not limited to:

- MySQL
- Oracle
- Hyperion Essbase
- Microsoft SQL Server, Access and Analysis Server
- IBM DB2 and Infomix
- SAP NetWeaver BW (Business Warehouse)

This enables you to expose data from many kinds of data sources through Query as a Web Service, thus making them accessible to Xcelsius.

You may get a little confused about why we need this data connectivity when we already have XML data and Web services, which can connect to almost any kind of data source. The advantage of this connectivity is that you need programming to retrieve data from your data source and wrap it into an XML string in the format required by Xcelsius, while Query as a Web Service is a product and all you need is some configuration to make it work, without any programming effort.

Query as a Web Service exposes data as a standard Web service, hosted in an SAP BusinessObjects environment by a web application server such as a Tomcat. It cannot function without an SAP BusinessObjects environment, which is responsible for processing its requests and responses.

Because Query as a Web Service exposes data as a standard Web service, you can use a Web service connectivity to connect to data, by pointing its WSDL URL to that of the Query as a Web Service. Xcelsius will successfully parse the WSDL to list the available methods, input parameters, and output values. However, we recommend that you connect to Query as a Web Service through a Web service connectivity. Why not use the one that's meant for it? Moreover, this only works if you are using Xcelsius Enterprise edition. Otherwise, if you are using Xcelsius Engage Server edition or Xcelsius Engage, though the WSDL can be parsed perfectly, the data from the underlying universe will not be returned.

7.1.1 When to Use Query as a Web Service

Deciding when to use a Query as a Web Service connectivity in your dashboard is quite straightforward: You want to use it when the data you need use is provided by this application. Then comes another question: When should you expose data through Query as a Web Service?

To answer this question, you need know what Query as a Web Service and its only direct data source, a universe, can do and their benefits.

Generally, a universe translates complex database fields into business terms that are familiar to the end business user, with aggregation supported. It acts as the bridge between the business user and the complex data source, enabling business users to create dashboards on their own, eliminating the effort spent on communication between the business and the IT department.

Query as a Web Service exposes some fields of a universe as a stand-alone Web service, thus allowing business intelligence (BI) data to be delivered to any user interface that can process and consume Web services.

In general, you may want to choose Query as a Web Service to expose your data when:

- It's better and easier for the client to consume Web service data.
- The data source can be connected to by a universe.
- You are inside an SAP BusinessObjects environment.

You can use this connectivity to connect to one or more universes and, consequently, one or more data sources. You can create as many such connectivities as you want in your dashboard. The relationship between Query as a Web Service connectivity and a universe is many to one. That is, one such connectivity can connects to only one universe, while many such connectivities can connect to the same universe. So it is with the relationship between a universe and a data source: One universe can connect to only one data source, while there can be multiple universes connected to the same data source.

Figure 7.1 shows the workflow from Xcelsius to the data source with this kind of connectivity.

A typical usage of Query as a Web Service is to create a trusted and attractive BI dashboard against SAP NetWeaver BW using Xcelsius, by building universes on top of SAP NetWeaver BW queries (one universe per BW query) and then building a query as a Web service for each universe. Inside Xcelsius, one or more Query as

7 | Advanced Data Connectivity

a Web Service connectivities can then be created to retrieve the actual business data stored in SAP NetWeaver BW.

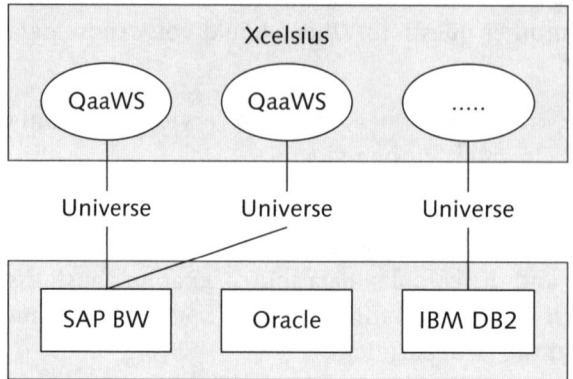

Figure 7.1 Workflow Using Query as a Web Service (QaaWS) in Xcelsius 2008

7.1.2 How to Use Query as a Web Service

To connect to Query as a Web Service, launch the Data Manager, click Add, and select Query as a Web Service from the dropdown list. You can create as many connectivities as you want in one dashboard.

The Properties panel for this connectivity are divided into two tabs, as described below.

Definition

This panel is very similar to that of a Web service connectivity.

- Name
  You give the connection a descriptive name instead of Connection 1 or Connection 2 to make it distinguishable when there are several connections in the list to the left.

- WSDL URL
  In the WSDL URL field, enter the WSDL URL of the Query as a Web Service. The WSDL URL should be provided by the person who has created the QaaWS. You can find the URL in Query as a Web Service, as displayed in Figure 7.2.

You can click the To Clipboard button to copy the WSDL URL onto a clipboard. Then in the Properties panel, you can paste it in the WSDL URL field.

Query as a Web Service | 7.1

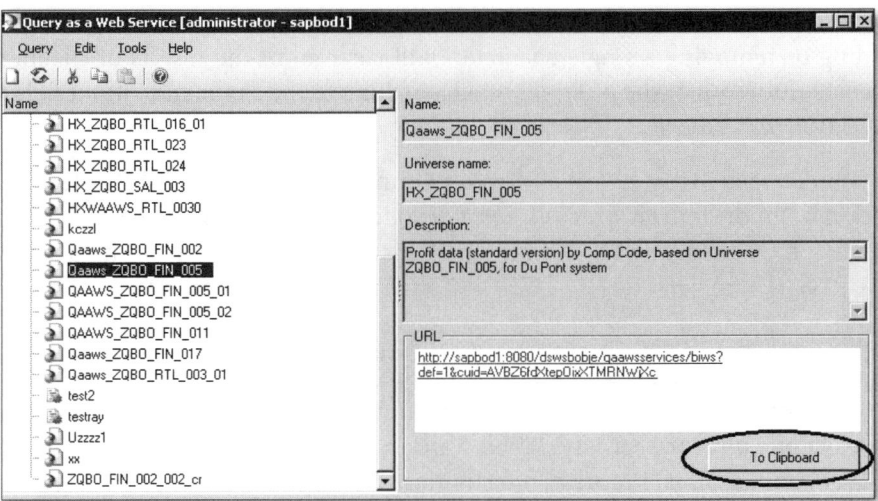

Figure 7.2 WSDL URL of a QaaWS Found Using this Client Tool

Clicking Import will trigger Xcelsius to connect to the specified WSDL URL and parse it. Here Query as a Web Service is just a normal Web service, and all of its available methods, input parameters, and output values will be displayed in the corresponding fields, as displayed in Figure 7.3.

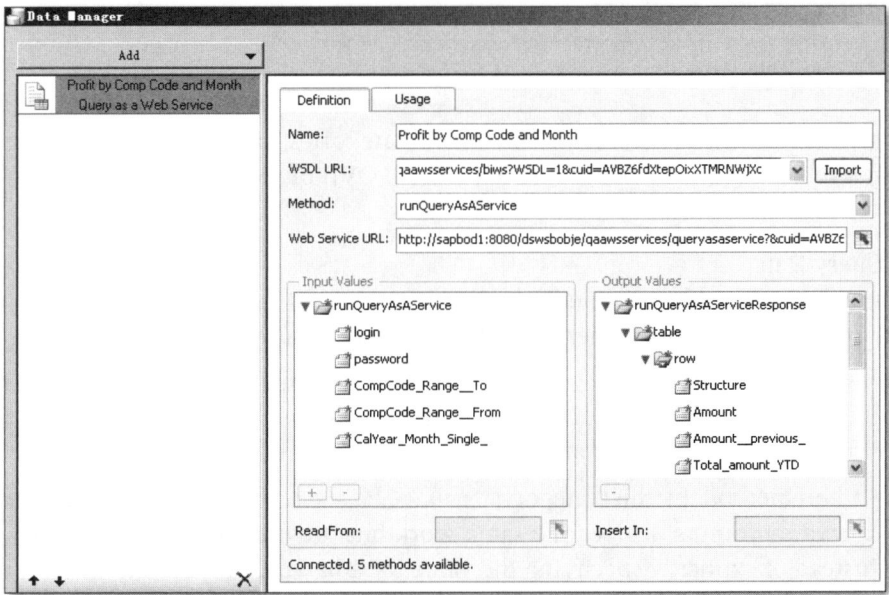

Figure 7.3 Metadata of a QaaWS after You Click Import

335

7 | Advanced Data Connectivity

As for a Web service connectivity, any change you made to the WSDL field, even just adding or removing a single character, will clear all of the results of clicking the Import button. All of the bindings you have done to the input and output fields of the QaaWS will be lost.

When you create a Query as a Web Service connectivity with a valid WSDL URL and click the Import button, you will see a dropdown arrow in this field each time you create a new connectivity. You can click this arrow to select from the history WSDL URLs.

- Method
  This field lists all methods contained in the Query as a Web Service. Each method corresponds to different input parameters and output values. You can only elect one per connectivity. If you want to use more methods of one Query as a Web Service, create more connectivities.

  You can click the dropdown arrow to see the available methods in this Query as a Web Service, as displayed in Figure 7.4.

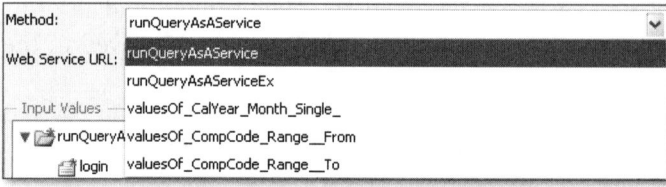

Figure 7.4 Available Methods of a Query as a Web Service

Generally, the methods are divided into two categories, one to query data and the other to list candidate values (list of values [LOV]) of each input parameter, if any.

- To Query Data
  This category, with the two methods `runQueryAsAService` and `runQueryAsAServiceEx`, is common to all Query as a Web Service resources.

  The method `runQueryAsAService` is selected by default, and you can use it to get the data most of the time. It retrieves the data defined in the Query as a Web Service application, with prompt values bound by the user for parameters.

  The other method in this category, `runQueryAsAServiceEx`, is generated for index-aware prompts. It does the same work but provides another functionality: Instead of explicitly specifying the value for a parameter, you can just enter its index. You can find the change in the Input Values area when switching from method `runQueryAsAService` to method `runQueryAsAServiceEx`.

For more info about these two methods, you can refer to the User Guide for Query as a Web Service.

▶ To Get LOV
You use the methods in this category to retrieve the candidate items, or list of values, of the input parameters. The method name is structured like `valueOf_xxx`, where `xxx` is the parameter name. For example, in Figure 7.4 above, there's one method called `valuesOf_CalYear_Month_Single_`, which is for parameter `CalYear_Month_Single` defined in the backend.

There will be one method for each parameter, no matter if it's optional or mandatory.

Naturally, this category contains no method if no parameter is defined in this Query as a Web Service.

You may use this method to help the user specify values of input parameters, to avoid wrong inputs or confusion caused by the user not knowing the valid format of each parameter value. For example, you can use this method to create a Query as a Web Service connectivity called "LOV of parameter XX" to retrieve the list of values of some parameter. You insert the result into a cell range and display it in the dashboard using a combo box. Then you create another Query as a Web Service connectivity to query the data with the method `runQueryAsAService`. You can bind the input parameter XX listed in the Input Values area to the cell that contains the selected value of the combo box. This way, the value selected from the combo box is always valid and thus can be accepted by `runQueryAsAService`.

▶ Input Values
This area lists all input parameters defined for the selected method of the Query as a Web Service. You can click on each parameter and set its value by either entering a constant text directly in the input field at the bottom of this area or click the Bind button to bind it to a single cell in the embedded spreadsheet.

As you can see from Figure 7.3 above, in Input Values, there are two parameters you need to specify values for: login and password. They indicate that to retrieve the data from the backend (from Query as a Web Service to a universe and then to the backend data source), you need to provide you're the values for these two parameters (in this case, your credentials for the SAP BusinessObjects Enterprise system hosting this QaaWS).

One more word here: If the parameter is to accept a range of values (requiring a From and a To value), Query as a Web Service will automatically break into two single-value parameters, one for From and the other for To, each of which can be bound to a single cell.

Sometimes there are some additional parameters other than user credentials. For example, to retrieve the number of products sold, you need to provide the calendar month to specify the date range. The parameter `valuesOf_CalYear_Month_Single_` in Figure 7.4 above is an example of this. When specifying a value for this parameter, either entering it directly or binding it to a cell, you need to specify the value format: If you want to see the number of products sold in a month, say, August 2009, should you enter 200908, 2009/08, or something else? If the parameter is an SAP variable, it may be something like [0CALMONTH].[200908]. To determine the exact format, you need to contact the person who created or developed the data source on which the universe is based. For example, in an SAP NetWeaver BW environment, you need to contact the person who created the BW queries.

If the parameter is optional, you can simply leave it empty if you don't want to specify any value for it. Clicking any folder node, such as the method name here, has no effect.

- Output Values
  This area lists all of the structures and data fields returned by the method selected above, including some metadata about the result of the query, such as a message indicating whether the query succeeded or failed. You can then select a data field or a structure to bind it to a cell or cell range in the embedded spreadsheet so that they can be further used by other UI components to display the data the user has requested.

  The data returned from the query is always a list of rows. A row is compose of several data fields, called columns. You can either click a single data field to bind all its values to a single cell, row, or column or click the row to insert all rows returned to a cell range. The number of cells of the target range should be equal to the number of data fields inside that row (structure), and the number of rows should be equal to the number of records returned, that is, how many records satisfy the query condition, defined by the values you specified for the input parameters in the Input Values area. If you don't know how many records will be returned, use the maximum number that will return, but don't exceed the limit specified by Xcelsius, as defined in menu FILE • PREFERENCE • EXCEL OPTIONS • MAXIMUM NUMBER OF ROWS.

For the Query as a Web Service we use in Figure 7.3 above, we bound rows to cell range Sheet1!$C$2:$F$8, with seven rows and four columns. We select seven rows because seven is the maximum number of rows of data we want to accept in Xcelsius, no matter how many there are in the backend. Similarly four is the number of fields in each row, including Structure, Amount, Amount_previoous, and Total_account_YTD.

Usage
In this tab you configure how and when to load the data, by setting the connection to be triggered when you load the dashboard, on intervals counted from the time when the dashboard is loaded, or by listing a certain cell in the embedded spreadsheet.

Also, you can set the load message and idle message here, which will inform the user about the connectivity's status. This functionality may be especially useful for this connectivity, because it often takes a long time to load data from the data source (such as SAP NetWeaver BW), in which case the data needs be processed by Query as a Web Service, Universe, and the database one by one.

The properties in this tab are exactly the same as those of a Web service or an XML data connectivity. For more details about their meanings and how to use them, please refer to the corresponding parts of Section 6.4.3 in Chapter 6, where we discussed the XML data connectivity.

7.2 Live Office Connection

SAP BusinessObjects Live Office Connection is used to connect to Live Office documents to retrieve data from SAP BusinessObjects, Crystal Reports, or SAP BusinessObjects Web Intelligence documents. The purpose is to create a dashboard based on data of one or more Crystal Reports or SAP BusinessObjects Web Intelligence documents, instead of from the data source directly, and to take advantages of these SAP BusinessObjects products.

SAP BusinessObjects Live Office is a product in the SAP BusinessObjects product suite that is an integration with Microsoft. It's an add-in of the Microsoft Office products family. With SAP BusinessObjects Live Office, you can insert Crystal Reports and SAP BusinessObjects Web Intelligence documents into a Microsoft Office document, including Word, Excel, Outlook, and PowerPoint. The inserted reports can be refreshed within your Microsoft Office document, which is why it's called SAP BusinessObjects Live Office. With SAP BusinessObjects Live Office, you access up-to-date information from your familiar Microsoft Office products that you use every day to do your job and make important business decisions. It gives you real-time data that is verifiable and easily refreshed. In a word, SAP BusinessObjects Live Office allows information workers to work in their most familiar environment: to consume live data within a Microsoft Office document.

When a Crystal Reports or SAP BusinessObjects Web Intelligence document is inserted into Microsoft Office Excel, the Excel document can then be used as the data source for Xcelsius 2008. Based on the Excel document, an SAP BusinessObjects Live Office Connection can be set up within Xcelsius so that the dashboard can display live report data. In this way, the Excel document with SAP BusinessObjects Live Office acts as the bridge between your visualization and an SAP BusinessObjects Business Objects report, making the visualization data Live.

In an enterprise deployment, the Xcelsius dashboards should be refreshable to reflect the latest data. There are many data connection types you can use to make the dashboard refreshable. However, SAP BusinessObjects Live Office works in the most "enterprise" way, meaning it connects to the SAP BusinessObjects Enterprise platform and consumes data from Crystal Reports and SAP BusinessObjects Web Intelligence documents. These infrastructures are all existing enterprise-level BI assets proven to be secure, performance scalable, and enterprise-class reporting tools that ensure you get the expected data format.

7.2.1 When to Use SAP BusinessObjects Live Office Connection

Briefly, you may choose an SAP BusinessObjects Live Office Connection when you want to create a dashboard on top of data in Crystal Reports or SAP BusinessObjects Web Intelligence documents. If somebody else created these documents, you only need go through this section to use them However, if you need create the Crystal Reports or Web Intelligence documents as middleware, some knowledge these two products is required.

Generally, there are two scenarios when you need choose this data connectivity type, as described below.

Security Restriction
One scenario in which you would use this connectivity is when the dashboard designer doesn't have the right to access the database directly but, for security's reasons, can only access other SAP BusinessObjects reports. In such cases, the

dashboard designer cannot retrieve data from the data source through any other connectivity. He can only see and access the data exposed from a Crystal Reports or SAP BusinessObjects Web Intelligence document, which has limited the data.

Special Data
Another scenario is when some data required in your dashboard cannot be provided directly in the data source, nor can it be calculated with Excel formulas in the embedded spreadsheet, but it can be generated with the help of Crystal Reports or SAP BusinessObjects Web Intelligence. This is a way to combine the strengths of all three of the SAP BusinessObjects reporting tools: Crystal Reports, SAP BusinessObjects Web Intelligence, and Xcelsius. To use this, you need know the strengths of each to make the best use of them.

For the first scenario (Security Restriction), it's often natural and obvious to use an SAP BusinessObjects Live Office Connection because the data is only available through SAP BusinessObjects Live Office documents. However, for this scenario (Special Data), whether to choose SAP BusinessObjects Live Office Connection is not that obvious at first. Usually, you'll try to connect to the data source directly through Query as a Web Service or XML data and later find it difficult or even impossible to fulfill all of the requirements, either in data or in format. After some tries, you may find SAP BusinessObjects Live Office Connection as the last resort to calculate the required data or expose data in the required format in Crystal Reports or SAP BusinessObjects Web Intelligence before consuming them in Xcelsius.

For example, let's say you're going to create a dashboard showing sales revenue by goods in different price ranges, That is, the profits of all goods sold at prices less than $10, between $10 and $20, more than $30, and so on. Suppose the backend data source is SAP NetWeaver BW, where such data is stored in an InfoCube. The sales revenue of each price range is not stored in the data source, because the range definition may change from time to time. Sometimes the user may want to further divide the range, for example, into less than $5, between $5 and $10, between $10 and $15, and so on. It's difficult to calculate such data in universe and then Query as a Web Service, nor can you do it inside the embedded Excel spreadsheet. So how do you do this?

If you are familiar with Crystal Reports, you may think to get the data using grouping with a specified order. Briefly, the steps to get such data in Crystal Reports are:

1. Connect to the data source with the corresponding driver (SAP NetWeaver BW MDX, for example).
2. Group on product price through Group Expert, and select In Specified Order in Group Options. Then create a group called "Less than $10" with the condition "Product Price Is Less Than $10." Similarly, create named groups for the other price ranges.
3. Create a summary field at Group Header as a sum of sales revenue.
4. Hide the Detail section.

Now the report has one row per price range. You can then insert this Crystal Reports report into an Excel document through the Live Office menu and connect to it through an SAP BusinessObjects Live Office Connection. This way, you get the data you want in Xcelsius by taking advantage of Crystal Reports.

In these circumstances, you have to generate the required fields in a Crystal Reports or SAP BusinessObjects Web Intelligence document and then connect to it from Xcelsius through an SAP BusinessObjects Live Office connection.

As mentioned in the previous section, you can also use a Query as a Web Service connection to connect to an SAP BusinessObjects platform. The difference is that QaaWS can only consume data from a query on top of a universe but cannot create new fields based on the existing fields.

In short, you need to use SAP BusinessObjects Live Office Connection when it's the only data source you can access or when you have to take advantage of Crystal Reports or SAP BusinessObjects Web Intelligence to get the data you need in your dashboard, and you cannot provide it otherwise.

7.2.2 How to Insert SAP BusinessObjects Reports to Excel

Before using SAP BusinessObjects Live Office Connection in your dashboard, you should know at least a little about how to create an Excel spreadsheet with Crystal Reports or how SAP BusinessObjects Web Intelligence documents are inserted. You can then use this Excel spreadsheet as the data source for Xcelsius.

After installing SAP BusinessObjects Live Office, you will see one more menu, called Live Office in Excel. You can click a submenu (for Excel 2003) or an icon in the ribbon area (for Excel 2007) to insert a Crystal Reports or SAP BusinessObjects Web Intelligence document or a universe query into your Excel spreadsheet. A running the Central Management Server (CMS) must be available now for you to choose a report or a universe from. The SAP BusinessObjects Web Service is used to verify the user to log him on to the CMS, so it must be also available.

For more information about how to create an Excel spreadsheet with Crystal Reports or SAP BusinessObjects Web Intelligence documents embedded, please refer to resources such as the user's guide for SAP BusinessObjects Live Office.

You can insert multiple reports, from one or multiple SAP BusinessObjects systems, into a single Excel file through the Live Office menu, in one or more sheets.

7.2.3 How to Use SAP BusinessObjects Live Office Connection

Unlike the data connectivities discussed previously, with the default embedded spreadsheet, selecting Live Office Connection from the Add dropdown list in the Data Manager will not add the connection to the list. Instead, this menu is used to detect all reports inserted into the Excel file after it has been imported.

Steps to Use SAP BusinessObjects Live Office Connection

The basic steps to use SAP BusinessObjects Live Office Connection from Xcelsius are as follows.

- Enable Live Office Compatibility.
  For the SAP BusinessObjects Live Office document to work, you need have enabled Live Office Compatibility through the menu FILE • PREFERENCE, as described in Chapter 2.

  If you have installed SAP BusinessObjects Live Office on your machine, Xcelsius will detect it and ask you if you want to enable it.

  Note that enabling Live Office Compatibility may affect the performance of other Microsoft Office programs. If you choose not to enable the Live Office Compatibility mode, you will need to work with SAP BusinessObjects Live Office in a spreadsheet outside of Xcelsius and then import you're the spreadsheet.

- Import Excel file with SAP BusinessObjects Live Office enabled.
  When you have created your Excel spreadsheet containing the required reports, you can click the Import or Import from Enterprise button in the Data menu to import it into Xcelsius. As mentioned in Chapter 2 when we discussed the Data menu, all data in that Excel file will be copied to the embedded spreadsheet, overwriting all changes you have made to it.

7 | Advanced Data Connectivity

- Add SAP BusinessObjects Live Office Connection.
  After importing the Excel file, you will see the data in the embedded spreadsheet, with all data and sheets included. You can then create dashboards based on this data. However, it is static and cannot be refreshed to retrieve live data, because by now, Xcelsius doesn't know that the data is from a Crystal Reports or SAP BusinessObjects Web Intelligence document or a universe query.

  To solve this, select Live Office Connection from the Add dropdown list in the Data Manager. Xcelsius will then detect all reports inserted into the Excel file and create a connection for each report object. You can then configure when to trigger these connections to get live data. The parameters of the reports will also prompt when the corresponding connection is triggered.

  One more word here: If you have inserted two different parts of a single report into the Excel file, the number of SAP BusinessObjects Live Office connections detected will be equal to the number of report parts, not the number of reports. That is, there will be two connections, not one, though the data is from one report.

Properties Panel

As mentioned above, selecting Live Office Connection in the Add dropdown list of the Data Manager will force Xcelsius to detect all SAP BusinessObjects reports contained in the imported Excel file and create a connection for each report. That's why you may get a little confused that nothing happened after clicking it, when no report is inserted into the Excel file.

Figure 7.5 shows the Properties panel after the SAP BusinessObjects Enterprise reports in the Excel file are detected. We have inserted two Crystal Reports documents into the Excel file, which is why you see two SAP BusinessObjects Live Office connections in the list.

If your Excel spreadsheet contains more than one view, you can choose one, some, or all of the views listed in the Views area of the Definition tab. Only the data from the views you choose will be refreshed when their corresponding SAP BusinessObjects Live Office connections are refreshed.

The properties in this tab are explained below.

- Name
  The Name field is disabled because it's carried over automatically from the definition of the SAP BusinessObjects Live Office report object, so you cannot change it.

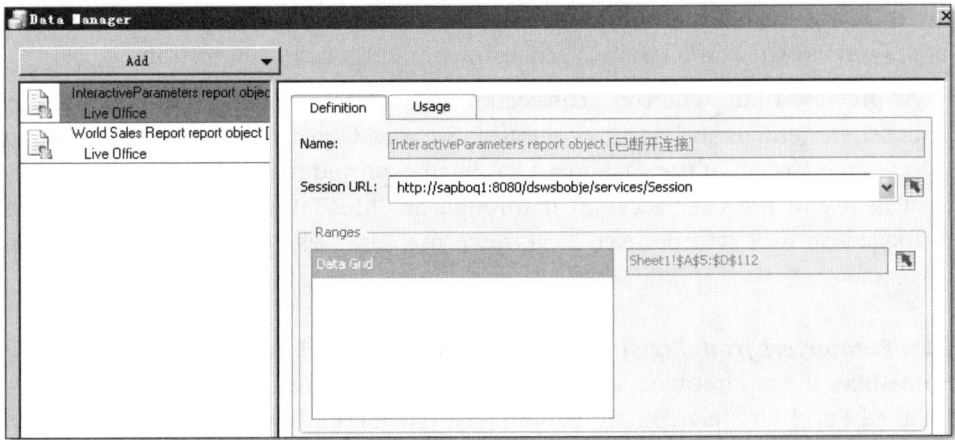

Figure 7.5 Properties of an SAP BusinessObjects Live Office Connection in Data Manager

- Session URL

  The Session URL points to the SAP BusinessObjects Enterprise Web service, which is used to connect to SAP BusinessObjects Live Office data at runtime. You will find an item "*http://<webserver>:8080/dswsbobje/services/session*" in the dropdown list, as a hint about the URL. In our example, we are using *http://sapboq1:8080/dswsbobje/services/Session*.

  Note that the first character of the last word, *Session* is capitalized, because the URL is case-sensitive here, in a Java Enterprise Edition application.

- Ranges

  In the Ranges area, you can bind data ranges of the SAP BusinessObjects Live Office–enabled Excel file into the embedded spreadsheet. By default, the bindings will be detected and configured automatically. There are two situations when you might want to bind the data to another range.

  On one hand, the auto-configured cell range may not be able to cover all possible values. For example, with default parameter values, the data from 10 sales regions is returned, which is bound to a cell range with 10 rows. However, with some parameter values, there may be more than 10 rows. So we need rebind the data to a cell range with the maximum number of rows we want to accept.

  On the other hand, we may want to bind the data to the same location as it is bound to in the old Excel file. For example, in the Excel file, the data is inserted into a range starting from the first row. But in the embedded spreadsheet, the some of the first rows are reserved for our other use, and we want to move them down.

The Usage tab is similar to that of other connectivities. Here, you can configure how to use the connectivity, such as how to trigger the connection.

At preview time, when the connection is triggered, you will be prompted to enter credentials to log on to the SAP BusinessObjects system to retrieve the report. However, if the dashboard has been exported to an SAP BusinessObjects system and the user accesses it through an InfoView, the credentials of the logged-on user will be used to retrieve the data, without the need to log on again.

Pass Parameters from Xcelsius to SAP BusinessObjects Live Office

Sometimes the report object you inserted into the SAP BusinessObjects Live Office–enabled Excel file may contain parameters. For the dashboard to work perfectly, you need to provide some way for the user to input values for those parameters and retrieve the corresponding data.

To make it work, you need to first bind the parameters of a Crystal Reports or SAP BusinessObjects Web Intelligence document to cells in the Excel file, before importing it into Xcelsius. To do this, go to the Live Office object and click Modify Object/Prompt Setting. You'll see the prompt options shown in Figure 7.6.

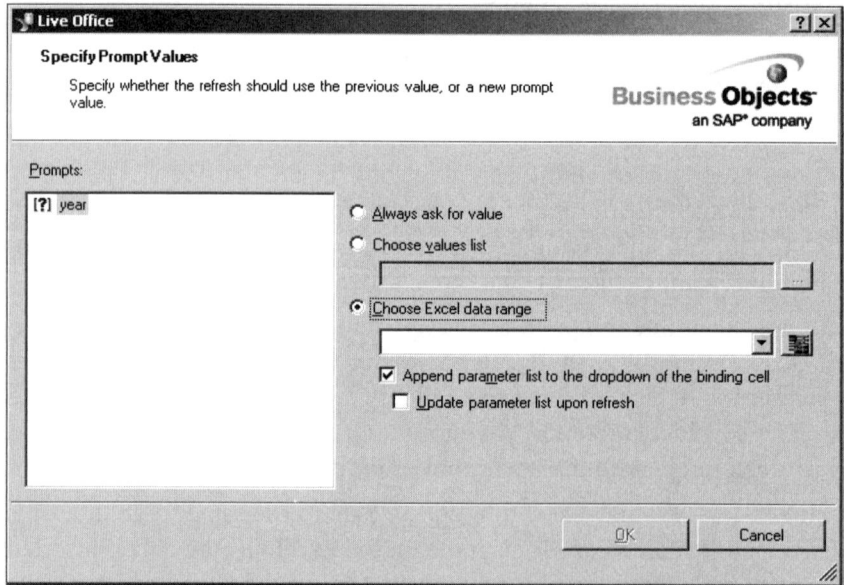

Figure 7.6 Prompt Settings for a Parameter in SAP BusinessObjects Live Office

For each parameter, the following three options are available:

- Always Ask for Value: Each time the document is refreshed, a prompt dialog will ask users for parameter values.
- Choose Values List: Parameter values are pre-specified here.
- Choose Excel Data Range: Bind parameter values to Excel range cells.

Obviously, the third option is the most flexible. Note that when import into Xcelsius, the report also retrieves values from these cells as its parameter values. This is the most important step to make it work. In Xcelsius, we can then bind some input UI components to the cell(s) that are bound to parameter values. The user can then change values through the UI components, triggering the SAP BusinessObjects Live Office connections and consequently refreshing the report objects.

Sometimes you'll note that the Prompt Setting menu item is grayed out. The prerequisites of an active Prompt Setting include:

- The reports inserted as SAP BusinessObjects Live Office object must include parameters.
- The SAP BusinessObjects Live Office object has been refreshed on demand and prompts have been brought out at least once.

The first prerequisite is ensured at report creation time. For the second item, let's take a look at SAP BusinessObjects Live Office refresh options. Go to the Live Office object, and select Refresh Options. A dialog will prompt you as displayed in Figure 7.7.

There are four refresh options you can choose from.

- Latest Instance: This option is applicable when the report has instances. Each time the object is refreshed, data will be retrieved from the last scheduled instance. In this case, no prompts are needed.
- On Demand: The object will be refreshed against the database, and prompts will show up if there are any.
- Use Report Saved Data: The object will be refreshed against data saved along with the report. No prompts are needed.
- Specific Instance: The object will be refreshed against the data from one specified instance. No prompts are needed.

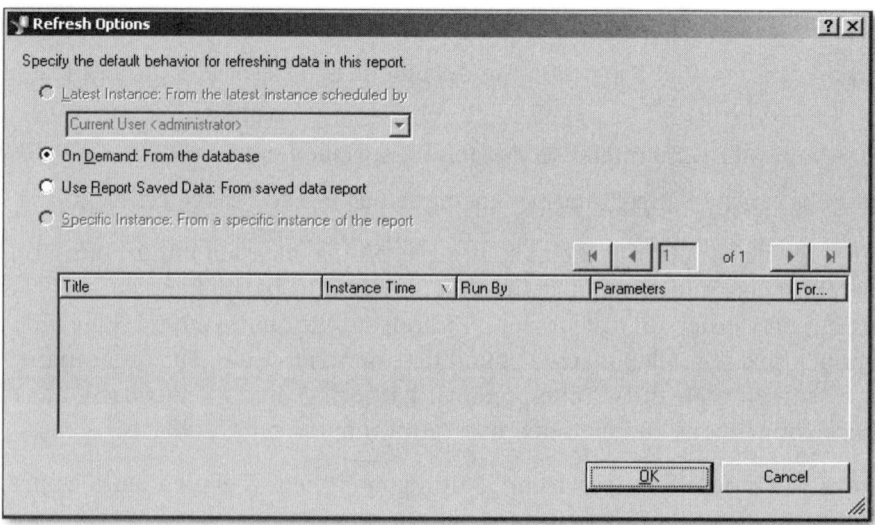

Figure 7.7 Refresh Options for a Parameter in SAP BusinessObjects Live Office

To activate the Prompt Setting menu item, we need to select On Demand. Then you need to refresh the object to bring up the prompt dialog and notify the program that this object has parameters.

7.2.4 Practice

Now let's go through a simple hands-on example to illustrate how to pass parameters from Xcelsius to SAP BusinessObjects Live Office so the user can set parameter values on the dashboard to retrieve corresponding data from the backend.

In this sample, the report is an SAP BusinessObjects Web Intelligence document with a parameter. The user can select one year and see the quantity sold across states for that selected year.

You can follow the steps below to complete this hands-on example.

1. Create an SAP BusinessObjects Web Intelligence document based on the eFashion sample universe from your SAP BusinessObjects system. It's a simple vertical table, including two objects: State and Quantity Sold. Add the Year object as a prompt query filter. Save this SAP BusinessObjects Web Intelligence document to SAP BusinessObjects Enterprise.

2. Create one SAP BusinessObjects Live Office–enabled Excel file, and insert the SAP BusinessObjects Web Intelligence report created in previous step.
3. Ensure that the Refresh option selected is On Demand, and refresh the Live Office object to bring up the prompt dialog.
4. Configure the Prompt Setting to bind prompt the values to cell $K$1, as shown in Figure 7.8.

	A	B	C	D	J	K	L
1	State	Quantity sold				2006	
2	California	17769					
3	Colorado	5116					
4	DC	6491					
5	Florida	4830					
6	Illinois	6519					
7	Massachusetts	5269					
8	New York	19109					
9	Texas	25193					

Figure 7.8 Data of the SAP BusinessObjects Live Office Document in the Embedded Spreadsheet

5. Save the Excel file to your local disk, and import it into a newly created Xcelsius dashboard.
6. Add SAP BusinessObjects Live Office Connections in the Data Manager. Specify a valid session URL. Leave the data binding as the default because this is a simple sample and we don't need to reserve extra space for potential data growing.
7. On the Usage tab of the SAP BusinessObjects Live Office Connection Propertyiessheet, configure the connection to refresh on trigger, and set the trigger cell to Sheet1!$K$1, which is the cell to hold parameter values. Specify it to refresh on value changes.
8. Add a column chart to the canvas. Add one series to bind to the Quantity Sold column, and bind the category labels to the State column. This column chart displays the quantity sold across states.
9. Add a cBox bo the canvas. Enter "2004," "2005," and "2006" to cells Sheet1!$D$1, $D$2, and $D$3, respectively, and bind labels to these three cells. This is a sample, so we'll just hardcode them. Actually, these candidate

items should be read from an SAP BusinessObjects Live Office object too, which could be refreshed when the visualization is loaded.

10. For the Data Insertion options of the combo box, select the insert typeLabel, and set the destination to cell Sheet1!$K$1, which is bound as the prompt value of the Live Office object, and is set as the trigger cell of SAP BusinessObjects Live Office Connection. At runtime, when the value of this critical cell changes, the SAP BusinessObjects Live Office Connection will be refreshed, and the value of this cell will be passed to the underlying report, to retrieve the accordant data.

Now we are done. You can click Preview to test the dashboard you have just created. Select among different year values, and you can see that the data in the column chart changes accordingly; it is processed by SAP BusinessObjects Live Office and then SAP BusinessObjects Web Intelligence behind it. The effect is illustrated in Figure 7.9.

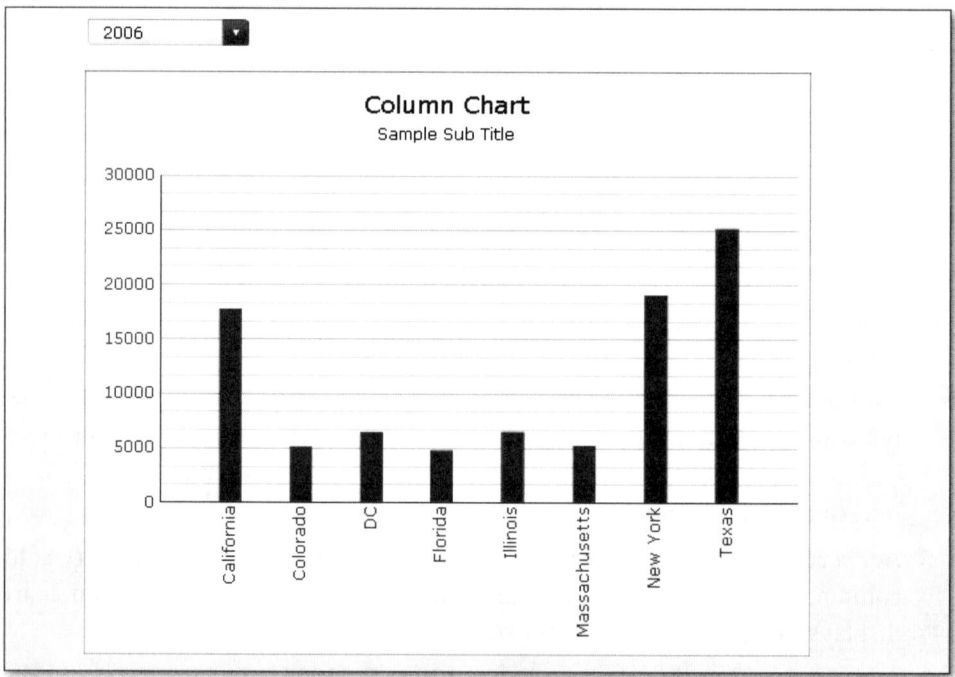

Figure 7.9 Final Effect of this Hands-On Example Using SAP BusinessObjects Live Office Connections

7.3 Crystal Reports Data Consumer

Crystal Reports is the SAP BusinessObjects flagship reporting product. It allows report designers to create highly formatted reports from virtually any data source and deliver them via email, Microsoft Office, Adobe PDF, or embedded in enterprise applications. With the release of the 2008 version, Crystal Reports greatly improves its interactivity feature, which empowers business users to easily manipulate data for deeper business insight.

The Crystal Reports data consumer connectivity allows you to insert Xcelsius dashboards into Crystal Reports 2008, and feed live data from them into Xcelsius. In this way you leverage and improve existing Crystal Reports documents or add the power of Xcelsius to new Crystal Reports documents. The integration of Xcelsius and Crystal Reports is one of the interactivity enhancements in Crystal Reports 2008. This integration enables report designers to embed Xcelsius visualization into Crystal Reports and link report data to the visualization, with the help of this connectivity defined in Xcelsius.

Figure 7.10 shows a simple report in the Crystal Reports 2008 designer environment, with an Xcelsius dashboard embedded.

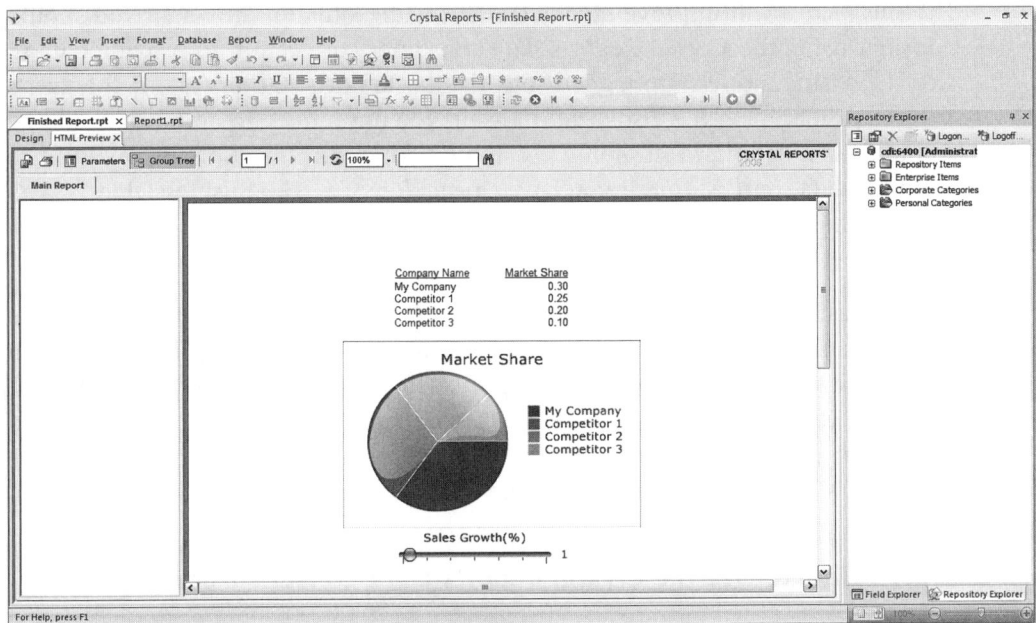

Figure 7.10 Insert an SWF File Created by Xcelsius 2008 in Crystal Reports

You need to be familiar with Crystal Reports to understand this section. You should already be able to create basic reports in Crystal Reports.

7.3.1 When to Use the Crystal Reports Data Consumer Connection

Xcelsius is primarily a data presentation tool, while Crystal Reports is better at data processing, complex formatting, and accurate printing. Because of their different features, they are used in different scenarios to meet different business requirements. Xcelsius often presents high-level data with rich interactivity to decision makers, and Crystal Reports can provide you with a solid starting point for your business intelligence strategy by helping you securely deliver the most requested pieces of information as highly formatted reports to end users.

Generally, you may choose such a connectivity if you want to combine the advantages of Crystal Reports and Xcelsius, providing intuitive analysis and formatted enterprise-level reporting into one single Crystal Reports document.

With the development of the business intelligence infrastructure, the end users' demands also grow. The consumers of the formatted reports may ask for more intuitive charts, easier data access, or even what-if scenario models inside the reports. Their primary concerns are still the detailed information, while the interactivity Xcelsius brings will improve efficiency. This is the situation in which you should consider using the Crystal Reports data consumer connection to provide data to Xcelsius visual models embedded into Crystal Reports. Otherwise, if the user's focus is primarily on the visualization itself, you don't need to bother embedding it into Crystal Reports. You should use another kind of connection to pull live data from the data sources. And if you have Crystal Reports, SAP BusinessObjects Web Intelligence, or universe data in place, Crystal Reports Live Office Connection may be your best choice.

Some other technical limitations could prevent you from using the Crystal Reports data consumer connections. Keep in mind that exporting and printing of Flash objects with connections to Crystal Reports data is not supported, and embedded Flash objects that do not have connections to Crystal Reports data can be exported to PDF only, so if you have a requirement to export and print, you may not be able to use the Crystal Reports data consumer connection.

7.3.2 How to Use the Crystal Reports Data Consumer Connection

To embed Xcelsius visualization into Crystal Reports, you need to work with both Xcelsius and Crystal Reports designer. Usually, you create a Crystal Reports report first to prepare data for Xcelsius. Then you design the dashboard in Xcelsius and configure the Crystal Reports data consumer connection, which is required for linking with Crystal Reports data later. Now that you have both the Crystal Reports and Xcelsius visual models ready, you insert the exported SWF document into the Crystal Reports document, and finally, you set your Xcelsius model to receive real-time Crystal Reports data. Again, we assume you already have adequate skills to build Xcelsius dashboards and Crystal Reports reports, so we'll focus on configuring the Crystal Reports Data Consumer connection and linking Crystal Reports data.

Connection

You add the Crystal Report data consumer connection in the Data Manager by selecting this type in the Add dropdown list, just like what you do for other connections. You can add only one connection of this type in a single dashboard, which is the same as Flash Variables and Portal Data.

Figure 7.11 shows the Properties panel of the Crystal Report data consumer connection.

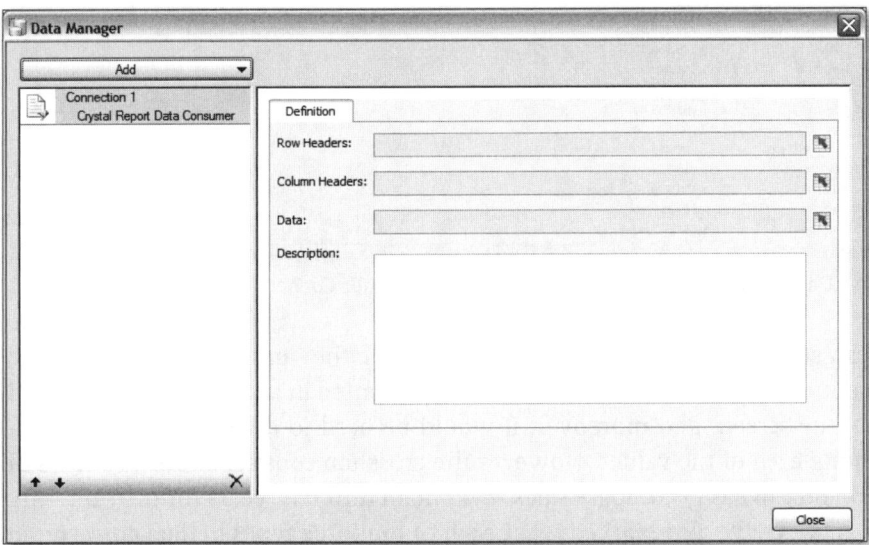

Figure 7.11 Definition of a Crystal Reports Data Consumer Connection

As shown in this figure, the Crystal Reports data consumer connection pulls three types of data from Crystal Reports and populates the embedded Excel spreadsheet with that data. These three types of data, Row Headers, Column Headers, and Data Range, essentially form a cross-tabulation, or cross-tab. A cross-tab is a very efficient way to display measures with two dimensions. It can provide greater insight than a simple vertical table or a horizontal table within a smaller space. If your work involves analyzing data in Excel, you must be familiar with the PivotTable functionality in Excel, which, in essence, creates a cross-tab.

Figure 7.12 shows an example comparing a vertical table with a cross-tab created by PivotTable functionality in Excel.

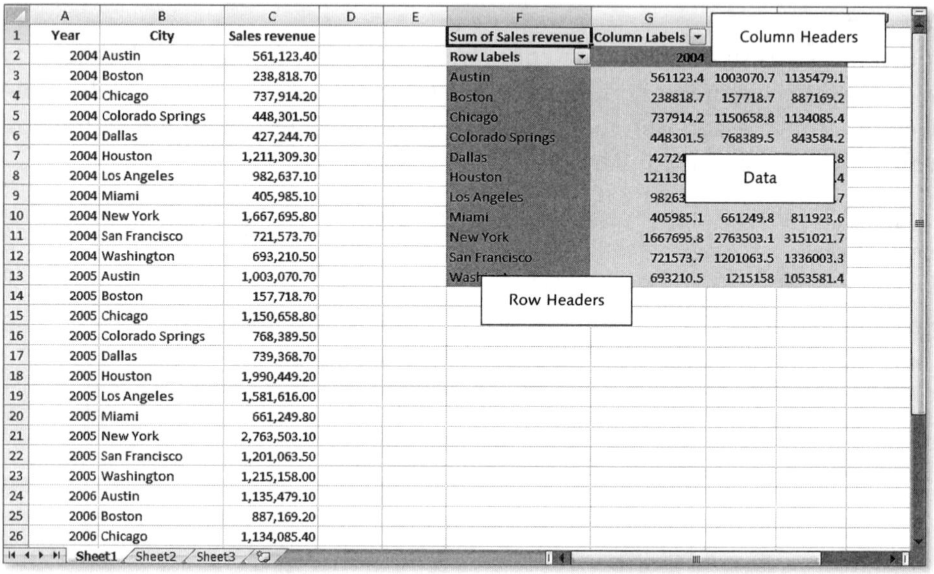

Figure 7.12 Data Bindings for a Crystal Reports Data Consumer Connection

As you can see from this figure, both tables provide the same information, that is, sales revenue by year and city. If the data was presented in a vertical table, it would not fit in one screen, and moreover, it would be hard to determine the relationships among each of the values. However the cross-tab consists of only 10 rows of data, and you can easily compare sales revenue in different years for the same city or vice versa . We've also marked what each of the three types of data correspond to in Figure 7.12. You can see that Xcelsius refers to column labels in a pivot table as column headers, and row labels as row headers.

Cross-tabs are very useful. Moreover, please also keep in mind that they are very important in Xcelsius. For example, when you bind data by range for a chart that supports multiple series of data, a column chart for instance, you can bind all of the information needed — the series name, values, category labels — all at once if you organize your data into a cross-tab. How are you going to create a similar column chart if your data is in a vertical table, as shown in Figure 7.12 above? It would be very hard or even impossible to achieve this.

Now let's consider the difference between Query as a Web Service connections and SAP BusinessObjects Live Office connections that we discussed in previous sections this chapter. QaaWS connections usually bring back data as vertical tables, while SAP BusinessObjects Live Office connections can leverage other SAP BusinessObjects reporting capabilities to receive data as cross-tabs. This can determine which type of connection to use, depending on whether a chart with multiple series of data is needed. For the Crystal Reports Data Consumer connection, a crosstab is the best way to organize your data. That's why we recommend that you always organize your data in cross-tabs if possible.

You may wonder what to do if your data has only one series. If that is the case, you can omit the binding for row headers or column headers to link to a vertical table or a horizontal data table. That being said, you should be aware that you don't need to bind all three of these types of data. You can even bind only row header, only column header, or only data, although that would be hardly useful.

In the Description text box, you can enter some information to describe how to bind the data later in Crystal Reports. This could become necessary if the Xcelsius designer and the Crystal Reports designer are not the same person or are in different development groups, so that the Crystal Reports designer may be confused about the format of the data the Xcelsius dashboard requires. It is best practice to document how to bind data in this text box.

Integration with Crystal Reports

After you've built the dashboard, with a Crystal Reports data consumer connection properly set up, you export it to an SWF file via the menu path FILE • EXPORT • SWF. Now you open a report in Crystal Reports 2008 Designer and insert the SWF file into the report by selecting Insert Flash in the Insert menu. A dialog box will pop up, as displayed in Figure 7.13, in which you can choose an SWF file and specify whether to embed it into the Crystal Reports document or create a link to the original SWF file only. To save you trouble when you migrate the Crystal Reports document to another environment, select the Embed option, though it may slightly increase the size of the Crystal Reports document.

Now that you've added the SWF file exported by Xcelsius into Crystal Reports, you need to link the Crystal Reports data. To do this, you launch Flash Data Expert in the context menu of the Flash Object. The Flash Data Expert interface is divided into two parts. On the left, available fields in the report are listed, and you can drag them into the boxes below to bind a field to row headers, column headers, or data. Each of these three boxes is only available if the corresponding part in the Crystal Reports data consumer is bound to cells in the Excel worksheet. For example, the Xcelsius designer needs a horizontal table of data, so he binds only the row headers and data in the Crystal Reports data consumer connection in Xcelsius. Then there will be only an Insert Row Label box and an Insert Data Values box in the Flash Data Expert for you to bind Crystal Reports data. On the right, a preview window shows what the Xcelsius dashboard looks like under the current binding configuration. The description entered in the Crystal Reports data consumer connection is displayed under the Preview window, which is useful for others to understand your idea.

Figure 7.13 Insert an SWF Object into Crystal Reports 2008

As displayed in Figure 7.14, we inserted the Year field into the column headers, the Store Name field into the row headers, and the Sales Revenue filed into the data values. The figure shows the preview of the data and the Xcelsius visual model.

The Flash Data Expert has a close relationship with the cross-tab feature in Crystal Reports. When you specify row headers, column headers, and data values in the Flash Data Expert, Crystal Reports generates the cross-tab data and passes it to the embedded Xcelsius dashboard. Note that some data values may not be directly available in the database. Crystal Reports has to summarize the data to calculate the aggregated values if that is the case.

Now let's see how a Crystal Reports native cross-tab is created. The cross-tab defined in the Crystal Reports data consumer connection should have the same properties as the Crystal Reports native cross-tab. Figure 7.15 shows the Cross-Tab Expert, which can create a native Crystal Reports cross-tab. To define the cross-tab data, you insert zero or more fields into rows, columns, and summarized fields. This means that for the Crystal Reports data consumer connection, you can also insert zero or more fields into row headers, column headers, and data.

Crystal Reports Data Consumer | **7.3**

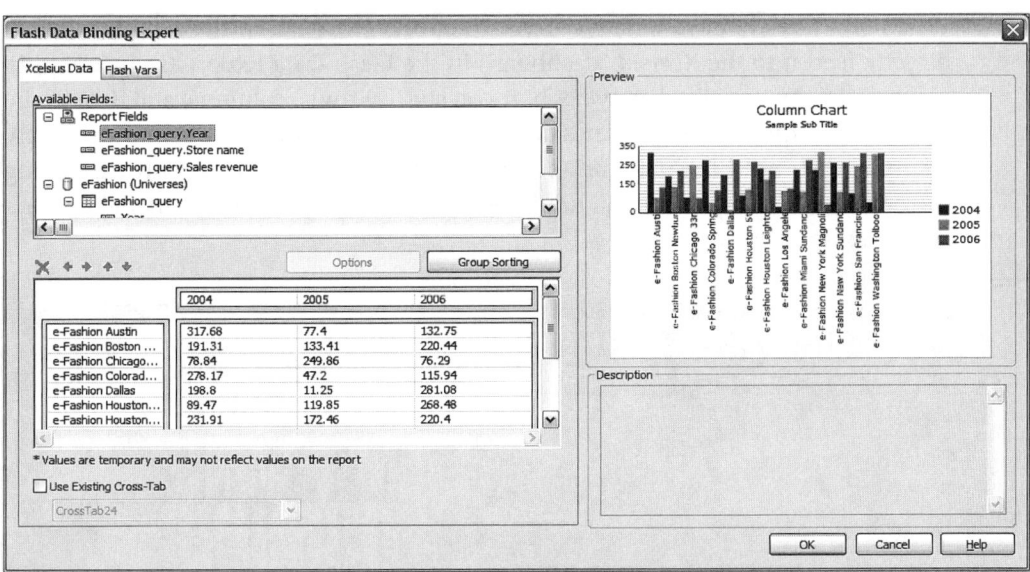

Figure 7.14 Data Mapping in the Data Binding Expert Inside Crystal Reports 2008

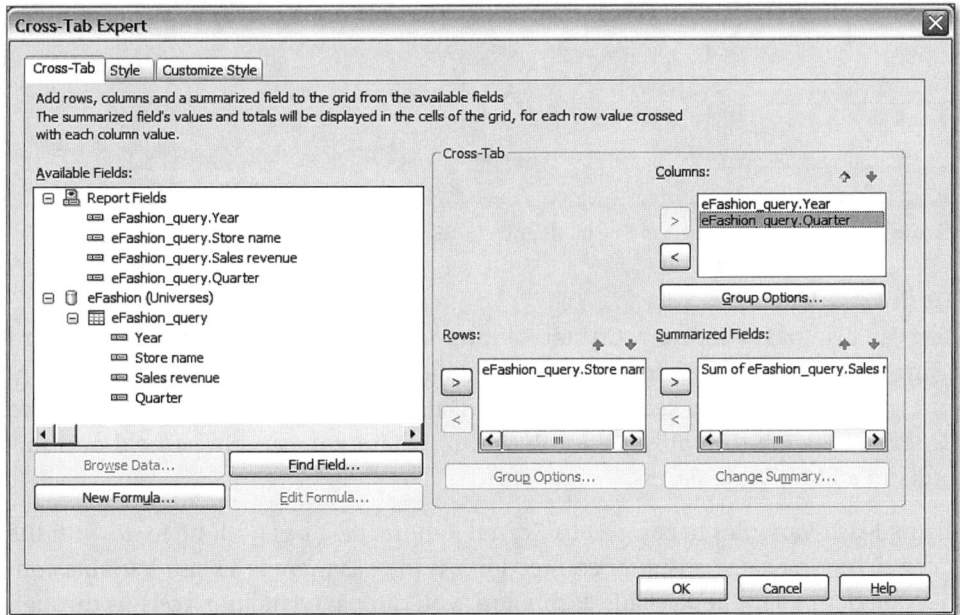

Figure 7.15 Cross-Tab Expert in Crystal Reports 2008

7 | Advanced Data Connectivity

When you already have a native Crystal Reports cross-tab in the report, you can directly feed it to the Xcelsius dashboard in the Flash Data Expert as illustrated in Figure 7.16. As explained above, when you specify rows, columns, and data in the Flash Data Expert, you're essentially creating a native Crystal Reports cross-tab, so if you only need the data for Xcelsius dashboard instead of actually displaying the cross-tab in the report, you don't need to create a cross-tab in Crystal Reports and use this option.

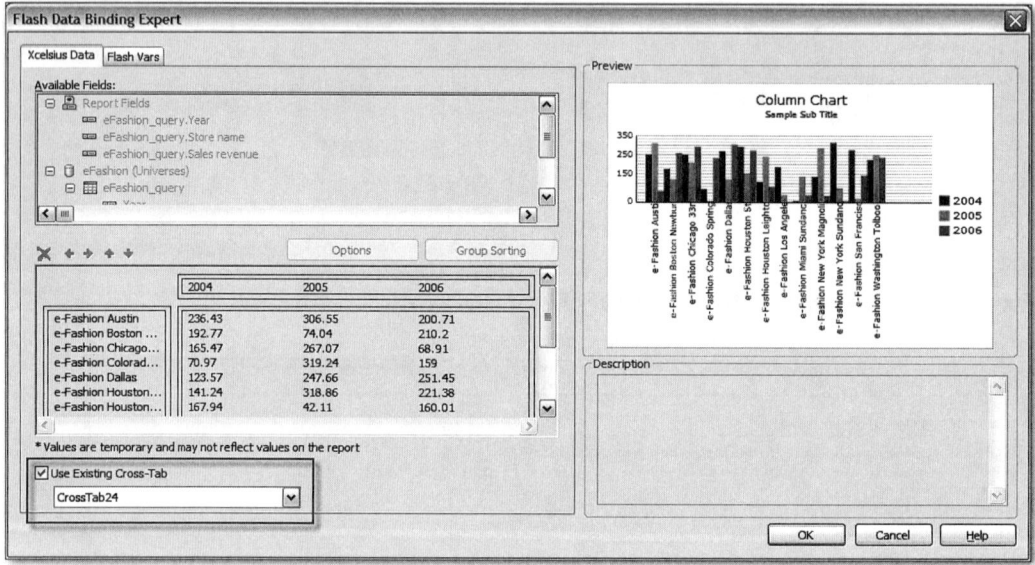

Figure 7.16 Flash Data Expert in Crystal Reports 2008

Flash Variables

You can also pass data from Crystal Reports to the embedded Xcelsius dashboard using Flash Variables if the Xcelsius dashboard has a Flash Variable connection. In Figure 7.17, you can see that the Flash Data Expert for this Flash object has no Xcelsius Data tab, but only a Flash Vars tab, where you can bind a field or a formula to a Flash Variable.

Using Flash Variables to connect to Crystal Reports data has nothing to do with the Crystal Reports data consumer connection. As long as there is a Flash Variable connection defined in the Xcelsius dashboard, you can pass data into Xcelsius through the Flash Data Expert using Flash Vars. This is primarily used with Xcelsius 4.5, the previous version of Xcelsius, in which the Crystal Reports data consumer connection was not yet provided.

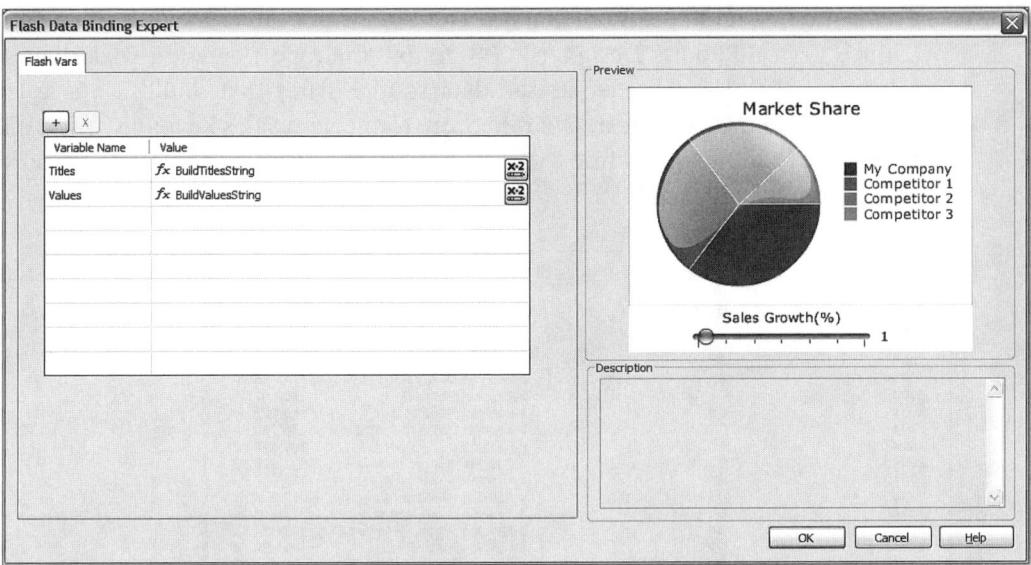

Figure 7.17 Data Binding as Flash Variables

Basically, to work with Xcelsius 2008, you can use these two methods interchangeably, but the Crystal Reports data consumer connection is easier to use. For the Flash Variables connection, you usually have to create Excel formulas to transform the data to the format the Flash Variable connection requires: either CSV or XML.

As a result, we recommend using the Crystal Reports data consumer connection instead of the Flash Variable connection for Xcelsius 2008 models. If you're still using Xcelsius 4.5, you have to use the Flash Variable connection.

7.3.3 Practice

Now let's go through a simple hands-on example to illustrate how to embed an Xcelsius dashboard into a Crystal Report document and connect live Crystal Reports data using the Crystal Reports data consumer connection.

In this practice, we'll create a Crystal Reports document connecting to the eFashion sample universe from your SAP BusinessObjects system. You can use any data source you'd like if you don't have access to an SAP BusinessObjects system. You'll also build a column chart that will display multiple series of data.

7 | Advanced Data Connectivity

1. Create the Crystal Reports document.

   Launch Crystal Reports Designer 2008, follow the report creation wizard, and select the eFashion universe as the data source. After that, build a query to include the four objects Year, Quarter, Store Name, and Sales Revenue. Insert all four fields from the query into the Details section in the report. Now the report should look like Figure 7.18.

   3/28/2010

Year	Quarter	Store name	Sales revenue
2004	Q1	e-Fashion Austin	197,890.70
2004	Q1	e-Fashion Boston Newbury	92,595.50
2004	Q1	e-Fashion Chicago 33rd	256,453.80
2004	Q1	e-Fashion Colorado Springs	131,796.90
2004	Q1	e-Fashion Dallas	150,687.00
2004	Q1	e-Fashion Houston 5th	166,035.00
2004	Q1	e-Fashion Houston Leighton	244,183.00
2004	Q1	e-Fashion Los Angeles	308,928.00
2004	Q1	e-Fashion Miami Sundance	137,529.70
2004	Q1	e-Fashion New York Magnolia	333,357.80
2004	Q1	e-Fashion New York Sundance	222,625.30
2004	Q1	e-Fashion San Francisco	210,292.40
2004	Q1	e-Fashion Washington Tolbo(	208,324.40
2004	Q2	e-Fashion Austin	154,038.50
2004	Q2	e-Fashion Boston Newbury	70,902.70
2004	Q2	e-Fashion Chicago 33rd	241,148.70
2004	Q2	e-Fashion Colorado Springs	129,076.30
2004	Q2	e-Fashion Dallas	114,990.60
2004	Q2	e-Fashion Houston 5th	145,045.50
2004	Q2	e-Fashion Houston Leighton	201,002.00
2004	Q2	e-Fashion Los Angeles	252,558.40
2004	Q2	e-Fashion Miami Sundance	121,170.30
2004	Q2	e-Fashion New York Magnolia	288,881.90
2004	Q2	e-Fashion New York Sundance	191,079.60
2004	Q2	e-Fashion San Francisco	188,935.80
2004	Q2	e-Fashion Washington Tolbo(	179,863.10
2004	Q3	e-Fashion Austin	81,982.20
2004	Q3	e-Fashion Boston Newbury	12,065.50
2004	Q3	e-Fashion Chicago 33rd	107,005.50
2004	Q3	e-Fashion Colorado Springs	85,620.90
2004	Q3	e-Fashion Dallas	73,164.10
2004	Q3	e-Fashion Houston 5th	74,144.10
2004	Q3	e-Fashion Houston Leighton	99,823.00
2004	Q3	e-Fashion Los Angeles	232,326.80
2004	Q3	e-Fashion Miami Sundance	50,926.20
2004	Q3	e-Fashion New York Magnolia	162,451.50
2004	Q3	e-Fashion New York Sundance	94,662.40
2004	Q3	e-Fashion San Francisco	161,981.80
2004	Q3	e-Fashion Washington Tolbo(	131,686.70
2004	Q4	e-Fashion Austin	127,212.00
2004	Q4	e-Fashion Boston Newbury	63,255.00
2004	Q4	e-Fashion Chicago 33rd	133,306.20
2004	Q4	e-Fashion Colorado Springs	101,807.40
2004	Q4	e-Fashion Dallas	88,403.00
2004	Q4	e-Fashion Houston 5th	143,853.90
2004	Q4	e-Fashion Houston Leighton	137,222.80
2004	Q4	e-Fashion Los Angeles	188,823.90
2004	Q4	e-Fashion Miami Sundance	96,358.90
2004	Q4	e-Fashion New York Magnolia	238,369.50
2004	Q4	e-Fashion New York Sundance	136,267.80
2004	Q4	e-Fashion San Francisco	160,363.70
2004	Q4	e-Fashion Washington Tolbo(	173,336.30
2005	Q1	e-Fashion Austin	263,162.20
2005	Q1	e-Fashion Chicago 33rd	334,296.80
2005	Q1	e-Fashion Colorado Springs	189,131.40
2005	Q1	e-Fashion Dallas	188,897.50
2005	Q1	e-Fashion Houston 5th	214,874.30
2005	Q1	e-Fashion Houston Leighton	347,358.90

Figure 7.18 Data in the Crystal Reports Document

2. Create the Xcelsius dashboard.

   Drag a column chart component onto the canvas, resize it to the size you want, and change the title of the chart to something descriptive, for example, "Sales Revenue by Store." Click the Fit Canvas to Components button in the toolbar to shrink the canvas to avoid unnecessary blanks. You can increase the canvas a little by clicking the Increase Canvas button in the toolbar for a better look and feel.

   The chart will display sales revenues from all of the e-fashion stores over several years. Each year will have its own series of data, and data will be in columns, so you'll put years on column headers and store names on row headers. Before you actually bind cells, you may want to go back to Crystal Reports to see how many years and how many stores are there so you'll know how big a data range to bind. In the report, you can find that there are 13 stores and 3 years of data. It's a good idea to bind a range bigger than this because the volume of data might increase in the future, and you can leverage the ignore end blanks feature of Xcelsius charts to avoid unnecessary blanks. So the range $B$1 to $F$5 will be column headers and will be filled with years; the range $A$2 to $A$16 will be row headers and will be filled with store names; the range $B$2 to $F$16 will be data values and will be filled with sales revenue data. Binding these ranges for the column chart is a little bit tedious. Because there is no data in the range, Xcelsius can't make a perfect guess if you bind by range, so you need to bind each series manually. You need to add five series. Each series name is bound to a cell in the column headers range. Each series' values are bound to a column in the data values range. The category labels will be bound to the row headers range. Don't forget to enable both the Ignore Values and Ignore Series options in the behavior Properties sheet.

   Now that the data is properly planned and bound to the column chart, you need to add a Crystal Reports data consumer connection and bind the column headers range, the row headers range, and the data range. This should be very easy. And you should leave some instruction in the description field to tell the Crystal Reports developer, yourself in this case, that the column headers should be years and the row headers should be store names.

   When you've finished, the workspace of your Xcelsius dashboard should look something like Figure 7.19. When everything is set, export the Xcelsius dashboard to an SWF document.

7 | Advanced Data Connectivity

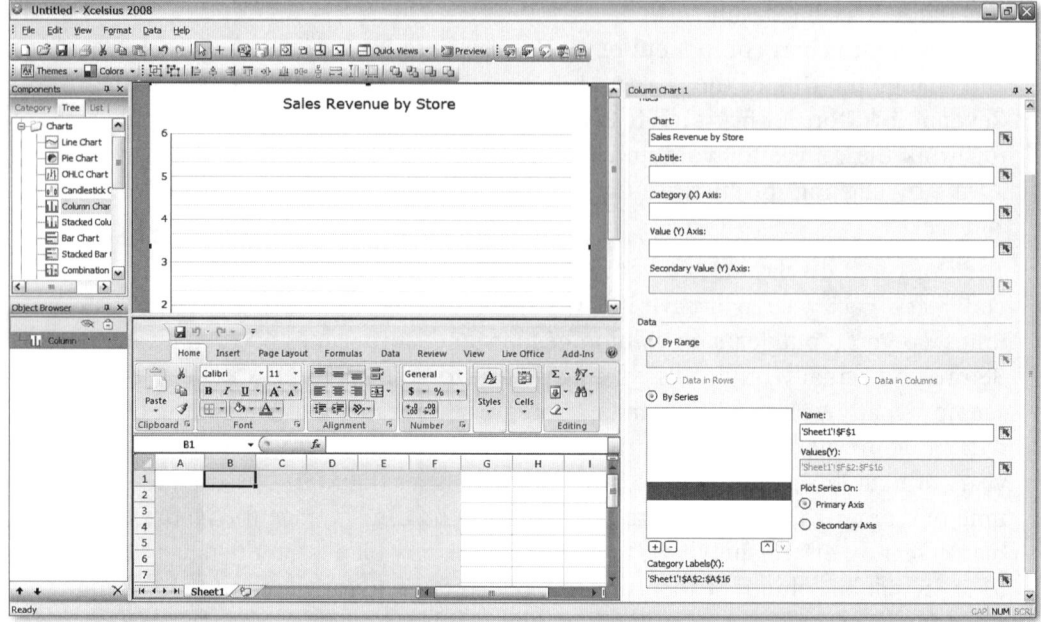

Figure 7.19 Data Binding in Xcelsius

3. Embed the Xcelsius model.

   Switch back to the Crystal Reports Designer. Now you'll insert the SWF file into the report. Select INSERT • FLASH to insert the SWF file into the Report Header section. Right-click the Flash object you have just added and launch the Flash Data Expert in the context menu. You then need to drag Year to the column header, Store Name to the row header, and Sales Revenue to the data to finish the data binding.

   You've finished this hands-on example. You can now preview the report to see the final result. It should look like Figure 7.20.

7.4 Flash Variables

Flash movies are usually hosted by a container, either the Adobe Flash Player or an HTML file. Thus, they are integrated with other parts of the container. If there is no way for Flash movies to communicate with the outer container that hosts them, the Flash technology will not be flexible. Adobe provides technologies for Flash movies to interact with their containers. Flash variables is one of those technologies, and it is an efficient method of importing variables into the Flash movies.

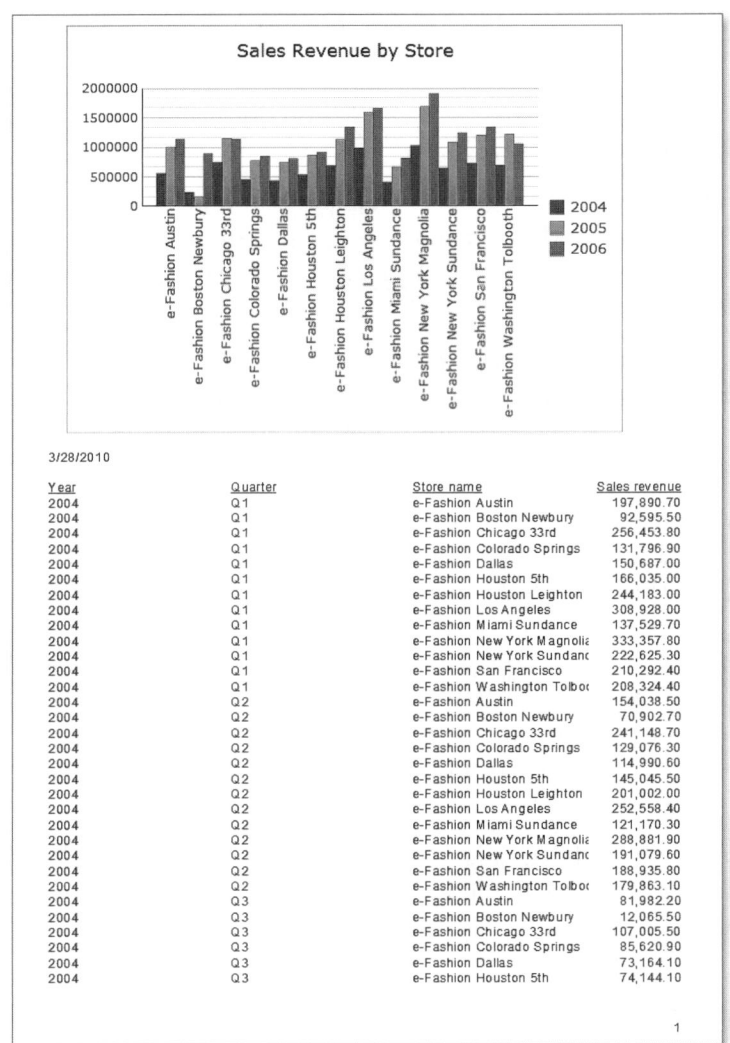

Figure 7.20 Final Effect of this Hands-On Example

Later in this chapter, you'll learn about more complicated technologies that enable interactivities such as method invocation.

In Xcelsius, the Flash Variables connectivity allows you to pass data to Xcelsius directly from the container. Flash variables itself is only a string of characters, but Xcelsius automatically encodes the variables for you so that the value of each variable can be mapped to a cell range in the embedded spreadsheet. Moreover, named ranges, which we mentioned in Chapter 6 when we discussed the XML data connectivity, are also supported to leverage your effort in Excel and reduce the time required to set up each variable.

7.4.1 When to Use Flash Variables

You usually use the Flash Variables technology when a Flash movie needs some information that is only available when the movie is first initialized. Usually, such information is provided by the container of the movie. This holds true for the Flash variables connections in Xcelsius.

For example, let's you are integrating an Xcelsius dashboard into a legacy web application. The dashboard will compare data pulled from the database with data the user enters on the page via HTML controls. You can use the Flash variables connection to import data into the dashboard from the HTML container.

You may think that you can use another connectivity such as XML data to retrieve such data on loading the dashboard. You can, but imagine another scenario where the data required by Xcelsius cannot be retrieved by any other data connectivity. For example, your dashboard is wrapped in an HTML file of a web application hosted on a web application server. The user needs to log on to the web application by entering his username and password before accessing the HTML file. Inside your dashboard, you need to retrieve the credentials such as username and password of the user who is currently accessing it. You have no other way to get his credentials but using Flash variables.

In such a case, you can use a Flash Variables connectivity to pass in the global session variables, so that the Flash movie can get the serialized session, token, user ID, and so on, and reuse them inside the Flash movie itself.

7.4.2 How to Use Flash Variables

To use a Flash Variables connection, launch the Data Manager and select Flash Variable in the Add dropdown list. In contrast to other connectivity types, to which many connections can be added in one dashboard, you can only add one Flash Variables connection. If one is already added, you'll find the Flash Variable option grayed out in the Add dropdown list.

This is easy to understand. Because a single Flash Variables connection can manage as many Flash variables as you want, there is essentially no need to create multiple Flash Variables connections for one Xcelsius dashboard.

The Properties panel of a Flash Variables connectivity is very simple, with only one tab, as displayed in Figure 7.21.

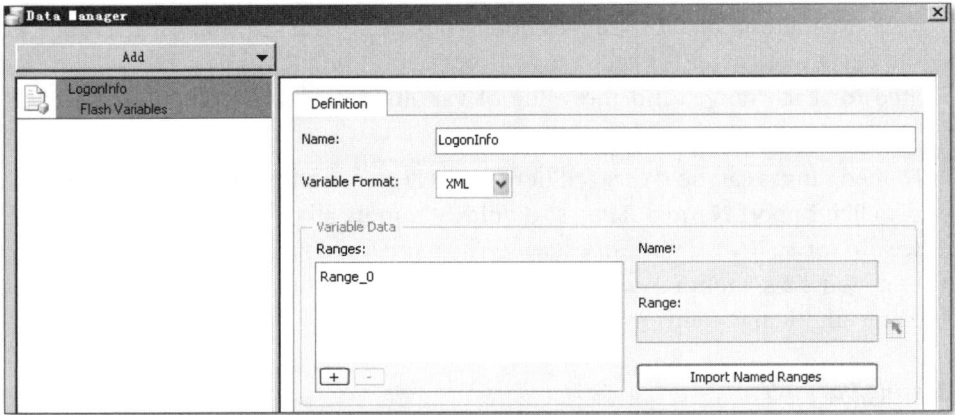

Figure 7.21 Definition of a Flash Variables Connection

The meanings of each property and how to use them are explained below.

Definition
▶ Name
You can enter a descriptive name for the connection. Although there will be only one Flash variables connection, a descriptive name will be helpful.

▶ Variable Format
We've mentioned that Flash variables are simple strings. When a single Flash variable is bound to a range of cells in the Excel worksheet, Xcelsius applies some kind of encoding method to the data. The variable format option is where you can specify this encoding method. You can select the CSV format or the XML format.

For example, let's say you have a range of three cells that the value of a Flash variable will fill in. Now let's show what the value of the Flash variable should be for both formats. In the CSV format, the value of the variable would be:

```
January,Febrary,March
```

In XML format, the value of the variable would be:

```
<data><row><column>FRANCE</column></row><row><column>SPAIN</column></row><row><column>COLOMBIA</column></row></data>
```

You can see that this format is identical to the one the XML data connection requires.

- Variable Data

  You can add one or more ranges here. You specify a name and bind a range in the Excel worksheet for each range. A corresponding Flash variable will be created for each range, and the value of variable will fill the range in the Excel worksheet.

  Named ranges can be leveraged here for easy creation of variables. You can simply click Import Named Ranges to quickly import all of the named ranges, like we did for an XML data connectivity. The names and ranges of all named ranges that you have defined will be automatically specified in the corresponding Name and Range fields.

Passing Variables

After setting up the Flash variables connection, you will not be able to see any effect without putting the generated SWF movie into a container. The easiest way is to use the Export to HTML functionality in Xcelsius to generate a default HMTL container of the movie. The user can then see your dashboard by accessing the HTML file through a web browser.

Normally, if you specify the file name of the exported HTML file as visualization.html, the generated HTML file will be similar to:

```
<HTML>
<HEAD>
<TITLE>visualization.swf</TITLE>
</HEAD>
<BODY>
<OBJECT classid="clsid:D27CDB6E-AE6D-11cf-96B8-444553540000"
codebase="http://fpdownload.adobe.com/pub/shockwave/cabs/flash/swflash.cab#version=9,0,0,0"
WIDTH="690" HEIGHT="490" id="myMovieName">
<PARAM NAME="movie" VALUE="visualization.swf">
<PARAM NAME="quality" VALUE="high">
<PARAM NAME="bgcolor" VALUE="#FFFFFF">
<PARAM NAME="play" VALUE="true">
<PARAM NAME="loop" VALUE="true">
<PARAM NAME=bgcolor VALUE="#FFFFFF">
<EMBED src="visualization.swf" quality=high bgcolor=#FFFFFF WIDTH="690" HEIGHT="490"
```

```
NAME="myMovieName" ALIGN="" TYPE="application/x-shockwave-flash"
play="true" loop="true"
PLUGINSPAGE="http://www.adobe.com/shockwave/download/index.cgi?P1_Prod_
Version=ShockwaveFlash">
</EMBED>
</OBJECT>
</BODY>
</HTML>
```

If the visualization.xlf file has a Flash variables connection defined inside it, the generated HTML will become:

```
<HTML>
<HEAD>
<TITLE>visualization.swf</TITLE>
</HEAD>
<BODY>
<OBJECT classid="clsid:D27CDB6E-AE6D-11cf-96B8-444553540000"
codebase="http://fpdownload.adobe.com/pub/shockwave/cabs/flash/swflash.
cab#version=9,0,0,0"
WIDTH="690" HEIGHT="490" id="myMovieName">
<PARAM NAME=FlashVars VALUE="COUNTRIES=%3Cdata%3E%3Crow%3E%3Ccolumn%3EF
RANCE%3C%2Fcolumn%3E%3C%2Frow%3E%3Crow%3E%3Ccolumn%3ESPAIN%3C%2Fcolumn%
3E%3C%2Frow%3E%3Crow%3E%3Ccolumn%3ECOLOMBIA%3C%2Fcolumn%3E%3C%2Frow%3E%
3C%2Fdata%3E">
<PARAM NAME="movie" VALUE="visualization.swf">
<PARAM NAME="quality" VALUE="high">
<PARAM NAME="bgcolor" VALUE="#FFFFFF">
<PARAM NAME="play" VALUE="true">
<PARAM NAME="loop" VALUE="true">
<PARAM NAME=bgcolor VALUE="#FFFFFF">
<EMBED src="visualization.swf" quality=high bgcolor=#FFFFFF WIDTH="690"
HEIGHT="490"
NAME="myMovieName" ALIGN="" TYPE="application/x-shockwave-flash"
play="true" loop="true"
FlashVars="COUNTRIES=%3Cdata%3E%3Crow%3E%3Ccolumn%3EFRANCE%3C%2Fcolumn%
3E%3C%2Frow%3E%3Crow%3E%3Ccolumn%3ESPAIN%3C%2Fcolumn%3E%3C%2Frow%3E%3Cr
ow%3E%3Ccolumn%3ECOLOMBIA%3C%2Fcolumn%3E%3C%2Frow%3E%3C%2Fdata%3E"
PLUGINSPAGE="http://www.adobe.com/shockwave/download/index.cgi?P1_Prod_
Version=ShockwaveFlash">
</EMBED>
</OBJECT>
</BODY>
</HTML>
```

We've highlighted the additional information in the second HTML file in red. You need an extra `PARAM` tag whose `NAME` attribute is always `FlashVars`, and the `VALUE` attribute is the variable key value pairs. The format is `variable_name=variable_value`. If there are multiple variables, they'll be concatenated by "&" signs, such as:

`variable_name1=variable_value1&variable_name2=variable_value2`.

In our example, there's only one parameter, named COUNTRIES, and its value is an encoded XML string, because we have chosen XML as the variable format.

The other thing to add is the `FlashVars` attribute in the `EMBED` tag. Its value should be the same as that of the VALUE attribute mentioned above. You must make these two changes simultaneously to make the Flash variable work on all browsers.

You may also notice that the texts have been URL encoded, which is an encoding scheme to avoid non-ASCII characters in URLs. For strings inside Flash variables, URL encoding is required, so special characters such as <, >, &, =, and spaces, will be changes to something like %3C and %20.

Now when you open this HTML document in your web browser, the SWF movie is loaded, and the values are assigned to the `COUNTRIES` Flash variable, the range corresponding to which will be updated. You can modify the values of the Flash variable in the HTML document to change what you want to see on the dashboard and, more practically, you can automatically generate the HTML document via a web application.

7.5 FS Command

FS Command is an Adobe Flash technology that enables Flash to communicate with either the Flash Player or the program hosting the Flash Player such as a web browser, through JavaScript. For example, a Flash file can use FS Command to execute a piece of JavaScript statement in a web browser.

Xcelsius provides an FS Command connection as one of its standard data connection types. With FS Command, your dashboard can invoke JavaScript code written in its container, either the Flash Player or a web browser.

If you are familiar with the Action Script language, you may know the function `fscommand` with the two parameters `command` and `parameters`. This data connectivity is similar to the Action Script function `fscommand`. You can refer to:

http://www.adobe.com/support/flash/action_scripts/actionscript_dictionary/action-script_dictionary372.html

for more info about its usage.

7.5.1 When to Use FS Command

You may choose an FS Command connectivity when you want to control the behavior of the dashboard's container (either the Flash Player or the host such as a web server) from inside the dashboard. For example, you can maximize the browser window or display an alert message using JavaScript when the user has done something, from within the dashboard.

Another scenario in which you might choose an FS Command connectivity is when you want to pass data from your dashboard to its container. For example, you can pass data about your dashboard, such as the currently selected value from a combo box, to a piece of JavaScript code run on the web server for further processing. This is faster than passing the data to a Web service or XMLL data connectivity running on a web application server. One disadvantage of it is that the JavaScript code may be interpreted differently by different web browsers such as Internet Explorer or Netscape.

7.5.2 How to Use FS Command

To use FS Command in your dashboard to call JavaScript codes, launch the Data Manager, click Add, and select FS Command from the dropdown list. You can create as many connectivities as you want in one dashboard.

The Property panel of an FS Command connectivity is very simple.

Definition

In this tab there are only three properties: Name, Command, and Parameters, as displayed in Figure 7.22.

- Name
  Like the other data connectivity methods mentioned in the sections above, you name the connection here with a description text instead of Connection 1 or Connection 2, to make it distinguishable when there are several connections in the list to the left. A typical name should indicate the purpose or functionality of that connectivity.

7 | Advanced Data Connectivity

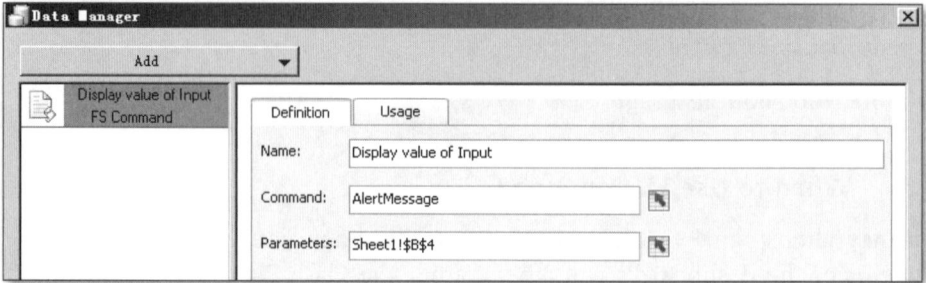

Figure 7.22 Definition of an FS Command Connection

▶ Command and Parameters
In these two fields you specify what command to invoke and the parameters. If your dashboard runs in Adobe Flash Player, the command can only be one of the predefined commands. However, if it's wrapped inside an HTML file and run in a web browser, you can use the name of any JavaScript function here, thus making it possible for your dashboard to call any JavaScript function.

For the latter case, at runtime, your dashboard doesn't call the command directly. Instead, in the HTML file with your dashboard embedded, you write a myMovie_DoFSCommand function using JavaScript with the parameters of command and properties, as shown below.

```
function myMovieName_DoFSCommand(command, args)
```

In this function, myMovieName is the ID of your dashboard as an embedded SWF object in the HTML, that is, the NAME attribute of the EMBED tag or the ID property of the OBJECT tag in the HTML file. When the connectivity is triggered, the command and parameters configured here will be passed to this function as command and args, respectively.

Now let's return to how to specify the values for these two fields. In the Command field, you specify the name of the JavaScript function that you want to call or invoke by either entering a text directly in the input field or clicking the Bind button to bind it to a single cell in the embedded spreadsheet. The Properties field works the same way. The accepted values of these two fields are different when the dashboard is run in an Adobe Flash Player or in a web browser, as explained below.

If the container of your dashboard is the Flash Player, you must enter the name of one of the predefined commands here and, correspondingly, the name of one of the supported parameters of that command, if any. The supported commands and their required parameters are listed below.

- `Quit`

  Parameter: no parameter accepted

  Purpose: Use this command if you want to close the Adobe Flash Player to terminate the presentation. You can provide a toggle button in your dashboard labeled Close for the user to close the Flash Player. Clicking the button will trigger the connectivity and thus close the Flash Player.

- `Fullscreen`

  Parameter: true or false

  Purpose: Use this command if you want to enable the user to set the Flash Player to full-screen mode or return it to normal menu view. Specify true for full-screen mode and false for normal view.

- `Allowscale`

  Parameter: true or false

  Purpose: Specifying false sets the Flash Player so that your dashboard is always drawn at its original size and is never scaled. Specifying true forces it to scale to 100% of the player.

- `Showmenu`

  Parameter: true or false

  Purpose: Specifying true enables the full set of context menu items in the Flash Player. If you want to restrict the user's access to them, specify false to hide all of the context menu items except About Flash Player.

- `Exec`

  Parameter: path to the application

  Purpose: Use this command if you want to execute an application from within the Flash Player. This command runs only in the subdirectory *fscommand*. In other words, if you use this command to call an application, the application must reside in a subdirectory called *fscommand*.

- `Trapallkeys`

  Parameter: true or false

  Purpose: Specifying true sends all key events, including accelerator keys, to the `onClipEvent(keyDown/keyUp)` handler in the Flash Player.

On the other hand, if your dashboard is wrapped by an HTML file and run in a web browser, you can send any message in the two parameters command and parameters. The messages are sent to the JavaScript function with the special name myMovieName_DoFSCommand in the HTML file, as mentioned before. This function can then either display or process the messages or call other JavaScript functions based on what command is passed in. This makes it possible for your dashboard to call any JavaScript function from within it, with myMovieName_DoFSCommand as the proxy.

Usage

An FS Command connectivity can only be triggered by a cell when its value has changed or has become equal to something. Unlike other connectivities such as Web services, it cannot be triggered on loading the dashboard or at intervals.

You trigger the FS Command connectivity the same way you would trigger any other connectivity mentioned above. You can refer to the corresponding sections for more info.

Figure 7.23 shows a sample Usage tab of an FS Command connectivity, where it's triggered when the value of cell Sheet1!$B$2 changes.

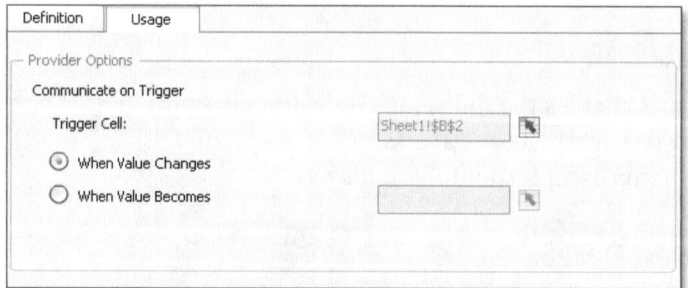

Figure 7.23 Trigger Option of an FS Command Connection

7.5.3 Practice

Let's go through a simple hands-on example to see how to use an FS Command connection. Suppose we are going to create a dashboard with an input text and a toggle button. When the user clicks the button, the text of that input text will be displayed with a JavaScript alert. You can follow the steps below to complete this hands-on example.

1. Set up the UI components.

   From the Components view, drag an input text and a toggle button onto the canvas. Bind the destination of the toggle button to cell Sheet1!$B$2. Bind the content and destination of input text to cell Sheet1!$B$4 so that its value is written to that cell.

2. Set up the FS Command connectivity.

   Launch the Data Manager to add an FS Command connection. On the Definition tab, enter "AlertMessage" for Command, and bind Parameters to cell Sheet1!$B$4, where the content of the input text is stored, as shown in Figure 7.24.

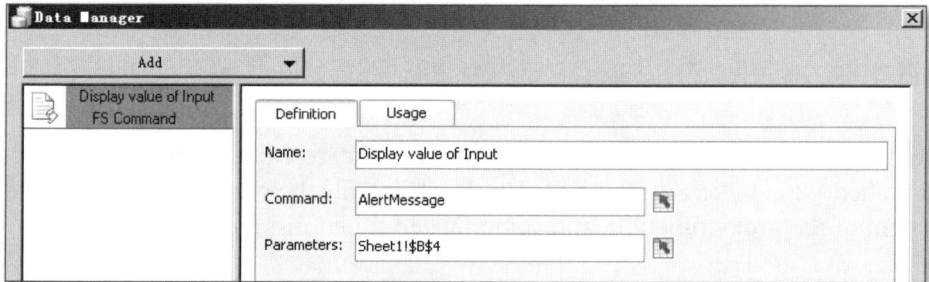

Figure 7.24 Definition of the FS Command Connection

On the Usage tab, bind the trigger cell to Sheet1!$B$2 and set it to trigger When Value Changes, as shown in Figure 7.23 above.

Now each time the user clicks the toggle button, the value in cell Sheet1!$B$2 is changed, and this FS Command connection is triggered.

3. Edit the JavaScript codes.

   We want to run the dashboard in a web browser, so we need write an HTML file containing it. To do this, follow the menu path FILE • EXPORT • HTML and specify its file name and location. An HTML file and an SWF file will be generated.

The proxy JavaScript function, named myMovieName_DoFSCommand above, will not be generated automatically. To add it, we need to find the name of the dashboard by opening the HTML file in a text editor and identify the NAME attribute of the EMBED tag or the ID property of the OBJECT tag, as displayed below.

<OBJECT classid="clsid:D27CDB6E-AE6D-11cf-96B8-444553540000" codebase="http://fpdownload.adobe.com/pub/shockwave/cabs/flash/swflash.cab#version=9,0,0,0"

7 | Advanced Data Connectivity

```
WIDTH="800" HEIGHT="600" id="myMovieName">
<PARAM NAME="movie" VALUE="fscommand_handson.swf">
...
</OBJECT>
```

Or:

```
<EMBED src="fscommand_handson.swf" quality=high bgcolor=#FFFFFF
WIDTH="800" HEIGHT="600"
NAME="myMovieName" ALIGN="" TYPE="application/x-shockwave-flash"
play="true" loop="true"
PLUGINSPAGE="http://www.adobe.com/shockwave/download/index.cgi?P1_Prod_
Version=ShockwaveFlash">
</EMBED>
```

Depending on your web browser, either the `OBJECT` or the `EMBED` tag will be used.

The ID of the dashboard is `myMovieName` in either case, so we add a JavaScript function called `myMovieName_DoFSCommand` in the HTML file, below the `<BODY>` tag. The content of the proxy function, and some related functions, are listed below.

```
<SCRIPT LANGUAGE="JavaScript">
function myMovieName_DoFSCommand(command, args) {
    alert ("The content in the Input Text is: " + args);
    if(command == "purpose1")
        func1();
    else if(command = "purpose2")
        func2(args);
}
function func1() {
    ...
}
function func2(args) {
    ...
}
</SCRIPT>
```

Note that the function `myMovieName_DoFSCommand()` can not only directly display or process the input parameters inside it, but can also call other JavaScript functions based on the input command to further process the parameters.

Now we are done. You can either open the HTML file directly, or put it on a web server so that others can access it through a web browser. Each time the user clicks the toggle button, the content of the input text will be displayed. Depending the real requirement, you can further process the passed-in value.

If you open the HTML file directly with a web browser, you will need set the SWF file as trusted so that it can access the HTML file, as we discussed in Chapter 6 when we covered the security issues involved with accessing external data.

Figure 7.25 displays a screenshot of the HTML file at runtime.

Figure 7.25 Final Effect of this Hands-On Example with an FS Command Connection

You can get the source file of this dashboard on this book's web page at *www.sap-press.com*.

7.6 External Interface Connection

Similar to FS Command, External Interface is an Adobe Flex technology that enables communication between Flash and its container such as an HTML page. It's a fantastic way to communicate with JavaScript directly from Flash. As we know, an Xcelsius dashboard is compiled into Flash. So this technology can be leveraged to enable communication between the dashboard and its container.

External Interface is very similar to FS Command but is more flexible, in that you can pass as many arguments as you want to any JavaScript function on the HTML page and receive a return value. It can work in the opposite direction as well, from JavaScript to Flash.

Xcelsius 2008 provides the External Interface connection as one of standard data connection types. With this connectivity, data from the SWF file can now be passed into or out of a specific cell range, using push/pull technology. Note that the communication is initialized by the container. In other words, it's the JavaScript that invokes the External Interface exposed by your dashboard.

7.6.1 When to Use an External Interface Connection

In some cases, you might want to control the dashboard from the outside. For example, you might retrieve a stock price from a provider over the Web (e.g., From Yahoo Stock), do some calculation using JavaScript, and then feed the result into your dashboard. In such a case, you can wrap the dashboard SWF file and JavaScript code in one HTML file. The output of the JavaScript is then sent to the SWF file via an External Interface connection.

One more powerful use of this connectivity is when you want to enable communication between two dashboards created by Xcelsius. For example, say you have created two fancy dashboards, one to display sales revenue for each branch and the other to display some info about a branch such as its map and images. You may want to use this connectivity to pass the selected branch between them.

In a word, you would choose this type of connectivity when you want to either pass external data into a cell or cell range of the dashboard or send data inside a cell or cell range of the dashboard to an external application.

7.6.2 How to Use and External Interface Connection

To add an External Interface connection, launch the Data Manager, click Add, and select External Interface Connection from the dropdown list. A connectivity of this type will be added to the Connections list with default properties. You can create as many connections of this type as you want in one dashboard.

As mentioned above, you pass external data into your dashboard or pass data inside your dashboard to external applications. To do so, you specify a cell range in the embedded spreadsheet as the source of the data sent out or the destination of the data passed in, and specify whether it can be read, written, or both. Once you understand this mechanism, you will know what to do with the Properties panel of an External Interface connection.

In the Properties panel, click the button with a plus (+) sign to add a range, which will be used as the source, the destination or both. The properties are per range, as explained below.

- Name

  You specify a name for the range by either entering a text directly in the Range Name field or clicking the Bind button to bind it to a single cell in the embedded spreadsheet. This name is not used only to make the range descriptive and easy to understand. It will be used in an external JavaScript function later.

- Range Type

  You then set the Range Type by selecting one from the dropdown list. If you want to pass a single value, select Cell and later bind Range to a single cell in the spreadsheet. Similarly, select Row/Column if you want to pass data in a one-dimensional array, and select Table if the data is two-dimensional, with multiple rows and columns.

- Range

  Depending on what range Type you have selected, you specify the range by clicking the Bind button to bind to a cell, a row or column, or a table in the embedded spreadsheet. For inbound communication, external data will be inserted here. For outbound communication, data in the specified cell range will be sent to external applications.

- Access

  Here you specify the access type of the cell range, by selecting either Read, Write, or Read/Write. If the data of the cell range will be sent to external applications, select Read. If the cell range is used as the destination of data passed in from external applications, select Write. If both might be used, select Read/Write.

You can add as many ranges as you want in one External Interface connection, by clicking the button with a + sign. To delete a range that you defined before, simply click to select it and click the button with a minus (-) sign.

Note that unlike the other connectivity types described above, you cannot change the name of the connectivity. You have to use the default names Connection 1, Connection 2, and so on.

Figure 7.26 shows a screenshot of the Properties page of an External Interface connection.

Note that there's no Usage tab here, where you might want to define when to trigger the connection. The reason for this is that this connectivity is not triggered by itself, but by JavaScript functions in its container HTML file.

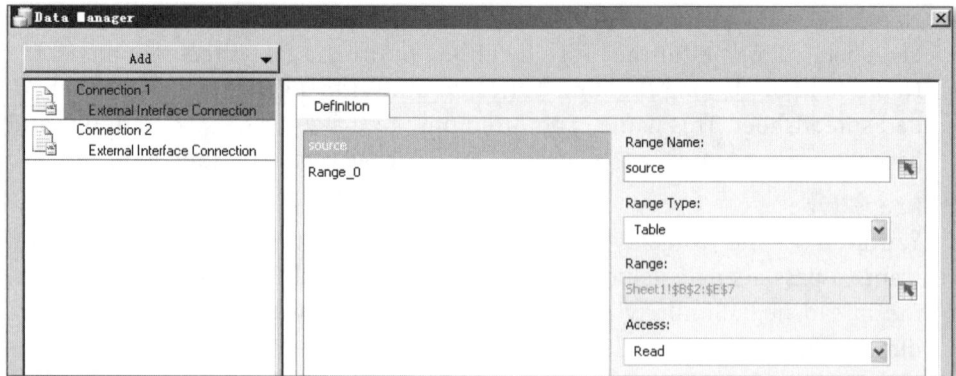

Figure 7.26 Definition of an External Interface Connection

7.6.3 Practice

Let's go through a simple hands-on example to demonstrate the use of External Interface connections in your dashboard. This hands-on example will cover how to write data from JavaScript to your dashboard (inbound) and how to read data from your dashboard to JavaScript (outbound). The user accesses the dashboard by visiting the HTML file containing the SWF file from a web browser.

1. Plan the data.

    We plan to use a cell range as both the source of and destination for data communication between our dashboard and its container, which is an HTML file in this hands-on example. For simplicity, we'll use a cell range with two rows and two columns, as displayed in Figure 7.27.

    Default values are filled in that cell range.

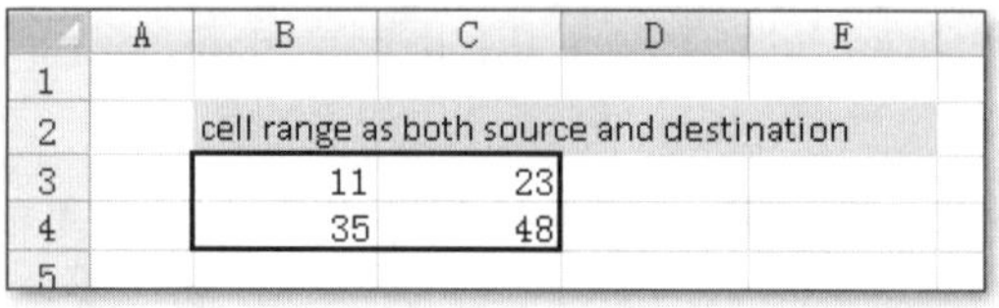

Figure 7.27 Data Structure in the Embedded Spreadsheet for this Hands-On Dashboard

2. Design your dashboard.

    To simulate both read and write, the user needs be able to see and manipulate the data in the cell range. To make it simple, we'll drag a grid component from the Components view, drop it onto the canvas, and bind its data to cell range

Sheet1!$B$3:$C$4. The data in this cell range is displayed in the grid component, and the user can change the data in the cell range within the grid.

The Properties panel of the grid is similar to that displayed in Figure 7.28.

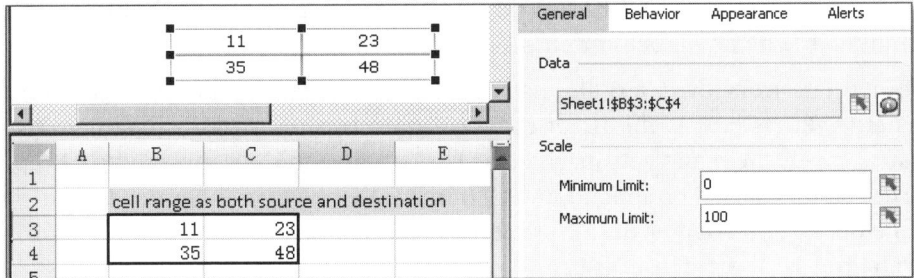

Figure 7.28 Bindings of the Grid

3. Set up an External Interface connection.

    In this step, we'll launch the Data Manager and add one External Interface connection. Its Properties panel is very simple. We bind its range to Sheet1!$B$3:$C$4, which stores the values of the grid component, set its range type to Table because it's a two-dimensional range, and set its access type to Read/Write to support both directions.

    Figure 7.29 displays the Properties panel of this connectivity.

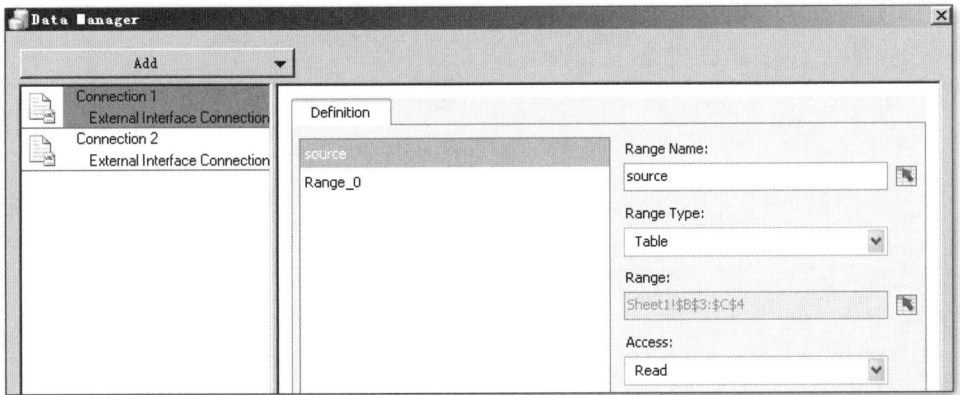

Figure 7.29 Definition of the External Interface Connection

4. Write the JavaScript code.

    Now the work on the dashboard is finished. Before going on to the JavaScript code, we need to export the dashboard to an HTML file. To do this, follow the menu path FILE • EXPORT • HTML and set the file location and name. An SWF file will be generated along with its HTML container.

The HTML file is designed to simulate the two communication directions between the SWF file and its HTML container. We'll use four input texts to display the value from the SWF file. The user can also manipulate the value in each input text, which will be written back to the SWF file.

To get data from the SWF file, use `myMovieName.getDataSource(rangeName)`, where `myMovieName` is the ID of the SWF object in the HTML container, and `rangeName` is the name you specified as Range Name in the connectivity's Properties panel. Like FS Command, the ID of the SWF object is either the NAME attribute of the EMBED tag or the ID property of the OBJECT tag, depending on what web browser the end user is using.

To write data back to the SWF file from the HTML file using JavaScript, use `myMovieName.setDataSource(rangeName, data)`.

The pieces of JavaScript code in the HTML file are illustrated below

```
<SCRIPT LANGUAGE="JavaScript">
    function writeToSWF() {
    ma = new Array(2);
    ma[0] = new Array(2);
    ma[0][0] = document.getElementById("a1").value;
    ma[0][1] = document.getElementById("b1").value;
    ma[1] = new Array(2);
    ma[1][0] = document.getElementById("a2").value;
    ma[1][1] = document.getElementById("b2").value;
      myMovieName.setDataSource("Data",ma);
    }

    function readFromSWF() {
    document.getElementById("a1").value = myMovieName.getDataSource("Data")[0][0];
    document.getElementById("b1").value = myMovieName.getDataSource("Data")[0][1];
    document.getElementById("a2").value = myMovieName.getDataSource("Data")[1][0];
    document.getElementById("b2").value = myMovieName.getDataSource("Data")[1][1];
    }

</SCRIPT>
```

```
<form id="f1">
    <input type="text" size="15" id="a1"/> <input type="text" size="15" id="b1"/> <p/>
    <input type="text" size="15" id="a2"/> <input type="text" size="15" id="b2"/> <p/>
    <input id="btn_write" type="button" value="Write" onclick="writeToSWF()"/>
    <input id="btn_read"  type="button" value="Read" onclick="readFromSWF()"/>
</form>
```

Four input texts are added to the HTML file to simulate the grid component.

The JavaScript function `writeToSWF()`, used to write the values of the four texts manipulated by the user through the web browser back to the SWF file, is triggered by clicking the Write button. Pay attention to the line `myMovieName.setDataSource("Data",ma)` in this method.

On the other hand, the JavaScript function `readFromSWF()` is used to read data from the SWF file into the four texts in the HTML file and is triggered by clicking the Read button. Pay attention to line `myMovieName.getDataSource("Data")[0][0]` in this method.

As a result, data between these four HTML texts and the dashboard is exchanged via an External Interface connection. Figure 7.30 shows the original state of the dashboard and the four HTML text fields on launching the HTML file, compared to the state when the Read button is clicked.

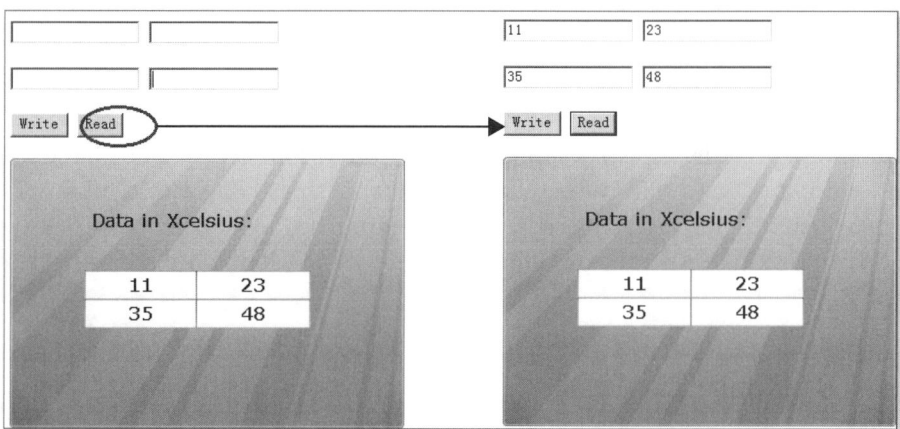

Figure 7.30 Data in the Xcelsius Dashboard is Read into the HTML Page

The user can modify the values in either the SWF file or the four HTML text fields. Clicking the Read button will fill the four HTML text fields with the values in the SWF file, and clicking the Write button will overwrite the SWF file with the values in the HTML text fields. Figure 7.31 shows the states before and after clicking the Write button.

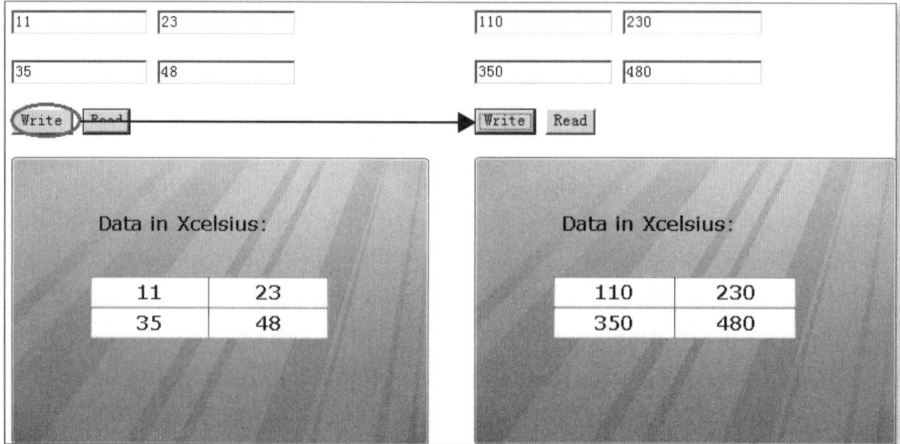

Figure 7.31 Data in the HTML Page is Written to the Xcelsius Dashboard

To make this work in your environment, you need set the SWF file as trusted so that it can access the HTML file. Do this in the Adobe Flash Player Settings Manager as described in Chapter 6, Section 6.3, Security Issues Related to Accessing External Data.

7.7 LCDS Connection

Xcelsius 2008 provides an LCDS connection for you to connect to Adobe LifeCycle Data Service (LCDS) to retrieve real-time data there. This is one aspect of integration between SAP Business-Objects and Adobe, similar to exporting your Xcelsius dashboard to Adobe AIR®, as mentioned previously in section 1.2.4 and later in section 8.4.2.

The Adobe LiveCycle® Data Services is a component of Adobe LifeCycle Enterprise Suite (ES), which provides an up-to-the-second view of your business data. In terms of programming, it is a scalable and optimized framework that abstracts the complexity of creating easy-to-use, personalized, and interactive applications of RIAs (rich Internet application). It runs on a web application server such as Tomcat or JBoss to provide real-time transactional services, enabling RIAs to pull and aggregate information from core enterprise applications and feeds outside the firewall. The supported protocol for data communication between LCDS and Xcelsius include HTTP, RMTP (Real-Time Messaging Protocol), and AMF (Action Message Format). For more information about LCDS, please refer to the Adobe website at *http://www.adobe.com/products/livecycle/dataservices/*.

LCDS needs some configuration before it can be accessed from Xcelsius. Very simply put, you need add the XLCDSServlet to the LCDS server and configure it in the Xcelsius-config files. Figure 7.32 shows the configurations you need for Xcelsius to connect to LCDS, cited from the Adobe website.

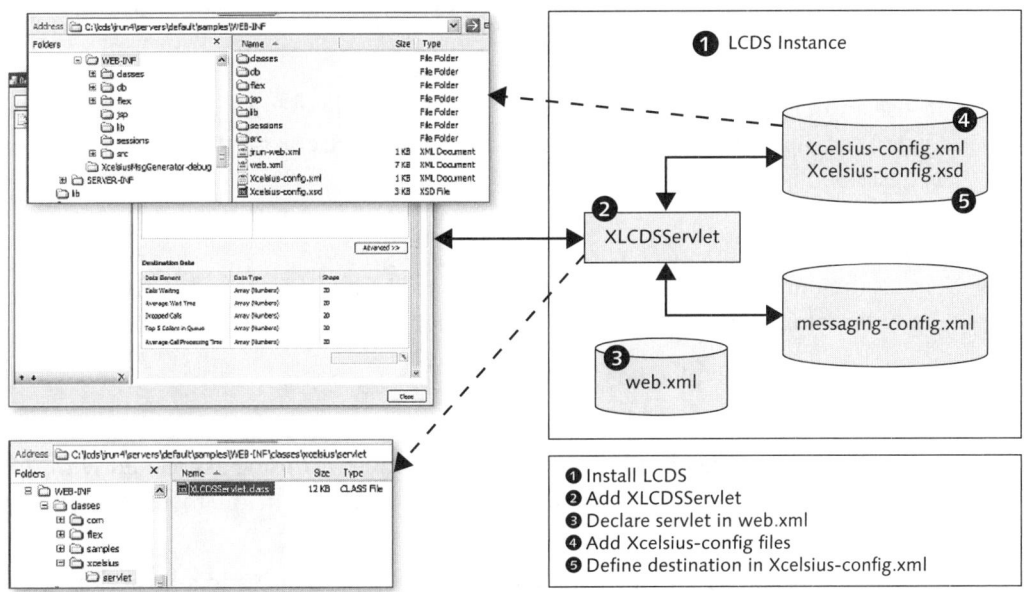

Figure 7.32 Required Configurations for the LCDS Server

With this connection you can stream real-time data from Adobe LifeCycle Data Service into your Xcelsius dashboard at runtime, thus creating low-latency, highly scalable, and data-consistent dashboards or widgets.

Most Xcelsius 2008 connectivities mentioned above, such as XML data and Web services, are used to retrieve live data from the server. An LCDS connection is used to retrieve real-time data, in that it must be able to quickly detect and respond to information, and the latency should be very low, sometimes within milliseconds. This is required by dashboards in real-time applications for stock trading or call center monitoring systems.

7.7.1 When to Use an LCDS Connection

You may choose an LCDS connection when the data is provided from the Adobe LifeCycle Data Service or when you want to create a real-time dashboard.

7.7.2 How to Use an LCDS Connection

To add this type of connection, launch the Data Manager and select LCDS Connection in the Add dropdown list. You can create as many connections of this type as you want in a single dashboard.

To use an LCDS connection, you need to be able to access the server hosting LifeCycle Data Service. You can configure this connectivity from its Properties panel, as described below.

Definition
This is the only tab in the Properties panel, as displayed in Figure 7.33. Similar to the External Interface connection, you cannot set the connection name.

The properties are explained as follows.

- Host
  You need to first select a host from the dropdown list to be associated with this LCDS connection. If no host exists, click the Host button to manage hosts, including add, edit, or delete a host.

  Figure 7.34 shows the hosts manager and the window to add a host after clicking Add.

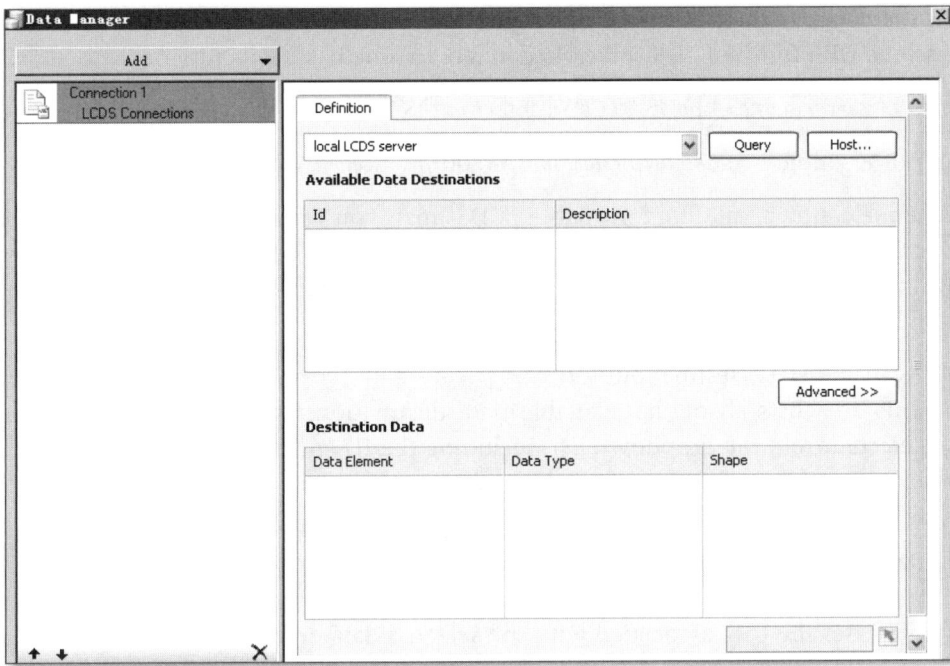

Figure 7.33 Definition of an LCDS Connection

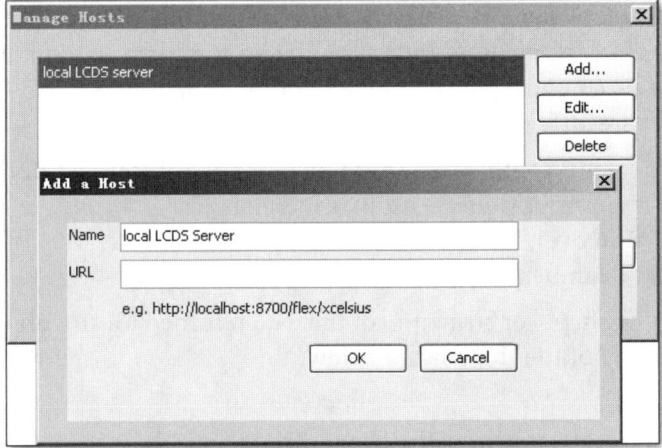

Figure 7.34 Add a Host through the Hosts Manager

As displayed in the figure, you specify a name for the host for easy identification and the URL for the LCDS server to connect to. The basic structure of the URL is:

http://<server name>:<port>/<LCDS context path>/xcelsius

In our example, we use *http://localhost:8700/flex/xcelsius*.

After selecting a valid and available LCDS host, you can click the Query button to trigger Xcelsius to retrieve information on what feed destinations are available from this host. All available data destinations and data elements of the LCDS host will be displayed in the corresponding area in this tab.

▶ Available Data Destinations
This area lists all of the available data destinations of the LCDS server you selected from the dropdown list, including the ID and description of each. You can then select one as the feed destination to bind to your dashboard.

You can click the Advanced button to make additional settings for the selected data destination. In Channel Type, you specify the type of channel, or communication protocol, that is currently being used. Similarly, the Channel URL field indicates the URL associated with the selected data destination.

You can click the Advanced button again to collapse these additional fields.

▶ Destination Data
This area lists all of the available data elements from the selected LCDS host. For each data element, you can click the Bind button on the bottom right to bind it to a single cell or a row or column or a cell range with multiple rows and columns in the embedded spreadsheet, which will be used to store the data.

The type of each data element is either Number (for numeric values), Txt (for string), or True/False (for Boolean values). It can also be an array of any type, for example, Numbers. Moreover, the type can be 3-dimensional as an array of array, for example, Array (Numbers).

The Shape field defines the shape, or structure, of the data returned for this element. The shape can be any of the three listed below.

▶ Singleton
This shape is for single values. You need to bind it to a single cell in the embedded spreadsheet.

▶ 1D
This shape is for one-dimensional data, that is, data in a row or column. The corresponding data type should be an array of some type, for example, Array

(Numbers). Its output data should be bound to a row or column in the embedded spreadsheet.

- 2D
  This is when the data is two-dimensional, that is, in a table of one or multiple rows and columns. The corresponding data type should be an array of an array of some type, for example, Array (Array (Txt)). Consequently, its returned data should be bound to a table in the embedded spreadsheet.

7.8 Portal Data

With Xcelsius 2008, you can create dashboards within the portal environment. Supported portals include IBM WebSphere and Microsoft SharePoint.

The portal data connectivity is for communication between dashboards (SWF) hosted in portals. One dashboard can provide some data to another as a provider, and the one using the data acts as the consumer. You can define some parameters in your dashboard so that the user can customize the values of those parameter within the portal.

With a portal data connection, you can connect your dashboard to SharePoint lists. Also, dashboards can communicate with one another, making it possible for users to adjust values in one dashboard and see the results in another. This is especially useful for a what-if analysis or when you need drill-down from one chart to another.

7.8.1 When to Use Portal Data

You may want to use this type of connectivity when your dashboard is to be hosted in a portal and you want to enable data communication between the dashboard and the portal or between the provider dashboard and the consumer. With the help of the portal, you can define some parameters inside your dashboard, the values of which the user can set through the portal. In this way, the user can customize the behavior and even the appearance of the dashboard. For example, you can define parameters that control colors in the dashboard, so the user can customize the color schema according to his preferences.

To use this type of connectivity, you need be able to access the portal hosting the dashboards.

7.8.2 How to Use Portal Data

To add a portal data connection, launch the Data Manager and select Portal Data from the Add dropdown list. Like Flash Variables, you can create only one portal data connection per dashboard. The connection will become disabled when there's already one such connection defined in your dashboard.

In the Properties panel of a portal data connection, what properties are available depends on the connection type. You can select a connection type from the dropdown list, which we'll explain below.

None
Choose this type if your dashboard doesn't need to communicate with another dashboard. Instead, define some parameters in your dashboard, and specify that you want the users to customize their values from within the portal. By specifying the values they want, different users can see different effects and/or different data of the same dashboard in the portal.

The Properties panel for this type of connection is displayed in Figure 7.35.

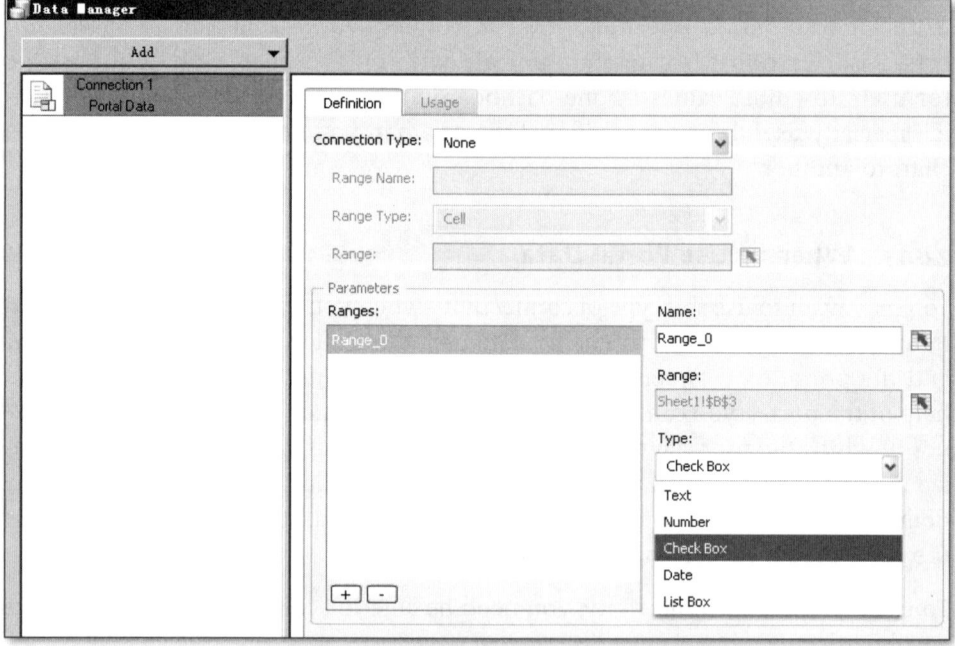

Figure 7.35 Definition of a Portal Data Connection with Type "None"

The Ranges area lists the definitions of all parameters of your dashboard. For each parameter, you need to configure three properties as listed below.

▶ Name
Here you define the name of the parameter, by either entering a text directly in the input field or clicking the Bind button to bind to a single cell in the embedded spreadsheet.

In SharePoint, the name will be displayed in the Properties dialog box for this dashboard. This parameter will not be listed as a parameter in SharePoint if its Name field is blank. That said, Name is a mandatory property.

▶ Range
Here you click the Bind button to select a cell range in the embedded spreadsheet, which will be used to store the values the user will specify for this parameter in the portal. Based on the parameter type, you can bind to a single cell or a cell range.

▶ Type
Here you set the type of the parameter. Depending on your scenario, you can choose from Text, Number, Check Box, Date, and List Box.

You could select Text to set any text-based data within your dashboard, for example, chart titles, greeting messages, and so on.

You use Number to set any numeric data. A typical usage of this type is to customize the alert thresholds used in the Alerts tab of a UI component such as a column chart or an icon. You can also select this type for the user to customize the number of major or minor divisions in a column chart.

Check Box is useful for toggling the value of a cell between 0 and 1. You may choose this type so the user can control whether to show certain components, using dynamic visibility.

You use Date to define a calendar date in your dashboard. It sets the format to Date and uses a true date value within the dashboard. For example, you can choose this type so the user can specify the date period he is interested in before requesting the data.

For the types listed above, the user can specify any value. The potential problem is that the user may not be clear about the accepted value format and thus may enter an invalid value, resulting in confusion or causing the application crash. To restrict the user input, you can select List Box, which enables the designer to build user selection options (a list of values) into the parameters.

This way, the user can select only from values provided at design time, which are always valid.

When List Box is selected, two more options become available. Entries sets what entries are available for the user to select. You can bind it to a row or column in the embedded spreadsheet, where the candidate items are stored. You use Default Selection for selecting which entry's value will be used by default if the user does not make a selection.

Consumer

Choose this type of connection if you want your dashboard to accept data from another web part within the portal, acting as a consumer. This will add a portal consumer connection to your dashboard. Figure 7.36 shows the Properties panel when Consumer is selected.

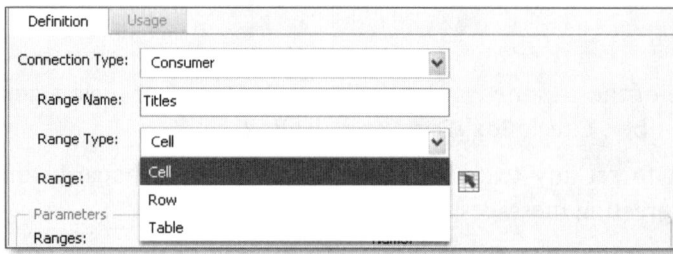

Figure 7.36 Definition of a Portal Data Connection with Type "Consumer"

As you can see from this figure, in addition to the properties in Parameters mentioned above, there are three important selections to configure in the Properties panel of the consumer connection: Range Name, Range Type, and Range, which we'll explain below.

- Range Name
  You set Range Name by entering a text directly. It will be displayed when connecting web parts together in portals. Like the Name property in Parameters mentioned above, Range Name is mandatory or the web parts cannot be connected.

- Range Type
  Range Type defines the amount of data that will be passed.
    - Cell consumes a single value from another web part.

- Row is a single row with multiple columns, which is similar to the shape type 1D described for LCDS connections. With this type, your dashboard consumes an array of data that will be passed in.
- Table represents data in multiple rows and columns, similar to the shape type 2D described for LCDS connections.

Usually, you will choose Cell or Row, to consume data from another dashboard. You may only want to choose Table to consume data from a portal list.

- Range
Range is the area in the embedded spreadsheet of your dashboard that the incoming data will be written to. Depending on what you select in Range Type, you may bind it to a single cell, a row or column, or a table with multiple rows and columns.

Provider

Choose this type of connection if you want the dashboard to provide data to another web part. In this case, only Xcelsius 2008 portal web parts can be used to consume information from a dashboard that is using the Provider connection.

The properties in the Definition tab are exactly the same as when you select Consumer. You an refer to the section above for info about how to use them.

One more tab, Usage, is activated only when you select Provider. Similar to many other types of connectivity, in the Usage tab you define whether you want your dashboard to send data based on the value of a single cell in the embedded spreadsheet, either when it changes or when it becomes equal to something.

7.9 Summary

In this chapter we discusses some advanced types of data connectivity provided by Xcelsius 2008, such as Query as a Web Service and Crystal Reports data consumer to an SAP BusinessObjects Enterprise environment, LCDS connection to the Adobe LifeCycle Data Service, and Flash Variable and FS Command to pass data from a container such as an HTML file or the Flash Player into Xcelsius. In Chapters 6 and 7, we have described all of the connections in Xcelsius 2008, so you should now have a big picture of them to help you choose the best ones to retrieve the data you need to create a powerful and efficient dashboard.

In the previous chapters, we discussed all of the UI components and data connectivity options available in Xcelsius. Some of the functionalities, such as drill-down and dynamic visibility, are common to most UI components and are very useful. In this chapter, let's consider them in terms of the dashboard.

8 Special Features

In Chapters 4 to 7, we discussed all of the UI components and types of data connectivity provided by Xcelsius 2008. Some features, such as drill-down and alerts, are common to multiple UI components and are useful enough to be widely used in creating dashboards using Xcelsius. When introducing each UI component, we talked a little bit about how to use these features in that particular UI component. This may help you understand that UI component, but may not be comprehensive enough for you to understand them in a higher level, as features on top of UI components.

In this chapter, we'll describe some special features that are not only useful but also widely used, from a general instead of a specific UI component's perspective.

After reading this chapter you will be able to:

▶ Describe those special features common to most UI components

▶ Be clear about what feature to use to achieve a requirement, before choosing the UI components

8.1 Drill-Down

You may already be very familiar with drill-down, which is a common feature for most charts such as pie charts. To drill down means to move from summary information to more detailed data to better focus on something. In a GUI environment, drilling down may involve clicking on some representative part to reveal more detailed information. Drill-down is a commonly used technique in reporting and analysis. For example, in a pie chart showing quarterly sales revenue, you can drill down from a quarter to see more detailed data, such as the monthly data, about that selected quarter.

A useful drill-down often occurs along a hierarchy, for example, from year to quarter to month, or from country to region to states. This is to some extent similar to navigating through the file system in your computer, from the high-level folders (e.g., My Computer) to the drivers (C:) to folders (My Documents) and files.

If you have ever used Crystal Reports 2008, which is also a product of SAP BusinessObjects for formatted enterprise reporting, you may know that the drill-down functionality is also supported in Crystal Reports, where the drill-down is defined by groups you have created through the Group Expert. The drill-down happens along the groups in their order. Each time you click (when you view the report through a web browser) or double-click (through the designer) a group, its child data is displayed in a separate window or tab.

Sometimes you might use drill-down along no hierarchy. Instead, you just use it as a selector. That is, you clicks on a slice on a pie chart, and some other information related to that selection is displayed on other components. The information changes according to your selection.

In Xcelsius, there's a Drill Down tab in the Properties panels of many UI components, and you need enable drill-down to use it. In this section, we'll take a closer look at how drill down is used in dashboard design with Xcelsius.

8.1.1 When to Use Drill-Down

Usually a dashboard is used to present high-level aggregated data with intuitive charts, to maximum the efficiency of information consumption for the end user. In a more sophisticated dashboard design, users can view detailed data from high-level data, along with a certain hierarchy. For example, users are first presented with a column chart displaying sales for each country. By selecting one country, users can view sales for each region of that country, and even a step further to each city in one region. This example is a classic drill-down path along the region hierarchy.

Sometimes you can also drill down along paths not within a hierarchy. For example, the user is first presented with a chart displaying the sales revenue of each country. On clicking one country, the user sees the graphic location or population or some other info about that country. In such scenarios, the drill-down feature is used as a selector.

In general, when you want to enable users to view data from high-level to details, this drill-down technique is your best-fit choice.

8.1.2 How to Use Drill-Down

Briefly, three elements are required to make a drill down.

- High-level aggregated data
- Detailed data
- The linkage between them

In Xcelsius, the high-level data and detailed data are represented with charts or table components, and the linkage between them is implemented with data insertion. When the use selects any part of the high-level data, data corresponding to the selection is inserted into some destination that will affect the detailed data.

Almost all chart components have a Drill Down tab on the Properties sheet. This chart component is where the high-level data is presented and data insertion is configured. Figure 8.1 shows a typical Drill Down tab.

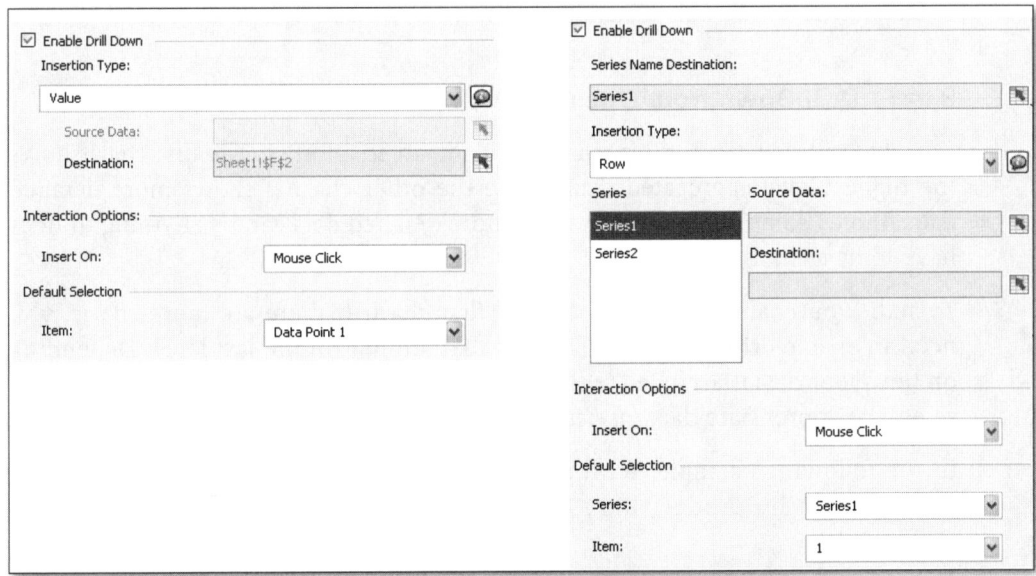

Figure 8.1 Drill Down Tab in the Properties Panel of Most UI Components

Some typical properties in this tab are briefly explained as follows.

- Enable Drill Down
  Select the Enable Drill Down checkbox to enable drill-down. Note that only after the data is configured in the General tab will this checkbox be active.
- Series Name Destination
  For a multiseries chart, the name of the series selected will be inserted into the destination cell specified here.
- Insertion Type
  Candidate types include position, value, row, column, and status list. You can refer to section 4.1.2 for detailed descriptions of these data insertion types.
- Source Data and Destination
  With a specified insertion type, bind the source data (if applicable) and destination here. If the component has multiple series, the source data and destination need to be configured for each series.
- Interaction Options
  Specify what action makes a drill-down selection: mouse click or mouse over.
- Default Selection
  Determine the default selection when the visualization is initially loaded.

8.1.3 Drill Down from One Chart to Another

Usually, drill-down is performed from one chart to another. The first chart shows the highest-level aggregated data, while the other chart(s) shows more detailed data. The UI component used to show more detailed data can be anything. It does have to be a chart.

To start, you enable drill-down for the first chart. If there are more charts, you need to enable drill-down for all charts that are not on the last level. Depending on how your data is arranged, either static or dynamic retrieved from a server, you select the appropriate data insertion type and source and destination data.

In the following example, we'll create two charts to display quarterly sales and a breakdown by product line. Follow the steps below to create this sample dashboard.

1. Plan the data.
   In this simple example, both the high-level and detailed data are stored in a

cell range in the embedded spreadsheet. You can regard it as returned from one connectivity such as a Web service connectivity.

Figure 8.2 shows how we store the data in the spreadsheet. The Total column is calculated within the embedded spreadsheet using Excel formulas to sum up values of the products.

	A	B	C	D	E	F	G	H
1								
2			Total	Phone	Desktop	Laptop	Service	
3		Q1	800	150	230	300	120	
4		Q2	830	190	220	280	140	
5		Q3	860	240	180	290	150	
6		Q4	900	260	200	280	160	
7								

Figure 8.2 High-Level Data in a Two-dimensional Cell Range for Drill-Down

If the data is dynamically retrieved from a connectivity at runtime, you can map it to a range from the second to the sixth row, for example, range Sheet1!$D$2:$I$6, with cells in the first row ($D$2:$I$2) storing the product names, and other cells ($D$3:$I$6) storing the values of all products in all quarters.

2. Set up the chart showing high-level data.
   We'll use a column chart to show and compare the sales revenue of all products in each quarter. To do this, drag a column chart from the Components view and drop it on the canvas, and bind its category label to column Sheet1!$B$3:$B$6 with quarter names and its values to column Sheet1!$C$3:$C$6 with sales revenues of all four quarters.

   What's more important in this step is to set up the drill-down behavior. When the user has clicked a quarter, the sales revenue for each product of that quarter should be picked out. To do this, set Insertion Type to Row, and insert a row from the cell range Sheet1!$B$3:$I$6 containing all products and their sales revenues in each quarter to the row Sheet1!$B$8:$I$8 as the destination.

   The Drill Down tab of this column chart is displayed in Figure 8.3.

3. Set up the chart showing detailed data.
   In the last step, we have inserted the data of each product for the selected quarter into a row. This step is very simple: Just use a chart to present the data. In this example, we'll use a pie chart to show the contribution of each product to the quarter's total sales revenue.

To do this, drop a pie chart onto the canvas and make it align with the bottom of the column chart. We'll bind its labels to row Sheet1!$D$2:$I$2, where the names of the available products are stored, and its values to row Sheet1!$D$8:$I$8, where the sales revenues of all products in that selected quarter are inserted. To indicate what quarter the pie chart is about, bind its subtitle to cell Sheet1!$B$8.

Figure 8.3 Workspace with Column Chart

Sometimes the last columns in Sheet1!$D$2:$I$2 and Sheet1!$D$8:$I$8 may be empty when there are less than six products. To avoid empty series, select IGNORE BLANK CELLS • IN VALUES in the Behavior tab.

Now we are done. Figure 8.4 below shows a screenshot of the dashboard at runtime. Q1 is selected by default, and the sales revenue of each product in Q1 is displayed in the pie chart. Whenever the user clicks another quarter, the data corresponding to that quarter is inserted into another row, causing the pie chart to change.

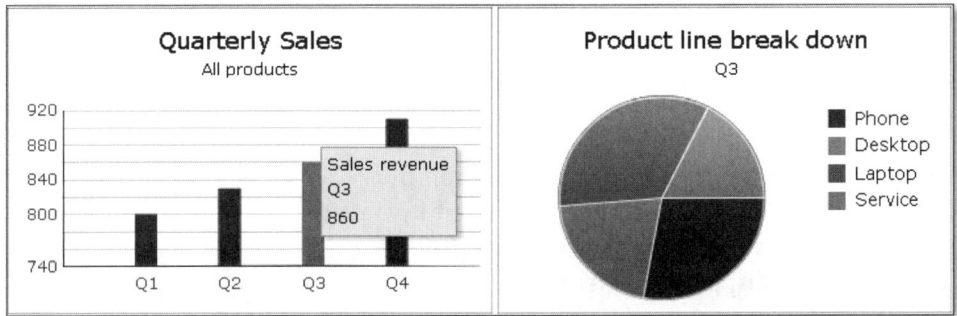

Figure 8.4 Effect of Drill-Down from One Chart to Another

This example is just a simple demonstration of how to create a dashboard with drill-down charts. You can easily extend or improve it to satisfy your real needs. For example, add one more chart to show more detailed data from a certain part of the second chart, making the dashboard a three-level drill-down.

8.1.4 Drill-Down on the Same Chart

Sometimes you might want to perform drill-down on the same chart. For example, a chart displays the yearly sales revenue, and users can drill down by clicking on one column to view the monthly sales for that year, on the same chart. Drill-down on the same pie chart is very attractive and intuitive to the user. This provides a more direct drill-down experience compared to that on multiple charts, which is more like data linking than drill-down.

Before you get very experienced with charts, you may take it for granted that drilling down on the same chart is very simple. Just use the single chart to represent data from high-level to detailed level. However, you will soon find out that something unexpected will occur. For example, let's say we want to create a dashboard where the user is first presented with the sales revenue of each quarter, and on clicking a quarter, the user will see the sales revenue by product lines in that quarter. On launching the dashboard, you may find that instead of displaying the high-level data, the chart just displays the sales revenue by products in the first quarter.

Briefly, this occurs because the chart automatically drills down to the lowest level, though there's been no user interaction. In the example mentioned above, the chart does display the high-level data, which is the sales revenue of each quarter, at first. However, because drill-down is enable and the first quarter is selected by default (if you haven't changed the Default Selection item in the Drill Down tab), the chart automatically drills down to display data in the lower level of the selected quarter. That's why you see the sales revenue by products in the first quarter instead of the high-level data of each quarter.

You may think this problem will not happen if we can set the Default Selection item to None. That is, if no item is selected by default, the auto drill-down will not happen. However, in versions before Xcelsius 2008 SP3, you have to select a default item, as displayed in Figure 8.5.

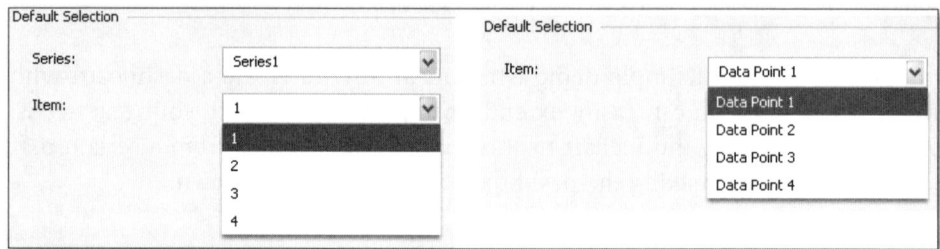

Figure 8.5 Default Selection for a Drill-Down

This book is targeted at Xcelsius 2008 SP1. However, at the time of writing this book, Xcelsius 2008 SP3 has been released. So one more word here: Xcelsius 2008 SP3 enables you to set the default selection to No Selection (-1), as displayed in Figure 8.6, which solves this problem.

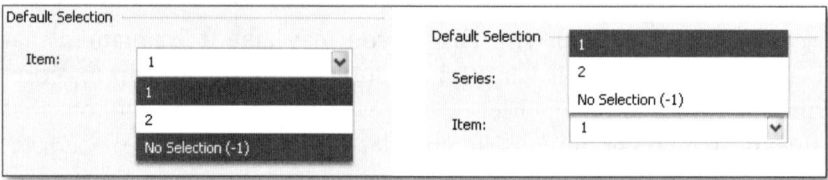

Figure 8.6 New Default Selection in Xcelsius 2008 SP3

However, this only solves the problem when the drill-down occurs on only the first level. That is, the drill-down only happens when the user clicks a data element in the first chart, but does not happen when the user clicks a data element in the second chart. If you want to provide a dashboard with four or more levels of drill-down, this problem will still occur.

One example requirement is that the user should first be presented with a chart showing the sales revenue of each quarter. On clicking a data element, the user should see the sales revenue of each product in that quarter. One step further, when the user clicks a product, the chart should display the weekly sales revenue of that product in that quarter. Figure 8.7 illustrates this requirement.

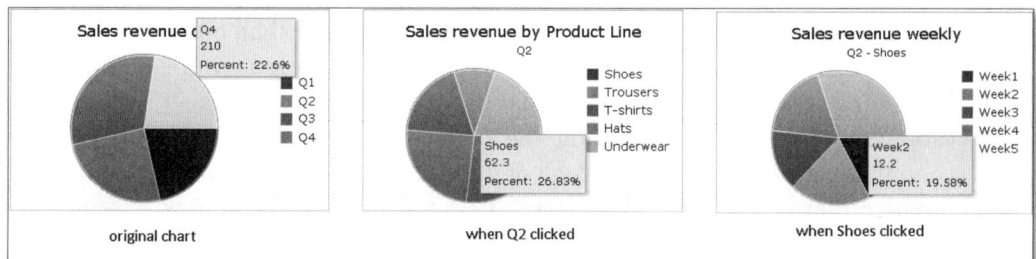

Figure 8.7 Three-Level Cascading Drill-Down on Three Charts

Setting the Default Selection item of the pie chart to No Selection results in the chart displaying the highest-level data to start, which is what we want. However, if you click any quarter, the chart displays the weekly sales revenue of some product, instead of the sales revenue of each product in that quarter. The reason is that when you click a quarter, the selected item of the pie chart changes from No Selection (-1) to the index of the selected quarter (for example, if Q2 is selected, the selected item is now 2). As a result, after displaying the sales revenue of each product, the chart immediately changes to display the weekly sales revenue of the second product, which is Trousers in our case.

Figure 8.8 illustrates what you will actually see. Let's ignore how to get the data for now. We'll explain it shortly.

Figure 8.8 Actual Behavior of the Three-Level Drill-Down on the Same Chart

8 | Special Features

So far, we have explained whether it's possible to achieve drill-down with one level or more on the same chart and how to achieve one-level drill-down. Enabling drill-down with more than one level on the same chart is more difficult, but is achievable with some workarounds.

Now let's see how to provide data for drill-down on more than one level. First, the data at each drill-down level needs be mapped to the same row or column in the embedded spreadsheet, because we have only one chart to display it. Second, you cannot retrieve all of the data at the start, map it to a cell range, and insert a row or column in data insertion. Instead, all of the data must be retrieved at runtime, with the identifier of the currently selected item passed to the server as a parameter. Figure 8.9 shows what the data should be like in the embedded spreadsheet.

	A	B	C	D	E	F	G	H	I	J	K
1											
2		insertion	live data	suppose there're at most 8 items, so D3:K5							
3			label								
4			value								
5			identifier if requried								
6											
7			base URL	http://server:port/services/.../getdata							
8			URL to fetch data	http://server:port/services/.../getdata?parentId=							
9											

Figure 8.9 Data in Embedded Spreadsheet for Multilevel Drill-Down

As Figure 8.9 shows, the data is always mapped to a single cell range of Sheet1!d3:k5, whether the user is currently on the first, second, or third drill-down level. (The number of columns in this range should be the maximum number of fields you want to accept, in all three levels. If your data contains more than eight fields, feel free to enlarge the range.) Consequently, we need do something to get the data to correspond to user's behavior through some kind of data connectivity and map it to that cell range. Simply speaking, we use an XML data connectivity that connects to a Java Servlet. As you can see from Figure 8.9 above, the URL for the connectivity is dynamically concatenated in cell Sheet1!$D$8 by adding the key of the currently selected item to the base URL. The steps to request the data are listed below.

1. At first, nothing is selected. The XML data connectivity is triggered on loading the dashboard with the URL *http://server:port/services/.../getdata?parentId=*.

2. On the server side, the servlet processing this request will find that the parentId is empty, so it will return the highest-level data, that is, the sales revenue of each quarter.
3. The user sees the sales revenues of all quarters and clicks on the one he is interested in, for example, Q2. The XML Data connectivity in our example is configured to be triggered when value of cell Sheet1!$D$8 changes. So when the user clicks Q2, the value of that cell changes to *http://server:port/services/.../getdata?parentId=Q2*, and the XML data connectivity is triggered with the new URL.
4. On the server side, the servlet processing this request will find that the parentId is Q2, so it returns the data of Q2, that is, the sales revenue of each product in Q2.
5. The user sees the sales revenue of all products in Q2. However, the user's selecting Q2 in step 3 makes the current selected item of the pie chart become item 2. As a result, the second product is selected automatically and immediately. Consequently, the value of cell Sheet1!$D$8 changes to *http://server:port/services/.../getdata?parentId=Product2*, and the XML data connectivity is triggered again with the new URL.
6. On the server side, the servlet processing this request will find that the parentId is now Product2, so it returns the data of Product2, that is, the sales revenue of each week in Q2 for Product2.
7. The user sees the sales revenue of Product2 for all weeks in Q2.

Auto drill-down happens again when the user clicks on the chart, though not for the first screen, which displays the highest-level data.

If you really want to enable drill-down for more than one level on the same chart, you can try the workaround explained below.

> **Note**
>
> The principle is to return one more item for the previously selected item, with a special identifier that the server will use and a value of 0 to make it invisible in the pie chart. On the server side, when receiving this special identifier, return nothing so that the content of the cell range remains unchanged, and thus the pie chart remains unchanged.

To illustrate this workaround, we'll go back through the steps of communication between the server and client, beginning from step 4, because the first three steps are the same.

8. On the server side, the servlet processing this request will find that the parentId is Q2 and the index of the selected item is 2, so it queries the data source for the data of Q2, that is, the sales revenue of each product in Q2.

   Instead of returning the data directly to Xcelsius, we'll add one more item here. As mentioned above, the item has a value of 0 and a special identifier, say, -1. This item is placed in the second position, because the index of the selected item (quarter) is 2.

   To help you understand it, the returned data is:

Shoes	-1	Trousers	T-shirts	Hats	Underwear
62.3	0	56.9	43.5	22.8	46.7

9. The user sees the sales revenue of all products in Q2. Because the value of the second item is 0, the user will not see it and thus cannot click it.

   Like the case explained previously, the user's selecting Q2 in step 3 makes the current selected item of the pie chart become item 2. As a result, the second product is selected automatically and immediately. However, the identifier of the second product is now -1, not Product2. Consequently, the value of cell Sheet1!$D$8 changes to *http://server:port/services/.../getdata?parentId=-1*, and the XML data connectivity is triggered again with the new URL.

10. On the server side, the servlet processing this request will find that the parentId is now -1. It then understands that this is triggered automatically by Xcelsius, not by user because it's invisible. So it returns nothing. As a result, content in cell range Sheet1!$C3$D5 remains unchanged. Consequently, the content of the chart is also unchanged. The user still sees the sales revenue of each product in Q2. In a word, the auto drill-down is bypassed in this way.

11. The user clicks on the product he is interested in, such as Product3. Consequently, the value of cell Sheet1!$D$8 changes to *http://server:port/services/.../getdata?parentId=Product3*, and the XML data connectivity is triggered again with the new URL.

12. On the server side, the servlet processing this request will find that the parentId is now Product3. It then returns the data of Product3, that is, the sales revenue of each week in Q2 for Product3.

8.2 Make Smart Use of Dynamic Visibility

As the name indicates, dynamic visibility is a feature that allows both the designer and the end user to show or hide a UI component dynamically, based on some condition at runtime. In Xcelsius 2008, this feature is common to most UI components. In other words, you define what components are displayed on the dashboard at what time.

You can define the dynamic visibility of either a single or a group of UI components at design time, by checking the value of a single cell in the embedded spreadsheet. The UI component(s) is only visible when the value is equal to a constant text value or that of another single cell. Note that the operator is always Equal To. You cannot define any other operator.

If you have some experience with the tab set component, you may find that it can also be used to define what components are displayed on the dashboard at what time. To achieve this, you put different UI components on different tabs, and when the user switches among tabs, different components are displayed on the single canvas. Figure 8.10 below what's displayed on the canvas when the user switches among the tabs of the tab set component.

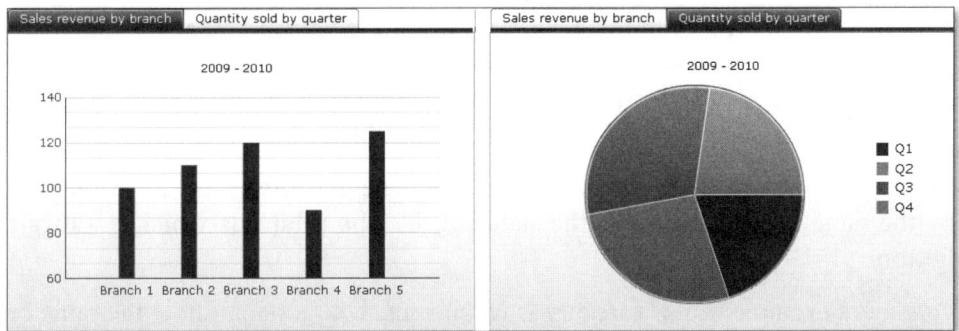

Figure 8.10 Dynamic Visibility Achieved with a Tab Set

This is a kind of dynamic visibility. In this section we'll ignore this type of usage of a tab set component and focus on how to show different UI components through the dynamic visibility property.

If you have ever used Crystal Reports 2008, you will find that it has a feature very similar to the dynamic visibility in Xcelsius. In Crystal Reports 2008, you can conditionally suppress a certain section with the Section Expert at runtime, based on the value of some data source fields or formulas.

8.2.1 When to Use Dynamic Visibility

Dynamic visibility is a very useful way for you to create an interactive dashboard. There are many situations where you can use it.

Give the User the Ability To Show or Hide a Single or Group of Components

This applies when you have some UI components in your dashboard as a supplement to those showing the main information, and you want the user to decide whether or not to see the additional info delivered by the supplementary components.

A typical use of this is the About or Help of the dashboard, which is a simple button at the corner of the dashboard. When it's clicked, a panel component appears showing what the dashboard is about or how to use it. Clicking the button again will hide the new component and return to the original screen.

Figure 8.11 shows an example of such a usage. At first, the dashboard shows the values in a line chart, as displayed in the left. When the user clicks the About button on the top right, the line chart becomes hidden, and a panel component appears, showing some basic info such as the version of the dashboard, displayed on the right. Meanwhile, the label of the About button becomes Close. Clicking on it again will revert the dashboard to its original state.

In this example, the visibilities of both the chart and the panel are controlled by the same cell, which stores the status of the About button, which is a toggle button.

One more example in this category is when some components show the same or similar data, but in different formats, and the user doesn't need see all of the components all of the time. The user can decide what kind of visualization he wants to see, and then the corresponding components are displayed and others become hidden. For example, you added two charts, one a column chart and the other a stacked column chart, to display sales for each region and/or sales trend. Users view either of these charts instead of viewing both simultaneously, by clicking a toggle button or selecting one from a combo box.

Make Smart Use of Dynamic Visibility | **8.2**

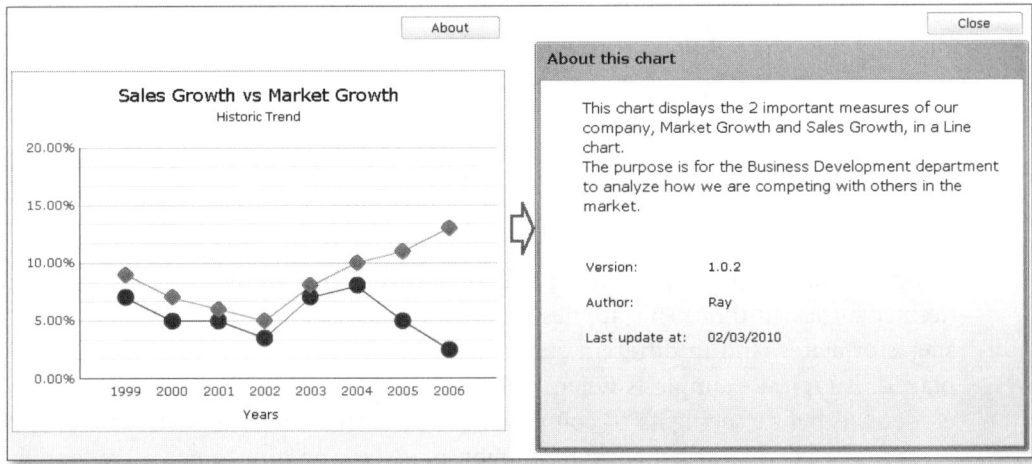

Figure 8.11 Show About the Dashboard Dynamically

Figure 8.12 illustrates this. The user can choose the visualization type from the combo box — a column chart or a pie chart.

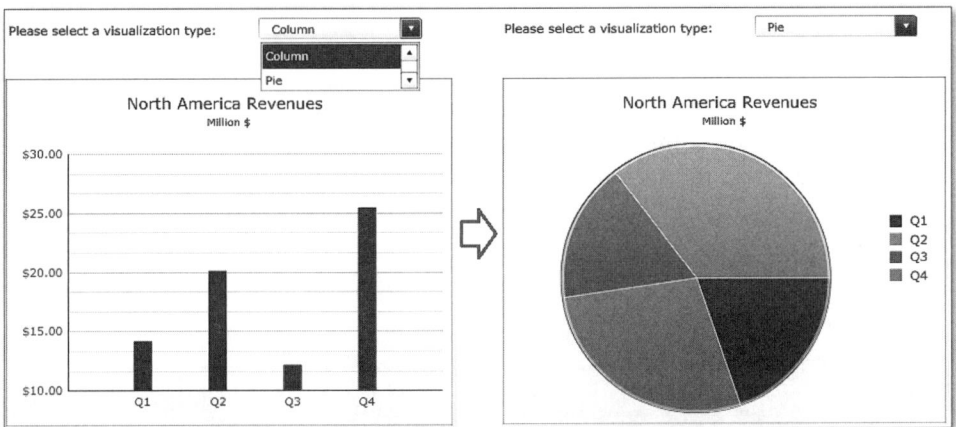

Figure 8.12 The User Can Decide to Show Different Components Based on Selection of a Combo Box

In this example, the visibilities are controlled dynamically by the combo box.

Another use of this is for the user to choose whether or not to see some supplementary information. Suppose you have some charts showing high-level aggregated data, such as the quarterly sales revenue of branches or product lines. As a supplement, you list some more detailed data, such as the daily sales revenue of

407

each product, in a list view or a spreadsheet component. At first, the component showing the detailed data is hidden. However, a button on the dashboard functions as a hide/display switch, and the user can click it to see the details when he wants to.

Show the UI Component that Should Be Shown

It's the difference between this and the situation described above is that whether or not to show a UI component is not controlled by the end user, but by the logic defined at design time. This applies when your dashboard is divided into several stages or states, and in different states, different UI components need to be displayed. A typical example is when your dashboard requires the user to enter his credentials before seeing its UI components with data. When the dashboard is first loaded, the user is presented with a logon panel asking him to enter credentials such as his access key. On a successful logon, the logon panel disappears, and the charts showing the confidential data are displayed.

We'll will see the effect of this and how to achieve it in the hands-on session shortly.

8.2.2 How to Use Dynamic Visibility

In Chapters 4 and 5 we have described how to use dynamic visibility to control the visibility of a UI component at runtime when talking about UI components. This property is common to most UI components. Figure 8.13 shows the typical properties related to Dynamic Visibility in the Properties panel.

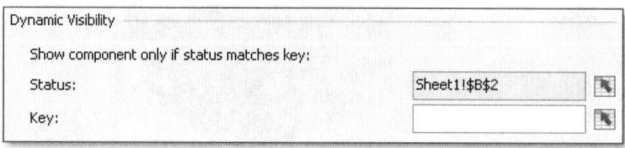

Figure 8.13 Dynamic Visibility Property in the Properties Panel

You need to specify two properties, as listed below.

- Status
  Bind Status to a cell that determines the visibility of the component. This cell is supposed to change at runtime.

▶ Key
Enter a value or bind it to a cell. The component is visible when the status matches the key.

The Key field is disabled until you have bound Status to a cell in the embedded spreadsheet. You can either enter a text directly in the field or click the Bind button to bind it to another cell.

The UI component is only displayed when the values of the two fields are equal.

Setting the dynamic visibility property of a single UI component is very straightforward. Sometimes, multiple UI components in your dashboard share the same dynamic visibility. For example, if your dashboard requires the user to enter his credentials before viewing any data, you need to provide one or more input fields for the user to enter his credentials, corresponding labels to indicate the purpose of each field, and a button to submit. All of these components share the same dynamic visibility property. Then we are faced with a question: How do you set this property for multiple components?

Of course, you can simply set dynamic visibility for each component and repeat the same steps for all of the components. This is a waste of time. Moreover, when the condition to show or hide them changes, you have to waste the time once more and try to avoid missing any component.

There are two better ways to do this, as explained below.

Multi-Select

Some properties are available in the Properties panel when multiple components are selected. Dynamic visibility is one of these. To do this, you hold down `Ctrl` on your keyboard and click to select multiple components. Then in the Properties panel, you can set the dynamic visibility property, once and for all.

However, when you need to update the status or key of the their dynamic visibility property, you should try to avoid missing any component before updating them.

You an further group those UI components by clicking the Group Components button on the toolbar after selecting them. In this way, when in the future you need to update the condition describing when to show or hide them, you can simply click on one the components to select them all. Thus, you will never miss a component.

Container

Another way is to include all of the components is to use a container component, described in Chapter 4, Section 4.4, and set the dynamic visibility property for the container only. The reason behind it is that when included in a container component such as a panel container, the UI components become part of the container and are shown or hidden along with it.

A typical usage of this is the logon panel when your dashboard requires the user to enter his credentials and click a Submit button before seeing the actual data, if he has the right to. To do this, we put all related components in a panel container and set its dynamic visibility instead of that of the related components. Figure 8.14 shows an example.

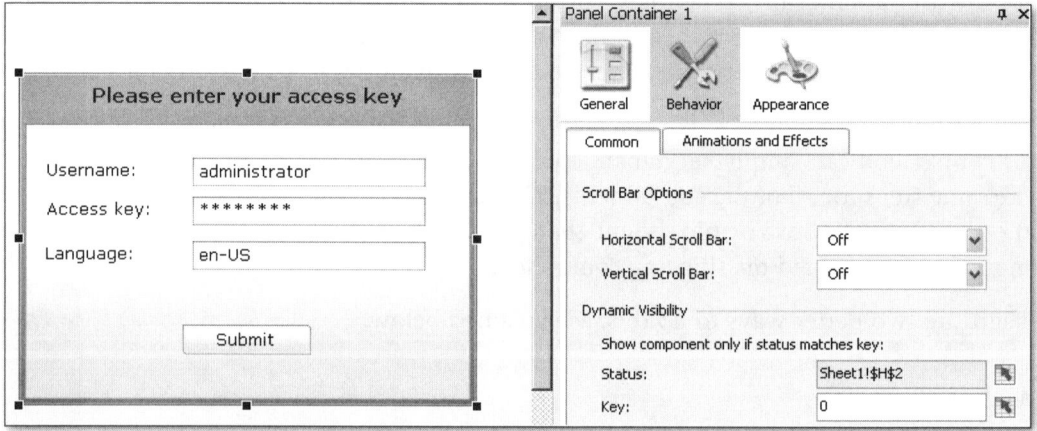

Figure 8.14 Set Dynamic Visibility Properties for Multiple Components in One Container

However, using an additional container changes the appearance of the dashboard. As you can see from Figure 8.14, the user will notice an extra header and borders around the labels, input texts, and button, which are part of the panel container. In the Properties panel of the container, you have no option to hide or remove the header or the borders. Therefore, you should not use this method if you don't want to display these extra spaces. Such a situation could occur when the components share the same dynamic visibility property logically but shouldn't be stand out in a container. For example, let's say you have a column and a pie chart to show the sales revenues of products and quarters together with some other components, which are visible after the user has entered correct credentials. They share the same dynamic visibility, but you don't want to wrap them inside a container. In this case, you have to use the method of selecting or grouping them all then setting the dynamic visibility property.

8.2.3 Practice

We'll go through a comprehensive hands-on example here to demonstrate the use of dynamic visibility for multiple UI components.

Suppose you are going to create a dashboard showing your company's retained profit of each quarter last year, which is very sensitive information. To help protect this information, you only show the data when the user has entered the correct credentials that have been granted access to it. For simplicity, we'll assume the data is secured with an access key, or shared secret. The user is granted permission to the data if he has entered correct key.

1. Plan the data.
   Basically, the data can be divided into four categories.
   - Metadata
     The purpose of the dashboard, the author, and the titles or labels
   - Logon data
     The access key the user has entered
   - Values
     The retained profit of each quarter
   - Indicating data
     Whether the log on is successful or not

Figure 8.15 shows what the data is like in the embedded spreadsheet in this sample dashboard. You can further customize it according to your requirements. For example, you can localize the labels and titles.

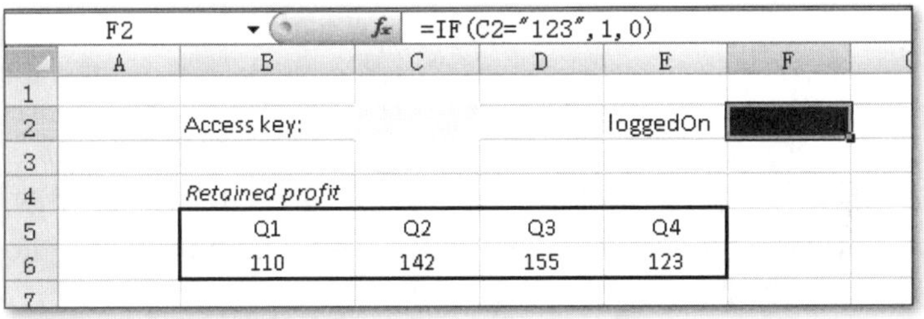

	A	B	C	D	E	F
1						
2		Access key:			loggedOn	
3						
4		Retained profit				
5		Q1	Q2	Q3	Q4	
6		110	142	155	123	
7						

F2: =IF(C2="123", 1, 0)

Figure 8.15 Data in the Embedded Spreadsheet for our Hands-On Example

As you can see from this figure, cell Sheet1!$C$2 is used to store the access key the user has entered, and cell range Sheet1!$B5$:$E$6 stores the confidential data.

A special cell, Sheet1!$F$2, is used to check whether the user's access key is valid, as the indicating data. It's calculated with Excel formulas by checking whether the user's access key is equal to 123, which is the key the designer and the granted end user have agreed on.

2. Set up the UI components for logon.

    Obviously, we need an input text component for the user to enter his access key and a label component for the input text. We'll bind the input text's destination under Data Insertion to cell Sheet1!$C$2 so that the text the user enters in this field will be inserted into that cell.

    When the user has entered his access key, there should be a button for him to say, "Hey, I have finished entering my access key, can you show me the retained profit now?" To do this, we add a toggle button component as the Submit button. Clicking on it will trigger the calculation of cell Sheet1!$F$2.

    By now, there's one label, one input text, and one toggle button on the canvas. You can move and position them as you like. Figure 8.16 shows the three components on the canvas and the Properties panel of the input text.

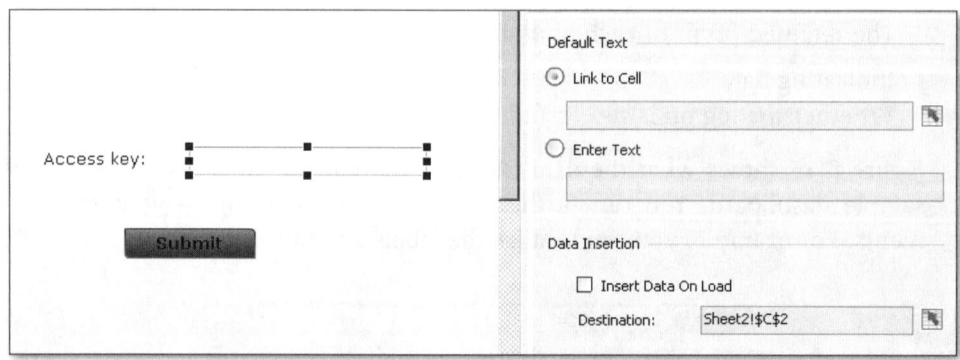

Figure 8.16 UI Components for the Logon Panel

We don't want the toggle button to look different with each click. To do this, we change its on and off labels to "Submit." Similarly, make the button and the labels the same color in both the on and off status.

3. Set up the chart for the data.

   Now let's set up the chart displaying the retained profit of each quarter. It's very simple. We'll drag and drop a pie chart onto the canvas, set its position, and bind its labels to range Sheet1!$B$5:$E$5 and its values to range Sheet1!$B$6:$E$6.

   Figure 8.17 shows the pie chart on the canvas and its Properties panel. Note that it has masked the three components defined in the last step, because we want to show it in the same position as the three components, both in the center of the canvas.

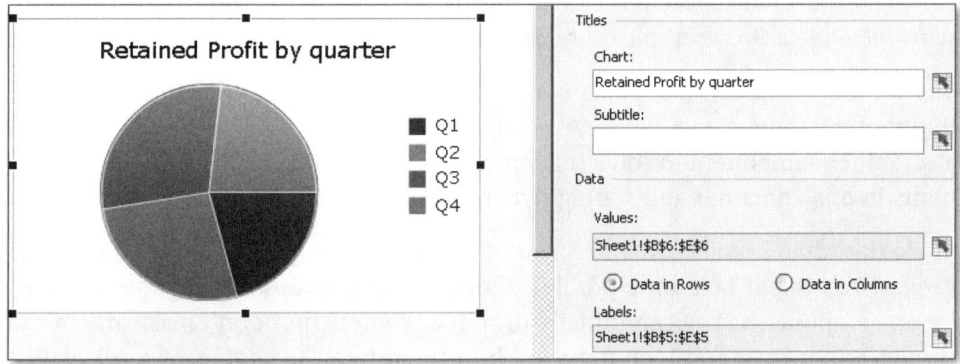

Figure 8.17 Data for the Pie Chart

4. Set up dynamic visibility.

   Now we come to the most important step in this hands-on example — setting the dynamic visibility of each component.

   As we have planned, cell Sheet1!$F$2 checks the user's access key and returns 1 if it's acceptable and 0 otherwise. You may want to bind Status to this cell and set Key to 0 in BEHAVIOR • COMMON • DYNAMIC VISIBILITY for the three logon components. For the pie chart, also bind Status to this cell but set Key to 1. That is, show the pie chart when the user has entered a correct access key and clicked the Submit button.

   Then the first problem you need solve is how to select each of the three logon components, because they have been masked by the pie chart. To do this, go to the Object Browser and click the Show/Hide button to hide the pie chart for now, as displayed in Figure 8.18. Note that you are only hiding the pie chart at design time, not at runtime.

8 | Special Features

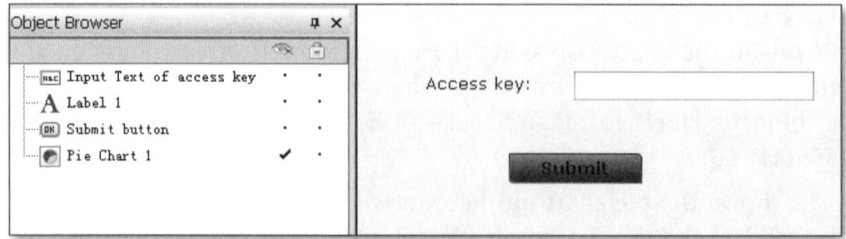

Figure 8.18 Hide Pie Chart with the Object Browser

To quickly find the UI component we want, we have renamed the text input and the toggle button to make them distinguishable. For a description of how to work with the Object Browser, please refer to Section 2.7 in Chapter 2.

The second problem is that you are repeating the same steps to set the dynamic visibility of the three components. As mentioned in the previous section, we can use a container component to solve this problem, by including all three of the components in one container and setting dynamic visibility for the container only.

To do this, drag a panel container from the Components view and drop it onto the canvas. You might be a little puzzled about where to drop it to include the three logon components. You can initially drop it anywhere, but don't mask any of the three components, and then move each of them into the container, as displayed in Figure 8.19.

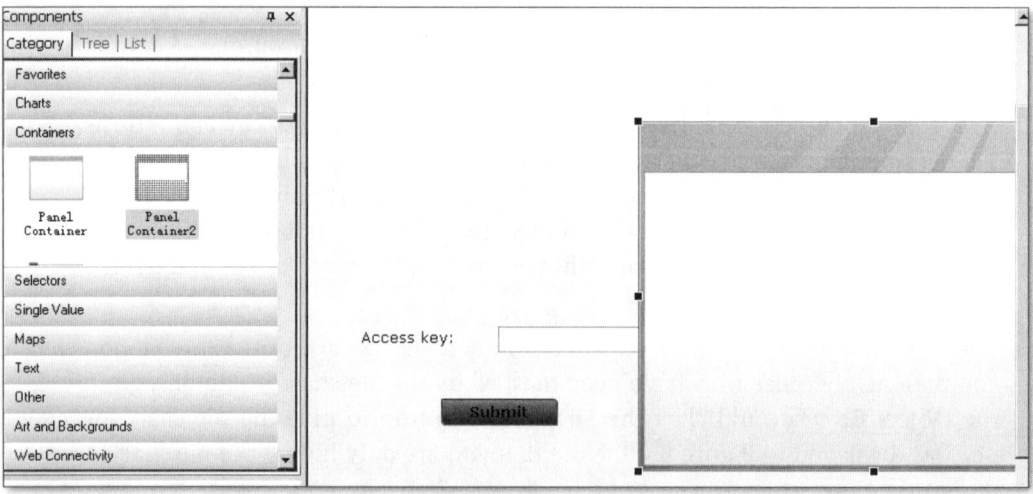

Figure 8.19 Drop the Panel Container Anywhere on the Canvas

414

Then, drag one of the components, move it into the container, and drop it there, as displayed in Figure 8.20.

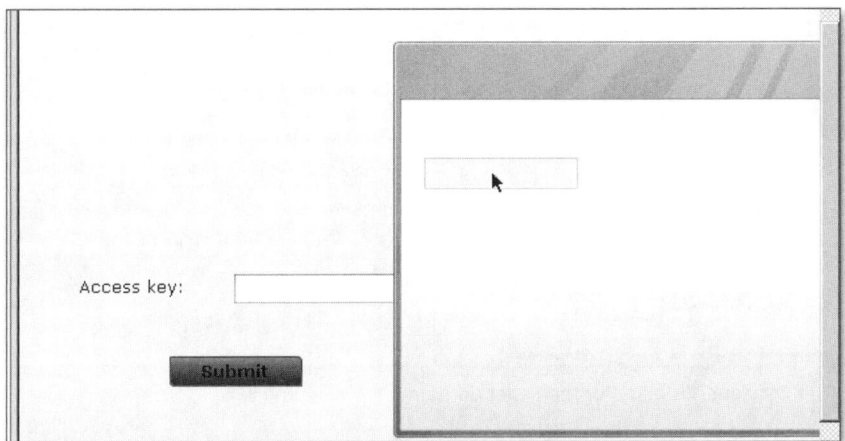

Figure 8.20 Drag the Three UI Components into the Panel Container

Repeat this step for the other two components. You may find that if you have grouped these components, you can move them all in one step and, furthermore, keep their relative positions during the move. This is a practical use of grouping components.

When you're finished, move the container to the center of the canvas and set its dynamic visibility property, as displayed in Figure 8.21.

Now the logon panel is done. The panel container, along with the label, the text input, and the toggle button, is only visible before the user has entered a valid access key, when the value in cell Sheet1!$F$2 is not equal to 0.

Setting dynamic visibility for the pie chart is very simple. You can select it in the Object Browser, select Behavior and then the Common tab, bind the Status field to cell Sheet1!$F$2, and set its Key to 1, which indicates a valid access key.

At runtime, the user is first presented with the logon screen. When the user clicks the Submit button, Xcelsius will calculate the value of cell Sheet1!$F$2. If it's 0, that is, if the user's access key doesn't match the agreed-on one, the dashboard remains on the logon screen, and nothing changes. However, when the user has entered a valid access key and then clicks the Submit button, the value in cell Sheet1!$F$2 becomes 1, causing the panel container to hide and the pie chart to show.

8 | Special Features

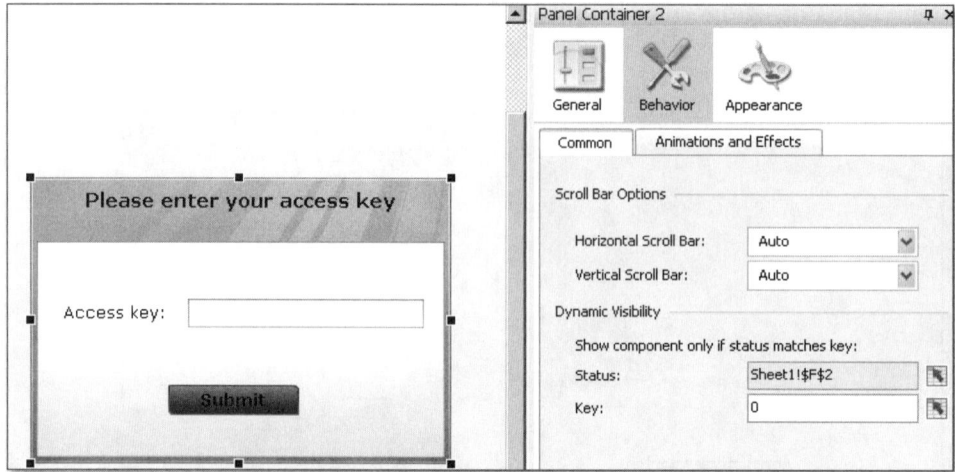

Figure 8.21 Set Dynamic Visibility for the Panel Container

Figure 8.22 shows the screen before and after the user clicks the Submit button with a valid access key entered in the input text.

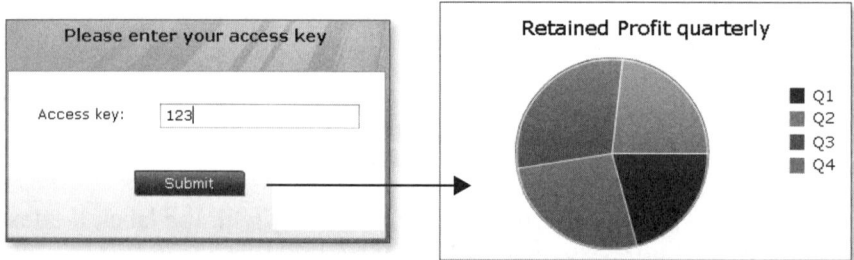

Figure 8.22 Screen Before and After the User Submits Valid Credentials

You can find the complete source file for this hands-on example on this book's web page at *www.sap-press.com*.

8.3 Alerts

Alerts are commonly used to call the user's attention to a specific item(s) that has reached some predefined limit by highlighting the item in a contrasting color. The user can then focus on these items and take action accordingly. These limits are often called thresholds, targets, budgets, or benchmarks and are the standards to which an item is compared to define what category it falls in.

Xcelsius provides an alert feature in a very user-friendly, easy-to-use and flexible way, so you can show different colors for different data items in a chart, icon, grid component, and so on.

Using alerts in your dashboard is very simple and easy, as we explained in Chapter 4 in the section on column charts, and as you will see in the next section. It's an important function because it allows the end user to quickly grasp the important items he should focus on with the help of your dashboard.

8.3.1 How to Use Alerts

Alerts can be enabled for UI components satisfying the following two conditions.

- The component is used to represent values. This includes most charts and single-value components but not selectors or containers.
- The component has only one series. That's why you cannot use alerts for pie charts or for charts with multiple series.

For example, you can configure alerts for a line chart with one series, but the Enable Alerts checkbox will become disabled if you add one more series to it.

You can define the alerts behavior in the Alerts tab in the Properties panel of the UI component. Briefly, the steps to configure alerts are as follows.

1. Select Enable Alerts in the Alerts tab to active alerts.
2. Select the alert method that suits your needs.
   If you want to define the status (good or bad) by the absolute value, select By Value. Otherwise, to define the status by the percentage of the absolute value against a base value, select By Percentage and then specify the target value as a constant number or bind it to a cell in the embedded spreadsheet.
3. Define alert thresholds.
   You can double-click a field to update the threshold of any existing range or enter a value and click Add to add a new threshold. If you want to dynamically define the thresholds, you can select Use a Range to bind the threshold definitions to a cell range, so the user can define what values are good at runtime, with the help of some other UI component such as a slider.

4. Define colors for each range.
   This step is as important as the last step of defining alert thresholds, because this is what the end user sees. In other words, the color you specify for each range here determines what items will get the user's attention. For example, if you highlight the values of certain range, you can define an outstanding color for that range so that the user can quickly focus on what you want him to.

   To take advantage of Xcelsius' built-in coloring mechanism, select Enable Auto Colors. In this case, you need tell Xcelsius what values are good by selecting the corresponding option in the Color Order area.

8.3.2 Practice

As you have seen above and in Chapter 4 when we discussed column charts, it's not difficult to use alerts in your dashboard. The hands-on example here is for you to better understand alerts as a common and useful feature of Xcelsius 2008, not just a property of some UI components.

Suppose you're going are to create a dashboard for the marketing department to find a range to define the "top-sold" product categories. To do this, you first create a column chart showing and comparing the quantities sold of all product categories. To highlight the top-sold categories with a very good market, you enable alerts to show them in different colors. The user can dynamically adjust the threshold at runtime. Meanwhile, for the top-sold categories, you want to know whether their total quantity sold takes up a reasonable proportion of the total quantity. As common sense, the total quantity sold is defined as "reasonable" if its percentage of the grand total is between 45% and 65%.

You don't know how to define a category as good or bad at design time, that is, how to define the top-sold product categories. Instead, you want the user to adjust the threshold at runtime to determine an appropriate threshold range, so that the total quantity sold of product categories above the threshold is reasonable. Now, let's begin.

You don't know how to define a category as good or bad at design time. Instead, you want the user to:

1. Plan the data.
   For simplicity, we won't use data connectivity here. We'll hardcode the data in the embedded spreadsheet.

The data in this hands-on example is very simple. We need a range to store the product categories and their corresponding quantities sold, which might be live data retrieved using some data connectivity, and a cell to store the threshold value of the "good" categories, which the user adjusts with a slider.

We also need to calculate some more data to determine the percentage of the quantity of the top-sold products against the grand total. To do this, we'll add a new row below the actual quantities sold by comparing the actual value with the threshold and returning the actual value for those above the threshold and 0 for others.

Your data should be similar to Figure 8.23.

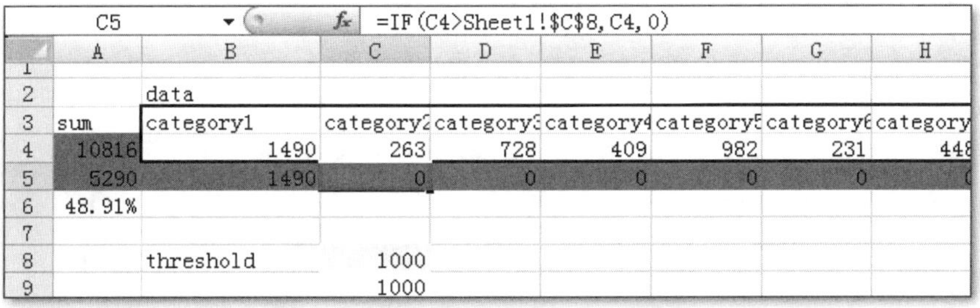

	A	B	C	D	E	F	G	H
1								
2		data						
3	sum	category1	category2	category3	category4	category5	category6	category
4	10816	1490	263	728	409	982	231	448
5	5290	1490	0	0	0	0	0	0
6	48.91%							
7								
8		threshold		1000				
9				1000				

(C5 = IF(C4>Sheet1!$C$8, C4, 0))

Figure 8.23 Data in the Embedded Spreadsheet

Note that only data in cell range Sheet1!$B$3:$R$4 is the actual data. Other data is calculated by Excel functions. So if you want to replace the hard-coded data in this hands-on example with your live data, simply map the output values of your data connectivity to cell range Sheet1!$B$3:$R$4.

2. Set up the UI components.

We need a column chart to show the quantity sold of each product category, a horizontal slider to define the threshold value of the good categories, and a gauge indicating whether the good categories are in a reasonable status.

For this, we'll drag these components onto the canvas and position them. Binding data is very simple, and we won't go into the details here. Briefly, the data of the column chart is bound to range Sheet1!$B$3:$R$4, the horizontal slider to cell Sheet1!$C$8, and the gauge to Sheet1!$A$5. Your canvas should be similar to what's displayed in Figure 8.24.

8 | Special Features

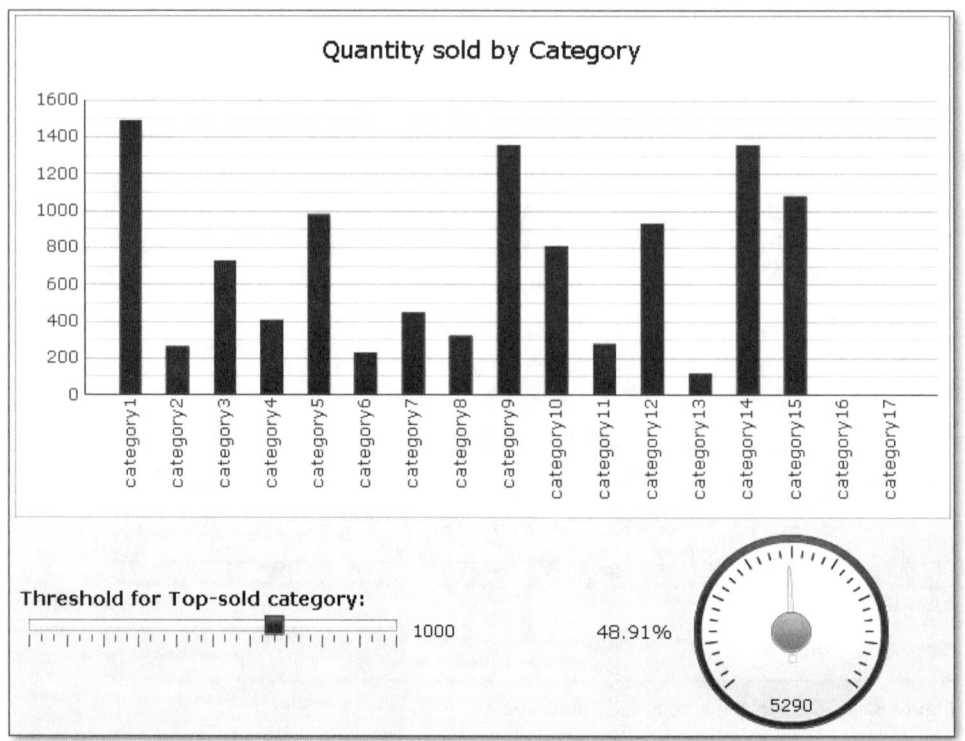

Figure 8.24 UI Components on the Canvas

3. Define alerts.

   This step is the focus of this hands-on example, to define appropriate alerts for each UI component.

   For the column chart, after selecting the Enable Alerts checkbox to activate the alerts tab, select By Value because we want to distinguish the categories by their absolute quantities sold.

   Only categories with a quantity sold above the user-defined value will be highlighted. To do this, select Use a Range, and bind the range to the cell where the user-defined threshold is stored. Xcelsius will then create two ranges at runtime based on the value of that cell: One range is from minimum to the value in the cell, and the other is from the value in the cell to the maximum.

   This may seem puzzling, because there are still three ranges defined in the Properties panel after binding the range to the cell, as displayed in Figure 8.25.

420

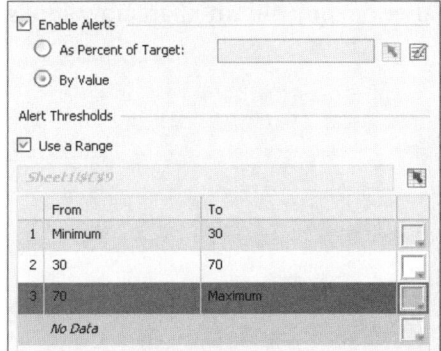

Figure 8.25 Three Ranges Displayed Only when One Threshold Is Defined

As a result, you cannot go on to set colors for each range because the cell is now empty. To solve this problem, give the cell a default value such as "1000." Xcelsius will detect the value and update the range definition immediately.

We want to customize the colors to highlight the good categories. To do this, unselect Enable Auto Colors and set the color of the first range to a neutral one (e.g., navy) and the color of the second range to something conspicuous, for example, green.

You can also customize the color to some user-defined value by clicking the color button to launch the color picker and then clicking the Bind button to bind the color to a cell in the embedded spreadsheet, as displayed in Figure 8.26.

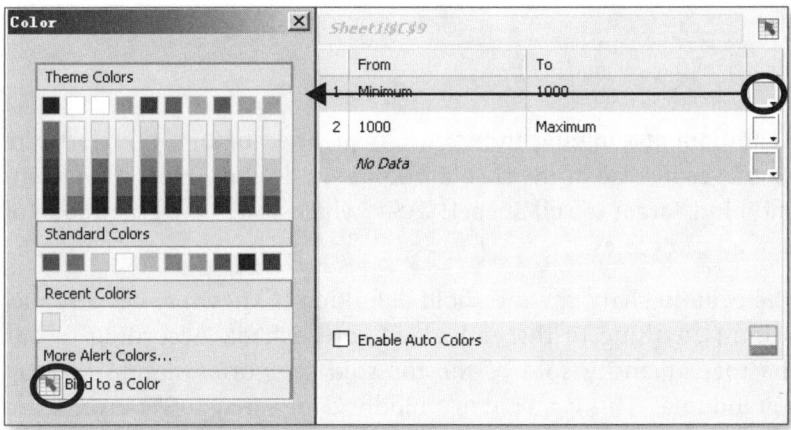

Figure 8.26 Bind a Color to a Cell in the Embedded Spreadsheet

That's all. The Alerts tab in the Properties panel of the column chart now looks like Figure 8.27.

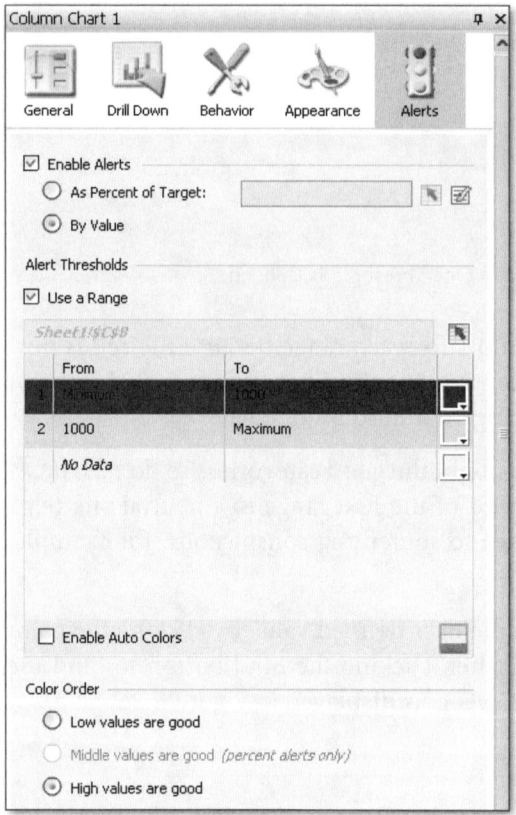

Figure 8.27 Alerts Tab for the Column Chart

For the gauge component showing the status, as planned before, the alerts are defined by percentages instead of the absolute value. To do this, select As Percentage of Target and bind Target to cell Sheet1!$A$4, which stores the grand total of quantities sold of all categories.

In contrast to the column chart, the threshold definition is known at design time, so we needn't bind anything to the embedded spreadsheet. According to our assumption, the total quantity sold of the top-sold categories should take up 45–65% of the grand total. This is a kind of "middle values are good" range. To do this, uncheck Enable Auto Colors, enter 20, 45, 65, and 80 in the Enter a Value field and click the Add button one by one. These four values will generate five ranges, of which less than 20% and greater than 80% are considered bad, 20–45% and 65–80% are warnings, and 45–65% is good. Click the Color button to specify colors for each, as displayed in Figure 8.28. In this example, we use red to indicate bad, yellow for warnings, and green for good.

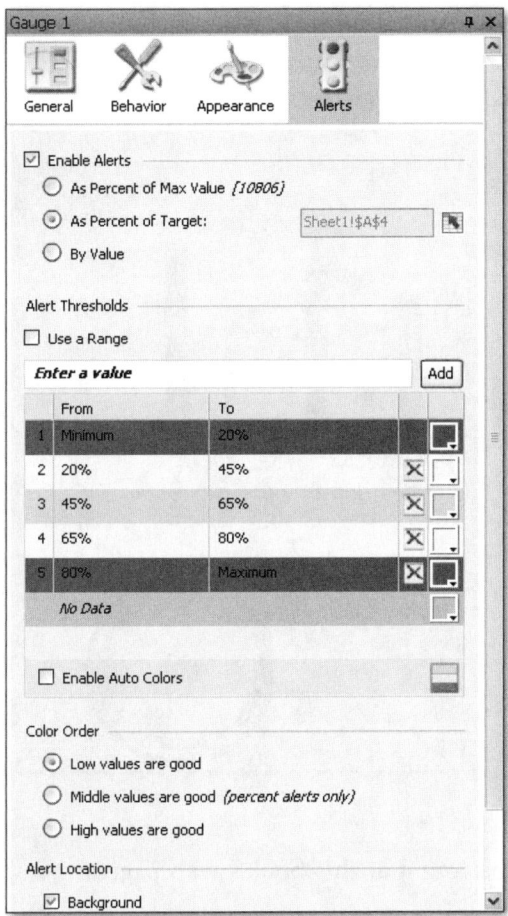

Figure 8.28 Alerts Tab for the Gauge

Now we are done. At runtime, the user moves the horizontal slider to adjust the threshold of top-sold categories. The colors of each column in the column chart will be updated accordingly based on the corresponding quantity sold, and the needle in the gauge moves to indicate whether the user's definition is reasonable. In this way the user can find an appropriate range to define the condition of a top-sold product category and make policies such as promotions and purchasing plans accordingly. In our example, we might find that it's appropriate to define the threshold between 900 and 1,100. That is, we can define any product category with a quantity sold larger than 900 and less than 1100 as a top-sold category.

Figure 8.29 shows a screenshot of the dashboard at runtime.

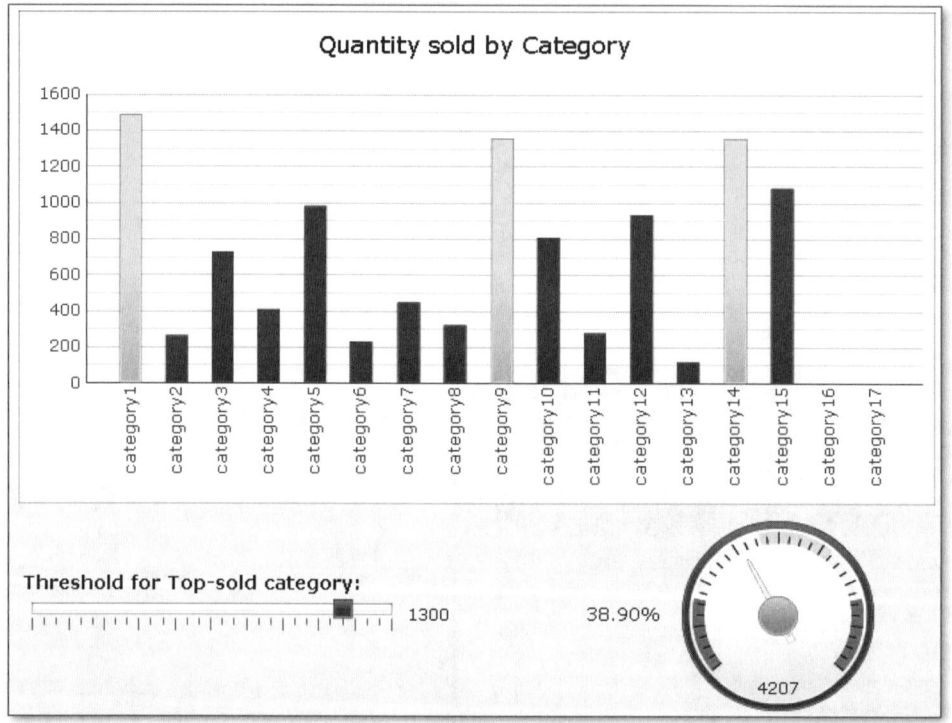

Figure 8.29 Our Dashboard at Runtime

The source file of this dashboard can be found at this book's web page at *www.sap-press.com*.

8.4 Export

Export is an important feature of Xcelsius. Basically, you create dashboards to illustrate data for information sharing and communication. Without the export functionality, you can only view the data inside the Xcelsius designer, which makes little sense in communication with others.

In Xcelsius 2008, you can export your dashboard as a local file, such as a PDF or Flash SWF file, or to an SAP BusinessObjects Enterprise system, thereby leveraging the power of this enterprise-level application. No matter what type you select, the exported dashboard is fully functional and interactive, instead of a plain image. The following sections will provide a detailed explanation of the various export types.

8.4.1 How to Use the Export Functionality

When you have come to the final stage in your dashboard design, you can export it by selecting FILE • EXPORT and choose an appropriate type. The toolbar also provides a quick way for you to export your dashboard to PowerPoint, Word, Outlook, PDF, and SAP BusinessObjects.

Flash

Adobe Flash, formerly known as Macromedia Flash, is now developed and distributed by Adobe. Flash files are generally in the SWF format, traditionally called ShockWave Flash movies, and usually have a .swf extension. It's widely used in web pages and other media types for animation. The benefits of exporting your dashboard to Adobe Flash is that it can run on almost all computers in the world and is operating system (OS) independent, so you needn't worry about whether the dashboard consumer can open your output, whether he is working on Windows, Linux, or Mac.

You can select this option if you want to export your dashboard into an Adobe Flash file, with a .swf extension, so that the user can double-click it to run when he has stand-alone Adobe Flash Player installed or access it via a web browser when the required plug-in is installed. You can send the Flash file as an attachment via email.

After clicking this command you will be prompted to enter the name you want to use for your Flash file and the folder to save it in.

AIR

AIR (Adobe Integrated Runtime) is a cross-platform, versatile runtime environment that can run Flash files. Before selecting Adobe AIR from the export options list, you need to have Java 2 Runtime Environment (J2EE) and Adobe Flex 3.0 SDK installed on your system and configured so that Xcelsius can find them.

The dashboard consumer needs have the Adobe AIR player installed. You can get it from the Adobe website at *http://get.adobe.com/air/*.

Both Flash and AIR are Adobe file formats that can run on your desktop. You can search the Internet to learn about the differences between them. Briefly, a Flash .swf file cannot access a local file until it's trusted by the consumer, as discussed in the section "Security Issues Related to Accessing External Data" in Chapter 6. On the other hand, AIR is browser-less and can access local storage and file systems, but it needs to be packaged, digitally signed, and installed on the consumer's local file system.

HTML

If you select this option, Xcelsius exports the dashboard to a Flash file and generates an HTML container. Then you can put the two files on a web server so that others can see your dashboard from a web browser. You can also integrate the dashboard with your web portal. You can further edit the HTML file to add more content, such as an introduction to the dashboard and users' comments about it.

If you have defined a Flash Variables connection in your dashboard, the Flash Variables will also be reflected in the HTML file. You can edit the HTML file to pass your customized values into the dashboard.

After clicking to select this option, you will be prompted to enter the file name and the folder to save the HTML file in. When you click OK, Xcelsius will generate one Flash file and one HTML file with the same name.

SAP BusinessObjects Platform

You can export your dashboard to an SAP BusinessObjects Enterprise platform as a Flash file so that other users in your company can see it in an InfoView or CMC (Central Management Console) through a web browser, and you can leverage SAP BusinessObjects Enterprise security in the meantime to control user access to your dashboard. Only users that have been granted the required rights in the SAP BusinessObjects system can access it.

After selecting this option, you will be prompted to enter the SAP BusinessObjects platform information in a dialog as shown in Figure 8.30.

Figure 8.30 Log on to SAP BusinessObjects Enterprise System Before Export

After entering the correct credentials, you need to select a folder to export your dashboard to. Then Xcelsius will generate a Flash SWF file and use an SAP BusinessObjects SDK to publish it to that folder. You can then specify who can access that SWF file in SAP BusinessObjects Enterprise. Note that this is the only way you can add a Flash SWF file to SAP BusinessObjects. You cannot directly upload the Flash file through SAP BusinessObjects BI portals such as InfoViews or CMC.

The benefit of this option is that you needn't export the dashboard and then send it to each consumer via email, which may be time-consuming and inconvenient to update. Instead, you export it to a specific folder in the SAP BusinessObjects Enterprise system. Then corporate users who have the required rights can access your dashboard and do further analyses.

Another benefit is that you can access other SAP BusinessObjects resources within your dashboard, without the need for the user to enter his credentials. For example, in your dashboard, if you are using Query as a Web Service, explained in Chapter 7, to access the source data, the end user needs to enter his credentials to log on to the SAP BusinessObjects Enterprise system before he can access the Query as a Web Service, which is deployed to an SAP BusinessObjects Enterprise system. However, when the dashboard has been exported to an SAP BusinessObjects platform, the platform will solve this problem when the user has logged on to the SAP BusinessObjects system.

For example, say you are in the IT department and have created one dashboard for the sales team and one for the HR team. You then export them to the corresponding folder. Within SAP BusinessObjects Enterprise you grant viewing rights to the folder for each team. When a user on the sales team logs on to SAP BusinessObjects Enterprise, he can see the dashboard in the sales folder.

To use this command, you need to have purchased an Xcelsius Enterprise license. Otherwise, this command will be disabled.

PDF

You can export your dashboard to PDF (Portable Document Format), a file format created by Adobe for creating documents in a manner independent of the application software, hardware, and operating system. Your dashboard will function completely the same everywhere, including the texts, fonts, images, and animations.

After selecting this option, you will be prompted to enter the file name and location for the PDF file. You can send it to consumers who can then view your dashboard in the PDF file. The dashboard in the PDF file is fully functional, not just an image.

You can also choose which version of Adobe Acrobat to use, either Acrobat 6 for PDF 1.5 or Adobe 9 for PDF 1.6. However, when exporting your dashboard to PDF through the toolbar, the exported document will always be in Acrobat 9 format.

Only one PDF file is generated in this case, with the Flash object embedded. It's different from exporting to HTML, which generates one SWF file and one HTML file.

PowerPoint Slide

Xcelsius can export your dashboard into a Microsoft PowerPoint file, thus making your presentation more attractive and interactive.

You may choose this option when you want to use the dashboard during a presentation using PowerPoint. For example, during a company conference, the sales manager can embed a dashboard showing global sales status in his presentation. In this way, he can show the sales info in different quarters or branches in the intuitive dashboard, without leaving the presentation.

After selecting this option you will be prompted to enter the file name and location for the PowerPoint file. Xcelsius will create a PowerPoint file with one slide where your dashboard is embedded, and automatically open it. Your dashboard may appear blank in PowerPoint in Edit mode, but don't worry; it will behave perfectly in Slide Show mode.

So what's behind the scenes? Xcelsius generates a temporary Flash file in your User directory (for example, *C:\Users\ray\AppData\Local\Temp*), and embeds it into a PowerPoint slide as a Macro Control.

Maybe you have noticed a limitation here. The generated PowerPoint file has only one slide, while usually we want to add the dashboard to an existing PowerPoint presentation. For example, say an HR manager is preparing his presentation for a year-end conference, and after the first few slides about some general info, he wants to add a dashboard to show the on-board and resignation status. To solve this problem, he can either copy the Flash object from the exported slide or manually insert the generated Flash file to PowerPoint. You can insert a Flash file into a PowerPoint slide either via the menu path INSERT • OBJECT or from the Developer tab.

Xcelsius is not required at runtime to display the dashboard inside the PowerPoint file. Only PowerPoint and Adobe Flash Player are.

Outlook

You can quickly send out your dashboard via email by exporting it to Outlook. When you select this option, Xcelsius generates a temp Flash file and launches Outlook to create a new mail message with that generated Flash file (.swf) as an attachment. You can then add more content to the message and send it out.

If you want to see the generated Flash file, go to the Temporary Internet Files folder on your computer, for example, *C:\Documents and Settings\Administrator\Local Settings\Temporary Internet Files\Content.Outlook\A9LU74IT\swfA.swf*.

Word

Xcelsius is tightly integrated with Microsoft Office products including Excel, PowerPoint, and Outlook. You can also export your dashboard to a Word document to make your document more attractive.

Similar to exporting to a PowerPoint slide, after selecting this option you will be prompted to enter a file name and location for the Word document. Xcelsius will generate a Word document embedding your dashboard, which will function the same as you see in Xcelsius. You can further edit the Word document to make it more meaningful, such as adding some words around the dashboard to explain its context and purpose.

8 | Special Features

In contrast to exporting your dashboard to Outlook or PowerPoint, when you select Word, the dashboard is embedded into the Word document as a ShockWave Flash object; it is not linked there. You will see that the size of the generated Word document is somewhat large — maybe over 1 megabyte.

8.5 Themes and Colors

When creating dashboards, you may wonder how Xcelsius colors the UI components. For example, how is the color of each data part of a pie chart defined. This is where themes and colors come into play.

Similar to many applications such as Microsoft Windows Operation System, in Xcelsius, a theme defines the global styles and properties of all components, including color, font styles and even behavior. It provides an easy way to customize the components and maintain a consistent look and feel among all components throughout your dashboard. This concept may be called skin in some other applications.

Color has a great impact on your dashboard. A misuse of color may negatively affect your dashboard and weaken the user experience. Colors define the color schema of your dashboard, that is, what color is used for each part of any UI component. The colors of the canvas background; the titles, labels, and values of a text component; and the mouse-over and selected colors are all defined in the color scheme. For example, a pie chart may have many parts, and the color of the first, second, and other parts is defined in the color scheme. A color scheme is also included in a theme, but you can further customize your components by changing the color scheme, within the same theme.

A theme also defines what colors are used to render the UI components. However, it is not just about colors. A theme also contains information about fonts and many other visual effects. When you have many UI components on the canvas, you can see the differences when switching to another theme. In fact, you can change the color scheme of a theme, thereby changing the colors of the UI components while maintaining the fonts and other visual effects.

8.5.1 How to Use Themes and Color

Generally, you can select from a list of themes and colors, which have been well-defined by Xcelsius 2008, to quickly make your dashboard attractive and professional. You can also switch among them, thus providing a different look and feel for your dashboard, without the need to modify your dashboard. You cannot create a new theme, but you can create your own customized color schemes.

How To Apply a Theme

Xcelsius provides some predefined themes such as Aqua, Aero, and Nova as displayed in Figure 8.31. The default theme is Nova.

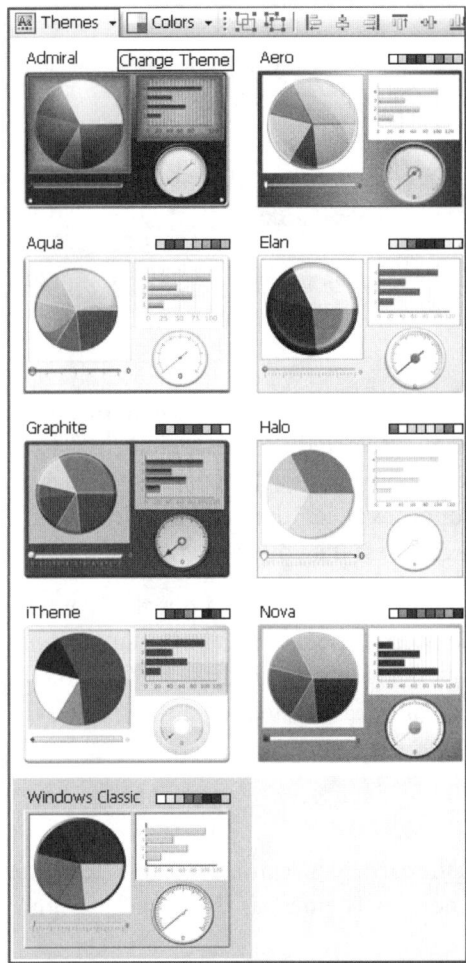

Figure 8.31 Available Themes from the Toolbar

As displayed in this figure, the themes are listed in two columns. Each theme's name is displayed on the top left, with the color scheme on the top right, and an

8 | Special Features

example on the bottom. You can get a rough idea about the styles of each theme from its colors and sample.

To apply a theme to your dashboard, simply select one from the Themes dropdown list, as displayed in Figure 8.31. You can also achieve this by electing FORMAT • THEMES and selecting one from the list window, as displayed in Figure 8.32.

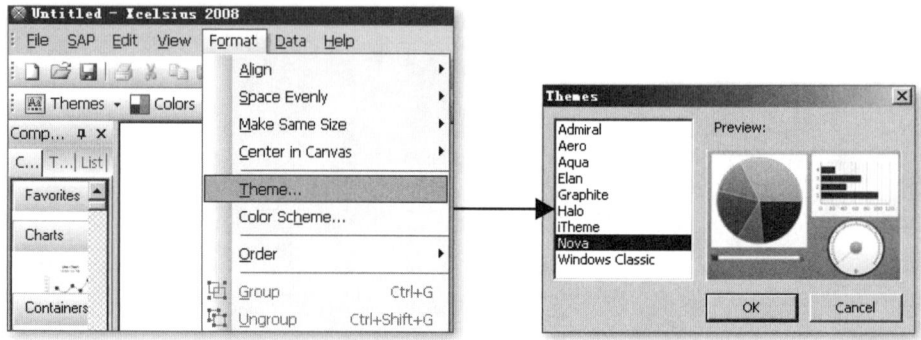

Figure 8.32 Available Themes from the Menu

When you change the theme of your dashboard, the look and feel of all of the UI components will be updated according to your selected theme, including colors, font family, font styles, and visual effects. If you have customized the colors or fonts of the UI components through the Properties sheet, they will be overwritten. You can test each theme to find out which one best fits your design.

You may underestimate the usefulness of themes when you find out that you can also customize the colors and fonts in the Properties panels. It is important to note that some other properties, such as lighting effects in some charts, are invisible in the Properties sheet. You may have noticed this when switching among different themes.

How To Apply a Color Scheme

To apply a new color scheme to your dashboard, you can select one from the Colors dropdown list in the toolbar area, next to Themes, as displayed in Figure 8.33.

The colors are listed vertically, with the name on the right and the sample colors on the left. Note that the first color scheme is Current Theme Colors, which are defined in themes and are what you are currently using for the UI components in your dashboard by default, if you haven't switched to another scheme.

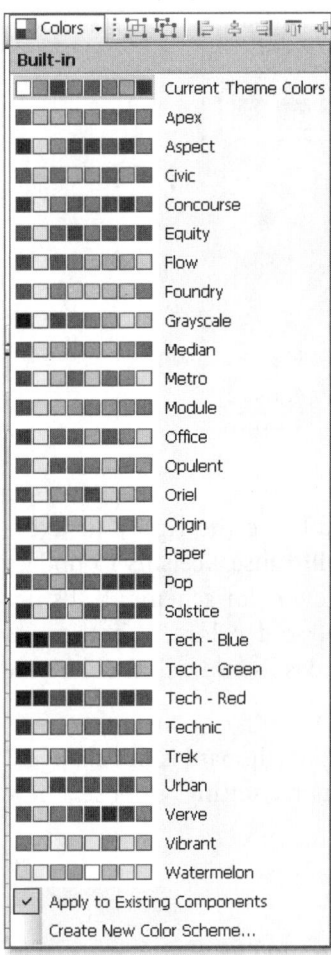

Figure 8.33 Available Color Schemes from Toolbar

You can also achieve this by going to FORMAT • COLOR SCHEMES and selecting a scheme in the list window, as shown in Figure 8.34.

You can click the Delete button on the bottom to delete a color scheme in the Custom category. However, those in the Built-In category cannot be deleted or edited.

You may wonder whether the order of the colors in a color scheme makes sense. We'll cover that in the next section when we create a color scheme of our own.

8 | Special Features

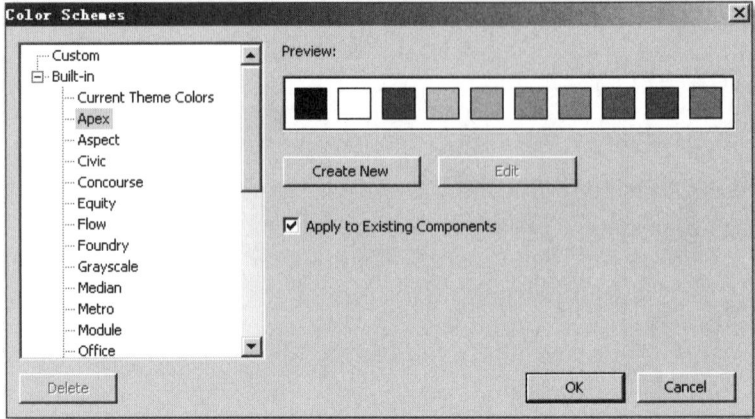

Figure 8.34 Available Color Schemes from the Menu

With both methods of selecting a color scheme you'll see the Apply to Existing Components checkbox, which, when selected, will cause Xcelsius to update the existing UI components on the canvas with the new color scheme. If it's not selected, the existing UI components will keep their old colors. Whether it's checked or not, any UI component you added to your dashboard will use the new color scheme.

When you apply a new color scheme, the theme of your dashboard is not changed. That is, the UI components retain their styles and property settings but use a new color palette.

How To Create a Customized Color Scheme

You cannot create a custom theme for Xcelsius, but you can create your own color schemes. The color schemes are XML files that define the color palette used to set the colors for each part of each component. You can find the XML files at *%XCEL-SIUS_DIR%/assets/themes*, for example, *C:\Program Files\Business Objects\Xcelsius\assets\themes*. In this folder is a subfolder called Built-In, which stores all of the built-in Xcelsius 2008 color schemes. You can take a look at the XML files for a better understanding of color schemes.

Sometimes you may want to create your own color scheme and reuse it in your dashboards. For example, to define a color scheme for your company so that all dashboards you and your colleagues design look similar, you create a color scheme first and then send it to others. Your colleagues will apply this color scheme when designing dashboards, thus ensuring a consistent look and feel.

To do this, you click Create New Color Scheme... in the Colors dropdown list in the toolbar area, or click the Create New button in the menu FORMAT • COLOR SCHEMES. A window will pop up for you to enter the name and select the colors of your color scheme, as shown in Figure 8.35.

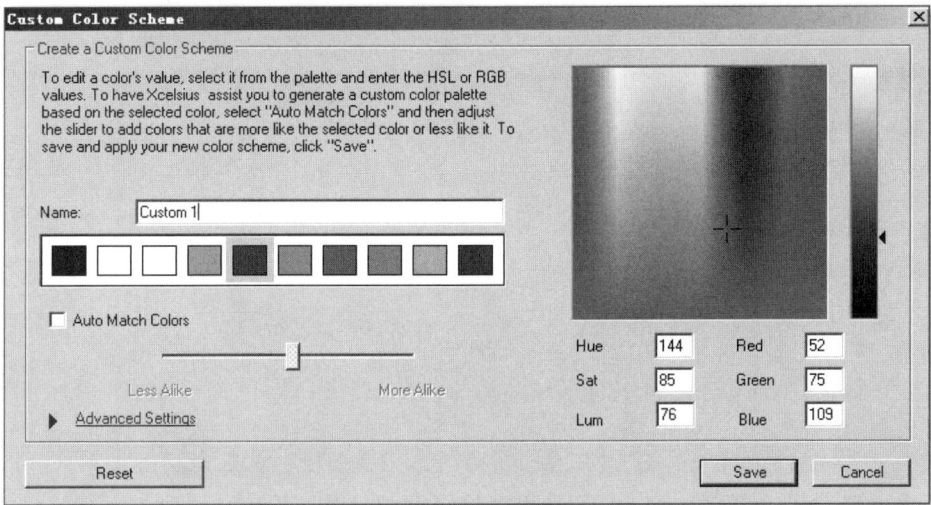

Figure 8.35 Create a New Color Scheme

Xcelsius can help you design your color scheme. To have Xcelsius assist you, click on the color palette to set a base color, and then select Auto Match Colors. Xcelsius will generate a custom color palette based on the selected color. You can then adjust the color palette by dragging the slider bar from Less Alike to More Alike. While you're dragging, the colors will be updated. Then, if you want to make some change to a certain color, unselect Auto Match Colors, select the color you want to change, and click on the right color palette to set a new color.

You can also set colors in more detail, by expanding Advanced Settings and setting the color for each item, as shown in Figure 8.36.

The color of each property is defined by the colors in the scheme. However, you can only configure 10 colors in a color scheme, although there are many more visual parts for which you want to configure colors. So what color among the 10 is used for what visual part? You can try them out by setting a conspicuous color for each of the 10 colors listed below Name, with Auto Match Colors unselected, and check what colors are updated in the Advanced Settings area. For example, as displayed in Figure 8.37, we'll set the first item of a custom color scheme to a very conspicuous color — red. When checking the colors of each tab in the Advanced

8 | Special Features

Settings area, we find out that this item in the color scheme controls the default colors of all items in the Text tab, all texts of charts, default and mouse-over colors of the label texts of selectors, the rick color of single-value components, the region border color of maps, and the button symbol color of scroll bars.

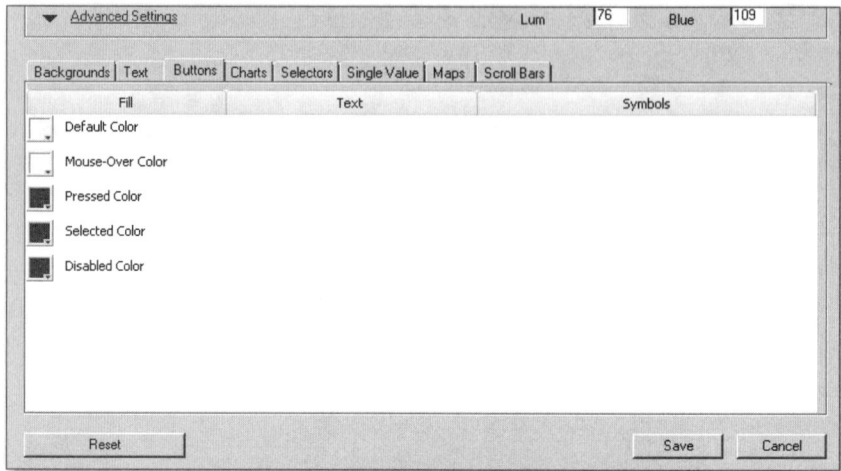

Figure 8.36 Advanced Settings When Editing a Custom Color Scheme

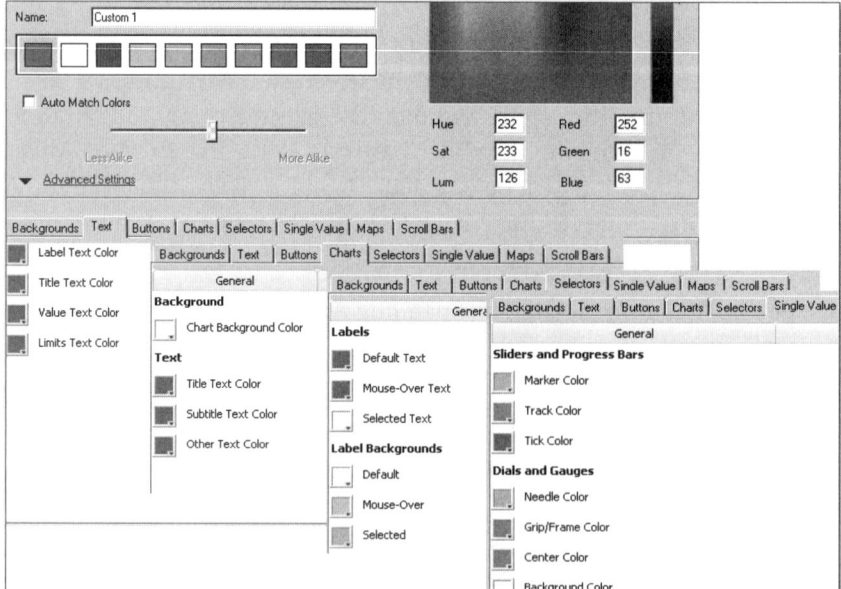

Figure 8.37 Usage of Each Color of the Scheme

To change a color in the color scheme, click to select it and choose one in the color picker to the right. Colors in the Advanced Settings will be updated accordingly, which may cost some time, during which period input is disabled.

The table below displays what UI components are affected by each color item in a color scheme, according to our investigation.

Item	Affected UI Components Parts
1	Texts of any part of all components
2	Default and mouse-over colors of buttons, chart background, selected text color of the label and default label background of selectors, dial and gauge background, default and mouse-over colors of maps, track and button color of scroll bars
3	Canvas background
4	Component background color, mouse-over color of selectors, selectable color of maps, thumb color of scroll bars
5	Chart series 1 (e.g., the first data part in a pie chart, the columns of the first series in a column chart, etc.), selected color of buttons, label background color of selectors when selected, marker color of sliders and progress bars, needle color of dials and gauges, region color of maps when selected
6	Chart series 2
7	Chart series 3
8	Chart series 4
9	Chart series 5
10	Disabled color of buttons, track color of sliders and progress bars, grip/frame color and center color of dials and gauges

You can specify any color, such as the background color of each chart, in Advanced Settings by selecting the Charts tab, clicking on the color next to Chart Background Color and customize your color from the color picker. Repeat these steps for any other color you want to customize.

To save your custom color scheme, click the Save button. It's then saved as an XML file in a custom subfolder beneath *%XCELSIUS_DIR%/assets/themes*, for example, in *C:\Program Files\BusinessObjects\Xcelsius\assets\themes\custom*.

To share your custom color scheme with others, send the XML file to them. They can then copy the XML file to the location on the file system where Xcelsius is installed, for example either "custom" or "built-in" under the folder *%XCELSIUS_*

DIR%/assets/themes. The difference lies in where they will see the custom color scheme when choosing among all of the available schemes — either in the category Built-In or the category Custom. The color scheme cannot be edited if it's placed in the subfolder Built-In.

If you are using Xcelsius 2008 SP3, things are a little different. The custom color scheme is not saved to the subfolder Custom, but to your personal folder such as *C:\Users\Ray\AppData\Roaming\XcelsiuscustomThemes*.

8.6　Summary

In this chapter, we explained some common and useful properties of most UI components from the perspective of an entire dashboard, not an individual component. The features we covered here are very useful in your design, and you will use them frequently to create professional dashboards. They include drill-down, alerts, color schemes, and so on. We hope you have gotten a big picture of these features, and will take them into consideration before choosing any UI component for your dashboard.

By now we've covered almost all aspects of Xcelsius 2008. Let's move on to a comprehensive hands-on example, to practice some of what we have learned.

9   A Comprehensive Hands-On Example

We have covered all that you need to create a dashboard with Xcelsius 2008, including all of the UI components and types of data connectivity. In this chapter, we will put everything together by leading you in creating a comprehensive dashboard. This sample dashboard will contain charts, selectors, single-value components, texts, art, backgrounds, and some data connections. It will give you the chance to practice most aspects of we've presented in previous chapters.

In the practice sections of some of the chapters, we went through simple examples. The difference between this chapter and those practice sections is that the previous practices focused on a single Xcelsius feature, but the example in this chapter is more comprehensive. You'll also learn about the workflow of building a real-world dashboard and some general best practices of working with Xcelsius.

After reading this chapter, you will be able to:

▸ Use all of the components you have learned about in this book

▸ Understand the workflow of building dashboards

▸ Apply general best practices while designing dashboards

Now suppose that it's 2007 and you work for eFashion, a successful retail store selling fashion merchandise in 11 U.S. cities. The company currently sells more than 200 products across 12 different product lines. You are an analyst working at eFashion headquarters in New York, and your job is to produce interactive dashboards and present them to the company's management team. You are currently designing a sales dashboard covering the past year, 2006, to help them analyze the sales status.

Basically, the workflow of building dashboards is often in the following sequence:

- Plan the dashboard.
- Prepare the data.
- Organize the data in Excel.
- Design the dashboard in Xcelsius.

You always start with planning. In the planning stage, you analyze user requirements and draw a first-draft design of what the dashboard will look like to the end user, including parameters, the canvas layout, and how the end-user will access it.

After that, you need to prepare the data that you need to present. This work can be done by either you, the dashboard designer, or the IT department after negotiation. In this step you need to understand the backend logic to retrieve live data, with the help of some data connectivity. In addition, you need to be very clear about the data structures of both the input and output. For example, how many rows and columns of data will be returned? This is important for you to map the output data and bind it to UI components later.

Before you start to actually work in Xcelsius, it is better to add a step to organize your data in the embedded Excel spreadsheet. Well-organized data in Excel greatly improves the design efficiency and makes the dashboard easy to maintain. What you need to go in this step includes highlighting different kinds of data in different colors and calculating some extra data with the help of Excel functions.

Finally, you design the dashboard in Xcelsius. You work with different kinds of UI components and data connectivities and set their properties. We'll discuss each of these steps in more detail in the following sections.

Now let's return to our hands-on example. The dashboard we're going to create will connect to live data through an SAP BusinessObjects Live Office connection, which in turn will fetch data via the eFashion universe deployed in an SAP BusinessObjects Enterprise system.

Maybe you cannot replicate the exact environment. For instance, you may not have an SAP BusinessObjects system, so the eFashion universe and SAP BusinessObjects Live Office are not available to you, but you can easily mock-up some data and use another connection type to follow this hands-on example. You can even insert the data directly into the embedded spreadsheet. Note that we are trying to give you the idea of how a professional dashboard is created. The workflow and design practices are the focus.

9.1 Planning the Dashboard

The first step of building a comprehensive dashboard is always planning, just like when you develop a piece of software, build a formatted report, or design a web page.

9.1.1 Plan the Workflow

For dashboard design, it is particularly important that you start from user requirements rather than from the data you are working with. Diving into the data at early stage can easily cause you to get lost and miss what you actually need to focus on. Basically, you should work with business users, communicate with them, and make sure you fully understand the following items:

- What primary business question they want the dashboard to answer
- What other questions may arise
- What actions they would like to take

Only when the user requirements are clear can you decide which components to use and what data each of them will display.

We recommend that you design with paper and pencil at the planning stage because this effectively removes you from the data you want to convey and the Xcelsius technologies, so you can focus on actual user requirements. It is also more efficient to communicate with business users through sketches on paper. It's quick and simple. More importantly, business users usually don't understand the technology you're using, even if it's as easy as Xcelsius, so designing on paper can be useful to get a general idea for the dashboard you want to create and to use to sign off the basic design of your dashboard.

In our sample dashboard project, however, we'll omit this step because our main purpose is to lead you through the process of creating a comprehensive dashboard. We'll assume that the communication with the end user has already been conducted and the user responses are as follows:

- This is a sales dashboard, so the primary metric is sales revenue.
- The company is expanding geographically. The dashboard should show sales revenue by U.S. states.
- There's a target sales revenue for each store. The dashboard should clearly illustrate the accomplishment status based on the target for each store.

- When a store has identified exceptions, more details on that store are needed, for example, the trend of the sales revenue and break-down of different product lines.

9.1.2 Plan the UI

Based on the above information, we can choose the appropriate visual presentation to tackle each problem, as explained below.

- Map
  A map is a very good way to display geographical data, so we'll use it to show revenue by region. From the map, we can drill down to a chart that displays the sales revenue of all of the stores in the state that is selected on the map.

- Column chart
  We'll use a column chart because we'll compare sales revenue across all of the stores. Alerts should be enabled to highlight the accomplishment of the revenue target. From the column chart, we can again drill down to a line chart and a pie chart.

- Line chart
  The line chart will display the monthly, quarterly, and year-to-date trends of the sales revenue. The user can choose which trend he wants to see.

- Pie chart
  The pie chart will display the distribution of the sales revenue across different product lines.

- Gauge
  We'll add a gauge to show the sales revenue of the selected state. This is not directly derived from user requirements, but it will help correct a small flaw in the map component: The values are not visible unless the mouse is pointing to a region. In addition, adding a single-value component increases the breadth of the components we use for this dashboard, which is good for demonstration and practice purposes in this sample dashboard project.

Figure 9.1 shows a mock-up of our dashboard. Please note that the mock-up is created in Xcelsius for simplicity in our sample dashboard project, but as we explained, you should do this with pen and paper.

Figure 9.1 MockUp of the Dashboard To Be Built

Pay attention to the way we placed the components. The layout of these components follows the logical relations among them. Information is presented from left to right, top to bottom, as it goes from high-level to more detailed. The map, at the upper left, carries the most high-level information, sales revenue by state. We can drill down to the store level in the column chart to the right of the map. Below the map and the column chart, we can drill down to information from single stores. This kind of layout is intuitive, so the user won't get confused by the information presented.

9.2 Preparing Data

Now that the initial design is completed, we need to consider what kind of data is needed for each component of the dashboard. The general best practice for a connected model is that you should build more connections returning fewer rows and columns instead of fewer connections returning more rows of data. The more data a connection returns, the slower your dashboard is. You will produce a very bad user experience if you are trying to pulling all of the data shown on the dashboard at once, which will probably make the user wait for tens of second or even minutes. Impatient users will close the dashboard before it finishes loading data.

A better way is to build more connections that return less data and trigger the connectivity only when required. Whenever more data is needed upon user interaction, more data is retrieved. The user may have to wait only a few seconds when he clicks on a chart or chooses a different item in a selector, which will be within the user's tolerance. If your databases and backend servers have enough power, this may be even unnoticeable.

We are now going to build queries that fetch only the data needed for each display component. SAP BusinessObjects Live Office is our chosen connection type in this sample dashboard project, so we are going to work in Excel and fetch data through SAP BusinessObjects Universe. If you are not using SAP BusinessObjects Live Office, you can create Web services for a Web service connection or develop a web application for an XML data connection.

Now let's launch Xcelsius and build connections for each component.

9.2.1 The U.S. Map

The U.S. map will display the sales revenue for each state, so we are going to build a query on the universe to get the sales revenue by state. We'll insert a universe query into Excel. The query includes the objects State and Sales Revenue, and it is filtered by Year as shown in Figure 9.2.

If you are not familiar with SAP BusinessObjects Universe, Listing 9.1 shows the generated SQL (Structured Query Language) statement for this query.

```
SELECT DISTINCT
  Agg_yr_qt_rn_st_ln_ca_sr.State,
  sum(Agg_yr_qt_rn_st_ln_ca_sr.Sales_revenue)
FROM
  Agg_yr_qt_rn_st_ln_ca_sr
WHERE
  (
  Agg_yr_qt_rn_st_ln_ca_sr.Yr  =  '2006'
  )
GROUP BY
  Agg_yr_qt_rn_st_ln_ca_sr.State
```

Listing 9.1 Generated SQL Statement for Sales Revenue by State

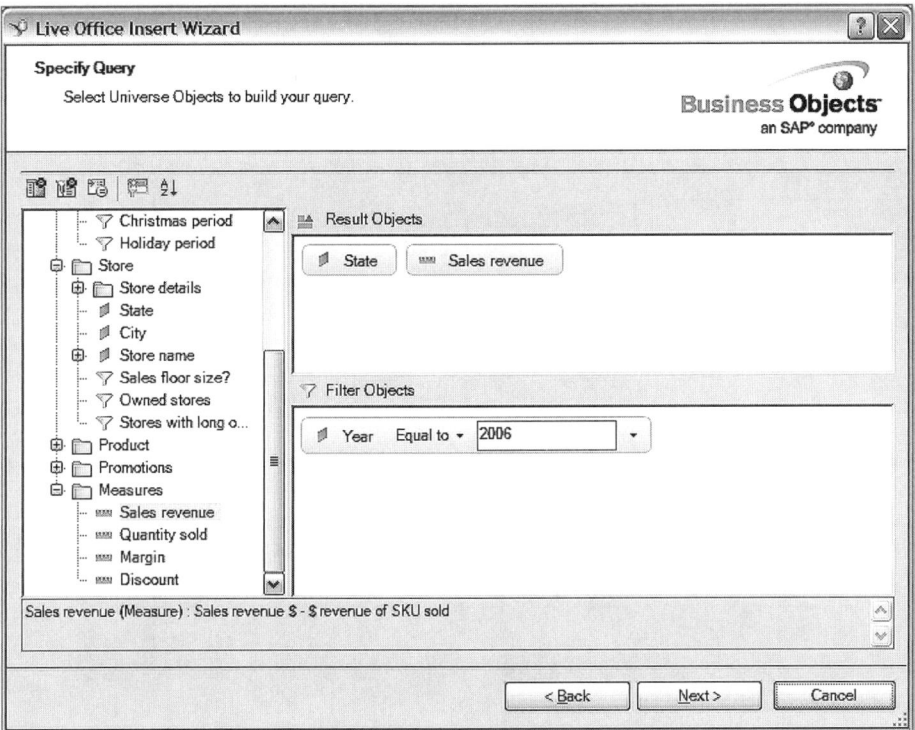

Figure 9.2 Revenue by State Query in Query Panel

9.2.2 The Gauge

This single-value component shows the sales revenue for the currently selected state on the map. Because the data for it is already included in the data for the map component, we don't need to build another query for the gauge alone. The data for the gauge is updated when the map component inserts the data for the state selected into the destination cell range.

9.2.3 The Column Chart

The user wants to see the sales revenue by store in a column chart, and only data for the stores in the selected state should be returned, so the universe query for the column chart includes the objects Store Name and Sales Revenue, and it is filtered by Year and State as shown in Figure 9.3.

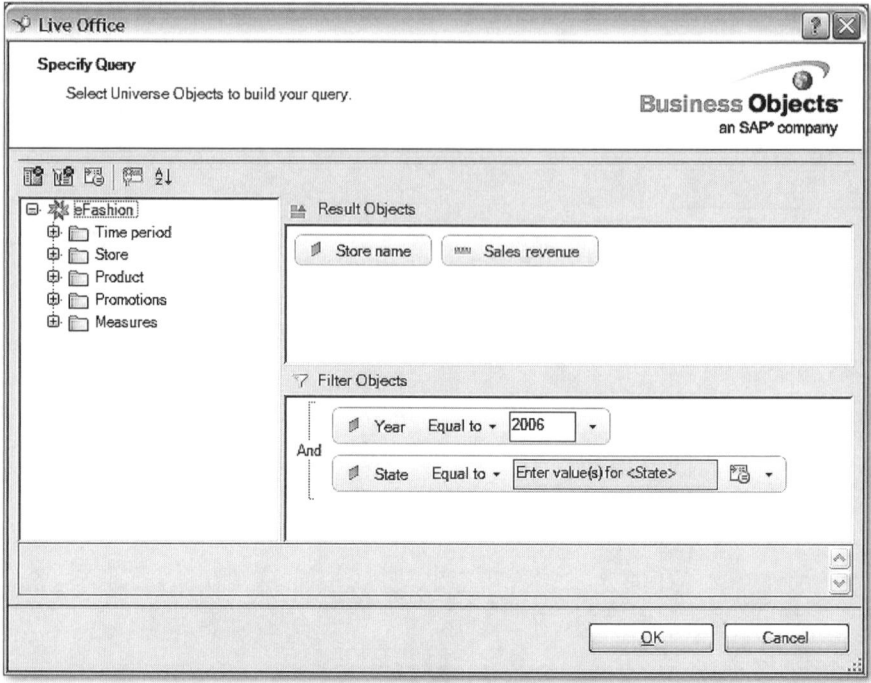

Figure 9.3 Revenue by Store Query in Query Panel

The generated SQL statement is displayed below. This SQL statement is a little bit longer than that of the sales revenue by state query because some table joins are involved. You may also notice that the Sale Revenue object and State object do not map to the same database fields for the two queries. The reason for this is that this query retrieves data from transactional tables, and the previous one retrieves data from a single aggregated table that is generated from transaction tables. SAP BusinessObjects Universe provides this aggregation awareness technology that can automatically determine which tables the data should be fetched from. The universe technology is beyond the scope of this book so we won't describe it here.

The SQL statement (Listing 9.2) merely gives you an idea of what data we are pulling from the database. Another interesting point in this SQL statement is the `@prompt` function in the `WHERE` clause. This is a universe function rather than an SQL function, which simply stands for a placeholder and will be replaced with a user response.

```sql
SELECT
  Outlet_Lookup.Shop_name,
  sum(Shop_facts.Amount_sold)
FROM
  Outlet_Lookup,
  Shop_facts,
  Calendar_year_lookup
WHERE
  ( Outlet_Lookup.Shop_id=Shop_facts.Shop_id  )
  AND  ( Shop_facts.Week_id=Calendar_year_lookup.Week_id  )
  AND
  (
  Calendar_year_lookup.Yr  =   '2006'
    AND
  Outlet_Lookup.State  =  @prompt('Enter State:','A','Store\State',Mono,Free,Persistent,,User:0)
  )
GROUP BY
  Outlet_Lookup.Shop_name
```

Listing 9.2 Generated SQL Statement for Sales Revenue by Store

9.2.4 The Line Chart

The line chart will display one of the monthly trends, the quarterly or the year-to-date (YTD) trends. We are going to utilize the dynamic visibility feature of Xcelsius to implement this switching, so instead of one line chart, we actually need three line charts. After further analyzing of the data, the universe in this case, we find that we can build a sales revenue by month query and a sales revenue by quarter query, but there is no YTD data. This problem will be solved by using Excel formulas to generate the YTD data based on the monthly data, which we'll demonstrated in the next section.

For sales revenue by month, the universe query includes the objects Month and Sales Revenue, and it is filtered by Year and Store Name, which again is a prompt, as illustrated in Figure 9.4.

9 | A Comprehensive Hands-On Example

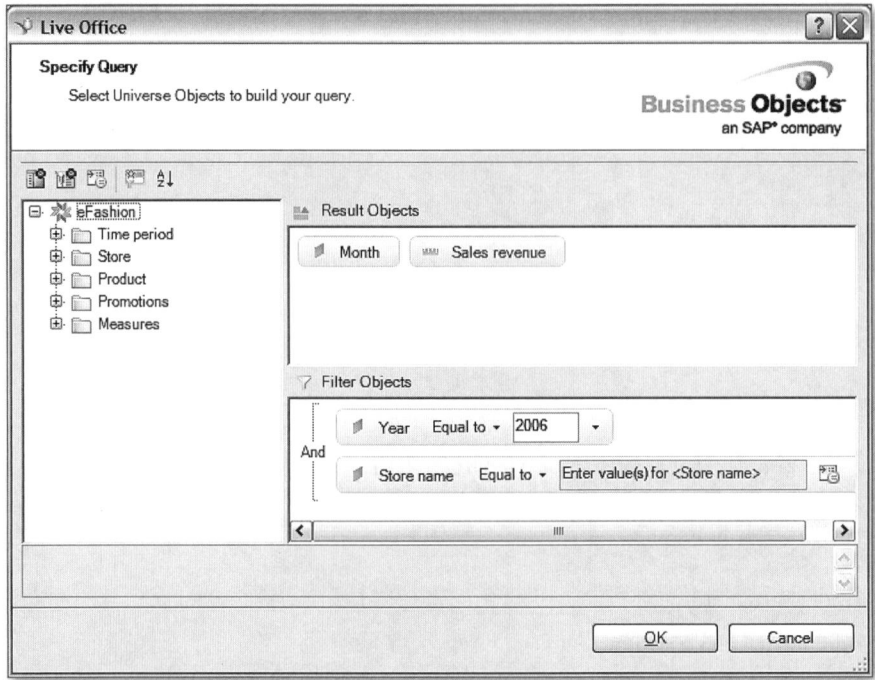

Figure 9.4 Revenue by Month Query in Query Panel

The SQL statement for this query is shown in Listing 9.3.

```
SELECT
  Agg_yr_qt_mt_mn_wk_rg_cy_sn_sr_qt_ma.Mth,
  sum(Agg_yr_qt_mt_mn_wk_rg_cy_sn_sr_qt_ma.Sales_revenue)
FROM
  Agg_yr_qt_mt_mn_wk_rg_cy_sn_sr_qt_ma
WHERE
  (
  Agg_yr_qt_mt_mn_wk_rg_cy_sn_sr_qt_ma.Yr  =  '2006'
   AND
  Agg_yr_qt_mt_mn_wk_rg_cy_sn_sr_qt_ma.Store_name  =  @prompt('Enter Store name:','A','Store\Store name',Mono,Free,Persistent,,User:0)
  )
GROUP BY
  Agg_yr_qt_mt_mn_wk_rg_cy_sn_sr_qt_ma.Mth
```

Listing 9.3 Generated SQL Statement for Sales Revenue by Month

We can easily build the revenue by quarter query (shown in Figure 9.5) by replacing the Month object with the Quarter object (Listing 9.4).

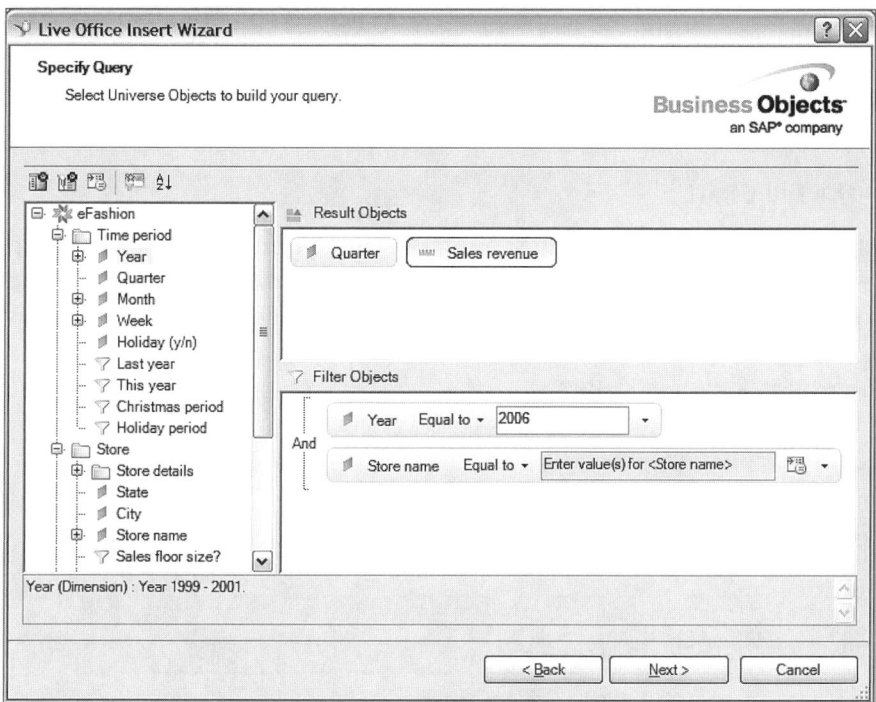

Figure 9.5 Revenue by Quarter Query in Query Panel

```
SELECT
  Agg_yr_qt_mt_mn_wk_rg_cy_sn_sr_qt_ma.Qtr,
  sum(Agg_yr_qt_mt_mn_wk_rg_cy_sn_sr_qt_ma.Sales_revenue)
FROM
  Agg_yr_qt_mt_mn_wk_rg_cy_sn_sr_qt_ma
WHERE
  (
  Agg_yr_qt_mt_mn_wk_rg_cy_sn_sr_qt_ma.Yr  =  '2006'
    AND
  Agg_yr_qt_mt_mn_wk_rg_cy_sn_sr_qt_ma.Store_name  =  @prompt('Enter Store name:','A','Store\Store name',Mono,Free,Persistent,,User:0)
  )
GROUP BY
  Agg_yr_qt_mt_mn_wk_rg_cy_sn_sr_qt_ma.Qtr
```

Listing 9.4 Generated SQL Statement for Sales Revenue by Quarter

9 | A Comprehensive Hands-On Example

9.2.5 The Radio Button

The radio button enables the user to switch the trend displayed in the line chart. A general best practice is to retrieve everything from the database if possible, including selector labels, but in this case the labels for this radio button cannot be retrieved from the database, so we'll simply hardcode them in the Excel worksheet.

9.2.6 The Pie Chart

Similar to the line chart we used to show the revenue trends, the pie chart also displays detailed information about a single store. It breaks the yearly revenue down to product lines. The universe query includes the objects Lines and Sales Revenue, and it is filtered by Year and Store Name as illustrated in Figure 9.6. The SQL statement is shown in Listing 9.5.

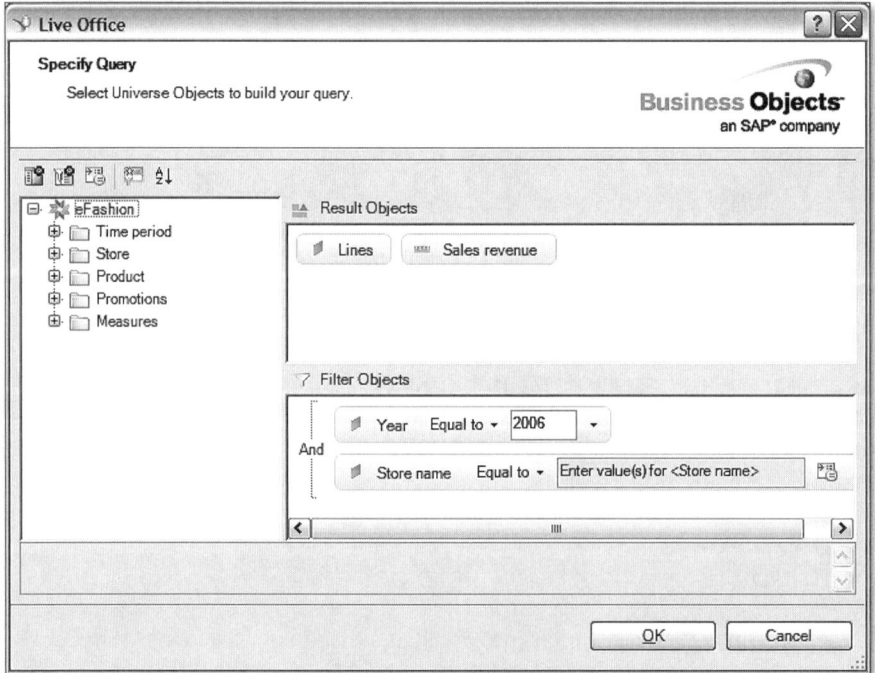

Figure 9.6 Revenue by Product Line Query in Query Panel

```
SELECT
  Article_lookup.Family_name,
  sum(Shop_facts.Amount_sold)
FROM
  Article_lookup,
  Shop_facts,
  Calendar_year_lookup,
  Outlet_Lookup
WHERE
  ( Outlet_Lookup.Shop_id=Shop_facts.Shop_id  )
  AND  ( Article_lookup.Article_id=Shop_facts.Article_id  )
  AND  ( Shop_facts.Week_id=Calendar_year_lookup.Week_id  )
  AND
  (
  Calendar_year_lookup.Yr  =  '2006'
    AND
  Outlet_Lookup.Shop_name  =  @prompt('Enter Store name:','A','Store\
Store name',Mono,Free,Persistent,,User:0)
  )
GROUP BY
  Article_lookup.Family_name
```

Listing 9.5 Generated SQL Statement for Sales Revenue by Product Line of a Certain Store

9.3 Organizing Data in Excel

In this phase, we are going to work with Excel to organize the data. Note that we are working in a standalone Excel instance with SAP BusinessObjects Live Office installed, not in the embedded Excel spreadsheet in Xcelsius. Later we'll import this Excel file into Xcelsius.

Because we are using the SAP BusinessObjects Live Office connection in this sample dashboard project, we already have a snapshot of data inside the embedded spreadsheet, which is helpful to the designer. However, for some other connection types, you will probably start with an empty spreadsheet. We recommend putting the data returned by each connectivity into the embedded spreadsheet and adding some dummy data so that later you can test charts and interactivity while you are designing in Xcelsius.

Figure 9.7 shows the current status of our spreadsheet. As you can see, we put the data for each component in separate worksheet, so we have five SAP BusinessObjects Live Office objects in four tabs in the embedded spreadsheet. You may find that the object doesn't start at cell $A$1. We intentionally left some space above and to the left of the data so that we'll have room if more logic is needed in the spreadsheet.

	A	B	C	D	E	F	G	H	I	J	K
1											
2											
3											
4											
5											
6				State	Sales revenue						
7				California	2992679						
8				Colorado	843584.2						
9				DC	1053581.4						
10				Florida	811923.6						
11				Illinois	1134085.4						
12				Massachusetts	887169.2						
13				New York	3151021.7						
14				Texas	4185098.3						
15											
16											
17											
18											
19											
20											
21											
22											
23											
24											

Figure 9.7 Excel Spreadsheet with SAP BusinessObjects Live Office Objects

Another best practice is adding a "control" sheet in Excel with the UI control logic inside, such as the data insertion, calculation mechanism, and when to trigger a connection.

The next few paragraphs list how we organize data in the embedded Excel spreadsheet for our sample dashboard:

- Adding the dashboard title
  We have a label component that is the dashboard title, so we'll enter the text "Sales Dashboard" in cell $E$6 and later bind it to the label component. If the title needs be updated, you can easily change it in this cell, without locating the label from among many components.

- Reserve cells for data insertion of the map component
  The data for the map component is a vertical range of sales revenue by state, so we'll select Row in the Insertion Type dropdown list in the Properties panel of the map component. Here, we'll highlight cell range $E$8 to $F$8 in yellow for the inserted row of data. Cell $F$8 contains the revenue of the selected state, which the gauge component will use later.

- Bind the prompt for the revenue by store SAP BusinessObjects Live Office connection
  Cell $E$8, which contains the currently selected state, will be used as the input parameter for the query retrieving the revenue by store of a state, so we need to bind the prompt for the revenue by store SAP BusinessObjects Live Office object to cell $E$8.

- Add the column chart title
  Enter the text "Revenue by Store" in cell $E$10.

- Reserve cells for data insertion of the column chart
  Similar to the map component, the drill-down functionality of the column chart should also be enabled. We'll highlight cell range $E$11 to $F$11 for data insertion of the column chart.

- Bind prompts for the rest of the queries
  There are three other queries: revenue by month, revenue by quarter, and revenue by product line. The store name is used as the input parameter for all of them, so bind their prompts to cell $E$11.

- Add the title for the line chart
  Enter "Revenue Trend" in cell $E$13.

- Add the pie chart title
  Enter "Revenue by Product Line" in cell $E$15.

- Add labels for the radio button
  Enter "Monthly," "Quarterly," and "YTD" in cells $E$17, $E$18, and $E$19, respectively, which will be used for a selector component.

- Reserve cells for data insertion of the radio button
  Highlight cell $E$20, where the selected label of the radio button is inserted so we can use the label of the radio button and this cell to control the dynamic visibility of the three line chart components.

9 | A Comprehensive Hands-On Example

Most of our control logic is now implemented in the Control tab of the Excel spreadsheet. Figure 9.8 shows the finished worksheet.

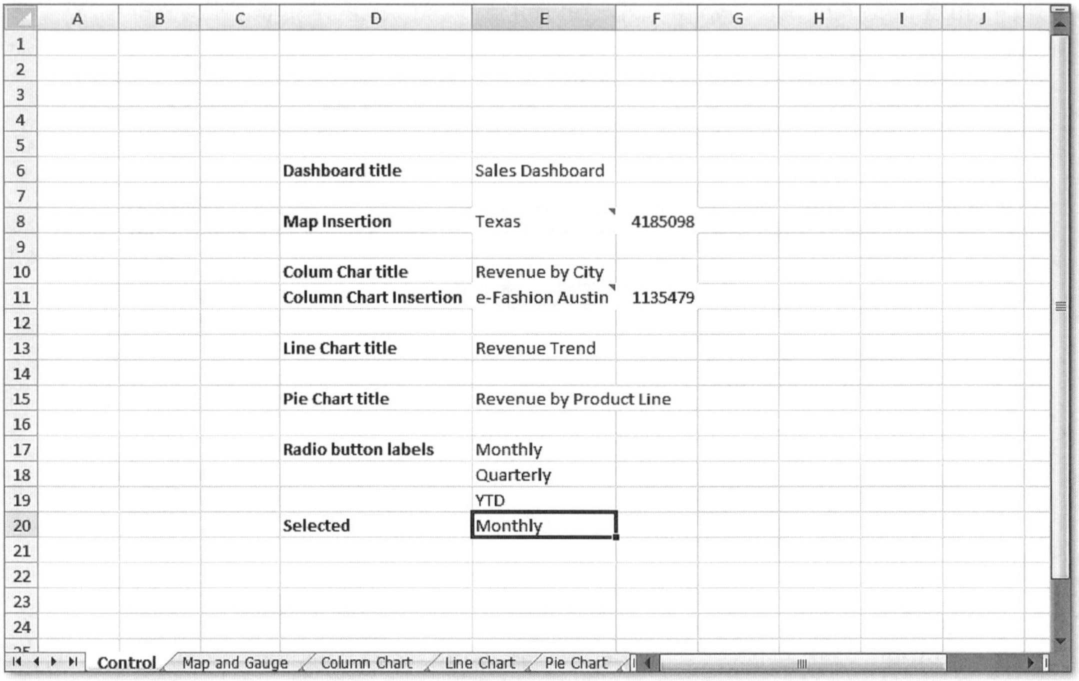

	A	B	C	D	E	F	G	H	I	J
1										
2										
3										
4										
5										
6				Dashboard title	Sales Dashboard					
7										
8				Map Insertion	Texas	4185098				
9										
10				Colum Char title	Revenue by City					
11				Column Chart Insertion	e-Fashion Austin	1135479				
12										
13				Line Chart title	Revenue Trend					
14										
15				Pie Chart title	Revenue by Product Line					
16										
17				Radio button labels	Monthly					
18					Quarterly					
19					YTD					
20				Selected	Monthly					
21										
22										
23										
24										

Tabs: Control / Map and Gauge / Column Chart / Line Chart / Pie Chart

Figure 9.8 Control Tab in the Excel Spreadsheet

There is one more thing to add in the Excel spreadsheet: the YTD trend data. We'll switch to the Line Chart tab in Excel and add an Excel formula to calculate the YTD trend based on the monthly trend data. The YTD revenue for January is just the revenue in January, so we'll make cell $F$7 equal to cell $E$7. Then, in cell $F$8, we'll add the formula SUM($E$7:E8). Notice that we've lock the first parameter of the sum function, which is the starting cell of the summation. This is necessary so that we can easily copy the formula to cells below.

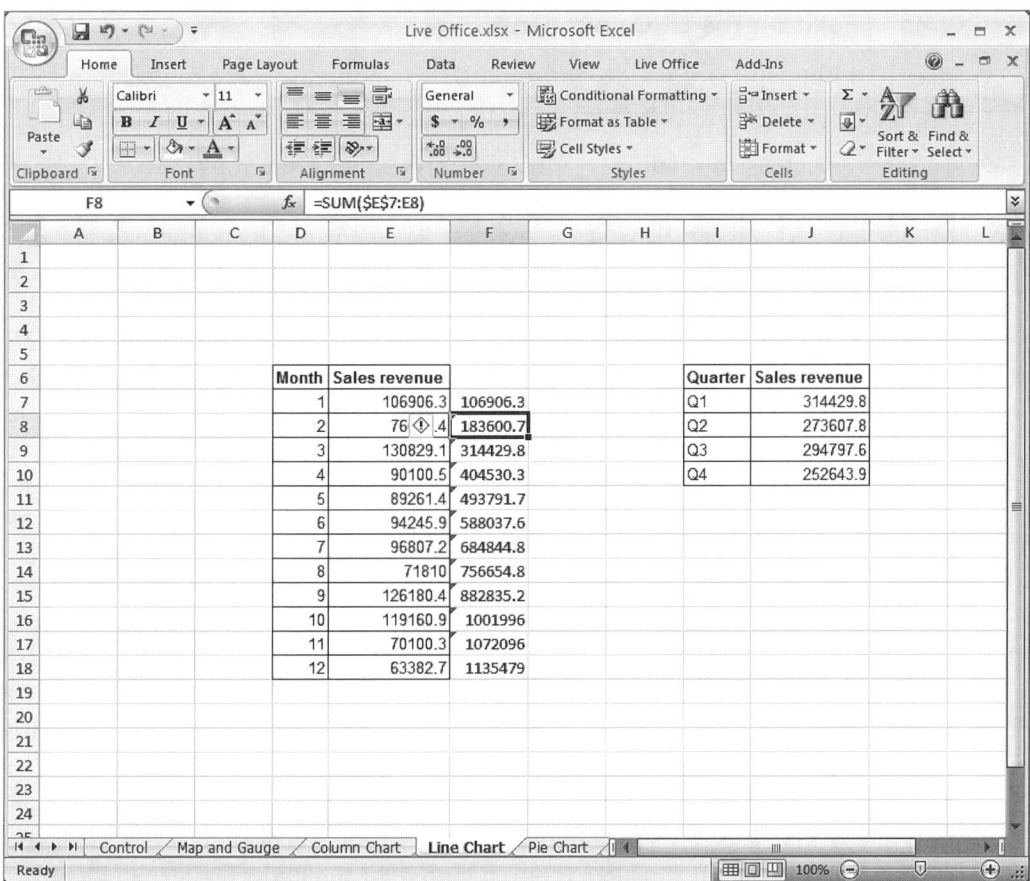

Figure 9.9 Formula to Calculate the YTD Trend

Now we've finished the data organization step. You can also do this in the embedded Excel spreadsheet in Xcelsius while you are designing the dashboard, but we recommend that you first deal with data itself so that you won't be distracted by the UI components. The result of this step is a well-organized Excel model that is clear and can be easily maintained.

9.4   Designing the Dashboard

Now that we have finished the plan and preparations, let's start building this dashboard.

455

9.4.1 Position the UI Components

The first thing you're going to do is add UI components to the canvas to implement the layout you've designed.

The first problem you will meet with will probably be the canvas size. The size of the canvas is 800 by 600 by default. You can change this size in the document properties, and you can also change the default canvas size by going to FILE · PREFERENCES, as described in Chapter 2. So how big should the canvas be? The answer depends on whether you have a rigid constraint on the canvas size, for example, if you're building a dashboard that will be integrated into a web page, and the web designer reserves an area, which has an accurate width and height, on the page for your dashboard. In that case, you should set the canvas to that specific size. Otherwise, you can freely choose the size. We recommend that you start with a relatively large canvas size and lay your components on it. When you finish designing the dashboard, if there is extra space, you can easily use Fit Canvas to Components to cut out the blank space. In this example, we'll use the default 800 by 600 canvas.

Laying the components on the canvas is quite straightforward with our planned layout. Usually you should follow the up-to-down, left-to-right order.

It is worth noting that the aligning and sizing tools in Xcelsius can really save you time in placing and sizing the components. For example, you can make the map and column chart the same height and align them at their top edges. Another example is that you can add three line charts to the canvas and make them the same width and height and align them to both their top and left edges so that they will exactly overlap each other. Alignment is very important for a clean appearance and for an agreeable user experience.

9.4.2 Import the Excel File

After we've added all of the required UI components, we'll import the Excel file that we edited in the previous step and continue setting the properties for each component. You can refer to the Properties panel of each component to get a clear idea what we are doing here.

The Label

Link the label's text to cell $E$6, which is Sales Dashboard.

The Map

First, remove the map title because it makes little sense. Then bind the Display data to the output value of the revenue by state query, which is in the cell range 'Map and Gauge'!$D$7:$E$14.

For data insertion, select Row as it's the insertion type and set the source data to the same range as the display data and the destination to cell range $E$8 to $F$8 in the Control tab. Be aware that in our database, District of Columbia is abbreviated to DC, so you need to edit the region key as shown in Figure 9.10.

Figure 9.10 Region Key Window

The Gauge

Bind the Data property to cell $F$8 in the Control tab and set the maximum to 5000000, which is the assumed maximum sales revenue a store can produce.

The Column Chart

Bind the column chart's title to cell $E$10 in the Control tab and its subtitle to cell $E$8 so that the title of the column chart will be Revenue by Store and the subtitle will be the state that is currently selected on the map. Bind the display data to the result of the revenue by store query.

Because we can't determine how many stores will be in the selected state, we'll bind more rows and select Ignore Blank Values in the Behavior tab in the chart's Properties panel.

Enable drill-down and select the row insertion type. Wet the source data to the same range as the display data and the destination to cell range $E$11 to $F$11 in the Control tab.

The Line Charts

The three line charts share a lot of common properties. Bind their titles to cell $E$13 in the Control tab and the subtitles to cell $E$11 so that the title of the line charts will be Revenue Trend and the subtitle will be the name of the store that is selected in the column chart.

Then bind their display data to the monthly trend data, quarterly trend data, and YTD trend data, respectively.

We also need to set the dynamic visibility properties for these line charts. To do this, in the Properties panel of each line chart, bind their keys to one cell in range $E$17 to $E$19, which are Monthly, Quarterly, and YTD, respectively, and bind the status to $E$20 so that when the radio button selection changes, it inserts one of the cells among $E$17 to $E$19 to cell $E$20, and the corresponding chart will be visible, with the other two2 hidden.

The Radio Button

Bind the label to cell range $E$17 to $E$19 in the Control tab. Select Label in the Insertion Type dropdown list and set Destination to $E$20.

The Pie Chart

Bind the title to cell $E$15 in the Control tab and the display data to the revenue by product line query result.

9.4.3 Connect to External Data

Now you can preview the dashboard and test the charts, the drill-down behavior, and the dynamic visibility with the sample data. If all is well, you can go on and configure the data connections.

We are using SAP BusinessObjects Live Office connections, so we'll simply use existing SAP BusinessObjects Live Office connections in the Data Manager. Xcelsius will then detect any existing SAP BusinessObjects Live Office connection contained in the Excel file and create one connection in the Data Manager for each that it detects.

For each connection, you can correct the session URL and set it to Refresh on Load. The only thing you need pay attention to is when to trigger each connectivity. For the SAP BusinessObjects Live Office connection called Revenue By Store, which corresponds to the revenue by store query, we set it to refresh when cell $E$8, the selected state, changes. We'll set the other three SAP BusinessObjects Live Office connections, corresponding to the revenue by month query, the revenue by quarter query, and the revenue by product line query, to refresh when cell $E$11, the selected store, changes.

At this point, you can preview your work again and test the data connections to see if the correct data is fetched upon user interaction.

9.4.4 Adjust the Appearance

Now the dashboard has complete functionality. If you like, you can make it look better by adjusting the components' appearances.

As the last step of this hands-on example, we'll change some styles of the components such as font size, color, and alignment. We'll add a background below the label component to highlight the purpose of this dashboard. We'll also change the theme and the color scheme for a cooler look and feel. The final result is displayed in Figure 9.11.

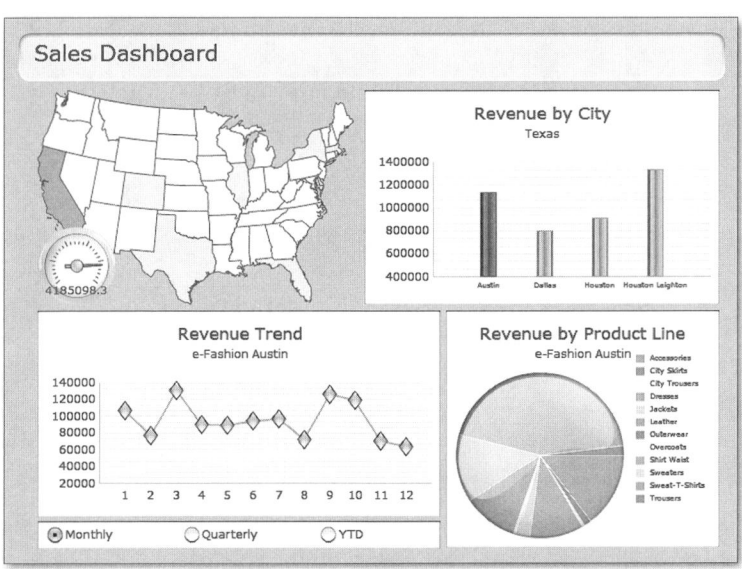

Figure 9.11 Final Version of the Dashboard

We've already explained how to change the appearance of each component, how to use the background, and how to change the theme or color scheme in previous chapters, so we'll ignore that here. According to your preferences, you can adjust the visual appearance of the dashboard, such as using different fonts or background colors.

You can get the source file of this dashboard from our website for reference.

9.5 Summary

Through this sample dashboard project, we hope that you have gained an understanding of the basic workflow of building a dashboard and the things you need to pay particular attention to. You plan the dashboard, prepare the data, organize the data in a separate Excel file or the embedded spreadsheet, and design your dashboard in Xcelsius. You can use a list view or some sample data to help debug and test your dashboard. When you're certain the dashboard is ready in both functionality and appearance after thorough testing, you can distribute it to the end users.

This chapter introduces the Xcelsius SDK and explains some of its core functionalities, highlights common cases where the SDK can be implemented, and gives an overview of the value that it can bring to your Xcelsius dashboard projects.

10 Introduction to the Xcelsius SDK

Xcelsius 2008 introduced a new level of overall dashboard power and control with the release of the Xcelsius Software Development Toolkit (referred to as an SDK). The Xcelsius 2008 SDK enables Xcelsius designers and developers to extend the value of their existing Xcelsius environments by creating custom components to address dashboard requirements that fall outside of the scope of inherent Xcelsius 2008 functionality. This chapter will get you familiar with the concept of the Xcelsius SDK and will also help you to understand the high-level value of the SDK and how to factor in the SDK when defining dashboard project specifications.

10.1 About the Xcelsius SDK

The Xcelsius SDK is built on Adobe's Flex technology and consists of a foundational set of software tools, fully functional code examples, documentation files and utilities that Flex developers can leverage to create and introduce custom components into the existing Xcelsius component library. The software technologies bundled with the SDK include a core Flex class library (.swc file) that facilitates communication to and from Xcelsius as well as a set of tools and compiler utilities that make packaging and distributing custom components for use in Xcelsius an easy process.

The Xcelsius SDK is made available to developers as a downloadable package from the SAP website. Xcelsius must be installed on the machine as a prerequisite to installing the SDK. For testing and debugging purposes it is strongly advised that developers have ready access to a licensed instance of Xcelsius 2008 that does not expire. To begin using the Xcelsius SDK risk free, a fully functional trial version of

Xcelsius may be installed as an alternative. Instructions on where to find the SDK are included below, in the *How to use the SDK* section.

10.2 About Flex

Flex is the technology behind the Xcelsius SDK and is the same technology that developers will use to build custom components for Xcelsius 2008.

Flex is an open source software framework developed by Adobe that allows developers to build rich, powerful cross-platform applications that run in the ubiquitous Adobe Flash Player. In addition to being supported by all major browsers, by leveraging the cross-operating system Adobe AIR runtime, Flex applications can also be designed to run on the desktop as well as mobile devices.

Flex provides developers with an intuitive way to create highly adaptable and functional application user interfaces as well as the logic behind them. Flex leverages a declarative markup language called MXML which is an XML-based syntax that enables developers to design and describe user interface layouts and behaviors. To power application functionality and to define application logic, Flex also leverages the object-oriented programming language ActionScript 3. All Flex applications compile out to a swf file, which can be deployed to a variety of environments. Developers new to Flex that are already familiar with languages such as XML and JavaScript will be able to pick up the Flex concept quickly.

The Flex framework also provides developers with complete access to over 100 built-in components that can be extended and customized in an infinite number of ways. From interactive layout components and a full charting library to components that provide intuitive access to web services and databases, the Flex component library is continuously evolving. These built in components provide developers with a measurable competitive advantage when developing applications by eliminating the need for custom development when implementing commonly used components. With a single line of code, developers can implement powerful, complex components in their applications.

To use the Flex framework, developers need access to the free SDK which is available for download from the Adobe website. However, for a more productive and complete development experience, it is recommended that developers also download Adobe Flex Builder. Flex Builder is an Integrated Development Environment that provides a complete framework for managing Flex projects and coding Flex applications. Features like intelligent coding, project linking and automatic code formatting are valuable time savers when developing Flex applications. Flex Builder is available as a free trial download as well as for purchase on the Adobe website. It should be noted that for the purpose of the Xcelsius 2008 SDK, Flex Builder 2 or 3 should be used as opposed to the newly named Flash Builder IDE which came out with the release of Flex 4. This recommendation is due to the current release of the Xcelsius SDK being built on an earlier version of the Flex framework.

10.3 When to Use the SDK

So often, due to rigid built-in functionality and dashboard component limitations, dashboard requirements are often scaled down, trimmed, or otherwise modified to make do with what is available in the dashboard technology package that has been bought into. This has always been problematic as seemingly harmless requests, such as altering axes on a given chart slightly outside of its inherent bounds begin to shed light on other potential stumbling blocks as dashboards begin to evolve and require finer control over the way users interact with, consume, navigate through and visualize their data.

Meeting every dashboard use case with a default toolset is an impossible order. The inevitable fact that unique requirements come along sooner or later that drive innovation and are not found in the core toolbox is a universal problem that can only be solved by empowering developers to satisfy their custom dashboard requirements with the use of an SDK. This is exactly what the Xcelsius 2008 SDK does: Empower developers to innovate and develop new components and concepts, satisfy the most demanding business requirements, and solve new and existing dashboard challenges in a creative way.

How and when the SDK is applied to a dashboard project is completely subjective and open on a project-by-project basis. However, listed below are a few common areas where the SDK can be implemented.

Create new data connections to connect to:

- CSV files
- Encrypted data repositories
- Customer Relationship Management Systems and legacy data stores
- Third party tools, such as Sales Force or MailChimp

- Text files
- Web site content
- Really Simple Syndication (RSS) feeds

Create new data visualizations

- Flash or Javascript Maps
- Specialty charts, such as Smith Charts or Gannt Charts
- New gauges, dials or heatmaps

Create new navigational controls

- Simple buttons
- Coverflow navigators
- Hierarchical trees
- Complex fish eye menus

Mathematic and data processing formulas

- Any math functions not supported natively by Xcelsius
- Any string or text functions not supported natively by Xcelsius
- Any statistical functions not supported natively by Xcelsius

These categories are common areas where the SDK can be applied, but it is important to remember that virtually any component that can be created in Flex can easily be purposed to function as an Xcelsius component. This new ability provides a great deal of creative latitude to the Xcelsius dashboard designer and the Flex developer alike.

10.4 How to Use the SDK

The introduction of a new SDK is always an exciting prospect, though it can be a confusing piece of functionality as well, especially for dashboard designers or dashboard stakeholders that are not necessarily aware of what SDK's are, how they bring value, and how they are actually used or applied in a real-world Xcelsius dashboard project. This lack of clarity that arises is for good reason, especially in the case of Xcelsius, due to the fact that the vast majority of Xcelsius designers and dashboard stakeholders are not and do not aspire to be Software Engineers. With that said, in the case of the Xcelsius 2008 SDK, it is much more important for dashboard designers and stakeholders to know that a mechanism exists that allows Software Engineers who are familiar with Flex, to inject custom functionality into their dashboard projects.

From a Software Engineer's perspective, the Xcelsius SDK and its foundational concepts and functionality that drive core value are fairly straight forward to understand and eventually master. At this point in the evolution of the Xcelsius SDK, functionality can be boiled down to a set of bare essentials that are highly adaptable and extremely powerful and flexible when properly applied. As the Xcelsius product and the SDK continue to evolve, we will certainly receive new pieces of functionality and potential down the road, but for now the SDK allows a Flex developer to create any Flex 2.0.1-compliant-component and import it for use into Xcelsius via a simple packaging process. The Flex component that you create can subsequently subscribe to data in the Xcelsius spreadsheet model in either a read, write, or read & write manner, opening the doors to the runtime data model that your Xcelsius 2008 dashboard relies on to consume, process, and display data.

This means that through Flex binding, that you can intercept, manipulate, and re-inject data to and from the Xcelsius 2008 model at will. With this powerful concept, it starts to become clear that with foundational hooks into the Xcelsius framework coupled with a powerful software tool (Flex), virtually anything and any component is possible.

From a nuts and bolts standpoint, getting setup to develop on the Xcelsius 2008 SDK is a fairly lightweight and straightforward process that can see you up and running in your very own environment within a few minutes. These steps assume a general familiarity with Flex basics, including MXML, ActionScript, and project setups. If you are not familiar with basic Flex project setup or Flex concepts in general, it is best to start learning, or at least to become familiar with Flex, before you begin using the SDK.

By following the steps below, you will be able to establish a Flex development environment for Xcelsius and will be primed to begin developing custom components for Xcelsius.

1. Download and Install Xcelsius 2008
    - *http://www.sap.com/solutions/sapbusinessobjects/sme/reporting-dashboarding/xcelsius/index.epx*
2. Download and Install the Xcelsius 2008 SDK
    - *www.sdn.sap.com/irj/boc/xcelsius-sdk*
    - **the Xcelsius Packager does not currently support 64-bit operating systems.

3. Download and Install Flex Builder

    ▸ *http://www.adobe.com/products/flex/*

4. Download and Install the Flex 2.0.1 Hotfix 3 SDK

    ▸ *http://labs.adobe.com/technologies/Flex/sdk/Flex2sdk.html*

5. Read the tutorials and the manuals. This is a critical step that is tempting to jump past to get started, but it will save significant amounts of time and energy if you take a day to familiarize yourself with the tutorials, source code, and other collateral that comes bundled with the SDK.

Once you have established your Flex development environment, implementing a custom component in Xcelsius is only a few steps away. Listed below is the high-level workflow (illustrated in Figure 10.1) for developing and injecting your custom component into Xcelsius 2008.

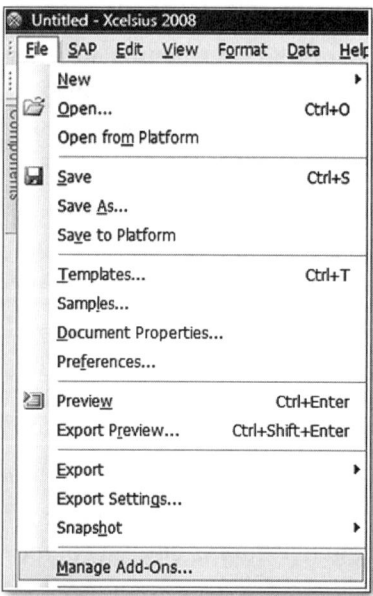

Figure 10.1 Managing and Installing Add-Ons

1. Create your component and Property Sheet applications in Flex, ultimately generating two swf files, one for the component, and one for the component's Property Sheet:

- Create a Flex project for your component
- Set your Flex project to compile using the Flex 2.0.1 Hotfix 3 SDK
- Add the Xcelsius SDK swc to your project's build path
- Develop and test your component
- Compile the applications

2. Package your component and Property Sheet swf files using the Xcelsius Packager, and build the package to generate an xlx installer file.
3. Open Xcelsius and install the xlx file generated as a result of step 2, using the Xcelsius Add-on manager.
4. Restart Xcelsius and begin using and testing your new component.

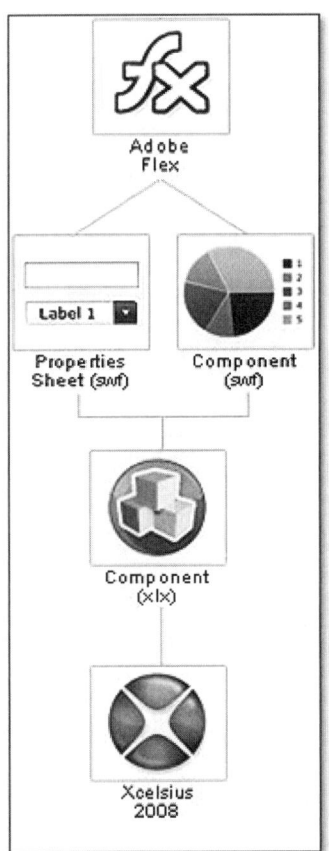

Figure 10.2 Xcelsius Custom Component Workflow

10.5 What Can be Done with the SDK?

Flex is a creative software tool with tremendous business value that provides developers with a virtually boundless canvas for innovating and creating components. Whether they are basic charts that satisfy simple outlying requirements, cutting-edge novel navigational elements or data visualizations that present data for interaction in a way that the Xcelsius components cannot accommodate, by combining the Xcelsius SDK and Flex, nearly anything is possible. A custom pie chart example with source code that illustrates the simplicity of a basic custom Flex component can be found below in Figure 10.4 and Listing 10.1 in this section.

Data Visualizations

- Data Visualizations with Custom ItemRenderers
- Heatmaps
- Geographical Mapping Components as shown in Figure 10.3

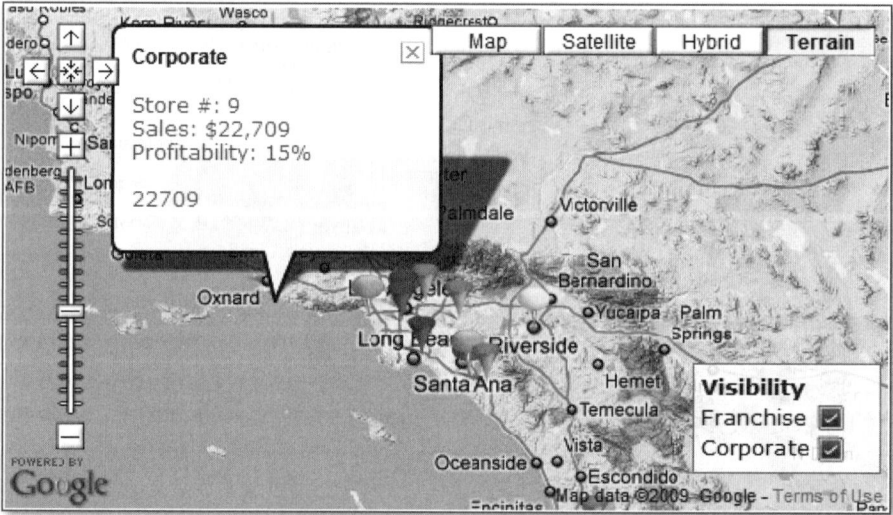

Figure 10.3 Custom Google Map

- 3d pie charts
- Hierarchical pie charts
- Multi-dial Gauges

- Data meters
- Sparkline collections, bullet charts, etc

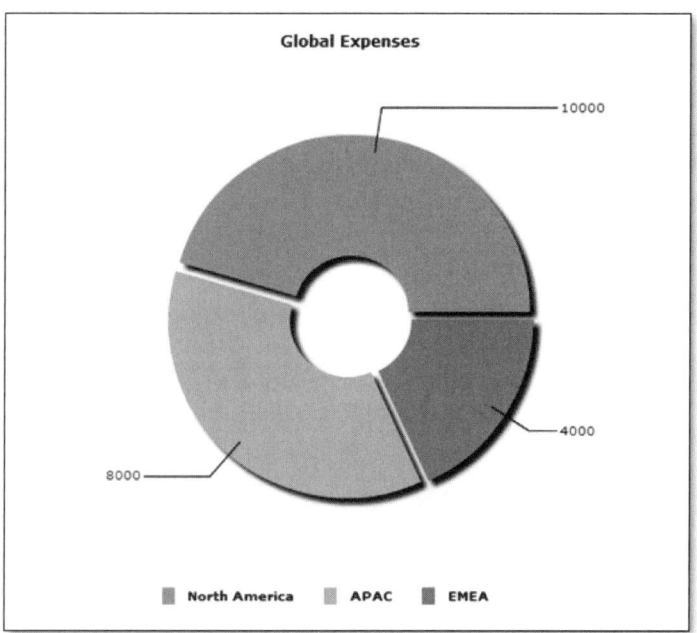

Figure 10.4 Sample Flex Pie chart + Slightly Modified Pie Series = Fast New Custom Pie Chart

```
<?xml version="1.0"?>
<mx:Application backgroundColor="0xffffff" xmlns:mx="http://www.adobe.
com/2006/mxml"
backgroundGradientAlphas="[1.0, 1.0]" backgroundGradientColors="[#FFFFF
F, #FFFFFF]">
  <mx:Script><![CDATA[
      import mx.collections.ArrayCollection;

      [Bindable]
      public var expenses:ArrayCollection = new    ArrayCollection([
        {Expense:"North America", Amount:10000},
        {Expense:"APAC", Amount:8000},
        {Expense:"EMEA", Amount:4000}
      ]);
  ]]></mx:Script>
  <mx:Label text="Global Expenses" fontWeight="bold"
        color="#000000" fontSize="12"/>
```

```
        <mx:PieChart id="myChart"
           dataProvider="{expenses}"
           showDataTips="true"
           innerRadius=".3">
           <mx:series>
              <mx:PieSeries
                 explodeRadius=".025"
                  field="Amount"
                  nameField="Expense"
                  labelPosition="callout"/>
           </mx:series>
        </mx:PieChart>
        <mx:Legend direction="horizontal"
              dataProvider="{myChart}" height="20"
              width="302" color="#000000"/>
</mx:Application>
```

Listing 10.1 Pie Chart Component Source Code

As you can see above, with a little bit of Flex code, you can create an exploded doughnut pie chart representation in just minutes.

Flex Applications

- Import entire Flex applications
- Import entire supporting dashboards or dashboard modules built in Flex
- Import Flex applications or modules that support data entry and write back to dashboard data marts or data warehouses

Data Processors, Connections and Functions

- Connect to Google Adwords
- Connect to homegrown data or Salesforce-type systems
- Connect to data cubes and expose MDX querying capabilities
- Sort and filter data using compound filters
- Mathematical, statistical and text/string functions can easily be created using the SDK

10.6 SDK Best Practices

As with any SDK, there are best practices that should be followed when scoping and developing your custom component. The best practices that we will be discussing below are specifically related to the Xcelsius SDK and workflow. It should be noted that at all times, Flex best practices should be followed as well, though they are outside of the scope of this discussion. A working knowledge of Flex best practices is advised before moving forward with your component development.

After developing numerous components for Xcelsius, there are a few common themes that should be adhered to, which will save time and will provide for much more rapid development, testing, and debugging cycles.

It should be noted that Xcelsius does not come with any kind of inherent debugging capabilities; therefore we must leverage what is available to gain insight into component runtime behavior.

Use Only What You Need

In general, using only what you need, cannot be overstated in software development and developing components purposed for Xcelsius 2008 is no exception. Below are some guidelines to keep in mind moving forward that should serve to expedite troubleshooting and testing cycles.

Bindings

The types of Binding Directions available to you as an SDK developer are; Input, Output, Both. These are the binding direction options that are available when subscribing to updates for a cell or a range of cells in the Xcelsius Excel data model. They are specified in the property sheet that accompanies your custom component, and should be used with care, specifically adjusted to suit the needs of a given component property.

- Input – Your component writes to Xcelsius
- Output – Your component reads from Xcelsius
- Both – Your component reads and writes from and to Xcelsius

Use Custom Property Sheets

The basic property sheet swf that is included with the Xcelsius SDK offers limited binding flexibility and virtually no customization or user experience control in the way a dashboard developer will interact with your component's properties, and should be avoided. Creating custom property sheets is an extra step but an extra step that is just as important as your custom component.

Don't Repeat Yourself

Since it is recommended to create your own custom property sheets, it is also recommended to create reusable property sheet patterns to prevent code duplication in every Property Sheet you create. We will explore some options around this concept in the chapter Implementing Advanced Custom Add-On Component Features.

Develop Test Containers

Debugging at Xcelsius runtime aside from trace statements and Alerts is currently non-existent. Therefore it is crucial that you create local Flex applications that allow you to test and manipulate your component's properties before testing your custom component in Xcelsius. This simple step will drastically cut down on your debugging revision cycles and will also allow you to leverage the inherent debugging capabilities of Flex Builder.

Trace and Alert

Often times it is not possible to replicate functionality in your local test container that occurs in Xcelsius, due to the fact that there is no shell or harness mechanism that the SDK provides to simulate data binding through the Xcelsius Excel model. Therefore, if you cannot troubleshoot through your test container and need to gain insight into what is happening at Xcelsius design or runtime, you may use Alerts or trace statements in your Flex component and capture the trace output via web browser tools or the Flash trace log.

Development Approaches (MXML vs. ActionScript)

When developing a visual component for Xcelsius that is either complex in layout or has the potential to evolve to a more complex visual layout using basic Flex components, MXML should be used wherever possible due to readability and design time editing WYSIWYG (what you see is what you get) advantages. Pure ActionScript may be favored for logic and data connectivity components or if you are developing a base class that other visual components will extend. However, if you are developing a composite component, MXML will save time in the long run and will be easier to read, maintain and edit, should the design further evolve or need to be changed in the future.

Styling

The current version of the SDK presents some challenges in preserving your design time styles at runtime. Often, when imported into Xcelsius and previewed, your component may lose some or all of its visual styles if you rely on inline MXML style directives.

A good approach to minimize the amount of style reapplication at runtime is to create your styles in a separate Cascading Style Sheet (CSS) file and to embed that CSS file for use in your component.

An alternate to the CSS file approach is manually reapplying styles through Action-Script style directives once your component has been initialized, though this approach often leads to a large amount of ActionScript style management code which is not necessarily ideal to have in your custom component's code base.

10.7 Summary

In this chapter, we introduced the Xcelsius SDK, explained some of its core functionality, highlighted common case where the SDK can be implemented and gave an overview of the value that it can bring to your Xcelsius dashboard projects. With the fundamental concept of the SDK in mind, the following chapters will build on this foundational knowledge to further illustrate and explain basic to advanced SDK implementation options and details.

This chapter will provide a detailed walkthrough of a full property sheet and corresponding custom Flex component for Xcelsius.

11   Get Started with Custom Component Basics

In this chapter, we will take a closer look into the core concepts of Xcelsius SDK development. We will cover the foundational pieces that compose a custom component and step through working concrete examples to get you up to speed and prepared for more advanced topics.

Let's start by gaining an understanding of the backbone of a custom component integration which facilitates all component data flow and binding communication; the custom component Property Sheet.

11.1   Developing Basic Add-On Property Sheets

Conceptually, Property Sheets will seem very similar to a developer who is familiar with Xcelsius and interacting with the Xcelsius components offered in the default component library. A Property Sheet is essentially a self-contained Flex application that serves as both a User Interface control and communication proxy between the Xcelsius design environment and your custom component's publicly exposed properties that you wish to give users control over.

Property sheets can serve many functions and since they are Flex-based applications, Property Sheets enable the custom component developer to exercise creativity in designing the most effective User Interface(s) that the business users who leverage the custom component will ultimately interact with.

The basic primary Property Sheet features that we will cover before moving to more advanced Property Sheet features are:

- Property Data Binding
- Property Value Setting/Getting

475

11.1.1 Property Sheet Data Binding

Perhaps the most powerful feature exposed by the Xcelsius SDK is the ability to bind to a variety of data ranges in the underlying Xcelsius Excel data model, to public properties that you specify in your custom Flex component. Binding types come in a handful of varieties and enable custom components to read, write or read and write to the Xcelsius Excel model in every way that is needed to fundamentally communicate with the two-dimensional data model (rows and columns) that is supported by the Xcelsius implementation of the Excel model.

Bindings can be adapted to suit a variety of basic to advanced use cases. In this section we will review the basic concepts of data binding that a custom component developer is most likely to encounter. Below are the fundamental concepts offered by the Xcelsius SDK binding mechanism.

Binding call example that specifies a read-only 2 dimensional array property binding of a custom component's xcChartData property:

```
proxy.bind("xcChartData", null, bindingID, BindingDirection.OUTPUT, "",
OutputBindings.ARRAY2D);
```

Binding Directions and Data Flow

When establishing a binding between Xcelsius and one of your custom component's properties, you are able to specify whether your property should be treated as read-only, write-only, or as both a read and write property.

Reading Values from the Spreadsheet

To specify your component's property as a read-only property, meaning that your property will be a consumer of data from the Xcelsius model, you will need to specify a binding direction type of "OUTPUT", as described below. By subscribing to the Xcelsius model through binding as a read-only or OUTPUT consumer, your component's property value will change any time the range or cell data your custom component is bound to in the Xcelsius data model changes, both at runtime as well as design time in the Xcelsius environment.

To access this binding direction type you may import the *xcelsius.binding.BindingDirection* namespace into your Property Sheet application. Below is the fully qualified path to the OUTPUT type.

```
xcelsius.binding.BindingDirection.OUTPUT
```

Writing Values to the Spreadsheet

To specify your component's property as a write-only property, meaning that your property will be a provider of data to the Xcelsius model, you will need to specify a binding direction type of "INPUT", as described below. By subscribing to the Xcelsius model through binding as a write-only or INPUT consumer, your component's property value will update the cell or range that it is bound to in the data model any time the data in your bound custom component property changes.

To access this binding direction type you may import the *xcelsius.binding.BindingDirection* namespace. Below is the fully qualified path to the INPUT type.

```
xcelsius.binding.BindingDirection.INPUT
```

Writing Values to and Reading Values from the Spreadsheet

To specify your component's property as both a read and write property, meaning that your property will be a provider and consumer of data via the Xcelsius Excel model, you will need to specify a binding direction type of "BOTH", as described below. By subscribing to the Xcelsius model in this manner, your component's property value will update the cell or range that it is bound to in the data model any time the data in your custom component property changes, and conversely, your component's property value will change anytime the Xcelsius Excel model is updated.

To access this binding direction type you may import the *xcelsius.binding.BindingDirection* namespace. Below is the fully qualified path to the BOTH type.

```
xcelsius.binding.BindingDirection.BOTH
```

Binding Types

Whether your custom component's property is read, write or both, it will need to specify what type of value it is in the proxy.bind() operation so the SDK can properly handle its data flow.

The options for InputBindings and OutputBindings are as follows in Figures 11.1 and 11.2:

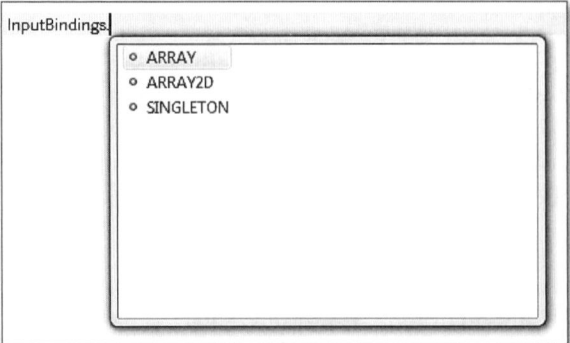

Figure 11.1 InputBinding options

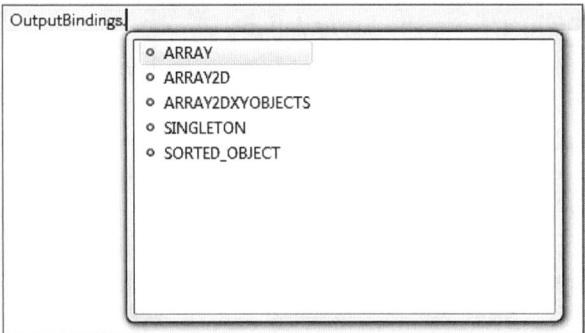

Figure 11.2 OutputBinding options

InputBindings

- ARRAY

    A type of ARRAY indicates that your custom component's property will be bound to and able to write to a set of cells in either a single column or row.

- ARRAY2D

    A type of ARRAY2D indicates that your custom component's property will be bound to and able to write to a set of cells in a row and column format.

- SINGLETON

    A type of SINGLETON indicates that your custom component's property will be bound to and able to write to a single cell.

OutputBindings
- ARRAY

  A type of ARRAY indicates that your custom component's property will be bound to and able to read from a set of cells in either a single column or row.

- ARRAY2D

  A type ofARRAY2D indicates that your custom component's property will be bound to and able to read from a set of cells in a row and column format.

- SINGLETON

  A type of SINGLETON indicates that your custom component's property will be bound to and able to read from a single cell.

- ARRAY2DXYOBJECTS

  A type of ARRAY2DXY indicates that your custom component's property will be bound to and able to read multiple columns or rows of cells output as a 2D array of Objects with x and y properties.

- SORTED_OBJECT

  A type of SORTED_OBJECT indicates that your custom component's property will be bound to and able to read a sorted object representation of a 2D table.

11.1.2 Explicitly Setting Property Values

Aside from the need to bind custom component properties to data in the Xcelsius Excel model, the ability also exists to read and write to a custom component's property directly through the Property Sheet, thus bypassing the Excel model altogether.

An example of this functionality would be if you have a Flex ColorPicker control on your Property Sheet that is responsible for setting a color property on your component. Assuming you had a custom Flex Canvas component with a public property named "xcBackgroundColor", you could write a value to that property by using the following command specified inline in the ColorPicker's "change" event handler, where "cp" represents the ID of your MXML ColorPicker in the Flex Property Sheet.

```
private var proxy:PropertySheetExternalProxy = new PropertySheetExternalProxy();

<mx:ColorPicker left="19" top="175" id="cp"
change="proxy.setProperty('xcChartColor',cp.selectedColor)"/>
```

11.1.3 Explicitly Getting Property Values

The ability to extract values from your custom component at Property Sheet design time exists as well and will be covered in the chapter Implementing Advanced Custom Add-On Component Features.

11.1.4 Property Sheet Styling

While certain factors need to be considered for styling custom components, Property Sheet styling is direct and enables developers to leverage common styling practices in Flex such as style sheet references, inline style directives and embedded style sheets.

11.1.5 Basic Property Sheet Overview

With some basic Property Sheet concepts in mind, let's take a walk through a functional example that highlights some of the fundamental aforementioned features. The full Property Sheet code is listed in breakout form of the code and accompanying code explanations in order from top to bottom.

This Property Sheet is designed as a basic example that is used to control a basic Flex AreaChart custom component with a handful of public properties. The full sample source code for the corresponding custom component is listed in the following section in this chapter: Developing Basic Add-On Components.

The image below in Figure 11.3 highlights the overall end result of the following Property Sheet and Component walk through by displaying the component, connected to data, and the data layout, inside of the Xcelsius designer.

Property Sheet Code Walkthrough
- Main property sheet initialization event handler
- Fundamental SDK import statements
- Private SDK variables
- Supporting SDK functions
- Proxy.Bind dissected

11.1 Developing Basic Add-On Property Sheets

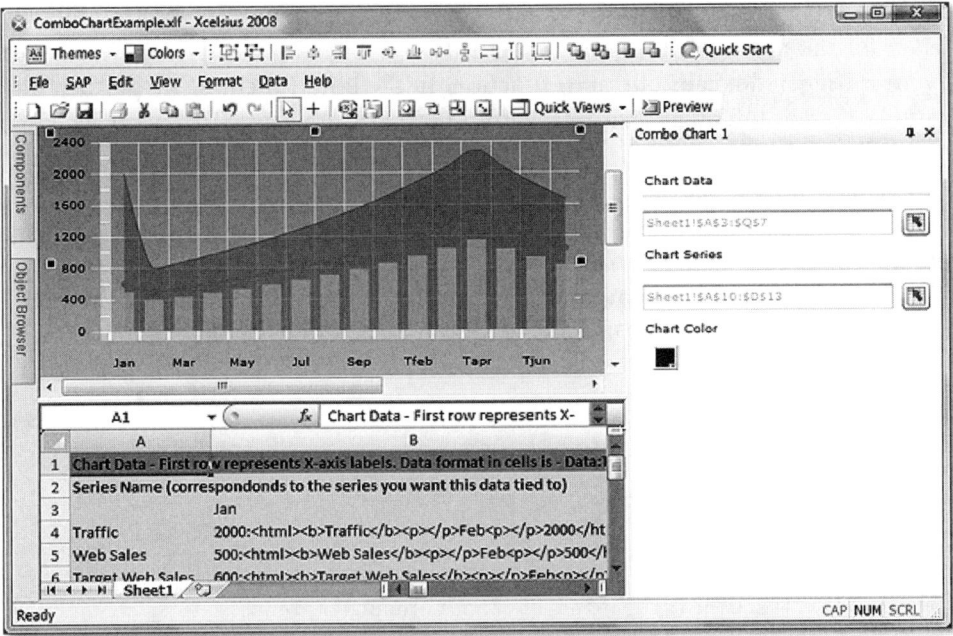

Figure 11.3 Custom Component and Property Sheet End Result

Figure 11.4 Property Sheet in Design Mode

Property Sheet Application Complete Event Listener
```
<?xml version="1.0" encoding="utf-8"?>
<mx:Application xmlns:mx="http://www.adobe.com/2006/mxml"
layout="absolute" applicationComplete="init();">
```

Get Started with Custom Component Basics

On line 2 of our Property Sheet which is a basic Flex Application MXML file, we listen for the native Flex Application event of "applicationComplete". When this event is triggered it calls our init() function. In the init() function, we perform the routine task of initializing and executing the basic Xcelsius SDK event listeners and callback functions needed to perform our custom component data binding and value setting tasks.

Fundamental SDK Import Statements

The import statements below provide us with a reference to the foundational classes and utilities in the SDK needed for our basic Property Sheet application.

```
<mx:Script>
<![CDATA[
import mx.containers.*;
import mx.controls.*;
import mx.core.Container;
import mx.events.FlexEvent;
import xcelsius.binding.BindingDirection;
import xcelsius.binding.tableMaps.input.InputBindings;
import xcelsius.binding.tableMaps.output.OutputBindings;
import xcelsius.propertySheets.impl.PropertySheetExternalProxy;
import xcelsius.propertySheets.interfaces.
PropertySheetFunctionNamesSDK;
```

Below, we call out and explain the import statements that are specifically related to the SDK.

```
import xcelsius.binding.BindingDirection;
```

The BindingDirection import statement enables you to call on Binding Direction constants from the Xcelsius SDK. The Binding Direction options (INPUT, OUTPUT, BOTH) specify the direction of data flow between your Xcelsius component properties and the Xcelsius Excel data model when performing a bind operation through the SDK.

```
import xcelsius.binding.tableMaps.input.InputBindings;
```

The InputBindings import statement enables you to call on Input Binding constants from the Xcelsius SDK. The Input Binding options (ARRAY, ARRAY2D, SINGLETON) specify the type of data range you wish to bind to between your Xcelsius component properties and the Xcelsius Excel data model when performing a bind operation through the SDK. InputBindings should be specified when a custom component property needs to input values into the Xcelsius Excel model.

```
import xcelsius.binding.tableMaps.output.OutputBindings;
```

The OutputBindings import statement enables you to call on Output Binding constants from the Xcelsius SDK. The Output Binding options (ARRAY, ARRAY2D, SINGLETON) specify the type of data range you wish to bind to between your Xcelsius component properties and the Xcelsius Excel data model when performing a bind operation through the SDK. OutputBindings should be specified when a custom component property needs to read values from the Xcelsius Excel model.

```
import xcelsius.propertySheets.impl.PropertySheetExternalProxy;
```

The PropertySheetExternalProxy import statement provides access to the PropertySheetExternalProxy class which is the backbone of the SDK integration performing all binding and value operations between the Property Sheet and custom component.

```
import xcelsius.propertySheets.interfaces.
PropertySheetFunctionNamesSDK;
```

The PropertySheetFunctionNamesSDK import statement provides access to a set of constants that tie to Xcelsius SDK function names.

Basic Private SDK Variables

The 3 private variables defined in this section are key to managing custom component property data binding and property value setting through the SDK.

```
private var proxy:PropertySheetExternalProxy = new
PropertySheetExternalProxy();
private var propertyToBind:String;

private var currentBindingID:String;
```

Below, we call out and explain the primary private variables related to the SDK.

```
private var proxy:PropertySheetExternalProxy
```

The proxy variable is responsible for performing the job that its class name indicates; to serve as a proxy between the custom component's properties and the Property Sheet. This variable is responsible for all key communication, property data binding and value setting in a custom component Property Sheet.

```
private var propertyToBind:String;
```

The propertyToBind variable serves as a string value that is responsible for holding the name of the custom component property that is currently being bound to during user-initiated binding operations. This value allows the developer to manage

UI controls, data binding for the given property, and any other housekeeping or special functionality associated with the property. This variable is used primarily in the initiateBind and continueBind functions listed in the following section Supporting SDK functions.

```
private var currentBindingID:String;
```

The currentBindingID variable serves as a string value that is responsible for holding the binding id of the custom component property that is currently being bound to during binding operations. This value allows the proxy to manage data bindings for the given property. This variable is used primarily in the initiateBind and continueBind functions listed in the following section Supporting SDK functions.

Supporting SDK Functions

A few common functions can be found across the majority of Property Sheet implementations. Those common functions are also included in this particular source code walkthrough as follows.

Initialize Values

The initValues function is responsible for retrieving the custom component's property values at property sheet initialization time and populating the Property Sheet's User Interface controls with their respective property values. In this particular implementation, we retrieve the 3 values exposed by our custom component and loop through them to initialize their corresponding property sheet controls. Listed below is the function code.

```
// Initializes Property Sheet on load to show the
current Xcelsius custom component property/style value.
private function initValues():void
{
   //Process the array of values for the Xcelsius custom
   //component properties.
   var propertyValues:Array = proxy.getProperties(
   ["xcChartData", "xcChartSeries", "xcChartColor"]);

   var propertyValuesLength:int = (propertyValues != null ?
                    propertyValues.length : 0);
   for (var i:int=0; i < propertyValuesLength; i++)
   {
      // Get the property name and value.
      var propertyObject:Object = propertyValues[i];
      var propertyName:String = propertyObject.name;
```

```
      var propertyValue:* = propertyObject.value;

      // Process the property by name, either show the
      //value or show the cell address if bound to the
      //Excel spreadsheet.
      var bindingText:String = "";
      switch (propertyName)
      {
         case "xcChartData":
            bindingText=
            getPropertyBindDisplayName(propertyName);
            if (bindingText != null)
            {
               // When bound the user cannot edit the value.
               tiChartData.enabled = false;
               // Show the address we are bound to.
               tiChartData.text = bindingText;
            }
            else
            {
               tiChartData.text = "";
            }
            break;
         case "xcChartSeries":
            bindingText =
            getPropertyBindDisplayName(propertyName);
            if (bindingText != null)
            {
               tiChartSeries.enabled = false;
               tiChartSeries.text = bindingText;
            }
            else
            {
               tiChartSeries.text = "";
            }
            break;
         case "xcChartColor":
            cpChartColor.selectedColor = propertyValue;
            break;
         default:
            break;
      }
   }
}
```

Get Bound Property Display Names

The getPropertyBindDisplayName function is a utility function that is responsible for returning the Excel range address that a given custom component property is bound to once a user-initiated binding operation has been completed. This cell address value is traditionally used in all custom Xcelsius components to visually indicate to the user through a text input control, where in the Excel model the property is bound to. Listed below is the function code.

```
// Returns the bind display name or null if not bound.
private function
   getPropertyBindDisplayName(propertyName:String):String
{
   // Get the array of bindings for this property.
   var propertyBindings:Array = proxy.getBindings([propertyName]);
   if ((propertyBindings != null)    &&
      (propertyBindings.length  > 0) &&
      (propertyBindings[0].length > 0))
   {
      // We have at least one binding for this
      //property so pick the 1st one.
      // Note: [0][0] is 1st property in the array,
      //then 1st binding for that property.
      var bindingID:String = propertyBindings[0][0];
      return proxy.getBindingDisplayName(bindingID);
   }
   return null;
}
```

Initiating End-User Interaction Binding Operations

The initiateBind function is a utility function that is responsible for launching the Xcelsius Binding Window as shown in Figure 11.5 and Excel range address that a given custom component property is bound to when the binding button for a particular property is clicked. This function allows the user to select or modify the range that a custom component's property is bound to. Listed below is the function code needed to launch this utility to initiate data binding operations for a given custom component property.

Figure 11.5 Initiate Bind Window

```
// Allows the user to select the Excel spreadsheet cell
//to bind to an Xcelsius custom component property.
private function initiateBind(propertyName:String):void
{
   //If there is an existing binding for this property
   //show that in the Excel binding selection window.
   //Store the currentBindingID (null if there is no
   //current binding), we need this for "continueBinding".

   currentBindingID = null;
   var propertyBindings:Array = proxy.getBindings([propertyName]);
   if ((propertyBindings != null) && (propertyBindings.length > 0))
   {
      //Use the 1st binding address for the property.
      currentBindingID = propertyBindings[0];
   }

   //Store the name of the property that we are binding,
   //we need this when we "continueBinding".
   propertyToBind = propertyName;

   //Let the user choose where to bind to in the
   //Excel spreadsheet.
   proxy.requestUserSelection(currentBindingID);
}
```

Finalizing User-Initiated Binding Operations

The continueBind function is a function called as a result of the user clicking the "OK" button in the Xcelsius binding control in Figure 11.6 once they have selected the desired range they would like to bind the custom component property to. This function performs the final steps via the "proxy" variable, needed to establish a binding of any type between the Xcelsius Excel model and a custom component property. Listed below is the function code needed to finalize or commit a data binding operation for a given custom component property. The remainder of the MXML code for this source code example is listed below the continueBind function code as well.

Figure 11.6 Clicking OK to Finalize Binding Operation

11 | Get Started with Custom Component Basics

```
// Completes the binding when the user has finished selecting
//the cell to bind to or cleared the binding.
private function continueBind(bindingID:String):void
{
   // Define common variables here.
   var propertyName:String = propertyToBind;
   var propertyValues:Array;
   var propertyObject:Object;
   var bindingAddresses:Array;

   // Clear any existing bindings - so we can re-bind.
   if (currentBindingID != null)
   {
      proxy.unbind(currentBindingID);
      currentBindingID = null;
   }

   // Process the property binding.
   switch (propertyName)
   {
      case "xcChartData":
         //User explicitly cleared binding,
         //do not create another.
         if ((bindingID == null) || (bindingID == ""))
         {

            //Fill the chart with an empty dataset
            propertyValues =
               proxy.getProperties([propertyName]);
            propertyObject =
               propertyValues[0];
            //Make sure we set the property
            //on the component as well.
            proxy.setProperty(propertyName,
                       propertyObject.value);
            return;
         }
         //Display the range address.
         tiChartData.text =
            proxy.getBindingDisplayName(bindingID);

         proxy.bind("xcChartData",
            null, bindingID,
```

```
              BindingDirection.OUTPUT, "",
              OutputBindings.ARRAY2D);
           break;
        case "xcChartSeries":
           //User explicitly cleared binding,
           //do not create another.
           if ((bindingID == null) || (bindingID == ""))
           {
              propertyValues =
                 proxy.getProperties([propertyName]);
              propertyObject = propertyValues[0];
              proxy.setProperty(propertyName,
                        propertyObject.value);
              return;
           }

           // Display the range address.
           tiChartSeries.text =
              proxy.getBindingDisplayName(bindingID);
           proxy.bind("xcChartSeries",
           null, bindingID,
           BindingDirection.OUTPUT, "",
           OutputBindings.ARRAY2D);
           break;
        default:
           break;
     }
  }
]]>
</mx:Script>
<mx:Canvas minWidth="268"  minHeight="350"
         width="100%" height="100%"
         backgroundColor="#FFFFFF">
   <mx:Label x="10" y="22" text="Chart Data"/>
   <mx:HRule y="39" height="10" right="10" left="10"/>
   <mx:TextInput id="tiChartData"
      y="57" right="42" left="10"/>
   <mx:Button y="56" right="10"  width="24"
      click="initiateBind('xcChartData');"
      icon="@Embed('com/assets/bind to cell.png')"/>
   <mx:Label x="10" y="87" text="Chart Series"/>
   <mx:Label x="10" y="152" text="Chart Color"/>
   <mx:HRule y="104" height="10" right="10" left="10"/>
```

```
        <mx:TextInput id="tiChartSeries" y="122"
                right="42" left="10"/>
        <mx:Button y="121" right="10"  width="24"
            click="initiateBind('xcChartSeries');"
            icon="@Embed('com/assets/bind to cell.png')"/>
        <mx:ColorPicker left="19" top="175"
        id="cpChartColor"
        change="proxy.setProperty('xcChartColor',
        cpChartColor.selectedColor)"/>
        </mx:Canvas>
</mx:Application>
```

11.1.6 Proxy.Bind Explained

The Xcelsius SDK bind function currently accepts 10 parameters, the last 5 of which are optional. Let's take a look at the fundamental first 5 parameters, in order.

1. Property
2. Chain
3. BindingID
4. Direction
5. InputMap
6. OutputMap

```
proxy.bind(
"xcChartData",            <- Property
null,                     <- Chain
bindingID,                <- BindingID
BindingDirection.OUTPUT,  <- Direction
"",                       <- InputMap
OutputBindings.ARRAY2D    <- OutputMap
);
```

- Property
  The name of the custom component property to be bound
- Chain
  An alternate array argument usually left blank for normal binding scenarios. This chain is usually reserved for Sub Element Binding.
- BindingID
  The Xcelsius-generated BindingID of the custom component property to be bound

- Direction
  The BindingDirection constant that indicates whether the property is read, write, or read and write
- InputMap
  The InputBindings constant that indicates whether the property is:
  SINGLETON, ARRAY OR ARRAY2D
- OutputMap
  The OutputBindings constant that indicates whether the property is:
  SINGLETON, ARRAY, ARRAY2D, ARRAY2DXYOBJECTS or SORTED_OBJECT

11.2 Developing Basic Add-On Components

With a basic Property Sheet implemented and connecting to our properties exposed by our custom component, we will take a look at how the custom component's public properties are exposed, consumed, set, and how they process their data output flow from Xcelsius, where applicable. The full component code is listed in breakout form of the code and accompanying code explanations in order from top to bottom.

This particular custom component is designed as a basic example that leverages a base Flex charting component, CartesianChart, to expose a simple yet powerful and highly adaptable chart that allows for multiple series types to be combined in a single chart implementation.

11.2.1 Custom Component Code Walkthrough

- Main component initialization event handler
- Private Variables
- Public Chart Color Variable
- Public Chart Series Variable
- Public Chart Data Variable
- Chart Building Function
- Tooltip Function
- MXML Markup

11 | Get Started with Custom Component Basics

Main Component Initialization Event Handler and Import Statements

On line 2 below, we listen for the native Flex Canvas event of "creationComplete". When this event is triggered, in the function buildSeries() we perform the fundamental operation of the component, which is to build up the Chart's data and series. Listed below is the complete import code.

```
<?xml version="1.0" encoding="utf-8"?>
<mx:Canvas verticalScrollPolicy="off" creationPolicy="all" creationComp
lete="buildSeries()"
horizontalScrollPolicy="off" xmlns:mx="http://www.adobe.com/2006/mxml"
width="400" height="400">
 <mx:Script>
 <![CDATA[
    import mx.charts.series.ColumnSet;
    import mx.graphics.RadialGradient;
    import mx.graphics.LinearGradient;
    import mx.managers.ToolTipManager;
    import mx.charts.renderers.LineRenderer;
    import mx.charts.renderers.CircleItemRenderer;
    import mx.charts.series.AreaSeries;
    import mx.charts.series.LineSeries;
    import mx.graphics.Stroke;
    import mx.charts.series.ColumnSeries;
    import mx.graphics.GradientEntry;
    import mx.collections.ArrayCollection;
```

Private Variables

The private variable _columnSet is responsible for clustering any specified ColumnSeries for our Cartesian Chart. The private variable _xcChartData is a Bindable ArrayCollection which serves as our Cartesian Chart's data provider. In the MXML code listed lastly in this section under MXML Markup: Grid Lines and Cartesian Chart, the Cartesian Chart's dataProvider property is bound to the _xcChartData variable. Listed below are the private variables for our basic component.

```
    private var _columnSet:ColumnSet = new ColumnSet();

    [Bindable]private var _xcChartData:ArrayCollection = new
    ArrayCollection();
```

Public Chart Color Variable- xcChartColor

The public variable xcChartColor is set up as a read and write variable and in each operation, it is responsible for setting or getting our Bindable internal variable _ xcChartColor. In the MXML code listed lastly in this section under MXML Markup: Grid Lines and Cartesian Chart, our Cartesian Chart's color property is bound to this private variable which controls the color property of the chart. Listed below is the public property function code.

```
[Bindable]private var _xcChartColor:Number = 0x000000;
public function get xcChartColor():Number
{
 return _xcChartColor;
}
public function set xcChartColor(value:Number):void
{
 _xcChartColor = value;;
}
```

Public Chart Series Variable

The public variable xcChartSeries is set up as a read and write variable and in each operation, it is responsible for setting or getting our internal variable _ xcChartSeries. In our Property Sheet, we have this variable defined as a 2D Array consumer and each time the public variable is set, we cycle through this 2D Array variable to build the chart series for our Cartesian Chart. Note that the function buildSeries() is called every time the xcChartSeries public set function is called, enabling the chart to completely redesign itself at Xcelsius runtime anytime the Xcelsius dashboard designer decides it should be redesigned, making it highly adaptable. Listed below is the function code.

```
private var _xcChartSeries:Array = new Array();
public function get xcChartSeries():Array
{
 return _xcChartSeries;
}

public function set xcChartSeries(value:Array):void
{
  try
  {
    _xcChartSeries = value;
    buildSeries();
  }
  catch(e:Error)
  {
    trace(e.getStackTrace());
```

            }
        }

Public Chart Data Variable

The public variable xcChartData is set up as a read and write variable and in each operation, it is responsible for setting or getting our internal variable _ xcChartData. In our Property Sheet, we have this variable defined as a 2D Array consumer and each time the public variable is set, we cycle through this 2D Array variable to build the data for our Cartesian Chart. Note that the building of the data is called every time the xcChartData public set function is called. Notice that we treat a 2D Array of data output from Xcelsius exactly like any other 2D Array would be treated in ActionScript. We access the data in Xcelsius by looping over the data, referencing rows and invidual cells by using their ordinal position, i.e. _ xcChartData[rowPosition][columnPosition] = a single cell in the Xcelsius Excel data model.

In this particular case, we always extract the user-specified series name for a given set of data, at position 0 on each row in the data. For brevity's sake, we then dynamically roll through each cell in any given row from position 1-N, to extract data values and associated tooltips. The data and tooltips values are specified as colon-separated in each given cell in the Xcelsius Excel model, i.e. [data:tooltip] or 5,000:My Tooltip. Listed below is the function code.

```
public function get xcChartData():Array
{
    return [];
}
/**
*Cycle through the 2D data Array,
*building data for each series
***/
public function set xcChartData(value:Array):void
{
    //Row[0]=SeriesName
    //Row[0-N]=Data:HTMLTooltip
    _xcChartData.removeAll();
    try
    {
        var columnStart:int = 0;
        var columnEnd:int = value[0].length;
        //Append each dataset to a
```

```
            //given month (month = key to each row)
            for (var i:int=columnStart; i<columnEnd; i++)
            {
               var data:Object = new Object();
               data.yLabel = value[0][i];
               if(data.yLabel == "" || data.yLabel == null)
                  continue;
               //Build data for each month
               for (var i2:int = 1;i2<value.length;i2++)
               {
                  //cell content format =
                  //[dataValue : toolTip];
                  var cell:String = String(value[i2][i]);
                  var seriesName:String = value[i2][0];
                  var dataValue:Number =
                     Number(cell.substring(
                        0,cell.indexOf(":")));
                  var toolTip:String =
                     cell.substring(
                     cell.indexOf(":") + 1, cell.length);

                  data[seriesName]= dataValue;
                  data[seriesName + data.yLabel] = toolTip;
               }
               _xcChartData.addItem(data);
            }
        }
        catch(e:Error)
        {
         trace(e.getStackTrace());
        }
}
```

Chart Building Function

The buildSeries function is responsible for looping through our publicly set private variable, xcChartSeries. In our Property Sheet, we have this variable defined as a 2D Array consumer and each time the public variable is set, we cycle through this 2D Array variable to build the series for our Cartesian Chart.

Notice that we treat a 2D Array of data output from Xcelsius exactly like any other 2D Array would be treated in ActionScript. We access the data in Xcelsius by looping over the data, referencing rows and individual cells by using their ordinal

Get Started with Custom Component Basics

position, i.e. _ xcChartSeries [rowPosition][columnPosition] = a single cell in the Xcelsius Excel data model.

For readability's sake, we have created an intermediary variable, called "series" that is an Array. Essentially, the series variable represents a row of data from the Xcelsius model and each cell in the row provides us with a singular piece of information about the type of series the user wants to see on the chart and how they want that series to be named and represented through the CartesianChart. In this particular case, we require the user to place the series type in position 0, the series name in position 1, the series color in position 2 and the series alpha in position 3 as show below.

`var series:Array = _xcChartSeries[i];`	→A row of data from Xcelsius
`var seriesType:String = series[0];`	→A cell (#1) of data from Xcelsius
`var seriesName:String = series[1];`	→A cell (#2) of data from Xcelsius
`var seriesColor:Number = series[2];`	→A cell (#3) of data from Xcelsius
`var seriesAlpha:Number = series[3];`	→A cell (#4) of data from Xcelsius

As we cycle through this data, in the switch statement below, we determine the type of series specified, style the series accordingly, and add the series on to the Cartesian Chart. Listed below is the function code.

```
/***
*Cycle through the 2D series Array,
*styling and adding specified series types
***/
private function buildSeries():void
{
   if(chart == null)
     return;
   chart.series=new Array();
   columnSet = new ColumnSet();
   columnSet.type = "clustered";
   var st:Stroke;
   for(var i:int=0;i<_xcChartSeries.length;i++)
   {
    var series:Array = _xcChartSeries[i];
    var seriesType:String = series[0];
    var seriesName:String = series[1];
    var seriesColor:Number = series[2];
```

```
var seriesAlpha:Number = series[3];
//Add the correct series based on the
//specified seriesType
switch (seriesType.toLowerCase())
{
   case "line":
      var ls:LineSeries = new LineSeries();
      ls.yField = seriesName;
         ls.name = seriesName;
         ls.displayName= seriesName;

         st = new Stroke();
         st.color=seriesColor;
         st.alpha=seriesAlpha;
         st.weight=2;
         st.pixelHinting=false;

      var linePointFill:RadialGradient =
         new RadialGradient();
      linePointFill.entries =
         [new GradientEntry(seriesColor,
                     0.33, .5),
         new GradientEntry(seriesColor,
                     0.65, seriesAlpha)]

         ls.setStyle("fill",linePointFill);
         ls.setStyle("lineStroke",st);
         ls.setStyle("stroke",st);
         ls.setStyle("radius",3);
         ls.setStyle("form","curve");
         ls.setStyle("itemRenderer",
         new ClassFactory(
         mx.charts.renderers.CircleItemRenderer));
          ls.setStyle ("lineSegmentRenderer",
         new ClassFactory(
         mx.charts.renderers.LineRenderer));

         //Add the series
         chart.series.push(ls);
   break;
   case "column":
      var cs:ColumnSeries = new ColumnSeries();
      cs.yField = seriesName;
```

```
            cs.name = seriesName;
            cs.displayName= seriesName;

        var columnFill:LinearGradient =
            new LinearGradient();
        columnFill.entries =
            [new GradientEntry(seriesColor,
                    0.33, seriesAlpha),
        new GradientEntry(seriesColor,
                    0.65, seriesAlpha)]

            cs.setStyle("fill",columnFill);
            cs.alpha=seriesAlpha;

            //Add the series
            columnSet.series.push(cs);
    break;
        case "area":
        var ar:AreaSeries = new AreaSeries();
        ar.yField = seriesName;
            ar.name = seriesName;
            ar.displayName= seriesName;

            st = new Stroke();
            st.color=seriesColor;
            st.alpha=1;
            st.weight=1;
            st.pixelHinting=false;

        var areaFill:LinearGradient =
            new LinearGradient();
        areaFill.entries =
            [new GradientEntry(seriesColor,
                0.33, .5),
                new GradientEntry(seriesColor,
                0.65, .6)]
            ar.setStyle("areaFill",areaFill);
            ar.setStyle("areaStroke",st);
            ar.setStyle("stroke",st);
            ar.setStyle("form","curve");
            //Add the series
            chart.series.push(ar);
        break;
```

```
        }
        chart.series.push(columnSet);
        }
}

private function formatDataTip(obj:Object):String
{
    return obj.item[obj.element.displayName +
            obj.item.yLabel];
}
```

Tooltip Function

The ability to finely control the information that an end user sees when they mouse over a given data point in an Xcelsius chart is an extremely important feature. By leveraging some standard Flex capabilities, we are able to return custom tooltips to our end users via this simple function which extracts information from the obj:Object parameter and returns our user-specified tooltip content, which may contain normal text as well as HTML. Listed below is the function code.

```
        private function formatDataTip(obj:Object):String
        {
return obj.item[obj.element.displayName + obj.item.yLabel];
        }
```

MXML Markup: Grid Lines and Cartesian Chart

The MXML specified in this part of the component provides us with the type of Grid Lines we want to use for our chart as well as the basic implementation of our Cartesian Chart's shell.

```
<mx:Array id="chartBg">
    <mx:GridLines alpha=".65" direction="both"/>
</mx:Array>
<mx:CartesianChart
      id="chart"
      width="100%" height="100%" showDataTips="true"
      color="{_xcChartColor}"
      dataTipFunction="formatDataTip"
      dataProvider="{_xcChartData}"
        backgroundElements="{chartBg}">
   <mx:horizontalAxis>
```

```
    <mx:CategoryAxis dataProvider="{_xcChartData}"
                categoryField="yLabel"/>
        </mx:horizontalAxis>
    </mx:CartesianChart>
</mx:Canvas>
```

11.3 Creating Basic Component Packages

As a continuation of the custom chart component highlighted in this chapter, let's build a packager for it as our final step in preparing it for consumption by Xcelsius.

Basic Component Packaging Steps

1. Open the Packager.exe application contained in the Xcelsius SDK install directory {Program Files}/BusinessObjects/Xcelsius/SDK.

2. Type in details related to your component as shown in Figure 11.7, including the component name.

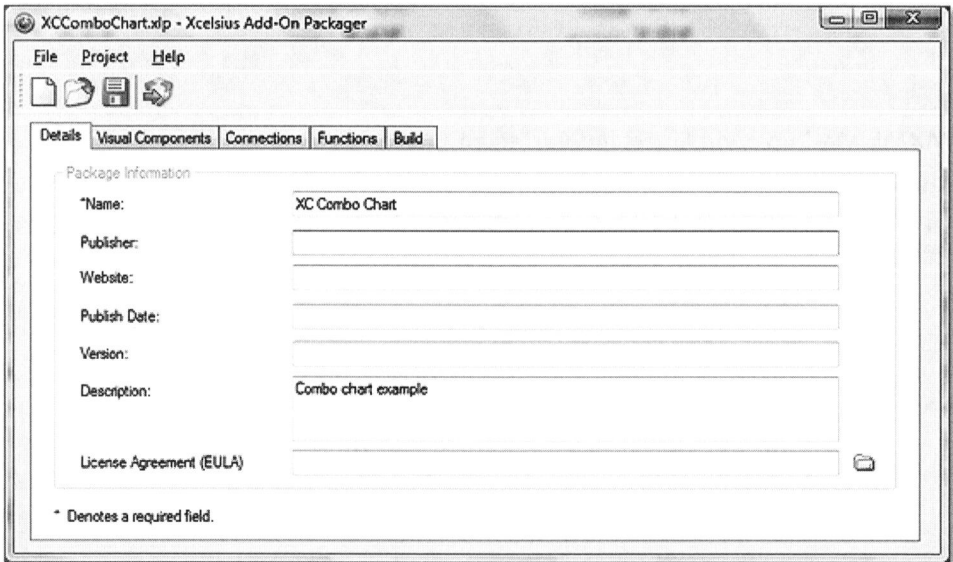

Figure 11.7 Enter your Component Details

3. Select the Visual Components tab and click Add New Component.
4. Enter the component's class name, including its full package path, as well as any additional information about the component, including the path to the Property Sheet swf file, component swf file and optional images you may define to represent the component in the Xcelsius Object Browser and Component List as shown in Figure 11.8.

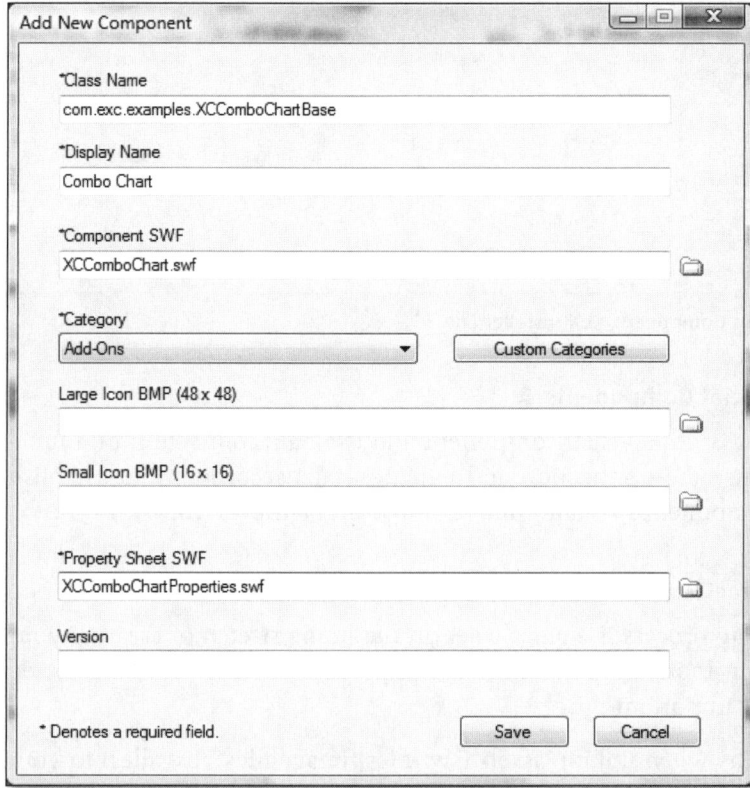

Figure 11.8 Enter your Component Class Name and SWF File Details

5. Save your packager file.
6. Build your XLX installer file and install it using the Xcelsius add-on manager (In Xcelsius, File -> Manage Add-Ons) as shown in Figure 11.9.

11 | Get Started with Custom Component Basics

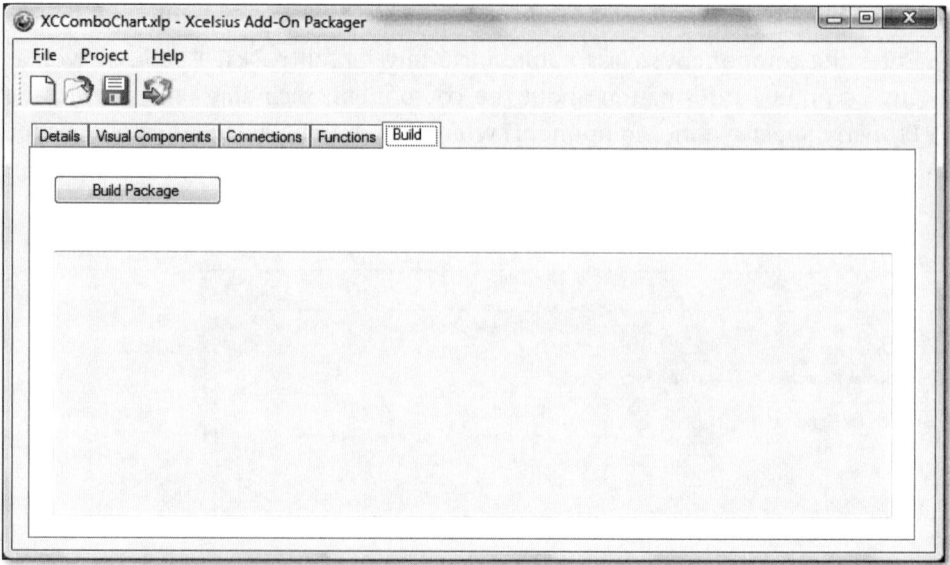

Figure 11.9 Build Your Component XLX Installer File

Packaging for Special Components

If your component is not a visual component and is a data connection or a function component, use the Connection and Function tabs accordingly to establish and build your component's installer file as shown in Figure 11.10.

Packaging Best Practices

While the packaging process is a simple act on the home stretch of creating your custom component, there are a handful of best practices that should be adhered to during this very important process.

- Use relative paths when linking assets (swf files, image files, text files) to your package.
- Use only one package per component to avoid installation conflicts in Xcelsius. Each package contains a unique ID value that Xcelsius inspects at install time and expects to be unique on a per-component basis.
- Do not copy components to avoid the conflict behavior described above.
- Save and backup your packages especially if you are developing products because if a package is lost or corrupted, you will once again run into the instal-

lation issue outlined above if you attempt to recreate the lost or corrupted package from the ground up.

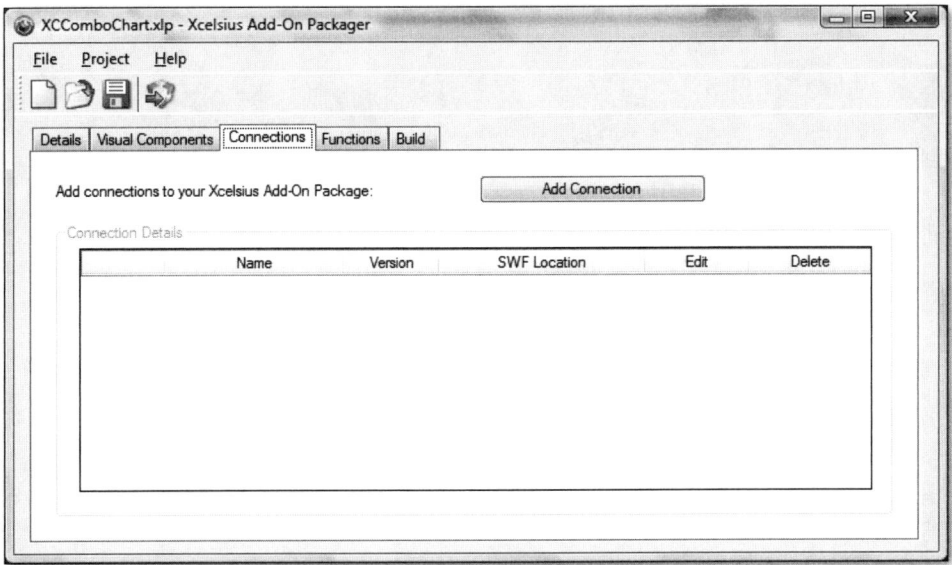

Figure 11.10 Connections Tab

11.4 Summary

In this chapter, we stepped through, in detail, a full Property Sheet and corresponding custom Flex component for Xcelsius. We also dived deeper into the details of certain core pieces of SDK functionality, highlighted common functions where the SDK can be implemented, and gave an overview of how to develop a basic custom component for your Xcelsius environment. With a functional component under our belts, in the following chapter Implementing Advanced Custom Add-On Component Features, we will take a tour of some more advanced yet less advertised, very powerful concepts and utilities exposed by the SDK.

> *A strong foundational knowledge of the advanced data binding and component communications abilities of the SDK will enable you to begin developing more advanced Property Sheet implementations.*

12   Implement Advanced Custom Add-On Component Features

With a good grasp on the fundamentals of the SDK, we will now take a look into the finer details of custom component development. We will also cover some less-advertised but very powerful SDK features, that when implemented, can give you a more granular level of control over the user experience and component functionality, enabling you to take your custom components to the next level.

12.1   Implementing Advanced Property Sheet Features

As your components begin to get slightly more complex, it is necessary to begin to use parts of the SDK that are not fully documented and are less obvious to understand and leverage. This section will go through several common scenarios that fall under this description and will explain how to use these powerful features with short and concise functional code snippets.

- Sub-element binding
- Persisting Property Sheet Values
- Retrieving Custom Component Property Values
- Setting Custom Component Property Values
- Generating Reusable Property Sheet Patterns
- Communicating with External Data Services

12.1.1   Sub-Element Binding

Sub element binding is the act of binding one or more data ranges in the Xcelsius Excel model to a single property in your custom component. A perfect example of this would be to define data for each series to a single component series property in an Xcelsius Column Chart component. Conceptually this seems very simple but as you get into the SDK is becomes less clear on how to actually implement this commonly-requested functionality.

For this example, we have a property called chartSeriesData that needs to accomplish the goals outlined above. Using the Xcelsius Column Chart's Property Sheet as a visual guide, let's take a look at how to setup the bindings and other functionality needed to support this feature through the SDK. Let's assume that the list containing the series names in the image below in Figure 12.1 has an ID in Flex of seriesList.

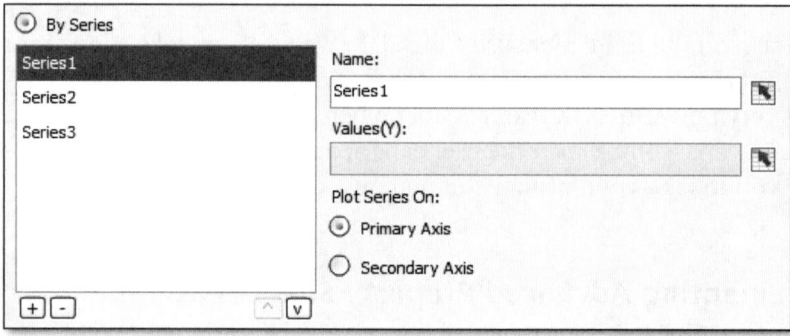

Figure 12.1 Series List Example

Sub Element properties leverage the same initiateBind and continueBind functions found in the previous chapter's Property Sheet code walkthrough with a few exceptions.

1. We need to establish a private Property Sheet variable called seriesBindingIDs whose function is to maintain a persistent list of Xcelsius Binding ID's associated with the chartSeriesData property.
   ```
   private var _seriesDataBindingIDs:Array = new Array();
   ```

2. In the initiateBind function, we need to set the currentBindingID equal to the stored bindingID that resides at the selected index of the list control (seriesList.selectedIndex) in our private variable above.
   ```
   if(propertyName == "chartSeriesData ")
   {
   currentBindingID =
       _seriesDataBindingIDs [seriesList.selectedIndex];
   proxy.requestUserSelection(
   ```

```
    _seriesDataBindingIDs [seriesList .selectedIndex]);
}
```

3. In the continueBind function, we need to perform some general UI housekeeping and most importantly pass the chain Array variable and the bindingID to the proxy.bind function. This notifies the SDK that you intend to bind the specified bindingID at the given index specified by the chain variable.

   ```
   case "chartSeriesData":
       //User explicitly cleared binding, do not create another.
       if ((bindingID == null) || (bindingID == ""))
       {
           txtSeriesData.enabled=false;
           txtSeriesData.text="";
           return;
       }

       txtSeriesData.enabled=false;

       //save this Binding ID in order to re-bind later
       _seriesDataBindingIDs[seriesList.selectedIndex] =
                                   bindingID;

       // create a chain to bind to
       //chartSeriesData[selectedIndex]
       var chain:Array = [seriesList.selectedIndex];

       proxy.bind("chartSeriesData", chain,
               bindingID, BindingDirection.OUTPUT,
               "", OutputBindings.ARRAY);

       break;
   ```

4. We also need to persist or save the private variable seriesDataBindingIDs stored ID's. This will enable us to save these values off for the given XLF so that the next time the user interacts with the component, all of the sub element binding ID's will be saved and ready for use. This concept will be covered for this particular example in the following Persisting Property Sheet Values and Retrieving Property Sheet Values sections.

These are the fundamental steps to establishing sub element binding. Other housekeeping operations should be performed based on the type of User Interface controls used to manage these bindings and the proxy calls proxy.unbind should also be used to clean up any legacy bindings, for example if the user were to hit the "-" button in the list control above, to remove a given series. A fully functional sub element binding example is provided in the SDK samples directory ({Program Files}\BusinessObjects\Xcelsius\SDK\samples) and is titled "RSSConnectorWithTrigger".

12.1.2 Persisting Property Sheet Values

One of the less advertised but tremendously helpful features of the SDK is the ability to save variable values across sessions for a given XLF file. For example, you may want to save the selected tab index if your property sheet has multiple tabs and you would like for your Property Sheet to auto-select the tab where the user was last working. This is a basic use case, though you can store much more complex values if you desire.

Let's take a look at what is needed to persist the binding ID's of our private _seriesDataBindingIDs variable mentioned in the Sub Element Binding section.

When the Property Sheet initializes, another event listener needs to be established along side of the standard SDK event listeners enumerated in Chapter 11.

proxy.addCallback(PropertySheetFunctionNamesSDK.GET_PROPERTIES_FUNCTION, getProperties);

The GET_PROPERTIES_FUNCTION event is triggered when the Property Sheet is closing or unloading and is responsible for saving off or persisting any variable values that you specify.

In the following example, we illustrate how to go about saving off the set of _seriesDataBindingIDs. The essential duty that this function performs is to return to the SDK an Array of name/value pair objects where the name is equal to the name of the property you want to persist and the value is equal to the value of the property you want to persist. It is important to note that the name property of the object may be named anything you desire and does not and should not be named with the name of the corresponding custom component property it is used to assist.

```
private function getProperties():Array
{
    var persist:Array = new Array();
    var persistObject:Object = new Object();
    var seriesDataBindings:Object = new Object();
    for (var i:int=0; i< _seriesDataBindingIDs.length; i++)
```

```
    {
        seriesDataBindings[i] =
            _seriesDataBindingIDs [i];
    }
    persistObject.name = "seriesDataBindingIDs";
    persistObject.value = seriesDataBindings;
    persist.push(persistObject);

    return persist;
}
```

12.1.3 Retrieving Persisted Property Sheet Values

Now that we have persisted a value to our XLF file, let's take a look at how to retrieve that value when the property sheet initializes.

When the Property Sheet initializes, as in the initValues() function referenced in Chapter 11, we need to make a call to our loadProperties function below.

In the loadProperties function, we use the proxy.getPersist function of the SDK to retrieve the object that we have persisted.

```
private function loadProperties():void
{
    //Get the property name and value of our seriesDataBindingIDs
    var propertyObject:Object = proxy.getPersist(["seriesDataBindingID
s"])[0];
    var propertyValue:* = persistProperties[0].value;
     for (var prop:String in propertyValue)
     {
         if (prop != null && prop != "")
         {
         _seriesDataBindingIDs[i] =
             propertyValue[prop];
         }
     }
}
```

The proxy.getPersist function of the SDK essentially accepts an Array of persisted property names and returns a corresponding Array of Objects with the previously stored name and value properties we established in the getProperties function referenced above.

With these basic functions it is possible to store and retrieve any number of property values to either serve advanced Property Sheet concepts such as Sub Element Binding, to store variable values for user experience management or for an unlimited variety of other purposes.

12.1.4 Setting Custom Component Property Values

Perhaps one of the most straightforward and concise concepts contained in the SDK, is the ability to set a Custom Component's property explicitly, not through the traditional binding mechanism.

For example, if had a property on our custom component by the name of fontSize that we wanted to set to value of 12, the one line of code below allows us to set the value of that component property. This operation can be done for any data type supported by the SDK, i.e. Arrays, Strings, 2D Arrays, etc.

```
proxy.setProperty('fontSize', 12);
```

12.1.5 Retrieving Custom Component Property Values

With the knowledge of how to set a custom component property, we will undoubtedly need to extract that component's property value for use in our Property Sheet. Let's use the fontSize property example to see how we would go about extracting the value of that property contained in our custom component.

Again, though not quite as concise, the process of extracting the currently stored value of a custom component property is fairly straight forward.

The proxy.getProperties function accepts an Array of property names (in this case just a single element Array) and returns an Array of property values. Since we are only getting one property value below, we can reference position 0 in the Array returned from proxy.getProperties and subsequently access its value property.

```
var fontSize:int = proxy.getProperties(['fontSize'])[0].value;
```

12.1.6 Generating Reusable Property Sheet Patterns

If you are creating a single component with no plans to develop future Xcelsius Flex components, it is hardly worth the effort to abstract away repetitive Property Sheet functionality into a set of base classes and controls. However, if you are creating or could see creating 3 or more custom components in the future, it is recommended to create at least some basic MXML components that abstract away the often repetitive boiler plate Property Sheet code necessary to facilitate binding operations and specifically Sub Element Binding operations. If you do not take the time to create these components, you will quickly find yourself deep in code that is repetitive in nature and difficult to debug and manage. By creating basic reusable patterns for Xcelsius Property Sheets, your Property Sheet code base can likely be cut in half and in some cases, by more than 70%.

At least a 20% savings can be attributed to creating a single MXML TextInput component that serves as a Bindable Xcelsius text input property facilitator. With a couple of View States and a handful of properties, you will quickly see that by leveraging the power and Flexibility of the Flex framework and layout structure, you can quickly generate huge code savings with a bit of effort.

The primary 3 items suggested for creating MXML components or base Action-Script classes for are:

1. The Property Sheet itself

    Create a new ActionScript class that extends mx.core.Application, and add the common event handlers, variables and repeated private and public functions found as a common thread through the majority of Property Sheets. i.e.

    ```
    package
    {
        import mx.core.Application;
        import xcelsius.propertySheets.impl.
            PropertySheetExternalProxy;
        import xcelsius.propertySheets.interfaces.
            PropertySheetFunctionNames;
        import xcelsius.propertySheets.interfaces.
            PropertySheetFunctionNamesSDK;

        public class MyXCPropertySheet extends Application
        {
            public function MyXCPropertySheet()
            {
                addEventListener(FlexEvent.CREATION_COMPLETE,
                    creationComplete);
                super();
            }

            protected function creationComplete(e:FlexEvent):void
            {
                proxy.addCallback(
    ```

12 | Implement Advanced Custom Add-On Component Features

```
    PropertySheetFunctionNamesSDK.RESPONSE_BINDING_ID,
    this.continueBind);

    proxy.callContainer(
    PropertySheetFunctionNames.INIT_COMPLETE_FUNCTION);

    proxy.addCallback(
    PropertySheetFunctionNamesSDK.GET_PROPERTIES_FUNCTION,
    getProperties);

    initValues();
}

/**
 * Fill the controls with the current values of the component.
 * **/
protected function initValues():void
{
   …….. .
}
…………………………………………
…………………………………………
}
```

2. initiateBind

    The initiateBind function, as your Property Sheet's grow in the number of custom component properties they are responsible for managing, becomes a large source and primary contributor to Property Sheet clutter and code duplication, specifically in instances where Sub Element Binding needs to be supported. By creating a generic initiateBind function with some additional embedded intelligence, you will likely be able to account for 90% of use cases. In outlying cases where the base class' initiateBind function is not suitable, you still have the option to override the base class' function, implement any custom logic for your outlying use case and then subsequently call the super class' initiateBind method to support the rest of your Property Sheet's initiateBind functionality, i.e. in your Property Sheet implementation that uses your ActionScript Property Sheet base class:

    ```
    override protected function initiateBind(propertyName:String):void
    {
        //Implement any custom needs here……
        super.initiateBind(propertyName);
    }
    ```

3. continueBind

The continueBind function, as your Property Sheet's grow in the number of custom component properties they are responsible for managing, also becomes an additional large source and primary contributor to Property Sheet clutter and code duplication, specifically in instances where Sub Element Binding needs to be supported. By creating a generic continueBind function with some additional embedded intelligence, this is another case where you will likely be able to account for 90% of use cases. In outlying cases where the base class' continueBind function is not suitable, you still have the option to override the base class' function, implement any custom logic for your outlying use case and then subsequently call the super class' continueBind method to support the rest of your Property Sheet's continueBind functionality, i.e. in your Property Sheet implementation that uses your ActionScript Property Sheet base class:

```
override protected function continueBind(bindingID:String):void
{
    //Implement any custom needs here......
    super.continueBind (bindingID);
}
```

12.1.7 Communicating with External Data Services

Communicating with external data sources is possible in your Flex property sheets, just as it is in your Flex components. You may use the HTTPService class from Flex, the WebService class, a URLLoader, or any other remote data service type offered in the currently supported version of Flex for Xcelsius. In the next section, Implementing Advanced Component Features, we will take a spin through a functional example of how to retrieve and display a simple remote XML file's contents through the Xcelsius Excel model.

12.1.8 Implementing Advanced Component Features

With advance Property Sheet functionality under our belts, let's take a look at how we can leverage the functionality where it matters most – in our custom component.

- Leveraging sub-element binding from Property Sheets
- Advanced Component Overview using sub-element binding + walkthrough of fully functional code
- Communicating with external data services

Leveraging Sub Element Binding from Property Sheets

Though the process of establishing Sub Element Binding for certain properties through the Property Sheet requires additional steps and binding management, using the Sub Element properties in your custom component is effortless and identical to the way you would interact with and process and other kind of Array or 2D Array normal binding implementation, i.e. where "subProperty" is a Sub Element Array:

```
for(var i:int = 0; i < subProperty.length; i++)
{
   //access each individual value just like usual
   var value:Object = subProperty[i];
}
```

Sub Element Array Tricks

One feature that is of quite significant impact, is the ability to write multiple data ranges simultaneously back to the Xcelsius Excel model through a single custom component property that leverages Sub Element Binding Direction type of BindingDirection.INPUT.

Let's say for example that we have created a Sub Element Property binding by the name of "numericLists" on our custom component. In this example, we are theoretically bound to 5 Xcelsius Excel columns, each with 5 cells of data. Our simple yet powerful objective is, through our custom component, to set the values of these 25 combined cells to hold the numbers 1-25, respectively.

Listed below is the source code that will construct the Sub Element numeric list in a manner that the Xcelsius SDK can bind it to the multiple list destinations. This is a fairly simple example though hopefully it sheds some light on more advanced, useful use cases.

This function cycles across 5 columns, creating a 5-element Array (or 5 cells), with each cell populated with its respective overall cell position in the entire collection, for each column Array. The contents of the numericListItems are shown below in Figure 12.2. At the end of the function, we dispatch a simple event to let Xcelsius know that our property has changed. Notifying Xcelsius can be done in a couple of different ways, this is the most concise for our short code example.

```
public var numericLists:Array = new Array();
private function generateSampleMultiList():void
{
   var numericListItems:Array = new Array();
```

```
var cellValue:Number = 1;
for(var numCols:int=0;numCols<5;numCols++)
{
   var tmpListArry:Array = new Array();
   for(var i:int = 0; i < 5; i++)
   {
      tmpListArry[i] = cellValue;
      cellValue++;
   }                         numericListItems.push(tmpListArry);
}
numericLists = numericListItems;
dispatchEvent(new Event("numericLists"));
}
```

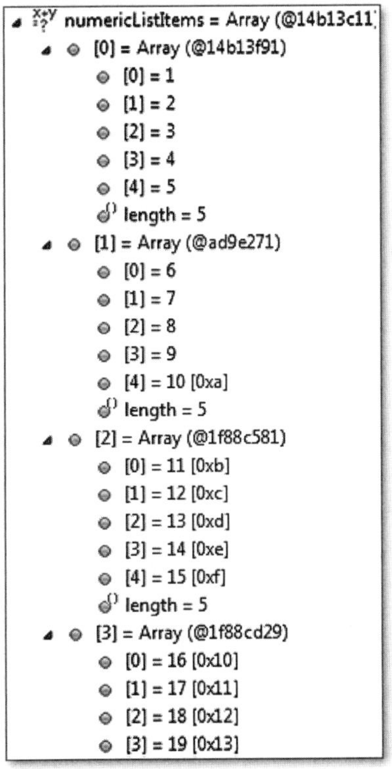

```
numericListItems = Array (@14b13c11)
  [0] = Array (@14b13f91)
    [0] = 1
    [1] = 2
    [2] = 3
    [3] = 4
    [4] = 5
    length = 5
  [1] = Array (@ad9e271)
    [0] = 6
    [1] = 7
    [2] = 8
    [3] = 9
    [4] = 10 [0xa]
    length = 5
  [2] = Array (@1f88c581)
    [0] = 11 [0xb]
    [1] = 12 [0xc]
    [2] = 13 [0xd]
    [3] = 14 [0xe]
    [4] = 15 [0xf]
    length = 5
  [3] = Array (@1f88cd29)
    [0] = 16 [0x10]
    [1] = 17 [0x11]
    [2] = 18 [0x12]
    [3] = 19 [0x13]
```

Figure 12.2 Numeric List Items Output from Flex Expressions Window

Communicating with External Data Services

Communicating with external data sources can be achieved using a variety of different mechanisms and utilities. For this functional example, we will connect to an XML feed on our C:\ drive and display its contents through a Bindable 2D input Array into the Xcelsius Excel model.

- Property Sheet Code
- Component Code
- End Result

Figure 12.3 Property Sheet in Design Mode

Since we have already taken a verbose spin through very similar property sheet code, a full description has been excluded and the full source code has been included for reference.

```
<?xml version="1.0" encoding="utf-8"?>
<mx:Application xmlns:mx="http://www.adobe.com/2006/mxml"
    layout="absolute" creationComplete="init()">
<mx:Script>
<![CDATA[
    import xcelsius.propertySheets.interfaces.
        PropertySheetFunctionNames;
    import xcelsius.propertySheets.interfaces.
        PropertySheetFunctionNamesSDK;
    import xcelsius.propertySheets.impl.
        PropertySheetExternalProxy;
    import xcelsius.binding.BindingDirection;
    import xcelsius.binding.tableMaps.input.InputBindings;
    import xcelsius.binding.tableMaps.output.OutputBindings;

    private var proxy:PropertySheetExternalProxy =
        new PropertySheetExternalProxy();
    private var propertyToBind:String;
```

```
    private var currentBindingID:String;

    private function init():void
    {
       proxy.addCallback(
        PropertySheetFunctionNamesSDK.RESPONSE_BINDING_ID,
        this.continueBind);
       proxy.callContainer(
        PropertySheetFunctionNames.INIT_COMPLETE_FUNCTION);
        initValues();
    }

    private function initValues():void
    {
       var props:Array =
          [
             "xmlUrl",
             "xmlData"
          ];

       // Process the array of values for the Xcelsius custom component
properties.
       var propertyValues:Array =
          proxy.getProperties(props);
       var propertyValuesLength:int =
          (propertyValues != null ?
          propertyValues.length : 0);
       for (var i:int=0; i < propertyValuesLength; i++)
       {
          // Get the property name and value.
          var propertyObject:Object = propertyValues[i];
          var propertyName:String = propertyObject.name;
          var propertyValue:* = propertyObject.value;

          //Process the property by name, either show the
          //value or show the cell address if
          // bound to the Excel spreadsheet.
          var bindingText:String = "";
          switch (propertyName)
          {
           case "xmlUrl":
             bindingText =
                getPropertyBindDisplayName(propertyName);
```

```
               if (bindingText != null)
               {
                  txtXmlUrl.enabled = false;
                  txtXmlUrl.text = bindingText;
               }
               else
               {
                  txtXmlUrl.enabled = true;
                  txtXmlUrl.text = propertyValue;
               }
            break;
         case "xmlData":
            bindingText =
               getPropertyBindDisplayName(propertyName);
            if (bindingText != null)
            {
               txtXmlData.enabled = false;
               txtXmlData.text = bindingText;
            }
            else
            {
               txtXmlData.text = "";
            }
            break;
         default:
            break;
      }
   }
}

/**
 * Allows the user to select the Excel spreadsheet
 * cell to bind to an Xcelsius custom component property.
 * **/
private function initiateBind(propertyName:String):void
{
   currentBindingID = null;
   var propertyBindings:Array =
      proxy.getBindings([propertyName]);
   if ((propertyBindings != null) &&
      (propertyBindings.length > 0))
   {
      // Use the 1st binding address for the property.
```

```
      currentBindingID = propertyBindings[0];
   }

   propertyToBind = propertyName;
   proxy.requestUserSelection(currentBindingID);
}


/**
 * Completes the binding when the user has finished
 * selecting the cell to bind to or cleared the binding.
 * **/
private function continueBind(bindingID:String):void
{
   var propertyName:String = propertyToBind;
   var propertyValues:Array;
   var propertyObject:Object;
   var bindingAddresses:Array;

   // Clear any existing bindings - so we can re-bind.
   if (currentBindingID != null)
   {
      proxy.unbind(currentBindingID);
      currentBindingID = null;
   }

   // Process the property binding.
   switch (propertyName)
   {
      case "xmlUrl":
         if ((bindingID == null) || (bindingID == ""))
         {
            txtXmlUrl.enabled=true;
            propertyValues = proxy.getProperties(
                     [propertyName]);
            propertyObject = propertyValues[0];
            txtXmlUrl.text = propertyObject.value;

            proxy.setProperty(propertyName,
                     propertyObject.value);
            return;
         }
         txtXmlUrl.enabled=false;
```

```
                    txtXmlUrl.text = proxy.getBindingDisplayName(
                              bindingID);
                    proxy.bind("xmlUrl", null,
                        bindingID, BindingDirection.OUTPUT,
                        "", OutputBindings.SINGLETON);
                    break;
                case "xmlData":
                    if ((bindingID == null) || (bindingID == ""))
                    {
                        txtXmlData.enabled=false;

                        propertyValues = proxy.getProperties(
                              [propertyName]);
                        propertyObject = propertyValues[0];
                        txtXmlData.text = "";
                        return;
                    }
                    txtXmlData.enabled=false;
                    txtXmlData.text = proxy.getBindingDisplayName(
                              bindingID);
                    proxy.bind("xmlData", null,
                        bindingID, BindingDirection.BOTH,
                        InputBindings.ARRAY2D,
                        OutputBindings.ARRAY2D);
                    break;
            default:
              break;
            }
        }

        /**
         * Returns the bind display name or null if not bound.
         * **/
        private function getPropertyBindDisplayName(propertyName:String):Str
ing
        {
            // Get the array of bindings for this property.
            var propertyBindings:Array = proxy.getBindings([propertyName]);
            if ((propertyBindings != null)     &&
                (propertyBindings.length > 0) &&
                (propertyBindings[0].length > 0))
            {
                // We have at least one binding for
```

```
            //this property so pick the 1st one.
            // Note: [0][0] is 1st property in the array,
            //then 1st binding for that property.
            var bindingID:String = propertyBindings[0][0];
            return proxy.getBindingDisplayName(bindingID);
        }
        return null;
    }

</mx:Script>
<mx:Canvas label="General" width="100%" height="100%" >
<mx:RadioButtonGroup id="radiogroup1"/>
<mx:VBox height="100%" top="0" width="100%" x="0">
    <mx:Canvas width="100%" height="100%" borderStyle="solid">
        <mx:Label text="XML Data Destination"
            width="131" enabled="true" left="10" top="70"/>
        <mx:Label text="XML URL" width="106"
            enabled="true" left="10" top="16"/>
        <mx:TextInput id="txtXmlData" enabled="false"
            y="85" right="69" left="10"/>
        <mx:TextInput id="txtXmlUrl" y="40"
            visible="true" right="69" left="10"
            change="proxy.setProperty('xmlUrl', txtXmlUrl.text)"/>
        <mx:Button y="40"  icon="@Embed('bind.png')"
            click="initiateBind('xmlUrl');"
            width="24" right="35"/>
        <mx:Button y="85"  icon="@Embed('bind.png')"
            click="initiateBind('xmlData');"
            width="24" right="35"/>
    </mx:Canvas>
</mx:VBox>
</mx:Canvas>
</mx:Application>
```

Component Code

Our custom XML Connector component, based on the Canvas object in Flex for simplicity so you can drag & drop the connector onto the Xcelsius designer. This component could very easily be turned into a data connection by using the Connection tab in the Xcelsius Packager. The objective of our custom XML component is to process a simple XML payload in the following format.

12 | Implement Advanced Custom Add-On Component Features

```
<root>
   <row cell1Value="1" cell2Value="1.2"/>
   <row cell1Value="2" cell2Value="2.2"/>
   <row cell1Value="3" cell2Value="3.2"/>
   <row cell1Value="4" cell2Value="4.2"/>
   <row cell1Value="5" cell2Value="5.2"/>
   <row cell1Value="6" cell2Value="6.2"/>
</root>
```

There is no doubt that Xcelsius has built-in utilities that are quite adept at processing XML, this demonstration however, is to serve as a primer for connecting to a remote data source and pushing that data up through to the Xcelsius Excel model through a custom component.

Import Statements and Public Component Variables for Xcelsius

In the first half of this component, we import our necessary namespaces so we can leverage the Flex HTTPService class. In this section we also specify our private HTTPService variable and also establish our public xmlUrl property as well as our 2D Array output property for Xcelsius, xmlData. xmlData's getter is tagged as a Bindable event to force Xcelsius Excel updates.

```
import flash.events.Event;
import flash.xml.XMLNode;
import mx.containers.Canvas;
import mx.controls.Alert;
import mx.rpc.events.FaultEvent;
import mx.rpc.events.ResultEvent;
import mx.rpc.http.HTTPService;

public class XmlConnector extends Canvas
{
   private var httpsvc:HTTPService = new HTTPService();

   private var _xmlUrl:String = "";
   public function set xmlUrl(value:String):void
   {
      _xmlUrl = value;
      getXML();
   }
   public function get xmlUrl():String
   {
      return _xmlUrl;
   }
```

```
private var _xmlData:Array = new Array();
public function set xmlData(value:Array):void
{
   _xmlData = value;
}
[Bindable(event="xmlData")]
public function get xmlData():Array
{
   return _xmlData;
}
```

Listening for our HTTPService Result
In this section we add the necessary event listeners to our HTTPService, call the super class' constructor in our constructur, and subsequently call the getXML() function so the service requests data on load. The getXML() function is a simple call out to the specified XML path. At line 64, we receive the result event of our HTTPService request. Listed below is the function code.

```
/**
 * Constructor
 * **/
public function XmlConnector()
{
   super();
   httpsvc.resultFormat = "xml";
   httpsvc.useProxy = false;
        httpsvc.addEventListener(ResultEvent.RESULT,httpserviceResult);
   httpsvc.addEventListener(FaultEvent.FAULT,httpFaultError);
   getXML();
}

/**
 * Call Http service
 ***/
private function getXML():void
{
   if(_xmlUrl == "" || _xmlUrl == null){return;}
   httpsvc.url = _xmlUrl;
   httpsvc.send();
}
```

HTTPService Result Processing

Once we receive the event result of the HTTPService call, we subsequently parse the XML, creating a 2D Array of cell data that Xcelsius can consume through binding via its Excel model. Listed below is the function code.

```
/**
* Http service result listener
***/
private function httpserviceResult(e:ResultEvent):void
{
   for each(var xn:XMLNode in e.result.childNodes)
   {
      var row:Array = new Array();
      row.push(xn.attributes.cell1Value);
      row.push(xn.attributes.cell2Value);
      _xmlData.push(row);
   }
   dispatchEvent(new Event("xmlData"));
}
```

HTTPService Fault Handling

The httpFaultError function catches any error encountered by the HTTPService call. Here we have implemented a simple Alert message, though something more sophisticated, like sending an error message to the Xcelsius model so the Xcelsius designer can define the user error experience, could easily be done as well. Listed below is the function code.

```
private function httpFaultError(e:FaultEvent):void
{
Alert.show("Unable to load the following file: " + _xmlUrl + "." +
"Please check to make sure that the specified  file " +
         "exists and is accessible.","I/O Error");
}
```

12.1.9 Additional Packaging Features

Packaging Visual Components and Connections through the Xcelsius Packager utility are very similar in process with a key difference being that custom components packaged using the Connections tab end up in the data menu as opposed to the component browser, for standard visual components. However, creating a Function Package or installer XLX is a bit different, yet even more concise. A good example of a simple Xcelsius function component, complete with source code and Packager can be found in the Xcelsius SDK Samples location under the following directory:

{Program Files }\Business Objects\Xcelsius\SDK\samples\XcelsiusSDKfunctions

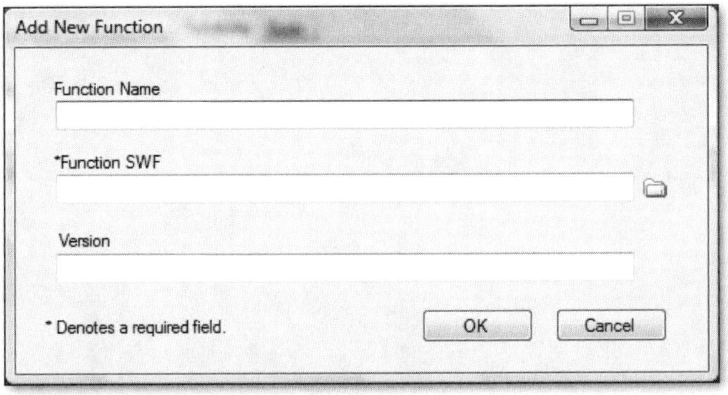

Figure 12.4 Add New Function Dialog

To use functions that have been created in your XLX installer file, add the custom component via the Add-On Manager and begin using the function in the Xcelsius Excel model just as you would a native Excel function.

Where to Go from Here: Tips, Tricks and Resources

As the SDK community continues to flourish, more resources are coming to the surface that will help developers who are new to the Xcelsius SDK.

Below are some useful links that cover fundamental SDK subject matter and provide a forum for Xcelsius SDK Q&A as well as helpful Flex links.

- Xcelsius Blog:
  EverythingXcelsius.com
- Forum:
  http://forums.sdn.sap.com/forum.jspa?forumID=466
- Getting Started with Flex:
  http://www.adobe.com/devnet/flex/

12.2 Summary

In this chapter, we enumerated some advanced yet commonly encountered and less documented features of the SDK. This introduction provides a foundational knowledge of the advanced data binding and component communications abilities of the SDK, enabling you to begin developing more advanced Property Sheet implementations.

After reading this chapter, you will know how to implement a Flex Bubble Chart with a runtime-controllable series color, tooltips (HTML or plain text), chart data and write back functionality to the Xcelsius Excel model.

13   Hands-On: Develop Your Custom Add-On Component

In this chapter we will take a hands-on step by step approach to creating a commonly implemented custom component type: a custom Flex chart. The component that will come as a result of this walkthrough is fairly short in the amount of source code required and concise, with a few key properties (listed and explained below) and quick-win benefits. The overall goal of the chart is to implement a Flex Bubble Chart with a runtime-controllable series color, tooltips (HTML or plain text), chart data and write back functionality to the Xcelsius Excel model in the way of a selected data and selected tooltip property.

13.1   Custom Properties Explained

- Bindable Chart Data: xcChartData
    - Binding Type: OutputBindings.ARRAY
    - Binding Direction: BindingDirection.OUTPUT
    - Purpose: To pass an array of cells to the bubble chart component, each cell with a CSV (comma separated value) format of:
    - valueX,valueY,radius,tooltip
    - valueX – The X position of a given bubble
    - valueY – The Y position of a given bubble
    - radius - The radius of a given bubble
    - tooltip – The tooltip, HTML or plain text, for a given bubble
- Bindable Series Color:
    - Binding Type: OutputBindings.SINGLETON

13 | Hands-On: Develop Your Custom Add-On Component

- Binding Direction: BindingDirection.OUTPUT
- Purpose: To pass a color value to control the chart's SolidColor color property.
- Bindable Selected Tooltip – Input
  - Binding Type: InputBindings.SINGLETON
  - Binding Direction: BindingDirection.INPUT
  - Purpose: To pass the selected tooltip value to a single cell in the Xcelsius Excel model.
- Bindable Selected Data – Input
  - Binding Type: InputBindings.SINGLETON
  - Binding Direction: BindingDirection.INPUT
  - Purpose: To pass the selected radius/value to a single cell in the Xcelsius Excel model.

13.2 Creating the Flex Component and Property Sheet Project

The first step in creating a custom component for Flex is to create a Flex project and file structure for your component, if one does not already exist.

Open Flex Builder and select from the top menu FILE • NEW • FLEX PROJECT as shown below in Figure 13.1.

Name your project CustomBubbleChart and select a logical location for the project to reside on your computer as shown below in Figure 13.2. Click Next.

Select the Library Path tab and click the Add SWC... button. Browse to locate the xcelsiusframework.swc file {Program Files }\BusinessObjects\Xcelsius\SDK\bin and click Open as shown below in Figures 13.3 and 13.4.

13.2 Creating the Flex Component and Property Sheet Project

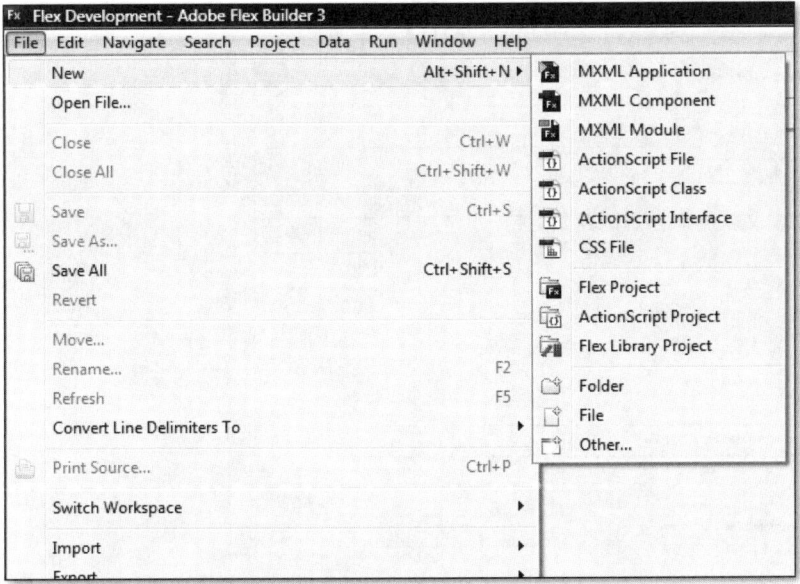

Figure 13.1 Creating a New Flex Project

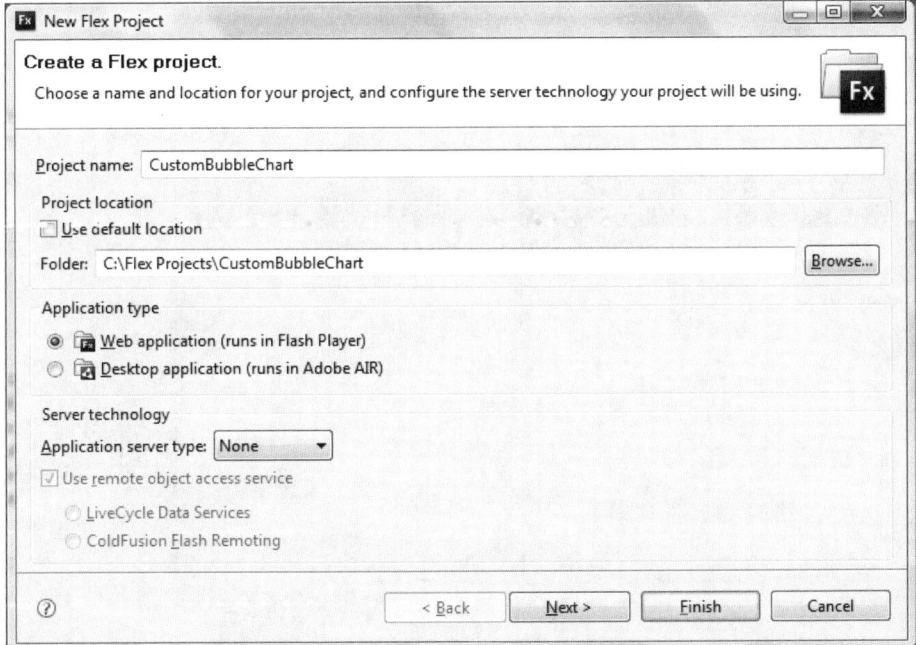

Figure 13.2 Name the Project and Select a Location

529

13 | Hands-On: Develop Your Custom Add-On Component

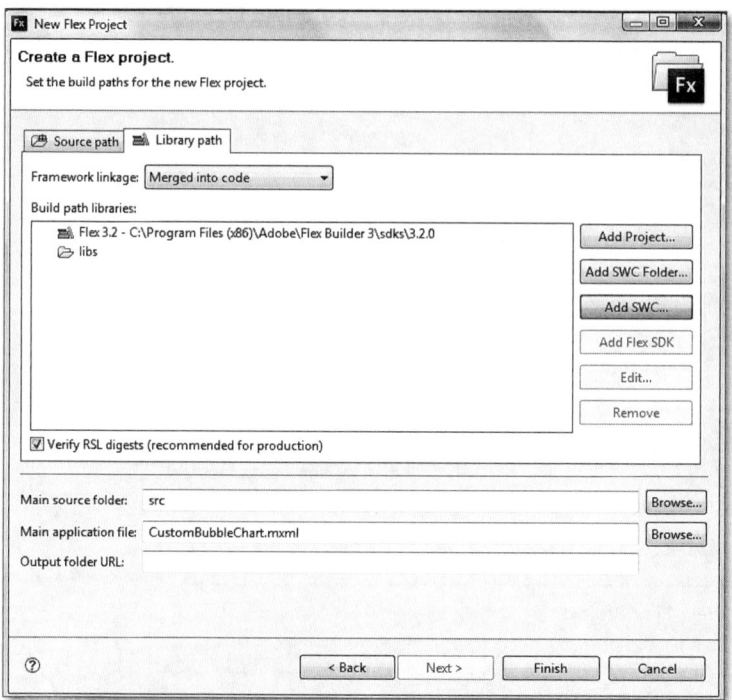

Figure 13.3 Add an SWC to the Flex Project

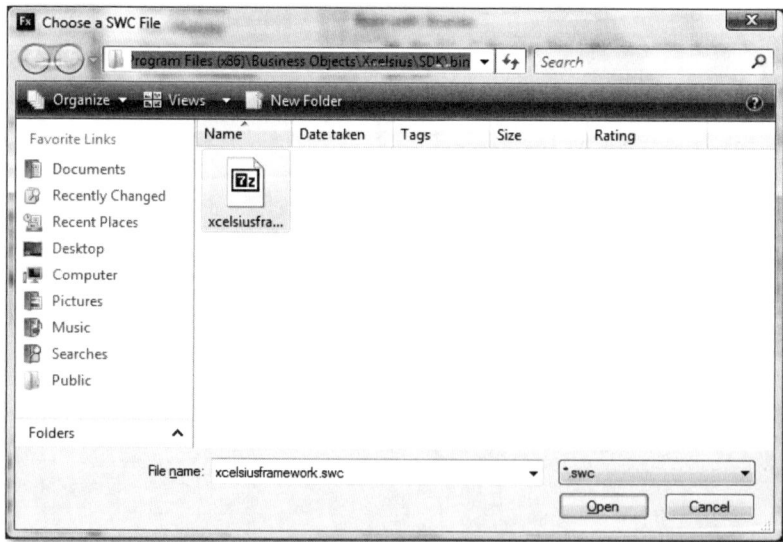

Figure 13.4 Locate and Select the XcelsiusFramework.swc Library

Click Finish to create your project as shown below in Figure 13.5.

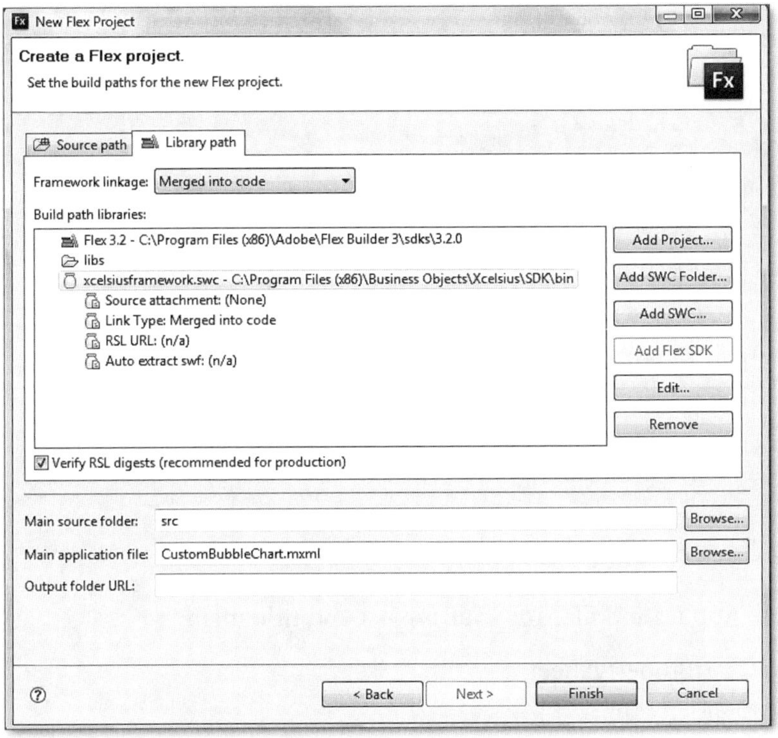

Figure 13.5 Click Finish to Create Your Flex Project

Select PROJECT • PROPERTIES as shown in Figure 13.6 in order to change the Flex compiler version to the 2.0.1 Hotfix 3 SDK version, if necessary. Click the Flex Compiler link in the left pane, select the Use a specific SDK option and select the proper SDK as shown in Figure 13.7. Click OK.

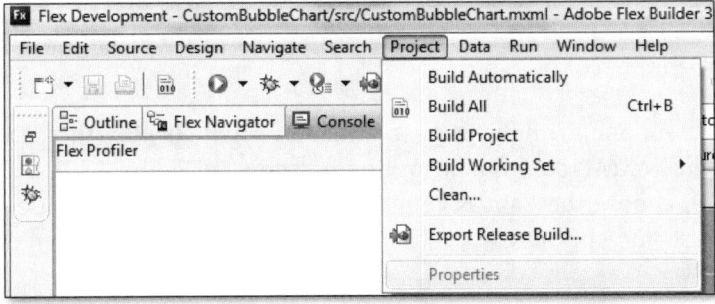

Figure 13.6 Navigating to Project Properties

13 | Hands-On: Develop Your Custom Add-On Component

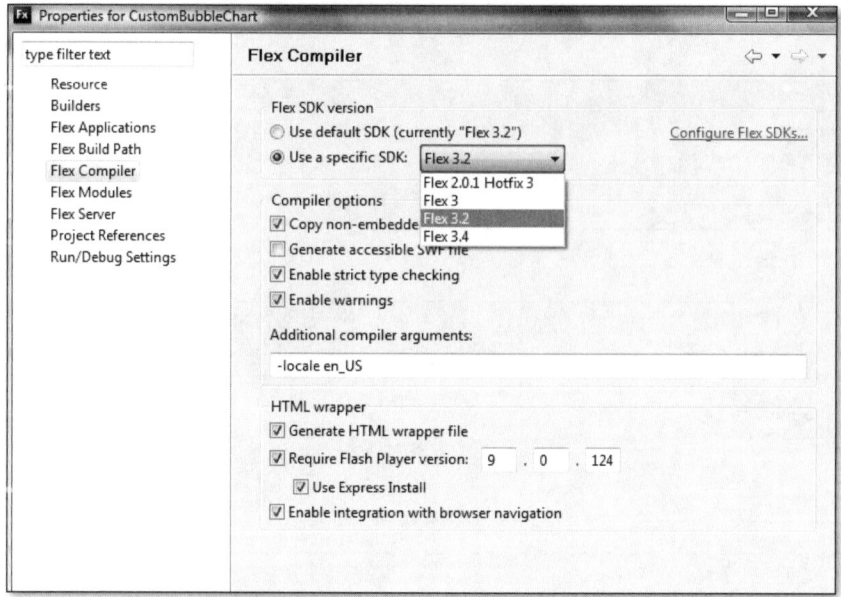

Figure 13.7 Setting the Proper SDK Version

Create 3 new Flex Application files for your project and title them:

- CustomBubbleChartPropertySheet
- CustomBubbleChart
- CustomBubbleChartTestContainer

Create a package structure under the src folder, to match Figure 13.8 below:

Figure 13.8 Project Folder Structure

Create a new MXML component under the exc folder by right-clicking the exc folder and selecting the MXML component option as show in Figure 13.9. As shown in Figure 13.10, choose the Canvas component as the component's base, name it BubbleChartBase and click OK.

13.2 Creating the Flex Component and Property Sheet Project

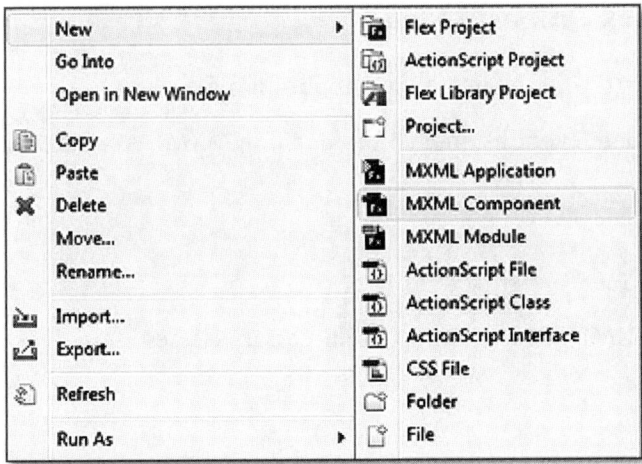

Figure 13.9 Create a New MXML Component

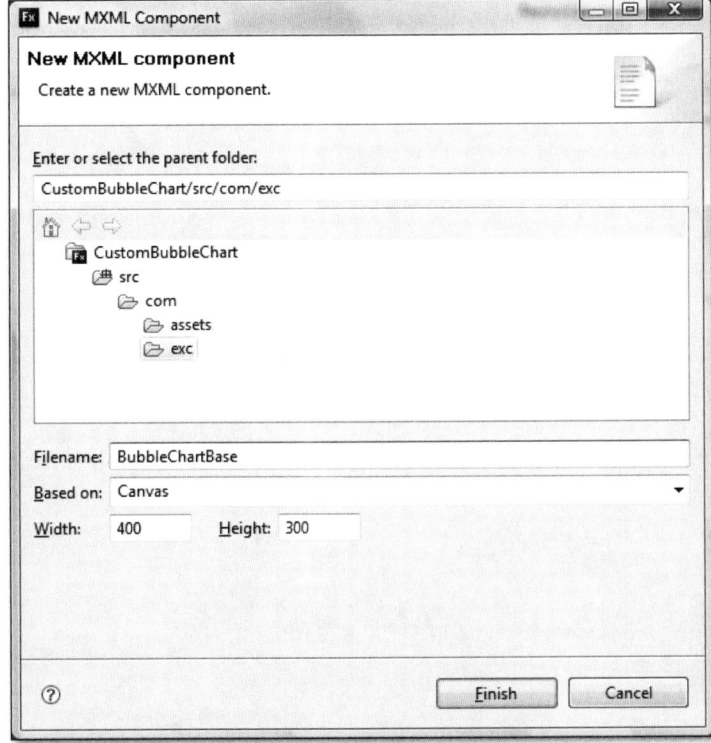

Figure 13.10 Choose the Component's Base and Name the Component

533

13 | Hands-On: Develop Your Custom Add-On Component

13.3 Creating the Flex Property Sheet

Open the CustomBubbleChartPropertySheet.mxml application file.

1. Add an applicationComplete event listener in the opening MXML Application tag.
   ```
   <?xml version="1.0" encoding="utf-8"?>
   <mx:Application xmlns:mx="http://www.adobe.com/2006/mxml"
   layout="absolute" applicationComplete="init();">
   ```

2. Insert a Script into the MXML file and import the necessary classes.
   ```
   <mx:Script>
   <![CDATA[
   
   import mx.containers.*;
   import mx.controls.*;
   import mx.core.Container;
   import mx.events.FlexEvent;
   import xcelsius.binding.BindingDirection;
   import xcelsius.binding.tableMaps.input.InputBindings;
   import xcelsius.binding.tableMaps.output.OutputBindings;
   import xcelsius.propertySheets.impl.PropertySheetExternalProxy;
   import xcelsius.propertySheets.interfaces.
   PropertySheetFunctionNamesSDK;
   ```

3. Create the necessary private variables for the SDK.
   ```
   private var proxy:PropertySheetExternalProxy = new
   PropertySheetExternalProxy();
   private var propertyToBind:String;
   private var currentBindingID:String;
   ```

4. Create the init() function that will fire when the Property Sheet's application-Complete event fires.
   ```
   private function init():void
   {
      proxy.addCallback(
         PropertySheetFunctionNamesSDK.RESPONSE_BINDING_ID,
         this.continueBind);
      proxy.callContainer(
         PropertySheetFunctionNamesSDK.INIT_COMPLETE_FUNCTION);
      initValues();
   }
   ```

5. Create the initValues() function that will extract the custom component public variable values and populate the Property Sheet's controls accordingly.

```
private function initValues():void
{
    var propertyValues:Array = proxy.getProperties(
            ["xcChartColor","xcChartData",
            "selectedData","selectedTooltip",
            "xcSeriesColor"]);

    var propertyValuesLength:int = (propertyValues != null ?
                        propertyValues.length : 0);
    for (var i:int=0; i < propertyValuesLength; i++)
    {
       var propertyObject:Object = propertyValues[i];
       var propertyName:String = propertyObject.name;

       var propertyValue:* = propertyObject.value;
       var bindingText:String = "";
       switch (propertyName)
       {
          case "xcChartColor":
             cpChartColor.selectedColor = propertyValue;
             break;
          case "xcChartData":
             bindingText = getPropertyBindDisplayName(
                        propertyName);
             if (bindingText != null)
             {
                tiChartData.text = bindingText;
             }
             else
             {
                tiChartData.text = "";
             }
             break;
          case "selectedData":
             bindingText =
                getPropertyBindDisplayName(propertyName);
             if (bindingText != null)
             {
                tiSelectedData.text = bindingText;
             }
```

```
            else
            {
                tiSelectedData.text = "";
            }
            break;
        case "selectedTooltip":
            bindingText =
                getPropertyBindDisplayName(propertyName);
            if (bindingText != null)
            {
                tiSelectedTooltip.text = bindingText;
            }
            else
            {
                tiSelectedTooltip.text = "";
            }
            break;
        case "xcSeriesColor":
            bindingText =
                getPropertyBindDisplayName(propertyName);
            if (bindingText != null)
            {
                tiSeriesColor.text = bindingText;
            }
            else
            {
                tiSeriesColor.text = "";
            }
            break;
        default:
            break;
        }
    }
}
```

6. Create our generic helper functions getPropertyBindDisplayName, and initiateBind.

```
private function getPropertyBindDisplayName
    (propertyName:String):String
{
    var propertyBindings:Array =
        proxy.getBindings([propertyName]);
    if ((propertyBindings != null)    &&
```

```
      (propertyBindings.length > 0) &&
      (propertyBindings[0].length > 0))
   {
      var bindingID:String = propertyBindings[0][0];
      return proxy.getBindingDisplayName(bindingID);
   }
   return null;
}

private function initiateBind(propertyName:String):void
{
   currentBindingID = null;
   var propertyBindings:Array =
      proxy.getBindings([propertyName]);
   if ((propertyBindings != null) &&
      (propertyBindings.length > 0))
   {
      currentBindingID = propertyBindings[0];
   }
   propertyToBind = propertyName;
   proxy.requestUserSelection(currentBindingID);
}
```

7. Create our binding commit function, continueBind.

```
private function continueBind(bindingID:String):void
{
   var propertyName:String = propertyToBind;
   var propertyValues:Array;
   var propertyObject:Object;
   var bindingAddresses:Array;

   if (currentBindingID != null)
   {
      proxy.unbind(currentBindingID);
      currentBindingID = null;
   }

   switch (propertyName)
   {
      case "xcChartData":
         if ((bindingID == null) || (bindingID == ""))
         {
```

```
            return;
        }
        tiChartData.text =
            proxy.getBindingDisplayName(bindingID);
        proxy.bind("xcChartData", null, bindingID,
            BindingDirection.OUTPUT, "",
            OutputBindings.ARRAY);
      break;
    case "selectedTooltip":
        if ((bindingID == null) || (bindingID == ""))
        {
            return;
        }
        tiChartData.text =
            proxy.getBindingDisplayName(bindingID);
        proxy.bind("selectedTooltip", null, bindingID,
            BindingDirection.INPUT,
            InputBindings.SINGLETON, "");
      break;
    case "selectedData":
        if ((bindingID == null) || (bindingID == ""))
        {
            return;
        }
        tiChartData.text =
            proxy.getBindingDisplayName(bindingID);
        proxy.bind("selectedData", null, bindingID,
            BindingDirection.INPUT,
            InputBindings.SINGLETON, "");
      break;
    case "xcSeriesColor":
        if ((bindingID == null) || (bindingID == ""))
        {
            return;
        }
        tiSeriesColor.text =
            proxy.getBindingDisplayName(bindingID);
        proxy.bind("xcSeriesColor", null, bindingID,
            BindingDirection.OUTPUT, "",
            OutputBindings.SINGLETON);
      break;
    default:
```

```
            break;
    }
}
```

8. Implement the XML layout and controls.

```
<mx:Canvas minWidth="268"  minHeight="350" width="100%" height="100%"
backgroundColor="#FFFFFF">
<mx:Label x="10" y="22" text="Chart Data"/>
<mx:Label x="10" y="277" text="Chart Color"/>
<mx:HRule y="39" height="10" right="10" left="92"/>
<mx:HRule y="295" height="10" right="10" left="92"/>
<mx:TextInput enabled="false" id="tiChartData" y="57" right="42"
left="92"/>
<mx:Button y="56" right="10"  width="24"
 click="initiateBind('xcChartData');"
 icon="@Embed('com/assets/bind.png')"/>
<mx:Label x="10" y="87" text="Selected Data Value"/>
<mx:HRule y="104" height="10" right="10" left="92"/>
<mx:TextInput enabled="false" id="tiSelectedData" y="122" right="42"
left="92"/>
<mx:Label x="10" y="152" text="Selected Tooltip Value"/>
<mx:HRule y="169" height="10" right="10" left="92"/>
<mx:TextInput enabled="false" id="tiSelectedTooltip" y="187"
right="42" left="92"/>
<mx:Button y="186" right="10"  width="24"
 click="initiateBind('selectedTooltip');"
 icon="@Embed('com/assets/bind.png')"/>
<mx:Label x="10" y="217" text="Series Color"/>
<mx:HRule y="234" height="10" right="10" left="92"/>
<mx:TextInput enabled="false" id="tiSeriesColor" y="252" right="42"
left="92"/>
<mx:Button y="251" right="10"  width="24"
 click="initiateBind('xcSeriesColor');"
 icon="@Embed('com/assets/bind.png')"/>
<mx:Button y="121" right="10"  width="24"
 click="initiateBind('selectedData');"
 icon="@Embed('com/assets/bind.png')"/>
<mx:ColorPicker id="cpChartColor"
 change="proxy.setProperty('xcChartColor',cpChartColor.
selectedColor)"
 x="92" y="313"/>
</mx:Canvas>
```

13.4 Creating the Flex Component

1. Open the BubbleChartBase.mxml component file.

2. Add an creationComplete event listener in the opening MXML tag.

   ```
   <?xml version="1.0" encoding="utf-8"?>
   <mx:Canvas creationComplete="buildChart()" xmlns:mx="http://www.
   adobe.com/2006/mxml" width="400" height="300">
   ```

3. Insert a Script into the MXML file and import the necessary classes.

   ```
   <mx:Script>
   <![CDATA[
    import mx.collections.ArrayCollection;
   ```

4. Create our chart data provider private variable for the custom component.

   ```
   [Bindable]private var _chartDp:ArrayCollection=new ArrayCollection();
   ```

5. Create the private and public custom component properties for Xcelsius.

   ```
   private var _xcChartData:Array=new Array();
   public function set xcChartData(value:Array):void
   {
       _xcChartData = value;
       buildChart();
   }
   public function get xcChartData():Array
   {
       return _xcChartData;
   }
   [Bindable]private var _xcChartColor:Number = 0x000000;
   public function get xcChartColor():Number
   {
       return _xcChartColor;
   }
   public function set xcChartColor(value:Number):void
   {
       _xcChartColor = value;;
   }
   [Bindable]private var _xcSeriesColor:Number = 0x0000ff;
   public function get xcSeriesColor():Number
   {
       return _xcSeriesColor;
   }
   public function set xcSeriesColor(value:Number):void
   ```

```
{
    _xcSeriesColor = value;;
}
private var _selectedTooltip:String="";
public function set selectedTooltip(value:String):void
{
    _selectedTooltip = value;
}
[Bindable(event="selectedTooltip")]
public function get selectedTooltip():String
{
    return _selectedTooltip;
}

private var _selectedData:Object;
public function set selectedData(value:Object):void
{
    _selectedData = value;
}
[Bindable(event="selectedData")]
public function get selectedData():Object
{
    return _selectedData;
}
```

6. Create our buildChart function to process the data from Xcelsius into data our Bubble Chart can display.

```
private function buildChart():void
{
    _chartDp.removeAll();
    for each(var s:String in _xcChartData)
    {
        var a:Array = s.split(",");
        var o:Object = new Object();
        o.valueX=a[0];
        o.valueY=a[1];
        o.radius=a[2];
        o.tooltip=a[3];
        _chartDp.addItem(o);
    }
}
```

7. Create our formatDataTip function to process mouse over tooltips for our bubble series and to push the selectedData and selectedTooltip Bindable properties to the Xcelsius Excel model.

```
private function formatDataTip(obj:Object):String
{
    _selectedTooltip = obj.item.tooltip;
    _selectedData = obj.item.radius;
    dispatchEvent(new Event("selectedTooltip"));
    dispatchEvent(new Event("selectedData"));
    return "<b>" + obj.element.displayName + "</b>" + "\n" + obj.item.tooltip;
}
```

8. Implement the XML layout and controls.

```
<mx:SolidColor id="sc1" color="{_xcSeriesColor}" alpha=".5"/>
<mx:BubbleChart dataTipFunction="formatDataTip" showDataTips="true"
color="{_xcChartColor}" dataProvider="{_chartDp}" id="bubbleChart"
width="100%" height="100%">
<mx:series>
   <mx:BubbleSeries
      fill="{sc1}"
            xField="valueX"
            yField="valueY"
            radiusField="radius"
            displayName="Bubble Series 1"

</mx:series>
<mx:verticalAxis >
            <mx:LinearAxis id="v1" />
       </mx:verticalAxis>
        <mx:horizontalAxis >
              <mx:LinearAxis id="h1" />
       </mx:horizontalAxis>
<mx:verticalAxisRenderer>
<mx:AxisRenderer tickLength="2" showLine="true" showLabels="true"/>
</mx:verticalAxisRenderer>
<mx:horizontalAxisRenderer>
<mx:AxisRenderer tickLength="2" showLine="true" showLabels="true"/>
</mx:horizontalAxisRenderer>
</mx:BubbleChart>
```

13.5 Creating the Flex Test Container

As specified in the SDK Best Practices, a local test container should always be established to test your custom component as thoroughly as possible before importing it for testing in the Xcelsius environment. In this case, the test container will be very lean but will enable you to step through its behavior at runtime to ensure everything is functioning as expected in Flex.

1. Open the CustomBubbleChartTestContainer.mxml component file and insert the following code, which sets the chart's data provider as expected from Xcelsius.

```
<?xml version="1.0" encoding="utf-8"?>
<mx:Application creationComplete="init()"
xmlns:mx="http://www.adobe.com/2006/mxml"
layout="absolute" xmlns:exc="com.exc.*">
<mx:Script>
    <![CDATA[
    private function init():void
    {
        bubbleChart.xcChartData =
            ["1,5,20,1,<html><i><b>tooltip0</b></i>",
            "10,20,50,1,tooltip1","10,10,30,1,tooltip2"]
    }
    ]]>
</mx:Script>
<exc:BubbleChartBase id="bubbleChart"/>
</mx:Application>
```

13.6 Creating the Packager and Xcelsius XLX Add-On

Now that we have our Property Sheet and custom component swf files ready, the next step is to create the packager file in order to generate our XLX installer file.

1. Open the Packager application and create a new Package called CustomBubbleChart.xlp
2. Select the Visual Components tab, click Add Component and specify the information as shown in Figure 13.11.

13 | Hands-On: Develop Your Custom Add-On Component

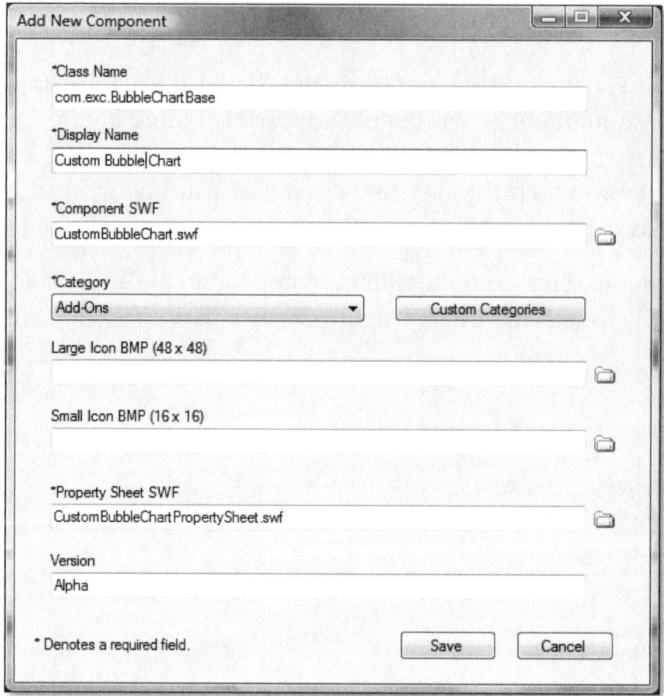

Figure 13.11 Specify your Component Details

3. Click Build to generate your XLX
4. Open Xcelsius, launch the Add-On Manager and browse to and install your newly created XLX installer file
5. Restart Xcelsius and drag your new add-on onto the Xcelsius designer. You are now ready to begin testing your new component.

13.7 Summary

In this chapter we presented a hands-on step by step approach to creating a commonly implemented custom component type: a custom Flex chart. You should now know how to implement a Flex Bubble Chart with a runtime-controllable series color, tooltips (HTML or plain text), chart data and write back functionality to the Xcelsius Excel model in the way of a selected data and selected tooltip property.

We want to share some additional tips for using Xcelsius and what you need to be aware of when using it in an SAP BusinessObjects Enterprise or other SAP environment.

A Tips for Using Xcelsius in SAP BusinessObjects Enterprise or other SAP Environment

In the previous chapters, we discussed almost every element of Xcelsius 2008 — its design environment including menus and toolbars, all of its rich UI components, and all kinds of data connectivity. In addition, we discussed the general workflow to create a dashboard and important features such as drill-down and alerts. This is enough information for you to create enterprise-level dashboards for your company.

We also covered the Xcelsius component SDK, with which you can create your custom UI components or data connectivities with the Adobe Flex programming language.

In this chapter, we'll discuss something that is not solely about Xcelsius but is very useful when building dashboards using Xcelsius in a reporting system.

After reading this chapter you will be able to:

▸ Describe how to use Xcelsius in an SAP BusinessObjects environment

▸ Know what license to choose when purchasing Xcelsius

A.1 Use Xcelsius in an SAP BusinessObjects Environment

Xcelsius is a product of SAP BusinessObjects, belonging to its BI (business intelligence) landscape and one of its query, reporting, and analysis products. Usually, Xcelsius is not used alone, but is used together with other SAP BusinessObjects products.

Xcelsius is often used in conjunction with SAP BusinessObjects products including:

- BI portals like InfoView/CMC (Central Management Console)
- Query as a Web Service
- SAP BusinessObjects Universe
- SAP BusinessObjects Live Office and consequently Crystal Reports/SAP BusinessObjects Web Intelligence
- Crystal Reports
- SAP BusinessObjects Web Intelligence

The following subsections will describe how Xcelsius is used with these other products.

A.1.1 How to Use Xcelsius with SAP BusinessObjects

InfoView/CMC
InfoView and CMC are portals of SAP BusinessObjects Enterprise, which can be used to host and manage the Xcelsius dashboards as Flash SWF objects. The portals can run on both Java and .Net web application servers, such as Apache Tomcat and Microsoft IIS (Internet Information Service).

To use this feature, you have to export your dashboard to the SAP BusinessObjects platform from the menu File. Keep in mind that this is the only way you can export your dashboard into an SAP BusinessObjects system as a Flash InfoObject. Though you can upload the source (.xlf) or output (.swf) into SAP BusinessObjects, it will not be recognized as a Flash file but as a plain file, which cannot be viewed but can only be downloaded. In the InfoView you will find that the object type of the uploaded SWF file is format-free, instead of Flash.

The benefits of accessing your dashboard through InfoView/CMC are easy and secure access.

- Easy access
  The end user can access the dashboard by logging on to InfoView and navigating to the folder in a web browser. You don't have to save the file locally on your computer. Figure A.1 shows the InfoView where the user accesses the dashboard.

  If you are familiar with InfoView, you will notice that fewer commands are available after right-clicking a Flash object. For example, you cannot schedule it.

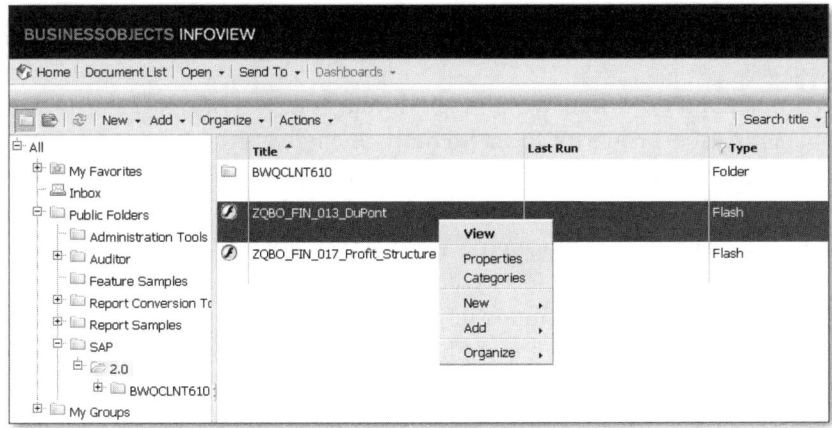

Figure A.1 To View an Xcelsius Dashboard in InfoView

Whenever the dashboard is updated, the designer can update it at the backend and export it to the SAP BusinessObjects platform after testing to overwrite the original version, without interrupting the end user. The end user knows nothing about this process. He just focuses on business analysis through this dashboard, which is always delivering the right information.

▶ Secure access
Within InfoView or CMC, you can configure who can access what dashboards with the enterprise-level permission control mechanism of SAP BusinessObjects. This way you can rest assured that only users who have been granted the required permissions can access the dashboard.

You can also store the source file (.xlf) of your dashboard design to the SAP BusinessObjects platform, from the menu path FILE • SAVE TO PLATFORM. Later you can open it from SAP BusinessObjects again, from the menu path FILE • OPEN FROM PLATFORM. This way you use the SAP BusinessObjects platform as a central storage place, similar to a version control application such as Microsoft VSS (Visual Source-Safe) or CVS (Concurrent Version System). For example, say you work with your colleagues to design a dashboard together. When you have come to a certain stage in the dashboard design, you save it to a folder in the SAP BusinessObjects platform. Your colleagues can then continue the design by opening it from that folder.

Query as a Web Service and SAP BusinessObjects Universe

Both of these are products of SAP BusinessObjects. The integration between Xcelsius and these two products is the Query as a Web Service connectivity in Xcelsius, with which you can connect to data exposed by SAP BusinessObjects Universe from your dashboard.

As mentioned in Chapter 7 when we discussed data connectivity, SAP BusinessObjects Universe is used primarily to map complex database fields into business terms that can be easily understood by non-IT business users. It can access several kinds of data sources, both relational and multidimensional. Many products of SAP BusinessObjects can access data through SAP BusinessObjects Universe, such as Crystal Reports and SAP BusinessObjects Web Intelligence. Query as a Web Service is used to expose partial or all data fields in a universe as a standard Web service, so that it can be consumed by any other application that can parse the Web service. This largely expands the usage of SAP BusinessObjects Universe.

If your company has SAP BusinessObjects Web Intelligence reports, some universes may have already been created. With Query as a Web Service connectivity, you leverage the existing universes to create Xcelsius dashboards.

Both products need be deployed to SAP BusinessObjects platforms to be available which means that at runtime, your SAP BusinessObjects Enterprise system, including a web application server such as Tomcat, the CMS, or some other related servers, must be running as well.

Live Office

SAP BusinessObjects Live Office is an integration between SAP BusinessObjects and the Microsoft Office product family. It allows you to insert Crystal Reports or SAP BusinessObjects Web Intelligence documents or universe queries into a Word, Excel, or PowerPoint document.

The integration between Xcelsius and SAP BusinessObjects Live Office goes in one direction only, allowing you to consume SAP BusinessObjects Live Office data inside Xcelsius. You do this by importing an SAP BusinessObjects Live Office–enabled Excel file and adding an SAP BusinessObjects Live Office connection. The user can see live data at runtime. If any parameter is defined in the Crystal Reports or Web Intelligence document or the universe query, the user will be prompted to enter values for them when accessing the dashboards.

Crystal Reports

The integration between Xcelsius and Crystal Reports exists in both products. In Xcelsius 2008, you configure a Crystal Reports data consumer connectivity to define what values are to be passed in from a Crystal Reports document. On the other hand, in Crystal Reports 2008, you insert the Xcelsius dashboard as a Flash object into the report and define how to pass values into it as Flash Vars, as explained in Chapter 7 as part of the discussion of the Crystal Reports data consumer connectivity.

You can also create charts within Crystal Reports 2008, but they are not as intuitive or attractive as those created in Xcelsius. With the help of this integration, you can include interactive Xcelsius dashboards in your Crystal Reports documents to provide a better user experience.

In Xcelsius you can also consume data from Crystal Reports by importing an SAP BusinessObjects Live Office–enabled Excel file with one or more Crystal Reports documents embedded and creating an SAP BusinessObjects Live Office connection in Xcelsius, as mentioned above and in Chapter 7 when we discussed the SAP BusinessObjects Live Office connectivity.

SAP BusinessObjects Web Intelligence

In contrast to the integration with Crystal Reports 2008, you cannot insert an Xcelsius dashboard into an SAP BusinessObjects Web Intelligence document. The integration goes only in one direction, for Xcelsius to consume data in an SAP BusinessObjects Web Intelligence document. Similar to Crystal Reports, you do this by importing an SAP BusinessObjects Live Office–enabled Excel file with one or more SAP BusinessObjects Web Intelligence documents embedded and creating an SAP BusinessObjects Live Office connection in Xcelsius for each SAP BusinessObjects Web Intelligence document. If you are working in an SAP BusinessObjects Enterprise XIR3 SP1 environment with Xcelsius 2008 SP1, this is the only way you can consume data from SAP BusinessObjects Web Intelligence documents within Xcelsius.

However, since SAP BusinessObjects Enterprise XIR3 SP2, you can make public the data in a block of an SAP BusinessObjects Web Intelligence document as a Query as a Web Service using standard WSDL and SOAP protocols and BI services. This is a new feature of SAP BusinessObjects Enterprise XI 3.1 SP2, and it is much easier than the traditional way of using SAP BusinessObjects Live Office. You can refer to the SAP website for more info about how to use it, at *http://help.sap.com/businessobject/product_guides/boexir31SP2/en/xi31_sp2_whats_new_en.pdf*.

Briefly, you need pay attention to the following items:

- You can only publish data from a block of the SAP BusinessObjects Web Intelligence document from the SAP BusinessObjects Web Intelligence Rich Client, not from InfoView.
- To publish the data, right-click the border of a block in either structure or results mode and select Publish Block in the context menu.
- After publishing, you can find the WSDL URL in the properties panel after selecting the Show BI Services checkbox. A typical WSDL URL might be *http://sapbod1:8080/dswsbobje/qaawsservices/biws?WSDL=1&cuid=AVXD17CR1ixHtGzSfTTShk8*.

Figure A.2 shows a screenshot of an SAP BusinessObjects Web Intelligence Rich Client, where the available BI services of the given SAP BusinessObjects Enterprise system are displayed, and the user has just selected a block and right-clicked.

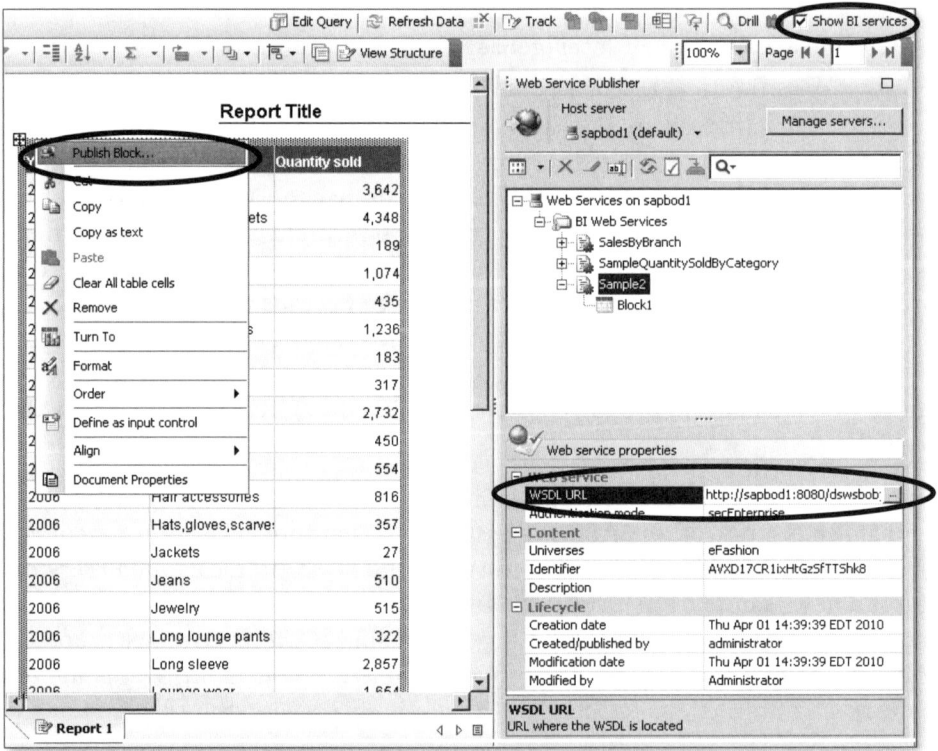

Figure A.2 Publish a Block of Data in a Web Intelligence Document as a Web Service in Web Intelligence Rich Client

To use the BI service in Xcelsius, you need to add a Query as a Web Service (or Web service) connection in the Data Manager, copy the WSDL URL from the Properties panel of the selected BI service in the SAP BusinessObjects Web Intelligence Rich Client, and paste it in the WSDL URL field. You can then bind input parameters and output values of this BI service, as displayed in Figure A.3.

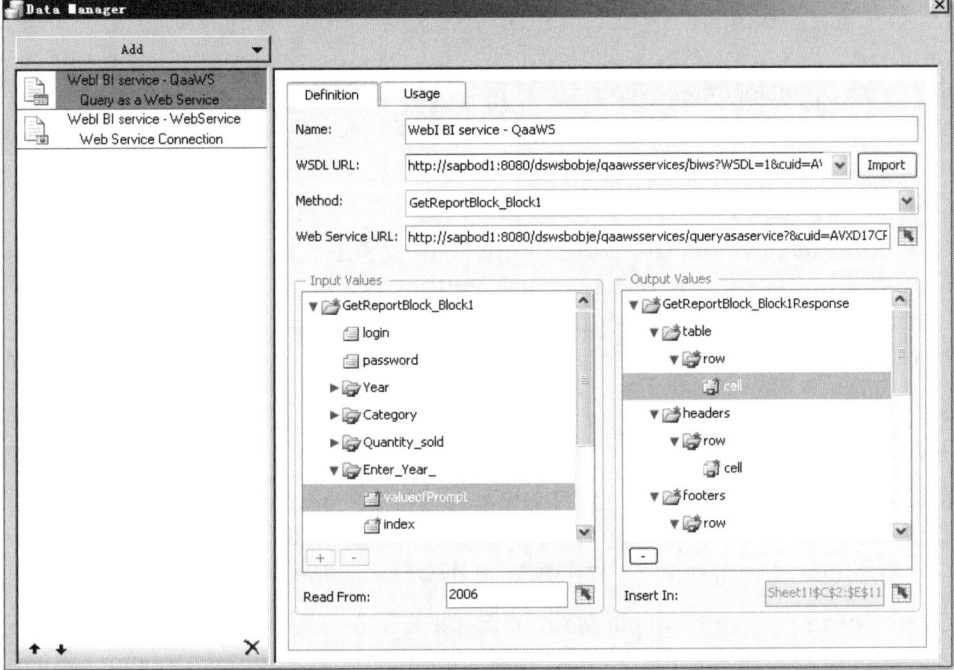

Figure A.3 Consuming Data from BI Services in Xcelsius

Parameters are also supported in this case. As displayed in Figure A.3, Enter_Year_ in the Input Values area is a parameter defined in the SAP BusinessObjects Web Intelligence document. You can use a selector component in the dashboard for the user to specify this parameter's value.

To use the returned data, you need to bind the output values to cell ranges in the embedded spreadsheet. To do this, bind the Cell of the nodes Table or Header in the Output Values area. Note that data in Header indicates the column name of each column, such as Sales Revenue, while that in Table indicates the actual value, such as $23.8. Though there's only one leaf node named Cell below Table or Header, you can bind it to a cell range with more columns, the number of which should be equal to that of the actual data. For example, in Figure A.3 above, the cell of Table is bound to cell range Sheet1!$C$2:$E$11 with three columns, because the data from the BI service contains the three columns Year, Category, and Quantity Sold.

The BI services are hosted in the SAP BusinessObjects Enterprise system, so you need credentials to log on to it. That's why you see two input parameters, Login and Password, in Figure A.3. You may or may not bind them to some input controls such as two input text components. If you are going to export the dashboard to an SAP BusinessObjects platform for end users to access through InfoView, CMC, or OpenDocument, you can simply ignore these two parameters because the user has already logged on to SAP BusinessObjects Enterprise.

Open Document

Open Document is web application provided by SAP BusinessObjects Enterprise for URL reporting, that is, to access an SAP BusinessObjects InfoObject with a URL. It can be used to view a Flash file created by Xcelsius, a Crystal Reports or Web Intelligence document, and so on. For example, you can view a Flash file with a URL like:

http://host:port/ OpenDocument/opendoc/openDocument.jsp?iDocID=6322

where 6322 for parameter iDocID is the ID of the Flash object in SAP BusinessObjects system. You may need to contact the administrator of your SAP BusinessObjects Enterprise system to find out the ID of your dashboard.

Open Document can be deployed to either a Java or .Net web application server, such as a Tomcat or IIS. You need to be certain about the required parameter values such as token to append to the URL. You can refer to the link below to see a list of available parameters in SAP BusinessObjects Enterprise XIR2.

http://devlibrary.businessobjects.com/businessobjectsxir2/en/en/BOE_SDK/boesdk_java_dg_doc/doc/boesdk_java_dg/Report_Linking13.html#1041621

With this feature, you can integrate Xcelsius dashboards into your own portal so that users can access them within their everyday portal instead of InfoView or CMC, by providing a link to the Open Document URL. A typical usage is to integrate Xcelsius with SAP Portal, by creating a URL iView, with its URL being an Open Document one, so that users can access the dashboards without leaving SAP Portal. For more info about this topic, please refer to the next section, where we'll discuss using Xcelsius in SAP Portal.

Deployment and Migration

When Xcelsius is used in conjunction with other SAP BusinessObjects products, you have to consider how to deploy your Xcelsius dashboards to the SAP BusinessObjects portal or SAP Portal and migrate them as part of your SAP BusinessObjects Enterprise system.

To deploy a dashboard to SAP BusinessObjects, you need to go to FILE • EXPORT • BUSINESS OBJECTS PLATFORM within Xcelsius 2008. Then you need to specify an appropriate folder to store the dashboard. In this case, the output is a Flash SWF file. Users can access it through InfoView or CMC or within another portal with Open Document.

Another issue is how to migrate your dashboards between SAP BusinessObjects systems, such as from a development environment to production, or when upgrading to a newer versions of SAP BusinessObjects Enterprise. You can use the Import Wizard provided by SAP BusinessObjects for the migration, treating the Xcelsius dashboards as common SAP BusinessObjects Enterprise objects such as a Crystal Reports document. However, if your dashboard consumes data from a Query as a Web Service, the WSDL URL of that connectivity will remain the same after migration. That is, at the development stage, you design your dashboard within Xcelsius 2008, consuming data by connecting to a Query as a Web Service that is deployed on the development environment of SAP BusinessObjects Enterprise. Now you migrate them to the production environment of SAP BusinessObjects Enterprise. Migrating the objects using the Import Wizard is not enough. You need go through the following steps to make the dashboard work perfectly after migration if it contains any data connectivity of type Query as a Web Service.

1. Update the universe connection.
   The connection of a universe defines where to retrieve the data — from the development database or the production database. After migration, the universe and its connection are copied to the production SAP BusinessObjects Enterprise system. However, it still connects to the old database.

2. Update the Query as a Web Service.
   The definition of the Query as a Web Service is copied to the production SAP BusinessObjects Enterprise system after migration. However, its URL still points to the old system, such as *http://boe_dev:8080/dswsbobje/*.... To reflect the environment change, you need re-edit it in the client tool provided by SAP BusinessObjects to deploy it to the new web application server of the production SAP BusinessObjects Enterprise system.

3. Update the WSDL URL within Xcelsius.
   The WSDL URL of the Query as a Web Service has changed, so you need to update it in Xcelsius 2008. To do this, you need the source file (.xlf) of the dashboard, not the Flash object.

4. After updating the WSDL URL of the Query as a Web Service connection, click the Import button again and rebind the Input and Output values.

5. When finished, follow the menu path FILE • EXPORT • BUSINESS OBJECTS PLATFORM again to deploy the dashboard to the production SAP BusinessObjects Enterprise system.

A.2　Use Xcelsius in an SAP Environment

Xcelsius, like most SAP BusinessObjects products, is platform-independent, that is, it can connect to almost any kind of data source and be deployed to almost any portal on any web application server. However, with SAP's acquisition, using Xcelsius within an SAP environment is more popular.

Generally, Xcelsius is used together with two SAP products.

- SAP NetWeaver Business Warehouse (BW):
- SAP NetWeaver Portal (formerly known as EP)

In the rest of this section, we'll discuss how Xcelsius is used with these products.

A.2.1　How to Use

SAP NetWeaver BW

SAP NetWeaver BW is the SAP data warehousing product that's used to store enterprise information in various types of structures including InfoCubes, InfoObjects, and Data Store Object. It's the foundation of reporting and analysis using SAP BusinessObjects products. We'll assume that you are familiar with SAP NetWeaver BW to continue with the following content.

In an SAP environment, Xcelsius is often used to create dashboards on top of the aggregated data stored in SAP NetWeaver BW. The typical steps are listed below in order.

1. Create a BW query with the necessary dimensions and measures.

   Depending on the business requirement, you can choose what dimensions (characteristics) and measures (key figures) of an InfoCube you want to show the end user. Sometimes you may need to create restricted or calculated key figures to show some special data to the user.

2. Create a universe based on the BW query.

   In this step you create a universe to connect to the BW query you just created. If multiple BW queries have to be queried to get the data for your dashboard, you need to create one universe for each BW query.

   Any variable defined in the BW query will be detected and mapped in the universe, as filters.

   You can also create a universe based on the InfoCube directly. However, this adds complexity for the user when creating a Query as a Web Service based on the universe in the next step, when he is faced with too many dimensions and measures. Moreover, think of the case when a restricted or calculated key figure is required. If the InfoCube is used each time in this step, many restricted or calculated key figures will be added to the InfoCube, which will confuse other users.

3. Create a Query as a Web Service based on the universe.

   In this step you create a Query as a Web Service to further specify what fields are to be exposed to Xcelsius. Pay attention to the order of the dimensions or measures in the Result area of Query as a Web Service. The result data will be in the same order when mapped to cell ranges in Xcelsius.

4. Create a dashboard with corresponding Query as a Web Service connectivity.

   Now you have created a Query as a Web Service, with which you can retrieve SAP NetWeaver BW data. This step is very straightforward. Just create a Query as a Web Service connectivity inside Xcelsius 2008 and do the bindings for both Input parameters and Output values.

For the input parameters, you can add some UI components to the dashboard for the user to specify the parameter values. You need to consider how to set dynamic visibility properties for them, so you can hide them when the result data has been returned. You can hardcode values for the parameters first, in the development or test stage, to focus on the functionality and visualization of your dashboard without a parameter prompt page. Finally, you need add the UI components for the user to input values, which is required for an interactive dashboard.

For the output values, pay attention to the order of the dimensions and measures defined in step 3 when do the bindings. They will appear in the same order in the cell range of the embedded spreadsheet.

Another way to connect to connect to data in SAP NetWeaver BW is through SAP BusinessObjects Live Office. First, you create a Crystal Reports document directly on top of an InfoCube or a BW query, or create an SAP BusinessObjects Web Intelligence document based on a universe on top of a BW query. Then you insert the Crystal Reports or SAP BusinessObjects Web Intelligence document into an SAP BusinessObjects Live Office–enabled Excel spreadsheet. Finally, import it into Xcelsius and create an SAP BusinessObjects Live Office connection, which we explained in Chapter 7.

Since Xcelsius 2008 SP2, you can connect to a BW query directly from within Xcelsius, with simply a few mouse clicks, which is much easier than the ways mentioned above. We won't cover how to use this feature here, because this book targets Xcelsius 2008 SP1.

SAP NetWeaver Portal

SAP NetWeaver Portal, formerly called Enterprise Portal (EP), is part of the SAP NetWeaver architecture. It provides a single point of access to information, enterprise applications, and services both inside and outside your company. It contains several components including knowledge management and collaboration. It's the platform for running custom Web Dynpro applications created either by SAP or by customers.

If the end users work with SAP NetWeaver Portal daily, you can use either of the two ways listed below to configure the portal so that the users can access Xcelsius dashboards within the company's SAP NetWeaver Portal system. The prerequisite is that you have deployed the dashboard onto the SAP BusinessObjects platform.

KM Integration

The first way is through the SAP BusinessObjects repository in knowledge management. After configuration, the portal user will be able to see a folder for the SAP BusinessObjects Enterprise system in knowledge management. He can then navigate to the dashboard and right-click to view it, just like he does from InfoView.

The SAP BusinessObjects Integrationfor SAP Solutions, commonly referred to as SAP IK, provides a BusinessObjectsKM.par file that you can upload into SAP NetWeaver Portal from the Administration Console within Portal Runtime. The

SAP NetWeaver Portal administrator can follow the steps listed in the Installation and Administration Guide of SAP IK to configure the SAP BusinessObjects repository to point to your SAP BusinessObjects Enterprise system.

URL iView

Another way is through a URL iView, with the help of Open Document, as mentioned in the section above. The user can click an iView from within SAP NetWeaver Portal to launch an Xcelsius dashboard.

SAP IK brings with it some .epa (Enterprise Portal Archive) files. After importing it to your SAP NetWeaver Portal system, you will see three iView templates added. You can duplicate any of them, or create a new URL iView, to point to a dashboard that has been exported into an SAP BusinessObjects platform. This is a big topic and is not the focus of this book, so we won't spend too much space on it. For example, you need configure single sign-on (SSO) between SAP NetWeaver Portal and your SAP BusinessObjects Enterprise system, so the user can access your dashboard from SAP NetWeaver Portal without entering credentials for the SAP BusinessObjects Enterprise system again, to achieve seamless integration.

A.3 Supported Excel Functions

As you have seen in the previous chapters and from your dashboard design experience, Excel plays a very important role in Xcelsius 2008. External data passed in from a data connectivity is mapped to the embedded Excel spreadsheet, which can in turn be mapped to UI components in the dashboard.

Sometimes the data you want to display in the dashboard is not passed in directly from the data connectivity. For example, let's say the sales revenues of the current and the previous months are returned from a Web service connectivity, but what you want to display is the growth rate. In such cases, you need to calculate the data in the embedded Excel spreadsheet, with the help of the powerful Excel functions.

Excel is popular thanks to its comprehensive and powerful functions. Xcelsius leverages this power of Excel and supports the most frequently used functions. If you are already familiar with Excel functions, you may find this functionality very useful. In the next section, we'll list and briefly explain these functions.

A.3.1 How Excel Functions Work in Xcelsius

At design time, you can enter Excel functions in the spreadsheet area and see the calculation results immediately. The embedded Excel spreadsheet in Xcelsius is actually a separate Excel process. If you launch the Task Manager by pressing [Ctrl] + [Alt] + [Del], you'll find an Excel process in the Process tab. So it's no surprise that functions at design time always return the same value as that of a stand-alone Excel program outside Xcelsius.

However, at runtime of the dashboard created in Xcelsius, no Excel process is running, and functions are calculated by Xcelsius itself. The Xcelsius function calculation engine tries to mimic Microsoft Excel. But you'll still find results from Xcelsius runtime differ from those of Excel in some cases. So you should preview the dashboard to test function results before you use a new Excel function for the first time.

A.3.2 Supported Functions

The Excel functions supported by Xcelsius 2008 can be divided into several categories as follows. For each category, the functions' names are listed with a brief introduction for you to get a rough idea about what it does. For more info about any function, you can search the Internet or refer to any help such as *office.microsoft.com*.

Two websites, *spreadsheets.about.com* and *www.techonthenet.com*, are very helpful for understanding certain functions.

Math and Trigonometry

- ABS
  Calculates the absolute value of a number.

- ACOS/ACOSH/ASIN/ASINH/ATAN/ATAN2/ATANH/COS/COSH/SIGN/SIGNH/TAN/TANH
  Calculates the direct/inverse trigonometric values.

- CEILING/FLOOR
  Rounds a number up or down based on a multiple of significance, which is a parameter of this function.

- COMBIN
  Returns the number of combinations by choosing N from M values. For example, COMBIN(10,3) = (10*9*8) / (3*2*1) = 120.

- DEGREES
  Changes radius into degrees.
- EVEN
  Rounds a number up to the closest even number. For example, EVEN(4.1) = 6.
- EXP
  Returns e raised to the N-th power, where e = 2.71828, which is the base of the natural logarithm.
- FACT
  Returns the factorial of a given number. For example, FACT(3) = 3*2*1 = 6.
- INT
  Returns the integer portion of a given number. For example, INT(2.8) = 2.
- Ln/LOG/LOG10
  Returns the logarithm of a given number.
- MOD
  Returns the remainder after a number is divided by a divisor. For example, MOD(13, 5) = 3.
- PI
  Returns the mathematical constant called pi (the ratio of the circumference to the diameter of a circle), which is 3.14159265358979.
- POWER
  Returns the result of a number raised to a given power. For example, POWER(2, 3) = 8.
- PRODUCT
  Multiples numbers and returns the product. For example, PRODUCT(2, 3, 4) = 24.
- QUOTIENT
  Divides a number. It differs from regular division in that it only returns the integer portion of a division operation. For example, QUOTIENT(5, 2) = 2.
- RADIANS
  Converts degrees into radians, in contrast to DEGREES. For example, RADIANS(120) = 2.094395102.
- RAND
  Returns a random number that is greater than or equal to 0 and less than 1. A new random number is returned each time the worksheet recalculates.

- **ROUND/ROUNDDOWN/ROUNDUP**
  Returns a number rounded to a specified number of digits. ROUNDUP rounds the number away from 0, while ROUNDDOWN rounds the number toward 0.
- **SIGN**
  Returns the sign of a number, which is 1 when the number is positive, -1 for a negative number, and 0 for 0.
- **SQRT**
  Returns the square root of a number. For example, SQRT(25) = 5.
- **SUM**
  Adds all numbers in a range of cells and returns the result.
- **SUMIF**
  Adds all numbers in a range of cells, based on a given criteria.
- **SUMPRODUCT**
  Multiplies the corresponding items in arrays and returns the sum of the results. For example, SUMPRODUCT({1,2;3,4}, {5,6;7,8}) = (1*5) + (2*6) + (3*7) + (4*8).
- **SUMSQ**
  Returns the sum of the squares of a series of values.
- **SUMX2MY2**
  Returns the sum of the difference of squares between two arrays.
- **SUMX2PY2**
  Returns the sum of the squares of corresponding items in the arrays and returns the sum of the results.
- **SUMXMY2**
  Returns the sum of the squares of the differences between corresponding items in the arrays and returns the sum of the results.
- **TRUNC**
  Returns a number truncated to a specified number of digits. For example, TRUNC(66.78,1) = 66.7.

Logical
- **AND**
  Returns TRUE only when both operands evaluate to TRUE. Otherwise returns FALSE.

- OR
  Returns FALSE only when both operands evaluate to FALSE. Otherwise returns TRUE.
- NOT
  Reverses the given Boolean value.
- IF
  Returns one value if a specified condition evaluates to TRUE or another value if it evaluates to FALSE. For example, IF(TRUE, 1, 2) = 1, and IF(FALSE, 1, 2) = 2.

Statistical
- AVEDEV
  Returns the average of the absolute deviations of the numbers provided.
- AVERAGE
  Returns the average (arithmetic mean) of the numbers provided.
- AVERAGEA
  Returns the average (arithmetic mean) of the numbers provided. The AverageA function is different from the Average function in that it treats TRUE as a value of 1 and FALSE as 0.
- BETADIST
  Returns the cumulative beta probability density function.
- COUNT
  Counts the number of cells that contain numbers and the number of arguments that contain numbers.
- COUNTA
  Counts the number of cells that are not empty and the number of arguments that contain values.
- COUNTIF
  Counts the number of cells in a range that meets a given criteria.
- DEVSQ
  Returns the sum of squares of deviations of data points from their sample mean.
- EXPONDIST
  Returns the exponential distribution.

- FISHER/FISHERINV
  Returns the direct/inverse Fisher transformation at the given number.
- FORECAST
  Returns a prediction of a future value based on existing values provided.
- GEOMEAN
  Returns the geometric mean of an array or range of positive data.
- HARMEAN
  Returns the harmonic mean of a data set.
- INTERCEPT
  Returns the Y-axis intersection point of a line using X-axis values and Y-axis values.
- KURT
  Returns the kurtosis of a data set.
- LARGE
  Returns the N-th largest value from a set of values.
- MAX/MEDIAN/MIN
  Returns the largest/median/smallest value from the numbers provided.
- NORMDIST
  Returns the normal cumulative distribution for a specified mean and standard deviation.
- NORMINV
  Returns the inverse of the normal cumulative distribution for the specified mean and standard deviation.
- NORMSINV
  Returns the inverse of the standard normal cumulative distribution. The distribution has a mean of zero and a standard deviation of one.
- RANK
  Returns the rank of a number in a list of numbers.
- SMALL
  Returns the k-th smallest value in a data set.
- STANDARDIZE
  Returns a normalized value from a distribution characterized by mean and standard deviation .

- STDEV
  Estimates the standard deviation based on a sample.
- VAR
  Estimates the variance based on a sample.

Lookup and Reference

These functions are expensive to calculate at runtime, so use them with care.

- CHOOSE
  Returns a value from a list of values based on a given position. For example, CHOOSE(2, "x", "y", "z") returns "y".
- HLOOKUP/VLOOKUP
  Searches for value in the top row/left column of table_array and returns the value in the same column/row based on the index_number.
- INDEX
  Returns either the value or the reference to a value from a table or range.
- LOOKUP
  Returns a value from a range (one row or one column) or from an array.
- MATCH
  Searches for a value in an array and returns the relative position of that item.
- OFFSET
  Returns a reference to a range that is offset a number of rows and columns from another range or cell.

Database and List Management

- DAVERAGE
  Averages the values in a field (column) of records in a list or database that match conditions you specify.
- DCOUNT
  Counts the cells that contain numbers in a field (column) of records in a list or database that match conditions that you specify.
- DCOUNTA
  Counts the nonblank cells in a field (column) of records in a list or database that match conditions that you specify.

- DGET

  Extracts a single value from a column of a list or database that matches conditions that you specify.

- DMAX/DMIN

  Returns the largest/smallest number in a field (column) of records in a list or database that matches conditions you that specify.

- DPRODUCT

  Multiplies the values in a field (column) of records in a list or database that match conditions that you specify.

- DSTDEV

  Estimates the standard deviation of a population based on a sample by using the numbers in a field (column) of records in a list or database that match conditions that you specify.

- DSUM

  Adds the numbers in a field (column) of records in a list or database that match conditions that you specify.

- DVAR

  Estimates the variance of a population based on a sample by using the numbers in a field (column) of records in a list or database that match conditions that you specify.

- DVARP

  Calculates the variance of a population based on the entire population by using the numbers in a field (column) of records in a list or database that match conditions that you specify.

Financial

You need some basic knowledge of finance to use these functions.

- DB

  Returns the depreciation of an asset for a specified period using the fixed-declining balance method.

- DDB

  Returns the depreciation of an asset for a specified period using the double-declining balance method or some other method you specify.

- FV

  Returns the future value of an investment based on periodic, constant payments and a constant interest rate.

- IPMT
  Returns the interest payment for a given period for an investment based on periodic, constant payments and a constant interest rate.
- IRR
  Returns the internal rate of return for a series of cash flows represented by the numbers in values.
- MIRR
  Returns the modified internal rate of return for a series of periodic cash flows. MIRR considers both the cost of the investment and the interest received on reinvestment of cash.
- NPER
  Returns the number of periods for an investment based on periodic, constant payments and a constant interest rate.
- NPV
  Calculates the net present value of an investment by using a discount rate and a series of future payments (negative values) and income (positive values).
- PMT
  Calculates the payment for a loan based on constant payments and a constant interest rate.
- PPMT
  Returns the payment on the principal for a given period for an investment based on periodic, constant payments and a constant interest rate.
- PV
  Returns the present value of an investment. The present value is the total amount that a series of future payments is worth now.
- RATE
  Returns the interest rate per period of an annuity.
- SLN
  Returns the straight-line depreciation of an asset for one period.
- SYD
  Returns the sum-of-years' digits depreciation of an asset for a specified period.
- VDB
  Returns the depreciation of an asset for any period you specify, including partial periods, using the double-declining balance method or some other method you specify.

Text and Data

- CONCATENATE
  Allows you to join two or more strings together. This is very useful in Xcelsius.

- DOLLAR
  Converts a number to text, using a currency format.

- EXACT
  Compares two strings and returns TRUE if both values are the same and FALSE otherwise.

- FIND
  Returns the location of a substring in a string. The search is case-sensitive.

- FIXED
  Returns a text representation of a number rounded to a specified number of decimal places.

- LEFT/RIGHT
  Allows you to extract a substring from a string, starting from the leftmost/rightmost character.

- LEN
  Returns the length of the specified string.

- LOWER
  Converts all letters in the specified string to lowercase. If there are characters in the string that are not letters, they are unaffected by this function.

- MID
  Extracts a substring from a string (starting at any position).

- REPLACE
  Replaces a sequence of characters in a string with another set of characters.

- REPT
  Returns a repeated text value a specified number of times.

- TEXT
  Returns a value converted to text with a specified format.

- VALUE
  Converts a text value that represents a number to a number.

Information

- ISNA
  Checks for a #N/A (value not available) error.
- ISNUMBER
  Checks for a numeric value.
- N
  Converts a value to a number.

Date and Time

- DATE
  Returns the number that represents an Excel date-time code.
- DATEVALUE
  Returns the serial number of a date.
- DAY
  Returns the day of the month (a number from 1 to 31) given a date value.
- DAYS360
  Returns the number of days between two dates based on a 360-day year.
- EDATE
  Returns the serial number representing the date that is the indicated number of months before or after a specified date (the start_date).
- EOMONTH
  Returns the serial number for the last day of the month that is the indicated number of months before or after start_date.
- HOUR
  Returns the hour of a time value (from 0 to 23).
- MINUTE
  Returns the minute of a time value (from 0 to 59).
- MONTH
  Returns the month (a number from 1 to 12) given a date value.
- NETWORKDAYS
  Returns the number of whole working days between start_date and end_date.
- NOW
  Returns the current system date and time. This function will refresh the date/time value whenever the worksheet recalculates.

- SECOND
  Returns the second of a time value (from 0 to 59).
- TIME
  Converts hours, minutes, and seconds given as numbers to an Excel serial number formatted with a time format.
- TIMEVALUE
  Converts a text time to an Excel serial number for a time.
- TODAY
  Returns the current system date. This function will refresh the date whenever the worksheet recalculates.
- WEEKDAY
  Returns a number representing the day of the week, given a date value.
- WEEKNUM
  Returns a number that indicates where the week falls numerically within a year.
- WORKDAY
  Returns a number that represents a date that is the indicated number of working days before or after a date (the starting date). For example, WORKDAY(DATE(2010,4,9),1) can be used to get the first work day after 2010/04/09. The result as a number is 40280, which is the date 2010/04/12 when viewed as Date. You may use this function to build a list of work days for the user to choose from.
- YEAR
  Returns a four-digit year (a number from 1900 to 9999) given a date value.
- YEARFRAC
  Calculates the fraction of the year represented by the number of whole days between two dates

A.4 Xcelsius Editions

Xcelsius 2008 is released in four editions: Enterprise, Server, Engage, and Present. You can choose what edition to use based on your requirements. Before purchasing, some knowledge of the differences among them will be helpful.

The basic functionalities of Xcelsius are available in all editions, such as creating a dashboard based on Excel data and exporting it to a Flash SWF file. Some advanced features, such as some advanced UI components and data connectivity types, are not available in some editions. Sometimes you cannot export your dashboard to some format such as to an SAP BusinessObjects platform, due to license constraints.

The installation files of all editions are the same. The editions, and consequently the different functionalities of each edition, are controlled by the license, or key code, you purchase.

Xcelsius 2008 can only be installed on a Windows operating system. After installation, the key code is written to the registry, at *HKEY_LOCAL_MACHINE\SOFTWARE\Business Objects\Suite 12.0\Xcelsius\Keycodes*. If you have installed Xcelsius on a 64-bit Windows system, the path may be slightly different, with an extra node, *Wow6432Node*, between *SOFTWARE* and *Business Objects*. The date following the key code in the registry value makes little sense.

The key code is written as-is, without any encryption. You can copy it for other uses or update it with another valid key code. Changes to the registry key will take effect the next time you launch Xcelsius 2008.

If you have key codes for different editions, you are free to switch among them by changing the key code in the registry.

A.4.1 Explanation of Each Edition

Very simply put, the Enterprise edition provides all of the functionalities of Xcelsius 2008 and consequently is the most expensive, while Present provides the fewest functionalities and is the cheapest. Engage Server is second to Enterprise in functionalities, and Engage is between Engage Server and Present.

Detailed explanations of each edition are presented in the following sections. You can compare them with your requirements and make an informed choice.

Enterprise

This is the complete edition of Xcelsius 2008, with all of the functionalities mentioned in this book supported. You can work freely with your dashboard and use whatever feature you think of with no limitation. To use all of the potentials of Xcelsius 2008 and create a powerful yet attractive dashboard, this edition is your best-fit choice.

As indicated by the name, this edition is primarily for enterprise use, where an SAP BusinessObjects Enterprise system might have been installed. Xcelsius Enterprise is added as the choice of reporting and analysis of a large and mature IT system.

Engage Server

This edition is quite similar to Enterprise, with most functionalities supported. All UI components are available in this edition. Its limitation is that it cannot connect to external data through any data connectivity related to SAP BusinessObjects, including:

- Query as a Web Service
- SAP BusinessObjects Live Office

These two types of connectivity are not listed in the Add dropdown list of the Data Manager, as displayed in Figure A.4.

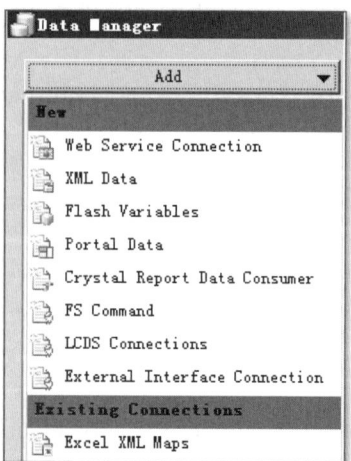

Figure A.4 Available Connection Types for Xcelsius Engage Server

However, Crystal Reports data consumer connectivity is included. That is, with the of Engage Server edition of Xcelsius 2008, you can still integrate with Crystal Reports 2008, to insert a dashboard into a crystal report and pass values into it there.

You may try to hack the system by creating a Web service connectivity to connect to the Query as a Web Service deployed in an SAP BusinessObjects Enterprise system. Though you can see the Input and Output values successfully after clicking

Import, the connection will not be triggered, and thus no SAP BusinessObjects Enterprise data will be returned.

Exporting to SAP BusinessObjects Enterprise is also disabled in this edition. In the menu FILE • EXPORT, you will find the option Business Objects Platform disabled.

The Engage Server edition is bundled with Flynet Web Service Generator, an easy way to generate Web services to expose data from database tables or applications. For more information, please refer to *http://www.flynetviewer.com*.

This edition is intended for users who want to create dashboards and deploy them to a portal environment by using its integration capabilities with web portals and reporting services. If you don't have an SAP Business Objects environment but want to deploy your dashboard to a portal or use most Xcelsius 2008 functionalities, Engage Server is your best choice.

SAP will stop providing technical support to Xcelsius Engage Server designer after December 31, 2011. So think againif you are going to purchase an Engage Server license.

Engage

Compared to Engage Server, the additional limitation of the Engage edition is that it lacks integration with any web portal or reporting services. That's why the connectivity's of portal data and LCDS are missing in the Add dropdown list in the Data Manager, as displayed in Figure A.5.

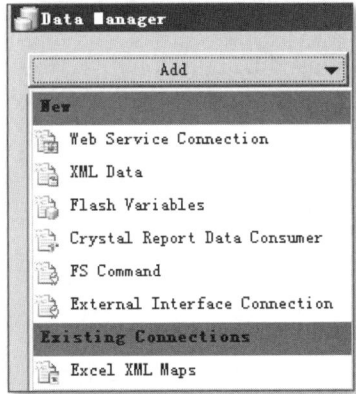

Figure A.5 Available Connection Types for Xcelsius Engage

Moreover, you'll find that you can create only one connectivity of the type Web service or XML data, while with a license for Enterprise or Server, you can create as many connectivities as you want of the types Web service or XML data, as mentioned in Chapter 6.

All UI components are available in this edition.

If you just need to connect to some external data source but not to deploy it to any portal or use the dashboards in an SAP BusinessObjects environment, you can choose Engage.

You can get an evaluation copy of Xcelsius Engage from the SAP website, at *http://www.businessobjects.com/campaigns/forms/downloads/xcelsius/engage/default.asp*.

Present
Xcelsius Present is the entry-level edition, with no connectivity to any external data source provided, and some of the UI components listed in this book are not included. It's intended for users who want to create dashboards with data in the embedded spreadsheet only and to present it with some common yet powerful UI components.

With this edition of Xcelsius, you cannot create any data connectivity through the Data Manager to connect to any external data source. In fact, the Data Manager cannot be launched within Xcelsius Present. The data should be known at design time and be inserted directly into the embedded spreadsheet.

Moreover, you cannot import data from an Excel file from an SAP BusinessObjects platform. In the Data menu, this item is disabled.

This edition has a robust suite of the most commonly used UI components. However, some advanced components are not available here. These can be divided into two categories as listed below.

- Selectors
  - Accordion menu
  - Sliding picture menu
  - List view
  - List builder
  - Ticker
  - Play selector

- Other
  - Calendar
  - History
  - Panel set
  - Source data
  - Trend analyzer

This edition features the most commonly used visualization export options, such as exporting to a PDF. With Xcelsius Present, you can only export your dashboard to PDF, PowerPoint, or Word, but not to Flash, AIR, HTML, Outlook, or an SAP BusinessObjects platform.

If your license is for Xcelsius Present, the edition info will be displayed in the window title of your Xcelsius workspace, such as UNTITLED XCELSIUS PRESENT 2008. This information is not included in menu HELP • ABOUT XCELSIUS.

A.5 Tips for Creating a Good Dashboard

In this section let's talk about some tips, or best practices, for creating a professional dashboard. Following these useful tips may save you a lot of time during your dashboard design and help you avoid some unnecessary mistakes.

Most of the tips in this section are based our experience. They can be divided into three categories, as listed below.

A.5.1 Tips for the Embedded Spreadsheet

Plan First

Plan first means plan what cells or cell ranges will be used for what purpose, prior to any data mapping or binding. In this step you need be clear about how many sheets (tabs) are needed, what data will be placed in what cells, the maximum number or rows and columns of external data, any data that will be calculated using Excel functions and how, and so on.

Name the Sheets

By default there are one to three sheets in the embedded spreadsheet, called Sheet1 and so on. These don't tell you much about what they're about. It's a best practice to give each sheet a descriptive name so that you or others can better understand your design thoughts, for example, Info, Labels, and Input Data.

Generally, you can use some of the following sheets in your dashboard.

Info

You can put some general metadata such as purpose, author, creation date, and some other assumptions like your coloring mechanism in a sheet called Info. If you are going to include Help or About in your dashboard, their content can also be stored here. Someone may prefer to write them in a separate sheet, and that's up to you.

If there are some known limitations of your current dashboard, or something that you want to update in future, you can document that here as well. This is a required sheet.

Data

You need this sheet to store the raw data from any data connectivity or the static data you entered at design time. The values passed in from the container at runtime can also be placed here, such as the data from FS Commands or Flash Variables. This is a required sheet.

Display

Many kinds of data for UI components can be stored in this sheet, including the titles, labels, candidate items of selectors, and destinations of data insertion of selectors or drill-down. For most UI components, either for user input or for displaying data, you should set the title properties or add a label component in front of each to tell the user about what they are. For example, you can add a label that says "Please enter your password (6-10 chars):" in front of an input text, telling the user that he needs to enter his password here, which is 6 to 10 characters long. You can use a dedicated sheet called something like Label to store such data, or include it in this sheet. The user can then bind the title or text of UI components to a cell or cell range in this sheet instead of entering the text directly in the Properties panel.

You can place the candidate items of selectors such as combo boxes in this tab if they are static.

Sometimes you need to display part of the raw data in a list view. For example, data of 10 rows and 4 columns is returned, but you want to display only the data in the first and the third columns in a list view. For the binding to work, you need to map data in the two columns into a cell range of 10 rows and 2 columns. You can put such data in this sheet, because it will be displayed in a list view or in the CalculatedData sheet, as mentioned below, because it's calculated from the raw data.

CalculatedData

Sometimes you need to create new data fields by making calculations based on the raw data. You can put them in the same Data sheet as the raw data if there are only a few fields or in a new sheet called something like CalculatedData when there are many calculated fields. For example, the sales revenues of each branch in two consecutive years are returned from a Web service connectivity, and you are going to use a trend icon to show whether the total sales revenue is going up or down on a yearly basis. You can calculate the difference using Excel functions and store the data in the sheet CalculatedData, so that you can easily make changes when the calculation method of some fields has changed.

We recommend that you include the calculation logic in this sheet as well, to explain how a new field is calculated.

Use Different Colors for Different Kinds of Data

There are many different kinds of data in the embedded spreadsheet: general info, input parameters, external data, calculated data, and so on. You can use different colors to highlight different kinds of data to keep things clear.

What color you use for what kind of data depends on your preferences. The only requirement is that you keep it consistent and define the colors in the Info sheet. Later, when another designer is not sure whether some data is from user input or from an external data source, he can refer to the color definition in the Info sheet.

In addition, you can use a thick box border to outline the area for certain data, such as the data returned from a Web service connection. In this way you or another designer can easily know the boundary of the data and avoid cell overlap.

Make Extensible Cell Ranges for Data Binding

When mapping the output of a data connectivity to a cell range in the embedded spreadsheet, usually you cannot know the accurate numbers of rows or columns. For example, you cannot be quite sure about how many branches there will be two years from now.

To make your dashboard usable several years later, you need make the cell range large enough to hold possible future entries.

When binding a UI component to this cell range, which may currently contain some blank rows or columns, remember to select Ignore Blank Cells in both values and series.

Explain the Cell Ranges

It's a good idea to write some explanative words about a cell to the top or left of a cell or cell range to show what it's about. Otherwise, you will have difficulty identifying the origin and target of that cell range.

Avoid Using Complex or Expensive Excel Functions

Flash is more complex than plain HTML and costs more time in loading. Using too many complex or expensive Excel functions will weaken performance, resulting in a worse user experience.

We recommend that you avoid using expensive Excel functions including SUMIF, COUNTIF, MATCH, and INDEX. If you really need this data, calculate it in the server and pass it to Xcelsius with some type of data connectivity, instead of calculating it in Xcelsius at runtime. Remember that Xcelsius is best at visualization, not calculation.

A.5.2 Tips for the UI Components

Use the Right UI Component

To choose the right UI component for your specific business scenario, you need have a good understanding of the advantages and disadvantages of all the components, which we discussed in Chapters 4 and 5. For example, you can choose a pie chart to visualize contribution, a panel to include a group of related components, or a gauge to indicate the status, but do not use a text Input when the user needs to select from a list of candidate items.

Keep a Consistent Look and Feel among Components

It looks ugly if the styles of the UI components on the canvas are inconsistent, for example, if the font size of one component is much bigger than that of some others.

The topic of look and feel includes font, colors, entry effects, alignments, and backgrounds. You can select a group of related components and align them to any direction (top, left, bottom, or right).

If you have defined an entry effect for a UI component, make sure others use the same one. For example, if some components fade-in in 2 seconds and others have no entry effect but appear on the canvas suddenly, this may look strange.

Use Custom Colors Carefully

To make a customized dashboard, you can use your preferred colors for UI components instead of the default ones. For example, you may want to customize the color of each slice of your pie chart. Furthermore, you can create your own color scheme.

An agreeable coloring mechanism will result in an outstanding and extremely attractive dashboard. A bad one will cause the user hesitate to give your dashboard a second look, making it completely useless despite its powerful functionality.

Figure A.6 displays some recommended colors that you can use in your dashboard. Generally, you may can use light and neutral colors for the banners, navigation tabs in a component like a tab set, and the borders. You can use brighter colors to display key messages. Light blue, light gray, or light beige are always good choices. And, of course, you need to ensure that the entire dashboard is consistent in color.

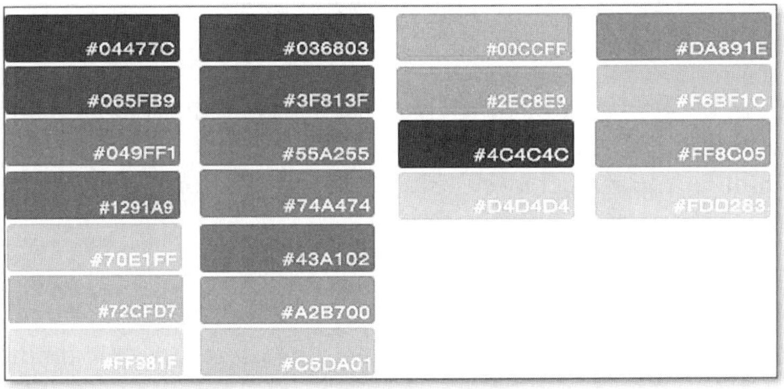

#04477C	#036803	#00CCFF	#DA891E
#065FB9	#3F813F	#2EC8E9	#F6BF1C
#049FF1	#55A255	#4C4C4C	#FF8C05
#1291A9	#74A474	#D4D4D4	#FDD283
#70E1FF	#43A102		
#72CFD7	#A2B700		
#FF981F	#C5DA01		

Figure A.6 Some Agreeable Colors for a Dashboard.

If you are not confident about your sense of colors, or aesthetic standard, you can fall back on the predefined color schemes in Xcelsius.

Use "Fit Canvas to Components" with an Extra Component to Define the Size

There are two ways to adjust the canvas size of your dashboard.

- Use the Increase Canvas, Decrease Canvas, Fit Canvas to Components, or Fit Canvas to Window buttons in the toolbar.
- Set the width and height from the menu FILE • DOCUMENT PROPERTIES • CANVAS SIZE in pixels

The best way to adjust the canvas size is use "Fit Canvas to Components" with the help of an extra component to define the border. The steps are as follows:

1. Drop a rectangle component onto the canvas.
2. Resize it to the size you want, with all existing UI components included in it.
3. Click the Fit Canvas to Components button in the toolbar.
4. Delete the rectangle.

The rectangle component here is used to define the border. An ellipse, a background, or even a chart can be used as well, but a container may not be a good choice, because it might include some existing UI components, adding difficulty to step 4 when you delete this extra component.

Add Help and/or About to Your Dashboard

From the end user's standpoint, it's good if the dashboard provides a Help or About for him to easily understand the dashboard, such as how to use it, what kind of input values are accepted, where the data is retrieved, how some data is calculated, and the meaning of each chart.

The Help or About can be displayed in a big label inside a container component. The user can click a button to show it and click it again or a click a Close button in the container to hide it. You can achieve this with a toggle button and dynamic visibility.

Prompt the User for each Input

Give user a hint about what he is to input or select and the format of a valid input. For selectors such as a checkbox or combo box, you an display the hint in its title. For a text input component, you can add an extra label.

A.5.3 Design Tips

Begin with a Pencil

Before working with your dashboard inside Xcelsius 2008, we strongly recommend getting away from the computer and designing with paper and pencil. As the saying goes, Think well before you act, and a pencil can help you think.

You should think thoroughly about your dashboard to start, from end to end. On the paper, you can illustrate the data flow and the mapping among UI components, the embedded spreadsheet, and external data. Also, you need to work out a draft of the layout and the interaction with the end user using the pencil, including what components are initially displayed, what become hidden or visible on what user interaction, and when to trigger what connection.

If Detail Is Required, Use a Link

Xcelsius is used to visualize high-level aggregated data, not details. However, sometimes the user may want to see the more detailed information to find out the root cause of something. For example, say the user has drilled down to a concrete store that contributes a lot to the company's total sales revenue, and then he want to see the sales info of each product every day for that store.

Instead of displaying these details in a list view or spreadsheet inside Xcelsius, you can create a Crystal Reports or SAP BusinessObjects Web Intelligence document for this purpose, with a parameter for the user to specify a store. After being deployed to SAP BusinessObjects Enterprise, the detailed report can be accessed with an Open Document URL, as explained in Chapter 8. In Xcelsius, a URL button is used to link to the report, with the ID of the currently selected store appended to the Open Document URL of the Crystal Reports or SAP BusinessObjects Web Intelligence document.

Use a Spreadsheet or List View for Debugging

Usually, the external data is not visualized directly in some UI components. Instead, it's reorganized or calculated before being bound to.

When previewing the dashboard to check the workflow, you may suspect something is wrong with the data but not be sure whether it's a problem with the original data from the external source or with your manual calculation or reorganization. In such circumstances, you can use a spreadsheet or list view component to help with debugging.

The original data, retrieved from some data connectivity, is mapped to a cell range in the embedded spreadsheet. You can use a spreadsheet, list view, or even a grid component to display this data in the canvas by binding its data to the range you are interested in. You can then compare what's displayed in the component in your dashboard with your original data to determine whether the problem lies here. For example, let's say you are creating a dashboard based on data from a BW query, with the help of SAP BusinessObjects Universe Builder and Query as a Web Service. You can use a list view to display the returned data from a Query as a Web Service connection and compare it with the data displayed in the Excel analyzer in SAP Business Explorer.

A.6 Summary

In this chapter, we discussed some extra information about using Xcelsius, including the available editions you can purchase, the supported Excel functions by Xcelsius 2008 SP1, and how to use Xcelsius with other SAP products. Our hope is to help you make more use of Xcelsius to help the decision-makers in your company understand the business and make wise decisions.

B   The Authors

Ray Li is a passionate business intelligence professional currently working for ByInsight Consulting as a BI consultant. He previously work for SAP BusinessObjects as a software engineer where he developed Xcelsius add-ons, designed and delivered Xcelsius dashboards in several projects and conducted trainings. Ray is well respected by his peers and was highly recommended by Mico Yuk, founder of the Xcelsius Gurus Network.

Evan DeLodder is a Software Engineer focused on applying cutting edge technologies in the Business Intelligence and data visualization space. Evan has led the development and implementation of numerous Business Intelligence software products and applications and continues to innovate and apply new ideas that compliment the SAP Business Intelligence platform. Evan is an Xcelsius SDK Guru on the popular website *EverythingXcelsius.com*, an SAP author, and a frequent contributor to the growing Xcelsius development community.

Index

A

About Xcelsius, 63
Accordion Menu, 210
ActionScript 3, 462, 465
Add-On Manager, 544
Ad-Hoc Query Designer, 28
Adjust the Appearance, 459
Adobe AIR runtime, 462
Adobe Flash, 17
Adobeís Flex, 461
Adobe LifeCycle Data Service, 391
Advanced Charts, 185
Advanced Component Features, 513
Advanced Custom Add-On Component Features , 505, 472
Advanced Data Connectivity, 331
Advanced Selectors, 210
Advanced Single-Value Components, 228
Alerts, 416
Alert Thresholds, 126
Align, 56
Appearance, 102
Area Chart, 144
Auto Play, 220

B

Backgrounds, 180
Bar Chart, 136
Behavior, 99, 114
Bindable Chart Data, 527
Bindable Selected Data, 528
Bindable Selected Tooltip, 528
Bindable Series Color, 527
Bind Data, 79
Binding Directions , 471
Binding Directions and Data Flow, 476

BindingID, 490
Binding Types, 477
Bubble Chart, 141
BubbleChartBase.mxml, 540
By Range, 111

C

Calendar, 225
Candlestick Chart, 202
Canvas, 71, 420, 468
Canvas and Spreadsheet, 54
Canvas Sizing, 38, 54
Cell, 81
Chain, 490
chartSeriesData, 506
Checkbox, 157
Column Chart, 110, 442
Combination Chart, 189
Common users, 18
Communicating with External Data Services, 505
Comparison, 23
Component Browser, 68
Component Code, 521
Components., 91
Components Browser, 31
Connections, 61
Connect to External Data, 458
Containers, 176, 410
Copy and Paste, 297
Copy/Paste/Cut/Delete/Select All, 51
Crystal Reports, 28
CSV files, 463
Currency, 107
Custom add-on component, 527
Custom Component Property Values, 510

Custom Components , 475
Custom Properties, 527

D

Data binding, 31, 53
Data Connectivity Basics, 293
Data Connectivity Capabilities, 26
Data Consumer Connection, 352
Data menu, 33
Data meters, 469
Data Point, 105
Data Visualization Capabilities, 20
Default Selection, 99
Description, 39
Developers, 18
Developing Basic Add-On Components, 480
Device Fonts, 40
Dial and Gauge, 172
Displaying Data in a Table, 235
Distribute the Output, 88
Distribution, 27
Divisions, 119
Document Properties, 38
Drill Down, 82, 83, 96, 393
Dual Slider, 229
Dynamic Visibility, 100, 405

E

Embedded Excel Spreadsheet, 71, 294
Enable Data Animation, 101
Encrypted data repositories, 463
Enterprise users, 18
Entry Effect, 101
Excel , 19, 31
Excel formulas, 54
Excel Options, 44
Excel XML Map, 326

Explicitly Getting Property Values, 480
Explicitly Setting Property Values, 479
Export, 46, 60, 424
Export Preview, 46
Export Settings, 47
External Data, 85
External Data Services, 513
External Interface Connection, 375

F

File, 31
Filled Radar Chart, 206
Filter, 153
Flash, 49
Flash Variables, 358
Flex applications , 462
Flex Builder , 462
Flex Component and Property Sheet Project, 528
Flex framework, 462
Flex Property Sheet, 534
Flex Test Container, 543
Font, 39
Format, 56, 66
Formatting, 85
FS Command, 368
Fundamental SDK import statements, 482

G

Gannt Charts, 464
Gauge, 442
Generating Reusable Property Sheet Patterns, 505
Get Bound Property Display Names, 486
Grid, 51
Grid Lines and Cartesian Chart, 499

H

Hierarchical pie charts, 468
Hotfix 3 SDK, 467
HTML, 49
HTTPService, 524
HTTPService Result, 523
Hyperion Essbase, 332

I

Icon, 217
IDE, 463
Image Component, 246
Implementing Advanced Custom Add-On Component Features , 505
Import, 59
Import Data from an Excel File, 298
Initialize Values, 484
Initiating End-User Interaction Binding Operations, 486
InputBindings, 478
InputMap, 491
Installation, 18
integrated development environment (IDE), 31
Interaction Options, 99
Interactivity, 24

J

JavaScript code, 379
Javascript Maps, 464

L

Languages, 43
LCDS Connection, 382
Legend, 104
License Manager, 63
Line Chart, 128, 442

Lines, 106, 252
List, 70
List Builder, 165
Live Office Compatibility, 45
Live Office Connection, 339

M

Manage Add-Ons, 49
Manual (Y) Axis, 117
Map, 442
MDX querying capabilities, 470
Menu, 31
Metadata, 411
Microsoft SQL Server, Access and Analysis Server, 332
Mouse Tracking, 173
Multi-dial Gauges, 468
Multi-Select , 409
MXML, 462
MXML Markup, 499
MySQL, 332
My workspace, 54

N

New command , 32

O

Object Browser, 52, 74
Object Elasticity, 173
OHLC Chart, 191
One-Dimensional Cell Range, 81
Open from Enterprise/Save To Enterprise, 34
Open/Save/Save As, 33
Oracle, 332
Organizing Data in Excel, 451
Outlook, 49
OutputBindings, 479

P

Packager and Xcelsius XLX Add-On, 543
Packaging best practices, 502
Panel Container, 177, 415
Percent, 108
Percentage, 22
Persisting Property Sheet Values, 505, 507
Picture Menus, 160
Pie Chart, 80, 92, 442
Planning the Dashboard, 441
Plan the UI, 442
Plan the Workflow, 441
Play Control, 231
Play Selector, 219
Plot Area, 103
Portal Data, 387
Position, 97
PowerPoint Slide, 49
Preferences, 41
Preparing Data, 443
Preview, 46
Private SDK variables, 480
Private Variables, 491
Progress Bar, 171
Properties, 52
Properties Panel, 329
Property Data Binding, 475
Property Sheet, 31, 72, 466, 475
Property Sheet Data Binding, 476
Property Sheet Styling, 480
Property Value Setting/Getting, 475
Proxy.Bind, 490
Proxy.Bind dissected, 480
proxy.getPersist function , 509
Public Chart Color Variable, 491
Public Chart Data Variable, 491

Q

Query as a Web Service, 331
Quick Start, 62

Quick Views, 52

R

Radar Chart, 203
Reading values from the spreadsheet, 476
Resize, 297
Retrieving Custom Component Property Values, 505
Retrieving Property Sheet Values, 507
Reusable Property Sheet Patterns, 510
Row/Column, 98
Run Locally, 300
Run on a Web Server, 300

S

Samples, 36
SAP BusinessObjects, 17
SAP BusinessObjects Enterprise, 34, 331
SAP BusinessObjects Live Office, 28
SAP BusinessObjects Portfolio, 28
SAP BusinessObjects Universe Designer, 28
SAP BusinessObjects Web Intelligence, 28
SAP NetWeaver BW (Business Warehouse), 332
Scale, 116
Security Issues Related to Accessing External Data, 299
Security Restriction, 340
Selectors, 147
Set Appearance, 135
Setting Custom Component Property Values, 505
Shapes, 248
Single Cell, 81
Slider, 167
Snapshot, 48
Space Evenly, 56

Spinner, 230
Spreadsheet, 81
Spreadsheet Table, 239
Stacked Column Chart, 186
Standard, 64
Status List, 97
Sub Element Array Tricks, 514
Sub-element binding, 505
Sub Element Binding , 514
Supporting SDK functions, 484
.swc file, 461

T

Tab Set, 178
Templates, 34
The Column Chart, 445
The Gauge, 445
The Line Chart, 447
Themes, 65
Themes and Colors, 430
The Pie Chart, 450
The Radio Button, 450
Ticker, 158
Title Area, 103
Toggle Button, 158
Toolbar, 56, 64
Tooltip Function, 491, 499
Transparency, 106
Tree Map, 208
Two-Dimensional Cell Range, 82

U

UI Components, 78, 393
UI controls, 20
UI elements, 20

Undo/Redo, 50
Use Current Excel Data, 48
User Interface, 475
Using Art, 246

V

Value, 97

W

Web Connectivity, 262
Web Service Connection, 20, 322, 323
Working with Charts, 92
Wrap Several Components, 176
Writing values to the spreadsheet, 477

X

Xcelsius, 17, 461
Xcelsius Column Chart , 506
Xcelsius SDK, 461
Xcelsius Workspace, 32
.xlf, 34
.xls, 32
.xlsx, 32
XML-based syntax, 462
XML, 462
XML Data, 301
XML File, 304
XML layout and controls, 539
XY Chart, 137

Y

(Y) Axis Scale, 118

www.sap-press.com

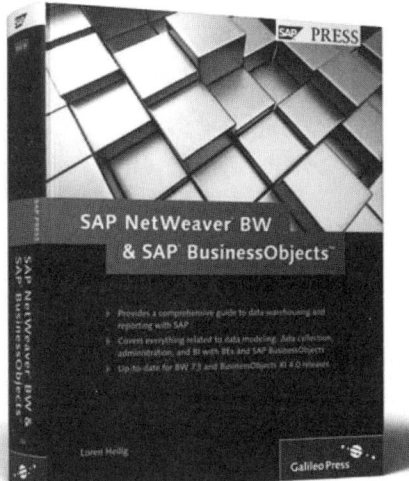

Provides a comprehensive guide to data warehousing and reporting with SAP

Covers everything related to data modeling, data collection, administration, and BI with BEx and SAP BusinessObjects

Up-to-date for BW 7.3 and BusinessObjects XI 4.x releases

Loren Heilig

SAP NetWeaver BW and SAP BusinessObjects

The Complete Guide to Business Intelligence with SAP

Finally—the entire SAP BI world comes in one volume! This comprehensive guide provides essential knowledge for a full staff of data warehousing/business intelligence SAP consultants, IT teams, DB managers, and end-users to efficiently work together. You will learn everything you need to know about SAP NetWeaver BW and BI, backend BW issues, end user intelligence tools, planning and consolidation tools from SAP, and more.

approx. 850 pp., 79,95 Euro / US$ 79.95
ISBN 978-1-59229-384-1, Nov 2011

>> www.sap-press.com

www.sap-press.com

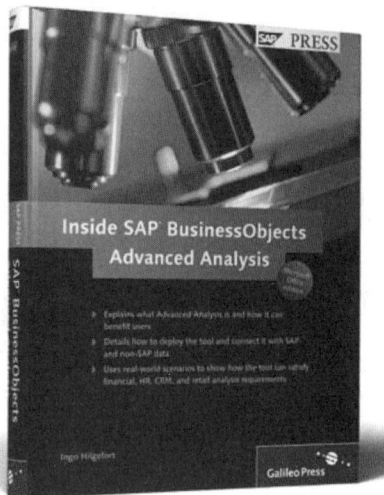

Explains what Advanced Analysis Office is and how it can benefit users

Details how to deploy the tool and connect it with SAP and non-SAP data

Uses real-world scenarios to show how the tool can work in financials, HR, CRM, and retail

Ingo Hilgefort

Inside SAP BusinessObjects Advanced Analysis

Offers a comprehensive review of the product features/functionalities, as well as targeted guidance on installation, delployment, data connectivity, and usage scenarios. It also provides a side-by-side comparison of SAP Advanced Analysis Office with SAP BEx Analyzer, and a product road that outlines the main topics in the SAP BI roadmap for the Advanced Analysis Office version and the Web version as well touch on the migration topic.

343 pp., 2010, 69,95 Euro / US$ 69.95
ISBN 978-1-59229-371-1

>> www.sap-press.com

www.sap-press.com

Provides step-by-step content for using the SAP Query Tool

Covers relevant content for all ERP components (SD, MM, PP, FI, CO, etc.)

Includes 100 ready-to-use Queries

Stephan Kaleske

SAP Query Reporting–Practical Guide

If you need to know how to deploy the SAP Query tool to create reports and extend the standard reporting capabilities of an ERP system, this book is for you. Through the use of many concrete, practical examples and solutions, you learn the main features of the SAP Query tool, including drill-down functionality, rankings, statistics, traffic symbols, calculated fields of information, and MS Office integration.

402 pp., 2011, 69,95 Euro / US$ 69.95
ISBN 978-1-59229-365-0

\>> www.sap-press.com

Your SAP Library is just a click away

1. Search
2. Buy
3. Read

Try now!

www.sap-press.com

- ✓ Easy and intuitive navigation
- ✓ Bookmarking
- ✓ Searching within the full text of all our books
- ✓ 24/7 access
- ✓ Printing capability

Galileo Press

Interested in reading more?

Please visit our Web site for all
new book releases from SAP PRESS.

www.sap-press.com